The Curriculum Studies Reader

Fourth Edition

For fifteen years, *The Curriculum Studies Reader* has been a field-defining anthology, bringing together the best scholarship from curriculum studies past and present. From John Dewey's nineteenth-century creed to Nel Noddings' twenty-first-century aims, this thoughtful combination of new and timely essays provides a complete survey of the discipline coupled with concrete examples of innovative curriculum and an examination of contemporary topics. New to this much-anticipated fourth edition are substantive updates to the selections of contemporary readings, including pieces by Thomas Misco and Peter Hlebowitsh, reflecting issues such as globalization and the reconciliation between reconceptualists and traditionalists in regard to curriculum.

Carefully balanced to engage with the history of curriculum studies while simultaneously looking ahead to its future, *The Curriculum Studies Reader* continues to be the most authoritative collection in the field.

David J. Flinders is Professor of Curriculum Studies in the School of Education at Indiana University, Bloomington, USA.

Stephen J. Thornton is Professor and Chair of the Department of Secondary Education at the University of South Florida, Tampa, USA.

The Curriculum Studies Reader

Fourth Edition

Edited by
David J. Flinders
Indiana University, Bloomington
and
Stephen J. Thornton
University of South Florida, Tampa

Routledge
Taylor & Francis Group
NEW YORK AND LONDON

Fourth edition published 2013
by Routledge
711 Third Avenue, New York, NY 10017

Simultaneously published in the UK
by Routledge
2 Park Square, Milton Park, Abingdon, Oxon OX14 4RN

Routledge is an imprint of the Taylor & Francis Group, an informa business

First edition published by RoutledgeFalmer 1998
Second edition published by RoutledgeFalmer 2004
Third edition published by Routledge 2009

Library of Congress Cataloging-in-Publication Data
The curriculum studies reader / [edited] by David J. Flinders & Stephen J. Thornton. – 4th ed.
p. cm.
Includes bibliographical references and index.
1. Education–Curricula–United States–Philosophy. 2. Curriculum planning–United States.
3. Curriculum change–United States. I. Flinders, David J., 1955– II. Thornton, Stephen J.
LB1570.C957 2012
375.000973–dc23
2012026849

ISBN: 978–0–415–52076–8 (hbk)
ISBN: 978–0–415–52075–1 (pbk)

Typeset in Minion
by Swales & Willis Ltd, Exeter, Devon

Contents

Preface ix
Introduction xi

Part One: Looking Back: A Prologue to Curriculum Studies 1

Introduction to Part One 3

1 Scientific Method in Curriculum-Making 11
Franklin Bobbitt

2 A Critical Consideration of the New Pedagogy in Its Relation to Modern Science 19
Maria Montessori

3 My Pedagogic Creed 33
John Dewey

4 The Public School and the Immigrant Child 41
Jane Addams

5 Dare the School Build a New Social Order? 45
George S. Counts

Part Two: Curriculum at Education's Center Stage 53

Introduction to Part Two 55

6 Basic Principles of Curriculum and Instruction 59
Ralph W. Tyler

7 The Rise of Scientific Curriculum-Making and Its Aftermath 69
Herbert M. Kliebard

8 Man: A Course of Study 79
Jerome S. Bruner

9 Objectives 95
W. James Popham

10 Educational Objectives—Help or Hindrance 109
Elliot W. Eisner

11 The Daily Grind 117
Philip W. Jackson

12 Curriculum and Consciousness 127
Maxine Greene

Part Three: Reconceptualizing Curriculum Theory 141

Introduction to Part Three 143

13 The Reconceptualization of Curriculum Studies 149
William F. Pinar

14 Pedagogy of the Oppressed 157
Paulo Freire

15 Controlling the Work of Teachers 167
Michael W. Apple

16 The Paideia Proposal 183
Mortimer J. Adler

17 The False Promise of the Paideia: A Critical Review of *The Paideia Proposal* 187
Nel Noddings

18 Implementation as Mutual Adaptation: Change in Classroom Organization 195
Milbrey Wallin McLaughlin

Part Four: After a Century of Curriculum Thought: Change and Continuity 207

Introduction to Part Four 209

19 The Four R's—An Alternative to the Tyler Rational 215
William E. Doll Jr.

20 Centripetal Thinking in Curriculum Studies 223
Peter Hlebowitsh

21 High-Stakes Testing and Curriculum Control: A Qualitative Metasynthesis 235
Wayne Au

22 Standardizing Knowledge in a Multicultural Society 253
Christine Sleeter and Jamy Stillman

23 Outside the Core: Accountability in Tested and Untested Subjects 269
Leslie Santee Siskin

24 What Does It Mean to Say a School Is Doing Well? 279
Elliot W. Eisner

25 Subtractive Schooling, Caring Relations, and Social Capital in the Schooling of U.S.–Mexican Youth 289
Angela Valenzuela

26 Teacher Experiences of Culture in the Curriculum 301
Elaine Chan

27 Interrupting Heteronormativity: Toward a Queer Curriculum Theory 315
Dennis Sumara and Brent Davis

28 Silence on Gays and Lesbians in Social Studies Curriculum 331
Stephen J. Thornton

29 Gender Perspectives on Educating for Global Citizenship 339
Peggy McIntosh

30 Moving Beyond Fidelity Expectations: Rethinking Curriculum Reform for Controversial Topics in Post-Communist Settings 353
Thomas Misco

31 Complementary Curriculum: The Work of Ecologically Minded Teachers 379
Christy M. Moroye

32 Curriculum for the 21st Century 399
Nel Noddings

Permissions 407
Index 411

Preface

This is the fourth edition of *The Curriculum Studies Reader*. The aim of the *Reader*, to provide a basic source book about the curriculum field, has not changed from its earlier editions. Nevertheless, such an aim has always been an ideal to reach for rather than something we could fully deliver on. There is not now and never has been entire agreement on the boundaries and proper content of the curriculum field.

Even a simple definition of "curriculum" such as "what educating institutions should teach" compels answering a vast, possibly overwhelming, set of questions including: what subject matter should be selected and by what criteria, how should the subject matter be organized, to whom should it be taught and by what methods and with what materials, how is it most effectively learned, and how might we judge the success of the undertaking. No one is an expert on the entirety of this still incomplete set of questions every curriculum designer answers, whether directly or tacitly.

This fourth edition is most like earlier editions in the first two parts of the book. We summarize the *Reader*'s four parts in the Introduction that follows. Here we want to make the point that Parts One and Two are chronologically older and these parts of the *Reader* have changed the least since the first edition appeared in 1998. These sections trace the emergence of curriculum as an area of scholarship and practice. Part One, in particular, introduces curriculum scholars from a hundred or more years ago. Their thinking laid foundations that are still discernible in the twenty-first century. Part Two takes up curriculum thought around the middle of the twentieth century, a time when curriculum scholarship focused most of all on models of curriculum development, including design, implementation, and evaluation, for K-12 schooling. In time, these curriculum scholars would become known as "traditionalists."

This focus was challenged by what came to be called the reconceptualists, who emerged in the 1970s. Part Three introduces some key writings by some reconceptualists. They were highly critical of the traditionalist focus: means of building better models as the main route to improving curriculum. Instead they raised issues of personal meaning, social criticism, and the like as the proper concerns of curriculum scholars. Part Three also looks at how curriculum scholars in the 1970s, who were not themselves reconceptualists, were increasingly critical of traditionalists for their emphasis on models that were expected to be followed but which ignored how schools actually work.

Part Four is concerned with recent developments and trends. In this part we survey some of the major issues in curriculum since the turn of the last century. This part changes most from edition to edition because we lack historical perspective and thus cannot be sure where recent developments will lead or whether they will endure.

Many changes in the curriculum field have taken place since the first edition of the *Reader* appeared. Two of these changes strike us as particularly significant when considering the contents of this volume. First, there has been some degree of reconciliation between the reconceptualists and traditionalists, seeking to identify what unites them in contrast to what separates them. Peter Hlebowitsh's reading in Part Four exemplifies this development, but the recent convergence of views has resulted from movement on both sides. In particular, first-generation reconceptualists (see the Introduction to Part Four) have recently begun efforts to identify "core" curriculum scholarship as well as other types of continuities within the field.

The second change is the continuing globalization of the curriculum field. Although national distinctiveness has scarcely disappeared, curriculum conferences and writings continue to grow more international in attendance and scope. So do trends such as accountability (Apple, 2011). To some extent, accountability and standards reflects schooling trends in post-industrial nations. It also reflects more longstanding tendencies such as portraying curriculum "gains" as a form of competition among nations, evidenced for example in international comparisons of student achievement in mathematics. In still another way, globalization reflects the reality of greater international connectedness with issues ranging from war and peace, the environment, trade, and digital technologies to drug trafficking and ethnic cleansing. These are all grist for the curricular mill.

What has not changed is that curriculum issues are ever present in education. They do not go away even when ignored. Thus, responsible educators must do their best in always-imperfect circumstances to deal with the trade-offs, potential, dilemmas, and challenges of the curriculum.

Reference

Apple, M. W. (2011). Global crises, social justice, and teacher education. *Journal of Teacher Education, 62*, 222–234.

Introduction

What do schools teach, what should they teach, and who should decide? Is the primary aim of education to instill basic skills or foster critical thinking? Should education aim to mold future citizens, transmit national values, engender personal development, or inspire academic achievement? Must education have an aim? And what beliefs, values, or attitudes are learned from the way classrooms are? That is, what lessons are taught but not planned, acquired but taken for granted? These are some of the perennial questions around which curriculum scholars have organized theory, research, teaching, and program evaluation. Collectively, such efforts constitute the academic study of curriculum and the focus of this book.

Although stating the book's focus implies a clearly delineated topic, the field of curriculum studies is anything but narrow. On the contrary, our topic sprawls out like the seemingly endless suburbs of a modern megalopolis. Its wide reach overlaps with every subject area; with cultural, political, and economic trends; with philosophical concerns; and with social issues. In addition, contemporary models of curriculum theory and research draw on increasingly diverse disciplinary perspectives and increasingly diverse inquiry methods. While this diversity can bewilder those unfamiliar with the field's intellectual terrain, others see both the need and the room for still greater diversity. Even without further development, the current range of work makes it useful to adopt broad perspectives from which to identify the field's various regions and familiar landmarks. No one can accurately represent the field from a single perspective. Yet, the trade-offs of accommodation are involved here as well. The more inclusive one's perspective, the more challenging it is to represent the field in ways that clearly illustrate its contributions to educational policy and practice.

Our choice in responding to this challenge is to portray the field, its various regions and familiar landmarks, through the genre of a "reader"—a collection of informed and influential writings. All of the writings in this reader are previously published articles, book chapters, research reports, or excerpts from larger works that sample the past and present trends of curriculum scholarship. The primary advantage of this approach is not comprehensiveness but rather the opportunity it allows for getting close to the ideas and debates that have inspired such wide interest in curriculum studies to begin with. Like other curriculum textbooks, this reader seeks to cast a broad net by attending to the field at large rather than to a certain type of curriculum work or area of specialization. However, the views and perspectives introduced in this collection do not stand above the fray of academic disagreements, arguments, and strongly held convictions.

On the contrary, the reader is intentionally designed to capture some of the contentious discourse and outright disputes for which the curriculum field is known. This animation of ideas and values plays an important role because it has nurtured the field in unlikely settings and through otherwise lean times. Surprisingly to some, the study of curriculum has held its own, even flourished, when no national crisis demanded an immediate educational response, when no vast infusion of federal dollars poured into research and development, when no mobs of angry parents clamored at the schoolhouse door, and when no technological marvels promised new ways to build better curricular mouse traps. All of these factors have had their day, and many are likely to recur in the future. Yet, with or without any added impetus, the questions of curriculum theory and practice are questions that have captured the imagination of educators and lay people from one generation to the next.

This enduring interest is found in both specific and general curriculum issues, and the writings in this volume also vary with respect to scope. Some readings are broadly conceived around the purposes and politics of schooling in general. Others focus on particular topics such as the use of instructional objectives, high-stakes testing, or heteronormativity. Even the most narrowly focused of these readings, however, illustrate recurrent themes and historical antecedents. Curricular debates, in short, represent intellectual traditions. Furthermore, the issues raised in curriculum studies often cut across a variety of subject areas and levels of education. One could reasonably argue that basic curriculum issues, or at least some of those issues, extend well beyond schooling to include the concerns of anyone interested in how people come to acquire the knowledge, skills, and values they do.

Be that as it may, our collection does focus mainly on the types of learning that are intended to take place in schools and classrooms. These institutional settings simply provide a window onto broader issues. Yet, our focus is still expansive, and as with any book of this kind, the difficult task has been to winnow down an extremely large body of material by selecting only a sample of that material. Having done so, we cannot claim to be representing the field in a comprehensive way. Our challenge reminds us of a common story told among cultural anthropologists. Seasoned ethnographers like to ask their fellow researchers just returning from fieldwork whether they have captured the entire culture of the particular group being studied. The question is asked tongue-in-cheek because all but the most naive know full well the impossibility of learning everything there is to know about other people. Like those returning anthropologists, we are unable to provide a complete or definitive account of all that is going on in the field—the norms, kinships, and relations of curriculum scholarship are simply too complex. This limitation of our work may sound harsh, but it can also be viewed together with another adage from ethnographic research—that we are not required to know everything in order to learn something.

To say that this book was created by sampling a much larger body of scholarship still leaves unanswered the questions of what criteria we used to select that sample. How did we choose some readings over others, and for what reasons? While this process was almost always more ambiguous than anticipated, three concerns stand out as having a prominent influence on our decisions. First, we sought to include work that is well recognized within the field. This criterion is not so much a matter of name recognition as it is a matter of a work's endurance or impact on how others think about curriculum issues. In a few cases, we have included authors (John Dewey or Paulo Freire, for example) who might not be considered curriculum scholars per se, but whose ideas have been so influential to curriculum studies that they can be considered part of the intellectual traditions on which others continue to build.

Writers who achieve this type of legacy also tend to be those who are grappling with ideas and problems that often surface in different areas of curriculum practice. Certain issues and problems are recurrent or even thematic to the point of being recognized as common to the field. We looked for writings that possess this thematic quality because they lend continuity to the particulars of practice, and without that continuity it would be difficult to connect the otherwise broad range of topics on which curriculum scholarship is carried out.

A second consideration in deciding the book's content has been our desire to include pivotal work. This consideration has played out in an effort to identify writings that most clearly signal turning points in the development of the field, or that serve as prototypes for exploring issues previously taken for granted. Exactly what constitutes ground-breaking work is conceptually difficult to pin down. Nevertheless, our aim is to represent not only the continuity of the field but also its dynamic qualities. The field is constantly changing, if not always in its underlying philosophical concerns, then in the field's ways of responding to concerns as they take on new shades of emphasis. Topics come and go as well, and some specific developments of current interest such as AIDS education or No Child Left Behind (NCLB) could not have been fully anticipated by earlier generations.

The first two considerations we have mentioned concern the conceptual foundations and development of the field. Our third consideration differs by emphasizing pedagogy. Because we teach curriculum courses at both the undergraduate and graduate levels, we often found our attention drawn to work that is accessible across a wide audience. In part, this means we have tried to select examples of scholarship that avoid the jargon of education and its associated disciplines. Much of the work in curriculum studies is and should be intellectually challenging, but some of that work (as in all fields) is challenging for reasons unnecessary to understanding its subject matter. We hope to have avoided the latter, sampling only from the most accessible work available.

The final issue we want to address concerns the organization of the book's content. Overall, the readings are divided chronologically into four parts. Part One, "Looking Back: A Prologue to Curriculum Studies," is centered on the work of five prominent figures: Franklin Bobbitt, Maria Montessori, John Dewey, Jane Addams, and George S. Counts. Their writings are brought together with a historical critique that introduces some of the early traditions of curriculum scholarship. Not only are all of these readings worth revisiting from time to time, but they also serve to provide enough historical information for beginning students of curriculum to start to appreciate the antecedents and changing social contexts in which the field's contemporary theories are rooted.

Part Two, "Curriculum at Education's Center Stage," sets out to illustrate the optimism and contradictions of an era marked by unparalleled national support for curriculum reform. Whatever complacency Americans had about education seemed to vanish with the launch of Sputnik I in 1957. For almost two decades after that event, hardly anyone questioned the need and urgency for large-scale curriculum reforms. Yet, this same period is remembered for an increasing sense of uneasiness within the field. Debates grew over how curriculum work should be carried out, earlier traditions became the targets of some criticism, and greater scrutiny was given to the field's underlying purposes.

These undertones of discontent were not short-lived. On the contrary, in many ways they presaged the soon-to-blossom critical and reconceptualist movements. Among other achievements, the reconceptualists, together with the open education movement, brought into focus the sociocultural and personal dimensions of curriculum with greater emphasis and clarity than had earlier generations. The efforts to achieve this are represented in Part Three, "Reconceptualizing Curriculum Theory." This section, however, is not limited to reconceptualist thought, which in and of itself is quite diverse. While curriculum studies had taken a reflective turn that is today very much alive and well, the field's most conventional scholarship did not stop simply because other ways of understanding that scholarship were made more readily available. To put this another way, the field seemed to annex new territory rather than move its location.

This annexation of various topics, ideas, and perspectives is examined as a contemporary issue in Part Four, "After a Century of Curriculum Thought." Our aim in this section is to suggest the various ways in which current scholarship reflects both the change and continuity of the field. The readings we have selected to represent these perspectives may at first seem unbridled, which is exactly how some people have come to view curriculum studies. Topics range from postmodernism to the growing debate over national standards. We have selected these readings to illustrate in as concrete a way as possible the breadth of issues on which today's curriculum scholars work, and at the same time, how this work builds on previous traditions.

If we were pressed to summarize what this final set of readings has to say about the current state of the field and its future directions, we would have to fall back on the truism that "much changes while staying the same." But that comment is not at all meant to be glib. Changes in both the tenor and focus of contemporary work make a difference in what receives attention and what does not. In this way, such trends make a difference in discussions of educational policy and practice, and in the levels of sophistication at which these discussions are carried out. In current decision making at the levels of research, policy and practice, informed points of view are valued by those engaged in such work. If anything, the need for informed scholarship today seems by past benchmarks to be increasingly urgent.

Part One

Looking Back: A Prologue to Curriculum Studies

Introduction to Part One

Curriculum theorizing and development are as old as educating institutions because any educational program must have a content. Although theorists and practitioners have (perhaps without conscious awareness) dealt with curriculum questions since at least the time of Plato's design for education in his ideal state, the notion of curriculum as a professional or scholarly field is recent. Historically, curriculum decisions were largely left to that small, usually elite, portion of the public most directly concerned with the operation of schools. In the United States, curriculum began to emerge as a field of scholarly inquiry and professional practice only toward the close of the nineteenth century, a time that roughly coincided with the rise of public schooling for the masses.

The burgeoning population of the public schools at the dawn of the twentieth century was only one of a number of tumultuous and consequential developments in American education. One result of such upheaval was the Progressive movement, a broad-based effort aimed at assuring the realization of American ideals in an increasingly urban-industrial and pluralistic nation (Cremin, 1964, pp. 8–10). Thus, the first self-conscious curriculum scholars saw their work as part of this broader reformation of American life. The responses of the progressive educational reformers were to institutionalize many of the now characteristic features of school curriculum, including such practices as tracking, standardized testing, and civic education (Tyack, 1974).

Although early curriculum specialists frequently perceived themselves as "progressives," these educational reformers, like their fellow progressives in politics and other fields, worked with diverse, even contradictory, conceptions of what "progressive" meant (see Curti, 1959; Kliebard, 1995; Lagemann, 2000). Thus, from its earliest days, the curriculum field has been characterized by vigorous disagreements about its proper aims and practices. For example, the various meanings assigned by curriculum specialists to terms such as "learning" and "democracy" are not merely esoteric concerns without consequences for the world of practice. To the contrary, how one defines terms to a great extent determines the resulting character of education.

The first set of readings we introduce includes five of the early formulations of the curriculum field as represented in the work of Franklin Bobbitt, Maria Montessori, John Dewey, Jane Addams, and George S. Counts. Each of these formulations retains an important contemporary presence in curriculum scholarship (see Eisner, 2002). In this sense, conflicting conceptions of curriculum have never been an aberration in the field. On the contrary, differing views have been present since the very first generation of curriculum scholarship. Indeed, the work of the first three early scholars we will encounter, Franklin Bobbitt, Maria Montessori and John Dewey, exemplify how different archetypes of the meaning of "curriculum" result in radically different views of educational aims and practice.

When he wrote *The Curriculum* (1918), Bobbitt was a professor at the University of Chicago as well as a sought-after curriculum consultant to school districts across the nation. He is an apt starting point for tracing the development of professional curriculum scholarship and practice in North America as the essentials of his approach to curriculum have been dominant in practice ever since. Moreover, Bobbitt was a self-proclaimed pioneer of the field. He asserts in the excerpt reproduced in this volume to be writing the "first" curriculum textbook. Although it is not self-evident what constitutes the "first" curriculum textbook, Bobbitt's claim is often conceded. In any case, there is no doubt that Bobbitt's *The Curriculum* has had enduring influence, particularly in its insistence that curriculum developers begin with the identification of proper goals. "Pioneer" implies finding one's way in unfamiliar terrain, but Bobbitt seems to have had few doubts that he was headed in the right direction. He epitomized the "can-do" attitude of the new professional elites of the Progressive era, a time when professionals in a variety of fields were increasingly considered the preferred means by which a forward-looking society addressed its problems. Bobbitt was quite sure of what ailed curriculum making: for too long it had been in the hands of amateurs and it was high time it became a professional undertaking.

Bobbitt was convinced that professional knowledge applicable to curriculum work could be found in the logic of "scientific management," which had been applied to raising worker productivity in industry (Callahan, 1962, pp. 79–94). In a nutshell, Bobbitt asserted that curriculum work, like work in industry, should be managed in the interests of efficiency and the elimination of waste. These same interests after all, it seemed obvious to Bobbitt and many of his contemporaries, in significant respects accounted for the world preeminence of the United States manufacturing industry. Use of the same methods would bring the same world-class standards to the school curriculum.

Bobbitt's claim that curriculum work was out of date, having not kept pace with other advances in schooling, is almost poignant. *The Curriculum* was Bobbitt's solution to this unfortunate state of affairs. As he makes plain in the preface, he proposed to lay out how curriculum can be constructed in a manner that honors scientific procedures. For Bobbitt, "scientific" suggested a systematic series of procedures, carried out by curriculum professionals, prior to implementation in a school district (see Eisner, 1985).

The content of any given curriculum, according to Bobbitt, could be "discovered" by a process of surveying what successful adults know and can do (Bobbitt, this volume, Chapter 1). In turn, the results of this process of discovery would be used to formulate educational objectives from which the curriculum scope and sequence (i.e., what is taught and in what order) would be derived to address where students fell short of successful adults. After instruction with this kind of curriculum, he believed, students would be prepared to lead successful lives in their adult years.

Efficiency, of course, suggests not only smooth operating procedures but minimization of "waste" as well. Thus, in addition to scientific curriculum making, Bobbitt wanted to minimize sources of wasted instructional time. He believed that diagnostic testing and other procedures proposed by behavioral psychologists such as Edward L. Thorndike would make possible prediction of the kind of errors students typically made. This would enable more efficient curriculum making as well as prevent unnecessary time being spent on the costly business of instruction, especially grade-level retention of students which Bobbitt considered enormously wasteful. As in industrial enterprises, Bobbitt wanted to maximize output (i.e., student learning) at minimum cost (i.e., paying teachers).

This outlook also held significance for the content of the curriculum. Bobbitt believed that "the shortcomings of children and men" in subjects such as spelling and grammar were "obvious" and hence these fields needed to be included in the curriculum. It was less apparent to Bobbitt, however, what shortcomings were overcome by "social" subjects such as literature, history, and geography. He urged attention to identifying significant educational objectives to which these social subjects could contribute (Bobbitt, this volume, Chapter 1).

Because Bobbitt's approach to curriculum work was based, he argued, on a dispassionate analysis of what youngsters needed to lead productive lives as adults, he dismissed arguments about the interests of children as irrelevant to the educational process. Moreover, Bobbitt did not question whether the existing social and economic order was just; he merely took that for granted. Hence, he saw the aim of schooling as matching individuals with the existing social and economic order (Lagemann, 2000, p. 107).

The second reading in Part One is by Italian educator and physician Maria Montessori. This figure shares at least one interest with Bobbitt: that being the relationship between science and education. Like Bobbitt, Montessori took a progressive stance in wanting to help design more modern conditions for schools via "scientific pedagogy." She saw education as following in the footsteps of medicine to "pass the purely speculative stage and base its conclusions on the positive results of experimentation" (this volume, Chapter 2). In addition, systematic inquiry is at the heart of what today has become widely known as the Montessori Method. Beyond these points, however, the similarities between Bobbitt and Montessori end and their differences begin.

Unlike Bobbitt, Montessori explicitly cautions against the dangers of applying science too literally to the education of children. Montessori locates these dangers in a tension that would follow curriculum work throughout the twentieth century. This tension is found in the differences between the specialized interests of the scientist and the social interests of the educator. For Montessori, educators needed the science of the clinician, not the science of aloof professionals removed from the day-to-day practical affairs of working with children. In the most useful view of science, child study through the fields of anthropology and psychology could inform but not substitute for sound pedagogy. By way of example, Montessori cites the extreme practice of designing student desks based purely on the measurements of children's physical characteristics. The result is children rigidly fastened in straight rows of desks with little or no room for natural movement. For Montessori, such artificial arrangements invoked the image of a display box of butterflies mounted on pins in their perfect lifelessness. She uses this image to emphasize that any use of science in education must be guided by broader purposes—purposes which she argues can be found in the concept of social liberty.

Another contrast with Bobbitt is that Montessori's approach elevates and transforms the role of classroom teachers. In Bobbitt's system, teachers were given a curriculum prior to instruction, a curriculum designed by a new brand of professional known as curriculum developers or curriculum workers. Montessori's teachers, on the other hand, were charged with creating developmental activities and classroom arrangements based on careful observations of the children in their care. For Montessori, it was not a matter of technical methods but rather attentive observations and the desire to learn that signaled the true spirit of scientific pedagogy.

A final point of difference between these two educational thinkers concerns the place of student interests. For Bobbitt, the needs of the individual were determined by the demands of adult life. Thus, curriculum designers looked to society while individual interests were largely irrelevant to their task. For Montessori, personal interests and talents represented important opportunities for development, and as such they should be nurtured. She makes this point specifically in relation to the use of rewards and prizes as ways to motivate or control children. Montessori (this volume, Chapter 2) writes:

> Everyone has as special tendency, a special vocation, modest perhaps, but certainly useful. The system of prizes may turn an individual aside from this vocation, may make him choose a false road, for him a vain one, and forced to follow it, the natural activity of a human being may be warped, lessened, even annihilated.

John Dewey's "My Pedagogic Creed," which follows Montessori's chapter, echoes similar concerns regarding the interests of students and their role in education. In doing so, Dewey's view of curriculum again provides a contrast with Bobbitt's industrial model. Where Bobbitt argued that adult society is the mold for the school curriculum, Dewey (this volume, Chapter 3) said such a view "results in subordinating the freedom of the individual to a preconceived social and political status." "True education," Dewey insisted, "comes through the stimulation of the child's powers by the demands of the social situations in which he finds himself." Reliance on behaviorist methods to Dewey signified external imposition whose effects "cannot truly be called educative." Indeed, Dewey pointed out that the worth of subject matter could only be determined by its educational uses. For example, Dewey (this volume, Chapter 3) questioned the value of history as school subject if it was the customary "inert" study of "the distant past." But Dewey maintained history "becomes full of meaning" if "taken as the record of man's social life and progress . . . as the child is introduced . . . directly into social life."

The distinctions Dewey drew, although consequential, are frequently subtle as Dewey spoke the unfamiliar language of reform, of education as a means of extending and reforming democratic, community life in the United States. The relative novelty of his language and views may help explain why Dewey's theory of curriculum has been often and widely misunderstood, even by those purporting to be his followers. In this regard, he wrote *Experience and Education* (1938) toward the end of his career because he believed, for example, his insistence on curriculum planning beginning with the experience of the child was being wrongly interpreted as disdain for the "progressive organization of subject-matter." Similarly, Dewey emphasized that starting with the experience of the child, far from producing laissez-faire classroom arrangements, increased rather than replaced the demands on judgment by the teacher in directing each pupil's learning toward worthwhile goals.

What would Dewey's ideal curriculum look like in practice? Although too lengthy a question to answer fully here, probably the most authentic answer can be obtained by examination of the laboratory school Dewey established and oversaw during his years at the University of Chicago (see Mayhew & Edwards, 1966; Tanner, 1997). In broad terms, Dewey's curriculum broke down the barriers, customary in schools a century ago as well as today, between children's life experiences and their experiences in the classroom. Hence, the heart of the curriculum would be activities based on a simplification of "existing social life." In this scheme of things, boundaries between traditional school subjects would be traversed. Children might, for example, examine how the local community deals with its problems and, in this context, develop measuring skills ordinarily assigned to mathematics, drawing skills ordinarily assigned to art, map skills ordinarily assigned to geography, and so forth. The logical organization of school subjects, Dewey insisted, was the organizational schema of adults; children require the "psychological" organization of subject matter, moving gradually toward adult modes of understanding associated with formal school subjects.

In sum, the school for Dewey was an integral part of community life; it was also an instrument for social reform. Whereas the followers of Bobbitt saw the school as an agent of social adaptation to the status quo, Dewey (this volume, Chapter 3) portrayed "the school as the primary and most effective interest of social progress and reform." Just as there should be no strict boundary between the curriculum and community life, Dewey believed the curriculum held the potential for society to remake itself.

Jane Addams, friend and collaborator of Dewey, also saw no sharp boundary between the curriculum and democratic community life. In 1889 Addams and her longtime associate, Helen Gates Starr, established a social settlement, Hull House, in Chicago's West Side slums. While Dewey's thoughts on the curriculum were mainly directed at formal schooling, the primary site of Addams' work was Hull House and its adjacent community. As Richard Bernstein (1967) observed, while Dewey brought "the theory and methods of social philosophy to bear on the concrete facts," Hull House "provided him with the 'facts'" (p. 37). Moreover, as Ellen Condliffe Lagemann (1994) has noted, Addams' location outside of the academy "enabled her to develop and sustain an approach to social analysis that was broad, synthetic, and problem- as opposed to discipline- or profession-centered" (p. xiii).

Hull House reached out to immigrants, to laborers, to mothers and children, to all in an urban-industrial community who needed or wanted its educational and social programs. Celebrated almost from the beginning, Hull House aimed through its educational programs to address the range of problems and aspirations of ordinary and needy people in an era when public schools often appeared inadequate to the task. Although Addams wrote and spoke widely about education, she considered these activities no substitute for the direct caring she saw as necessary (Noddings, 2001, p. 184). As Addams wrote in her autobiographical *Twenty Years at Hull-House*, first published in 1910, she believed she was filling educational needs that were otherwise neither recognized nor met:

> It sometimes seems that the men of substantial scholarship were content to leave to the charlatan the teaching of those things which deeply concern the welfare of mankind. . . . A settlement soon discovers that simple people are interested in large and vital subjects. . . .
>
> (Addams, 1961, p. 282)

Hull House strove to value both the traditions immigrants brought to the United States and the necessary adjustments to their new environment. "The ignorant teacher," Addams wrote, "cuts [immigrant children] off" from their parents and their parents' traditions, while "the cultivated teacher fastens them because his own mind is open to the charm and beauty of the old-country life." It is therefore not surprising that Addams understood that a one-size-fits-all curriculum to "Americanize" immigrants may not fit the needs of any individual. Coercion was not part of her stock in trade.

Rather, through provision of choice and individualization, the extraordinary breadth of the Hull House curricular offerings aimed to both expand student horizons and connect to their aspirations and needs. But these ambitious goals were as far as possible harmonized with the community. Courses were offered in cooking, arithmetic, history, athletics, clay modeling, English for Italians, and many other subject matters. There were classes on writers such as Dante, Browning, and Shakespeare, and also a Plato club. Dr. Dewey lectured on social psychology to "groups consisting largely of people from the immediate neighborhood" (Addams, this volume, Chapter 4). Although fully supportive of the exceptional community member who was college-bound, more fundamentally Hull House aimed to "connect him with all sorts of people by his ability to understand them as well by his power to supplement their present surroundings with the historic background" (Addams, 1961, pp. 284–285).

Since at least Addams' time, great significance and considerable disagreement has been attached to the connection of cultural pluralism and the school curriculum. The educational program enacted at Hull House in this regard has always held the potential to inform discussion of this issue. Its curriculum modeled how to foster intergenerational and intercultural communication, open-minded and balanced debate, and the relationship of education to community betterment. As Nel Noddings (2001, p. 185) writes:

> Life at Hull House was proof that people could cooperate, actually live together, despite differences of religion, nationality and economic status. There were no ideological tests at Hull House beyond the common commitment to improve the neighborhood, Chicago and, more generally, the lives of working people.

If building a more humane and democratic society was integral to Dewey's and Addams' theories of curriculum, it was almost the singular goal of George S. Counts. From the time of his earliest, major works in the 1920s, Counts was concerned with the injustices of democracy and capitalism in the United States, particularly as they played out in the context of schooling (see Kliebard, 1995, pp. 158–159). Like Dewey, Counts grew increasingly restive with "child-centered," progressive educators who appeared to be ignoring the social context of education in the business-dominated atmosphere of the 1920s. For Counts, the seemingly dominant stream of progressive education spoke to the "needs" of the child as though these had meaning outside of the society in which education unfolded.

The catastrophic economic slump of the 1930s ushered in a much more receptive environment for the disenchanted intellectual critics of the business orientation of the 1920s. American social thought became more polarized, and collectivist thought enjoyed possibly its most widespread popularity in the history of the United States (see Bowers, 1969). Counts (this volume, Chapter 5) caught the spirit of the times when he remarked in *Dare the School Build a New Social Order?* (1932) that "the so-called 'practical' men of our generation—the politicians, the financiers, the industrialists" had acted selfishly and bungled the well-being of Americans. Counts appealed for teachers to lead the schools and the public toward "social regeneration." For Counts and his fellow social reconstructionists (several of the most prominent of whom such as Harold Rugg were Counts' colleagues at Teachers College, Columbia University), it seemed apparent that the age of collectivism had arrived.

Aspects of Counts' vision of a regulated and directed economy in order to serve more than society's elite were, of course, consistent with the more radical elements of the

New Deal yet to come. Indeed, it is a sign of how Counts was in touch with the times that later some of his main ideas were to find their parallels in the words and policies of President Franklin D. Roosevelt during the early New Deal years. Nevertheless, given what he viewed as the failure of individualism in American life, Counts looked to the school curriculum as a place to inculcate collectivist ideas. Counts maintained that all school programs already inculcated ideas, but those ideas had been ones that primarily served the interests of the ruling classes. As Counts (this volume, Chapter 5) put it, "the real question is not whether imposition will take place, but rather from what source it will come."

Counts' theory of curriculum found a ready audience during the depths of the Great Depression in the early 1930s. For example, he and his colleague, the historian Charles A. Beard, were dominant forces in the Commission on the Social Studies, which had been established by the American Historical Association to make recommendations for the schools. The commission's reports, although stopping short of formulating an actual curriculum, nonetheless leaned heavily toward an activist-oriented social studies curriculum consonant with the tenets of social reconstructionism. Furthermore, beginning in the 1920s, Rugg oversaw the development of social studies curriculum materials that were based to some extent on social reconstructionist principles. In contrast to most available materials, their explicit focus was on the problems of American life (see Thornton, 2001). Rugg's materials became bestsellers and were widely adopted across the United States. This is all the more remarkable given the fiscal retrenchment faced by school districts during the 1930s.

Rugg's social studies materials probably mark the greatest success of the social reconstructionists in the implementation of their ideas in school programs. As the Great Depression and the New Deal waned, however, Rugg's textbooks came under growing fire from conservative groups. For this and other reasons, the series eventually fell out of favor. Almost the same fate befell social reconstructionism itself as the 1930s wore on and World War II approached. Conservative criticism and the changing climate of educational opinion increasingly shifted Counts and other social reconstructionists from at or near the center of educational debate to a more peripheral position (Kliebard, 1995, pp. 176–178). Nevertheless, the flame of social reconstructionism in educational thought was never entirely extinguished and was, as we shall see, visible again in the 1970s and thereafter.

Before leaving Counts, however, it should be noted that his view of curriculum attracted criticism not only from educational and political traditionalists. No less a progressive figure than Dewey, while sympathizing with some of Counts' collectivist goals, found parts of Counts' curriculum thinking worrisome. For example, Dewey always championed teaching students to think for themselves. From this perspective, the preordained ends of Counts' "imposition" seemed hard to distinguish from indoctrination. This tension too is embedded in the field's historical continuity.

References

Addams, J. (1961). *Twenty years at Hull-House.* New York: Signet Classic.

Bernstein, R. J. (1967). *John Dewey.* New York: Washington Square Press.

Bowers, C. A. (1969). *The progressive educator and the Depression.* New York: Random House.

Callahan, R. E. (1962). *Education and the cult of efficiency.* Chicago: University of Chicago Press.

Counts, George S. (1932) *Dare the school build a new social order?* New York: John Day.

Cremin, L. A. (1964). *The transformation of the school.* New York: Vintage.

Curti, M. (1959). *The social ideas of American educators, with a new chapter on the last twenty-five years.* Totowa, NJ: Littlefield, Adams.

Dewey, J. (1938). *Experience and education.* New York: Macmillan.

Eisner, E. W (1985). Franklin Bobbitt and the "science" of curriculum making. In E. W. Eisner (Ed.), *The art of educational evaluation* (pp. 13–28). London: Falmer.

Eisner, E. W. (2002). *The educational imagination* (3rd ed.). Upper Saddle River, NJ: Merrill/Prentice Hall.

Kliebard, H. M. (1995). *The struggle for the American curriculum, 1893–1958* (2nd ed.). New York: Routledge.

Lagemann, E. C. (1994). Introduction to the Transaction edition: Why read Jane Addams? In Jane Addams, *On education* (pp. vii-xvii). New Brunswick, NJ: Transaction Publishers.

Lagemann, E. C. (2000). *An elusive science: The troubling history of education research.* Chicago: University of Chicago Press

Mayhew, K. C., & Edwards, A. C. (1966). *The Dewey school.* New York: Atherton.

Noddings, N. (2001). Jane Addams, 1860–1935. In J. A. Palmer (Ed.), *Fifty major thinkers on education: From Confucius to Dewey* (pp. 182–187). London: Routledge.

Tanner, L. M. (1997). *Dewey's laboratory school.* New York: Teachers College Press.

Thornton, S. J. (2001). Harold Rugg, 1886–1960. In J. A. Palmer (Ed.), *Fifty modern thinkers on education: From Piaget to the present* (pp. 10–15). London: Routledge.

Tyack, D. B. (1974). *The one best system.* Cambridge, MA: Harvard University Press.

1
Scientific Method in Curriculum-Making

Franklin Bobbitt

Since the opening of the twentieth century, the evolution of our social order has been proceeding with great and ever-accelerating rapidity. Simple conditions have been growing complex. Small institutions have been growing large. Increased specialization has been multiplying human interdependencies and the consequent need of coordinating effort. Democracy is increasing within the Nation; and growing throughout the world. All classes are aspiring to a full human opportunity. Never before have civilization and humanization advanced so swiftly.

As the world presses eagerly forward toward the accomplishment of new things, education also must advance no less swiftly. It must provide the intelligence and the aspirations necessary for the advance; and for stability and consistency in holding the gains. Education must take a pace set, not by itself, but by social progress.

The present program of public education was mainly formulated during the simpler conditions of the nineteenth century. In details it has been improved. In fundamentals it is not greatly different. A program never designed for the present day has been inherited.

Any inherited system, good for its time, when held to after its day, hampers social progress. It is not enough that the system, fundamentally unchanged in plan and purpose, be improved in details. In education this has been done in conspicuous degree. Our schools today are better than ever before. Teachers are better trained. Supervision is more adequate. Buildings and equipment are enormously improved. Effective methods are being introduced, and time is being economized. Improvements are visible on every hand. And yet to do the nineteenth-century task better than it was then done is not necessarily to do the twentieth-century task.

New duties lie before us. And these require new methods, new materials, new vision. The old education, except as it conferred the tools of knowledge, was mainly devoted to filling the memory with facts. The new age is more in need of facts than the old; and of more facts; and it must find more effective methods of teaching them. But there are now other functions. Education is now to develop a type of wisdom that can grow only out of participation in the living experiences of men, and never out of mere memorization of verbal statements of facts. It must, therefore, train thought and judgment in connection with actual life-situations, a task distinctly different from the cloistral activities of the past. It is also to develop the goodwill, the spirit of service, the social valuations, sympathies, and attitudes of mind necessary for effective group-action where specialization has created endless interdependency. It has the function of training every citizen, man or woman, not for knowledge about citizenship, but for proficiency in citizenship;

not for knowledge about hygiene, but for proficiency in maintaining robust health; not for a mere knowledge of abstract science, but for proficiency in the use of ideas in the control of practical situations. Most of these are new tasks. In connection with each, much is now being done in all progressive school systems; but most of them yet are but partially developed. We have been developing knowledge, not function; the power to reproduce facts, rather than the powers to think and feel and will and act in vital relation to the world's life. Now we must look to these latter things as well.

Our task in this volume is to point out some of the new duties. We are to show why education must now undertake tasks that until recently were not considered needful; why new methods, new materials, and new types of experience must be employed. We here try to develop a point of view that seems to be needed by practical school men and women as they make the educational adjustments now demanded by social conditions; and needed also by scientific workers who are seeking to define with accuracy the objectives of education. It is the feeling of the writer that in the social reconstructions of the post-war years that lie just ahead of us, education is to be called upon to bear a hitherto undreamed-of burden of responsibility; and to undertake unaccustomed labors. To present some of the theory needed for the curriculum labors of this new age has been the task herein attempted.

This is a first book in a field that until recently has been too little cultivated. For a long time, we have been developing the theory of educational method, both general and special; and we have required teachers and supervisors to be thoroughly cognizant of it. Recently, however, we have discerned that there is a theory of curriculum-formulation that is no less extensive and involved than that of method; and that it is just as much needed by teachers and supervisors. To know what to do is as important as to know how to do it. This volume, therefore, is designed for teacher-training institutions as an introductory textbook in the theory of the curriculum; and for reading circles in the training of teachers in service. It is hoped also that it may assist the general reader who is interested in noting recent educational tendencies.

The technique of curriculum-making along scientific lines has been but little developed. The controlling purposes of education have not been sufficiently particularized. We have aimed at a vague culture, an ill-defined discipline, a nebulous harmonious development of the individual, an indefinite moral character-building, an unparticularized social efficiency, or, often enough nothing more than escape from a life of work. Often there are no controlling purposes; the momentum of the educational machine keeps it running. So long as objectives are but vague guesses, or not even that, there can be no demand for anything but vague guesses as to means and procedure. But the era of contentment with large, undefined purposes is rapidly passing. An age of science is demanding exactness and particularity.

The technique of scientific method is at present being developed for every important aspect of education. Experimental laboratories and schools are discovering accurate methods of measuring and evaluating different types of educational processes. Bureaus of educational measurement are discovering scientific methods of analyzing results, of diagnosing specific situations, and of prescribing remedies. Scientific method is being applied to the fields of budget-making, child-accounting, systems of grading and promotion, etc.

The curriculum, however, is a primordial factor. If it is wrongly drawn up on the basis merely of guess and personal opinion, all of the science in the world applied to the factors above enumerated will not make the work efficient. The scientific task preceding all others is the determination of the curriculum. For this we need a scientific technique. At present this is being rapidly developed in connection with various fields of training.

The central theory is simple. Human life, however varied, consists in the performance of specific activities. Education that prepares for life is one that prepares definitely and adequately for these specific activities. However numerous and diverse they may be for any social class, they can be discovered. This requires only that one go out into the world of affairs and discover the particulars of which these affairs consist. These will show the abilities, attitudes, habits, appreciations, and forms of knowledge that men need. These will be the objectives of the curriculum. They will be numerous, definite, and particularized. The curriculum will then be that series of experiences which children and youth must have by way of attaining those objectives.

The word *curriculum* is Latin for a *race-course*, or the *race* itself—a place of deeds, or a series of deeds. As applied to education, it is that *series of things which children and youth must do and experience* by way of developing abilities to do the things well that make up the affairs of adult life; and to be in all respects what adults should be.

The developmental experiences exist upon two levels. On the one hand, there is the general experience of living the community life, without thought of the training values. In this way, through participation, one gets much of his education for participation in community life. In many things this provides most of the training; and in all essential things, much of it. But in all fields, this incidental or undirected developmental experience leaves the training imperfect. It is necessary, therefore, to supplement it with the conscious directed training of systematized education. The first level we shall call undirected training; and the second, directed training.

The curriculum may, therefore, be defined in two ways: (1) it is the entire range of experiences, both undirected and directed, concerned in unfolding the abilities of the individual; or (2) it is the series of consciously directed training experiences that the schools use for completing and perfecting the unfoldment. Our profession uses the term usually in the latter sense. But as education is coming more and more to be seen as a thing of experiences, and as the work- and play-experiences of general community life are being more and more utilized, the line of demarcation between directed and undirected training experience is rapidly disappearing. Education must be concerned with both, even though it does not direct both.

When the curriculum is defined as including both directed and undirected experiences, then its objectives are the total range of human abilities, habits, systems of knowledge, etc., that one should possess. These will be discovered by analytic survey. The curriculum- discoverer will first be an analyst of human nature and of human affairs. His task at this point is not at all concerned with "the studies"—later he will draw up appropriate studies as *means*, but he will not analyze the tools to be used in a piece of work as a mode of discovering the objectives of that work. His first task rather, in ascertaining the education appropriate for any special class, is to discover the total range of habits, skills, abilities, forms of thought, valuations, ambitions, etc., that its members need for the effective performance of their vocational labors; likewise, the total range needed for their civic activities; their health activities; their recreations; their language; their parental, religious, and general social activities. The program of analysis will be no narrow one. It will be wide as life itself. As it thus finds all the things that make up the mosaic of full-formed human life, it discovers the full range of educational objectives.

Notwithstanding the fact that many of these objectives are attained without conscious effort, the curriculum-discoverer must have all of them before him for his labors. Even though the scholastic curriculum will not find it necessary to aim at all of them, it is the function of education to see that all of them are attained. Only as he looks to the entire series can he discover the ones that require conscious effort. He will be content to let as much as possible be taken care of through undirected experiences. Indeed he will strive for such conditions that a maximum amount of the training can be so taken care of.

The curriculum of the schools will aim at those objectives that are not sufficiently attained as a result of the general undirected experience. This is to recognize that the total range of specific educational objectives breaks up into two sets: one, those arrived at through one's general experiences without his taking thought as to the training; the other, those that are imperfectly or not at all attained through such general experience. The latter are revealed, and distinguished from the former, by the presence of imperfections, errors, shortcomings. Like the symptoms of disease, these point unerringly to those objectives that require the systematized labors of directed training. Deficiencies point to the ends of conscious education. As the specific objectives upon which education is to be focused are thus pointed out, we are shown where the curriculum of the directed training is to be developed.

Let us illustrate. One of the most important things in which one is to be trained is the effective use of the mother-tongue. It is possible to analyze one's language activities and find all of the things one must do in effectively and correctly using it. Each of these things then becomes an objective of the training. But it is not necessary consciously to train for each of them. Let an individual grow up in a cultivated language-atmosphere, and he will learn to do, and be sufficiently practiced in doing, most of them, without any directed training. Here and there he will make mistakes. *Each mistake is a call for directed training.*

The curriculum of the directed training is to be discovered in the shortcomings of individuals after they have had all that can be given by the undirected training. This principle is recognized in the recent work of many investigators as to the curriculum of grammar. One of the earliest studies was that of Professor Charters.[1] Under his direction, the teachers of Kansas City undertook to discover the errors made by pupils in their oral and written language. For the oral errors the teachers carried notebooks for five days of one week and jotted down every grammatical error which they heard made by any pupil at any time during the day. For the errors in writing they examined the written work of the pupils for a period of three weeks. They discovered twenty-one types of errors in the oral speech and twenty-seven types in the written. The oral errors in the order of their frequency were as follows:—

1.	Confusion of past tense and past participle	24
2.	Failure of verb to agree with its subject in number and person	14
3.	Wrong verb	12
4.	Double negative	11
5.	Syntactical redundance	10
6.	Wrong sentence form	5
7.	Confusion of adjectives and adverbs	4
8.	Subject of verb not in nominative case	4
9.	Confusion of demonstrative adjective with personal pronoun	3
10.	Predicate nominative not in nominative case	2
11.	First personal pronoun standing first in a series	2

12. Wrong form of noun or pronoun	2
13. Confusion of past and present tenses	2
14. Object of verb or preposition not in the objective case	1
15. Wrong part of speech due to a similarity of sound	1
16. Incorrect comparison of adjectives	1
17. Failure of the pronoun to agree with its antecedent	0.3
18. Incorrect use of mood	0.3
19. Misplaced modifier	0.3
20. Confusion of preposition and conjunction	0.2
21. Confusion of comparatives and superlatives	0.1

Each error discovered is a symptom of grammatical ignorance, wrong habit, imperfect valuation, or careless attitude toward one's language. The nature of the deficiency points to the abilities and dispositions that are to be developed in the child by way of bringing about the use of the correct forms. Each grammatical shortcoming discovered, therefore, points to a needed objective of education. It points to a development of knowledge or attitude which the general undirected language experience has not sufficiently accomplished; and which must therefore be consciously undertaken by the schools.

Scientific method must consider both levels of the grammar curriculum. One task is to provide at the school as much as possible of a cultivated language-atmosphere in which the children can live and receive unconscious training. This is really the task of major importance, and provides the type of experience that should accomplish an ever-increasing proportion of the training. The other task is to make children conscious of their errors, to teach the grammar needed for correction or prevention, and to bring the children to put their grammatical knowledge to work in eliminating the errors. In proportion as the other type of experience is increased, this conscious training will play a diminishing role.

In the spelling field, Ayres, Jones, Cook and O'Shea, and others have been tabulating the words that children and adults use in writing letters, reports, compositions, etc. In this way they have been discovering the particularized objectives of training in spelling. But words are of unequal difficulty. Most are learned in the course of the reading and writing experience of the children without much conscious attention to the spelling. But here and there are words that are not so learned. Investigations, therefore, lay special emphasis upon the words that are misspelled. Each misspelled word reveals a directed-curriculum task. Here, as in the grammar, error is the symptom of training need; and the complete error-list points unerringly to the curriculum of conscious training.

In the vocational field, and on the technical side only, Indianapolis has provided an excellent example of method of discovering the objectives of training. Investigators, without pre-suppositions as to content of vocational curriculum, set out to discover the major occupations of the city, the processes to be performed in each, and the knowledge, habits and skills needed for effective work. They talked with expert workmen; and observed the work-processes. In their report, for each occupation, they present: (1) a list of tools and machines with which a workman must be skillful; (2) a list of the materials used in the work with which workers need to be familiar; (3) a list of items of general knowledge needed concerning jobs and processes; (4) the kinds of mathematical operations actually employed in the work; (5) the items or portions of science needed for control of processes; (6) the elements of drawing and design actually used in the work; (7) the characteristics of the English needed where language is vitally involved in one's work, as in commercial occupations; (8) elements of hygiene needed for keeping one's self up to the physical standards demanded by the work; and (9) the needed facts of economics.

Many of the things listed in such a survey are learned through incidental experience. Others cannot be sufficiently learned in this way. It is by putting the workers to work, whether adolescent or adult, and by noting the kinds of shortcomings and mistakes that show themselves when training is absent or deficient, that we can discover the curriculum tasks for directed vocational education.

The objectives of education are not to be discovered within just any kind or quality of human affairs. Occupational, civic, sanitary, or other activity may be poorly performed and productive of only meager results. At the other end of the scale are types of activity that are as well performed as it is in human nature to perform them, and which are abundantly fruitful in good results. Education is established upon the presumption that human activities exist upon different levels of quality or efficiency; that performance of low character is not good; that it can be eliminated through training; and that only the best or at least the best attainable is good enough. Whether in agriculture, building-trades, housekeeping, commerce, civic regulation, sanitation, or any other, education presumes that the best that is practicable is what ought to be. Education is to keep its feet squarely upon the earth; but this does not require that it aim lower than the highest that is practicable.

Let us take a concrete illustration. The curriculum-discoverer wishes, for example, to draw up a course of training in agriculture. He will go out into the practical world of agriculture as the only place that can reveal the objectives of agricultural education. He will start out without prejudgment as to the specific objectives. All that he needs for the work is pencil, notebook, and a discerning intelligence. He will observe the work of farmers; he will talk with them about all aspects of their work; and he will read reliable accounts which give insight into their activities. From these sources he will discover the particular things that the farmers do in carrying on each piece of work; the specific knowledge which the farmers employ in planning and performing each specific task; the kinds of judgments at which they must arrive; the types of problems they must solve; the habits and skills demanded by the tasks; the attitudes of mind, appreciations, valuations, ambitions, and desires, which motivate and exercise general control.

Facts upon all of these matters can be obtained from a survey of any agricultural region, however primitive or backward. But primitive agriculture is the thing which exists without any education. It is the thing education is to eliminate. The curriculum-discoverer, therefore, will not investigate just any agricultural situation. He will go to the farms that are most productive and most successful from every legitimate point of view. These will often be experimental or demonstration farms which represent what is practicable for the community, but which may not be typical of actual practices in that community. Where such general practices are inferior, agricultural education is to aim not at what is but at what ought to be.

When the farming practices are already upon a high plane, education has but a single function: it is to hand over these practices unchanged to the members of the new generation.

Where the practices of a region are primitive or backward, education has a double function to perform. It is not only to hand over to the new generation a proficiency that is equal to that of their fathers, but it is also to lift the proficiency of the sons to a height much beyond that of their fathers. Within such a region, therefore, agricultural

science, which shall, as does Medicine, cover a broad and varied field of comparative study.

And among the branches affliated with it will most certainly be found Pedagogical Hygiene, Pedagogical Anthropology, and Experimental Psychology.

Truly, Italy, the country of Lombroso, of De-Giovanni, and of Sergi, may claim the honour of being pre-eminent in the organisation of such a movement. In fact, these three scientists may be called the founders of the new tendency in Anthropology: the first leading the way in criminal anthropology, the second in medical anthropology, and the third in pedagogical anthropology. For the good fortune of science, all three of them have been the recognised leaders of their special lines of thought, and have been so prominent in the scientific world that they have not only made courageous and valuable disciples, but have also prepared the minds of the masses to receive the scientific regeneration which they have encouraged. (For reference, see my treatise "Pedagogical Anthropology.")[2]

Surely all this is something of which our country may be justly proud.

Today, however, those things which occupy us in the field of education are the interests of humanity at large, and of civilisation, and before such great forces we can recognise only one country—the entire world. And in a cause of such great importance, all those who have given any contribution, even though it be only an attempt not crowned with success, are worthy of the respect of humanity throughout the civilised world. So, in Italy, the schools of Scientific Pedagogy and the Anthropological Laboratories, which have sprung up in the various cities through the efforts of elementary teachers and scholarly inspectors, and which have been abandoned almost before they became definitely organised, have nevertheless a great value by reason of the faith which inspired them, and because of the doors they have opened to thinking people.

It is needless to say that such attempts were premature and sprang from too slight a comprehension of new sciences still in the process of development. Every great cause is born from repeated failures and from imperfect achievements. When St. Francis of Assisi saw his Lord in a vision, and received from the Divine lips the command—"Francis, rebuild my Church!"—he believed that the Master spoke of the little church within which he knelt at that moment. And he immediately set about the task, carrying upon his shoulders the stones with which he meant to rebuild the fallen walls. It was not until later that he became aware of the fact that his mission was to renew the Catholic Church through the spirit of poverty. But the St. Francis who so ingenuously carried the stones, and the great reformer who so miraculously led the people to a triumph of the spirit, are one and the same person in different stages of development. So we, who work toward one great end, are members of one and the same body; and those who come after us will reach the goal only because there were those who believed and laboured before them. And, like St. Francis, we have believed that by carrying the hard and barren stones of the experimental laboratory to the old and crumbling walls of the school, we might rebuild it. We have looked upon the aids offered by the materialistic and mechanical sciences with the same hopefulness with which St. Francis looked upon the squares of granite, which he must carry upon his shoulders.

Thus we have been drawn into a false and narrow way, from which we must free ourselves, if we are to establish true and living methods for the training of future generations.

To prepare teachers in the method of the experimental sciences is not an easy matter. When we shall have instructed them in anthropometry and psychometry in the most minute manner possible, we shall have only created machines, whose usefulness will be most doubtful. Indeed, if it is after this fashion that we are to initiate our teachers into experiment, we shall remain forever in the field of theory. The teachers of the old school, prepared according to the principles of metaphysical philosophy, understood the ideas of certain men regarded as authorities, and moved the muscles of speech in talking of them, and the muscles of the eye in reading their theories. Our scientific teachers, instead, are familiar with certain instruments and know how to move the muscles of the hand and arm in order to use these instruments; besides this, they have an intellectual preparation which consists of a series of typical tests, which they have, in a barren and mechanical way, learned how to apply.

The difference is not substantial, for profound differences cannot exist in exterior technique alone, but lie rather within the inner man. Not with all our initiation into scientific experiment have we prepared *new masters*, for, after all, we have left them standing without the door of real experimental science; we have not admitted them to the noblest and most profound phase of such study,—to that experience which makes real scientists.

And, indeed, what is a scientist? Not, certainly, he who knows how to manipulate all the instruments in the physical laboratory, or who in the laboratory of the chemist handles the various reactives with deftness and security, or who in biology knows how to make ready the specimens for the microscope. Indeed, it is often the case that an assistant has a greater dexterity in experimental technique than the master scientist himself. We give the name scientist to the type of man who has felt experiment to be a means guiding him to search out the deep truth of life, to lift a veil from its fascinating secrets, and who, in this pursuit, has felt arising within him a love for the mysteries of nature, so passionate as to annihilate the thought of himself. The scientist is not the clever manipulator of instruments, he is the worshipper of nature and he bears the external symbols of his passion as does the follower of some religious order. To this body of real scientists belong those who, forgetting, like the Trappists of the Middle Ages, the world about them, live only in the laboratory, careless often in matters of food and dress because they no longer think of themselves; those who, through years of unwearied use of the microscope, become blind; those who in their scientific ardour inoculate themselves with tuberculosis germs; those who handle the excrement of cholera patients in their eagerness to learn the vehicle through which the diseases are transmitted; and those who, knowing that a certain chemical preparation may be an explosive, still persist in testing their theories at the risk of their lives. This is the spirit of the men of science, to whom nature freely reveals her secrets, crowning their labours with the glory of discovery.

There exists, then, the "spirit" of the scientist, a thing far above his mere "mechanical skill," and the scientist is at the height of his achievement when the spirit has triumphed over the mechanism. When he has reached this point, science will receive from him not only new revelations of nature, but philosophic syntheses of pure thought.

It is my belief that the thing which we should cultivate in our teachers is more the *spirit* than the mechanical skill of the scientist; that is, the *direction* of the *preparation* should be toward the spirit rather than toward the mechanism. For example, when we considered the scientific preparation of teachers to be simply the acquiring of the technique of science, we did not attempt to make these elementary teachers perfect anthropologists, expert experimental psychologists, or masters of infant hygiene; we wished only to *direct them* toward the field of experimental science, teaching them to manage the various instruments with a certain degree of skill. So now, we wish to *direct* the teacher, trying to awaken in him, in connection with his own particular field, the school, that scientific *spirit* which opens the door for him to broader and bigger possibilities. In other words, we wish to awaken in the mind and heart of the educator an *interest in natural phenomena* to such an extent that, loving nature, he shall understand the anxious and expectant attitude of one who has prepared an experiment and who awaits a revelation from it.[3]

The instruments are like the alphabet, and we must know how to manage them if we are to read nature; but as the book, which contains the revelation of the greatest thoughts of an author, uses in the alphabet the means of composing the external symbols or words, so nature, through the mechanism of the experiment, gives us an infinite series of revelations, unfolding for us her secrets.

Now one who has learned to spell mechanically all the words in his spelling-book, would be able to read in the same mechanical way the words in one of Shakespeare's plays, provided the print were sufficiently clear. He who is initiated solely into the making of the bare experiment, is like one who spells out the literal sense of the words in the spelling-book; it is on such a level that we leave the teachers if we limit their preparation to technique alone.

We must, instead, make of them worshippers and interpreters of the spirit of nature. They must be like him who, having learned to spell, finds himself, one day, able to read behind the written symbols the *thought* of Shakespeare, or Goethe, or Dante. As may be seen, the difference is great, and the road long. Our first error was, however, a natural one. The child who has mastered the spelling-book gives the impression of knowing how to read. Indeed, he does read the signs over the shop doors, the names of newspapers, and every word that comes under his eyes. It would be very natural if, entering a library, this child should be deluded into thinking that he knew how to read the *sense* of all the books he saw there. But attempting to do this, he would soon feel that "to know how to read mechanically" is nothing, and that he needs to go back to school. So it is with the teachers whom we have thought to prepare for scientific pedagogy by teaching them anthropometry and psychometry.

But let us put aside the difficulty of preparing scientific masters in the accepted sense of the word. We will not even attempt to outline a programme of such preparation, since this would lead us into a discussion which has no place here. Let us suppose, instead, that we have already prepared teachers through long and patient exercises for the *observation* of *nature*, and that we have led them, for example, to the point attained by those students of natural sciences who rise at night and go into the woods and fields that they may surprise the awakening and the early activities of some family of insects in which they are interested. Here we have the scientist who, though he may be sleepy and tired with walking, is full of watchfulness, who is not aware that he is muddy or dusty, that the mist wets him, or the sun burns him; but is intent only upon not revealing in the least degree his presence, in order that the insects may, hour after hour, carry on peacefully those natural functions which he wishes to observe. Let us suppose these teachers to have reached the standpoint of the scientist who, half blind, still watches through his microscope the spontaneous movements of some particular infusory animalcule. These creatures seem to this scientific watcher, in their manner of avoiding

the school. The schools were at first furnished with the long, narrow benches upon which the children were crowded together. Then came science and perfected the bench. In this work much attention was paid to the recent contributions of anthropology. The age of the child and the length of his limbs were considered in placing the seat at the right height. The distance between the seat and the desk was calculated with infinite care, in order that the child's back should not become deformed, and, finally, the seats were separated and the width so closely calculated that the child could barely seat himself upon it, while to stretch himself by making any lateral movements was impossible. This was done in order that he might be separated from his neighbour. These desks are constructed in such a way as to render the child visible in all his immobility. One of the ends sought through this separation is the prevention of immoral acts in the schoolroom. What shall we say of such prudence in a state of society where it would be considered scandalous to give voice to principles of sex morality in education, for fear we might thus contaminate innocence? And, yet, here we have science lending itself to this hypocrisy, fabricating machines! Not only this; obliging science goes farther still, perfecting the benches in such a way as to permit to the greatest possible extent the immobility of the child, or, if you wish, to repress every movement of the child.

It is all so arranged that, when the child is well-fitted into his place, the desk and chair themselves force him to assume the position considered to be hygienically comfortable. The seat, the foot-rest, the desks are arranged in such a way that the child can never stand at his work. He is allotted only sufficient space for sitting in an erect position. It is in such ways that schoolroom desks and benches have advanced toward perfection. Every cult of the so-called scientific pedagogy has designed a model scientific desk. Not a few nations have become proud of their "national desk,"—and in the struggle of competition these various machines have been patented.

Undoubtedly there is much that is scientific underlying the construction of these benches. Anthropology has been drawn upon in the measuring of the body and the diagnosis of the age; physiology, in the study of muscular movements; psychology, in regard to perversion of instincts; and, above all, hygiene, in the effort to prevent curvature of the spine. These desks were indeed scientific, following in their construction the anthropological study of the child. We have here, as I have said, an example of the literal application of science to the schools.

I believe that before very long we shall all be struck with great surprise by this attitude. It will seem incomprehensible that the fundamental error of the desk should not have been revealed earlier through the attention given to the study of infant hygiene, anthropology, and sociology, and through the general progress of thought. The marvel is greater when we consider that during the past years there has been stirring in almost every nation a movement toward the protection of the child.

I believe that it will not be many years before the public, scarcely believing the descrip- tions of these scientific benches, will come to touch with wondering hands the amazing seats that were constructed for the purpose of preventing among our school children curvature of the spine!

The development of these scientific benches means that the pupils were subjected to a régime, which, even though they were born strong and straight, made it possible for them to become humpbacked! The vertebral column, biologically the most primitive, fundamental, and oldest part of the skeleton, the most fixed portion of our body, since the skeleton is the most solid portion of the organism—the vertebral column, which resisted and was strong through the desperate struggles of primitive man when he fought against the desert-lion, when he conquered the mammoth, when he quarried the solid rock and shaped the iron to his uses, bends, and cannot resist, under the yoke of the school.

It is incomprehensible that so-called *science* should have worked to perfect an instrument of slavery in the school without being enlightened by one ray from the movement of social liberation, growing and developing throughout the world. For the age of scientific benches was also the age of the redemption of the working classes from the yoke of unjust labour.

The tendency toward social liberty is most evident, and manifests itself on every hand. The leaders of the people make it their slogan, the labouring masses repeat the cry, scientific and socialistic publications voice the same movement, our journals are full of it. The underfed workman does not ask for a tonic, but for better economic conditions which shall prevent malnutrition. The miner who, through the stooping position maintained during many hours of the day, is subject to inguinal rupture, does not ask for an abdominal support, but demands shorter hours and better working conditions, in order that he may be able to lead a healthy life like other men.

And when, during this same social epoch, we find that the children in our schoolrooms are working amid unhygienic conditions, so poorly adapted to normal development that even the skeleton becomes deformed, our response to this terrible revelation is an orthopedic bench. It is much as if we offered to the miner the abdominal brace, or arsenic to the underfed workman.

Some time ago a woman, believing me to be in sympathy with all scientific innovations concerning the school, showed me with evident satisfaction *a corset or brace for pupils*. She had invented this and felt that it would complete the work of the bench.

Surgery has still other means for the treatment of spinal curvature. I might mention orthopedic instruments, braces, and a method of periodically suspending the child, by the head or shoulders, in such a fashion that the weight of the body stretches and thus straightens the vertebral column. In the school, the orthopedic instrument in the shape of the desk is in great favour today; someone proposes the brace—one step farther and it will be suggested that we give the scholars a systematic course in the suspension method!

All this is the logical consequence of a material application of the methods of science to the decadent school. Evidently the rational method of combating spinal curvature in the pupils is to change the form of their work—so that they shall no longer be obliged to remain for so many hours a day in a harmful position. It is a conquest of liberty which the school needs, not the mechanism of a bench.

Even were the stationary seat helpful to the child's body, it would still be a dangerous and unhygienic feature of the environment, through the difficulty of cleaning the room perfectly when the furniture cannot be moved. The foot-rests, which cannot be removed, accumulate the dirt carried in daily from the street by the many little feet. Today there is a general transformation in the matter of house furnishings. They are made lighter and simpler so that they may be easily moved, dusted, and even washed. But the school seems blind to the transformation of the social environment.

It behooves us to think of what may happen to the *spirit* of the child who is condemned to grow in conditions so artificial that his very bones may become deformed. When we speak of the redemption of the working man, it is always understood that beneath the most apparent form of suffering, such as poverty of the blood, or ruptures, there exists that other wound from which the soul of the man who is subjected to any form of slavery must suffer. It is at this deeper wrong that we aim when we say that the workman must be redeemed through liberty. We know only too well that when a man's very blood has been consumed or his intestines wasted away through his work, his soul must have lain oppressed in darkness, rendered insensible, or, it may be, killed within him. The *moral* degradation of the slave is, above all things, the weight that opposes the progress of humanity—humanity striving to rise and held back by this great burden. The cry of redemption speaks far more clearly for the souls of men than for their bodies.

What shall we say then, when the question before us is that of *educating children?*

We know only too well the sorry spectacle of the teacher who, in the ordinary schoolroom, must pour certain cut and dried facts into the heads of the scholars. In order to succeed in this barren task, she finds it necessary to discipline her pupils into immobility and to force their attention. Prizes and punishments are ever-ready and efficient aids to the master who must force into a given attitude of mind and body those who are condemned to be his listeners.

It is true that today it is deemed expedient to abolish official whippings and habitual blows, just as the awarding of prizes has become less ceremonious. These partial reforms are another prop approved of by science, and offered to the support of the decadent school. Such prizes and punishments are, if I may be allowed the expression, the *bench* of the soul, the instrument of slavery for the spirit. Here, however, these are not applied to lessen deformities, but to provoke them. The prize and the punishment are incentives toward unnatural or forced effort, and, therefore we certainly cannot speak of the natural development of the child in connection with them. The jockey offers a piece of sugar to his horse before jumping into the saddle, the coachman beats his horse that he may respond to the signs given by the reins; and, yet, neither of these runs so superbly as the free horse of the plains.

And here, in the case of education, shall man place the yoke upon man?

True, we say that social man is natural man yoked to society. But if we give a comprehensive glance to the moral progress of society, we shall see that little by little, the yoke is being made easier, in other words, we shall see that nature, or life, moves gradually toward triumph. The yoke of the slave yields to that of the servant, and the yoke of the servant to that of the workman.

All forms of slavery tend little by little to weaken and disappear, even the sexual slavery of woman. The history of civilisation is a history of conquest and of liberation. We should ask in what stage of civilisation we find ourselves and if, in truth, the good of prizes and of punishments be necessary to our advancement. If we have indeed gone beyond this point, then to apply such a form of education would be to draw the new generation back to a lower level, not to lead them into their true heritage of progress.

Something very like this condition of the school exists in society, in the relation between the government and the great numbers of the men employed in its administrative departments. These clerks work day after day for the general national good, yet they do not feel or see the advantage of their work in any immediate reward. That is, they do not realise that the state carries on its great business through their daily tasks, and that the whole nation is benefited by their work. For them the immediate good is promotion, as passing to a higher class is for the child in school. The man who loses sight of the really big aim of his work is like a child who has been placed in a class below his real standing: like a slave, he is cheated of something which is his right. His dignity as a man is reduced to the limits of the dignity of a machine which must be oiled if it is to be kept going, because it does not have within itself the impulse of life. All those petty things such as the desire for decorations or medals, are but artificial stimuli, lightening for the moment the dark, barren path in which he treads.

In the same way we give prizes to school children. And the fear of not achieving promotion, withholds the clerk from running away, and binds him to his monotonous work, even as the fear of not passing into the next class drives the pupil to his book. The reproof of the superior is in every way similar to the scolding of the teacher. The correction of badly executed clerical work is equivalent to the bad mark placed by the teacher upon the scholar's poor composition. The parallel is almost perfect.

But if the administrative departments are not carried on in a way which would seem suitable to a nation's greatness; if corruption too easily finds a place; it is the result of having extinguished the true greatness of man in the mind of the employee, and of having restricted his vision to those petty, immediate facts, which he has come to look upon as prizes and punishments. The country stands, because the rectitude of the greater number of its employees is such that they resist the corruption of the prizes and punishments, and follow an irresistible current of honesty. Even as life in the social environment triumphs against every cause of poverty and death, and proceeds to new conquests, so the instinct of liberty conquers all obstacles, going from victory to victory.

It is this personal and yet universal force of life, a force often latent within the soul, that sends the world forward.

But he who accomplishes a truly human work, he who does something really great and victorious, is never spurred to his task by those trifling attractions called by the name of "prizes," nor by the fear of those petty ills which we call "punishments." If in a war a great army of giants should fight with no inspiration beyond the desire to win promotion, epaulets, or medals, or through fear of being shot, if these men were to oppose a handful of pygmies who were inflamed by love of country, the victory would go to the latter. When real heroism has died within an army, prizes and punishments cannot do more than finish the work of deterioration, bringing in corruption and cowardice.

All human victories, all human progress, stand upon the inner force.

Thus a young student may become a great doctor if he is spurred to his study by an interest which makes medicine his real vocation. But if he works in the hope of an inheritance, or of making a desirable marriage, or if indeed he is inspired by any material advantage, he will never become a true master or a great doctor, and the world will never make one step forward because of his work. He to whom such stimuli are necessary, had far better never become a physician. Everyone has a special tendency, a special vocation, modest, perhaps, but certainly useful. The system of prizes may turn an individual aside from this vocation, may make him choose a false road, for him a vain one, and forced to follow it, the natural activity of a human being may be warped, lessened, even annihilated.

We repeat always that the world *progresses* and that we must urge men forward to obtain progress. But progress comes from the *new things that are born*, and these, not being foreseen, are not rewarded with prizes: rather, they often carry the leader to martyrdom. God forbid that poems should ever be born of the desire to be crowned in the Capitol! Such a vision need only come into the heart of the poet and the muse will vanish. The poem must spring from the soul of the poet, when he thinks neither of himself nor of the prize. And if he does win the laurel, he will feel the vanity of such a prize. The true reward lies in the revelation through the poem of his own triumphant inner force.

There does exist, however, an external prize for man; when, for example, the orator sees the faces of his listeners change with the emotions he has awakened, he experiences something so great that it can only be likened to the intense joy with which one discovers that he is loved. Our joy is to touch, and conquer souls, and this is the one prize which can bring us a true compensation.

Sometimes there is given to us a moment when we fancy ourselves to be among the great ones of the world. These are moments of happiness given to man that he may continue his existence in peace. It may be through love attained or because of the gift of a son, through a glorious discovery or the publication of a book; in some such moment we feel that there exists no man who is above us. If, in such a moment, someone vested with authority comes forward to offer us a medal or a prize, he is the important destroyer of our real reward—"And who are you?" our vanished illusion shall cry, "Who are you that recalls me to the fact that I am not the first among men? Who stands so far above me that he may give me a prize?" The prize of such a man in such a moment can only be Divine.

As for punishments, the soul of the normal man grows perfect through expanding, and punishment as commonly understood is always a form of *repression*. It may bring results with those inferior natures who grow in evil, but these are very few, and social progress is not affected by them. The penal code threatens us with punishment if we are dishonest within the limits indicated by the laws. But we are not honest through fear of the laws; if we do not rob, if we do not kill, it is because we love peace, because the natural trend of our lives leads us forward, leading us ever farther and more definitely away from the peril of low and evil acts.

Without going into the ethical or metaphysical aspects of the question, we may safely affirm that the delinquent before he transgresses the law, has, *if he knows of the existence of a punishment*, felt the threatening weight of the criminal code upon him. He has defined it, or he has been lured into the crime, deluding himself with the idea that he would be able to avoid the punishment of the law. But there has occurred within his mind, a *struggle between the crime and the punishment*. Whether it be efficacious in hindering crime or not, this penal code is undoubtedly made for a very limited class of individuals; namely, criminals. The enormous majority of citizens are honest without any regard whatever to the threats of the law.

The real punishment of normal man is the loss of the consciousness of that individual power and greatness which are the sources of his inner life. Such a punishment often falls upon men in the fullness of success. A man whom we would consider crowned by happiness and fortune may be suffering from this form of punishment. Far too often man does not see the real punishment which threatens him.

And it is just here that education may help.

Today we hold the pupils in school, restricted by those instruments so degrading to body and spirit, the desk—and material prizes and punishments. Our aim in all this is to reduce them to the discipline of immobility and silence,—to lead them,—where? Far too often toward no definite end.

Often the education of children consists in pouring into their intelligence the intellectual contents of school programmes. And often these programmes have been compiled in the official department of education, and their use is imposed by law upon the teacher and the child.

Ah, before such dense and wilful disregard of the life which is growing within these children, we should hide our heads in shame and cover our guilty faces with our hands!

Sergi says truly: "Today an urgent need imposes itself upon society: the reconstruction of methods in education and instruction, and he who fights for this cause, fights for human regeneration."

Notes

1. Trevisini, 1892.
2. Montessori: "L'Antropologia Pedagogica." Vallardi.
3. See in my treatise on Pedagogical Anthropology the chapter on "The Method Used in Experimental Sciences."

3

My Pedagogic Creed

John Dewey

Article One: What Education Is

I Believe that—all education proceeds by the participation of the individual in the social consciousness of the race. This process begins unconsciously almost at birth, and is continually shaping the individual's powers, saturating his consciousness, forming his habits, training his ideas, and arousing his feelings and emotions. Through this unconscious education, the individual gradually comes to share in the intellectual and moral resources which humanity has succeeded in getting together. He becomes an inheritor of the funded capital of civilization. The most formal and technical education in the world cannot safely depart from this general process. It can only organize it or differentiate it in some particular direction.

- The only true education comes through the stimulation of the child's powers by the demands of the social situations in which he finds himself. Through these demands he is stimulated to act as a member of a unity, to emerge from his original narrowness of action and feeling, and to conceive of himself from the standpoint of the welfare of the group to which he belongs. Through the responses which others make to his own activities he comes to know what these mean in social terms. The value which they have is reflected back into them. For instance, through the response which is made to the child's instinctive babblings the child comes to know what those babblings mean; they are transformed into articulate language, and thus the child is introduced into the consolidated wealth of ideas and emotions which are now summed up in language.
- This educational process has two sides, one psychological and one sociological, and that neither can be subordinated to the other, or neglected, without evil results following. Of these two sides, the psychological is the basis. The child's own instincts and powers furnish the material and give the starting-point for all education. Save as the efforts of the educator connect with some activity which the child is carrying on of his own initiative independent of the educator, education becomes reduced to a pressure from without. It may, indeed, give certain external results, but cannot truly be called educative. Without insight into the psychological structure and activities of the individual, the educative process will, therefore, be haphazard and arbitrary. If it chances to coincide with the

child's activity it will get a leverage; if it does not, it will result in friction, or disintegration, or arrest of the child's nature.

- Knowledge of social conditions, of the present state of civilization, is necessary in order properly to interpret the child's powers. The child has his own instincts and tendencies, but we do not know what these mean until we can translate them into their social equivalents. We must be able to carry them back into a social past and see them as the inheritance of previous race activities. We must also be able to project them into the future to see what their outcome and end will be. In the illustration just used, it is the ability to see in the child's babblings the promise and potency of a future social intercourse and conversation which enables one to deal in the proper way with that instinct.
- The psychological and social sides are organically related, and that education cannot be regarded as a compromise between the two, or a superimposition of one upon the other. We are told that the psychological definition of education is barren and formal—that is gives us only the idea of a development of all the mental powers without giving us any idea of the use to which these powers are put. On the other hand, it is urged that the social definition of education, as getting adjusted to civilization, makes of it a forced and external process, and results in subordinating the freedom of the individual to a preconceived social and political status.
- Each of these objections is true when urged against one side isolated from the other. In order to know what a power really is we must know what its end, use, or function is, and this we cannot know save as we conceive of the individual as active in social relationships. But, on the other hand, the only possible adjustment which we can give to the child under existing conditions is that which arises through putting him in complete possession of all his powers. With the advent of democracy and modern industrial conditions, it is impossible to foretell definitely just what civilization will be twenty years from now. Hence it is impossible to prepare the child for any precise set of conditions. To prepare him for the future life means to give him command of himself; it means so to train him that he will have the full and ready use of all his capacities that his eye and ear and hand may be tools ready to command, that his judgment may be capable of grasping the conditions under which it has to work, and the executive forces be trained to act economically and efficiently. It is impossible to reach this sort of adjustment save as constant regard it had to the individual's own powers, tastes, and interests—that is, as education is continually converted into psychological terms.

In sum, I believe that the individual who is to be educated is a social individual, and that society is an organic union of individuals. If we eliminate the social factor from the child we are left only with an abstraction; if we eliminate the individual factor from society, we are left only with an inert and lifeless mass. Education, therefore, must begin with a psychological insight into the child's capacities, interests, and habits. It must be controlled at every point by reference to these same considerations. These powers, interests, and habits must be continually interpreted—we must know what they mean. They must be translated into terms of their social equivalents—into terms of what they are capable of in the way of social service.

Article Two: What the School Is

I Believe that—the school is primarily a social institution. Education being a social process, the school is simply that form of community life in which all those agencies are concentrated that will be most effective in bringing the child to share in the inherited resources of the race, and to use his own powers for social ends.

- Education, therefore, is a process of living and not a preparation for future living.
- The school must represent present life—life as real and vital to the child as that which he carries on in the home, in the neighborhood, or on the playground.
- That education which does not occur through forms of life, forms that are worth living for their own sake, is always a poor substitute for the genuine reality, and tends to cramp and to deaden.
- The school, as an institution, should simplify existing social life; should reduce it, as it were, to an embryonic form. Existing life is so complex that the child cannot be brought into contact with it without either confusion or distraction; he is either overwhelmed by the multiplicity of activities which are going on, so that he loses his own power of orderly reaction, or he is so stimulated by these various activities that his powers are prematurely called into play and he becomes either unduly specialized or else disintegrated.
- As such simplified social life, the school life should grow gradually out of the home life; that it should take up and continue the activities with which the child is already familiar in the home.
- It should exhibit these activities to the child, and reproduce them in such ways that the child will gradually learn the meaning of them, and be capable of playing his own part in relation to them.
- This is a psychological necessity, because it is the only way of securing continuity in the child's growth, the only way of giving a background of past experience to the new ideas given in school.
- It is also a social necessity because the home is the form of social life in which the child has been nurtured and in connection with which he has had his moral training. It is the business of the school to deepen and extend his sense of the values bound up in his home life.
- Much of present education fails because it neglects this fundamental principle of the school as a form of community life. It conceives the school as a place where certain information is to be given, where certain lessons are to be learned, or where certain habits are to be formed. The value of these is conceived as lying largely in the remote future; the child must do these things for the sake of something else he is to do; they are mere preparations. As a result they do not become a part of the life experience of the child and so are not truly educative.
- The moral education centers upon this conception of the school as a mode of social life, that the best and deepest moral training is precisely that which one gets through having to enter into proper relations with others in a unity of work and thought. The present educational systems, so far as they destroy or neglect this unity, render it difficult or impossible to get any genuine, regular moral training.

- The child should be stimulated and controlled in his work through the life of the community.
- Under existing conditions far too much of the stimulus and control proceeds from the teacher, because of neglect of the idea of the school as a form of social life.
- The teacher's place and work in the school is to be interpreted from this same basis. The teacher is not in the school to impose certain ideas or to form certain habits in the child, but is there as a member of the community to select the influences which shall affect the child and to assist him in properly responding to these influences.
- The discipline of the school should proceed from the life of the school as a whole and not directly from the teacher.
- The teacher's business is simply to determine, on the basis of larger experience and riper wisdom, how the discipline of life shall come to the child.
- All questions of the grading of the child and his promotion should be determined by reference to the same standard. Examinations are of use only so far as they test the child's fitness for social life and reveal the place in which he can be of the most service and where he can receive the most help.

Article Three: The Subjectmatter of Education

I Believe that—the social life of the child is the basis of concentration, or correlation, in all his training or growth. The social life gives the unconscious unity and the background of all his efforts and of all his attainments.

- The subjectmatter of the school curriculum should mark a gradual differentiation out of the primitive unconscious unity of social life.
- We violate the child's nature and render difficult the best ethical results by introducing the child too abruptly to a number of special studies, of reading, writing, geography, etc., out of relation to this social life.
- The true center of correlation on the school subjects is not science, nor literature, nor history, nor geography, but the child's own social activities.
- Education cannot be unified in the study of science, or so-called nature study, because apart from human activity, nature itself is not a unity; nature in itself is a number of diverse objects in space and time, and to attempt to make it the center of work by itself is to introduce a principle of radiation rather than one of concentration.
- Literature is the reflex expression and interpretation of social experience; that hence it must follow upon and not precede such experience. It, therefore, cannot be made the basis, although it may be made the summary of unification.
- Once more that history is of educative value in so far as it presents phases of social life and growth. It must be controlled by reference to social life. When taken simply as history it is thrown into the distant past and becomes dead and inert. Taken as the record of man's social life and progress it becomes full of meaning. I believe, however, that it cannot be so taken excepting as the child is also introduced directly into social life.
- The primary basis of education is in the child's powers at work along the same general constructive lines as those which have brought civilization into being.

- The only way to make the child conscious of his social heritage is to enable him to perform those fundamental types of activity which make civilization what it is.
- In the so-called expressive or constructive activities as the center of correlation.
- This gives the standard for the place of cooking, sewing, manual training, etc., in the school.
- They are not special studies which are to be introduced over and above a lot of others in the way of relaxation or relief, or as additional accomplishments. I believe rather that they represent, as types, fundamental forms of social activity; and that it is possible and desirable that the child's introduction into the more formal subjects of the curriculum be through the medium of these constructive activities.
- The study of science is educational in so far as it brings out the materials and processes which make social life what it is.
- One of the greatest difficulties in the present teaching of science is that the material is presented in purely objective form, or is treated as a new peculiar kind of experience which the child can add to that which he has already had. In reality, science is of value because it gives the ability to interpret and control the experience already had. It should be introduced, not as so much new subjectmatter, but as showing the factors already involved in previous experience and as furnishing tools by which that experience can be more easily and effectively regulated.
- At present we lose much of the value of literature and language studies because of our elimination of the social element. Language is almost always treated in the books of pedagogy simply as the expression of thought. It is true that language is a logical instrument, but it is fundamentally and primarily a social instrument. Language is the device for communication; it is the tool through which one individual comes to share the ideas and feelings of others. When treated simply as a way of getting individual information, or as a means of showing off what one has learned, it loses its social motive and end.
- There is, therefore, no succession of studies in the ideal school curriculum. If education is life, all life has, from the outset, a scientific aspect, an aspect of art and culture, and an aspect of communication. It cannot, therefore, be true that the proper studies for one grade are mere reading and writing, and that at a later grade, reading, or literature, or science, may be introduced. The progress is not in the succession of studies, but in the development of new attitudes towards, and new interests in, experience.
- Education must be conceived as a continuing reconstruction of experience; that the process and the goal of education are one and the same thing.
- To set up any end outside of education, as furnishing its goal and standard, is to deprive the educational process of much of its meaning, and tends to make us rely upon false and external stimuli in dealing with the child.

Article Four: The Nature of Method

I Believe that—the question of method is ultimately reducible to the question of the order of development of the child's powers and interests. The law for presenting and treating material is the law implicit within the child's own nature. Because this is so I believe the following statements are of supreme importance as determining the spirit in which education is carried on.

- The active side precedes the passive in the development of the child-nature; that expression comes before conscious impression; that the muscular development precedes the sensory; that movements come before conscious sensations; I believe that consciousness is essentially motor or impulsive; that conscious states tend to project themselves in action.
- The neglect of this principle is the cause of a large part of the waste of time and strength in school work. The child is thrown into a passive, receptive, or absorbing attitude. The conditions are such that he is not permitted to follow the law of his nature; the result is friction and waste.
- Ideas (intellectual and rational processes) also result from action and devolve for the sake of the better control of action. What we term reason is primarily the law of order or effective action. To attempt to develop the reasoning powers, the powers of judgment, without reference to the selection and arrangement of means in action, is the fundamental fallacy in our present methods of dealing with this matter. As a result we present the child with arbitrary symbols. Symbols are a necessity in mental development, but they have their place as tools for economizing effort; presented by themselves they are a mass of meaningless and arbitrary ideas imposed from without.
- The image is the great instrument of instruction. What a child gets out of any subject presented to him is simply the images which he himself forms with regard to it.
- If nine-tenths of the energy at present directed towards making the child learn certain things were spent in seeing to it that the child was forming proper images, the work of instruction would be indefinitely facilitated.
- Much of the time and attention now given to the preparation and presentation of lessons might be more wisely and profitably expended in training the child's power of imagery and in seeing to it that he was continually forming definite vivid, and growing images of the various subjects with which he comes in contact in his experience.
- Interests are the signs and symptoms of growing power. I believe that they represent dawning capacities. Accordingly the constant and careful observation of interests is of the utmost importance for the educator.
- These interests are to be observed as showing the state of development which the child has reached.
- They prophesy the stage upon which he is about to enter.
- Only through the continual and sympathetic observation of childhood's interests can the adult enter into the child's life and see what it is ready for, and upon what material it could work most readily and fruitfully.
- These interests are neither to be humored nor repressed. To repress interest is to substitute the adult for the child, and so to weaken intellectual curiosity and alertness, to suppress initiative, and to deaden interest. To humor the interests is to substitute the transient for the permanent. The interest is always the sign of some power below; the important thing is to discover this power. To humor the interest is to fail to penetrate below the surface, and its sure result is to substitute caprice and whim for genuine interest.

- The emotions are the reflex of actions.
- To endeavor to stimulate or arouse the emotions apart from their corresponding activities is to introduce an unhealthy and morbid state of mind.
- If we can only secure right habits of action and thought, with reference to the good, the true, and the beautiful, the emotions will for the most part take care of themselves.
- Next to deadness and dullness, formalism and routine, our education is threatened with no greater evil than sentimentalism.
- This sentimentalism is the necessary result of the attempt to divorce feeling from action.

Article Five: The School and Social Progress

I Believe that—education is the fundamental method of social progress and reform.

- All reforms which rest simply upon the enactment of law, or the threatening of certain penalties, or upon changes in mechanical or outward arrangements, are transitory and futile.
- Education is a regulation of the process of coming to share in the social consciousness; and that the adjustment of individual activity on the basis of this social consciousness is the only sure method of social reconstruction.
- This conception has due regard for both the individualistic and socialistic ideals. It is duly individual because it recognizes the formation of a certain character as the only genuine basis of right living. It is socialistic because it recognizes that this right character is not to be formed by merely individual precept, example, or exhortation, but rather by the influence of a certain form of institutional or community life upon the individual, and that the social organism through the school, as its organ, may determine ethical results.
- In the ideal school we have the reconciliation of the individualistic and the institutional ideals.
- The community's duty to education is, therefore, its paramount moral duty. By law and punishment, by social agitation and discussion, society can regulate and form itself in a more or less haphazard and chance way. But through education society can formulate its own purposes, can organize its own means and resources, and thus shape itself with definiteness and economy in the direction in which it wishes to move.
- When society once recognizes the possibilities in this direction, and the obligations which these possibilities impose, it is impossible to conceive of the resources of time, attention, and money which will be put at the disposal of the education.
- It is the business of everyone interested in education to insist upon the school as the primary and most effective interest of social progress and reform in order that society may be awakened to realize what the school stands for, and arouse to the necessity of endowing the educator with sufficient equipment properly to perform his task.
- Education thus conceived marks the most perfect and intimate union of science and art conceivable in human experience.

- The art of thus giving shape to human powers and adapting them to social service is the supreme art; one calling into its service the best of artists; that no insight, sympathy, tact, executive power, is too great for such service.
- With the growth of psychological service, giving added insight into individual structure and laws of growth; and with growth of social science, adding to our knowledge of the right organization of individuals, all scientific resources can be utilized for the purposes of education.
- When science and art thus join hands the most commanding motive for human action will be reached, the most genuine springs of human conduct aroused, and the best service that human nature is capable of guaranteed.
- The teacher is engaged, not simply in the training of individuals, but in the formation of the proper social life.
- Every teacher should realize the dignity of his calling; that he is a social servant set apart for the maintenance of proper social order and the securing of the right social growth.
- In this way the teacher always is the prophet of the true God and the usherer in of the true kingdom of God.

4

The Public School and the Immigrant Child

Jane Addams

I am always diffident when I come before a professional body of teachers, realizing as I do that it is very easy for those of us who look on to bring indictments against result; and realizing also that one of the most difficult situations you have to meet is the care and instruction of the immigrant child, especially as he is found where I see him, in the midst of crowded city conditions.

And yet in spite of the fact that the public school is the great savior of the immigrant district, and the one agency which inducts the children into the changed conditions of American life, there is a certain indictment which may justly be brought, in that the public school too often separates the child from his parents and widens that old gulf between fathers and sons which is never so cruel and so wide as it is between the immigrants who come to this country and their children who have gone to the public school and feel that they have there learned it all. The parents are thereafter subjected to certain judgment, the judgment of the young which is always harsh and in this instance founded upon the most superficial standard of Americanism. And yet there is a notion of culture which we would define as a knowledge of those things which have been long cherished by men, the things which men have loved because thru generations they have softened and interpreted life, and have endowed it with value and meaning. Could this standard have been given rather than the things which they see about them as the test of so-called success, then we might feel that the public school has given at least the beginnings of culture which the child ought to have. At present the Italian child goes back to its Italian home more or less disturbed and distracted by the contrast between the school and the home. If he throws off the control of the home because it does not represent the things which he has been taught to value he takes the first step toward the Juvenile Court and all the other operations of the law, because he has prematurely asserted himself long before he is ready to take care of his own affairs.

We find in the carefully prepared figures which Mr. Commons and other sociologists have published that while the number of arrests of immigrants is smaller than the arrests of native born Americans, the number of arrests among children of immigrants is twice as large as the number of arrests among the children of native born Americans. It would seem that in spite of the enormous advantages which the public school gives to these children it in some way loosens them from the authority and control of their parents, and tends to send them, without a sufficient rudder and power of self-direction, into the perilous business of living. Can we not say, perhaps, that the schools ought to do more to connect these children with the best things of the past, to make them realize something of the beauty and charm of the language, the history, and the traditions which their parents represent. It is easy to cut them loose from their parents, it requires cultivation to tie them up in sympathy and understanding. The ignorant teacher cuts them off because he himself cannot understand the situation, the cultivated teacher fastens them because his own mind is open to the charm and beauty of that old-country life. In short, it is the business of the school to give to each child the beginnings of a culture so wide and deep and universal that he can interpret his own parents and countrymen by a standard which is worldwide and not provincial.

The second indictment which may be brought is the failure to place the children into proper relation toward the industry which they will later enter. Miss Arnold has told us that children go into industry for a very short time. I believe that the figures of the United States census show the term to be something like six years for the women in industry as against twenty-four years for men, in regard to continuity of service. Yet you cannot disregard the six years of the girls nor the twenty-four years of the boys, because they are the immediate occupation into which they enter after they leave the school—even the girls are bound to go thru that period—that is, the average immigrant girls are—before they enter the second serious business of life and maintain homes of their own. Therefore, if they enter industry unintelligently, without some notion of what it means, they find themselves totally unprepared for their first experience with American life, they are thrown out without the proper guide or clue which the public school might and ought to have given to them. Our industry has become so international, that it ought to be easy to use the materials it offers for immigrant children. The very processes and general principles which industry represents give a chance to prepare these immigrant children in a way which the most elaborated curriculum could not present. Ordinary material does not give the same international suggestion as industrial material does.

Third, I do not believe that the children who have been cut off from their own parents are going to be those who, when they become parents themselves, will know how to hold the family together and to connect it with the state. I should begin to teach the girls to be good mothers by teaching them to be good daughters. Take a girl whose mother has come from South Italy. The mother cannot adjust herself to the changed condition of housekeeping, does not know how to wash and bake here, and do the other things which she has always done well in Italy, because she has suddenly been transported from a village to a tenement house. If that girl studies these household conditions in relation to the past and to the present needs of the family, she is undertaking the very best possible preparation for her future obligations to a household of her own. And to my mind she can undertake it in no better way. Her own children are mythical and far away, but the little brothers and sisters pull upon her affections and her loyalty, and she longs to have their needs recognized in the school so that the school may give her some help. Her mother complains that the baby is sick in America because she cannot milk her own goat; she insists if she had her own goat's milk the baby would be quite well and flourishing, as the children were in Italy. If that girl can be taught that the milk makes the baby ill because it is not clean and be provided with a simple test that she may know when milk is clean, it may take her into the study not only of the milk within the four walls of the tenement house, but into the inspection of the milk of her district. The milk, however, remains good educational material, it makes even more concrete the connection which you would be glad to use between the household and the affairs of the American city. Let her not follow the mother's example of complaining about changed conditions; let her rather make the adjustment for her mother's entire household. We cannot tell what adjustments the girl herself will be called upon to make ten years from now; but we can give her the clue and the aptitude to adjust the family with which she is identified to the constantly changing conditions of city life. Many of us feel that, splendid as the public schools are in their relation to the immigrant child, they do not understand all of the difficulties which surround that child—all of the moral and emotional perplexities which constantly harass him. The children long that the school teacher should know something about the lives their parents lead and should be able to reprove the hooting children who make fun of the Italian mother because she wears a kerchief on her head, not only because they are rude but also because they are stupid. We send young people to Europe to see Italy, but we do not utilize Italy when it lies about the schoolhouse. If the body of teachers in our great cities could take hold of the immigrant colonies, could bring out of them their handicrafts and occupations, their traditions, their folk songs and folk lore, the beautiful stories which every immigrant colony is ready to tell and translate; could get the children to bring these things into school as the material from which culture is made and the material upon which culture is based, they would discover that by comparison that which they give them now is a poor, meretricious and vulgar thing. Give these children a chance to utilize the historic and industrial material which they see about them and they will begin to have a sense of ease in America, a first consciousness of being at home. I believe if these people are welcomed upon the basis of the resources which they represent and the contributions which they bring, it may come to pass that these schools which deal with immigrants will find that they have a wealth of cultural and industrial material which will make the schools in other neighborhoods positively envious. A girl living in a tenement household, helping along this tremendous adjustment, healing over this great moral upheaval which the parents have suffered and which leaves them bleeding and sensitive—such a girl has a richer experience and a finer material than any girl from a more fortunate household can have at the present moment.

I wish I had the power to place before you what it seems to me is the opportunity that the immigrant colonies present to the public school: the most endearing occupation of leading the little child, who will in turn lead his family, and bring them with him into the brotherhood for which they are longing. The immigrant child cannot make this demand upon the school because he does not know how to formulate it; it is for the teacher both to perceive it and to fulfil it.

5

Dare the School Build a New Social Order?

George S. Counts

3

If we may now assume that the child will be imposed upon in some fashion by the various elements in his environment, the real question is not whether imposition will take place, but rather from what source it will come. If we were to answer this question in terms of the past, there could, I think, be but one answer: on all genuinely crucial matters the school follows the wishes of the groups or classes that actually rule society; on minor matters the school is sometimes allowed a certain measure of freedom. But the future may be unlike the past. Or perhaps I should say that teachers, if they could increase sufficiently their stock of courage, intelligence, and vision, might become a social force of some magnitude. About this eventuality I am not over-sanguine, but a society lacking leadership as ours does, might even accept the guidance of teachers. Through powerful organizations they might at least reach the public conscience and come to exercise a larger measure of control over the schools than hitherto. They would then have to assume some responsibility for the more fundamental forms of imposition which, according to my argument, cannot be avoided.

That the teachers should deliberately reach for power and then make the most of their conquest is my firm conviction. To the extent that they are permitted to fashion the curriculum and the procedures of the school they will definitely and positively influence the social attitudes, ideals, and behavior of the coming generation. In doing this they should resort to no subterfuge or false modesty. They should say neither that they are merely teaching the truth nor that they are unwilling to wield power in their own right. The first position is false and the second is a confession of incompetence. It is my observation that the men and women who have affected the course of human events are those who have not hesitated to use the power that has come to them. Representing as they do, not the interests of the moment or of any special class, but rather the common and abiding interests of the people, teachers are under heavy social obligation to protect and further those interests. In this they occupy a relatively unique position in society. Also since the profession should embrace scientists and scholars of the highest rank, as well as teachers working at all levels of the educational system, it has at its disposal, as no other group, the knowledge and wisdom of the ages. It is scarcely thinkable that these men and women would ever act as selfishly or bungle as badly as have the so-called "practical" men of our generation—the politicians, the financiers, the industrialists. If all of these facts are taken into account, instead of shunning power, the profession should rather seek power and then strive to use that power fully and wisely and in the interests of the great masses of the people.

The point should be emphasized that teachers possess no magic secret to power. While their work should give them a certain moral advantage, they must expect to encounter the usual obstacles blocking the road to leadership. They should not be deceived by the pious humbug with which public men commonly flatter the members of the profession. To expect ruling groups or classes to give precedence to teachers on important matters, because of age or sex or sentiment, is to refuse to face realities. It was one of the proverbs of the agrarian order that a spring never rises higher than its source. So the power that teachers exercise in the schools can be no greater than the power they wield in society. Moreover, while organization is necessary, teachers should not think of their problem primarily in terms of organizing and presenting a united front to the world, the flesh, and the devil. In order to be effective they must throw off completely the slave psychology that has dominated the mind of the pedagogue more or less since the days of ancient Greece. They must be prepared to stand on their own feet and win for their ideas the support of the masses of the people. Education as a force for social regeneration must march hand in hand with the living and creative forces of the social order. In their own lives teachers must bridge the gap between school and society and play some part in the fashioning of those great common purposes which should bind the two together.

This brings us to the question of the kind of imposition in which teachers should engage, if they had the power. Our obligations, I think, grow out of the social situation. We live in troublous times; we live in an age of profound change; we live in an age of revolution. Indeed it is highly doubtful whether man ever lived in a more eventful period than the present. In order to match our epoch we would probably have to go back to the fall of the ancient empires or even to that unrecorded age when men first abandoned the natural arts of hunting and fishing and trapping and began to experiment with agriculture and the settled life. Today we are witnessing the rise of a civilization quite without precedent in human history—a civilization founded on science, technology, and machinery, possessing the most extraordinary power, and rapidly making of the entire world a single great society. Because of forces already released, whether in the field of economics, politics, morals, religion, or art, the old molds are being broken. And the peoples of the earth are everywhere seething with strange ideas and passions. If life were peaceful and quiet and undisturbed by great issues, we might with some show of wisdom center our attention on the nature of the child. But with the world as it is, we cannot afford for a single instant to remove our eyes from the social scene or shift our attention from the peculiar needs of the age.

In this new world that is forming, there is one set of issues which is peculiarly fundamental and which is certain to be the center of bitter and prolonged struggle. I refer to those issues which may be styled economic. President Butler has well stated the case: "For a generation and more past," he says, "the center of human interest has been moving from the point which it occupied for some four hundred years to a new point which it bids fair to occupy for a time equally long. The shift in the position of the center of gravity in human interest has been from politics to economics; from considerations that had to do with forms of government, with the establishment and protection of individual liberty, to considerations that have to do with the production, distribution, and consumption of wealth."

Consider the present condition of the nation. Who among us, if he had not been reared amid our institutions, could believe his eyes as he surveys the economic situation, or his ears as he listens to solemn disquisitions by our financial and political leaders on the cause and cure of the depression! Here is a society that manifests the most extraordinary contradictions: a mastery over the forces of nature, surpassing the wildest dreams of antiquity, is accompanied by extreme material insecurity; dire poverty walks hand in hand with the most extravagant living the world has ever known; an abundance of goods of all kinds is coupled with privation, misery, and even starvation; an excess of production is seriously offered as the underlying cause of severe physical suffering; breakfastless children march to school past bankrupt shops laden with rich foods gathered from the ends of the earth; strong men by the million walk the streets in a futile search for employment and with the exhaustion of hope enter the ranks of the damned; great captains of industry close factories without warning and dismiss the workmen by whose labors they have amassed huge fortunes through the years; automatic machinery increasingly displaces men and threatens society with a growing contingent of the permanently unemployed; racketeers and gangsters with the connivance of public officials fasten themselves on the channels of trade and exact toll at the end of the machine gun; economic parasitism, either within or without the law, is so prevalent that the tradition of honest labor is showing signs of decay; the wages paid to the workers are too meager to enable them to buy back the goods they produce; consumption is subordinated to production and a philosophy of deliberate waste is widely proclaimed as the highest economic wisdom; the science of psychology is employed to fan the flames of desire so that men may be enslaved by their wants and bound to the wheel of production; a government board advises the cotton-growers to plow under every third row of cotton in order to bolster up the market; both ethical and aesthetic considerations are commonly overridden by "hard-headed business men" bent on material gain; federal aid to the unemployed is opposed on the ground that it would pauperize the masses when the favored members of society have always lived on a dole; even responsible leaders resort to the practices of the witch doctor and vie with one another in predicting the return of prosperity; an ideal of rugged individualism, evolved in a simple pioneering and agrarian order at a time when free land existed in abundance, is used to justify a system which exploits pitilessly and without thought of the morrow the natural and human resources of the nation and of the world. One can only imagine what Jeremiah would say if he could step out of the pages of the Old Testament and cast his eyes over this vast spectacle so full of tragedy and of menace.

The point should be emphasized, however, that the present situation is also freighted with hope and promise. The age is pregnant with possibilities. There lies within our grasp the most humane, the most beautiful, the most majestic civilization ever fashioned by any people. This much at least we know today. We shall probably know more tomorrow. At last men have achieved such a mastery over the forces of nature that wage slavery can follow chattel slavery and take its place among the relics of the past. No longer are there grounds for the contention that the finer fruits of human culture must be nurtured upon the toil and watered by the tears of the masses. The limits to achievement set by nature have been so extended that we are today bound merely by our ideals, by our power of self-discipline, by our ability to devise social arrangements suited to an industrial age. If we are to place any credence whatsoever in the word of our engineers, the full utilization of modern technology at its present level of development should enable us to produce several times as much goods as were ever produced at the very peak of prosperity, and with the working day, the working year, and the working life reduced by half. We hold within our hands the power to usher in an age of plenty, to make secure the lives of all, and to banish poverty forever from the land. The only cause for doubt or pessimism lies in the question of our ability to rise to the stature of the times in which we live.

Our generation has the good or the ill fortune to live in an age when great decisions must be made. The American people, like most of the other peoples of the earth, have come to the parting of the ways; they can no longer trust entirely the inspiration which came to them when the Republic was young; they must decide afresh what they are to do with their talents. Favored above all other nations with the resources of nature and the material instrumentalities of civilization, they stand confused and irresolute before the future. They seem to lack the moral quality necessary to quicken, discipline, and give direction to their matchless energies. In a recent paper Professor Dewey has, in my judgment, correctly diagnosed our troubles: "the schools, like the nation," he says, "are in need of a central purpose which will create new enthusiasm and devotion, and which will unify and guide all intellectual plans."

This suggests, as we have already observed, that the educational problem is not wholly intellectual in nature. Our Progressive schools therefore cannot rest content with giving children an opportunity to study contemporary society in all of its aspects. This of course must be done, but I am convinced that they should go much farther. If the schools are to be really effective, they must become centers for the building, and not merely for the contemplation, of our civilization. This does not mean that we should endeavor to promote particular reforms through the educational system. We should, however, give to our children a vision of the possibilities which lie ahead and endeavor to enlist their loyalties and enthusiasms in the realization of the vision. Also our social institutions and practices, all of them, should be critically examined in the light of such a vision.

4

In *The Epic of America* James Truslow Adams contends that our chief contribution to the heritage of the race lies not in the field of science, or religion, or literature, or art but rather in the creation of what he calls the "American Dream"—a vision of a society in which the lot of the common man will be made easier and his life enriched and ennobled. If this vision has been a moving force in our history, as I believe it has, why should we not set ourselves the task of revitalizing and reconstituting it? This would seem to be the great need of our age, both in the realm of education and in the sphere of public life, because men must have something for which to live. Agnosticism, skepticism, or even experimentalism, unless the last is made flesh through the formulation of some positive social program, constitutes an extremely meager spiritual diet for any people. A small band of intellectuals, a queer breed of men at best, may be satisfied with such a spare ration, particularly if they lead the sheltered life common to their class; but the masses, I am sure, will always demand something more solid and substantial. Ordinary men and women crave a tangible purpose towards which to strive and which lends richness and dignity and meaning to life. I would consequently like to see our profession come to grips with the problem of creating a tradition that has roots in American soil, is in harmony with the spirit of the age, recognizes the facts of industrialism, appeals to the most profound impulses of our people, and takes into account the emergence of a world society.[1]

The ideal foundations on which we must build are easily discernible. Until recently the very word America has been synonymous throughout the world with democracy and symbolic to the oppressed classes of all lands of hope and opportunity. Child of the revolutionary ideas and impulses of the eighteenth century, the American nation became the embodiment of bold social experimentation and a champion of the power of environment to develop the capacities and redeem the souls of common men and women. And as her stature grew, her lengthening shadow reached to the four corners of the earth and everywhere impelled the human will to rebel against ancient wrongs. Here undoubtedly is the finest jewel in our heritage and the thing that is most worthy of preservation. If America should lose her honest devotion to democracy, or if she should lose her revolutionary temper, she will no longer be America. In that day, if it has not already arrived, her spirit will have fled and she will be known merely as the richest and most powerful of the nations. If America is not to be false to the promise of her youth, she must do more than simply perpetuate the democratic ideal of human relationships: she must make an intelligent and determined effort to fulfill it. The democracy of the past was the chance fruit of a strange conjunction of forces on the new continent; the democracy of the future can only be the intended offspring of the union of human reason, purpose, and will. The conscious and deliberate achievement of democracy under novel circumstances is the task of our generation.

Democracy of course should not be identified with political forms and functions—with the federal constitution, the popular election of officials, or the practice of universal suffrage. To think in such terms is to confuse the entire issue, as it has been confused in the minds of the masses for generations. The most genuine expression of democracy in the United States has little to do with our political institutions: it is a sentiment with respect to the moral equality of men: it is an aspiration towards a society in which this sentiment will find complete fulfillment. A society fashioned in harmony with the American democratic tradition would combat all forces tending to produce social distinctions and classes; repress every form of privilege and economic parasitism; manifest a tender regard for the weak, the ignorant, and the unfortunate; place the heavier and more onerous social burdens on the backs of the strong; glory in every triumph of man in his timeless urge to express himself and to make the world more habitable; exalt human labor of hand and brain as the creator of all wealth and culture; provide adequate material and spiritual rewards for every kind of socially useful work; strive for genuine equality of opportunity among all races, sects, and occupations; regard as paramount the abiding interests of the great masses of the people; direct the powers of government to the elevation and the refinement of the life of the common man; transform or destroy all conventions, institutions, and special groups inimical to the underlying principles of democracy; and finally be prepared as a last resort, in either the defense or the realization of this purpose, to follow the method of revolution. Although these ideals have never been realized or perhaps even fully accepted anywhere in the United States and have always had to struggle for existence with contrary forces, they nevertheless have authentic roots in the past. They are the values for which America has stood before the world during most of her history and with which the American people have loved best to associate their country. Their power and authority are clearly revealed in the fact that selfish interests, when grasping for some special privilege, commonly wheedle and sway the masses by repeating the words and kneeling before the emblems of the democratic heritage.

It is becoming increasingly clear, however, that this tradition, if its spirit is to survive, will have to be reconstituted in the light of the great social trends of the age in which we live. Our democratic heritage was largely a product of the frontier, free land, and a simple agrarian order. Today a new and strange and closely integrated industrial economy is rapidly sweeping over the world. Although some of us in our more sentimental moments talk wistfully of retiring into the more tranquil society of the past, we could scarcely induce many of our fellow citizens to accompany us. Even the most hostile critics of industrialism would like to take with them in their retirement a few such fruits of the machine as electricity, telephones, automobiles, modern plumbing, and various labor-saving devices, or at least be assured of an abundant supply of slaves or docile and inexpensive servants. But all such talk is the most idle chatter. For better or for worse we must take industrial civilization as an enduring fact: already we have become parasitic on its institutions and products. The hands of the clock cannot be turned back.

If we accept industrialism, as we must, we are then compelled to face without equivocation the most profound issue which this new order of society has raised and settle that issue in terms of the genius of our people—the issue of the control of the machine. In whose interests and for what purposes are the vast material riches, the unrivaled industrial equipment, and the science and technology of the nation to be used? In the light of our democratic tradition there can be but one answer to the question: all of these resources must be dedicated to the promotion of the welfare of the great masses of the people. Even the classes in our society that perpetually violate this principle are compelled by the force of public opinion to pay lip-service to it and to defend their actions in its terms. No body of men, however powerful, would dare openly to flout it. Since the opening of the century the great corporations have even found it necessary to establish publicity departments or to employ extremely able men as public relations counselors in order to persuade the populace that regardless of appearances they are lovers of democracy and devoted servants of the people. In this they have been remarkably successful, at least until the coming of the Great Depression. For during the past generation there have been few things in America that could not be bought at a price.

If the benefits of industrialism are to accrue fully to the people, this deception must be exposed. If the machine is to serve all, and serve all equally, it cannot be the property of the few. To ask these few to have regard for the common weal, particularly when under the competitive system they are forced always to think first of themselves or perish, is to put too great a strain on human nature. With the present concentration of economic power in the hands of a small class, a condition that is likely to get worse before it gets better, the survival or development of a society that could in any sense be called democratic is unthinkable. The hypocrisy which is so characteristic of our public life today is due primarily to our failure to acknowledge the fairly obvious fact that America is the scene of an irreconcilable conflict between two opposing forces. On the one side is the democratic tradition inherited from the past; on the other is a system of economic arrangements which increasingly partakes of the nature of industrial feudalism. Both of these forces cannot survive: one or the other must give way. Unless the democratic tradition is able to organize and conduct a successful attack on the economic system, its complete destruction is inevitable.

If democracy is to survive, it must seek a new economic foundation. Our traditional democracy rested upon small-scale production in both agriculture and industry and a rather general diffusion of the rights of property in capital and natural resources. The driving force at the root of this condition, as we have seen, was the frontier and free land. With the closing of the frontier, the exhaustion of free land, the growth of population, and the coming of large-scale production, the basis of ownership was transformed. If property rights are to be diffused in industrial society, natural resources and all important forms of capital will have to be collectively owned. Obviously every citizen cannot hold title to a mine, a factory, a railroad, a department store, or even a thoroughly mechanized farm. This clearly means that, if democracy is to survive in the United States, it must abandon its individualistic affiliations in the sphere of economics. What precise form a democratic society will take in the age of science and the machine, we cannot know with any assurance today. We must, however, insist on two things: first, that technology be released from the fetters and the domination of every type of special privilege; and, second, that the resulting system of production and distribution be made to serve directly the masses of the people. Within these limits, as I see it, our democratic tradition must of necessity evolve and gradually assume an essentially collectivistic pattern. The only conceivable alternative is the abandonment of the last vestige of democracy and the frank adoption of some modern form of feudalism.

Notes

Chapters 3 and 4, in George S. Counts, *Dare the School Build a New Social Order?* New York: John Day, 1932. Reprinted by permission of Martha L. Counts. Copyright renewed 1959 by George S. Counts.

1. In the remainder of the argument I confine attention entirely to the domestic situation. I do this, not because I regard the question of international relations unimportant, but rather because of limitations of space. All I can say here is that any proper conception of the world society must accept the principle of the moral equality of races and nations.

Part Two

Curriculum at Education's Center Stage

Introduction to Part Two

The readings in this part of the book lead into and reflect the reform efforts of the 1950s and 1960s. As the 1950s wore on, concerns arose that the curriculum lacked academic rigor and, as a consequence, academically talented young people were failing to realize their potential. This was especially worrisome to many Americans during the cold war in which the services of technological and scientific elites were deemed vital to national security. The popular belief that school programs in the Soviet Union were particularly rigorous only heightened public concern. James Conant (1959), former president of Harvard, was one of a number of well-publicized critics of school programs. Central to his recommendations was the consolidation of small high schools in order to provide greater numbers of advanced, specialized courses for gifted and academically inclined students.

These concerns nourished unprecedented federal and private support for curriculum development projects. The life cycle of these projects alternated between crisis and optimism. Mathematics, science, and foreign language curricula, especially programs for academically talented students, were perceived as directly relevant to national defense, and thus the first to receive attention.

Taking the lead in curriculum change efforts were subject matter specialists such as physicists and mathematicians as well as a healthy number of psychologists. They had faith that the specialists, armed with specialized knowledge and modern techniques, could set American schools back on track. They set out to construct curriculum materials that would form a foundation for transforming U.S. school programs.

From these heady beginnings, the curriculum reform movement took hold in universities and educational publishing for at least a decade. Yet, the movement was to end in controversy. On the one hand, its political aftermath is symbolized by what eventually came to be an open attack on the National Science Foundation for its role in the development of an elementary social studies curriculum, "Man: A Course of Study" (MACOS). Although this program had been designed to develop concepts through a process of discovery, its content, the nature of humans as a species, came to be seen as a repudiation of mainstream American values (Schaffarzick, 1979). As Jerome Bruner (2006, p. 4), who headed the MACOS project, observed many years later, "comparing the human condition in different cultures is, alas, too easily interpreted as finding fault with our own." On the other hand, scholarly rather than political controversy came from within academe, symbolized by Joseph Schwab's pronouncement that for all practical purposes, the curriculum field had reached a moribund state (Schwab, 1969).

This first two readings in Part Two look back to the field of curriculum leading up to the national reform movement. We begin with excerpts from Ralph Tyler's 1949 *Basic Principles of Curriculum and Instruction.* Tyler's slim book, a mere 128 pages cover to cover, signalled both a precursor to reform and a culmination of progressive educational thought. In particular, Tyler's rationale reaches back to the work of Franklin Bobbitt and others who sought to bring the field into the modern, scientific age. Their strategy for doing so was to develop curricula using a means–ends model. Tyler specifically organized the process around four questions: What are the purposes of an educational program? What experiences will further these purposes? How shall the program be organized? And, how shall it be evaluated?

These questions represent four design elements, the first of which Tyler gives special emphasis. "All aspects of the educational program," he writes, "are really means to accomplish basic educational purposes" (this volume, Chapter 6). Tyler's book does not venture to suggest specific objectives, but almost half of its pages are devoted to describing sources of information that support the selection of objectives. Three primary sources are discussed early on. The first is the study of learners, including their social and psychological needs. The second source, echoing Bobbitt's approach, includes studies of contemporary life to help identify "critical knowledge" and aid in the transfer of training. The third source of information includes suggestions from subject matter specialists. Tyler cites the Committee of Ten as an example, but not as an exemplar, of using subject matter specialists to identify educational objectives. This committee was formed in 1892 by the National Education Association, and was charged with the task of recommending objectives for secondary education. The committee organized its work around particular subjects such as geography, mathematics, and Latin. In this sense, subject matter expertise was foregrounded. From Tyler's perspective, however, the Committee of Ten misunderstood the role of subject matter in general education. For example, Tyler (this volume, Chapter 6) observes that the committee's "report in Mathematics outlines objectives for the beginning courses in the training of a mathematician" rather than asking: "What can your subject contribute to the education of young people who are not going to be specialists in your field?"

Following Tyler we have included a well-known essay by curriculum historian Herbert Kliebard (1975) dealing with the formative years of the curriculum field. Kliebard's focus is the influence of "scientific" curriculum making. We have already noted that the scientific strain of curriculum thought has tended to be dominant ever since the field's inception, and although Kliebard's piece is now over thirty years old, it is particularly relevant today. Specifically, Kliebard concludes that "scientific" approaches to curriculum and other educational matters have come to pervade and continue to shape contemporary educational thought. We need only cite current uses of standardized testing and the No Child Left Behind legislation as examples of Kliebard's point.

The next reading by Jerome Bruner suggests another approach with its own contemporary relevance. In 1959 the National Academy of Sciences organized a special conference on science curriculum change, especially how it pertained to gifted students, at Woods Hole, Massachusetts. Bruner directed the meeting and the attendees were scientists, psychologists interested in learning, and educators. The following year Bruner published an account of the proceedings as *The Process of Education* (1960). It quickly became a bestseller. The principles enunciated in this brief text—at less than 100 pages even shorter than Tyler's *Basic Principles*—were to prove cornerstones of the curriculum reform movement.

Three of the most important of these principles can be glimpsed in the opening paragraphs of the reading on MACOS. First he proclaims that children will learn more effectively if they discover ideas for themselves rather than the familiar method of being told those ideas. Second he asserts that children are capable of engaging in authentic intellectual activity from an early age; he rejects the popular notion that children cannot think until instruction has inculcated information to think with. Third he argues that children should focus on the structure of disciplines, how things are related, rather than on acquisition of mere information. All in all, Bruner contended, skill in discovery and grasp of disciplinary structures made possible significant transfer of training. Rather than commit to memory actual information, of which there was too much and it would soon be dated anyway, children would learn how to learn.

As noted, although MACOS was planned to be an elementary social studies curriculum, it did not fit neatly with how knowledge is conventionally carved up into school subjects. It drew on anthropology, biology, and linguistics, fields not well represented in elementary school curriculum, and dealt with possibly unfamiliar cultural practices without being judgmental. Thus MACOS's subject matter marked a bold departure from the intellectual habits and content of elementary social studies education in the United States. In effect, as one of Bruner's collaborators (Dow, 1991) put it, MACOS created a "parallel curriculum" which teachers were ill-prepared to implement. Moreover, this new curriculum was more single-mindedly academic, as the reading by Philip Jackson (this volume, Chapter 11) tellingly reveals, than teacher norms and student expectations for "the daily grind" of classrooms.

Both Tyler's rationale and Bruner's innovative curriculum package serve to underscore questions of educational purpose, and doing so sets the stage for the next pair of readings. These readings represent the great objectives debate. By the late 1960s, this debate had come to focus not on whether specific objectives should be used in curriculum planning, but on how objectives should be used, the form they should take, and the functions they should be expected to serve. The dominant camp again worked from a means–ends perspective that required curriculum developers to state clearly the objectives of a program prior to deciding its content or organization. Proponents of this approach, such as W. James Popham and others (e.g., Mager, 1962) argued that pre-specified, clearly stated, and measurable objectives are essential to curriculum planning for at least two reasons. First, educators without such objectives would not know the outcomes they seek to realize, and thus have little basis for deciding how to select or organize classroom activities. Second, without objectives, an evaluator would not know what to look for in determining a program's success or failure. Under the influence of this logic, thousands of American teachers learned to write behavioral objectives in the 1970s using standardized and tightly specified formats.

A dissenting position to the objectives movement is represented by Elliot Eisner's article, "Educational Objectives—Help or Hindrance?" Eisner questioned both the practicality of pre-specified objectives and the underlying assumptions on which they are based. On the practical side, he saw two problems. First, the potential outcomes of instruction are usually so numerous that it would be difficult to anticipate all of these objectives with a high degree of specificity. Second, the objectives-first sequence does not seem to be borne out in practice. That is, while teachers often begin with explicit objectives, they also allow the selection of content and activities to inform and modify objectives as instructional activities unfold in the classroom. To put this another way, Eisner argued that the rationality of teaching is more dynamic, more interactive, and less mechanistic than the proponents of behavioral objectives had assumed. Moreover, Eisner asserts that evaluators have confused objectives with standards. Standards can be applied in a fairly routine manner, but using objectives as criteria for assessment unavoidably entails an element of judgment on the part of the evaluator.

A related criticism was that the objectives movement jumped too quickly from objectives to outcomes, thereby by-passing practice altogether. This concern made Philip Jackson's book, *Life in Classrooms*, particularly distinctive. Jackson did not vault over classrooms, but jumped right into them. In the brief excerpts we have taken from his book, Jackson offers a number of arguments for why the daily routines of practice should be of paramount concern for those interested in school curriculum. These routines are often overshadowed because they are commonplace, repetitive, and ordinary. Herein we find an interesting paradox; for if Jackson is right, practice is ignored for the very reasons that it is so important. Classroom routines have an enduring influence specifically because they are commonplace, repetitive, and ordinary. In addition, Jackson argues that these routines are more than simply ways of delivering subject matter or acquiring academic skills. Rather, "the daily grind" itself teaches a hidden curriculum of unspoken expectations, and these expectations are what most often determine a student's school success or failure. If researchers or evaluators were to examine an educational program solely on the basis of its stated objectives, the hidden curriculum would in all likelihood remain just that—hidden.

The final reading of Part Two is by the philosopher of education Maxine Greene. Like Jackson, Greene is concerned with the implicit and hidden messages of school curricula while openly displaying disenchantment with conventional curriculum designs. Greene argues that existing school programs are largely irrelevant to the existential desires for meaning and direction salient in the lives of young people. Moreover, such desires could not be addressed by rearrangement of the existing curriculum or its better presentation. Instead, Greene argued that the curriculum must engage students in an "interior journey," adding that:

> Not only may it [an interior journey] result in the effecting of new syntheses within experience; it may result in an awareness of the process of knowing, of believing, of perceiving. It may even result in an understanding of the ways in which meanings have been sedimented in an individual's own personal history. . . . But then there opens up the possibility of presenting curriculum in such a way that it does not impose or enforce. (this volume, Chapter 12)

Thus, Greene sees educational possibilities for countering Jackson's "daily grind."

References

Bruner, J. S. (1960). *The process of education.* Cambridge, MA: Harvard University Press.

Bruner, J. S. (2006). *In search of pedagogy, Volume I.* New York: Routledge.

Conant, J. B. (1959). *The American high school today.* New York: McGraw-Hill.

Dow, P. B. (1991). *Schoolhouse politics.* Cambridge, MA: Harvard University Press.

Mager, R. F. (1962). *Preparing instructional objectives.* Palo Alto, CA: Fearon.

Schaffarzick, J. (1979). Federal curriculum reform: A crucible for value conflict. In J. Schaffarzick & G. Sykes (Eds.), *Value conflicts and curriculum issues* (pp. 1–24). Berkeley: McCutchan.

Schwab, Joseph J. (1969). The practical: A language for curriculum. *School Review, 78(1),* 1–23.

6
Basic Principles of Curriculum and Instruction

Ralph W. Tyler

Introduction

This small book[1] attempts to explain a rationale for viewing, analyzing and interpreting the curriculum and instructional program of an educational institution. It is not a textbook, for it does not provide comprehensive guidance and readings for a course. It is not a manual for curriculum construction since it does not describe and outline in detail the steps to be taken by a given school or college that seeks to build a curriculum. This book outlines one way of viewing an instructional program as a functioning instrument of education. The student is encouraged to examine other rationales and to develop his own conception of the elements and relationships involved in an effective curriculum.

The rationale developed here begins with identifying four fundamental questions which must be answered in developing any curriculum and plan of instruction. These are:

1. What educational purposes should the school seek to attain?
2. What educational experiences can be provided that are likely to attain these purposes?
3. How can these educational experiences be effectively organized?
4. How can we determine whether these purposes are being attained?

This book suggests methods for studying these questions. No attempt is made to answer these questions since the answers will vary to some extent from one level of education to another and from one school to another. Instead of answering the questions, an explanation is given of procedures by which these questions can be answered. This constitutes a rationale by which to examine problems of curriculum and instruction.

1. What Educational Purposes should the School Seek to Attain?

Many educational programs do not have clearly defined purposes. In some cases one may ask a teacher of science, of English, of social studies, or of some other subject what objectives are being aimed at and get no satisfactory reply. The teacher may say in effect that he aims to develop a well-educated person and that he is teaching

English or social studies or some other subject because it is essential to a well-rounded education. No doubt some excellent educational work is being done by artistic teachers who do not have a clear conception of goals but do have an intuitive sense of what is good teaching, what materials are significant, what topics are worth dealing with and how to present material and develop topics effectively with students. Nevertheless, if an educational program is to be planned and if efforts for continued improvement are to be made, it is very necessary to have some conception of the goals that are being aimed at. These educational objectives become the criteria by which materials are selected, content is outlined, instructional procedures are developed and tests and examinations are prepared. All aspects of the educational program are really means to accomplish basic educational purposes. Hence, if we are to study an educational program systematically and intelligently we must first be sure as to the educational objectives aimed at.

But how are objectives obtained? Since they are consciously willed goals, that is, ends that are desired by the school staff, are they not simply matters of personal preference of individuals or groups? Is there any place for a systematic attack upon the problem of what objectives to seek?

It is certainly true that in the final analysis objectives are matters of choice, and they must therefore be the considered value judgments of those responsible for the school. A comprehensive philosophy of education is necessary to guide in making these judgments. And, in addition, certain kinds of information and knowledge provide a more intelligent basis for applying the philosophy in making decisions about objectives. If these facts are available to those making decisions, the probability is increased that judgments about objectives will be wise and that the school goals will have greater significance and greater validity. For this reason, a large part of the so-called scientific study of the curriculum during the past thirty years has concerned itself with investigations that might provide a more adequate basis for selecting objectives wisely. The technical literature of the curriculum field includes hundreds of studies that collected information useful to curriculum groups in selecting objectives.

Accepting the principle that investigations can be made which will provide information and knowledge useful in deciding about objectives, the question is then raised what sources can be used for getting information that will be helpful in this way. A good deal of controversy goes on between essentialists and progressives, between subject specialists and child psychologists, between this group and that school group over the question of the basic source from which objectives can be derived. The progressive emphasizes the importance of studying the child to find out what kinds of interests he has, what problems he encounters, what purposes he has in mind. The progressive sees this information as providing the basic source for selecting objectives. The essentialist, on the other hand, is impressed by the large body of knowledge collected over many thousands of years, the so-called cultural heritage, and emphasizes this as the primary source for deriving objectives. The essentialist views objectives as essentially the basic learnings selected from the vast cultural heritage of the past.

Many sociologists and others concerned with the pressing problems of contemporary society see in an analysis of contemporary society the basic information from which objectives can be derived. They view the school as the agency for helping young people to deal effectively with the critical problems of contemporary life. If they can determine what these contemporary problems are then the objectives of the school are to provide those knowledges, skills, attitudes, and the like that will help people to deal intelligently with these contemporary problems. On the other hand, the educational philosophers recognize that there are basic values in life, largely transmitted from one generation to another by means of education. They see the school as aiming essentially at the transmission of the basic values derived by comprehensive philosophic study and hence see in educational philosophy the basic source from which objectives can be derived.

The point of view taken in this course is that no single source of information is adequate to provide a basis for wise and comprehensive decisions about the objectives of the school. Each of these sources has certain values to commend it. Each source should be given some consideration in planning any comprehensive curriculum program. Hence, we shall turn to each of the sources in turn to consider briefly what kinds of information can be obtained from the source and how this information may suggest significant educational objectives.

Studies of the Learners Themselves as a Source of Educational Objectives

Education is a process of changing the behavior patterns of people. This is using behavior in the broad sense to include thinking and feeling as well as overt action. When education is viewed in this way, it is clear that educational objectives, then, represent the kinds of changes in behavior that an educational institution seeks to bring about in its students. A study of the learners themselves would seek to identify needed changes in behavior patterns of the students which the educational institution should seek to produce.

An investigation of children in the elementary school in a certain community may reveal dietary deficiency and inadequate physical condition. These facts may suggest objectives in health education and in social studies but they suggest objectives only when viewed in terms of some conception of normal or desirable physical condition. In a society which takes dietary deficiencies for granted, there would be little likelihood of inferring any educational objectives from such data. Correspondingly, studies of adolescence during the depression indicated that a considerable number were greatly perturbed over the possibility that they would be unable to find work upon graduation. This does not automatically suggest the need for vocational guidance or occupational preparation. Studies of the learner suggest educational objectives only when the information about the learner is compared with some desirable standards, some conception of acceptable norms, so that the difference between the present condition of the learner and the acceptable norm can be identified. This difference or gap is what is generally referred to as a need.

There is another sense in which the term "need" is used in the psychological writings of Prescott, Murray, and others. They view a human being as a dynamic organism, an energy system normally in equilibrium between internal forces produced by the energy of the oxidation of food and external conditions. To keep the system in equilibrium it is necessary that certain "needs" be met. That is, certain tensions are produced which result in disequilibrium unless these tensions are relieved. In this sense every organism is continually meeting its needs, that is, reacting in such a way as to relieve these forces that bring about imbalance. In these terms one of the problems of education is to channel the means by which these needs are met so that the resulting behavior is socially acceptable, yet at the same time the needs are met and the organism is not under continuous, unrelieved tensions. Prescott classifies these needs into three types: physical needs such as the need for food, for water, for activity, for sex and the like; social needs such as the need for affection, for belonging, for status or respect from this social group; and integrative needs, the need to relate one's self to something larger and beyond one's self, that is, the need for a philosophy of life. In this sense all children have the same needs and it is the responsibility of the school as with every other social institution to help children to get these needs met in a way which is not only satisfying but provides the kind of behavior patterns that are personally and socially significant. A study of such needs in a given group of children would involve identifying those needs that are not being properly satisfied and an investigation of the role the school can play in helping children to meet these needs. This may often suggest educational objectives in the sense of indicating certain knowledge, attitudes, skills, and the like, the development of which would help children to meet these needs more effectively. These studies may also suggest ways in which the school can help to give motivation and meaning to its activities by providing means for children to meet psychological needs that are not well satisfied outside the school.

Studies of Contemporary Life Outside the School

The effort to derive objectives from studies of contemporary life largely grew out of the difficulty of accomplishing all that was laid upon the schools with the greatly increased body of knowledge which developed after the advent of science and the Industrial Revolution. Prior to this time the body of material that was considered academically respectable was sufficiently small so that there was little problem in selecting the elements of most importance from the cultural heritage. With the tremendous increase in knowledge accelerating with each generation after the advent of science, the schools found it no longer possible to include in their program all that was accepted by scholars. Increasingly the question was raised as to the contemporary significance of particular items of knowledge or particular skills and abilities. Herbert Spencer in his essay on *What Knowledge Is of Most Worth?* attempted to deal with this problem in a way that has characterized many of the efforts over the past century. Although this represented the interpretation of informal observations rather than systematic studies, the technique used by Spencer in some respects is very similar to techniques used by investigators today.

When the First World War required the training of a large number of people in the skilled trades, training that must take place in a relatively short period of time, the older and slower apprentice systems were no longer adequate. The idea of job analysis developed and was widely used to work out training programs in World War I which would speed up the training of people for the skilled trades and various types of technology. In essence, job analysis is simply a method of analyzing the activities carried on by a worker in a particular field in order that a training program can be focused upon those critical activities performed by this worker. In essence, most studies of contemporary life have a somewhat similar "logic."

Today there are two commonly used arguments for analyzing contemporary life in order to get suggestions for educational objectives. The first of these arguments is that because contemporary life is so complex and because life is continually changing, it is very necessary to focus educational efforts upon the critical aspects of this complex life and upon those aspects that are of importance today so that we do not waste the time of students in learning things that were important fifty years ago but no longer have significance at the same time that we are neglecting areas of life that are now important and for which the schools provide no preparation.

A second argument for the study of contemporary life grows out of the findings relating to transfer of training. As long as educators believed that it was possible for a student to train his mind and the various faculties of the mind in general and that he could use these faculties under whatever conditions might be appropriate, there was less need for analyzing contemporary life to suggest objectives. According to this view the important objectives were to develop the several faculties of the mind and as life developed the student would be able to use this trained mind to meet the conditions that he encountered. Studies of transfer of training, however, indicated that the student was much more likely to apply his learning when he recognized the similarity between the situations encountered in life and the situations in which the learning took place. Furthermore, the student was more likely to perceive the similarity between the life situations and the learning situations when two conditions were met: (1) the life situations and the learning situations were obviously alike in many respects, and (2) the student was given practice in seeking illustrations in his life outside of school for the application of things learned in school. These findings are used to support the value of analyzing contemporary life to identify learning objectives for the school that can easily be related to the conditions and opportunities of contemporary life for use of these kinds of learning.

Using studies of contemporary life as a basis for deriving objectives has sometimes been criticized particularly when it is the sole basis for deriving objectives. One of the most frequent criticisms has been that the identification of contemporary activities does not in itself indicate their desirability. The finding, for example, that large numbers of people are engaged in certain activities does not per se indicate that these activities should be taught to students in the school. Some of these activities may be harmful and in place of being taught in the school some attention might need to be given to their elimination. The second type of criticism is the type made by essentialists who refer to studies of contemporary life as the cult of "presentism." These critics point out that because life is continually changing, preparing students to solve the problems of today will make them unable to deal with the problems they will encounter as adults because the problems will have changed. A third kind of criticism is that made by some progressives who point out that some of the critical problems of contemporary life and some of the common activities engaged in by adults are not in themselves interesting to children nor of concern to children, and to assume that they should become educational objectives for children of a given age neglects the importance of considering the children's interests and children's needs as a basis for deriving objectives.

These criticisms in the main apply to the derivation of objectives solely from studies of contemporary life. When objectives derived from studies of contemporary life are checked against other sources and in terms of an acceptable educational philosophy, the first criticism is removed. When studies of contemporary life are used as a basis for indicating important areas that appear to have continuing importance, and when the studies of contemporary life suggest areas in which students can have opportunity to practice what they learn in school, and also when an effort is made to develop in students an intelligent understanding of the basic principles involved in these matters, the claim that such a procedure involves a worship of "presentism" is largely eliminated. Finally, if studies of contemporary life are used to indicate directions in which educational objectives may aim, while the choice of particular objectives for given children takes into account student interests and needs, these studies of contemporary life can be useful without violating relevant criteria of appropriateness for students of particular age levels. Hence, it is worthwhile to utilize data obtained from studies of contemporary life as one source for suggesting possible educational objectives.

Suggestions About Objectives from Subject Specialists

This is the source of objectives most commonly used in typical schools and colleges. School and college textbooks are usually written by subject specialists and largely reflect their views. Courses of study prepared by school and college groups are usually worked out by subject specialists and represent their conception of objectives that the school should attempt to attain. The reports of the Committee of Ten that appeared at the turn of the century had a most profound effect upon American secondary education for at least twenty-five years. Its reports were prepared by subject specialists and the objectives suggested by them were largely aimed at by thousands of secondary schools.

Many people have criticized the use of subject specialists on the grounds that the objectives they propose are too technical, too specialized, or in other ways are inappropriate for a large number of the school students. Probably the inadequacy of many previous lists of objectives suggested by subject specialists grows out of the fact that these specialists have not been asked the right questions. It seems quite clear that the Committee of Ten thought it was answering the question: What should be the elementary instruction for students who are later to carry on much more advanced work in the field? Hence, the report in History, for example, seems to present objectives for the beginning courses for persons who are training to be historians. Similarly the report in Mathematics outlines objectives for the beginning courses in the training of a mathematician. Apparently each committee viewed its job as outlining the elementary courses with the idea that these students taking these courses would go on for more and more advanced work, culminating in major specialization at the college or university level. This is obviously not the question that subject specialists should generally be asked regarding the secondary school curriculum. The question which they should be asked runs somewhat like this: What can your subject contribute to the education of young people who are not going to be specialists in your field; what can your subject contribute to the layman, the garden variety of citizen? If subject specialists can present answers to this question, they can make an important contribution, because, presumably, they have a considerable knowledge of the specialized field and many of them have had opportunity both to see what this subject has done for them and for those with whom they work. They ought to be able to suggest possible contributions, knowing the field as well as they do, that it might make to others in terms of its discipline, its content, and the like.

Some of the more recent curriculum reports do indicate that subject specialists can make helpful suggestions in answers to this question. The various reports published by the Commission on the Secondary School Curriculum of the Progressive Education

Association beginning with "Science in General Education," including "Mathematics in General Education," "Social Studies in General Education," and other titles have been very useful and have thrown some light on the question, "What can this subject contribute to the education of young people who are not to specialize in it?" Other groups have recently prepared somewhat similar reports which also seem promising. Committee reports from the National Council of Mathematics Teachers, the National Council of English Teachers, the National Council of Social Studies Teachers, are cases in point. In general, they recognize much more clearly than did the committee preparing reports for the Committee of Ten that the subject is expected to make contributions to a range of students not considered in the earlier reports. In general, the more recent reports will be found useful as an additional source for suggestions about objectives.

Most of the reports of subject groups do not stop with objectives and many of them do not list objectives specifically. Most of them begin with some outline indicating their conception of the subject field itself and then move on to indicate ways in which it can be used for purposes of general education. Persons working on the curriculum will find it necessary to read the reports in some detail and at many places draw inferences from the statements regarding objectives implied. In general, two kinds of suggestions can be got from the reports as far as objectives are concerned. The first is a list of suggestions regarding the broad functions a particular subject can serve, the second is with regard to particular contributions the subject can make to other large functions which are not primarily functions of the subject concerned.

Let me illustrate these two types of suggestions that can be got from these reports. Recent reports of English groups, for example, have suggested educational functions of English as a study of language. The first function is to develop effective communication including both the communication of meaning and the communication of form. The second type of contribution is to effective expression, including in expression the effort of the individual to make internal adjustments to various types of internal and external pressures. A third function of language is to aid in the clarification of thought as is provided, for example, by the use of basic English as a means of aiding students to see whether they understand ideas clearly enough to translate them into operational words. This last function of clarification of thought is well illustrated by the statement of George Herbert Palmer that when confused he used to write himself clearheaded.

In the realm of literature these English committees see various kinds of contributions in terms of major functions literature can serve. Some emphasize its value in personal exploration. Literature in this sense can provide an opportunity for the individual to explore kinds of life and living far beyond his power immediately to participate in, and also give him a chance to explore vicariously kinds of situations which are too dangerous, too fraught with consequences for him to explore fully in reality. A number of committee reports speak of the general function of literature in providing greater extension to the experience of young people, not limited by geographic opportunities, nor limited in time nor limited in social class or types of occupations or social groups with which they can participate. In this case literature becomes the means of widely extending the horizon of the reader through vicarious experience. Another function of literature is to develop reading interests and habits that are satisfying and significant to the reader. Some English committees stress as an important objective to develop increasing skill in interpreting literary material, not only skill in analyzing the logical development and exposition of ideas but also the whole range of things including human motives which are formulated in written language and can therefore be subject to study and critical interpretation. Finally, some English committees propose that literature serves the function of appreciation, including both an opportunity for significant emotional reactions to literary forms and also opportunities for critical appraisal both of form and content, and a means thereby of developing standards of taste in literature.

These suggestions with regard to possible major functions of language and literature provide large headings under which to consider possible objectives which the school can aim at through language and literature. Such an analysis indicates the pervasive nature of the contribution that language and literature might possibly make to the development of children, adolescents, or adults. They suggest objectives that are more than knowledge, skills, and habits; they involve modes of thinking, or critical interpretation, emotional reactions, interests and the like.

Another illustration of the suggestions of major functions a subject may serve can be obtained from recent reports of science committees. One such report suggests three major functions science can serve for the garden variety of citizen. The first of these is to contribute to the improvement of health, both the individual's health and public health. This includes the development of health practices, of health attitudes, and of health knowledge, including an understanding of the way in which disease is spread and the precautions that can be taken by the community to protect itself from disease and from other aspects of poor health. The second suggested function of science is the use and conservation of natural resources; that is, science can contribute to an understanding of the resources of matter and energy that are available, the ways in which matter and energy can be obtained and utilized so as not greatly to deplete the total reserves, an understanding of the efficiency of various forms of energy transformation, and an understanding of plant and animal resources and the ways in which they can be effectively utilized. The third function of science is to provide a satisfying world-picture, to get clearer understanding of the world as it is viewed by the scientist and man's relation to it, and the place of the world in the larger universe. From these suggested functions of science, again it is possible to infer a good many important objectives in the science field, objectives relating to science, knowledge, attitudes, ability to solve problems, interests and the like.

Recent art reports illustrate another example of suggestions regarding major functions a subject might serve in general education. Some five functions have been proposed in these reports. The first, and in terms of Monroe's writing the most important, is the function of art in extending the range of perception of the student. Through art one is able to see things more clearly, to see them through the eyes of the artist, and thus to get a type of perception he is not likely to obtain in any other way. Both art production and art criticism are likely to extend perception. A second function proposed for art is the clarification of ideas and feelings through providing another medium for communication in addition to verbal media. There are students who find it possible to express themselves and communicate more effectively through art forms than through writing or speaking. For them this is an important educational function of art. A third function is personal integration. This refers to the contribution art has sometimes made to the relieving of tensions through symbolic expression. The making of objects in the studio and shop and expression through dancing and through music have long been known to produce an opportunity for personal expression and personal release from tension that is important in providing for the better integration of some young people. A fourth function is the development of interests and values. It is maintained that aesthetic values are important both as interesting qualities for the student and also as expressing very significant life values in the same category with the highest ultimate values of life. On this basis the contribution art can make in providing satisfaction of these interests and in developing an understanding of and desire to obtain these art values is an important educational function of art. Finally, a fifth function of art is the development of technical competence, a means of acquiring skill in painting or drawing or music, or some other art form which can have meaning and significance to the art student. These art reports are another illustration of material from which a number of significant suggestions regarding educational objectives can be inferred from a statement of functions.

A second type of suggestion that can be got from reports of subject specialists are the particular contributions that a subject can make to other large educational functions, that may not be thought of as unique functions of the subject itself. *The Report of the Committee on Science in General Education* is an excellent illustration of this type of suggestion. This report is organized in terms of suggested contributions science can make in each of the major areas of human relationships. In personal living, for example, suggestions are made as to ways in which science can help to contribute to personal health, to the need for self assurance, to a satisfying world picture, to a wide range of personal interests, and to aesthetic satisfaction. In the area of personal-social relations, suggestions are made as to ways in which science may help to meet student needs for increasingly mature relationships in home and family life and with adults outside the family, and for successful and increasingly mature relationships with age mates of both sexes. In the area of social-civic relations suggestions are made as to how science may help to meet needs for responsible participation in socially significant activities, and to acquire social recognition. In the area of economic relations suggestions are made as to how science may help to meet needs for emotional assurance of progress toward adult status, to meet the need for guidance in choosing an occupation and for vocational preparation, to meet the need for the wise selection and use of goods and services, and to meet the needs for effective action in solving basic economic problems.

The volume *Science in General Education* then goes on to outline the ways in which science can be taught to encourage reflective thinking and to develop other characteristics of personality such as creative thinking, aesthetic appreciation, tolerance, social sensitivity, self-direction. Critics have questioned the depths of contributions that science might make on a number of these points, but it is clear that these suggestions are useful in indicating possible objectives that a school might wish to aim at, using science or other fields as a means for attaining these objectives. Other subject groups have, in similar fashion, made suggestions regarding specific contributions these subjects might make to areas that are not uniquely the responsibility of these subjects. It is then through the drawing of inferences from reports of this sort regarding both the major functions that specialists think the subject can make and also the more specific contributions that the subject might make to other major functions that one is able to infer objectives from the reports of subject specialists.

I would suggest in order to get some taste of the kind of thing that can be obtained from these reports that you read at least one subject report at the level in which you are interested and jot down your interpretation of the major functions the committee believes that this subject can serve and the more specific contributions it can make to other educational functions. Then, formulate a list of the educational objectives you infer from these statements. This will give you some idea of the kinds of objectives that are likely to be suggested by the reports that are being made by various subject groups.

Note

1. From Ralph W. Tyler, *Basic Principles of Curriculum and Instruction.* Chicago: University Chicago Press, 1949: pp. 1–7, 16–19, 25–33.

7
The Rise of Scientific Curriculum-Making and Its Aftermath

Herbert M. Kliebard

When Boyd Bode published *Modern Educational Theories* in 1927, he took on what had already become the entrenched establishment of the curriculum world. With his trenchant criticism of Franklin Bobbitt in the chapter, "Curriculum Construction and Consensus of Opinion" and of W. W. Charters in the succeeding chapter, "Curriculum Making and the Method of Job Analysis," Bode was attacking not only the work of two men who had established themselves as the prototypes of the curriculum specialist, but the very foundations on which curriculum as a field of specialization had been based. Bode probably did not suspect, however, that the notion of careful pre-specification of educational objectives (with variations in terminology and technique) and the notion of activity analysis as the means toward their "discovery" (also with variations in terminology and technique) would become the foundations on which, almost half a century later, many books would be written, Ph.D.s awarded, careers established, and millions of dollars expended. Certainly Bode never dreamed that legislation embodying these principles would be enacted across the United States and that the very ideas he was attacking would become semi-official doctrine in federal and state agencies as well as in many educational institutions.

The Scientific Curriculum Making of Bobbitt and Charters

Bobbitt and Charters lived in auspicious times. Mental discipline as a theoretical basis for the curriculum was almost dead by the early twentieth century. The bright flame of American Herbartianism, which had for a time captured the imagination of the educational world, was flickering. An educational ideology true to the times was needed, and nothing was more appropriate than scientific curriculum making. This doctrine, with its promise of precision and objectivity, had an immediate appeal. Certainly there was no reason why scientific principles applied to education would not meet with the same success as science applied to business in the form of scientific management. The general notion of applied science, as well as the particular model of scientific arrangement, is in fact evident throughout the work of Bobbitt and Charters.

Of the two, Bobbitt was perhaps the first to strike this rich vein. As a young instructor in educational administration at the University of Chicago, he effectively drew the parallel between business techniques and education in a lengthy article in the *Twelfth Yearbook of the National Society for the Study of Education* (Bobbitt 1913). But Bobbitt, unlike other educators who turned to scientific management, was not content merely to apply certain management techniques to education, such as maximum utilization of the school plant; he provided the professional educators in the twentieth century with the concepts and metaphors—indeed, the very language—that were needed to create an aura of technical expertise without which the hegemony of professional educators could not be established. Science was not simply a tool with which to carve out exactitude in educational affairs generally and in the curriculum in particular; it was a means by which one could confer professional status and exclude the uninitiated. Even the term "curriculum specialist" implied a particular set of technical skills unavailable to the untrained. While the notion of science implies a certain aura of exclusiveness, Bobbitt was probably not explicitly aware of such a political use of his technical language. In his two major works, *The Curriculum* (1918) and *How to Make a Curriculum* (1924), as well as in numerous articles on the techniques of curriculum making, he seems simply to have believed that science had the key that idle speculation and even philosophy failed to provide.

Like Bobbitt, W. W. Charters was already a major leader in education by the time Bode's work was published. Charters had written *Methods of Teaching* in 1909 and *Teaching the Common Branches* in 1913, both popular books; but with *Curriculum Construction* in 1923, he established himself in the forefront of curriculum thinking. (In the preface to this book, Charters gives particular thanks to his "former colleague, B. H. Bode" for "his criticism of theoretical principles.") Like Bobbitt also, Charters approached the problems of curriculum from the perspective of functional efficiency. Through the method of activity analysis (or job analysis, as it was also called), Charters was able to apply professional expertise to the development of curricula in many diverse fields, including secretarial studies, library studies, pharmacy, and especially teacher education (with *The Commonwealth Teacher-Training Study* in 1929). Activity analysis was so universally applicable a technique of curriculum development that Charters was even able to use it to develop a curriculum for being a woman. As with other occupations, one simply had to analyze the particular activities that defined the role and then place these in relationship to the ideals that would control these activities. The training involved in performing the activities well would then become the curriculum (Charters 1921, 1925). Out of the work and thought of Bobbitt and Charters, as well as their contemporaries and disciples, arose a new rationale and a modus operandi for the curriculum field that were to prevail to the present day. So dominant did scientific curriculum making become that Bode's *Modern Educational Theories* stands as one of the few direct assaults on some of its principal tenets and certainly the most important.

Preparing for Adulthood

One of the most basic tenets of scientific curriculum making is a principle enunciated early in Bobbitt's *How to Make a Curriculum*: "Education is primarily for adult life, not for child life. Its fundamental responsibility is to prepare for the fifty years of adulthood, not for the twenty years of childhood and youth" (1924, p. 8). Education, in other words, consists in preparing to become an adult. There is probably no more crucial notion in the entire theory. Without it, there would be no point, for example, in such careful analysis of adult activities and their ultimate transformation into minute and explicit curricular objectives. Moreover, much curriculum policy, such as the strong emphasis on curriculum differentiation with its basis in predicting the probable destination of children as to their adult lives, rests squarely on education as preparation. If education is for what lies ahead, then it becomes of utmost importance to state with reasonable accuracy what that future holds. Bode's criticism is most telling in making the distinction between a prediction by, for example, an astronomer as to the curve of a comet and an educator constructing a future ideal in schooling. Curriculum making, in other words, is a form of utopian thinking, not of crystal-ball gazing. But Dewey, whom Bode cites favorably in this context, had gone even further in attacking the notion of preparation. In "My Pedagogic Creed," Dewey took pains to define education as "a process of living and not a preparation for future living" (1929, p. 292), and he undertook specifically in *Democracy and Education* to point up other deficiencies in the idea. To think of children as merely getting ready for a remote and obscure world, Dewey thought, is to remove them as social members of the community. "They are looked upon as candidates," he said; "they are placed on the waiting list" (1916, p. 63). Furthermore, since children are not directed and stimulated by what is so remote in time, the educator must introduce, on a large scale, extrinsic rewards and punishments. Bode's criticism of education as preparation rests largely on the assumption that it would lead to a social status quo rather than social improvement. While Dewey would no doubt agree, his criticism is more far-reaching and devastating. He considered not only its social significance but its impact on the child and the pedagogical process itself.

A curious sidelight to the importance of education as preparation in scientific curriculum making is Bobbitt's own developing ambivalence toward the idea. In setting forth his curriculum theory in the epic *Twenty-Sixth Yearbook of the National Society for the Study of Education*, Bobbitt says, "Education is not primarily to prepare for life at some future time. Quite the reverse; it purposes to hold high the current living.... In a very true sense, life cannot be 'prepared for.' It can only be lived" (1926, p. 43). Later, when asked to write his summary theory of curriculum, Bobbitt declared, "While there are general guiding principles that enable parents and teachers to foresee in advance the long general course that is normally run, yet they cannot foresee or foreknow the specific and concrete details of the course that is to be actualized" (1934, p. 4). In these passages, he sounds more like Kilpatrick than himself. But if Bobbitt was ambivalent, even self-contradictory, on the subject of education as preparation, his disciples and present intellectual heirs are not. If anything is ingrained in curriculum thinking today, it is the notion that it is the job of curriculum planners to anticipate the exact skills, knowledge, and—to use today's most fashionable term—"competencies" that will stand one in good stead at an imagined point in the future. These predictions about what one will need in the future become the bases of curriculum planning.

Specificity of Objectives

A concomitant of the emphasis on preparation is the insistence that the end products of the curriculum be stated with great particularity. Vague Delphic prophecies simply won't do. " 'Ability to care for one's health' . . ." declared Bobbitt, "is too general to be useful. It must be reduced to particularity: ability to manage the ventilation of one's sleeping room, ability to protect one's self against micro-organisms, ability to care for the teeth, and so on" (1924, p. 32). If science is to be identified with exactitude, then scientific curriculum making must demonstrate its elevated status through the precision with which objectives are stated. It is at this point that Bode's criticism is both astute and telling. He points out, for example, that under the guise of scientific objectivity,

Bobbitt inserts a submerged ideology. Scientific objectivity, it turns out, becomes a way of preserving the tried and true values of the society as well as making explicit the prevailing practical skills of the contemporary world.

Bode, of course, would not object to a philosophy of education governing curriculum; his objection is that the values of the scientific curriculum makers are disguised and covert. Furthermore, even a cursory examination of Bobbitt's most famous list of objectives would indicate wide latitude in the degree of specificity with which the objectives are stated. Alongside "the ability to keep one's emotional serenity, in the face of circumstances however trying" (1924, p. 25), "an attitude and desire of obedience to the immutable and eternal laws which appear to exist in the nature of things," and "confidence in the beneficence of these laws" (1924, p. 26), we find "ability to read and interpret facts expressed by commonly used types of graphs, diagrams, and statistical tables" (1924, p. 12), as well as "ability to care properly for the feet" (1924, p. 14). Although the injunction to be specific and explicit is unqualified, there seems to be some difficulty in carrying it out simply as a practical matter. In considering the efficient functioning of the human body, for example, we have no guidance as to whether to begin with the leg, the foot, the toe, or the toenail. The same problem would arise if we were dealing with the ability to swing a hammer or the ability to solve quadratic equations. The scientific curriculum makers' allegiance to specificity was allied to Thorndike's conception of the mind as consisting of multitudinous separate and individual functions (1901, p. 249), whereas Bode seems committed to a much broader conception of thought processes as well as a more optimistic view of transfer of training.

Making a Choice

If the practical problem of specificity were somehow resolved, perhaps by extending the list of objectives into the thousands or the hundreds of thousands, another issue would become even more apparent: how would we decide, objectively of course, which objectives to keep and which to leave out? As Bode indicates, one of Bobbitt's solutions was to throw the matter open to a vote or at least to a panel. In his famous Los Angeles study, Bobbitt asserted that his list of objectives "represent[ed] the practically unanimous judgment of some twenty-seven hundred well-trained and experienced adults" (1924, p. 10), a claim about which Bode is clearly skeptical. As Bode points out, the twelve hundred Los Angeles teachers, who were charged with reviewing the list drawn up by the fifteen hundred graduate students at the University of Chicago, were in a dilemma. All of the objectives listed unquestionably represented desirable traits and skills, from "keeping razor in order" (Bobbitt 1922, p. 21) to "ability to tell interesting stories interestingly—and many of them" (p. 26).

The wide agreement, Bode suspects, was probably achieved by a combination of specificity when practical and clearly desirable skills were involved and vagueness or ambiguity when value issues were broached. Inspection of Bobbitt's list of objectives indicates that Bode is essentially correct, thereby accounting in part for the obvious discrepancies in the level of specificity with which the objectives are stated as well as the near unanimity of agreement among twenty-seven hundred adult human beings. State legislators, educators, and the general public frequently find themselves in the same position today when they are asked to give their assent to such educational goals as "self-realization" and "mental health." One can hardly be against them.

A Standard for Living

Although Bode's criticism of the method of consensus is certainly convincing, he considers only indirectly another of Bobbitt's ways of dealing with the seemingly limitless scope of a curriculum defined by the full range of human activity. While the task of the "curriculum discoverer" did involve, according to Bobbitt, a full catalog of the activities of mankind, Bobbitt was careful to indicate that much of what has to be learned is acquired by "undirected experience." "*The curriculum of the directed training,*" Bobbitt insisted, "*is to be discovered in the shortcomings of individuals after they have had all that can be given by the undirected training*" (1918, p. 45, original emphasis). Bobbitt's understanding of "shortcomings," actually, is quite similar to the contemporary notion of "needs." A standard is set, a norm; and the curriculum consists of the ways of treating deviations from the standard. Thus the curriculum seems cut down to manageable proportions without resort to the method of consensus. (It is a deceptively simple solution.) The fundamental issue, however, is not whether the list of objectives is derived from this or that method: more basic is the question of whether objectives ought to be prespecified at all. One might argue, therefore, that Bode, in skillfully demolishing the method of consensus, did not quite strike the jugular vein of scientific curriculum making. The central question is whether the curriculum should be a blueprint for what people should be like, not how the blueprint is drawn.

But even if one were to concede prespecification of objectives in such areas as arithmetic, grammar, and spelling, how far could one go in justifying the "social shortcomings" of which Bobbitt speaks (1918, p. 50)? As many of Bobbitt's objectives imply, there was literally no activity of mankind—social, intellectual, or practical—that was not potentially, at least, a curricular objective. Bode correctly identified Herbert Spencer as having anticipated the trend toward specificity in stating objectives, but of at least equal importance is Spencer's role in identifying the scope of the school curriculum with life itself. Spencer, like Bobbitt and Charters, considered the best curriculum to be the one that demonstrated the highest utility. Spencer, it should be remembered, asked the question, "What knowledge is of most worth?," not merely, "What shall the schools teach?" In a subtle way, then, he was reconstructing a basic curriculum question. To the scientific curriculum makers, the two questions were essentially the same; thus by posing their question in this way, scientific curriculum makers were determining the kind of answer that could be given. The answer to the scientific curriculum maker is likely to be phrased in terms of high survival value and functional utility rather than in terms of intellectual virtues. In this sense, the curriculum became the ultimate survival kit for the modern world. For example, in the state of Oregon today, certain districts have instituted requirements for high school graduation of such "survival" skills as listing birth-control methods in order of effectiveness, or demonstrating ability to officiate at two different sports and perform two basic dance steps (*Newsweek*, January 25, 1975, p. 69). Any sense of a distinctive function for the schools is lost.

Limitations of the School

Two serious but often unexamined questions are raised by such a conception of the school curriculum. The first relates to the extent to which the school as one institution of society can as a purely practical matter devote itself to the full range of human activity that man engages in. A second question, perhaps even more fundamental than the first, is whether all activity can be reduced to particular components.

From the days of the *Cardinal Principles* report to the present, the conventional way to begin the process of curriculum development has been to agree on a set of broad goals which in fact represents a categorization of human activity generally. The next step, of course, is to "operationalize" these goals by translating them into numerous minute and specific objectives—in effect, creating a catalog of human activity. Surely if Charters were able to identify the activities that constitute being a secretary or a librarian, it was only a step further to identify all the other activities of mankind. In this way the most urgent of these activities may be identified (e.g., earning a living) and the most pressing social problems addressed (e.g., drug addiction).

The missing ingredient in all this is some attention to the nature of the school. If there is one serious omission in Bode's analysis, it is the failure to recognize the limitations of the institution of schooling. The knowledge that is of the most worth may not be the kind of knowledge that can be transmitted in a school context. The place of the school in the social structure, the makeup of its inhabitants, and the characteristic activities that take place within its boundaries must be considered along with the power of schooling as we know it to produce fundamental and direct changes in human attitudes and behavior. Hence if curriculum makers do not temper the question of what is most important to know with the question of what schools can accomplish, their claims for programs designed to reduce crime, improve human relations, prevent drunken driving, ensure economic independence, or remove sexual inhibitions are unreliable.

Analyzing Human Activity

Furthermore, while it may be true that a limited number of human activities may be anticipated and therefore practiced in advance, the extension of the method of job analysis from the limited realm of routine and replicative behavior into the full universe of human activity represents perhaps the most fundamental fallacy in the whole scientific curriculum-making movement. The source of this assumption, as is the case with other elements of scientific curriculum making, is the example of industry. Just as the global and complex process of building an automobile can be broken down into a series of minute and simple operations, so presumably can the activities of a mother or a teacher. But we do not learn language, for example, by anticipating all of the sentences we will utter in our adult lives and then rehearsing them as part of our preparation to become adults. Instead, we learn or assimilate or perhaps even inherit the governing principles of language that permit us to create or invent sentences that we have never before heard expressed. Similarly, in mathematics we do not scientifically catalog all of the mathematical operations we will perform as adults as a direct rehearsal for the performance of those mathematical operations.

Here Bode's criticism of job analysis as the universal technique of curriculum making is particularly cogent. The analogy between definite operations which imply simply replicative activity and activities that involve, let us say, judgment, simply will not hold. As he puts it, friendliness, courtesy, and honesty "are not reducible to 'definite operations' " (Bode 1927, p. 109). The process of educating a teacher to conduct himself or herself wisely and judiciously in the classroom is not, as current programs of teacher training so often imply, a process of first anticipating the particular situations that will arise in the classroom and then directing the teachers to conduct themselves in a particular way relative to these specific situations. Rather, teacher education can involve the examination, analysis, and adaptation of some broad principles which at some unknown point in the future and in some unanticipated circumstances may provide a guide to keen judgment and wise action.

Scientific Curriculum Making in Teacher Education

Bode's astute criticism of the scientific curriculum makers notwithstanding, it should be clear to anyone familiar with the current state of the art in the curriculum world that the scientific curriculum movement, with few adaptations and modifications, has been triumphant. It is true that behaviorism has provided a few refinements of language in stating objectives, and certain so-called academic subjects such as mathematics and science have perhaps more respectability than in the days of Bobbitt and Charters. But the key ingredients and analogies remain the same. While this modern version of scientific curriculum making is well established in virtually all sectors of the curriculum world, it exists, not surprisingly, in its most virulent form in the area of teacher education. The vogue movements which go under the names of competency-based teacher education (CBTE) and performance-based teacher education (PBTE) are prime examples of what has evolved from the basic principles enunciated by Bobbitt and Charters. Charters himself helped direct a major study begun in 1925 which had all the earmarks of the PBTE (or CBTE) ideology.

The Commonwealth Teacher-Training Study

As is the case with the current programs, the *Commonwealth Teacher-Training Study* was to be based on scientific research into the teaching process as opposed to mere speculation and tradition. As a first step, Charters and Waples "ascertained the traits that characterize excellent teachers" (1929, p. 4). Adapting the consensus approach, the investigators used two methods: analyzing the professional literature and interviewing "expert judges." Working from a list of eighty-three traits, ranging alphabetically from Accuracy through Foresight and Magnetism all the way to Wittiness (pp. 56–61), "translators" were given the task of interpreting statements made in writing or in the interviews. Thus, "knows how to meet people" could become translated into the traits, "adaptability" or "approachability." Reliability among the translators was determined by applying the Spearman prophecy formula. Finally, after some of the original traits of teachers were telescoped, scientifically determined lists were prepared indicating that senior high school teachers should be characterized by twenty-six traits including Good Taste and Propriety, junior high school teachers by Conventionality (morality) and Open-mindedness, and so on.

Next, in an adaptation of the job analysis technique, the investigators collected a master list of 1,001 teacher activities. Perhaps one of these activities is worth quoting in its entirety:

> 788. Securing cordial relations with superintendent
> Maintaining cordial relations with superintendent. This involves being loyal to and respecting

> the superintendent. Becoming acquainted with superintendent and working in harmony with him. Performing friendly acts for superintendent; remembering superintendent at Christmas; making designs and drawings for superintendent; making lamp shades for superintendent's wife. (Charters and Waples 1929, p. 423)

Thus, after three years of research by trained investigators and a grant of $42,000 from the Commonwealth Fund, was a blow dealt to fuzzy thinking in teacher education and a major stride taken in the direction of a scientifically determined teacher-education curriculum.

The Contemporary Aftermath

One of the most persistent and puzzling questions in this, the aftermath of the scientific curriculum-making movement, is why we retain, even revere, the techniques and assumptions we have inherited from Bobbitt and Charters, at the same time as we reject, implicitly at least, the actual outcomes of their research. Few people read Bobbitt's famous study, *Curriculum-Making in Los Angeles*, or his magnum opus, *How to Make a Curriculum*, or have even heard of Charters and Waples's *Commonwealth Teacher-Training Study*. If they did read these works, the most likely reaction would be one of amusement. And yet we pursue with sober dedication the techniques on which these works are based. Admittedly, performance-based teacher education may just be a slogan system resting only on a foundation of high-sounding rhetoric and pious promises and covered with a gloss of false novelty; but if it means anything, it surely implies that one can identify the particular components of teaching activity that make for good teachers and that these characteristics (Charters would call them traits) or behaviors (Charters would call them activities) can form the basis of a program of teacher training. Research takes the form of identifying the particular components of teaching that will ensure success. While there seems to be some caution in stating the characteristics and behaviors with the same degree of conviction as Bobbitt and Charters did, an abiding faith in the efficacy of the approach remains. The persistence of this faith in the face of a record of over a half century of failure is a mystery that probably even Bode could not fathom.

Is Teaching a Technology?

At the heart of some of our most fundamental problems in the field of curriculum and of teacher education as well is the question of whether teaching is a technology by which carefully fashioned products in the form of learning or behavior are made. These products would have to be designed with the exactitude and specificity that Bobbitt and Charters called for. Teaching would be the application of standardized means by which predictable results would be achieved, and curriculum development the specification of the end-products and the rules for their efficient manufacture. Teacher education, in turn, would be the process by which persons are transformed into efficient manufacturers. The research evidence that presumably would support such an analogy between the teaching and the manufacturing process, however, has been disappointing to the proponents. For example, a recent thorough examination of the research basis for performance-based teacher education led to the conclusion that eleven process variables previously identified as "promising"—such as "clarity," "variability," and "enthusiasm"—were indeed notably unpromising, leading the authors to conclude that "an empirical basis for performance-based teacher education does not exist" (Heath and Nielson 1974, p. 475). Moreover, pessimism about the ultimate success of the approach was not based simply on flaws in statistical analysis or research design. The more fundamental problem was the framework in which such research was cast—a framework which, by the way, has held sway since the days of Bobbitt, Charters, and the scientific curriculum-making movement.

Bode as Prophet

The point of all this is not simply that Bobbitt, Charters, and their likeminded contemporaries were mistaken in their faith in a given approach; the age in which they lived was one where optimism about the power of science to solve a multitude of human and social problems was near its peak. If they were naive or mistaken, one can hardly blame them. What is almost unforgivable, however, is that the half century since the zenith of their influence has produced little more by way of sophistication and refinement. With few exceptions, Bode's criticism of 1927 would carry as much force today were it directed against the present-day heirs of scientific curriculum making.

Particularly disappointing are the precipitous efforts to convert highly tentative and limited research findings into immediate prescriptions. This may be a function of the large constituency of teachers and school administrators who want immediate and concrete answers to such global questions as What is a good teacher? and What is a good curriculum? Part of the problem, undoubtedly, with the era of the scientific curriculum makers and with ours is the failure to recognize the complexity of the phenomena with which we deal. There is the same confusion between science and desert empiricism, the same naiveté about the nature of the teaching process, the same neglect of conceptual analysis. To be critical of scientific curriculum making, as Bode was, is not to be critical of science or even the importance of scientific inquiry into educational processes: it is to be critical of a simplistic and vulgar scientism. Its persistence is a source of embarrassment.

References

Bobbitt, Franklin. (1913). "Some General Principles of Management Applied to the Problems of City-School Systems." In *The Supervision of City Schools. Twelfth Yearbook of the National Society for the Study of Education*, Part 1, pp. 7–96. Bloomington, Ill.: Public School Publishing Co.

——. (1918). *The Curriculum.* Boston: Houghton Mifflin.

——. (1922). *Curriculum-making in Los Angeles.* Supplementary Educational Monographs, no. 20. Chicago: University of Chicago Press.

——. (1924). *How to Make a Curriculum.* Boston: Houghton Mifflin.

——. (1926). "The Orientation of the Curriculum-maker." In *The Foundations and Technique of Curriculum-construction. Twenty-Sixth Yearbook of the National Society for the Study of Education*, Part 2, pp. 41–55. Bloomington, Ill.: Public School Publishing Co.

——. "A Summary Theory of the Curriculum." *Society for Curriculum Study News Bulletin* 5 (January 12, 1934): 2–4.

Bode, Boyd H. (1927). *Modern Educational Theories.* New York: Macmillan.

Charters, Werrett W. (1909). *Methods of Teaching: Developed from a Functional Standpoint.* Chicago: Row, Peterson & Co.

——. (1913). *Teaching the Common Branches.* Boston: Houghton Mifflin.

——. "The Reorganization of Women's Education." *Educational Review* 62 (October 1921): 224–231.

——. (1923). *Curriculum Construction.* New York: Macmillan.

——. (1925). "Curriculum for Women." In *Proceedings of the High School Conference.* Urbana, Ill.: University of Illinois.

Charters, Werrett W., and Waples, Douglas. (1929). *The Commonwealth Teacher-training Study.* Chicago: University of Chicago Press.

Dewey, John. (1916). *Democracy and Education: An Introduction to the Philosophy of Education.* New York: Macmillan.

——. "My Pedagogic Creed." *Journal of the National Education Association* 18, no. 9 (December 1929): 291–295.

Heath, Robert W., and Nielson, Mark A. "The Research Basis for Performance-based Teacher Education." *Review of Educational Research* 44, no. 4 (Fall 1974): 463–484.

National Education Association Commission on the Reorganization of Secondary Education. (1918). *Cardinal Principles of Secondary Education: A Report.* Washington: Government Printing Office.

Spencer, Herbert. (1860). "What Knowledge Is of Most Worth?" In *Education: Intellectual, Moral and Physical*, pp. 1–96. New York: D. Appleton and Co.

"Survival Test." *Newsweek*, January 25, 1975, p. 69.

Thorndike, E. L., and Woodworth, R. S. "The Influence of Improvement in One Mental Function upon the Efficiency of Other Functions," Part 1. *Psychological Review* 8, no. 3 (May 1901): 247–261.

8
Man: A Course of Study

Jerome S. Bruner

There is a dilemma in describing a course of study.

One must begin by setting forth the intellectual substance of what is to be taught, else there can be no sense of what challenges and shapes the curiosity of the student. Yet the moment one succumbs to the temptation to "get across" the subject, at that moment the ingredient of pedagogy is in jeopardy. For it is only in a trivial sense that one gives a course to "get something across," merely to impart information. There are better means to that end than teaching. Unless the learner also masters himself, disciplines his taste, and deepens his view of the world, the "something" that is got across is hardly worth the effort of transmission.

The more "elementary" a course and the younger its students, the more serious must be its pedagogical aim of forming the intellectual powers of those whom it serves. It is as important to justify a good mathematics course by the intellectual discipline it provides or the honesty it promotes as by the mathematics it transmits. Indeed, neither can be accomplished without the other.

We begin this article with an account of the substance or structure of a course in "social studies" now in the process of construction. A discussion of pedagogy follows. The aim of the exercise is to write a transitional first draft of the course, a common focus for those of us who have been trying to compose the course, trying to teach parts of it to children in Grade V. If the exercise is finally successful, we shall end with a completed course—with the materials, guides, films, and the other things that must be in the student's hands and on the teacher's shelf. There will be drafts in between. The exercise, we hope, will allow us to be clearer about what we are doing. In the final section we shall consider how we propose to get from a first draft such as this to a course that is ready for teaching.

Structure of the Course

The content of the course is man: his nature as a species, the forces that shaped and continue to shape his humanity. Three questions recur throughout:

What is human about human beings?
How did they get that way?
How can they be made more so?

We seek exercises and materials through which our pupils can learn wherein man is distinctive in his adaptation to the world, and wherein there is discernible continuity between him and his animal forbears. For man represents that crucial point in evolution where adaptation is achieved by the vehicle of culture and only in a minor way by further changes in his morphology. Yet there are chemical tides that run in his blood that are as ancient as the reptiles. We make every effort at the outset to *tell* the children where we hope to travel with them. Yet little of such recounting gets through. It is much more useful, we have found, to pose the three questions directly to the children so that their own views can be brought into the open and so that they can establish some points of view of their own.

In pursuit of our questions we shall explore five matters, each closely associated with the evolution of man as a species, each defining at once the distinctiveness of man and his potentiality for further evolution. The five great humanizing forces are, of course, tool-making, language, social organization, the management of man's prolonged childhood, and man's urge to explain. It has been our first lesson in teaching that no pupil, however eager, can appreciate the relevance of, say, tool-making in human evolution without first grasping the fundamental concept of a tool, or what a language is, or a myth, or social organization. These are not obvious matters. So we are involved in teaching not only the role of tools or language in the emergence of man, but as a necessary precondition for doing so, setting forth the fundamentals of linguistics or the theory of tools. And it is as often the case as not that (as in the case of the "theory of tools") we must solve a formidable intellectual problem ourselves in order to be able to help our pupils do the same.

While one readily singles out these five massive contributors to man's humanization, under no circumstances can they be put into airtight compartments. Human kinship is distinctively different from primate mating patterns precisely because it is classificatory and rests on man's ability to use language. Or, if you will, tool use enhances the division of labor in a society which in turn affects kinship. And language itself is more clearly appreciated by reference to its acquisition in the uniquely human interaction between child and parent. Obviously, the nature of man's world view, whether formulated in myth or in science, depends upon, and is constrained by, the nature of human language. So while each domain can be treated as a separate set of ideas, as we shall see, success in teaching depends upon making it possible for children to have a sense of their interaction.

Language

Teaching the essentials of linguistics to children in the elementary grades has limits, but they are wider than we had expected. There are certain pedagogic precautions to be respected if ten-year-olds are to be captivated by the subject. It must not, to begin with, be presented as a normative subject—as an exercise in how things *should* be written or said. It must, moreover, be disassociated from such traditional "grammar" as the child has encountered. There is nothing so deadening as to have a child handle the "type and order" problem by "recognizing" one category of words as "nouns" and parroting, upon being asked what he means by a noun, that it is a "person, place, or thing." It is not that he is either "right" or "wrong," but rather that he is as remote from the issue as he would be if he attempted to account for grief over the assassination of a President by citing the Constitution on the division of powers. And finally, the discussion needs to remain close to the nature of language in use, its likely origin, and the functions to which it is put.

Whether it is true or not that a ten-year-old has a complete grammatical repertory, he is certainly capable of, and delighted in, recognizing all linguistic features when confronted with instances of them. The chief aid to such recognition is contrast—the opportunity to observe the oppositional features that are so much a feature of human language. What comes hard is to formulate these features conceptually; to go beyond the intuitive grasp of the native speaker to the more self-conscious understanding of the linguist. It is this task—getting children to look at and to ponder the things they can notice in their language long enough to understand them—that is most difficult and it should not be pushed to the point of tedium.

Our section on language includes a consideration of what communication is—by contrasting how humans and animals manage to send and receive messages. The early sessions have proved lively and in the course of them nearly every major issue of linguistics is raised and allowed to go begging. This preliminary exercise has the great virtue that it can be repeated on later occasions, when students have achieved varying levels of sophistication, with the result that they readily recognize how much progress they have made.

The opening session (or sessions, for students often want to continue the arguments over animals and humans) usually indicates which among several openings can be best pursued in later units. The instance which follows is influenced by far too little experience to be considered the general rule, but it is at least one example.

The discussion led naturally to the design features of a language. We designed a language game based on bee language, requiring the children to find hidden objects by using messages in this bee-like language. The children are encouraged to design similar languages and to improve on the design of the language used. They take to this readily and are eager to discuss and make clearer such design features as semanticity, voice-ear link, displacement, and cultural transmission. The game, of course, is a lead into the demonstration of bee language as presented in the von Frisch film (which is not altogether satisfactory). We were struck, however, at how much more interested the children were in talking about their own language than in discussing bee language or von Frisch's analysis of it. It is as if the bee linguistics were interesting as an introduction into the closer analysis of their own language.

Our next objective is to present the powerful ideas of arbitrariness, of productivity, and of duality of patterning, the latter the exclusive property of human language. We have approached arbitrariness by the conventional route of comparing how pictures, diagrams, charades, and words refer to things. There are nice jokes to be used, as in the example given by Hockett of the tiny word *whale* referring to a big thing, while the large word *microorganism* refers to a tiny one. With respect to productivity, we have had considerable initial success with two exercises. The first is with a language containing four types (how, what, when, where) with a limited number of tokens of each type (e.g., by hand, by weapon, by trap, as tokens of the "how" type) and with a highly constrained set of orders each referring to a different kind of food-related activity. By this means we readily establish the idea of *type* and *order* as two basic ideas. They readily grasp the idea of substitutivity of tokens within a type. (Indeed, given the interest in secret codes based on substitution of words or letters for code breaking, they need little instruction on this score.)

Once the ideas of type and order are established, we begin the following amusing exercises to illustrate the interchangeability of language frames. We present:

1	2	3	4	5
The	man	ate	his	lunch
A	lady	wore	my	hat
This	doctor	broke	a	bottle
My	son	drove	our	car

and the children are now asked to provide "matching" examples. They can do so readily. They soon discover that so long as they pick words in the order 1 2 3 4 5, from any place in each column, something "sensible" can be got—even if it is silly or not true like, "My doctor wore a car," or, "A lady ate a bottle," it is at least not "crazy" like, "Man the lunch his ate."

The students need no urging to construct new frames and to insert additional types into frames already set up (like a new first column the tokens of which include, *did, can, has,* etc.). Interesting discoveries are made—such as the relative openness of some positions and the closed nature of others. We hope to devise methods to help the children discover some of the deeper features of grammar, better to grasp what a language is—for example, that one can start with relatively simple sentence frames, "kernel sentences," and transform them progressively into negatives, queries, and passives or any two or even three of these, and that more complex forms can be returned to simpler forms by applying the transformations in reverse.

Finally, a game has been devised (a game involving signaling at sea) to illustrate duality of patterning, that most difficult feature of human language. It involves developing a language initially with a very limited set of building blocks (as with human languages, each of which combines intrinsically meaningless sound elements, phones, into a unique system that renders them into meaningful phonemes, a change in one of which will alter the meaning of a word so that, in English, *rob* and *lob* are different words, but not so in Japanese where /r/ and /1/ are allophones of the same phoneme just as plosive /p/ *(pin)* and non-plosive /p/ *(spin)* are "the same" for us but not for others). Three kinds of word blocks can be arranged in a frame, making twenty-seven possible "words" or lexemes. But there must be rules as to which combinations mean things and which do not. It is very quickly apparent to the children that the blocks as such "mean" nothing, but the frames do—or some do and some do not. We are in progress of going from this point toward other aspects of duality at this time.

It is a natural transition to go from syntax to the question of how language is acquired by young humans and other primates. We shall use the considerable resources provided by recent studies of language acquisition to show the manner in which syntax emerges from certain very elementary forms such as the pivot-plus-open-class and the head-plus- attribute. The idea of "writing a grammar" for any form of speech encountered will also be presented. In addition, the child-adult "expansion-idealization" cycle will be explored as an example of a powerful form of social grouping that is crucial for transmitting the language. For contrast, we hope to examine the problems of language development of Vicki, a chimpanzee raised by a family along with their own child of like age. The subtle problem of "traditional" and "hereditary" transmission is bound to emerge.

Finally, and with the benefit of their newly gained insight into the nature of language, we shall return to the question of the origins of human language and its role in shaping human characteristics. We hope first to cover the newly available materials on the universal characteristics of all human languages—first getting the children to make some informed guesses on the subject. Then we shall consider the role of language in the organization of the early human group and the effectiveness it might add to such group activities as hunting, given its design features and its universals. To go from this point to a consideration of myth and its nature is not a difficult step.

We have examined these matters in some detail here (though not closely enough). Our hope is to give the reader a concrete sense of how far we wish to go. It is plain that the section on language can take as much of a year as one wishes. We are overproducing materials to give us some better idea of what is possible and how to combine what is possible. Some schools may want to devote much time to language, and we hope to make it possible for them to do so. But above all, we hope to provide enough variety so that a teacher can choose an emphasis of his own, whether it be to increase self-consciousness about language or to impart a livelier sense of some distinctively human aspect of human language. In the first stages of our work, the tendency is to concentrate more on "getting the subject right"—in this case linguistics—than on getting the whole course constructed. And just as there is a tension between the requirements of the subject itself and those imposed by the need to teach it to children, so is there a necessary tension between the parts of our course (the five topics) and the whole (the nature and evolution of man). We shall return to this matter in discussing the summer workshop in a later section.

The section on language has required the collaboration of a variety of linguists of different stripe—pure, anthropological, psychological—and of teachers, psychologists, film-makers, artists, and children. At that, it is hardly a quarter done. Gloria Cooper of Harvard has directed the unit, with the aid of David McNeill of Harvard, Mary Henle of the New School, John Mickey of Colorado State, Betsy Dunkman of the Newton Schools, and Florence Jackson of the New York City Schools.

Tool Making

One starts with several truths about children and "tools." They have usually not used many of them, and in general, tools will not be of much interest. This may derive from the deeper truth that, in general, children (like their urban parents) think of tools as set pieces that are to be bought in hardware stores. And finally, children in our technologically mature society usually have little notion of the relation between tools and our way of life. Production takes place in factories where they have never been, its products are packaged to disguise the production process that brought them into being.

The tool unit is still under discussion. What follows are some of the leading ideas that animate the design of the unit.

We begin with a philosophical approach to the nature of tool-using. What is most characteristic of any kind of tool-using is not the tools themselves, but rather the program that guides their use. It is in this broader sense that tools take on their proper meaning as amplifiers of human capacities and implementers of human activity.

Seen as amplifiers, tools can fall into three general classes—amplifiers of sensory capacities, of motor capacities, and of ratiocinative capacities. Within each type there are many subspecies. There are sensory amplifiers like microscopes and ear horns that are "magnifiers," others, like spirit levels and bobs, that are "reference markers," etc. Some implement systems "stretch out" time (slow motion cinematography) and others condense it (time-lapse registration). In the realm of motor amplifiers, some tools provide a basis for binding, some for penetrating, some even for steadying—as when one of our pupils described a draughtsman's compass as a "steadying tool." And, of course, there are the "soft tools" of ratiocination such as mathematics and logic and the "hard tools" they make possible, ranging from the abacus to the high speed digital computer and the automaton.

Once we think of tools as imbedded in a program of use—as implementers of human activity—then it becomes possible to deal with the basic idea of substitutability, an idea as crucial to language as it is to tools. If one cannot find a certain word or phrase, a near equivalent can be substituted in its place. So too with tools: if a skilled carpenter happens not to have brought his chisel to the job, he can usually substitute something else in its place—the edge of a plane blade, a pocket knife, etc. In short, tools are not fixed, and the "functional fixedness" found by so many psychologists studying problem-solving comes finally because so much thinking about tools fixes them to the convention—a hammer is for nails and nothing but nails.

Our ultimate object in teaching about tools is, as noted before, not so much to explicate tools and their significance, but to explore how tools affected man's evolution. The evidence points very strongly to the central part in evolution played by natural selection favoring the user of spontaneous pebble tools over those proto-hominids who depended upon their formidable jaws and dentition. In time, survival depended increasingly on the capacities of the tool-user and tool-maker—not only his opposable forefinger and thumb, but the nervous system to go with them. Within a few hundred thousand years after the first primitive tool-using appears, man's brain size more than doubles. Evolution (or more simply, survival) favored the larger brained creatures capable of adapting by the use of tools, and brain size seems to have been roughly correlated with that capacity. There are many fascinating concomitants to this story. Better weapons meant a shift to carnivorousness. This in turn led to leisure—or at least less food-gathering—which in turn makes possible permanent or semipermanent settlement. Throughout, the changes produced lead to changes in way of life, changes in culture and social organization, changes in what it is possible to do.

All of these matters are now superbly documented in Leaky's excavations in Olduvai Gorge in East Africa. We have consulted with him and he has expressed eagerness to edit four films for us on tool-making and its subsequent effects on the emergence of a new way of life. These are scheduled for the fall of 1965. If we are successful in getting our pupils to speculate about the changes in a society that accompany changes in technology, we will at least have fulfilled one of the original aims of the Social Studies Program: to get across the idea that a technology requires a counterpart in social organization before it can be used effectively by a society.

There happen also to be new materials available on the burgeoning technology of the Magdalenian period when more decorative features appear and tool-makers begin to specialize. We are exploring this work to see whether it too can be used in the same spirit.

A few of the exercises being planned to the "tool section" give some flavor of the pedagogy. One unit calls for the taking of a "census of skills"—the tasks that children know how to perform, along with some effort to examine how they were learned (including tool skills). Another unit consists of trying to design an "all-purpose" tool so that the children can have some notion of the programmatic questions one asks in designing a tool and why specialized use has a role.

There will also be an opportunity (of which more in a later section) for the children to compare "tool play" of an Eskimo boy and Danai boy of New Guinea with the play of immature free-ranging baboons, macaques, and chimpanzees. We are also in process of obtaining films on the technique of manufacture of flint implements and hope also to obtain inexpensive enough materials to have our pupils try their hand at flint knapping and other modes of instrument making, guided possibly by films on the subject by the distinguished French archeologist, Dr Bordes.

There will also be some treatment in the course of tools to make tools as well as of tools that control various forms of natural power. A possible route into this discussion is an overview of the evolution of tool-making generally—from the first "spontaneous" or picked-up tools, to the shaped ones, to those shaped to a pattern, to modern conceptions of man-machine relations as in contemporary systems research. Indeed, if we do follow this approach we shall also explore the design of a game of tool design involving variables such as cost, time, gain, specificity of function, and skill required, with the object of making clear the programmatic nature of tools and the manner in which tools represent a selective extension of human powers.

Social Organization

The section on social organization is still in preliminary planning, save in one respect where work is quite well advanced. The unit has as its objective to make children aware that there is a structure in a society and that this structure is not fixed once and for all. It is an integrated pattern and you cannot change one part of the pattern without other parts of the society changing with it. The way a society arranges itself for carrying out its affairs depends upon a variety of factors ranging from its ecology at one end to the irreversible course of its history and world view at the other.

A first task is to lead children to recognize explicitly certain basic patterns in the society around them, patterns they know well in an implicit, intuitive way—the distinction between kin and others, between face-to-face groups and secondary groups, between reference groups and ones that have corporate being. These, we believe, are distinctions that children easily discover. We should also like the children to grasp the rather abstract fact that within most human groups beyond the immediate family, continuity depends not so much upon specific people, but upon "roles" filled by people—again, as with language and tool-use, there are structures with substitutability.

Such social organization is marked by reciprocity and exchange—cooperation is compensated by protection, service by fee, and so on. There is always giving and getting. There are, moreover, forms of legitimacy and sanction that define the limits of possible behavior in any given role. They are the bounds set by a society and do not depend upon the individual's choice. Law is the classic case, but not the only one. One cannot commit theft legally, but then too one cannot ignore friends with impunity and law has nothing to do with it.

A society, moreover, has a certain world view, a way of defining what is "real," what is "good," what is "possible." To this matter we turn in a later section, mentioning it here only to complete our catalogue of aspirations of ideas we hope to introduce in this part of the course.

We believe that these matters can be presented to children in a fashion that is gripping, close to life, and intellectually honest. The pedagogy is scarcely clear, but we are on the track of some interesting ways of operating. One difficulty with social organization is its ubiquity. Contrast may be our best way of saving social organization from obviousness—

by comparing our own forms of social organization with those of baboon troops, of Eskimo, of Bushmen, of prehistoric man as inferred from excavated living floors in Europe and East Africa. But beyond this we are now developing a "family" of games designed to bring social organization into the personal consciousness of the children.

The first of these games, "Hunting," is designed to simulate conditions in an early human group engaged in hunting and is patterned on the life and ecology of the Bushmen of the Kalahari Desert. The elements of the game are Hunters, Prey, Weapons, Habitats, Messages, Predators, and Food. Without going into detail, the game simulates (in the manner of so-called Pentagon games used for increasing the sensitivities of generals) the problem of planning how far one wishes to go in search of various kinds of game, how resources need to be shared by a group to go beyond "varmint" hunting to larger game, how differentiation of labor can come about in weapon-making and weapon-using, how one must decide among different odds in hunting in one terrain or another. Given the form of the game (for which we are principally grateful to Dr Clark Abt), its content can be readily varied to fit the conditions of life of other hunting groups, such as the Eskimo, again with the object of contrast.

What has proved particularly interesting in our early work with the game is that it permits the grouping of a considerable amount of "real" material around it—accounts of the life of the Kalahari Bushmen (of which there is an extraordinarily rich record on film and in both literary and monographic form), their myths and art, the "forbiddingly" desert ecology that is their environment. And so too with the Eskimo; should we go ahead to construct an analogue game for them, for we are in possession of an equally rich documentation on the Netsilik Eskimo of Pelly Bay. Indeed, one of the documentary films made by the ESI Studio in collaboration with the Canadian Film Board and Dr Asen Balikci of the University of Montreal (one of seven half-hour films to be "cut" from our 100,000 feet of film) has already received international acclaim.

Finally, and again by contrast, there now exists a vast store of material on the social organization of higher primates—a considerable portion of which is also in film shot by a crew under Dr Irven DeVore of Harvard for ESI—that serves extremely well to provoke discussion on what is uniquely human about human social organization.

The group now at work on Social Organization consists of Edwin Dethlefsen of Harvard, Richard McCann, on leave from the Newton Schools, and Mrs Linda Braun of the ESI staff.

Child Rearing

This unit has just begun to take shape at the time of writing. It is proceeding on three general themes in the hope of clarifying them by reference to particular materials in the areas of language, of social organization, of tool-making, and of childhood generally. The first general theme is the extent to which and the manner in which the long human childhood (assisted as it is by language) leads to the dominance of sentiment in human life, in contrast to instinctual patterns of gratification and response found to predominate at levels below man. That is to say, affect can now be aroused and controlled by symbols—human beings have an attitude about anger rather than just anger or not anger. The long process of sentiment formation requires both an extended childhood and access to a symbolized culture through language. Without sentiment (or values or the "second signal system" or whatever term one prefers) it is highly unlikely that human society or anything like it would be possible.

A second theme is organized around the human (perhaps primate) tendency toward mastery of skill for its own sake—the tendency of the human being, in his learning of the environment, to go beyond immediate adaptive necessity toward innovation. Recent work on human development has underlined this "push toward effectance," as it has been called. It is present in human play, in the increased variability of human behavior when things get under control. Just as William James commented three-quarters of a century ago that habit was the fly-wheel of society, we can now say that the innovative urge is the accelerator.

The third theme concerns the shaping of the man by the patterning of childhood—that while all humans are intrinsically human, the expression of their humanity is affected by what manner of childhood they have experienced.

The working out of these themes has only begun. One exercise now being tried out is to get children to describe differences between infancy, childhood, and adulthood for different species—using live specimens brought to class (in the case of non-human species) or siblings for humans. For later distribution, of course, the live specimens (and siblings) will be rendered on film. Yet the success of a session, say, with a ten-day-old, stud-tailed macaque suggests that the real thing should be used whenever possible.

Dr Balikci will be cutting a film on Eskimo childhood from the Netsilik footage, and comparable films on baboon and Japanese macaque childhood will also be in preparation. Beyond this there is still little to report. Dr Richard Jones of Brandeis is in charge of the unit, assisted by Miss Catherine Motz, on leave from Germantown Friends School, and Mrs Kathy Sylva and Mrs Phyllis Stein of ESI.

World View

The fifth unit in preparation concerns itself with man's drive to explicate and represent his world. While it concerns itself with myth, with art, with primitive legend, it is only incidentally designed to provide the stories, the images, the religious impulses, and the mythic romance of man's being. It would be more accurate to describe the unit as "beginning philosophy" in both senses of that expression—philosophy at the beginning and, perhaps, philosophy for young beginners.

Central to the unit is the idea that men everywhere are humans, however advanced or "primitive" their civilization. The difference is not one of more or less than human, but of how particular human societies express their human capacities. A remark by the French anthropologist, Levi-Strauss, puts it well.

> Prevalent attempts to explain alleged differences between the so-called primitive mind and scientific thought have resorted to qualitative differences between the working processes of the mind in both cases, while assuming that the entities which they were studying remained very much the same. If our interpretation is correct, we are led toward a completely different view—namely, that the kind of logic in mythical thought is as rigorous as that of modern science, and that the difference lies, not in the quality of the intellectual process, but in the nature of things to which it is applied. This is well in agreement with the situation known to prevail in the field of technology: What makes a steel ax superior to a stone ax is not that the first one is better made than the second. They are equally well made, but steel is quite different from stone. In the same way we may be able to show that the same logical processes operate in myth as in science, and that man has always been thinking equally well; the improvement lies, not

> in the alleged progress of man's mind, but in the discovery of new areas to which it may apply its unchanged and unchanging powers.

All cultures are created equal. One society—say, that of Eskimos—may have only a few tools, but they are used in a versatile way. The woman's knife does what our scissors do, but it also serves to scrape hides, and to clean and thin them. The man's knife is used for killing and skinning animals, carving wood and bone, cutting snow for building blocks for the igloo, chopping meat into bites. Such simple weapons are "the mother of tools," and by specialization a number of tools derive from them. What is "lost" in variety of tools is won in the versatility of uses; in brief, an Eskimo man and wife have tools for all their tasks and can carry most of these tools about with them at all times.

So too with symbolic systems. The very essence of being human is in the use of symbols. We do not know what the hierarchy of primacy is between speech, song, dance, and drawing; but, whichever came first, as soon as it stood for something else other than the act itself, man was born; as soon as it caught on with another man, culture was born, and as soon as there were two symbols, a system was born. A dance, a song, a painting, and a narrative can all symbolize the same thing. They do so differently. One way of searching for the structure of a world view is to take an important narrative and to see what it ultimately tells. A narrative, or at least a corpus of narratives, may be what philosophy used to be. It may reflect what is believed about the celestial bodies and their relation to man, it may tell how man came into being, how social life was founded, what is believed about death and about life after death, it may codify law and morals. In short, it may give expression to the group's basic tenets on astronomy, theology, sociology, law, education, even esthetics.

In studying symbolic systems, we want the students to understand myths rather than to learn them. We will give them examples from simple cultures for the same reason for which the anthropologist travels into an isolated society. Our hope is to lead the children to understand how man goes about explaining his world, making sense of it and that one kind of explanation is no more human than another.

We have selected for our starting point some hunting societies. An Eskimo society, a Bushman society, and an Australian aboriginal society will certainly suffice to show what the life experience of hunting peoples is. From the scrutiny of the myths of these groups, it is immediately clear that you can tell a society by the narratives it keeps. The ecology, the economy, the social structure, the tasks of men and women, and the fears and anxieties are reflected in the stories, and in a way which the children can handle them. One good example of Eskimo narrative or Eskimo poetry, if skillfully handled in class, can show the child that the problems of an Eskimo are like our problems: to cope with his environment, to cope with his fellow men, and to cope with himself. We hope to show that wherever man lives, he manages not only to survive and to breed, but also to think and to express his thoughts. But we can also let the children enjoy the particulars of a given culture—the sense of an alien ecology, the bush, or ice and snow, and a participant understanding for alien styles.

We introduce an origin myth, things taking their present order, the sun shining over the paths of the Bushmen, and the Bushmen starting to hunt. But we should equip the children with some possible theories to make the discussion profitable, theories not in words, but in ways of reading and understanding a myth. If the narrative is to be called a myth, it should portray conditions radically different from the way things are now. It is possible to devise ways for children to analyze a plot. If done with one story variant only, such an analysis may yield something akin to a phrase-structure grammar; if done with a group of myths, something comparable to a transformational grammar may result. It is intriguing to see how stories change. Children know such things intuitively and can be helped to appreciate them more powerfully.

One last thing: why should such things be taught so early? Why not postpone them until the student can handle the "theory" itself, not only the examples? There is a reason: if such things are new to a twenty-year-old, there is not only a new view to learn, but an old established view to unlearn. We want the children to recognize that man is constantly seeking to bring reason into his world, that he does so with a variety of symbolic tools, and that he does so with a striking and fully rational humanity. The unit on world view is under the direction of Dr Elli Maranda, aided by Mr Pierre Maranda and assisted by Miss Bonnie McLane.

Pedagogy

The most persistent problem in social studies is to rescue the phenomena of social life from familiarity without, at the same time, making it all seem "primitive" and bizarre. Three techniques are particularly useful to us in achieving this end. The first is contrast, of which much has already been said. The second is through the use of "games" that incorporate the formal properties of the phenomena for which the game is an analogue. In this sense, a game is like a mathematical model—an artificialized but often powerful representation of reality. Finally, we use the ancient approach of stimulating self-consciousness about assumptions—going beyond mere admonition to think. We believe there is a learnable strategy for discovering one's unspoken assumptions.

Before considering each of these, a word is in order about a point of view quite different from ours. It holds that one should begin teaching social studies by presenting the familiar world of home, the street, and the neighborhood. It is a thoroughly commendable ideal; its only fault is its failure to recognize how difficult it is for human beings to see generality in what has become familiar. The "friendly postman" is indeed the vicar of federal powers, but to lead the child to the recognition of such powers requires many detours into the realm of what constitutes power, federal or otherwise, and how, for example, constituted power and willfully exercised force differ. We would rather find a way of stirring the curiosity of our children with particulars whose intrinsic drama and human significance are plain—whether close at hand or at a far remove. If we can evoke a feeling for bringing order into what has been studied, the task is well started.

A word first about contrast. We hope to use four principal sources of contrast: man *versus* higher primates, man *versus* prehistoric man, contemporary technological man *versus* "primitive" man, and man *versus* child. We have been gathering materials relevant to each of the contrasts—films, stories, artifacts, readings, pictures, and above all, ideas for pointing up contrasts in the interest of achieving clarity.

Indeed, we often hope to achieve for our pupils a sense of continuity by presenting them first with what seems like contrast and letting them live with it long enough to sense that what before seemed different is, in fact, closely akin to things they understand from their own lives. So it is particularly with our most extensive collection of material, a film record taken through the full cycle of the year of a family of Netsilik Eskimo. The ecology and the externals are full of contrast to daily life in an American or European setting. But there is enough material available to go into depth, to work into the year's cycle of a single family so that our pupils can get a sense of the integrity not only of a family, but of a culture. It is characteristic of Netsilik Eskimo, for example, that they make a few beautifully specialized tools and weapons, such as their fishing lester or spear. But it is also apparent that each man can make do with the stones he finds around him, that the Eskimo is a superbly gifted *bricoleur*. Whenever he needs to do something, improvised tools come from nowhere. A flat stone, a little fish oil, a touch of arctic cotton and he has a lamp. So while the Eskimo film puts modern technological man in sharp contrast, it also serves perhaps even better, to present the inherent, internal logic of any society. Each society has its own approach to technology, to the use of intelligence.

Games go a long way toward getting children involved in understanding language and social organization; they also introduce, as we have already noted, the idea of a theory of these phenomena. We do not know to what extent these games will be successful, but we shall give them a careful try-out. The alleged success of these rather sophisticated games in business management and military affairs is worth extrapolating!

As for stimulating self-consciousness about thinking, we feel that the best approach is through stimulating the art of getting and using information—what is involved in going beyond the information given and what makes it possible to take such leaps. Crutchfield has produced results in this sphere by using nothing more complicated than a series of comic books in which the adventures of a detective, aided by his nephew and niece, are recounted. The theme is using clues cleverly. As children explore the implications of clues encountered, their general reasoning ability increases, and they formulate more and better hypotheses. We plan to design materials in which children have an opportunity to do this sort of thinking with questions related to the course—possibly in connection with prehistoric materials where it will be most relevant. If it turns out to be the case that the clothing that people wore was made from the skins of the ibex, what can they "postdict" about the size of a hunting party and how would they look for data? Professor Leaky informs us that he has some useful material on this subject.

Children should be at least as self-conscious about their strategies of thought as they are about their attempts to commit things to memory. So too the "tools" of thought—what is explanation and "cause." One of those tools is language—perhaps the principal one. We shall try to encourage children to have a look at language in this light.

The most urgent need of all is to give our pupils the experience of what it is to use a theoretical model, with some sense of what is involved in being aware that one is trying out a theory. We shall be using a fair number of rather sophisticated theoretical notions, in intuitively rather than formally stated form, to be sure, but we should like to give children the experience of using alternative models. This is perhaps easiest to do in the study of language, but it can also be done elsewhere.

We shall, of course, try to encourage students to discover on their own. Children surely need to discover generalizations on their own. Yet we want to give them enough opportunity to do so to develop a decent competence at it and a proper confidence in their ability to operate on their own. There is also some need for the children to pause and review in order to recognize the connections within the structure they have learned—the kind of internal discovery that is probably of highest value. The cultivation of such a sense of connectedness is surely the hub of our curriculum effort.

If we are successful, we would hope to achieve five ideals:

1. To give our pupils respect for and confidence in the powers of their own mind.

2. To give them respect, moreover, for the powers of thought concerning the human condition, man's plight, and his social life.
3. To provide them with a set of workable models that make it simpler to analyze the nature of the social world in which they live and the condition in which man finds himself.
4. To impart a sense of respect for the capacities and plight of man as a species, for his origins, for his potential, for his humanity.
5. To leave the student with a sense of the unfinished business of man's evolution.

The Form of the Course

It is one thing to describe the nature of a course in terms of its underlying discipline and its pedagogical aims, and quite another to render these hopes into a workable form for real teachers in real classes. Teachers are sufficiently constrained by their work loads so that it would be vain to hope they might read generally and widely enough in the field to be able to give form to the course in their own terms. The materials to be covered in this particular course, moreover, are so vast in scope as to be forbidding. The materials, in short, have got to be made usable and attractive not only to the highly gifted teacher, but to teachers in general, and to teachers who live with the ordinary fatigue of coping with younger pupils day by day. They cannot be overburdened with reading, nor can the reading be of such an order as to leave them with a feeling of impotence. At the same time, the material presented should be woven loosely enough to permit the teacher to satisfy his interests in forming a final product to be presented to children.

That much said, we can state what we mean by a *unit*, the elements of which the course is made. A unit is a body of materials and exercises that may occupy as much as several days of class time or as little as half a class period. In short, it can be played to the full and consume a considerable amount of the course content, or be taken *en passant*. Indeed, some units will surely be skipped and are intended only for those teachers who have a particular interest in a topic or a particular kind of exercise. There will be more units than can possibly be fitted into a year's course and teachers will be encouraged to put them together in a form that is commodious to their own intent.

In a manner of speaking, a collection of such units constitutes a course of study. But the image is unfortunate, connoting as it does so many beads strung together by some principle of succession. It is our hope that after a certain number of units have been got through, a unit can then be introduced to "recode" what has gone before, to exploit connection. Some units only review and present no new material.

A unit also sits on the teacher's ready shelf, and consists of six constituent elements.

1 *Talks to teachers.* These consist of lively accounts of the nature of the unit—particularly the nature of its mystery, what about it impels curiosity and wonder. Our experience in preparing these indicates the importance of staying close to the great men in the field, if possible to find a great article that can be presented in somewhat abridged form. The design of a language (taken from Hockett) or the nature of kinship (taken from Radcliffe-Brown) or how a thing should be called (Roger Brown)—these

are examples. The genre needs further study and we are exploring the kind of writing required—something that is at once science and poetry. If it should turn out that a student finds "talks to teachers" worth reading, so much the better.

2 *Queries and contrasts.* In trying out materials to be taught, we have learned certain ways of getting ideas across or getting the students to think out matters on their own. Often these can be embodied in devices—pictures, reading, and diagrams. But sometimes they are best stated as hints to teachers about questions to use and contrasts to invoke.

"How could you improve the human hand?" turns out to be a useful question. So does the question, "What are the different ways something can 'stand for' something else, like a red light 'standing for' *stop?*"

We have already spoken of our tactical fondness for contrasts, and we are coming up with useful ones in our designing. One such is to have students contrast a cry of pain with the words, "It hurts." Another is to compare the usual words from which phonemes may be inferred—hit, hat, hate, hut, hot, etc. Or the difference to be found in the two allophones of the phoneme /p/ in the words *spit* and *pit*—the the latter of which will blow out a match held to the lips, the former will not. Yet the two are regarded as the "same letter" or the "same sound" whereas *hot* and *hut* are "different."

3 *Devices.* This part of the unit contains the "stuff"—the material for students. Principal among the devices is, of course, reading material and we are, like others, struggling to get such material prepared. In good season we hope to understand this obscure matter better. Currently, we are operating, much as others have, to find, or cause to be written, material that is interesting, informative, and in a decent style.

But there are many devices beyond reading that are in need of developing for different units. One is the film loop for use with the Technicolor cartridge projectors that we use increasingly. We are putting together four-minute loops constructed from Eskimo and baboon footage, with the intention of *asking* questions or *posing* riddles. Too often, films have a way of producing passivity. Can we devise ones to do the opposite? Why does *Last Year at Marienbad* abrade the curiosity so well?

We are also exploring what can be done with games, as already noted, and with animation and graphics and maps. We shall get help where we can find it within ESI and outside.

4 *Model exercises.* From time to time in devising a unit it becomes plain that the problem we face is less in the subject matter and more in the intellectual habits of children in ordinary schools. We have commented on some of these problems already—the difficulty many children and not a few adults have in distinguishing necessary from necessary and sufficient conditions, the tendency of children to be lazy in using information, not exploiting its inferential power to nearly the degree warranted.

Model exercises are designed to overcome such intellectual difficulties. We think they are best kept imbedded in the very materials one is teaching. But it is often helpful to provide the teacher with additional special devices. We intend to use puzzles, conundrums, games—a kind of pedagogical first-aid kit.

5 *Documentaries.* These are accounts, or even tape recordings, of ordinary children at work with the materials in the unit. We would like the documentary to be both exemplary and at the same time typical enough to be within reach of a teacher in his own work.

Along with the documentary goes a more analytic description. The analytic documentary is designed to serve dual purposes. The first is to make it plainer both to ourselves and to teachers what in fact are the psychological problems involved in particular kinds of intellectual mastery that we hope to stimulate in children. In this sense, the analytic documentary is a further clarification of our pedagogical objectives. But in another sense, they represent an attempt on our part to accustom teachers to thinking in more general terms about the intellectual life of children. The second objective—call it educational—is to provide teachers with what might be a more useful educational psychology than the kind that is found conventionally in textbooks dedicated to that obscure subject.

It is our hope that as we proceed in our work there will be spin-offs in the form of general research problems that can be worked on by research centers not directly geared to the daily routines of curriculum building and curriculum testing. The work of such centers, as well as research in the regular literature on intellectual development, will constitute a continuing font from which we can draw material for the analytic documentaries.

6 *Supplementary materials.* The final section of the unit "kit" consists of such supplementary materials as paperbacks (and lists of related paperbacks), additional film and game materials, and such other devices as might attract the attention of either a diligent student or an aspiring teacher. Without question, it will become clearer what is needed by way of supplement once we have gone further into providing what will be our standard fare.

A final word about the unit materials. We hope to issue them in such a form that each year's experience can be added to the previous year's kit. That is to say, we believe that as new experience is gained in teaching the course, new editions of the kits should be made available to all our teachers. We intend to gather the wisdom of teachers who try out the course so that it may be made available later to others, to gather in new materials for teaching, new documentaries, new analyses of the scholarly literature, and fresh attempts through our talks to teachers to lend a still more compelling mystery to those topics that deserve to be taught. Indeed, it is probably obvious by now that the six-sectioned unit kit, stretched from one end of the teacher's shelf to the other, is our proposed substitute for that normally most unhelpful genre, the teacher's manual.

Teacher Training

No plans for teacher training have yet been established, save that we hope within the next two years to bring together for a summer session a group of master teachers to help advise us about proper steps. Our staff now includes several highly gifted and experienced teachers, all now brooding over this very issue.

Try-out and Shaping

The "course," such as it is, will be "taught" to three classes this coming summer (1965) at the Underwood School in Newton. The classes will be fourth, fifth, and sixth grades, with the object of discovering at what level to pitch the material, how to take account of the slow and fast learners, and so on. But teaching is in this case part of a summer workshop effort to get material written, drawn, readied. It will also provide an opportunity to do the kind of intensive interviewing of children to determine what they are making of the material and how their grip may be strengthened.

In short, the summer ahead is a first effort to do an intensive summer workshop on the course.

9
Objectives

W. James Popham

A key feature of any rational planning, educational or otherwise, is the possession of some idea of what is to be accomplished. Educators, of course, characteristically describe these intended accomplishments as their goals or objectives. Some people use the terms "goal" or "objective" interchangeably, as well as such synonyms as "aims," "intents," etc. Other people employ a much more distinctive meaning of the terms, using "goal" to describe a broader description of intent and "objective" to denote a more specific spelling out of the goal. Because there is currently no overwhelmingly preferred usage of these terms, be sure to seek clarification from an educator regarding the manner in which he is using the many terms which may be employed to describe educational goals. In this guidebook, the terms will be employed interchangeably.

Measurability and Clarity

One of the most prominent arenas of educational activity during the 1960s concerned the form in which instructional objectives should be stated. As a consequence of the programmed instruction movement which captured the attention of many educators during the early sixties, we heard more and more about the merits of stating objectives in precise, measurable terms. Programmed instruction enthusiasts pointed out again and again that such objectives were requisite for a proper instructional design. A number of other instructional specialists also began to support the worth of explicitly stated objectives. What was the point of this activity?

For years educators have been specifying their objectives in rather general language such as, "At the end of the year the student will become familiar with important literary insights." There is nothing intrinsically wrong with such an objective, for it probably provides one with a general idea of what is to be done during the year. However, for instructional or evaluation purposes, such an objective is almost useless since it identifies no specific indicator for determining whether or not the objective has been achieved. As a consequence, in recent years an increasing number of educators have urged that in order for objectives to function effectively in instructional and evaluation situations, they must be stated in terms of *measurable learner behavior.* In other words, since educational systems are designed to improve the learner in some way, an educational objective should describe the particular kind of behavior changes which will reflect such improvement. An example of objectives which would satisfy this measurability criterion would be the following: "When given previously unencountered selections from different authors, the student can, by style and other cues, correctly name the writer." The main attribute of a properly stated instructional objective is that it describes what the learner *will do* or is *able to do* at the end of instruction which he could not prior to instruction. Another way of putting it is that a usefully stated objective will invariably be measurable in such a way that an unequivocal determination can be made as to whether the objective has been accomplished.

The major advantages of such objectives is that they promote increased *clarity* regarding educational intents, whereas vague and unmeasurable objectives yield considerable ambiguity and, as a consequence, the possibility of many interpretations not only of what the objective means but, perhaps more importantly, whether it has been accomplished.

During the past several years many books and papers and audiovisual aids have been published[1] which guide the practitioner regarding how instructional objectives should be stated. Some of these guides focus considerable attention on the choice of verb used to describe the hoped-for post-instruction status of the learner. For instance, instead of saying "The learner *will know* the chief battles of the Civil War," the educator is advised to put it this way: "The learner *will list* in writing the chief battles of the Civil War." Note that the only difference is that in the second objective a verb is employed which describes a specific type of action or *behavior* on the part of the learner, in contrast to the verb "know" which can mean many things to many people. In the preferred objective a phrase, "in writing," has also been added which ties down the meaning of the objective even more. Since the essential feature of a properly stated objective is that it unambiguously communicates an educational intent, we might also have used such phrases as:

will recite aloud
will select from a list
will write the names of the opposing generals

One can think of different verbs which might be employed to communicate what is intended in an objective. At a very general level there are "internal state" verbs such as "understand." At a more specific level we can think of action verbs such as "identify" or "distinguish." But even these verbs permit some difference in interpretations as to the precise manner in which the learner will identify or distinguish. Even more specific behavioral phrases such as "pointing to" or "reciting aloud" further reduce the ambiguity. In general, the evaluator should employ phrases with sufficient specificity for the task at hand. Usually, that will mean more rather than less specific language.

Because a well formed instructional objective describes the type of learner behavior which is to be produced by the instructional treatment, such statements have often been referred to as *behavioral objectives* or *performance objectives.* The reason why so many educators have recently been advocating such goal statements is that the reduced ambiguity of the objectives yields a significant increase in the clarity needed both for (1) deciding on the *worth* of the objective and (2) determining whether the objective has been *achieved.*

Another important attribute of a well stated instructional objective is that it refers to the *learner's* behavior, not that of the *teacher.* Statements such as "the teacher will introduce the class to the basic elements of set theory" do not qualify as educational objectives, for they merely describe the nature of the educational treatment (in this case provided by the teacher), not what that treatment is to accomplish in terms of modifications in the learner.

An additional element of a usefully formulated instructional objective is that it should refer to the learner's *post-instruction* behavior, not his behavior during instruction. For instance, we might imagine a group of children working furiously on practice problems in a mathematics class. Now it is not on the basis of the learners' skill with these practice problems that the teacher will judge the adequacy of his instruction, but on later problems given as part of an end-of-unit or end-of-course examination. Thus, the type of learner behavior to be described in a properly stated educational objective must definitely occur after the instruction designed to promote it.

The term "post-instruction" should be clarified, however. Certainly we are interested in what is happening to learners during the course of a school year, not merely at its conclusion. Thus, we test or otherwise observe pupils at numerous points during the year. Similarly, we might conceive of a one week or single day instructional period for our treatment. A useful objective, useful in the sense that we can determine whether it has been achieved by the learner, might be promoted by an extremely short instructional period.

Guideline Number 1. The educational evaluator should encourage the use of instructional objectives which provide explicit descriptions of the post-instruction behavior desired of learners.

All, or Nothing at All?

As the evaluator becomes conversant with the advantages of measurable goals he sometimes becomes excessive in his advocacy of such objectives. Educators will ask him, "Must *all* my goals be stated in measurable terms? Aren't there some objectives that I can pursue even if I can't describe precisely how I will measure them?"

For *evaluation purposes*, the response should be that unmeasurable goals are of little or no use. Yet, for instructional purposes a more conciliatory response is warranted. There are undoubtedly some objectives, e.g., promoting a student's appreciation of art, which may currently be unassessable yet are so intrinsically meritorious that they are worth the risk of some instructional investment. Such high-risk high-gain goals might reasonably command a segment of our instructional time, but it is the *proportion* of instruction devoted to the pursuit of such goals which is at issue. Currently, the vast majority of our educational efforts are devoted to the pursuit of such non-measurable aims. We need to alter the proportion so that most of our goals are of a measurable nature, thus permitting us to determine whether they have been accomplished and, consequently, allowing us to get better at achieving them. Some proportion of instructional resources might, on the other hand, because of great potential dividends, be devoted to the pursuit of non-measurable objectives. From an evaluator's point of view, the unmeasurable goals will be of no use, thus he should attempt to reduce the proportion of such non-behavioral goals to a reasonable number. At the same time, of course, we should increase our sophistication in measuring those goals which are important but currently elusive so that in the future we can measure even these.

Guideline Number 2. While recognizing that non-measurable goals will be of limited use for his purposes, the educational evaluator must be aware that instructors may wish to devote a reasonable proportion of their efforts to the pursuit of important but currently unassessable objectives.

Selected and Constructed Learner Responses

When describing the myriad forms of learner behavior which educators might be interested in achieving you will find that the learner is engaging in acts which can be classified under two headings, that is, he is either *selecting* from alternatives or *constructing*. He is *selecting* when he chooses "true" or "false" to describe a statement or when he picks the answer to a multiple choice question. He is *constructing* when he writes an essay, gives an impromptu speech, or performs a free exercise routine in a gymnastics class. In a sense the difference between selected and constructed responses is somewhat similar to the difference between "recognition" and "recall" as used by measurement specialists in connection with customary achievement testing. When the learner is asked to recognize a correct answer from among multiple choice alternatives, he must select the correct response. When he is asked to recall a correct answer, he must construct his own response, presumably based on his recollection of what the correct answer should be. Beyond this difference, however, the selection versus construction distinction can be applied to all types of learner response, noncognitive as well as cognitive, and therefore is more useful.

The distinction between selected and constructed responses becomes important when we realize that with selected response objectives it is relatively simple to determine whether the learner's responses are acceptable, for we merely identify in advance which alternatives are the correct ones. With constructed responses, however, the task is far more difficult since we must identify in advance the criteria by which we will distinguish between acceptable and unacceptable learner responses. To illustrate, if the objective concerns the learner's skill in writing essays, then unless we can specify the standard which all acceptable essays must satisfy, we have an objective which is difficult if not impossible to measure.

The importance of this point cannot be overemphasized, for many educators who zealously proclaim the merits of measurable objectives end up by offering the following type of goal as an example of a well written objective:

> At the conclusion of the course the student will describe the major contributions of each novelist studied during the semester.

The difficulty with such objectives is that the elements needed to render a description satisfactory are not delineated. How will the teacher, in examining the various descriptions prepared by her students, decide which ones are good enough? This should not suggest that such criteria cannot be isolated or described. They definitely can, but it is hard work. Many teachers who rely heavily on constructed response student behavior prefer the work-evading tactic of relying on a "general impression" of the quality of a student's efforts. The unreliability of such general impressions, of course, has been amply documented through the years.

The major point of this discussion is that if an objective is based upon a learner's constructed response, the *criteria of adequacy must be given*, that is, the standards for judging the acceptability of a learner's response must be supplied. The criteria of adequacy should be included in the objective, or at least referred to in the objective. For example, the following objective would be acceptable:

> The learner will deliver a 15 minute extemporaneous speech violating no more than two of the twelve "rules for oral presentation" supplied in class, as judged by a panel of three randomly selected classmates using the standard rating form.

Ideally, the evaluator would prefer a set of crisply stated criteria by which to determine the adequacy of a constructed response. In practice, however, it may be necessary to state such criteria in terms of a group of judges being satisfied. For instance, even without explicating a single criterion, one can frame a satisfactory objective which indicates that a judge (or judges) will consider satisfactory greater proportions of post-instruction learner responses than those which occurred prior to instruction.

An example of this stratagem may prove helpful. Suppose an elementary teacher wants to improve her pupils' abilities to prepare watercolor prints, but has difficulty in describing criteria of adequacy for determining the quality of colors. She might give a particular assignment at the start of instruction, next teach the children, then give an *identical* watercolor assignment after instruction. The two productions of each child are then randomly paired after first having been secretly coded so that the teacher knows which was pre-instruction and which was post-instruction. The pairs are then given to a competent judge who is asked simply to designate which of any pair is better. No criteria at all need be described. The hope, of course, would be that more of the post-instruction watercolors would be judged superior. The objective for such a situation might be phrased like this:

> When compared with pre-instruction watercolor preparations based on an identical assignment, at least 75 per cent of the pupils' post-instruction watercolor productions will be considered superior by an external judge who is not aware of the point at which the watercolors were prepared.

It is important to use an external judge in these situations to avoid bias, conscious or subconscious, on the part of the teacher or, for that matter, anyone involved heavily in the instruction.

Anytime anyone engaged in educational evaluation encounters a constructed response objective without clearly explicated criteria of adequacy, the deficiency should be remedied or the objective discarded.

Guideline Number 3. The educational evaluator must identify criteria of adequacy when using instructional objectives which require constructed responses from learners.

Content Generality

In the early 1960s any objective which explicitly described the learner's post-instruction behavior was considered to be an acceptable goal statement. Such objectives as the following were frequently found in sets of recommended goals:

> The pupil will be able to identify at least three elements in *Beowulf* which are characteristic of the epic form.

Yet, upon examining such objectives it becomes clear that the statement is nothing more than a test item concerning the particular literary work, *Beowulf.* Such objectives, while sufficiently precise, are not very economical to use. To teach a semester or year long course with this type of objectives one might be obliged to have dozens or even hundreds of such statements. At any rate, what most educators wish to accomplish is not so limited in scope, but covers a broad range of learner behaviors, behaviors which hopefully can be employed profitably in many situations. Professor Eva Baker[2] has offered a useful distinction between objectives according to whether they possess content *generality* or *test* item *equivalence.* The former *Beowulf* example, since it dealt with a single test item, possessed test item equivalence and is of limited utility. To possess content generality, that is, to describe a broader range of learner behavior, the objective could be rewritten as follows:

> The pupil will be able to identify at least three elements in any epic which are characteristic of that form.

By referring to *any epic,* rather than a particular epic, the objective takes on a more general form, and, as such, can be more parsimoniously employed by educational evaluators. If only to avoid the necessity of dealing with innumerable objectives, educational evaluators should foster the use of content-general objectives and eschew the use of test item equivalent goals.

One of the most vexing problems for those who work with instructional objectives is deciding *just how specific* or *just how general* they should be stated. Although there are no absolute guides here, or even consensus preference, it has become clear that the level of generality for objectives should probably vary from situation to situation. A teacher in the classroom may wish to use extremely explicit objectives. Yet, if the evaluator is attempting to secure reactions from community people regarding their estimates of the worth of certain objectives, then more general statements may be preferable. There are experimental techniques which can be used to cope with the generality level question, but until we have definitive evidence regarding what level works best in given situations, it would be wise for the evaluator to remain flexible on this point.

Guideline Number 4. The educational evaluator should foster the use of measurable objectives which possess content generality rather than test item equivalence.

Proficiency Levels

Once a measurable objective has been formulated, there is another question which should be answered by those framing the objective, namely, *how well* should the learner perform the behavior specified in the objectives. A convenient way of thinking about this question is to consider two kinds of minimal proficiency levels which can be associated with an objective.

First, we are interested in the degree of proficiency which must be displayed by an individual learner. This is called the *student minimal level* and is illustrated by the *italicized* section in the following objective:

> The learner will be able to multiply correctly *at least nine out of ten* of any pair of two digit multiplication problems randomly generated by the instructor.

This student minimal level asserts that the learner must perform with at least a 90 per cent proficiency.

A second decision needs to be made with respect to the proportion of the *group* of learners who must master the objective. Does everyone need to achieve the objective? Only half the class? This is established through the *class minimal level* which is illustrated by the *italicized* section of the following objective:

> *Eighty per cent or more* of the learners will be able to multiply correctly at least nine out of ten of any pair of two digit multiplication problems randomly generated by the instructor.

Here we see that for the objective to be achieved at the desired levels of proficiency at least 80 per cent of the learners must perform 90 per cent or better on the multiplication problems. Sometimes this is referred to as an 80–90 proficiency level.

Now the advantage, particularly to the evaluator, of specifying class and student minimal levels *prior to instruction* is that the power of the instructional treatment can then be tested against such standards in producing the hoped-for results. Too often the designers of an instructional system will, after instruction, settle for mediocre levels of proficiency. By pre-setting performance standards those involved in the design and implementation of the instructional treatment are forced to put their pedagogical proficiency on the line.

But it's easier to say how to state minimal proficiency levels than it is to decide just what they should be. Too many educators merely pluck them from the air if they're used at all, e.g., "We want 90–90 levels on all our objectives." Obviously, this would be unthinking, for there are certain objectives which we would hope that *all* of our learners would achieve with 100 per cent proficiency. Examples of these might be in the field of health, rudimentary intellectual skills, etc.

Probably the best we can do now is to seek the wisdom of many people, certainly including those who have experience in the education of the learners with whom we are working. Careful analysis of how well learners have done in the past, coupled with our most insightful appraisal of how well each individual *should* perform with respect to the objective, can yield an approximation of defensible class and student minimal levels.

An important consideration for establishing some proficiency levels is the initial skill of the learner prior to instruction, sometimes referred to as his "entry behavior." For certain instructional situations, e.g., remedial math, learners who commence an instructional sequence with abysmally low entry behaviors might not be expected to perform as well at the close of instruction as other learners who headed into the instruction with an advantage. For other situations, the criterion levels are not so malleable, thus we would expect students in a driver training course to achieve the desired minimal levels irrespective of their entry behavior.

Now it is always possible, of course, to alter performance standards after the instructional treatment has either proven to be ineffectual or more effective than we thought.

But this should be done very cautiously, only after pushing the instructional treatment to the limits of its potency.

Guideline Number 5. Prior to the introduction of the instructional treatment educational evaluators should strive to establish minimal proficiency levels for instructional objectives.

The Taxonomies of Educational Objectives

A technique for analyzing objectives which many evaluators find useful stems from the work of Benjamin Bloom and a group of university examiners who in 1956 published a scheme[3] for classifying educational objectives according to the kinds of learner behavior they were attempting to promote. An extension of the classification scheme by David Krathwohl and others appeared in 1964.[4] These two *taxonomies* (classification schemes) of educational objectives first divided instructional goals into three groups or *domains*, the cognitive, affective, and psychomotor. *Cognitive* objectives deal with intellectual learner outcomes such as whether a pupil can analyze sentences into their component parts or can recall the names of the 50 states. *Affective* objectives are concerned with attitudinal, valuing, emotional learner actions such as promoting a pupil's interest in literature or strengthening his esteem for democratic processes. *Psychomotor* objectives describe intended learner outcomes of a largely physical skill nature such as learning to use a typewriter or how to swim the breaststroke.

Each of these three domains has been further subdivided into several levels of learner behaviors which are sought in each domain. For instance, in the cognitive domain we find *knowledge* objectives which, briefly, describe those goals that require the learner to recall information of one sort or another. Another type of objective in the cognitive domain is *analysis* which refers to the learner's ability to subdivide a complex whole into its constituent segments. Within each domain the several levels of objectives are arranged more or less hierarchically so that, for example, analysis objectives are ranked higher than knowledge objectives. Lower levels within a domain are generally considered prerequisite to higher levels.

To the evaluator, the major utility of a taxonomic analysis of the objectives with which he is dealing is that he can detect unsuspected omissions or overemphasis. For example, he might subject a group of objectives under consideration by a school faculty to an analysis according to the taxonomies and discover that there were no affective objectives present or that all of the cognitive objectives were at the lowest levels of the cognitive domain. Once apprised of this situation the school faculty might wish to select the objectives anyway, but at least they have a better idea of the types of goals they are adopting.

Although each of the three domains has been broken down into multiple levels, six for the cognitive, five for the affective and five for the psychomotor,[5] the evaluator may find the use of all of these levels too sophisticated for some of the tasks he must accomplish. Many educators report sufficient utility is gained by using the three major domain headings, i.e., cognitive, affective, and psychomotor, coupled with a rough two-level break-down in each domain, such as "lowest level" and "higher than lowest level." However, there may be some situations in which a more fine grained analysis is required.[6] Accordingly, brief descriptions of each level in each of the three domains are presented below. An evaluator should, however, regroup the levels into a system of sufficient precision for the task at hand.

Cognitive Domain

The cognitive domain has six levels. They move from knowledge, the lowest level, to evaluation, the highest level.

Knowledge. Knowledge involves the recall of specifics or universals, the recall of methods and processes, or the recall of a pattern, structure, or setting. It will be noted that the essential attribute at this level is *recall.* For assessment purposes, a recall situation involves little more than "bringing to mind" appropriate material.

Comprehension. This level represents the lowest form of understanding and refers to a kind of apprehension that indicates that a student knows what is being communicated and can make use of the material or idea without necessarily relating it to other material or seeing it in its fullest implications.

Application. Application involves the use of abstractions in particular or concrete situations. The abstractions used may be in the form of procedures, general ideas, or generalized methods. They may also be ideas, technical principles, or theories that must be remembered and applied to novel situations.

Analysis. Analysis involves the breakdown of a communication into its constituent parts such that the relative hierarchy within that communication is made clear, that the relations between the expressed ideas are made explicit, or both. Such analyses are intended to clarify the communication, to indicate how it is organized and the way in which the communication managed to convey its effects as well as its basis and arrangement.

Synthesis. Synthesis represents the combining of elements and parts so that they form a whole. This operation involves the process of working with pieces, parts, elements, and so on, and arranging them so as to constitute a pattern or structure not clearly present before.

Evaluation. Evaluation requires judgments about the value of material and methods for given purposes. Quantitative and qualitative judgments are made about the extent to which material and methods satisfy criteria. The criteria employed may be those determined by the learner or those given to him.

Affective Domain

The affective domain is subdivided into five levels. These levels, in particular, may cause the evaluator much difficulty in classifying objectives. Once more, the five levels may have some value in that they encourage one to think about different forms of objectives, but it is not recommended that the evaluator devote too much time in attempting to classify various objectives within these levels.

Receiving (Attending). The first level of the affective domain is concerned with the learner's sensitivity to the existence of certain phenomena and stimuli, that is, with his willingness to receive or to attend to them. This category is divided into three subdivisions which reflect three different levels of attending to phenomena—namely, awareness of the phenomena, willingness to receive phenomena, and controlled or selected attention to phenomena.

Responding. At this level one is concerned with responses that go beyond merely attending to phenomena. The student is sufficiently motivated that he is not just "willing to attend," but is actively attending.

Valuing. This category reflects the learner's holding of a particular value. The learner displays behavior with sufficient consistency in appropriate situations that he actually is perceived as holding this value.

Organization. As the learner successively internalizes values, he encounters situations in which more than one value is relevant. This requires the necessity of organizing his values into a system such that certain values exercise greater control.

Characterization by a Value or Value Complex. At this highest level of the affective taxonomy internalization has taken place in an individual's value hierarchy to the extent that we can actually characterize him as holding a particular value or set of values.

Psychomotor Domain

Simpson's psychomotor taxonomy, although not as widely used as the cognitive and affective taxonomies, rounds out our three domain picture. Like the affective taxonomy, this domain consists of five levels.

Perception. The first step in performing a motor act is the process of becoming aware of objects, qualities or relations by way of the sense organs. It is the main portion of the situation-interpretation-action chain leading to motor activity.

Set. Set is a preparatory adjustment for a particular kind of action or experience. Three distinct aspects of set have been identified, namely, mental, physical, and emotional.

Guided Response. This is an early step in the development of a motor skill. The emphasis is upon the abilities that are components of the more complex skill. Guided response is the overt behavioral act of an individual under the guidance of another individual.

Mechanism. At this level the learner has achieved a certain confidence and degree of skill in the performance of an act. The habitual act is a part of his repertoire of possible responses to stimuli and the demands of situations where the response is appropriate.

Complex Overt Response. At this level, the individual can perform a motor act that is considered complex because of the movement pattern required. The act can be carried out efficiently and smoothly, that is, with minimum expenditure of energy and time.

Another way in which these taxonomies may be of use to the evaluator is as an aid in generating new objectives. The evaluator may suggest to the educator who is formulating objectives a wider variety of learner behaviors which might be incorporated in the objectives.

Guideline Number 6. The educational evaluator will often find the Taxonomies of Educational Objectives useful both in describing instructional objectives under consideration and in generating new objectives.

Constructing Versus Selecting Objectives

Thus far in the discussion it has been emphasized that the educational evaluator will find the use of measurable instructional objectives invaluable in his work. Recalling that the two major roles of educational evaluation occur in connection with needs assessment and assessing treatment adequacy, the evaluator will find that measurable goals are literally indispensable in properly carrying out either of these two roles. As we continue to examine additional techniques which may be used by evaluators this will become even more evident. Yet, there is a major problem to be faced by the evaluator, namely, where do such measurable goals come from?

Suppose, for example, that an evaluation consultant is called upon by a local school district to help in determining whether a new treatment, in this case a series of new text books, is sufficiently effective. The first thing he does is to ask what objective the treatment is supposed to accomplish. If he discovers that no objectives arise, at least none beyond a few nebulous general goals, what is he to do? Should he refuse to assist the district until they put their objectives in order? Obviously not. Should he prepare the objectives himself? Well, for any extended treatment that requires a tremendous amount of work and, besides, the school staff may not agree with the objectives he constructs. Should he give the school faculty a crash course in how to write objectives, then help them as they spell out their own measurable goals? So far, this seems like the best alternative, but the evaluator had best recognize that most school personnel—teachers through administrators—are already heavily committed to other assignments. Too many evaluators who have used this "help them construct their own objectives" approach will recount frustrating experiences in getting already harassed teachers to write out their own measurable objectives.

A better alternative would seem to be to ask the school faculty to *select* objectives from a set of alternatives rather than to ask them to construct their own. Selecting measurable objectives from a wide ranging set of alternatives represents a task that can reasonably be accomplished by most educators. Asking those same educators to *construct* their own measurable objectives is, generally speaking, an unrealistic request.

During the past few years several agencies have been established to collect large pools of instructional objectives and test measures. In general, these item banks and objectives banks have been assembled to permit educators to employ their resources in activities related to instruction or evaluation. A directory of extant collections of instructional objectives[7] is now available and should be of considerable use to an educational evaluator.

Illustrative of agencies established to collect and distribute educational objectives is the Instructional Objectives Exchange (IOX), founded in 1968. The Exchange has assembled an extensive collection of measurable instructional objectives in grades K-12 in all fields. These objectives were usually contributed to IOX by school districts, Title III projects, curriculum development teams, or individual teachers. Some were developed in the Instructional Objectives Exchange. As soon as a reasonably extensive group of objectives have been assembled in a given field at a given grade range, these are published as an IOX *collection*. Each collection consists of a set of objectives plus one or more measuring devices which may be used to assess the attainment of each objective. The Exchange intends to have at least a half dozen or so test items (broadly defined) for all their objectives so that they can be readily used to constitute pretests, posttests, etc.

By consulting the current listing of IOX objective collections[8] an evaluator can secure a set of alternative objectives from which the educators with whom he is working can select those appropriate for their own instructional situations. It is assumed that only a portion of any collection will be selected. Of course, if all the objectives which are sought are not included in a collection, the local educators can augment those available by writing some of their own. Since this should, in general, be a reasonably small number, the objective construction task should therefore not be too onerous.

Either for needs assessment or assessing treatment adequacy the use of extant objectives collections can prove invaluable. Although we shall be examining the specifics of the process in more detail later, it can be seen how in assessing the current perceptions of students, teachers, and community representatives regarding needed objectives, reactions to a list of possible objectives (selected from extant collections) would represent an economic way to secure such perceptions. Similarly, in assessing the adequacy of a new instructional procedure it should be relatively straightforward to select from an available collection those objectives which the procedure seemed best suited to accomplish. Since in many of the agencies currently distributing objectives a number of test items accompany each objective, it is apparent that it would be relatively simple to assess whether the objective had been accomplished.

To give the reader some idea of the kinds of materials available in these collections, Figure 9.1 includes an example from one of the IOX collections. Although the objectives from other objective pools may be organized somewhat differently, they are essentially comparable. In Figure 9.2 some affective objectives from two recently developed[9] collections, namely, (1) attitude toward school and (2) self-concept, are presented to illustrate the type of non-cognitive goals available in such collections.

Although the objective collections currently available at various locations throughout the country represent an extremely useful resource for the educational evaluator, there may be situations for which an evaluator finds no already prepared objectives available. The most likely alternatives for him to follow have been previously described, and they usually require his heavy involvement in construction of the objectives. Another option, however, is to try to pool the resources of several groups who have similar interests in order to produce a new objective pool. For instance, several of the health professions, notably nursing and dental education, have lately shown considerable interest in

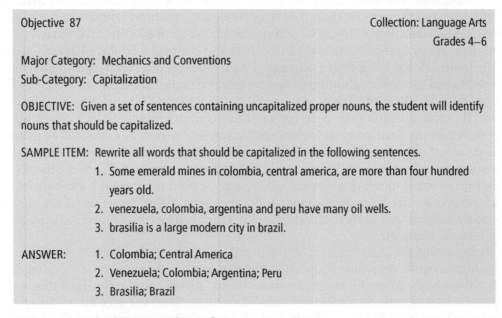

Objective 87 — Collection: Language Arts, Grades 4–6

Major Category: Mechanics and Conventions

Sub-Category: Capitalization

OBJECTIVE: Given a set of sentences containing uncapitalized proper nouns, the student will identify nouns that should be capitalized.

SAMPLE ITEM: Rewrite all words that should be capitalized in the following sentences.

1. Some emerald mines in colombia, central america, are more than four hundred years old.
2. venezuela, colombia, argentina and peru have many oil wells.
3. brasilia is a large modern city in brazil.

ANSWER:

1. Colombia; Central America
2. Venezuela; Colombia; Argentina; Peru
3. Brasilia; Brazil

Figure 9.1 Sample objective and item from an IOX collection.

Attitude Toward School

(Attitude Toward School Subjects) Students will indicate relative preferences for five subject areas (aesthetics—art and music; language arts—spelling, oral participation, listening, writing; mathematics; reading; science), when given sets of three verbal descriptions of classroom activities in specific subject areas and three corresponding pictures, by marking one of the pictures to indicate in which activity they would most like to participate.

(General Attitude) Students will indicate favorable attitudes toward school, in a global sense, by incurring a minimum of absenteeism from school during a specified time period, as observed from teacher or school records.

(Attitude Toward School Subjects) Students will reveal relative preferences for seven subject areas (English, arithmetic, social studies, art, music, physical education, science) by selecting, from among sets of seven "headlines" (each representing one of the subject areas noted above), those that appear most and least interesting to read about.

Self Concept

Given a contrived situation in which the teacher describes several factitiously esteemed students, class members will demonstrate positive self concepts by voluntarily identifying themselves as students who have won the teacher's esteem.

The students will display unconditionally positive self concepts by responding to a 10-item inventory, entitled *Parental Approval Index*, which asks how the child's mother would feel about him as a person if he engaged in certain actions which would normally be expected to yield disapproval of the act.

Students will display an expectation for future success by checking a higher percentage of want ad job requests from the *Choose a Job Inventory* which offer more prestigious, socially approved occupations.

Figure 9.2 Examples of objectives from two IOX collections in the affective domain.

establishing objective banks which are specifically designed for their own instructional situations.

As these recently developed objective collections are revised and updated, as different forms of data (e.g., consumer value ratings) are assembled to guide the selector, and as more sophisticated storage and retrieval systems (e.g., computer-based) are established, these objectives/measures banks should provide an increasingly useful set of tools for an educational evaluator.

Guideline Number 7. The educational evaluator should consider the possibility of selecting measurable objectives from extant collections of such objectives.

In reviewing the section regarding the uses of instructional objectives by educational evaluators, we have examined (1) the role of measurability as an aid to clarity, (2) selected versus constructed learner responses, (3) content general versus test item equivalent objectives, (4) the proportion of objectives which must be measurable, (5) performance standards, (6) taxonomic analysis of objectives, and (7) selecting objectives from extant collections. For each of those points a guideline was presented which, briefly, suggested a course of action for educational evaluators.

Notes

1. See, for example, Popham, W.J. and Baker, E.L. *Establishing Instructional Goals*, Prentice Hall, Inc., Englewood Cliffs, N.J., 1970, as well as the numerous citations in the selected references section of this guidebook. A series of filmstrip-tape programs distributed by Vimcet Associates, P.O. Box 24714, Los Angeles, California 90024, will also be helpful for training evaluation personnel.
2. Baker, E.L. *Defining Content for Objectives*, Vimcet Associates, Box 24714, Los Angeles, California, 1968.
3. Bloom, Benjamin, et al. *The Taxonomy of Educational Objectives, Handbook I: The Cognitive Domain*, David McKay, New York, 1956.
4. Krathwohl, David, et al. *The Taxonomy of Educational Objectives, Handbook II: The Affective Domain*, David McKay, New York, 1964.
5. Simpson, Elizabeth J. *The Classification of Educational Objectives: Psychomotor Domain*, Research Project No. OE-5-85-104, University of Illinois, Urbana, 1966.
6. It should be noted that in order to make accurate classifications according to the *Taxonomies* it is often necessary to know the nature of the instructional events preceding the point at which the learner's behavior is measured. For example, a given learner behavior might reflect only recall if the topic had been previously treated, but something quite different if not previously encountered in class.
7. The *Directory of Measurable Objectives Sources* at one time could be obtained from the Upper Midwest Regional Educational Laboratory in Minneapolis, Minnesota or in care of Mr. Arthur Olson, Colorado State Department of Education, State Office Building, Denver, Colorado 80203. Objectives and related tests of the Wisconsin Design for Reading Skill Development, an individualized reading system, are also available from National Computer Systems, 4401 West 76th St., Minneapolis, Minnesota 55435.
8. Available from IOX, Box 24095, Los Angeles, California 90024.
9. Support for the development of these affective objective collections was contributed in a cooperative effort of the state level ESEA Title III programs of the following states: Arizona, Colorado, Florida, Hawaii, Idaho, Iowa, Kansas, Massachusetts, Minnesota, Missouri, Montana, North Dakota, Ohio, Rhode Island, South Carolina, Texas and Wisconsin.

10

Educational Objectives—Help or Hindrance?[1]

Elliot W. Eisner

If one were to rank the various beliefs or assumptions in the field of curriculum that are thought most secure, the belief in the need for clarity and specificity in stating educational objectives would surely rank among the highest. Educational objectives, it is argued, need to be clearly specified for at least three reasons: first, because they provide the goals toward which the curriculum is aimed; second, because once clearly stated they facilitate the selection and organization of content; third, because when specified in both behavioral and content terms they make it possible to evaluate the outcomes of the curriculum.

It is difficult to argue with a rational approach to curriculum development—who would choose irrationality? And, if one is to build curriculum in a rational way, the clarity of premise, end or starting point, would appear paramount. But I want to argue in this paper that educational objectives clearly and specifically stated can hamper as well as help the ends of instruction and that an unexamined belief in curriculum as in other domains of human activity can easily become dogma which in fact may hinder the very functions the concept was originally designed to serve.

When and where did beliefs concerning the importance of educational objectives in curriculum development emerge? Who has formulated and argued their importance? What effect has this belief had upon curriculum construction? If we examine the past briefly for data necessary for answering these questions, it appears that the belief in the usefulness of clear and specific educational objectives emerged around the turn of the century with the birth of the scientific movement in education.

Before this movement gained strength, faculty psychologists viewed the brain as consisting of a variety of intellectual faculties. These faculties, they held, could be strengthened if exercised in appropriate ways with particular subject matters. Once strengthened, the faculties could be used in any area of human activity to which they were applicable. Thus, if the important faculties could be identified and if methods of strengthening them developed, the school could concentrate on this task and expect general intellectual excellence as a result.

This general theoretical view of mind had been accepted for several decades by the time Thorndike, Judd, and later Watson began, through their work, to chip away the foundations upon which it rested. Thorndike's work especially demonstrated the specificity of transfer. He argued theoretically that transfer of learning occurred if and only if elements in one situation were identical with elements in the other. His empirical work supported his theoretical views, and the enormous stature he enjoyed in education as well as in psychology influenced educators to approach curriculum development in ways consonant with his views. One of those who was caught up in the scientific movement in education was Franklin Bobbitt, often thought of as the father of curriculum theory. In 1918 Bobbitt published a signal work titled simply, *The Curriculum.*[2] In it he argued that educational theory is not so difficult to construct as commonly held and that curriculum theory is logically derivable from educational theory. Bobbitt wrote in 1918:

> The central theory is simple. Human life, however varied, consists in its performance of specific activities. Education that prepares for life is one that prepares definitely and adequately for these specific activities. However numerous and diverse they may be for any social class, they can be discovered. This requires that one go out into the world of affairs and discover the particulars of which these affairs consist. These will show the abilities, habits, appreciations, and forms of knowledge that men need. These will be the objectives of the curriculum. They will be numerous, definite, and particularized. The curriculum will then be that series of experiences which childhood and youth must have by way of attaining those objectives.[3]

In *The Curriculum*, Bobbitt approached curriculum development scientifically and theoretically: study life carefully to identify needed skills, divide these skills into specific units, organize these units into experiences, and provide these experiences to children. Six years later, in his second book, *How To Make a Curriculum*,[4] Bobbitt operationalized his theoretical assertions and demonstrated how curriculum components—especially educational objectives—were to be formulated. In this book Bobbitt listed nine areas in which educational objectives are to be specified. In these nine areas he listed 160 major educational objectives which run the gamut from "Ability to use language in all ways required for proper and effective participation in community life" to "Ability to entertain one's friends, and to respond to entertainment by one's friends."[5]

Bobbitt was not alone in his belief in the importance of formulating objectives clearly and specifically. Pendleton, for example, listed 1,581 social objectives for English, Guiler listed more than 300 for arithmetic in grades 1–6, and Billings prescribed 888 generalizations which were important for the social studies.

If Thorndike was right, if transfer was limited, it seemed reasonable to encourage the teacher to teach for particular outcomes and to construct curriculums only after specific objectives had been identified.

In retrospect it is not difficult to understand why this movement in curriculum collapsed under its own weight by the early 1930's. Teachers could not manage fifty highly specified objects, let alone hundreds. And, in addition, the new view of the child, not as a complex machine but as a growing organism who ought to participate in planning his own educational program, did not mesh well with the theoretical views held earlier.[6]

But, as we all know, the Progressive movement too began its decline in the forties, and by the middle fifties, as a formal organization at least, it was dead.

By the late forties and during the fifties, curriculum specialists again began to remind us of the importance of specific educational objectives and began to lay down guidelines for their formulation. Rationales for constructing curriculums developed by Ralph Tyler[7] and Virgil Herrick[8] again placed great importance on the specificity of objectives. George Barton[9] identified philosophic domains which could be used to select objectives. Benjamin Bloom and his colleagues[10] operationalized theoretical assertions by building a taxonomy of educational objectives in the cognitive domain; and in 1964, Krathwohl, Bloom, and Masia[11] did the same for the affective domain. Many able people for many years have spent a great deal of time and effort in identifying methods and providing prescriptions for the formulation of educational objectives, so much so that the statement "Educational objectives should be stated in behavioral terms" has been elevated—or lowered—to almost slogan status in curriculum circles. Yet, despite these efforts, teachers seem not to take educational objectives seriously—at least as they are prescribed from above. And when teachers plan curriculum guides, their efforts first to identify over-all educational aims, then specify school objectives, then identify educational objectives for specific subject matters, appear to be more like exercises to be gone through than serious efforts to build tools for curriculum planning. If educational objectives were really useful tools, teachers, I submit, would use them. If they do not, perhaps it is not because there is something wrong with the teachers but because there might be something wrong with the theory.

As I view the situation, there are several limitations to theory in curriculum regarding the functions educational objectives are to perform. These limitations I would like to identify.

Educational objectives are typically derived from curriculum theory, which assumes that it is possible to predict with a fair degree of accuracy what the outcomes of instruction will be. In a general way this is possible. If you set about to teach a student algebra, there is no reason to assume he will learn to construct sonnets instead. Yet, the outcomes of instruction are far more numerous and complex for educational objectives to encompass. The amount, type, and quality of learning that occurs in a classroom, especially when there is interaction among students, are only in small part predictable. The changes in pace, tempo, and goals that experienced teachers employ when necessary and appropriate for maintaining classroom organization are dynamic rather than mechanistic in character. Elementary school teachers, for example, are often sensitive to the changing interests of the children they teach, and frequently attempt to capitalize on these interests, "milking them" as it were for what is educationally valuable.[12] The teacher uses the moment in a situation that is better described as kaleidoscopic than stable. In the very process of teaching and discussing, unexpected opportunities emerge for making a valuable point, for demonstrating an interesting idea, and for teaching a significant concept. The first point I wish to make, therefore, is that the dynamic and complex process of instruction yields outcomes far too numerous to be specified in behavioral and content terms in advance.

A second limitation of theory concerning educational objectives is its failure to recognize the constraints various subject matters place upon objectives. The point here is brief. In some subject areas, such as mathematics, languages, and the sciences, it is possible to specify with great precision the particular operation or behavior the student is to perform after instruction. In other subject areas, especially the arts, such specification is frequently not possible, and when possible may not be desirable. In a class in mathematics or spelling, uniformity in response is desirable, at least insofar as it indicates that students are able to perform a particular operation adequately, that is, in accordance with accepted procedures. Effective instruction in such areas enables students to function with minimum error in these fields. In the arts and in subject matters where, for example, novel or creative responses are desired, the particular behaviors to be developed cannot easily be identified. Here curriculum and instruction should yield behaviors and products which are unpredictable. The end achieved ought to be something of a surprise to both teacher and pupil. While it could be argued that one might formulate an educational objective which specified novelty, originality, or creativeness as the desired outcome, the particular referents for these terms cannot be specified in advance; one must judge after the fact whether the product produced or the behavior displayed belongs in the "novel" class. This is a much different procedure than is determining whether or not a particular word has been spelled correctly or a specific performance, that is, jumping a 3-foot hurdle, has been attained. Thus, the second point is that theory concerning educational objectives has not taken into account the particular relationship that holds between the subject matter being taught and the degree to which educational objectives can be predicted and specified. This, I suppose, is in part due to the fact that few curriculum specialists have high degrees of intimacy with a wide variety of subject matters and thus are unable to alter their general theoretical views to suit the demands that particular subject matters make.

The third point I wish to make deals with the belief that objectives stated in behavioral and content terms can be used as criteria by which to measure the outcomes of curriculum and instruction. Educational objectives provide, it is argued, the standard against which achievement is to be measured. Both taxonomies are built upon this assumption since their primary function is to demonstrate how objectives can be used to frame test items appropriate for evaluation. The assumption that objectives can be used as standards by which to measure achievement fails, I think, to distinguish adequately between the application of a standard and the making of a judgment. Not all—perhaps not even most— outcomes of curriculum and instruction are amenable to measurement. The application of a standard requires that some arbitrary and socially defined quantity be designated by which other qualities can be compared. By virtue of socially defined rules of grammar, syntax, and logic, for example, it is possible to quantitatively compare and measure error in a discursive or mathematical statement. Some fields of activity, especially those which are qualitative in character, have no comparable rules and hence are less amenable to quantitative assessment. It is here that evaluation must be made, not primarily by applying a socially defined standard, but by making a human qualitative judgment. One can specify, for example, that a student shall be expected to know how to extract a square root correctly and in an unambiguous way, through the application of a standard, determine whether this end has been achieved. But it is only in a metaphoric sense that one can measure the extent to which a student has been able to produce an aesthetic object or an expressive narrative. Here standards are unapplicable; here judgment is required. The making of a judgment in distinction to the application of a standard implies that valued qualities are not merely socially defined and arbitrary in character. The judgment by which a critic determines the value of a poem, novel, or play is not achieved merely by applying standards already known to the particular product being judged; it requires that the critic—or teacher—view the product with respect to the unique properties it displays and then, in relation to his experience and sensibilities, judge its value in terms which are incapable of being reduced to quantity or rule.

This point was aptly discussed by John Dewey in his chapter on "Perception and Criticism" in *Art as Experience.*[13] Dewey was concerned with the problem of identifying the means and ends of criticism and has this to say about its proper function:

> The function of criticism is the reeducation of perception of works of art; it is an auxiliary process, a difficult process, of learning to see and hear. The conception that its business is to appraise, to judge in the legal and moral sense, arrests the perception of those who are influenced by the criticism that assumes this task.[14]

Of the distinction that Dewey makes between the application of a standard and the making of a critical judgment, he writes:

> There are three characteristics of a standard. It is a particular physical thing existing under specifiable conditions; it is *not* a value. The yard is a yard-stick, and the meter is a bar deposited in Paris. In the second place, standards are measures of things, of lengths, weights, capacities. The things measured are not values, although it is of great social value to be able to measure them, since the properties of things in the way of size, volume, weight, are important for commercial exchange. Finally, as standards of measure, standards define things with respect to *quantity*. To be able to measure quantities is a great aid to further judgments, but it is not a mode of judgment. The standard, being an external and public thing, is applied *physically*. The yard-stick is physically laid down upon things to determine their length.[15]

And I would add that what is most educationally valuable is the development of that mode of curiosity, inventiveness, and insight that is capable of being described only in metaphoric or poetic terms. Indeed, the image of the educated man that has been held in highest esteem for the longest period of time in Western civilization is one which is not amenable to standard measurement. Thus, the third point I wish to make is that curriculum theory which views educational objectives as standards by which to measure educational achievement overlooks those modes of achievement incapable of measurement.

The final point I wish to make deals with the function of educational objectives in curriculum construction.

The rational approach to curriculum development not only emphasizes the importance of specificity in the formulation of educational objectives but also implies when not stated explicitly that educational objectives be stated prior to the formulation of curriculum activities. At first view, this seems to be a reasonable way to proceed with curriculum construction: one should know where he is headed before embarking on a trip. Yet, while the procedure of first identifying objectives before proceeding to identify activities is logically defensible, it is not necessarily the most psychologically efficient way to proceed. One can, and teachers often do, identify activities that seem useful, appropriate, or rich in educational opportunities, and from a consideration of what can be done in class, identify the objectives or possible consequences of using these activities. MacDonald argues this point cogently when he writes:

> Let us look, for example, at the problem of objectives. Objectives are viewed as directives in the rational approach. They are identified prior to the instruction or action and used to provide a basis for a screen for appropriate activities.
>
> There is another view, however, which has both scholarly and experiential referents. This view would state that our objectives are only known to us in any complete sense after the completion of our act of instruction. No matter what we thought we were attempting to do, we can only know what we wanted to accomplish after the fact. Objectives by this rationale are heuristic devices which provide initiating consequences which become altered in the flow of instruction.
>
> In the final analysis, it could be argued, the teacher in actuality asks a fundamentally different question from "What am I trying to accomplish?" The teacher asks "What am I going to do?" and out of the doing comes accomplishment.[16]

Theory in curriculum has not adequately distinguished between logical adequacy in determining the relationship of means to ends when examining the curriculum as a *product* and the psychological processes that may usefully be employed in building curriculums. The method of forming creative insights in curriculum development, as in the sciences and arts, is as yet not logically prescribable. The ways in which curriculums can be usefully and efficiently developed constitute an empirical problem; imposing logical requirements upon the process because they are desirable for assessing the product is, to my mind, an error. Thus, the final point I wish to make is that educational objectives need not precede the selection and organization of content. The means through which imaginative curriculums can be built is as open-ended as the means through which scientific and artistic inventions occur. Curriculum theory needs to allow for a variety of processes to be employed in the construction of curriculums.

I have argued in this paper that curriculum theory as it pertains to educational objectives has had four significant limitations. First, it has not sufficiently emphasized the extent to which the prediction of educational outcomes cannot be made with accuracy. Second, it has not discussed the ways in which the subject matter affects precision in stating educational objectives. Third, it has confused the use of educational objectives as a standard for measurement when in some areas it can be used only as a criterion for judgment. Fourth, it has not distinguished between the logical requirement of relating means to ends in the curriculum as a product and the psychological conditions useful for constructing curriculums.

If the arguments I have formulated about the limitations of curriculum theory concerning educational objectives have merit, one might ask: What are their educational consequences? First, it seems to me that they suggest that in large measure the construction of curriculums and the judgment of its consequences are artful tasks. The methods of curriculum development are, in principle if not in practice, no different from the making of art—be it the art of painting or the art of science. The identification of the factors in the potentially useful educational activity and the organization or construction of sequence in curriculum are in principle amenable to an infinite number of combinations. The variable teacher, student, class group, require artful blending for the educationally valuable to result.

Second, I am impressed with Dewey's view of the functions of criticism—to heighten one's perception of the art object—and believe it has implications for curriculum theory. If the child is viewed as an art product and the teacher as a critic, one task of the teacher would be to reveal the qualities of the child to himself and to others. In addition, the teacher as critic would appraise the changes occurring in the child. But because the teacher's task includes more than criticism, he would also be responsible, in part, for the improvement of the work of art. In short, in both the construction of educational means (the curriculum) and the appraisal of its consequences, the teacher would become an artist, for criticism itself when carried to its height is an art. This, it seems to me, is a dimension to which curriculum theory will someday have to speak.

Notes

1. This is a slightly expanded version of a paper presented at the fiftieth annual meeting of the American Educational Research Association, Chicago, February, 1966.
2. Franklin Bobbitt, *The Curriculum* (Boston: Houghton Mifflin Co., 1918).
3. *Ibid.*, p. 42.
4. Franklin Bobbitt, *How To Make a Curriculum* (Boston: Houghton Mifflin Co., 1924).
5. *Ibid.*, pp. 11–29.
6. For a good example of this view of the child and curriculum development, see *The Changing Curriculum, Tenth Yearbook*, Department of Supervisors and Directors of Instruction, National Education Association and Society for Curriculum Study (New York: Appleton-Century Crofts Co., 1937).
7. Ralph W. Tyler, *Basic Principles of Curriculum and Instruction* (Chicago: University of Chicago Press, 1951).

8. Virgil E. Herrick, "The Concept of Curriculum Design," *Toward Improved Curriculum Theory,* (eds.). Virgil E. Herrick and Ralph W. Tyler (Supplementary Educational Monographs, No. 71 [Chicago: University of Chicago Press, 1950]), pp. 37–50.
9. George E. Barton, Jr., "Educational Objectives: Improvement of Curriculum Theory about Their Determination," *ibid.*, pp. 26–35.
10. Benjamin Bloom et al. (ed.), *Taxonomy of Educational Objectives, Handbook I:* The Cognitive Domain (New York: Longmans, Green & Co., 1956).
11. David Krathwohl, Benjamin Bloom, and Bertram Masia, *Taxonomy of Educational Objectives, Handbook II: The Affective Domain* (New York: David McKay, Inc., 1964).
12. For an excellent paper describing educational objectives as they are viewed and used by elementary school teachers, see Philip W. Jackson and Elizabeth Belford, "Educational Objectives and the Joys of Teaching," *School Review,* LXXIII (1965), 267–291.
13. John Dewey, *Art as Experience* (New York: Minton, Balch & Co., 1934).
14. *Ibid.*, p. 324.
15. *Ibid.*, p. 307.
16. James B. MacDonald, "Myths about Instruction," *Educational Leadership,* XXII, No. 7 (May, 1965), 613–614.

11

The Daily Grind

Philip W. Jackson

On a typical weekday morning between September and June some 35 million Americans kiss their loved ones goodbye, pick up their lunch pails and books, and leave to spend their day in that collection of enclosures (totalling about one million) known as elementary school classrooms. This massive exodus from home to school is accomplished with a minimum of fuss and bother. Few tears are shed (except perhaps by the very youngest) and few cheers are raised. The school attendance of children is such a common experience in our society that those of us who watch them go hardly pause to consider what happens to them when they get there. Of course our indifference disappears occasionally. When something goes wrong or when we have been notified of his remarkable achievement, we might ponder, for a moment at least, the meaning of the experience for the child in question, but most of the time we simply note that our Johnny is on his way to school, and now, it is time for our second cup of coffee.

Parents are interested, to be sure, in how *well* Johnny does while there, and when he comes trudging home they may ask him questions about what happened today or, more generally, how things went. But both their questions and his answers typically focus on the highlights of the school experience—its unusual aspects—rather than on the mundane and seemingly trivial events that filled the bulk of his school hours. Parents are interested, in other words, in the spice of school life rather than in its substance.

Teachers, too, are chiefly concerned with only a very narrow aspect of a youngster's school experience. They, too, are likely to focus on specific acts of misbehavior or accomplishment as representing what a particular student did in school today, even though the acts in question occupied but a small fraction of the student's time. Teachers, like parents, seldom ponder the significance of the thousands of fleeting events that combine to form the routine of the classroom.

And the student himself is no less selective. Even if someone bothered to question him about the minutiae of his school day, he would probably be unable to give a complete account of what he had done. For him, too, the day has been reduced in memory into a small number of signal events—"I got 100 on my spelling test," "We went to gym," "We had music." His spontaneous recall of detail is not much greater than that required to answer our conventional questions.

This concentration on the highlights of school life is understandable from the standpoint of human interest. A similar selection process operates when we inquire into or recount other types of daily activity. When we are asked about our trip downtown or our day at the office we rarely bother describing the ride on the bus or the time spent in front of the watercooler. Indeed, we are more likely to report that nothing happened than to catalogue the pedestrian actions that took place between home and return. Unless something interesting occurred there is little purpose in talking about our experience.

Yet from the standpoint of giving shape and meaning to our lives these events about which we rarely speak may be as important as those that hold our listener's attention. Certainly they represent a much larger portion of our experience than do those about which we talk. The daily routine, the "rat race," and the infamous "old grind" may be brightened from time to time by happenings that add color to an otherwise drab existence, but the grayness of our daily lives has an abrasive potency of its own. Anthropologists understand this fact better than do most other social scientists, and their field studies have taught us to appreciate the cultural significance of the humdrum elements of human existence. This is the lesson we must heed as we seek to understand life in elementary classrooms.

I

School is a place where tests are failed and passed, where amusing things happen, where new insights are stumbled upon, and skills acquired. But it is also a place in which people sit, and listen, and wait, and raise their hands, and pass out paper, and stand in line, and sharpen pencils. School is where we encounter both friends and foes, where imagination is unleashed and misunderstanding brought to ground. But it is also a place in which yawns are stifled and initials scratched on desktops, where milk money is collected and recess lines are formed. Both aspects of school life, the celebrated and the unnoticed, are familiar to all of us, but the latter, if only because of its characteristic neglect, seems to deserve more attention than it has received to date from those who are interested in education.

In order to appreciate the significance of trivial classroom events it is necessary to consider the frequency of their occurrence, the standardization of the school environment, and the compulsory quality of daily attendance. We must recognize, in other words, that children are in school for a long time, that the settings in which they perform are highly uniform, and that they are there whether they want to be or not. Each of these three facts, although seemingly obvious, deserves some elaboration, for each contributes to our understanding of how students feel about and cope with their school experience.

The amount of time children spend in school can be described with a fair amount of quantitative precision, although the psychological significance of the numbers involved is another matter entirely. In most states the school year legally comprises 180 days. A full session on each of those days usually lasts about six hours (with a break for lunch), beginning somewhere around nine o'clock in the morning and ending about three o'clock in the afternoon. Thus, if a student never misses a day during the year, he spends a little more than one thousand hours under the care and tutelage of teachers. If he has attended kindergarten and was reasonably regular in his attendance during the grades, he will have logged a little more than seven thousand classroom hours by the time he is ready for junior high school.

The magnitude of 7,000 hours spread over six or seven years of a child's life is difficult to comprehend. On the one hand, when placed beside the total number of hours the child has lived during those years it is not very great—slightly more than one-tenth of his life during the time in question, about one-third of his hours of sleep during that period. On the other hand, aside from sleeping, and perhaps playing, there is no other activity that occupies as much of the child's time as that involved in attending school. Apart from the bedroom (where he has his eyes closed most of the time) there is no single enclosure in which he spends a longer time than he does in the classroom. From the age of six onward he is a more familiar sight to his teacher than to his father, and possibly even to his mother.

Another way of estimating what all those hours in the classroom mean is to ask how long it would take to accumulate them while engaged in some other familiar and recurring activity. Church attendance provides an interesting comparison. In order to have had as much time in church as a sixth grader has had in classrooms we would have to spend all day at a religious gathering every Sunday for more than 24 years. Or, if we prefer our devotion in smaller doses, we would have to attend a one-hour service every Sunday for 150 years before the inside of a church became as familiar to us as the inside of a school is to a twelve-year-old.

The comparison with church attendance is dramatic, and perhaps overly so. But it does make us stop and think about the possible significance of an otherwise meaningless number. Also, aside from the home and the school there is no physical setting in which people of all ages congregate with as great a regularity as they do in church.

The translation of the child's tenure in class into terms of weekly church attendance serves a further purpose. It sets the stage for considering an important similarity between the two institutions: school and church. The inhabitants of both are surrounded by a stable and highly stylized environment. The fact of prolonged exposure in either setting increases in its meaning as we begin to consider the elements of repetition, redundancy, and ritualistic action that are experienced there.

A classroom, like a church auditorium, is rarely seen as being anything other than that which it is. No one entering either place is likely to think that he is in a living room, or a grocery store, or a train station. Even if he entered at midnight or at some other time when the activities of the people would not give the function away, he would have no difficulty understanding what was *supposed* to go on there. Even devoid of people, a church is a church and a classroom, a classroom.

This is not to say, of course, that all classrooms are identical, anymore than all churches are. Clearly there are differences, and sometimes very extreme ones, between any two settings. One has only to think of the wooden benches and planked floor of the early American classroom as compared with the plastic chairs and tile flooring in today's suburban schools. But the resemblance is still there despite the differences, and, more important, during any particular historical period the differences are not that great. Also, whether the student moves from first to sixth grade on floors of vinyl tile or oiled wood, whether he spends his days in front of a black blackboard or a green one, is not as important as the fact that the environment in which he spends these six or seven years is highly stable.

In their efforts to make their classrooms more homelike, elementary school teachers often spend considerable time fussing with the room's decorations. Bulletin boards are changed, new pictures are hung, and the seating arrangement is altered from circles to rows and back again. But these are surface adjustments at best, resembling the work of the inspired housewife who rearranges the living room furniture and changes the color of the drapes in order to make the room more "interesting." School bulletin boards may be changed but they are never discarded, the seats may be rearranged but thirty of them are there to stay, the teacher's desk may have a new plant on it but there it sits, as ubiquitous as the roll-down maps, the drab olive waste-basket, and the pencil sharpener on the window ledge.

Even the odors of the classroom are fairly standardized. Schools may use different brands of wax and cleaning fluid, but they all seem to contain similar ingredients, a sort of universal smell which creates an aromatic background that permeates the entire building. Added to this, in each classroom, is the slightly acrid scent of chalk dust and the faint hint of fresh wood from the pencil shavings. In some rooms, especially at lunch time, there is the familiar odor of orange peels and peanut butter sandwiches, a blend that mingles in the late afternoon (following recess) with the delicate pungency of children's perspiration. If a person stumbled into a classroom blindfolded, his nose alone, if he used it carefully, would tell him where he was.

All of these sights and smells become so familiar to students and teachers alike that they exist dimly, on the periphery of awareness. Only when the classroom is encountered under somewhat unusual circumstances, does it appear, for a moment, a strange place filled with objects that command our attention. On these rare occasions when, for example, students return to school in the evening, or in the summer when the halls ring with the hammers of workmen, many features of the school environment that have merged into an undifferentiated background for its daily inhabitants suddenly stand out in sharp relief. This experience, which obviously occurs in contexts other than the classroom, can only happen in settings to which the viewer has become uncommonly habituated.

Not only is the classroom a relatively stable physical environment, it also provides a fairly constant social context. Behind the same old desks sit the same old students, in front of the familiar blackboard stands the familiar teacher. There are changes, to be sure—some students come and go during the year and on a few mornings the children are greeted at the door by a strange adult. But in most cases these events are sufficiently uncommon to create a flurry of excitement in the room. Moreover, in most elementary classrooms the social composition is not only stable, it is also physically arranged with considerable regularity. Each student has an assigned seat and, under normal circumstances, that is where he is to be found. The practice of assigning seats makes it possible for the teacher or a student to take attendance at a glance. A quick visual sweep is usually sufficient to determine who is there and who is not. The ease with which this procedure is accomplished reveals more eloquently than do words how accustomed each member of the class is to the presence of every other member.

An additional feature of the social atmosphere of elementary classrooms deserves at least passing comment. There is a social intimacy in schools that is unmatched elsewhere in our society. Buses and movie theaters may be more crowded than classrooms, but people rarely stay in such densely populated settings for extended periods of time and while there, they usually are not expected to concentrate on work or to interact with each other. Even factory workers are not clustered as close together as students in a standard classroom. Indeed, imagine what would happen if a factory the size of a typical elementary school contained three or four hundred adult workers. In all likelihood the unions would not allow it. Only in schools do thirty or more people spend several hours each day literally side by side. Once we leave the classroom we seldom again are required to have contact with so many people for so long a time. This fact will become particularly relevant in a later chapter in which we treat the social demands of life in school.

A final aspect of the constancy experienced by young students involves the ritualistic and cyclic quality of the activities carried on in the classroom. The daily schedule, as an instance, is commonly divided into definite periods during which specific subjects are to be studied or specific activities engaged in. The content of the work surely changes from day to day and from week to week, and in this sense there is considerable variety amid the constancy. But spelling still comes after arithmetic on Tuesday morning, and when the teacher says, "All right class, now take out your spellers," his announcement comes as no surprise to the students. Further, as they search in their desks for their spelling textbooks, the children may not know what new words will be included in the day's assignment, but they have a fairly clear idea of what the next twenty minutes of class time will entail.

Despite the diversity of subject matter content, the identifiable forms of classroom activity are not great in number. The labels: "seatwork," "group discussion," "teacher demonstration," and "question-and-answer period" (which would include work "at the board"), are sufficient to categorize most of the things that happen when class is in session. "Audiovisual display," "testing session," and "games" might be added to the list, but in most elementary classrooms they occur rarely.

Each of these major activities are performed according to rather well-defined rules which the students are expected to understand and obey—for example, no loud talking during seatwork, do not interrupt someone else during discussion, keep your eyes on your own paper during tests, raise your hand if you have a question. Even in the early grades these rules are so well understood by the students (if not completely internalized) that the teacher has only to give very abbreviated signals ("Voices, class," "Hands, please.") when violations are perceived. In many classrooms a weekly time schedule is permanently posted so that everyone can tell at a glance what will happen next.

Thus, when our young student enters school in the morning he is entering an environment with which he has become exceptionally familiar through prolonged exposure. Moreover, it is a fairly stable environment—one in which the physical objects, social relations, and major activities remain much the same from day to day, week to week, and even, in certain respects, from year to year. Life there resembles life in other contexts in some ways, but not all. There is, in other words, a uniqueness to the student's world. School, like church and home, is someplace special. Look where you may, you will not find another place quite like it.

There is an important fact about a student's life that teachers and parents often prefer not to talk about, at least not in front of students. This is the fact that young people have to be in school, whether they want to be or not. In this regard students have something in common with the members of two other of our social institutions that have involuntary attendance: prisons and mental hospitals. The analogy, though dramatic, is not intended to be shocking, and certainly there is no comparison between the unpleasantness of life for inmates of our prisons and mental institutions, on the one hand, and the daily travails of a first or second grader, on the other. Yet the school child, like the incarcerated adult, is, in a sense, a prisoner. He too must come to grips with the inevitability of his experience. He too must develop strategies for dealing with the conflict that frequently arises between his natural desires and interests on the one hand and institutional expectations on the other. Several of these strategies will be discussed in the chapters that follow. Here it is sufficient to note that the thousands of hours spent in the highly stylized environment of the elementary classroom are not, in an ultimate sense, a matter of choice, even though some children might prefer school to play. Many seven-year-olds skip happily to school, and as parents and teachers we are glad they do, but we stand ready to enforce the attendance of those who are more reluctant. And our vigilance does not go unnoticed by children.

In sum, classrooms are special places. The things that happen there and the ways in which they happen combine to make these settings different from all others. This is not to say, of course, that there is no similarity between what goes on in school and the students' experiences elsewhere. Classrooms are indeed like homes and churches and hospital wards in many important respects. But not in all.

The things that make schools different from other places are not only the paraphernalia of learning and teaching and the educational content of the dialogues that take place there, although these are the features that are usually singled out when we try to portray what life in school is really like. It is true that nowhere else do we find blackboards and teachers and textbooks in such abundance and nowhere else is so much time spent on reading, writing, and arithmetic. But these obvious characteristics do not constitute all that is unique about this environment. There are other features, much less obvious though equally omnipresent, that help to make up "the facts of life," as it were, to which students must adapt. From the standpoint of understanding the impact of school life on the student some features of the classroom that are not immediately visible are fully as important as those that are.

The characteristics of school life to which we now turn our attention are not commonly mentioned by students, at least not directly, nor are they apparent to the casual observer. Yet they are as real, in a sense, as the unfinished portrait of Washington that hangs above the cloakroom door. They comprise three facts of life with which even the youngest student must learn to deal and may be introduced by the key words: *crowds, praise*, and *power*.

Learning to live in a classroom involves, among other things, learning to live in a crowd. This simple truth has already been mentioned, but it requires greater elaboration. Most of the things that are done in school are done with others, or at least in the presence of others, and this fact has profound implications for determining the quality of a student's life.

Of equal importance is the fact that schools are basically evaluative settings. The very young student may be temporarily fooled by tests that are presented as games, but it doesn't take long before he begins to see through the subterfuge and comes to realize that school, after all, is a serious business. It is not only what you do there but what others think of what you do that is important. Adaptation to school life requires the student to become used to living under the constant condition of having his words and deeds evaluated by others.

School is also a place in which the division between the weak and the powerful is clearly drawn. This may sound like a harsh way to describe the separation between teachers and students, but it serves to emphasize a fact that is often overlooked, or touched upon gingerly at best. Teachers are indeed more powerful than students, in the sense of having greater responsibility for giving shape to classroom events, and this sharp difference in authority is another feature of school life with which students must learn how to deal.

In three major ways then—as members of crowds, as potential recipients of praise or reproof, and as pawns of institutional authorities—students are confronted with aspects of reality that at least during their childhood years are relatively confined to the hours spent in classrooms. Admittedly, similar conditions are encountered in other environments. Students, when they are not performing as such, must often find themselves lodged within larger groups, serving as targets of praise or reproof, and being bossed around or guided by persons in positions of higher authority. But these kinds of experiences are particularly frequent while school is in session and it is likely during this time that adaptive strategies having relevance for other contexts and other life periods are developed.

In the sections of this chapter to follow, each of the three classroom qualities that have been briefly mentioned will be described in greater detail. Particular emphasis will be given to the manner in which students cope with these aspects of their daily lives. The goal of this discussion, as in the preceding chapters, is to deepen our understanding of the peculiar mark that school life makes on us all. [. . .]

V

As implied in the title of this chapter, the crowds, the praise, and the power that combine to give a distinctive flavor to classroom life collectively form a hidden curriculum which each student (and teacher) must master if he is to make his way satisfactorily through the school. The demands created by these features of classroom life may be contrasted with the academic demands—the "official" curriculum, so to speak—to which educators traditionally have paid the most attention. As might be expected, the two curriculums are related to each other in several important ways.

As has already been suggested in the discussion of praise in the classroom, the reward system of the school is linked to success in both curriculums. Indeed, many of the rewards and punishments that sound as if they are being dispensed on the basis of academic success and failure are really more closely related to the mastery of the hidden curriculum. Consider, as an instance, the common teaching practice of giving a student credit for trying. What do teachers mean when they say a student tries to do his work? They mean, in essence, that he complies with the procedural expectations of the institution. He does his homework (though incorrectly), he raises his hand during class discussion (though he usually comes up with the wrong answer), he keeps his nose in his book during free study period (though he doesn't turn the page very often). He is, in other words, a "model" student, though not necessarily a good one.

It is difficult to imagine any of today's teachers, particularly those in elementary schools, failing a student who tries, even though his mastery of course content is slight. Indeed, even at higher levels of education rewards sometimes go to the meek as well as the mighty. It is certainly possible that many of our valedictorians and presidents of our honor societies owe their success as much to institutional conformity as to intellectual prowess. Although it offends our sensibilities to admit it, no doubt that bright-eyed little girl who stands trembling before the principal on graduation day arrived there at least in part because she typed her weekly themes neatly and handed her homework in on time.

This manner of talking about educational affairs may sound cynical and may be interpreted as a criticism of teachers or as an attempt to subvert the virtues of neatness, punctuality, and courteous conduct in general. But nothing of that kind is intended. The point is simply that in schools, as in prisons, good behavior pays off.

Just as conformity to institutional expectations can lead to praise, so can the lack of it lead to trouble. As a matter of fact, the relationship of the hidden curriculum to student difficulties is even more striking than is its relationship to student success. As an instance, consider the conditions leading to disciplinary action in the classroom. Why do teachers scold students? Because the student has given a wrong answer? Because, try as he might, he fails to grasp the intricacies of long division? Not usually. Rather, students are commonly scolded for coming into the room late or for making too much noise or for not listening to the teacher's directions or for pushing while in line. The teacher's wrath, in other words, is more frequently triggered by violations of institutional regulations and routines than by signs of his students' intellectual deficiencies.

Even when we consider the more serious difficulties that clearly entail academic failure, the demands of the hidden curriculum lurk in the background. When Johnny's parents are called in to school because their son is not doing too well in arithmetic, what explanation is given for their son's poor performance? Typically, blame is placed on motivational deficiencies in Johnny rather than on his intellectual shortcomings. The teacher may even go so far as to say that Johnny is *un*motivated during arithmetic period. But what does this mean? It means, in essence, that Johnny does not even try. And not trying, as we have seen, usually boils down to a failure to comply with institutional expectations, a failure to master the hidden curriculum.

Testmakers describe a person as "test-wise" when he has caught on to the tricks of test construction sufficiently well to answer questions correctly even though he does not know the material on which he is being examined. In the same way one might think of students as becoming "school-wise" or "teacher-wise" when they have discovered how to respond with a minimum amount of pain and discomfort to the demands, both official and unofficial, of classroom life. Schools, like test items, have rules and traditions of their own that can only be mastered through successive exposure. But with schools as with tests all students are not equally adroit. All are asked to respond but not everyone catches on to the rules of the game.

If it is useful to think of there being two curriculums in the classroom, a natural question to ask about the relationship between them is whether their joint mastery calls for compatible or contradictory personal qualities. That is, do the same strengths that contribute to intellectual achievement also contribute to the student's success in conformity to institutional expectations? This question likely has no definite answer, but it is thought-provoking and even a brief consideration of it leads into a thicket of educational and psychological issues.

It is probably safe to predict that general ability, or intelligence, would be an asset in meeting all of the demands of school life, whether academic or institutional. The child's ability to understand causal relationships, as an instance, would seem to be of as much service as he tries to come to grips with the rules and regulations of classroom life as when he grapples with the rudiments of plant chemistry. His verbal fluency can be put to use as easily in "snowing" the teacher as in writing a short story. Thus, to the extent that the demands of classroom life call for rational thought, the student with superior intellectual ability would seem to be at an advantage.

But more than ability is involved in adapting to complex situations. Much also depends upon attitudes, values, and lifestyle—upon all those qualities commonly grouped under the term: *personality*. When the contribution of personality to adaptive strategy is considered, the old adage of "the more, the better," which works so well for general ability, does not suffice. Personal qualities that are beneficial in one setting may be detrimental in another. Indeed, even a single setting may make demands that call upon competing or conflicting tendencies in a person's makeup.

We have already seen that many features of classroom life call for patience, at best, and resignation, at worst. As he learns to live in school our student learns to subjugate his own desires to the will of the teacher and to subdue his own actions in the interest of the common good. He learns to be passive and to acquiesce to the network of rules, regulations, and routines in which he is embedded. He learns to tolerate petty frustrations and accept the plans and policies of higher authorities, even when their rationale is unexplained and their meaning unclear. Like the inhabitants of most other institutions, he learns how to shrug and say, "That's the way the ball bounces."

But the personal qualities that play a role in intellectual mastery are very different from those that characterize the Company Man. Curiosity, as an instance, that most fundamental of all scholarly traits, is of little value in responding to the demands of conformity. The curious person typically engages in a kind of probing, poking, and exploring that is almost antithetical to the attitude of the passive conformist. The scholar must develop the habit of challenging authority and of questioning the value of tradition. He must insist on explanations for things that are unclear. Scholarship requires discipline, to be sure, but this discipline serves the demands of scholarship rather than the wishes and desires of other people. In short, intellectual mastery calls for sublimited forms of aggression rather than for submission to constraints.

This brief discussion likely exaggerates the real differences between the demands of institutional conformity and the demands of scholarship, but it does serve to call attention to points of possible conflict. How incompatible are these two sets of demands? Can both be mastered by the same person? Apparently so. Certainly not all of our student council presidents and valedictorians can be dismissed as weak-willed teacher's pets, as academic Uriah Heeps. Many students clearly manage to maintain their intellectual aggressiveness while at the same time acquiescing to the laws that govern the social traffic of our schools. Apparently it *is* possible, under certain conditions, to breed "docile scholars," even though the expression seems to be a contradiction in terms. Indeed, certain forms of scholarship have been known to flourish in monastic settings, where the demands for institutional conformity are extreme.

Unfortunately, no one seems to know how these balances are maintained, nor even how to establish them in the first place. But even more unfortunate is the fact that few if any school people are giving the matter serious thought. As institutional settings multiply and become for more and more people the areas in which a significant portion of their life is enacted, we will need to know much more than we do at present about how to achieve a reasonable synthesis between the forces that drive a person to seek individual expression and those that drive him to comply with the wishes of others. Presumably what goes on in classrooms contributes significantly to this synthesis. The school is the first major institution, outside the family, in which almost all of us are immersed. From kindergarten onward, the student begins to learn what life is really like in The Company.

The demands of classroom life discussed in this chapter pose problems for students and teachers alike. As we have seen, there are many methods for coping with these demands and for solving the problems they create. Moreover, each major adaptive strategy is subtly transformed and given a unique expression as a result of the idiosyncratic characteristics of the student employing it. Thus, the total picture of adjustment to school becomes infinitely complex as it is manifested in the behavior of individual students.

Yet certain commonalities do exist beneath all the complexity created by the uniqueness of individuals. No matter what the demand or the personal resources of the person facing it there is at least one strategy open to all. This is the strategy of psychological withdrawal, of gradually reducing personal concern and involvement to a point where neither the demand nor one's success or failure in coping with it is sharply felt. In order to better understand student tactics, however, it is important to consider the climate of opinion from which they emerge. Before focusing on what they do in the classroom, we must examine how students feel about school.

12
Curriculum and Consciousness

Maxine Greene

Curriculum, from the learner's standpoint, ordinarily represents little more than an arrangement of subjects, a structure of socially prescribed knowledge, or a complex system of meanings which may or may not fall within his grasp. Rarely does it signify possibility for him as an existing person, mainly concerned with making sense of his own life-world. Rarely does it promise occasions for ordering the materials of that world, for imposing "configurations"[1] by means of experiences and perspectives made available for personally conducted cognitive action. Sartre says that "knowing is a moment of praxis," opening into "what has not yet been."[2] Preoccupied with priorities, purposes, programs of "intended learning"[3] and intended (or unintended) manipulation, we pay too little attention to the individual in quest of his own future, bent on surpassing what is merely "given," on breaking through the everyday. We are still too prone to dichotomize: to think of "disciplines" or "public traditions" or "accumulated wisdom" or "common culture" (individualization despite) as objectively existent, external to the knower—there to be discovered, mastered, learned.

Quite aware that this may evoke Dewey's argument in *The Child and the Curriculum*, aware of how times have changed since 1902, I have gone in search of contemporary analogies to shed light on what I mean. ("Solution comes," Dewey wrote, "only by getting away from the meaning of terms that is already fixed upon and coming to see the conditions from another point of view, and hence in a fresh light."[4]) My other point of view is that of literary criticism, or more properly philosophy of criticism, which attempts to explicate the modes of explanation, description, interpretation, and evaluation involved in particular critical approaches. There is presently an emerging philosophic controversy between two such approaches, one associated with England and the United States, the other with the Continent, primarily France and Switzerland; and it is in the differences in orientation that I have found some clues.

These differences are, it will be evident, closely connected to those separating what is known as analytic or language philosophy from existentialism and phenomenology. The dominant tendency in British and American literary criticism has been to conceive literary works as objects or artifacts, best understood in relative isolation from the writer's personal biography and undistorted by associations brought to the work from the reader's own daily life. The new critics on the Continent have been called "critics of consciousness."[5] They are breaking with the notion that a literary work can be dealt with objectively, divorced from experience. In fact, they treat each work as a manifestation of an individual writer's experience, a gradual growth of consciousness into expression. This is in sharp contrast to such a view as T.S. Eliot's emphasizing the autonomy and the "impersonality" of literary art. "We can only say," he wrote in an introduction to *The Sacred Wood*, "that a poem, in some sense, has its own life; that its parts form something quite different from a body of neatly ordered biographical data; that the feeling, or emotion, or vision resulting from the poem is something different from the feeling or emotion or vision in the mind of the poet."[6] Those who take this approach or an approach to a work of art as "a self-enclosed isolated structure"[7] are likely to prescribe that purely aesthetic values are to be found in literature, the values associated with "significant form"[8] or, at most, with the contemplation of an "intrinsically interesting possible."[9] M.H. Abrams has called this an "austere dedication to the poem *per se*,"[10] for all the enlightening analysis and explication it has produced. "But it threatens also to commit us," he wrote, "to the concept of a poem as a language game, or as a floating Laputa, insulated from life and essential human concerns in a way that accords poorly with our experience in reading a great work of literature."

For the critic of consciousness, literature is viewed as a genesis, a conscious effort on the part of an individual artist to understand his own experience by framing it in language. The reader who encounters the work must recreate it in terms of *his* consciousness. In order to penetrate it, to experience it existentially and empathetically, he must try to place himself within the "interior space"[11] of the writer's mind as it is slowly revealed in the course of his work. Clearly, the reader requires a variety of cues if he is to situate himself in this way; and these are ostensibly provided by the expressions and attitudes he finds in the book, devices which he must accept as orientations and indications—"norms," perhaps, to govern his recreation. *His* subjectivity is the substance of the literary object; but, if he is to perceive the identity emerging through the enactments of the book, he must subordinate his own personality as he brackets out his everyday, "natural" world.[12] His objective in doing so, however, is not to analyze or explicate or evaluate; it is to extract the experience made manifest by means of the work. Sartre says this more concretely:

> Reading seems, in fact, to be the synthesis of perception and creation. . . . The object is essential because it is strictly transcendent, because it imposes its own structures, and because one must wait for it and observe it; but the subject is also essential because it is required not only to disclose the object (that is, to make *there be* an object) but also that this object might *be* (that is, to produce it). In a word, the reader is conscious of disclosing in creating, of creating by disclosing. . . . If he is inattentive, tired, stupid, or thoughtless most of the relations will escape him. He will never manage to "catch on" to the object (in the sense in which we see that fire "catches" or "doesn't catch"). He will draw some phrases out of the shadow, but they will appear as random strokes. If he is at his best, he will project beyond the words a synthetic form, each phrase of which will be no more than a partial function: the "theme," the "subject," or the "meaning."[13]

There must be, he is suggesting, continual reconstructions if a work of literature is to become meaningful. The structures involved are generated over a period of time, depending upon the perceptiveness and attentiveness of the reader. The reader, however, does not simply regenerate what the artist intended. His imagination can move him beyond the artist's traces, "to project beyond the words a synthetic form," to constitute a new totality. The autonomy of the art object is sacrificed in this orientation; the reader, conscious of lending his own life to the book, discovers deeper and more complex levels than the level of "significant form." (Sartre says, for instance, that "Raskolnikov's waiting is *my* waiting, which I lend him. Without this impatience of the reader he would remain only a collection of signs. His hatred of the police magistrate who questions him is my hatred which has been solicited and wheedled out of me by signs, and the police magistrate himself would not exist without the hatred I have for him via Raskolnikov."[14])

Disclosure, Reconstruction, Generation

The reader, using his imagination, must move within his own subjectivity and break with the common sense world he normally takes for granted. If he could not suspend his ordinary ways of perceiving, if he could not allow for the possibility that the horizons of daily life are not inalterable, he would not be able to engage with literature at all. As Dewey put it: "There is work done on the part of the percipient as there is on the part of the artist. The one who is too lazy, idle, or indurated in convention to perform this work will not see or hear. His 'appreciation' will be a mixture of scraps of learning with conformity to norms of conventional admiration and with a confused, even if genuine, emotional excitation."[15] The "work" with which we are here concerned is one of disclosure, reconstruction, generation. It is a work which culminates in a bringing something into being by the reader—in a "going beyond" what he has been.[16]

Although I am going to claim that learning, to be meaningful, must involve such a "going beyond," I am not going to claim that it must also be in the imaginative mode. Nor am I going to assert that, in order to surpass the "given," the individual is required to move into and remain within a sealed subjectivity. What I find suggestive in the criticism of consciousness is the stress on the gradual disclosure of structures by the reader. The process is, as I have said, governed by certain cues or norms perceived in the course of reading. These demand, if they are to be perceived, what Jean Piaget has called a "continual 'decentering' without which [the individual subject] cannot become free from his intellectual egocentricity."[17]

The difference between Piaget and those interested in consciousness is, of course, considerable. For one thing, he counts himself among those who prefer not to characterize the subject in terms of its "lived experience." For another thing, he says categorically that "the 'lived' can only have a very minor role in the construction of cognitive structures, for these do not belong to the subject's *consciousness* but to his operational *behavior,* which is something quite different."[18] I am not convinced that they are as different as he conceives them to be. Moreover, I think his differentiation between the "individual subject" and what he calls "the epistemic subject, that cognitive nucleus which is common to all subjects at the same level,"[19] is useful and may well shed light on the problem of curriculum, viewed from the vantage point of consciousness. Piaget is aware that his stress on the "epistemic subject" looks as if he were subsuming the individual under some impersonal abstraction;[20] but his discussion is not far removed from those of Sartre and the critics of consciousness, particularly when they talk of the subject entering into a process of generating structures whose being (like the structures Piaget has in mind) consists in their "coming to be."

Merleau-Ponty, as concerned as Piaget with the achievement of rationality, believes that there is a primary reality which must be taken into account if the growth of "intellectual consciousness" is to be understood. This primary reality is a perceived life-world; and the structures of the "perceptual consciousness"[21] through which the child first comes in contact with his environment underlie all the higher level structures which develop later in his life. In the prereflective, infantile stage of life he is obviously incapable of generating cognitive structures. The stage is characterized by what Merleau-Ponty calls "egocentrism" because the "me" is part of an anonymous collectivity, unaware of itself, capable of living "as easily in others as it does in itself."[22] Nevertheless, even then, before meanings and configurations are imposed, there is an original world, a natural and social world in which the child is involved corporeally and affectively. Perceiving that world, he effects certain relations within his experience. He organizes and "informs" it before he is capable of logical and predicative thought. This means for Merleau-Ponty that consciousness exists primordially—the ground of all knowledge and rationality.

The growing child assimilates a language system and becomes habituated to using language as "an open system of expression" which is capable of expressing "an indeterminate number of cognitions or ideas to come."[23] His acts of naming and expression take place, however, around a core of primary meaning found in "the silence of primary consciousness." This silence may be understood as the fundamental awareness of being present in the world. It resembles what Paulo Freire calls "background awareness"[24] of an existential situation, a situation actually lived before the codifications which make new perceptions possible. Talking about the effort to help peasants perceive their own reality differently (to enable them, in other words, to learn), Freire says they must somehow make explicit their "real consciousness" of their worlds, or what they experienced while living through situations they later learn to codify.

The point is that the world is constituted for the child (by means of the behavior called perception) prior to the "construction of cognitive structures." This does not imply that he lives his life primarily in that world. He moves outward into diverse realms of experience in his search for meaning. When he confronts and engages with the apparently independent structures associated with rationality, the so-called cognitive structures, it is likely that he does so as an "epistemic subject," bracketing out for the time his subjectivity, even his presence to himself.[25] But the awareness remains in the background; the original perceptual reality continues as the ground of rationality, the base from which the leap to the theoretical is taken.

Merleau-Ponty, recognizing that psychologists treat consciousness as "an object to be studied," writes that it is simply not accessible to mere factual observation:

> The psychologist always tends to make consciousness into just such an object of observation. But all the factual truths to which psychology has access can be applied to the concrete subject only after a philosophical correction. Psychology, like physics and the other sciences of nature, uses the method of induction, which starts from facts and then assembles them. But it is very evident that this induction will remain blind if we do not know in some other way, and indeed from the inside of consciousness itself, what this induction is dealing with.[26]

Induction must be combined "with the reflective knowledge that we can obtain from ourselves as conscious objects." This is not a recommendation that the individual engage in introspection. Consciousness, being intentional, throws itself outward *towards* the world. It is always consciousness of something—a phenomenon, another person, an object in the world: Reflecting upon himself as a conscious object, the individual—the learner, perhaps—reflects upon his relation to the world, his manner of comporting himself with respect to it, the changing perspectives through which the world presents itself to him. Merleau-Ponty talks about the need continually to rediscover "my actual presence to myself, the fact of my consciousness which is in the last resort what the word and the concept of consciousness mean."[27] This means remaining in contact with one's own perceptions, one's own experiences, and striving to constitute their meanings. It means achieving a state of what Schutz calls "*wide-awakeness* . . . a plane of consciousness of highest tension originating in an attitude of full attention to life and its requirements."[28] Like Sartre, Schutz emphasizes the importance of attentiveness for arriving at new perceptions, for carrying out cognitive projects. All this seems to me to be highly suggestive for a conception of a learner who is "open to the world,"[29] eager, indeed *condemned* to give meaning to it—and, in the process of doing so, recreating or generating the materials of a curriculum in terms of his own consciousness.

Some Alternative Views

There are, of course, alternative views of consequence for education today. R.S. Peters, agreeing with his philosophic precursors that consciousness is the hallmark of mind and always "related in its different modes to objects," asserts that the "objects of consciousness are first and foremost objects in a public world that are marked out and differentiated by a public language into which the individual is initiated."[30] (It should be said that Peters is, *par excellence*, the exponent of an "objective" or "analytic" approach to curriculum, closely related to the objective approach to literary criticism.) He grants that the individual "represents a unique and unrepeatable viewpoint on this public world"; but his primary stress is placed upon the way in which the learning of language is linked to the discovery of that separately existing world of "objects in space and time." Consciousness, for Peters, cannot be explained except in connection with the demarcations of the public world which meaning makes possible. It becomes contingent upon initiation into public traditions, into (it turns out) the academic disciplines. Since such an initiation is required if modes of consciousness are to be effectively differentiated, the mind must finally be understood as a "product" of such initiation. The individual must be enabled to achieve a state of mind characterized by "a mastery of and care for the worthwhile things that have been transmitted, which are viewed in some kind of cognitive perspective."[31]

Philip H. Phenix argues similarly that "the curriculum should consist entirely of knowledge which comes from the disciplines, for the reason that the disciplines reveal knowledge in its teachable forms."[32] He, however, pays more heed to what he calls "the experience of reflective self-consciousness,"[33] which he associates specifically with "concrete existence in direct personal encounter."[34] The meanings arising out of such an encounter are expressed, for him, in existential philosophy, religion, psychology, and certain dimensions of imaginative literature. They are, thus, to be considered as one of the six "realms of meaning" through mastery of which man is enabled to achieve self-transcendence. Self-transcendence, for Phenix, involves a duality which enables the learner to feel himself to be agent and knower, and at once to identify with what he comes to know. Self-transcendence is the ground of meaning; but it culminates in the engendering of a range of "essential meanings," the achievement of a hierarchy in which all fundamental patterns of meaning are related and through which human existence can be fulfilled. The inner life of generic man is clearly encompassed by this scheme; but what is excluded, I believe, is what has been called the "subjectivity of the actor," the *individual* actor ineluctably present to himself. What is excluded is the feeling of separateness, of strangeness when such a person is confronted with the articulated curriculum intended to counteract meaninglessness.

Schutz writes:

> When a stranger comes to the town, he has to learn to orientate in it and to know it. Nothing is self-explanatory for him and he has to ask an expert . . . to learn how to get from one point to another. He may, of course, refer to a map of the town, but even to use the map successfully he must know the meaning of the signs on the map, the exact point within the town where he stands and its correlative on the map, and at least one more point in order correctly to relate the signs on the map to the real objects in the city.[35]

The prestructured curriculum resembles such a map; the learner, the stranger just arrived in town. For the cartographer, the town is an "object of his science," a science which has developed standards of operation and rules for the correct drawing of maps. In the case of the curriculum-maker, the public tradition or the natural order of things is "the object" of his design activities. Here too there are standards of operation: the subject matter organized into disciplines must be communicable; it must be appropriate to whatever are conceived as educational aims. Phenix has written that education should be understood as "a guided recapitulation of the processes of inquiry which gave rise to the fruitful bodies of organized knowledge comprising the disciplines."[36] Using the metaphor of the map, we might say that this is like asking a newcomer in search of direction to recapitulate the complex processes by which the cartographer made his map. The map may represent a fairly complete charting of the town; and it may ultimately be extremely useful for the individual to be able to take a cartographer's perspective. When that individual first arrives, however, his peculiar plight ought not to be overlooked: his "background awareness" of being alive in an unstable world; his reasons for consulting the map; the interests he is pursuing as he attempts to orient himself when he can no longer proceed by rule of thumb. He himself may recognize that he will have to come to understand the signs on the map if he is to make use of it. Certainly he will have to decipher the relationship between those signs and "real objects in the city." But his initial concern will be conditioned by the "objects" he wants to bring into visibility, by the landmarks he needs to identify if he is to proceed on his way.

Learning—A Mode of Orientation

Turning from newcomer to learner (contemporary learner, in our particular world), I am suggesting that his focal concern is with ordering the materials of his own life-world when dislocations occur, when what was once familiar abruptly appears strange. This may come about on an occasion when "future shock" is experienced, as it so frequently is today. Anyone who has lived through a campus disruption, a teachers' strike, a guerilla theatre production, a sit-in (or a be-in, or a feel-in) knows full well what Alvin Toffler means when he writes about the acceleration of change. "We no longer 'feel' life as men did in the past," he says. "And this is the ultimate difference, the distinction that separates the truly contemporary man from all others. For this acceleration lies behind the impermanence—the transience—that penetrates and tinctures our consciousness, radically affecting the way we relate to other people, to things, to the entire universe of ideas, art and values."[37] Obviously, this does not happen in everyone's life; but it is far more likely to occur than ever before in history, if it is indeed the case that change has speeded up and that forces are being released which we have not yet learned to control. My point is that the contemporary learner is more likely than his predecessors to experience moments of strangeness, moments when the recipes he has inherited for the solution of typical problems no longer seem to work. If Merleau-Ponty is right and the search for rationality is indeed grounded in a primary or perceptual consciousness, the individual may be fundamentally aware that the structures of "reality" are contingent upon the perspective taken and that most achieved orders are therefore precarious.

The stage sets are always likely to collapse.[38] Someone is always likely to ask unexpectedly, as in Pinter's *The Dumb Waiter*, "Who cleans up after we're gone?"[39] Someone is equally likely to cry out, "You seem to have no conception of where we stand! You won't find the answer written down for you in the bowl of a compass—I can tell you that."[40] Disorder, in other words, is continually breaking in; meaninglessness is recurrently overcoming landscapes which once were demarcated, meaningful. It is at moments like these that the individual reaches out to reconstitute meaning, to close the gaps, to make sense once again. It is at moments like these that he will be moved to pore over maps, to disclose or generate structures of knowledge which may provide him unifying perspectives and thus enable him to restore order once again. His learning, I am saying, is a mode of orientation—or reorientation in a place suddenly become unfamiliar. And "place" is a metaphor, in this context, for a domain of consciousness, intending, forever thrusting outward, "open to the world." The curriculum, the structures of knowledge, must be presented to such a consciousness as possibility. Like the work of literature in Sartre's viewing, it requires a subject if it is to be disclosed; it can only *be* disclosed if the learner, himself engaged in generating the structures, lends the curriculum his life. If the curriculum, on the other hand, is seen as external to the search for meaning, it becomes an alien and an alienating edifice, a kind of "Crystal Palace" of ideas.[41]

There is, then, a kind of resemblance between the ways in which a learner confronts socially prescribed knowledge and the ways in which a stranger looks at a map when he is trying to determine where he is in relation to where he wants to go. In Kafka's novel, *Amerika*, I find a peculiarly suggestive description of the predicament of someone who is at once a stranger and a potential learner (although, it eventually turns out, he never succeeds in being taught). He is Karl Rossmann, who has been "packed off to America" by his parents and who likes to stand on a balcony at his Uncle Jacob's house in New York and look down on the busy street:

> From morning to evening and far into the dreaming night that street was a channel for the constant stream of traffic which, seen from above, looked like an inextricable confusion, for ever newly improvised, of foreshortened human figures and the roofs of all kinds of vehicles, sending into the upper air another confusion, more riotous and complicated, of noises, dusts and smells, all of it enveloped and penetrated by a flood of light which the multitudinous objects in the street scattered, carried off and again busily brought back, with an effect as palpable to the dazzled eye as if a glass roof stretched over the street were being violently smashed into fragments at every moment.[42]

Karl's uncle tells him that the indulgence of idly gazing at the busy life of the city might be permissible if Karl were traveling for pleasure; "but for one who intended to remain in the States it was sheer ruination." He is going to have to make judgments which will shape his future life; he will have, in effect, to be reborn. This being so, it is not enough for him to treat the unfamiliar landscape as something to admire and wonder at (as if it were a cubist construction or a kaleidoscope). Karl's habitual interpretations (learned far away in Prague) do not suffice to clarify what he sees. If he is to learn, he must identify what is questionable, try to break through what is obscure. Action is required of him, not mere gazing; *praxis*, not mere reverie.

If he is to undertake action, however, he must do so against the background of his original perceptions, with a clear sense of being present to himself. He must do so, too, against the background of his European experience, of the experience of rejection, of being "packed off" for reasons never quite understood. Only with that sort of awareness will he be capable of the attentiveness and commitment needed to engage with the world and make it meaningful. Only with the ability to be reflective about what he is doing will he be brave enough to incorporate his past into the present, to link the present to a future. All this will demand a conscious appropriation of new perspectives on his experience and a continual reordering of that experience as new horizons of the "Amerika" become visible, as new problems arise. The point is that Karl Rossmann, an immigrant in an already structured and charted world, must be conscious enough of himself to strive towards rationality; only if he achieves rationality will he avoid humiliations and survive.

As Kafka tells it, he never does attain that rationality; and so he is continually manipulated by forces without and within. He never learns, for example, that there can be no justice if there is no good will, even though he repeatedly and sometimes eloquently asks for justice from the authorities—always to no avail. The ship captains and pursers, the business men, the head waiters and porters all function according to official codes of discipline which are beyond his comprehension. He has been plunged into a public world with its own intricate prescriptions, idiosyncratic structures, and hierarchies; but he has no way of appropriating it or of constituting meanings. Throughout most of the novel, he clings to his symbolic box (with the photograph of his parents, the memorabilia of childhood and home). The box may be egocentrism; it may signify his incapacity to embark upon the "decentering" required if he is to begin generating for himself the structures of what surrounds.

In his case (and, I would say, in the case of many other people) the "decentering" that is necessary is not solely a cognitive affair, as Piaget insists it is. Merleau-Ponty speaks of a "lived decentering,"[43] exemplified by a child's learning" "to relativise the notions of the youngest and the eldest" (to learn, e.g., to become the eldest in relation to the newborn child) or by his learning to think in terms of reciprocity. This happens, as it would have to happen to Karl, through actions undertaken within the "vital order," not merely through intellectual categorization. It does not exclude the possibility that a phenomenon analogous to Piaget's "epistemic subject" emerges, although there appears to be no reason (except, perhaps, from the viewpoint of empirical psychology) for separating it off from the "individual subject." (In fact, the apparent difference between Piaget and those who talk of "lived experience" may turn upon a definition of "consciousness." Piaget, as has been noted,[44] distinguishes between "consciousness" and "operational behavior," as if consciousness did *not* involve a turning outward to things, a continuing reflection upon situationality, a generation of cognitive structures.) In any case, every individual who consciously seeks out meaning is involved in asking questions which demand essentially epistemic responses.[45] These responses, even if incomplete, are knowledge claims; and, as more and more questions are asked, there is an increasing "sedimentation" of meanings which result from the interpretation of past experiences looked at from the vantage point of the present. Meanings do not inhere in the experiences that emerge; they have to be constituted, and they can only be constituted through cognitive action.

Returning to Karl Rossmann and his inability to take such action, I have been suggesting that he *cannot* make his own "primary consciousness" background so long as he clings to his box; nor can he actively interpret his past experience. He cannot (to stretch Piaget's point somewhat) become or will himself to be an "epistemic subject." He is, as Freire puts it, submerged in a "dense, enveloping reality or a tormenting blind alley" and will be unless he can "perceive it as an objective-problematic situation."[46] Only then will he be able to intervene in his own reality with attentiveness, with awareness—to act upon his situation and make sense.

It would help if the looming structures which are so incomprehensible to Karl were somehow rendered cognitively available to him. Karl might then (with the help of a teacher willing to engage in dialogue with him, to help him pose his problems) reach out to question in terms of what he feels is thematically relevant or "worth questioning."[47] Because the stock of knowledge he carries with him does not suffice for a definition of situations in which porters manhandle him and women degrade him, in which he is penalized for every spontaneous action, he cannot easily refer to previous situations for clues. In order to cope with this, he needs to single out a single relevant element at first (from all the elements in what is happening) to transmute into a theme for his "knowing consciousness." There is the cruel treatment meted out to him, for example, by the Head Porter who feels it his duty "to attend to things that other people neglect." (He adds that, since he is in charge of all the doors of the hotel [including the "doorless exits"], he is "in a sense placed over everyone," and everyone has to obey him absolutely. If it were not for his repairing the omissions of the Head Waiter in the name of the hotel management, he believes, "such a great organization would be unthinkable."[48]) The porter's violence against Karl might well become the relevant element, the origin of a theme.

Making Connections

"What makes the theme to be a theme." Schutz writes, "is determined by motivationally relevant interest-situations and spheres of problems. The theme which thus has become relevant has now, however, become a problem to which a solution, practical, theoretical, or emotional, must be given."[49] The problem for Karl, like relevant problems facing any individual, is connected with and a consequence of a great number of other perplexities, other dislocations in his life. If he had not been so badly exploited by authority figures in times past, if he were not so childishly given to blind trust in adults, if he were not so likely to follow impulse at inappropriate moments, he would never have been assaulted by the Head Porter. At this point, however, once the specific problem (the assault) has been determined to be thematically relevant for him, it can be detached from the motivational context out of which it derived. The mesh-work of related perplexities remains, however, as an outer horizon, waiting to be explored or questioned when necessary. The thematically relevant element can then be made interesting in its own right and worth questioning. In the foreground, as it were, the focus of concern, it can be defined against the background of the total situation. The situation is not in any sense obliterated or forgotten. It is *there*, at the fringe of Karl's attention while the focal problem is being solved; but it is, to an extent, "bracketed out." With this bracketing out and this foreground focusing, Karl may be for the first time in a condition of wide-awakeness, ready to pay active attention to what has become so questionable and so troubling, ready to take the kind of action which will move him ahead into a future as it gives him perspective on his past.

The action he might take involves more than what is understood as problem-solving. He has, after all, had some rudimentary knowledge of the Head Porter's role, a knowledge conditioned by certain typifications effected in the prepredicative days of early childhood. At that point in time, he did not articulate his experience in terms of sense data or even in terms of individual figures standing out against a background. He saw typical structures according to particular zones of relevancy. This means that he probably saw his father, or the man who was father, not only as bearded face next to his mother, not only as large figure in the doorway, but as over-bearing, threatening, incomprehensible Authority who was "placed over everyone" and had the right to inflict pain. Enabled, years later, to confront something thematically relevant, the boy may be solicited to recognize his present knowledge of the porter as the sediment of previous mental processes.[50] The knowledge of the porter, therefore, has a history beginning in primordial perceptions; and the boy may succeed in moving back from what is seemingly "given" through the diverse mental processes which constituted the porter over time. Doing so, he will be exploring both the inner and outer horizons of the problem, making connections within the field of his consciousness, interpreting his own past as it bears on his present, reflecting upon his own knowing.

And that is not all. Having made such connections between the relevant theme and other dimensions of his experience, he may be ready to solve his problem; he may even feel that the problem is solved. This, however, puts him into position to move out of his own inner time (in which all acts are somehow continuous and bound together) into the intersubjective world where he can function as an epistemic subject. Having engaged in a reflexive consideration of the activity of his own consciousness, he can now shift his attention back to the life-world which had been rendered so unrecognizable by the Head Porter's assault. Here too, meanings must be constituted; the "great organization" must be understood, so that Karl can orient himself once again in the everyday. Bracketing out his subjectivity for the time, he may find many ways of engaging as a theoretical inquirer with the problem of authority in hotels and the multiple socioeconomic problems connected with that. He will voluntarily become, when inquiring in this way, a partial self, an inquirer deliberately acting a role in a community of inquirers. I am suggesting that he could not do so as effectively or as authentically if he had not first synthesized the materials within his inner time, constituted meaning in his world.

The analogy to the curriculum question, I hope, is clear. Treating Karl as a potential learner, I have considered the hotels and the other structured organizations in his world as analogous to the structures of prescribed knowledge—or to the curriculum. I have suggested that the individual, in our case the student, will only be in a position to learn when he is committed to act upon his world. If he is content to admire it or simply accept it as given, if he is incapable of breaking with egocentrism, he will remain alienated from himself and his own possibilities; he will wander lost and victimized upon the road; he will be unable to learn. He may be conditioned; he may be trained. He may even have some rote memory of certain elements of the curriculum; but no matter how well devised is that curriculum, no matter how well adapted to the stages of his growth, learning (as disclosure, as generating structures, as engendering meanings, as achieving mastery) will not occur.

At once, I have tried to say that unease and disorder are increasingly endemic in contemporary life, and that more and more persons are finding the recipes they habitually use inadequate for sense-making in a changing world. This puts them, more and more frequently, in the position of strangers or immigrants trying to orient themselves in an unfamiliar town. The desire, indeed the *need*, for orientation is equivalent to the desire to constitute meanings, all sorts of meanings, in the many dimensions of existence. But this desire, I have suggested, is not satisfied by the authoritative confrontation of student with knowledge structures (no matter how "teachable" the forms in which the knowledge is revealed). It is surely not satisfied when the instructional situation is conceived to be, as G.K. Plochmann has written, one in which the teacher is endeavoring "with respect to his subject matter, to bring the understanding of the learner in equality with his own understanding."[51] Described in that fashion, with "learner" conceived generically and the "system" to be taught conceived as preexistent and objectively real, the instructional situation seems to me to be one that alienates because of the way it ignores both existential predicament and primordial consciousness. Like the approach to literary criticism Abrams describes, the view appears to commit us to a concept of curriculum "as a floating Laputa, insulated from life and essential human concerns. . . ."[52]

The cries of "irrelevance" are still too audible for us to content ourselves with this. So are the complaints about depersonalization, processing, and compulsory socialization into a corporate, inhuman world. Michael Novak, expressing some of this, writes that what our institutions "decide is real is enforced as real." He calls parents, teachers, and psychiatrists (like policemen and soldiers) "the enforcers of reality"; then he goes on to say:

> When a young person is being initiated into society, existing norms determine what is to be considered real and what is to be annihilated by silence and disregard. The good, docile student accepts the norms; the recalcitrant student may lack the intelligence—or have too much; may lack maturity—or insist upon being his own man.[53]

I have responses like this in mind when I consult the phenomenologists for an approach to curriculum in the present day. For one thing, they remind us of what it means for an individual to be present to himself; for another, they suggest to us the origins of significant quests for meaning, origins which ought to be held in mind by those willing to enable students to be themselves.

If the existence of a primordial consciousness is taken seriously, it will be recognized that awareness begins perspectively, that our experience is always incomplete. It is true that we have what Merleau-Ponty calls a "prejudice" in favor of a world of solid, determinate objects, quite independent of our perceptions. Consciousness does, however, have the capacity to return to the precognitive, the primordial, by "bracketing out" objects as customarily seen. The individual can release himself into his own inner time and rediscover the ways in which objects arise, the ways in which experience develops. In discussing the possibility of Karl Rossmann exploring his own past, I have tried to show what this sort of interior journey can mean. Not only may it result in the effecting of new syntheses within experience; it may result in an awareness of the process of knowing, of believing, of perceiving. It may even result in an understanding of the ways in which meanings have been sedimented in an individual's own personal history. I can think of no more potent mode of combatting those conceived to be "enforcers of the real," including the curriculum designers.

But then there opens up the possibility of presenting curriculum in such a way that is does not impose or enforce. If the student is enabled to recognize that reason and order may represent the culminating step in his constitution of a world, if he can be enabled to see that what Schutz calls the attainment of a "reciprocity of perspectives"[54] signifies the achievement of rationality, he may realize what it is to generate the structures of the disciplines on his own initiative, against his own "background awareness." Moreover, he may realize that he is projecting beyond his present horizons each time he shifts his attention and takes another perspective on his world. "To say there exists rationality," writes Merleau-Ponty, "is to say that perspectives blend, perceptions confirm each other, a meaning emerges."[55] He points out that we witness at every moment "the miracles of related experiences, and yet nobody knows better than we do how this miracle is worked, for we are ourselves this network of relationships." Curriculum can offer the possibility for students to be the makers of such networks. The problem for their teachers is to stimulate an awareness of the questionable, to aid in the identification of the thematically relevant, to beckon beyond the everyday.

> I am a psychological and historical structure, and have received, with existence, a manner of existence, a style. All my actions and thoughts stand in a relationship to this structure, and even a philosopher's thought is merely a way of making explicit his hold on the world, and what he is. The fact remains that I am free, not in spite of, or on the hither side of these motivations, but by means of them. For this significant life, this certain significance of nature and history which I am, does not limit my access to the world, but on the contrary is my means of entering into communication with it. It is by being unrestrictedly and unreservedly what I am at present that I have a chance of moving forward; it is by living my time that I am able to understand other times, by plunging into the present and the world by taking on deliberately what I am fortuitously, by willing what I will and doing what I do, that I can go further.[56]

To plunge in; to choose; to disclose; to move: this is the road, it seems to me, to mastery.

Notes

1. Maurice Merleau-Ponty, *The Primary of Perception.* James M. Edie, (ed.) Evanston, Ill.: Northwestern University Press, 1964, p. 99.
2. Jean Paul Sartre, *Search for a Method.* New York: Alfred A. Knopf, 1963, p. 92.
3. Ryland W. Crary, *Humanizing the School Curriculum: Development and Theory.* New York: Alfred A. Knopf, 1969, p. 13.
4. John Dewey, "The Child and the Curriculum." Martin S. Dworking, (ed.) *Dewey on Education.* New York: Teachers College Bureau of Publications, 1959, p. 91.
5. Sarah Lawall, *Critics of Consciousness.* Cambridge, Mass.: Harvard University Press, 1968.
6. T.S. Eliot, *The Sacred Wood.* New York: Barnes & Noble University Paperbacks, 1960, p. x.
7. Dorothy Walsh. "The Cognitive Content of Art." Francis J. Coleman, (ed.) *Aesthetics.* New York: McGraw-Hill, 1968, p. 297.
8. Clive Bell, *Art.* London: Chatto & Windus, 1914.
9. Walsh, *op. cit.*
10. M.H. Abrams, "Belief and the Suspension of Belief." M.H. Abrams, (ed.) *Literature and Belief.* New York: Columbia University Press, 1957, p. 9.
11. Maurice Blanchot. *L'Espace littéraire.* Paris: Gallimard, 1955.
12. See, e.g., Alfred Schutz, "Some Leading Concepts of Phenomenology." Maurice Natanson, (ed.) *Collected Papers I.* The Hague: Martinus Nijhoff, 1967, pp. 104–105.
13. Jean Paul Sartre. *Literature and Existentialism.* 3rd ed. New York: The Citadel Press, 1965, p. 43.
14. *Ibid.* p. 15.
15. John Dewey. *Art as Experience.* New York: Minton, Balch & Company, 1934, p. 54.
16. Sartre. *Search for a Method. op. cit.*, p. 91.
17. Jean Piaget. *Structuralism.* New York: Basic Books, 1970, p. 139.

18. *Ibid.*, p. 68.
19. *Ibid.*, p. 139.
20. *Ibid.*
21. Maurice Merleau-Ponty. *Phenomenology of Perception.* London: Routledge Kegan Paul Ltd., 1962.
22. Merleau-Ponty. *The Primacy of Perception, op. cit.*, p. 119.
23. *Ibid.*, p. 99.
24. Paulo Freire. *Pedagogy of the Oppressed.* New York: Herder and Herder, 1970, p. 108.
25. Schutz. "On Multiple Realities." *op. cit.*, p. 248.
26. Merleau-Ponty. *The Primacy of Perception, op. cit.*, p. 58.
27. Merleau-Ponty. *Phenomenology of Perception, op. cit.*, p. xvii.
28. Schutz. "On Multiple Realities." *op. cit.*
29. Merleau-Ponty, *op. cit.*, p. xv.
30. R.S. Peters. *Ethics and Education.* London: George Allen and Unwin, 1966, p. 50.
31. R.S. Peters. *Ethics and Education.* Glenview, Ill.: Scott Foresman and Co., 1967, p. 12.
32. Philip H. Phenix, "The Uses of the Disciplines as Curriculum Content." Donald Vandenberg, (ed.) *Theory of Knowledge and Problems of Education.* Urbana, Ill.: University of Illinois Press, 1969, p. 195.
33. Philip H. Phenix. *Realms of Meaning.* New York: McGraw-Hill, 1964, p. 25.
34. *Ibid.*
35. Schutz. "Problem of Rationality in the Social World." Natanson, (ed.) *Collected Papers II.* The Hague: Martinus Nijhoff, 1967, p. 66.
36. Phenix, "Disciplines as Curriculum Content," *op. cit.*, p. 195.
37. Alvin Toffler. *Future Shock.* New York: Random House, 1970, p. 18.
38. Albert Camus. *The Myth of Sisyphus.* New York: Alfred A. Knopf, 1955, p. 72.
39. Harold Pinter. *The Dumb Waiter.* New York: Grove Press, 1961, p. 103.
40. Tom Stoppard. *Rosencrantz and Guildenstern are Dead.* New York: Grove Press, 1967, pp. 58–59.
41. Cf. Fyodor Dostoevsky. *Notes from Underground*, in *The Short Novels of Dostoevsky.* New York: Dial Press, 1945. "You believe in a palace of crystal that can never be destroyed . . . a palace at which one will not be able to put out one's tongue or make a long nose on the sly." p. 152.
42. Franz Kafka. *Amerika.* Garden City, N.Y.: Doubleday Anchor Books, 1946, p. 38.
43. Merleau-Ponty. *The Primacy of Perception, op. cit.*, p. 110.
44. Piaget, *op. cit.*
45. Richard M. Zaner. *The Way of Phenomenology.* New York: Pegasus Books, 1970, p. 27.
46. Freire, *op. cit.*, p. 100.
47. Schutz. "The Life-World." Natanson, (ed.) *Collected Papers, III.* The Hague: Martinus Nijhoff, 1967, p. 125.
48. Kafka, *op. cit.*, p. 201.
49. Schutz. "The Life-World." *op. cit.*, p. 124.
50. Schutz, "Leading Concepts of Phenomenology," *op. cit.*, p. 111.
51. G.K. Plochmann. "On the Organic Logic of Teaching and Learning." Vandenberg, *op. cit.*, p. 244.
52. Cf. footnote 10.
53. Michael Novak. *The Experience of Nothingness.* New York: Harper & Row, 1970, p. 94.
54. Schutz. "Symbols, Reality, and Society." *Collected Papers I, op. cit.*, p. 315.
55. Merleau-Ponty, *Phenomenology of Perception, op. cit.*, p. xix.
56. *Ibid.*, pp. 455–56.

Part Three

Reconceptualizing Curriculum Theory

Introduction to Part Three

As the curriculum reform movement was drawing to a close with the 1960s, writers such as Maxine Greene were pressing the curriculum field in new directions. An important manifestation of change was attention in the 1970s through most of the 1990s to why the preceding national curriculum change efforts had failed to effect reform in the ways envisaged (e.g., McLaughlin, this volume, Chapter 18). As a result, the 1970s and early 1980s may be characterized as a period of renewed experimentation in the wake of the curriculum reform movement. Looking back, Nel Noddings (2001, pp. 38–39) listed some of the significant experiments: continuous progress programs, modular scheduling, media-centered education, individualized instruction, behavioral objectives, mastery learning, discovery learning, interdisciplinary studies, and learning centers. By the 1970s, as the preceding list implies, experimentation increasingly stressed curricular choice rather than standardization. Students were often provided, for example, with multiple courses, even "mini-courses," which they could elect to meet standard requirements in academic subjects.

Thus one of the themes most important in Part Three is choice, of students having some significant say in what they study or how they study it or both. Choice suggests its alternative, curriculum standardization. Because what schools teach is a political as well as an educational decision, intertwined with issues of choice or standardization are questions of power, as George Counts had so well understood (see Part One). Curriculum scholars in the 1970s returned with greater vigor to issues of power than had been evident since the Great Depression. Power became a complementary theme to choice and standardization for this period. In a sense, then, the period from the late 1960s until well after the alarmist *A Nation at Risk* (National Commission on Excellence in Education, 1983) was a competition between the forces of curriculum standardization and curriculum choice. The powers of standardization would win out.

The politics of education and the battles over who controlled what schools teach largely came to overshadow the possibilities unleashed by experimentation. Under the circumstances, innovations may have been insufficiently tested to establish if they "worked." Some innovations, as is evident in the readings, harked back to the centrality John Dewey (this volume, Chapter 4) ascribed to the individualization of instruction: "What a child gets out of any subject presented to him is simply the images which he himself forms with regard to it." Unlike the standards movement and its associated testing movement, which secured dominance in U.S. public education in the 1990s, many of the curricular innovations of the 1970s valued the various outcomes that resulted from diversification of standard curricula in the interests of personal relevance.

Subsequent insistence by policymakers on the desirability of a standardized curriculum with uniform outcomes has been widely criticized as a policy, particularly concerning what outcomes should be valued, how it should be implemented, whether it is properly aligned with tests, and so forth. Oddly, however, less attention seems to have been devoted to critiquing the premises of standardization with questions such as why uniform outcomes are desirable in the first place and what opportunity costs they entail. The readings in Part Three contribute to an now ongoing critique of these premises.

The first essay, by William Pinar, responded to the perception that established approaches to curriculum were inadequate, incomplete, or both. While maintaining that established approaches to curriculum were "reliant" on each other, Pinar was in the forefront of a new "reconceptualist" movement. He argued that the two other main currents of curriculum thought, perspectives of "traditionalists" and "conceptual-empiricists" (or employers of a "social science" perspective) were inherently incomplete. Two important elements that reconceptualist curriculum theories add, Pinar argued, were their "value-laden perspective" and their "politically emancipatory intent." In large part, however, he distinguishes the movement by what it is not.

According to Pinar, traditionalists, working in the traditions of Franklin Bobbitt and Ralph Tyler, were immersed in the assumptions of schools and society as they are—the traditionalists' task is to describe how curriculum improvement could be secured without fundamental alterations to existing institutional and societal arrangements. To do so, Pinar maintained, traditionalists engaged in curriculum theorizing that "is theoretical only in the questionable sense that it is abstract and usually at variance with what occurs in schools" (this volume, Chapter 13).

Pinar described conceptual-empiricists as curriculum scholars who applied the questions and methods of social science to curricular phenomena. Although he saw this group as an "heir" or successor to the traditionalists, he found their attention to the normative element of their work perfunctory as conceptual-empirical "research in education, in many instances, has become indistinguishable from social science research" (this volume, Chapter 13). This concern echoes Montessori's (this volume, Chapter 2) apprehension about the specialized interests of science versus the social interests of education. For Pinar's part, he seems to have held out hope that the conceptual-empiricists might move toward the reconceptualist position. For instance, he credited the conceptual-empiricist Decker Walker with building on calls for deliberation rather than remaining preoccupied with "prescriptive curriculum theories" that Pinar viewed as integral to the Tyler rationale. Pinar also praised Walker's work because, even though it incorporated traditionalist elements such as "the practical concerns of school people and school curriculum," Walker's use of anthropological research methods placed "his work . . . closer to some reconceptualists than . . . other mainstream conceptual-empiricists." Pinar, in other words, urged "value-laden," politicized curriculum theorizing, which he thought more likely to occur through anthropological means than in social sciences such as "political science or psychology" (this volume, Chapter 13).

The next reading turns decidedly political. It is by Paulo Freire, who had longtime involvements with social movements and adult education, particularly in his native Brazil and other parts of Latin America. By the 1970s his writings were becoming widely read in the United States where he attracted a devoted and enduring set of disciples. Freire's curriculum thought is not easily summarized. Indeed, Freire was always worried that his ideas would become a recipe-like method to be followed uncritically (Apple, Gandin, & Hypolito, 2001, p. 132). His overarching aim was to teach the oppressed classes to bring about social justice in capitalist societies. He vigorously opposed the transmission model of curriculum, what he referred to as "banking education," because it reinforced the established knowledge already used to oppress the disadvantaged. Instead, he believed that "emancipatory" curriculum must grow out of lived experience and their social circumstances. Freire made no clear divide between education and politics:

> The starting point for organizing the program content of education or political action must be the present, existential, concrete situation, reflecting the aspirations of the people. Utilizing certain basic contradictions, we must pose this existential, concrete, present situation to the people as a problem which challenges them and requires a response—not just at the intellectual level, but at the level of action. (this volume, Chapter 14)

Such problem-posing education could be achieved not by anyone "liberating" a social class, but rather through dialogue among educators and the oppressed. In the particular excerpts included here in Part Three, Freire describes what he views as the essential characteristics of such dialogue.

The next reading, by Michael Apple, again evokes the theme of power common to Freire's work and the early reconceptualists. As a critical theorist, Apple decries teachers being "de-skilled" as workers by patriarchal, undemocratic policymakers. Teachers' work, he argues further, has intensified while their control over its quality has declined. Certainly much of what Apple described here in the mid-1980s subsequently became, as evident in Part Four, ever more relevant and pressing for teachers. As Apple puts this:

> I claimed that they [teachers] were more and more faced with the prospect of being deskilled because of the encroachment of technical control procedures into the curriculum. The integration together of management systems, reductive behaviorally based curriculum, pre-specified teaching "competencies" and procedures and student responses, and pre and post testing, was leading to a loss of control and a separation of conception from execution. (this volume, Chapter 15)

Mortimer Adler, the philosopher who contributes the next essay, was interested in curriculum theorizing as a means for promoting what he took for granted as the "best" knowledge and thus the knowledge of most worth. On this point he stood in contrast to the more varied and multifaceted concerns of the preceding three contributors to Part Three who, for all their differences, nonetheless agreed the traditional intellectual foundations of the "best" knowledge were an insufficient basis for sound curriculum theorizing. Adler, on the other hand, was a perennialist, boldly declaring that the best knowledge was unchanging and concerned with great questions such as what is the nature of truth and justice. He quoted his one-time associate, Robert Maynard Hutchins (1953), for the central plank of his beliefs: "The best education for the best is the best education for all."

Because in Adler's words, "we are a politically classless society," he believed that all young people in a democracy should study the same curriculum. Adler asserted that this democratic view of schooling has been generally agreed upon in American education, exemplified by thinkers such as Hutchins, Dewey, and Horace Mann. Thus, Adler (and Hutchins) argued the curriculum traditionally preserved for the elite was the best for everyone: "The innermost meaning of social equality is substantially the same quality of life for all. That calls for the same quality of schooling for all." Although

Adler acknowledged the curriculum needed to be taught well and "children are educable in varying degrees," he still argued that choice in the curriculum would cause "a certain number of students to voluntarily downgrade their own education" (this volume, Chapter 16).

In the next essay, the philosopher of education Nel Noddings roundly disputes Adler's theory of curriculum. To begin with, she questions that we, except in the most narrow and technical sense, live in a politically classless society. So for Adler to imply that giving everyone the same knowledge appreciably compensates for other inequalities, Noddings thinks, is misleading, even dangerous. Moreover, she notes, as Adler must have known but fails to mention, Dewey and Hutchins vigorously disagreed on curriculum matters. Further, Noddings contests that social equality should be equated with everyone living (or being educated) in the same way. In fact, Noddings contends along with Dewey that equality suggests individual differences should be respected and education build on these legitimate differences.

Noddings allows that Adler's recommendations "follow inexorably" from his assumptions, but she challenges his assumptions. She takes issue, for instance, with Adler's assumption that the "intellectually best" person is the ideal for all persons: "What the schools need to do, instead, is to legitimize multiple models of excellence," with the most important thing being "ethical goodness," which "we need far more urgently than intellectual prowess." Moreover, Noddings rejects Adler's dismissal of divergence from his prescribed subjects in the curriculum as equivalent to "downgrading" one's education:

> I am simply pointing out what John Dewey counseled again and again: Any subject freely undertaken as an occupation—as a set of tasks requiring goal-setting, means-ends analysis, choice of appropriate tools and materials, exercise of skills, living through the consequences, and evaluating the results—is educative. . . . It is not the subjects offered that make a curriculum properly a part of education but how those subjects are taught, how they connect to the personal interests and talents of the students who study them, and how skillfully they are laid out against the whole continuum of human experience. (this volume, Chapter 17)

The final reading in Part Three recasts Noddings arguments in the context of classroom implementation. Its author, Milbrey McLaughlin, was like many of the authors in Part Three writing in the aftermath of a national reform movement (see Part Two) that was generally judged to have failed in significantly improving school currriulum. McLaughlin explained that most of the curricular innovations of that period had concentrated on "technological" change. She suggested that "organizational" change in the structure of the institutional setting or the culture of the school might be a more significant factor in effecting educational change. "Innovations in classroom organization such as open education, multiage grouping, integrated day, differentiated staffing, and team teaching," McLaughlin noted by way of illustration, "are not based on a 'model' of classroom organization change to be strictly followed, but a common set of convictions about the nature of learning and the purpose of teaching." Rather than the conventional assumption that implementation consists of "the direct and straightforward application of an educational technology or plan," McLaughlin was suggesting change that matters is associated with "mutual adaptation" or "modification of both the project design and changes in the institutional setting and individual participants during the course of implementation" (this volume, Chapter 18).

If mutual adaptation is the hallmark of successful reform, a "teacher-proof" curriculum would be ineffectual from the start. To state this more broadly, McLaughlin's research is instructive on the nature of meaningful curriculum change. To illustrate, she examined open education projects in two settings. The settings were "similar in almost every aspect—resources, support and interest, target group, background characteristics"—but differed significantly in implementation strategy and implementation outcomes:

> The Eastown open education project had extensive and ongoing staff training, spent a lot of staff time and energy on materials development, arranged for staff to meet regularly, and engaged in regular formative evaluation. This project was also well implemented, ran smoothly, and met its objectives. . . . Implementation in this [the Seaside] project was only pro forma—largely because of the absence of implementation strategies that would allow learning, growth, and development or mutual adaptation to take place. (this volume, Chapter 18)

McLaughlin was perhaps writing in less conservative times than Michael Apple, but because each approached teaching and curriculum for a different theoretical perspective, it is instructive to compare their views on what came to be know in the 1970s and 1980s as the implementation problem.

References

Apple, M. W., Gandin, L. A. & Hypolito, A. M. (2001). "Paulo Freire, 1921–1997." In J. Palmer (Ed.) *Fifty modern thinkers on education: From Piaget to the present* (pp. 128–133). London: Routledge.

Hutchins, R. M. (1953). *The conflict in education in a democratic society.* New York: Harper.

National Commission on Excellence in Education, (1983). *A nation at risk: The imperative for educational reform.* Washington, DC: U.S. Department of Education.

Noddings, N. (2001). Care and coercion in school reform. *Journal of Educational Change, 2,* 35–43.

13
The Reconceptualization of Curriculum Studies

William F. Pinar

What some observers have designated a "movement" is visible in the field of curriculum studies in the United States. Some have termed it "reconceptualism," others "the new curriculum theory." Both terms suggest more thematic unity among the curriculum writing characterized as the "reconceptualization" than, upon close examination, appears to exist. Nonetheless, some thematic similarities are discernible, though insufficient in number to warrant a characterization like "ideology" or composite, agreed-upon point of view. What can be said, without dispute, is that by the summer of 1978, there will have been six conferences and five books[1] in the past six years which are indications of a socio-intellectual phenomenon in this field, and a phenomenon which clearly functions to reconceptualize the field of curriculum studies. Thus, while the writing published to date may be somewhat varied thematically, it is unitary in its significance for the field. If this process of transformation continues at its present rate, the field of curriculum studies will be profoundly different in 20 years time than it has been during the first 50 years of its existence.

What is this reconceptualization? The answer, at this point, is a slippery one, and to gain even an inchoate grip, one looks to the field as it is. This will indicate, in part, what is not. To a considerable extent, the reconceptualization is a reaction to what the field has been, and what it is seen to be at the present time.

Traditionalists

Most curricularists at work in 1977 can be characterized as *traditionalists.* Their work continues to make use of the "conventional wisdom" of the field, epitomized still by the work of Tyler. More important in identifying traditionalists than the allusion to Tyler is citing the *raison d'être* for traditional curriculum work. Above all, the reason for curriculum writing, indeed curriculum work generally, is captured in the phrase "service to practitioners." Curriculum work tends to be field-based and curriculum writing tends to have school teachers in mind. In short, traditional curriculum work is focused on the schools. Further, professors of curriculum have tended to be former school people. In fact, school service of some sort, ordinarily classroom teaching, is still viewed as a prerequisite for a teaching post in the field in a college or university. To an extent not obvious in certain of the other subfields of education (for instance, philosophy and psychology of education, recently in administration and the "helping services"), curricularists are former school people whose intellectual and subcultural ties tend to be with school practitioners. They tend to be less interested in basic research, in theory development, in related developments in allied fields, than in a set of perceived realities of classrooms and school settings generally.

There is, of course, an historical basis for traditional curriculum work. Cremin suggests that it was after superintendent Newlon's work in curriculum revision, in the early 1920s in Denver, that the need for a curriculum specialist became clear.[2] It is plausible to imagine school administrators like Newlon asking teachers who demonstrated an interest in curriculum and its development to leave classroom teaching and enter an administrative office from which they would attend full-time to matters curricular. There were no departments of curriculum in colleges of education in the 1920s; Newlon and other administrators could go nowhere else but to the classroom for curriculum personnel. When the training of curriculum personnel began at the university level in the 1930s, it surfaced in departments of administration and secondary education, indicating further the field's origin in and loyalty to the practical concerns of school personnel. This affiliation, more tenuous and complex at the present time than it was in the 1920s and 1930s, is evident in the programmes of the largest professional association of curricularists in the United States, the Association for Supervision and Curriculum Development. The programmes of ASCD annual meetings indicate a considerable and growing presence of school personnel. Further, the workshops and papers listed, the authors of which are university teachers, tend to have an explicit thematic focus on whatever school concerns are *au courant*.

There is another sense in which traditionalists carry forward the tradition of the field. The curriculum field's birth in the 1920s was understandably shaped by the intellectual character of that period. Above all it was a time of an emerging scientism when so-called scientific techniques from business and industry were finding their way into educational theory and practice. The early curricularist came to employ what Kliebard has termed the "bureaucratic model."[3] This model is characterized by its ameliorative orientation, ahistorical posture, and an allegiance to behaviourism and to what Macdonald has termed a "technological rationality." The curriculum worker is dedicated to the "improvement" of schools. He honours this dedication by accepting the curriculum structure as it is. "Curriculum change" is measured by comparing resulting behaviours with original objectives. Even humanistic educators tend to accept many of these premises, as they introduce, perhaps, "values clarification" into the school curriculum. Accepting the curriculum structure as it is, and working to improve it, is what is meant by the "technician's mentality." In a capsule way, it can be likened to adjusting an automobile engine part in order to make it function more effectively. This is also technological rationality, and its manifestations in school practice run the gamut from "competency-based teacher education" to "modular scheduling." The emphasis is on design, change (behaviourally observable), and improvement.

What has tended to be regarded as curriculum theory in the traditional sense, most notably Tyler's rationale,[4] is theoretical only in the questionable sense that it is abstract and usually at variance with what occurs in schools. Its intent is clearly to guide, to be of assistance to those in institutional positions who are concerned with curriculum. Of course, this is a broad concern. Most teachers share it, at least in terms of daily lesson planning. But as well as an element of teaching, curriculum is traditionally thought to include considerations such as evaluation, supervision, and also curriculum development and implementation. The boundaries of the field are fuzzy.

Thematically there is no unity. From Tyler to Taba and Saylor and Alexander to the current expression of this genre in Daniel and Laurel Tanner's book, Neil's and Zais' writing (all of which attempt an overview of considerations imagined pertinent to a curriculum worker) to the humanistic movement (for instance the work of such individuals as Fantini, Jordan, Simon, Weinstein) is a broad thematic territory.[5] What makes this work one territory is its fundamental interest in working with school people, with revising the curricula of schools. Traditional writing tends to be journalistic, necessarily so, in order that it can be readily accessible to a readership seeking quick answers to pressing, practical problems. The publications of the Association for Supervision and Curriculum Development also exemplify, to a considerable extent, this writing. ASCD is the traditionalists' professional organization. Relatively speaking, there exists a close relationship between traditional curricularists and school personnel.

Conceptual-Empiricists

A relationship between school personnel and the other two groups of curricularists—*conceptual-empiricists* and *reconceptualists*—also exists. But the nature of this relationship differs from the alliance historically characteristic of the field. This difference becomes clearer as we examine, momentarily, a second group of curricularists, a group which, until reconceptualists appeared, seemed to be the only heir to the field.

I use the word heir advisedly, for the traditional curriculum field has been declared terminally ill or already deceased by several influential observers, among them Schwab and Huebner.[6] What has caused, in the past 15 to 20 years, the demise of the field? A comprehensive answer to this important question is inappropriate in the present context. What can be pointed to is two-fold. First, the leadership of the so-called curriculum reform movement of the 1960s was outside the field. This bypass was a crippling blow to its professional status. If those whose work was curriculum development and implementation were called on primarily as consultants and only rarely at that, then clearly their claim to specialized knowledge and expertise was questionable. Second, the economic situation of the past six years has meant a drying up of funds for in-service work and for curriculum proposals generally. A field whose professional status was irreparably damaged now lost the material basis necessary for its functioning. How could curricularists work with school people without money or time for in-service workshops? How could curriculum proposals be implemented without requisite funds?

With the traditional, practical justification of the field attenuated—even teacher-training efforts have slowed dramatically—new justifications appeared. Curriculum and other education subfields have become increasingly vulnerable to criticisms regarding scholarly standards by colleagues in so-called cognate fields. Particularly the influence of colleagues in the social sciences is evident, paralleling the political ascendency of these disciplines in the university generally. In fact, research in education, in many instances, has become indistinguishable from social science research. The appearance and proliferation of conceptual-empiricists in the curriculum field is a specific instance of this general phenomenon. There remains, of course, the notion that research has implications for classroom practice, but it is usually claimed that many years of extensive research are necessary before significant implications can be obtained.

This development has gone so far that, examining the work done by a faculty in a typical American college of education, one has little sense of education as a field with its own identity. One discovers researchers whose primary identity is with the cognate field. Such individuals view themselves as primarily psychologists, philosophers, or sociologists with "research interests" in schools and education-related matters. By 1978, it is accurate to note that the education field has lost whatever (and it was never complete of course) intellectual autonomy it possessed in earlier years, and now is nearly tantamount to a colony of superior, imperialistic powers.

The view that education is not a discipline in itself but an area to be studied by the disciplines is evident in the work of those of curricularists I have called conceptual-empiricists. The work of this group can be so characterized, employing conceptual and empirical in the sense social scientists typically employ them. This work is concerned with developing hypotheses to be tested, and testing them in methodological ways characteristic of mainstream social science. This work is reported, ordinarily, at meetings of the American Educational Research Association. Just as the Association for Supervision and Curriculum Development is the traditionalists' organization, AERA tends to be the organization of conceptual-empiricists. (In relatively small numbers traditionalists and reconceptualists also read papers at AERA annual meetings.)

An illustrative piece of conceptual work from this second group of curricularists was published in the AERA-sponsored *Review of Educational Research.* It is George Posner's (with Kenneth Strike) "A categorization scheme for principles of sequencing content." A prefatory paragraph indicates that his view is a social scientist's one, reliant upon hypothesis-making, data collection, and interpretation.

> We have very little information, based on hard data, regarding the consequences of alternative content sequences and will need a good deal more research effort before we are able to satisfactorily suggest how content *should* be sequenced. Our intention here is to consider the question, What are the alternatives?[7]

The article is a conceptual one, concerned with what the authors view as logically defensible content sequencing alternatives, and it is empirical in its allegiance to the view of empirical research, one yielding "hard data," typical of social science at the present time.

In a recently published essay, Decker F. Walker, another visible conceptual-empiricist, moves away somewhat from strict social science as exemplified in Posner's work.[8] His essay, or case study as he terms it, is more anthropological in its methodological form, demonstrating a type of curriculum research which Walker's co-editor Reid endorses.[9] Anthropology, it should be noted, while regarded as not as "pure" a social science as political science or psychology, is nonetheless generally categorized as a social science.

Taking his cue from Schwab, Walker argues that prescriptive curriculum theories, (partly because they do not reflect the actual process of curriculum change), are not useful. Rather than focus on why curriculum developers did not follow the Tyler rationale, Walker concentrates on how, in fact, the developers did proceed. In his study he finds little use for terms like objectives and important use for terms such as platform and deliberation. He concludes that curricularists probably ought to abandon the attempt to make actual curriculum development mirror prescriptive theories, accept "deliberation" as a core aspect of the development process, and apply the intellectual resources of the field toward improving the quality of deliberation and employing it more effectively.

This work I find significant to the field in two ways. First it deals another hard blow to the Tyler rationale and its influence. Second, Walker is moving away from social science. His work remains social science, but it is closer to the work of some reconceptualists than it is to that of Posner, and other mainstream conceptual-empiricists. Walker retains the traditional focus upon the practical concerns of school people and school curriculum, and no doubt he has and will spend a portion of his professional time on actual curriculum projects. Further, his methods seem more nearly those of the ethnomethodologist whose approaches do not easily fit the picture of conventional theories of the middle range, as projected by individuals such as the sociologist Robert Merton, who has influenced so many conceptual-empirical studies in the field of sociology. Walker appears to be moving outside mainstream conceptual-empiricism.

Also in the Reid and Walker book is work by another visible conceptual-empiricist, Ian Westbury. With his co-author Lynn McKinney, Westbury studies the Gary, Indiana school system during the period 1940–1970.[10] Like Walker's study of the art project, McKinney and Westbury's study would seem to be outside mainstream conceptual-empiricism, even close to work characteristic of the humanities. The structure of the study, however, indicates its allegiance to social science, thus warranting its categorization as conceptual-empirical. The work is an historical study done in the service of generalization, work that has interest in the particular (the Gary district) as it contributes to understanding of the general. The "general" in this instance is the phenomenon of stability and change, which the authors "now believe are the two primary functions of the administrative structure which surround the schools."[11] Finally what the study demonstrates is "that a concern for goals without a concomitant concern for organizational matters addresses only a small part of the problem of conceiving new designs for schools."[12] This use of the specific to illustrate a general, ahistorical "law" is, of course, a fundamental procedure of mainstream social science.

Reconceptualists

This concern for generalization is not abandoned in the work of the third group of curricularists, the reconceptualists. For example, at the fourth conference at the University of Wisconsin-Milwaukee, Professor Apple reported the results of a study he and a colleague conducted in a kindergarten, substantiating claims he has made before regarding the socio-political functions of classroom behaviour.[13] His case study is distinguishable from the work of a typical conceptual-empiricist in two significant respects: (1) his acknowledged "value-laden" perspective, and (2) a perspective with a politically emancipatory intent. That is, in contrast to the canon of traditional social science, which prescribes data collection, hypothesis substantiation or disconfirmation in the disinterested service of building a body of knowledge, a reconceptualist tends to see research as an inescapably political as well as intellectual act. As such, it works to suppress, or to liberate, not only those who conduct the research, and those upon whom it is conducted, but as well those outside the academic subculture. Mainstream social science research, while on the surface seemingly apolitical in nature and consequence, if examined more carefully can be seen as contributing to the maintenance of the contemporary social-political order, or contributing to its dissolution. Apple and Marxists and neo-Marxists go further and accept a teleological view of historical movement, allying themselves with the lower classes, whose final emergence from oppression is seen to be inevitable. A number of reconceptualists, while not Marxists, nonetheless accept some variation of this teleological historical view. And many of these, at least from a distance, would seem to be "leftists" of some sort. Nearly all accept that a political dimension is inherent in any intellectual activity.

This political emphasis distinguishes the work of Apple, Burton, Mann, Molnar, some of the work of Huebner and Macdonald, from the work of traditionalists and conceptual-empiricists.[14] It is true that Reid and Walker in their *Case Studies in Curriculum Change* acknowledge that curriculum development is political, but the point is never developed, and never connected with a view of history and the contemporary social order. The focus of Walker's case study and of other case studies in the book is limited to literal curriculum change, without historicizing this change, indicating its relationship to contemporary historical movement generally. In the 1975 ASCD year-book, on the other hand, which is edited by Macdonald and Zaret, with essays also by Apple, Burton, Huebner, and Mann, this sitting of curriculum issues in the broad intellectual-historical currents of twentieth-century life is constant.[15] Macdonald speaks, for instance, of technological rationality, an intellectual mode comparable in its pervasiveness and taken-for-grantedness to the ascendency of technology in human culture at large.[16] Such individuals would argue that comprehension of curriculum issues is possible only when they are situated historically.

The 1975 ASCD year-book speaks to school people. It is not that reconceptualists do not speak to this constituency of the curriculum field. But there is a conscious abandonment of the "technician's mentality." There are no prescriptions or traditional rationales. What this year-book offers, instead, is heightened awareness of the complexity and historical significance of curriculum issues. Because the difficulties these reconceptualists identify are related to difficulties in the culture at large, they are not "problems" that can be "solved." That concept created by technological rationality, is itself problematic. Thus, what is necessary, in part, is fundamental structural change in the culture. Such an aspiration cannot be realized by "plugging into" the extant order. That is why an elective or two on Marx in high-school social studies classes, or the teaching of autobiographical reflection in English classes, bring indifference and often alarm to most reconceptualists. That "plugging into," "co-opting" it was termed in the 1960s during the student protests, accepts the social order as it is. What is necessary is a fundamental reconceptualization of what curriculum is, how it functions, and how it might function in emancipatory ways. It is this commitment to a comprehensive critique and theory development that distinguishes the reconceptualist phenomenon.

To understand more fully the efforts of the individuals involved in inquiry of this kind requires some understanding of metatheory and philosophy of science. Without such grounding, it is difficult, if not impossible, for curricularists to see clearly their work in the context of the growth of knowledge in general. Max van Manen's paper at the 1976 Wisconsin conference was a significant effort to analyse various structures of theoretic knowledge as they related to dominant modes of inquiry in the field of curriculum.[17] His work builds on basic analyses undertaken by philosophers of science such as Radnitzky and Feyerabend.[18] More work needs to be done along this line.

The reconceptualization, it must be noted, is fundamentally an intellectual phenomenon, not an interpersonal-affiliative one. Reconceptualists have no organized group, such as ASCD or AERA. Individuals at work, while sharing certain themes and motives, do not tend to share any common interpersonal affiliation. (In this one respect their work parallels that of the so-called romantic critics of the 1960s. But here any such comparison stops.) Conferences have been held yearly; the most recent on the campus of Rochester Institute of Technology, Rochester, New York. A journal and a press emphasizing this work are scheduled to appear by 1979.

Conclusion

As an interpreter of metatheories, Richard Bernstein recently analysed, in detail, individuals at work in four areas—empirical research, philosophical analysis, phenomenology and critical theory of society.[19] (The first category corresponds to conceptual-empirical, the third and fourth to reconceptualist work.) He ends his study with this conviction:

> In the final analysis we are not confronted with exclusive choices: either empirical or interpretative theory or critical theory. Rather there is an internal dialectic in the restructing of social political theory: when we work through any one of these movements we discover the others are implicated.[20]

This is so in the field of curriculum studies also. We are not faced with an exclusive choice: either the traditional wisdom of the field, or conceptual-empiricism, or the reconceptualization. Each is reliant upon the other. For the field to become vital and significant to American education it must nurture each "moment," its "internal dialectic." And it must strive for synthesis, for a series of perspectives on curriculum that are at once empirical, interpretative, critical, emancipatory.

But such nurturance and synthesis do not characterize, on the whole, the field today. Some of the issues raised by the British sociologist David Silverman are germane here.[21] As a prologue to more adequate social science theorizing, Silverman proposes that we learn how to read Castaneda's account of his apprenticeship to Don Juan in order that we may come to know the kinds of questions that need to be asked. He is convinced that mainstream conceptual-empiricists, regardless of field, do not now know what questions to ask, and are, indeed, intolerant of reconceptualizations that differ from their own. This intolerance is discernible in the American curriculum field. To some extent it can be found in each group of curricularists.

I am convinced that this intolerance among curricularists for work differing from one's own must be suspended to some extent if significant intellectual movement in the field is to occur. Becoming open to another genre of work does not mean loss of one's capacity for critical reflection. Nor does it mean, necessarily, loss of intellectual identity. One may remain a traditionalist while sympathetically studying the work of a reconceptualist. One's own point of view may well be enriched. Further, an intellectual climate may become established in which could develop syntheses of current perspectives, regenerating the field, and making more likely that its contribution to American education be an important one.

Acknowledgment

This is a revised version of a paper presented at the Annual Meeting of the American Educational Research Association in New York in April, 1977.

Notes

1. Conferences have been held at the University of Rochester (1973), Xavier University of Cincinnati (1974), the University of Virginia (1975), the University of Wisconsin at Milwaukee (1976), Kent State University (1977), and the Rochester Institute of Technology (1978). Books include: Pinar, W. (Ed) *Heightened Consciousness, Cultural Revolution and Curriculum Theory* (McCutchan Publishing Corp., Berkeley, CA, 1974); IDEM, *Curriculum Theorizing: The Reconceptualists* (McCutchan Publishing Corp., Berkeley, CA, 1975); Pinar, W., and Grumet, M. R. *Toward a Poor Curriculum* (Kendall/Hunt Publishing Co., Dubuque, IA, 1976). At a 1976 conference held at the State University of New York at Geneseo; Professors Apple, Greene, Kliebard and Huebner read papers. Each of these persons has been associated with the reconceptualists although the chairmen of this meeting, Professors DeMarte and Rosarie, did not see this seminar as being in the tradition of the others. The papers from this seminar were published in *Curriculum Inquiry*, Vol. 6, No. 4 (1977).
2. Cremin, L. "Curriculum-making in the United States." In Pinar, W. (ed.), *Curriculum Theorizing*, pp. 19–35.
3. Kliebard, H. M. "Persistent curriculum issues in historical perspective," and "Bureaucracy and curriculum theory." In Pinar, W. (ed.) *Curriculum Theorizing*, pp. 39–69.
4. Tyler, R. W., *Basic Principles of Curriculum and Instruction* (University of Chicago Press, Chicago, 1950).
5. Taba, H. *Curriculum Development: Theory and Practice* (Harcourt, Brace and World, New York, 1962); Saylor, G., and Alexander, W. *Curriculum Planning for Modern Schools* (Holt, Rinehart and Winston, New York, 1966); Tanner, D., and Tanner, L. N. *Curriculum Development: Theory into Practice* (MacMillan, New York, 1975); Neil, J. D. *Curriculum: A Comprehensive Introduction* (Little, Brown and Co., Boston, 1977); Zais, R. S. *Curriculum: Principles and Foundations* (Thomas Y. Browell, New York, 1976); Weinstein, G., and Fantini, M. D. *Toward Humanistic Education: A Curriculum of Affect* (Praeger Publishers, New York, 1971); Simon, S., et al. *Values Clarification* (Hart, New York, 1972); Jordan, D. "The ANISA Model." Paper presented to conference on curriculum at the University of Virginia, 1975 (available from Charles W. Beegle, Curry Memorial School of Education, University of Virginia, Charlottesville, VA 22903, USA).
6. Schwab, J. J. *The Practical: A Language for Curriculum* (National Education Association, Washington, D.C., 1970); Huebner, D. "The moribund curriculum field: Its wake and our work." *Curriculum Inquiry*, Vol. 6, No. 2 (1976).
7. Posner, G. J. and Strike, K. A. "A categorization scheme for principles of sequencing content." *Review of Educational Research*, Vol. 46, No. 4 (1976).
8. Walker, D. F. "Curriculum development in an art project." In Reid, W. A., and Walker, D. F. (eds.) *Case Studies in Curriculum Change* (Routledge and Kegan Paul, London, 1975).
9. Reid, W. A. "The changing curriculum: theory and practice." In Reid and Walker, op. cit.
10. McKinney, W. L., and Westbury, I. "Stability and change; the public schools of Gary, Indiana, 1940–70." In Reid and Walker, op. cit.
11. Ibid., p. 44.
12. Ibid., p. 50.
13. Apple, M. W., and King, N. "What do schools teach?" Paper presented at the University of Wisconsin and Milwaukee Conference.
14. For discussion of this point see my prefatory remarks in *Curriculum Theorizing* (Note 1). See also: Klohr, P. R. "The State of the Field." Paper presented at the Xavier University Conference on Curriculum; Miller, J. L. "Duality: Perspectives on the reconceptualization." Paper presented to University of Virginia Conference; Macdonald, J. B. "Curriculum Theory as intentional activity." Paper presented to University of Virginia Conference (see Note 5); Macdonald, J. B. "Curriculum Theory and human interests." In Pinar, W. (ed.) *Curriculum Theorizing*; Benham, B. J. "Curriculum Theory in the 1970s: the reconceptualist movement." Texas Technical University, 1976, unpublished paper.
15. Zaret, E., and Macdonald, J. B. *Schools in Search of Meaning* (Association for Supervision and Curriculum Development, Washington, D.C., 1975).
16. Macdonald, J. B. "The quality of everyday life in schools." In Zaret and Macdonald, op. cit.
17. Van Manen, M. "Linking ways of knowing with ways of being practical." *Curriculum Inquiry*, Vol. 6, No. 3 (1977).
18. Radnitzky, G. *Contemporary Schools of Metascience* (Henry Regnery Co., Chicago, 1973); Feyerbend P. K. "Against method; outline of an anarchist theory of knowledge." In *Minnesota Studies in the Philosophy of Science*, Vol. 4 (University of Minnesota Press, Minneapolis, 1970).
19. Bernstein, R. J. *The Restructuring of Social and Political Theory* (Harcourt, Brace, Jovanovich, New York, 1976).
20. Ibid., 235.
21. Silverman, D. *Reading Castaneda: A Prologue to the Social Sciences* (Routledge and Kegan Paul, London, 1975).

14
Pedagogy of the Oppressed

Paulo Freire

As we attempt to analyze dialogue as a human phenomenon, we discover something which is the essence of dialogue itself: *the word.* But the word is more than just an instrument which makes dialogue possible; accordingly, we must seek its constitutive elements. Within the word we find two dimensions, reflection and action, in such radical interaction that if one is sacrificed—even in part—the other immediately suffers. There is no true word that is not at the same time a praxis.[1] Thus, to speak a true word is to transform the world.[2]

An unauthentic word, one which is unable to transform reality, results when dichotomy is imposed upon its constitutive elements. When a word is deprived of its dimension of action, reflection automatically suffers as well; and the word is changed into idle chatter, into *verbalism,* into an alienated and alienating "blah." It becomes an empty word, one which cannot denounce the world, for denunciation is impossible without a commitment to transform, and there is no transformation without action.

On the other hand, if action is emphasized exclusively, to the detriment of reflection, the word is converted into *activism.* The latter—action for action's sake—negates the true praxis and makes dialogue impossible. Either dichotomy, by creating unauthentic forms of existence, creates also unauthentic forms of thought, which reinforce the original dichotomy.

Human existence cannot be silent, nor can it be nourished by false words, but only by true words, with which men transform the world. To exist, humanly, is to *name* the world, to change it. Once named, the world in its turn reappears to the namers as a problem and requires of them a new *naming.* Men are not built in silence,[3] but in word, in work, in action-reflection.

But while to say the true word—which is work, which is praxis—is to transform the world, saying that word is not the privilege of some few men, but the right of every man. Consequently, no one can say a true word alone—nor can he say it *for* another, in a prescriptive act which robs others of their words.

Dialogue is the encounter between men, mediated by the world, in order to name the world. Hence, dialogue cannot occur between those who want to name the world and those who do not wish this naming—between those who deny other men the right to speak their word and those whose right to speak has been denied them. Those who have been denied their primordial right to speak their word must first reclaim this right and prevent the continuation of this dehumanizing aggression.

If it is in speaking their word that men, by naming the world, transform it, dialogue imposes itself as the way by which men achieve significance as men. Dialogue is thus an existential necessity. And since dialogue is the encounter in which the united reflection and action of the dialoguers are addressed to the world which is to be transformed and humanized, this dialogue cannot be reduced to the act of one person's "depositing" ideas in another, nor can it become a simple exchange of ideas to be "consumed" by the discussants. Nor yet is it a hostile, polemical argument between men who are committed neither to the naming of the world, nor to the search for truth, but rather to the imposition of their own truth. Because dialogue is an encounter among men who name the world, it must not be a situation where some men name on behalf of others. It is an act of creation; it must not serve as a crafty instrument for the domination of one man by another. The domination implicit in dialogue is that of the world by the dialoguers; it is conquest of the world for the liberation of men.

Dialogue cannot exist, however, in the absence of a profound love for the world and for men. The naming of the world, which is an act of creation and re-creation, is not possible if it is not infused with love.[4] Love is at the same time the foundation of dialogue and dialogue itself. It is thus necessarily the task of responsible Subjects and cannot exist in a relation of domination. Domination reveals the pathology of love: sadism in the dominator and masochism in the dominated. Because love is an act of courage, not of fear, love is commitment to other men. No matter where the oppressed are found, the act of love is commitment to their cause—the cause of liberation. And this commitment, because it is loving, is dialogical. As an act of bravery, love cannot be sentimental; as an act of freedom, it must not serve as a pretext for manipulation. It must generate other acts of freedom; otherwise, it is not love. Only by abolishing the situation of oppression is it possible to restore the love which that situation made impossible. If I do not love the world—if I do not love life—if I do not love men—I cannot enter into dialogue.

On the other hand, dialogue cannot exist without humility. The naming of the world, through which men constantly re-create that world, cannot be an act of arrogance. Dialogue, as the encounter of men addressed to the common task of learning and acting, is broken if the parties (or one of them) lack humility. How can I dialogue if I always project ignorance onto others and never perceive my own? How can I dialogue if I regard myself as a case apart from other men—mere "its" in whom I cannot recognize other "I"s? How can I dialogue if I consider myself a member of the in-group of "pure" men, the owners of truth and knowledge, for whom all non-members are "these people" or "the great unwashed?" How can I dialogue if I start from the premise that naming the world is the task of an elite and that the presence of the people in history is a sign of deterioration, thus to be avoided? How can I dialogue if I am closed to—and even offended by—the contribution of others? How can I dialogue if I am afraid of being displaced, the mere possibility causing me torment and weakness? Self-sufficiency is incompatible with dialogue. Men who lack humility (or have lost it) cannot come to the people, cannot be their partners in naming the world. Someone who cannot acknowledge himself to be as mortal as everyone else still has a long way to go before he can reach the point of encounter. At the point of encounter there are neither utter ignoramuses nor perfect sages; there are only men who are attempting, together, to learn more than they now know.

Dialogue further requires an intense faith in man, faith in his power to make and remake, to create and re-create, faith in his vocation to be more fully human (which is not the privilege of an elite, but the birthright of all men). Faith in man is an *a priori* requirement for dialogue; the "dialogical man" believes in other men even before he meets them face to face. His faith, however, is not naïve. The "dialogical man" is critical and knows that although it is within the power of men to create and transform, in a concrete situation of alienation men may be impaired in the use of that power. Far from destroying his faith in man, however, this possibility strikes him as a challenge to which he must respond. He is convinced that the power to create and transform, even when thwarted in concrete situations, tends to be reborn. And that rebirth can occur—not gratuitously, but in and through the struggle for liberation—in the supersedence of slave labor by emancipated labor which gives zest to life. Without this faith in man, dialogue is a farce which inevitably degenerates into paternalistic manipulation.

Founding itself upon love, humility, and faith, dialogue becomes a horizontal relationship of which mutual trust between the dialoguers is the logical consequence. It would be a contradiction in terms if dialogue—loving, humble, and full of faith—did not produce this climate of mutual trust, which leads the dialoguers into ever closer partnership in the naming of the world. Conversely, such trust is obviously absent in the anti-dialogics of the banking method of education. Whereas faith in man is an *a priori* requirement for dialogue, trust is established by dialogue. Should it founder, it will be seen that the preconditions were lacking. False love, false humility, and feeble faith in man cannot create trust. Trust is contingent on the evidence which one party provides the others of his true, concrete intentions; it cannot exist if that party's words do not coincide with his actions. To say one thing and do another—to take one's own word lightly—cannot inspire trust. To glorify democracy and to silence the people is a farce; to discourse on humanism and to negate man is a lie.

Nor yet can dialogue exist without hope. Hope is rooted in men's incompletion, from which they move out in constant search—a search which can be carried out only in communion with other men. Hopelessness is a form of silence, of denying the world and fleeing from it. The dehumanization resulting from an unjust order is not a cause for despair but for hope, leading to the incessant pursuit of the humanity denied by injustice. Hope, however, does not consist in crossing one's arms and waiting. As long as I fight, I am moved by hope; and if I fight with hope, then I can wait. As the encounter of men seeking to be more fully human, dialogue cannot be carried on in a climate of hopelessness. If the dialoguers expect nothing to come of their efforts, their encounter will be empty and sterile, bureaucratic and tedious.

Finally, true dialogue cannot exist unless the dialoguers engage in critical thinking—thinking which discerns an indivisible solidarity between the world and men and admits of no dichotomy between them—thinking which perceives reality as process, as transformation, rather than as a static entity—thinking which does not separate itself from action, but constantly immerses itself in temporality without fear of the risks involved. Critical thinking contrasts with naïve thinking, which sees "historical time as a weight, a stratification of the acquisitions and experiences of the past,"[5] from which the present should emerge normalized and "well-behaved." For the naïve thinker, the important thing is accommodation to this normalized "today." For the critic, the important thing is the continuing transformation of reality, in behalf of the continuing humanization of men. In the words of Pierre Furter:

> The goal will no longer be to eliminate the risks of temporality by clutching to guaranteed space, but rather to temporalize space. . . . The universe is revealed to me not as space, imposing a massive presence to which I can but adapt, but as a scope, a domain which takes shape as I act upon it.[6]

For naïve thinking, the goal is precisely to hold fast to this guaranteed space and adjust to it. By thus denying temporality, it denies itself as well.

Only dialogue, which requires critical thinking, is also capable of generating critical thinking. Without dialogue there is no communication, and without communication there can be no true education. Education which is able to resolve the contradiction between teacher and student takes place in a situation in which both address their act of cognition to the object by which they are mediated. Thus, the dialogical character of education as the practice of freedom does not begin when the teacher-student meets with the students-teachers in a pedagogical situation, but rather when the former first asks himself *what* he will dialogue with the latter *about*. And preoccupation with the content of dialogue is really preoccupation with the program content of education.

For the anti-dialogical banking educator, the question of content simply concerns the program about which he will discourse to his students; and he answers his own question, by organizing his own program. For the dialogical, problem-posing teacher-student, the program content of education is neither a gift nor an imposition—bits of information to be deposited in the students—but rather the organized, systematized, and developed "re-presentation" to individuals of the things about which they want to know more.[7]

Authentic education is not carried on by "A" *for* "B" or by "A" *about* "B," but rather by "A" *with* "B," mediated by the world—a world which impresses and challenges both parties, giving rise to views or opinions about it. These views, impregnated with anxieties, doubts, hopes, or hopelessness, imply significant themes on the basis of which the program content of education can be built. In its desire to create an ideal model of the "good man," a naïvely conceived humanism often overlooks the concrete, existential, present situation of real men. Authentic humanism, in Pierre Furter's words, "consists in permitting the emergence of the awareness of our full humanity, as a condition and as an obligation, as a situation and as a project."[8] We simply cannot go to the laborers—urban or peasant[9]—in the banking style, to give them "knowledge" or to impose upon them the model of the "good man" contained in a program whose content we have ourselves organized. Many political and educational plans have failed because their authors designed them according to their own personal views of reality, never once taking into account (except as mere objects of their action) the *men-in-a-situation* to whom their program was ostensibly directed.

For the truly humanist educator and the authentic revolutionary, the object of action is the reality to be transformed by them together with other men—not other men themselves. The oppressors are the ones who act upon men to indoctrinate them and adjust them to a reality which must remain untouched. Unfortunately, however, in their desire to obtain the support of the people for revolutionary action, revolutionary leaders often fall for the banking line of planning program content from the top down. They approach the peasant or urban masses with projects which may correspond to their own view of the world, but not to that of the people.[10] They forget that their fundamental objective is to fight alongside the people for the recovery of the people's stolen humanity, not to "win the people over" to their side. Such a phrase does not belong in the vocabulary of revolutionary leaders, but in that of the oppressor. The revolutionary's role is to liberate, and be liberated, with the people—not to win them over.

In their political activity, the dominant elites utilize the banking concept to encourage passivity in the oppressed, corresponding with the latter's "submerged" state of consciousness, and take advantage of that passivity to "fill" that consciousness with slogans which create even more fear of freedom. This practice is incompatible with a truly liberating course of action, which, by presenting the oppressors' slogans as a problem, helps the oppressed to "eject" those slogans from within themselves. After all, the task of the humanists is surely not that of pitting their slogans against the slogans of the oppressors, with the oppressed as the testing ground, "housing" the slogans of first one group and then the other. On the contrary, the task of the humanists is to see that the oppressed become aware of the fact that as dual beings, "housing" the oppressors within themselves, they cannot be truly human.

This task implies that revolutionary leaders do not go to the people in order to bring them a message of "salvation," but in order to come to know through dialogue with them both their *objective situation* and their *awareness* of that situation—the various levels of perception of themselves and of the world in which and with which they exist. One cannot expect positive results from an educational or political action program which fails to respect the particular view of the world held by the people. Such a program constitutes cultural invasion,[11] good intentions notwithstanding.

The starting point for organizing the program content of education or political action must be the present, existential, concrete situation, reflecting the aspirations of the people. Utilizing certain basic contradictions, we must pose this existential, concrete, present situation to the people as a problem which challenges them and requires a response—not just at the intellectual level, but at the level of action.[12]

We must never merely discourse on the present situation, must never provide the people with programs which have little or nothing to do with their own preoccupations, doubts, hopes, and fears—programs which at times in fact increase the fears of the oppressed consciousness. It is not our role to speak to the people about our own view of the world, not to attempt to impose that view on them, but rather to dialogue with the people about their view and ours. We must realize that their view of the world, manifested variously in their action, reflects their *situation* in the world. Educational and political action which is not critically aware of this situation runs the risk either of "banking" or of preaching in the desert.

Often, educators and politicians speak and are not understood because their language is not attuned to the concrete situation of the men they address. Accordingly, their talk is just alienated and alienating rhetoric. The language of the educator or the politician (and it seems more and more clear that the latter must also become an educator, in the broadest sense of the word), like the language of the people, cannot exist without thought; and neither language nor thought can exist without a structure to which they refer. In order to communicate effectively, educator and politician must understand the structural conditions in which the thought and language of the people are dialectically framed.

It is to the reality which mediates men, and to the perception of that reality held by educators and people, that we must go to find the program content of education. The investigation of what I have termed the people's "thematic universe"[13]—the complex of their "generative themes"—inaugurates the dialogue of education as the practice of freedom. The methodology of that investigation must likewise be dialogical, affording the opportunity both to discover generative themes and to stimulate people's awareness in regard to these themes. Consistent with the liberating purpose of dialogical education, the object of the investigation is not men (as if men were anatomical fragments), but rather the thought-language with which men refer to reality, the levels at which they perceive that reality, and their view of the world, in which their generative themes are found.

Equally appropriate for the methodology of thematic investigation and for problem-posing education is this effort to present significant dimensions of an individual's contextual reality, the analysis of which will make it possible for him to recognize the interaction of the various components. Meanwhile, the significant dimensions, which in their turn are constituted of parts in interaction, should be perceived as dimensions of total reality. In this way, a critical analysis of a significant existential dimension makes possible a new, critical attitude towards the limit-situations. The perception and comprehension of reality are rectified and acquire new depth. When carried out with a methodology of *conscientização* the investigation of the generative theme contained in the minimum thematic universe (the generative themes in interaction) thus introduces or begins to introduce men to a critical form of thinking about their world.

In the event, however, that men perceive reality as dense, impenetrable, and enveloping, it is indispensable to proceed with the investigation by means of abstraction. This method does not involve reducing the concrete to the abstract (which would signify the negation of its dialectical nature), but rather maintaining both elements as opposites which interrelate dialectically in the act of reflection. This dialectical movement of thought is exemplified perfectly in the analysis of a concrete, existential, "coded" situation.[14] Its "decoding" requires moving from the abstract to the concrete; this requires moving from the part to the whole and then returning to the parts; this in turn requires that the Subject recognize himself in the object (the coded concrete existential situation) and recognize the object as a situation in which he finds himself, together with other Subjects. If the decoding is well done, this movement of flux and reflux from the abstract to the concrete which occurs in the analysis of a coded situation leads to the supersedence of the abstraction *by* the critical perception of the concrete, which has already ceased to be a dense, impenetrable reality.

When an individual is presented with a coded existential situation (a sketch or photograph which leads by abstraction to the concreteness of existential reality), his tendency is to "split" that coded situation. In the process of decoding, this separation corresponds to the stage we call the "description of the situation," and facilitates the discovery of the interaction among the parts of the disjoined whole. This whole (the coded situation), which previously had been only diffusely apprehended, begins to acquire meaning as thought flows back to it from the various dimensions. Since, however, the coding is the representation of an existential situation, the decoder tends to take the step from the representation to the very concrete situation in which and with which he finds himself. It is thus possible to explain conceptually why individuals begin to behave differently with regard to objective reality, once that reality has ceased to look like a blind alley and has taken on its true aspect: a challenge which men must meet.

In all the stages of decoding, men exteriorize their view of the world. And in the way they think about and face the world—fatalistically, dynamically, or statically—their generative themes may be found. A group which does not concretely express a generative thematics—a fact which might appear to imply the nonexistence of themes—is, on the contrary, suggesting a very dramatic theme: *the theme of silence.* The theme of silence suggests a structure of mutism in face of the overwhelming force of the limit-situations.

I must re-emphasize that the generative theme cannot be found in men, divorced from reality; nor yet in reality, divorced from men; much less in "no man's land." It can only be apprehended in the men-world relationship. To investigate the generative theme is to investigate man's thinking about reality and man's action upon reality, which is his praxis. For precisely this reason, the methodology proposed requires that the investigators and the people (who would normally be considered objects of that investigation) should act as *co-investigators.* The more active an attitude men take in regard to the exploration of their thematics, the more they deepen their critical awareness of reality and, in spelling out those thematics, take possession of that reality.

Some may think it inadvisable to include the people as investigators in the search for their own meaningful thematics: that their intrusive influence (N.B., the "intrusion" of those who are most interested—or ought to be—in their own education) will "adulterate" the findings and thereby sacrifice the objectivity of the investigation. This view mistakenly presupposes that themes exist, in their original objective purity, outside men—as if themes were *things.* Actually, themes exist in men in their relations with the world, with reference to concrete facts. The same objective fact could evoke different complexes of generative themes in different epochal sub-units. There is, therefore, a relation between the given objective fact, the perception men have of this fact, and the generative themes.

A meaningful thematics is expressed by men, and a given moment of expression will differ from an earlier moment, if men have changed their perception of the objective facts to which the themes refer. From the investigator's point of view, the important thing is to detect the starting point at which men visualize the "given" and to verify whether or not during the process of investigation any transformation has occurred in their way of perceiving reality. (Objective reality, of course, remains unchanged. If the perception of that reality changes in the course of the investigation, that fact does not impair the validity of the investigation.)

We must realize that the aspirations, the motives, and the objectives implicit in the meaningful thematics are *human* aspirations, motives, and objectives. They do not exist "out there" somewhere, as static entities; *they are occurring.* They are as historical as men themselves; consequently, they cannot be apprehended apart from men. To apprehend these themes and to understand them is to understand both the men who embody them and the reality to which they refer. But—precisely because it is not possible to understand these themes apart from men—it is necessary that the men concerned understand them as well. Thematic investigation thus becomes a common striving towards awareness of reality and towards self-awareness, which makes this investigation a starting point for the educational process or for cultural action of a liberating character.

The real danger of the investigation is not that the supposed objects of the investigation, discovering themselves to be co-investigators, might "adulterate" the analytical results. On the contrary, the danger lies in the risk of shifting the focus of the investigation from the meaningful themes to the people themselves, thereby treating the people as objects of the investigation. Since this investigation is to serve as a basis for developing an educational program in which teacher-student and students-teachers combine their cognitions of the same object, the investigation itself must likewise be based on reciprocity of action.

Thematic investigation, which occurs in the realm of the human, cannot be reduced to a mechanical act. As a process of search, of knowledge, and thus of creation, it requires the investigators to discover the interpenetration of problems, in the linking of meaningful themes. The investigation will be most educational when it is most critical, and most critical when it avoids the narrow outlines of partial or "focalized" views of reality, and sticks to the comprehension of *total* reality. Thus, the process of searching for the meaningful thematics should include a concern for the links between themes, a concern to pose these themes as problems, and a concern for their historical-cultural context.

Just as the educator may not elaborate a program to present *to* the people, neither may the investigator elaborate "itineraries" for researching the thematic universe, starting from points which *he* has predetermined. Both education and the investigation designed to support it must be "sympathetic" activities, in the etymological sense of the word. That is, they must consist of communication and of the common experience of a reality perceived in the complexity of its constant "becoming."

The investigator who, in the name of scientific objectivity, transforms the organic into something inorganic, what is becoming into what is, life into death, is a man who fears change. He sees in change (which he does not deny, but neither does he desire) not a sign of life, but a sign of death and decay. He does want to study change—but in order to stop it, not in order to stimulate or deepen it. However, in seeing change as a sign of death and in making people the passive objects of investigation in order to arrive at rigid models, he betrays his own character as a killer of life.

Notes

1. $\left.\begin{array}{l}\text{Action}\\ \text{Reflection}\end{array}\right\}$ word = work = praxis
   Sacrifice of action = verbalism
   Sacrifice of reflection = activism
2. Some of these reflections emerged as a result of conversations with Professor Ernani Maria Fiori.
3. I obviously do not refer to the silence of profound meditation, in which men only apparently leave the world, withdrawing from it in order to consider it in its totality, and thus remaining with it. But this type of retreat is only authentic when the meditator is "bathed" in reality; not when the retreat signifies contempt for the world and flight from it, in a type of "historical schizophrenia."
4. I am more and more convinced that true revolutionaries must perceive the revolution, because of its creative and liberating nature, as an act of love. For me, the revolution, which is not possible without a theory of revolution—and therefore science—is not irreconcilable with love. On the contrary: the revolution is made by men to achieve their humanization. What, indeed, is the deeper motive which moves men to become revolutionaries, but the dehumanization of man? The distortion imposed on the word "love" by the capitalist world cannot prevent the revolution from being essentially loving in character, nor can it prevent the revolutionaries from affirming their love of life. Guevara (while admitting the "risk of seeming ridiculous") was not afraid to affirm it: "Let me say, with the risk of appearing ridiculous, that the true revolutionary is guided by strong feelings of love. It is impossible to think of an authentic revolutionary without this quality." *Venceremos—The Speeches and Writings of Che Guevara*, edited by John Gerassi (New York, 1969), p.398.
5. From the letter of a friend.
6. Pierre Furter, *Educação e Vida* (Rio, 1966), pp. 26–27.
7. In a long conversation with Malraux, Mao-Tse-Tung declared, "You know I've proclaimed for a long time: we must teach the masses clearly what we have received from them confusedly." André Malraux, *Anti-Memoirs* (New York, 1968), pp. 361–362. This affirmation contains an entire dialogical theory of how to construct the program content of education, which cannot be elaborated according to what the *educator* thinks best for *his* students.
8. Furter, *op. cit.*, p. 165.
9. The latter, usually submerged in a colonial context, are almost umbilically linked to the world of nature, in relation to which they feel themselves to be component parts rather than shapers.
10. "Our cultural workers must serve the people with great enthusiasm and devotion, and they must link themselves with the masses, not divorce themselves from the masses. In order to do so, they must act in accordance with the needs and wishes of the masses. All work done for the masses must start from their needs and not from the desire of any individual, however well-intentioned. It often happens that objectively the masses need a certain change, but

subjectively they are not yet conscious of the need, not yet willing or determined to make the change. In such cases, we should wait patiently. We should not make the change until, through our work, most of the masses have become conscious of the need and are willing and determined to carry it out. Otherwise we shall isolate ourselves from the masses. . . . There are two principles here: one is the actual needs of the masses rather than what we fancy they need, and the other is the wishes of the masses, who must make up their own minds instead of our making up their minds for them." From the *Selected Works of Mao-Tse-Tung*, Vol. III. "The United Front in Cultural Work" (October 30, 1944) (Peking, 1967), pp. 186–187.

11. This point will be analyzed in detail in Chapter 4.
12. It is as self-contradictory for true humanists to use the banking method as it would be for rightists to engage in problem-posing education. (The latter are always consistent—they never use a problem-posing pedagogy.)
13. The expression "meaningful thematics" is used with the same connotation.
14. The coding of an existential situation is the representation of that situation, showing some of its constituent elements in interaction. Decoding is the critical analysis of the coded situation.

15
Controlling the Work of Teachers

Michael W. Apple

Proletarianization: Class and Gender

An examination of changes in class composition over the past two decades points out something quite dramatically. The process of proletarianization has had a large and consistent effect. There has been a systematic tendency for those positions with relatively little control over their labor process to expand during this time period. At the same time, there was a decline in positions with high levels of autonomy.[1]

This should not surprise us. In fact, it would be unusual if this did not occur, especially now. In a time of general stagnation and of crises in accumulation and legitimation, we should expect that there will also be attempts to further rationalize managerial structures and increase the pressure to proletarianize the labor process. This pressure is not inconsequential to educators, both in regard to the kinds of positions students will find available (or not available) after completing (or not completing) schooling, and also in regard to the very conditions of working within education itself. The labor of what might be called "semi-autonomous employees" will certainly feel the impact of this. Given the fiscal crisis of the state, this impact will be felt more directly among state employees such as teachers as well. One should expect to see a rapid growth of plans and pressures for the rationalization of administration and labor within the state itself.[2] This is one of the times when one's expectations will not be disappointed.

In earlier work, I argued that teachers have been involved in a long but now steadily increasing restructuring of their jobs. I claimed that they were more and more faced with the prospect of being de-skilled because of the encroachment of technical control procedures into the curriculum in schools. The integration together of management systems, reductive behaviorally based curricula, pre-specified teaching "competencies" and procedures and student responses, and pre- and post-testing, was leading to a loss of control and a separation of conception from execution. In sum, the labor process of teaching was becoming susceptible to processes similar to those that led to the proletarianization of many other blue-, pink-, and white-collar jobs. I suggested that this restructuring of teaching had important implications given the contradictory class location of teachers.[3]

When I say that teachers have a contradictory class location, I am *not* implying that they are by definition within the middle classes, or that they are in an ambiguous position somehow "between" classes. Instead, along with Wright, I am saying that it is wise to think of them as located simultaneously in two classes. They thus share the interests of both the petty bourgeoisie and the working class.[4] Hence, when there is a fiscal crisis in which many teachers are faced with worsening working conditions, layoffs, and even months without being paid—as has been the case in a number of urban areas in the United States—and when their labor is restructured so that they lose control, it is possible that these contradictory interests will move closer to those of other workers and people of color who have historically been faced with the use of similar procedures by capital and the state.[5]

Yet, teachers are not only classed actors. They are gendered actors as well—something that is too often neglected by investigators. This is a significant omission. A striking conclusion is evident from the analyses of proletarianization. In every occupational category, *women* are more apt to be proletarianized than men. This could be because of sexist practices of recruitment and promotion, the general tendency to care less about the conditions under which women labor, the way capital has historically colonized patriarchal relations, the historical relation between teaching and domesticity, and so on. Whatever the reason, it is clear that a given position may be more or less proletarianized depending on its relationship to the sexual division of labor.[6]

In the United States, it is estimated that over 90 percent of women's (paid) work falls into four basic categories: (1) employment in "peripheral" manufacturing industries and retail trades, and considerably now in the expanding but low-paid service sector of the economy; (2) clerical work; (3) health and education; and (4) domestic service. Most women in, say, the United States and the United Kingdom are concentrated in either the lowest-paid positions in these areas or at the bottom of the middle-pay grades when there has been some mobility.[7] One commentator puts it both bluntly and honestly: "The evidence of discrimination against women in the labour market is considerable and reading it is a wearing experience."[8]

This pattern is, of course, largely reproduced within education. Even given the years of struggle by progressive women and men, the figures—most of which will be quite familiar to many of you—are depressing. While the overwhelming majority of school teachers are women (a figure that becomes even higher in the primary and elementary schools), many more men are heads or principals of primary and elementary schools, despite the proportion of women teachers.[9] As the vertical segregation of the workforce increased, this proportion actually increased in inequality. In the United States in 1928, women accounted for 55 percent of the elementary school principalships. Today, with nearly 90 percent of the teaching force in elementary schools being women, they account for only 20 percent of principals.[10] This pattern has strong historical roots—roots that cannot be separated from the larger structures of class and patriarchy outside the school.

In this chapter, I shall want to claim that unless we see the connections between these two dynamics—class and gender—we cannot understand the history of and current attempts at rationalizing education or the roots and effects of proletarianization on teaching itself. Not all teaching can be unpacked by examining it as a labor process or as a class phenomenon, though as I have tried to demonstrate in some of my previous work much of it is made clearer when we integrate it into theories of and changes in class position and the labor process. Neither can all of teaching be understood as totally related to patriarchy, though why it is structured the way it is is due in very large part to the history of male dominance and gender struggles,[11] a history I shall discuss in considerably more detail in the next chapter. The two dynamics of class and gender (with race, of course) are not reducible to each other, but intertwine, work off, and codetermine the terrain on which each operates. It is at the intersection of these two dynamics that one can begin to unravel some of the reasons why procedures for rationalizing the work of teachers have evolved. As we shall see, the ultimate effects of these procedures, with the loss of control that accompanies them, can bear in important ways on how we think about the "reform" of teaching and curriculum and the state's role in it.

Academic Knowledge and Curricular Control

So far I have made a number of general claims about the relationship between proletarianization and patriarchy in the constitution of teaching. I want to go on to suggest ways we can begin to see this relationship in operation. Some sense of the state's role in sponsoring changes in curricular and teaching practice in the recent past is essential here.

The fact that schools have tended to be largely organized around male leadership and female teachers is simply that—a social fact—unless one realizes that this means that educational authority relations have been formally patriarchal. As in the home and the office, male dominance is there; but teachers—like wives, mothers, clerical workers, and other women engaged in paid and unpaid labor—have carved out spheres of power and control in their long struggle to gain some autonomy. This autonomy only becomes a problem for capital and the state when what education is for needs revision.

To take one example outside of education: in offices clerical work is in the process of being radically transformed with the introduction of word-processing technologies, video display terminals, and so on. Traditional forms of control—ones usually based on the dominance of the male boss—are being altered. Technical control, where one's work is de-skilled and intensified by the "impersonal" machinery in the office, has made significant inroads. While certainly not eliminating patriarchal domination, it has in fact provided a major shift in the terrain on which it operates. Capital has found more efficient modes of control than overt patriarchal authority.[12]

Similar changes have occurred in schools. In a time when the needs of industry for technical knowledge and technically trained personnel intersect with the growth in power of the new petty bourgeoisie (those people in technical and middle management positions) and the reassertion of academic dominance in the curriculum, pressures for curricular reform can become quite intense. Patience over traditional forms of control will lessen.

Patriarchal relations of power, therefore, organized around the male principal's relations to a largely female teaching staff, will not necessarily be progressive for capital or the state. While they once served certain educational and ideological ends, they are less efficient than what has been required recently. Gender relations must be partly subverted to create a more efficient institution. Techniques of control drawn from industry will tend to replace older styles which depended more on a sexual division of power and labor within the school itself.

Perhaps an example will document the long and continuing history of these altered relationships. In the United States, for instance, during the late 1950s and the 1960s, there was rather strong pressure from academics, capital, and the state to reinstitute academic disciplinary knowledge as the most "legitimate" content for schools. In the areas of mathematics and science especially, it was feared that "real" knowledge was not being taught. A good deal of effort was given to producing curricular programs that were systematic, based on rigorous academic foundations, and, in the elementary school material in particular, were teacher-proof. Everything a teacher was to deal with was provided and prespecified. The cost of the development of such programs was socialized by the state (i.e., subsidized by tax dollars). The chance of their being adopted by local school districts was heightened by the National Defense Education Act, which reimbursed school districts for a large portion of the purchase cost. That is, if a school system purchased new material of this type and the technology which supported it, the relative cost was minimal. The bulk of the expense was repaid by the state. Hence, it would have seemed irrational not to buy the material—irrational in two ways: (1) the chance of getting new curricula at low cost is clearly a rational management decision within industrial logic, and (2) given its imprimatur of science and efficiency, the material itself seemed rational.

All of this is no doubt familiar to anyone who lived through the early years of this movement, and who sees the later, somewhat less powerful, effects it had in, say, England and elsewhere. Yet this is not only the history of increasing state sponsorship of and state intervention in teaching and curriculum development and adoption. *It is the history of the state, in concert with capital and a largely male academic body of consultants and developers, intervening at the level of practice into the work of a largely female workforce.* That is, ideologies of gender, of sex-appropriate knowledge, need to be seen as having possibly played a significant part here. The loss of control and rationalization of one's work forms part of a state/class/gender "couplet" that works its way out in the following ways. Mathematics and science teaching are seen as abysmal. "We" need rapid change in our economic responsiveness and in "our" emerging ideological and economic struggle with the Soviet Union.[13] Teachers (who just happen to be almost all women at the elementary level) aren't sophisticated enough. Former ways of curricular and teaching control are neither powerful nor efficient enough for this situation. Provide both teacher-proof materials and financial incentives to make certain that these sets of curricula actually reach the classroom.

One must integrate an analysis of the state, changes in the labor process of state employees, and the politics of patriarchy to comprehend the dynamics of this history of curriculum. It is not a random fact that one of the most massive attempts at rationalizing curricula and teaching had as its target a group of teachers who were largely women. I believe that one cannot separate out the fact of a sexual division of labor and the vision of who has what kinds of competence from the state's attempts to revamp and make more "productive" its educational apparatus. In so doing, by seeing these structurally generated relationships, we can begin to open up a door to understanding part of the reasons behind what happened to these curriculum materials when they were in fact introduced.

As numerous studies have shown, when the material was introduced into many schools, it was not unusual for the "new" math and "new" science to be taught in much the same manner as the old math and old science. It was altered so that it fitted into both the existing regularities of the institution and the prior practices that had proven successful in teaching.[14] It is probably wise to see this as not only the result of a slow-to-change bureaucracy or a group of consistently conservative administrators and teachers. Rather, I think it may be just as helpful to think of this more structurally in labor process and gender terms. The supposed immobility of the institution, its lack of significant change in the face of the initial onslaught of such material, is at least partly tied to the resistances of a female workforce against external incursions into the practices they had evolved over years of labor. It is in fact more than a little similar to the history of ways in which other women employees in the state and industry have reacted to past attempts at altering traditional modes of control of their own labor.[15]

A Note on the State

The points I have just made about the resistances of the people who actually work in the institutions, about women teachers confronted by external control, may seem straightforward. However, these basic arguments have very important implications not only about how we think about the history of curriculum reform and control, but more importantly about how many educators and political theorists have pictured the larger issue of the state's role in supporting capital. In the historical example I gave, state intervention on the side of capital and for "defense" is in opposition to other positions within the state itself. The day-to-day interests of one occupational position (teachers) contradict the larger interests of the state in efficient production.[16] Because of instances such as this, it is probably inappropriate to see the state as a homogeneous entity, standing above day-to-day conflicts.

Since schools *are* state apparatuses, we should expect them to be under intense pressure to act in certain ways, especially in times of both fiscal and ideological crises. Even so, this does not mean that people employed in them are passive followers of policies laid down from above. As Roger Dale has noted:

> Teachers are not merely "state functionaries" but do have some degree of autonomy, and [this] autonomy will not necessarily be used to further the proclaimed ends of the state apparatus. Rather than those who work there fitting themselves to the requirements of the institutions, there are a number of very important ways in which the institution has to take account of the interests of the employees and fit itself to them. It is here, for instance, that we may begin to look for the sources of the alleged inertia of educational systems and schools, that is to say what appears as inertia is not some immutable characteristic of bureaucracies but is due to various groups within them having more immediate interests than the pursuit of the organization's goals.[17]

Thus, the "mere" fact that the state wishes to find "more efficient" ways to organize teaching does not guarantee that this will be acted upon by teachers who have a long history of work practices and self-organization once the doors to their rooms are closed. As we shall see in a moment, however, the fact that it is primarily women employees who have faced these forms of rationalization has meant that the actual outcomes of these attempts to retain control of one's pedagogic work can lead to rather contradictory ideological results.

Legitimating Intervention

While these initial attempts at rationalizing teaching and curricula did not always produce the results that were anticipated by their academic, industrial, and governmental proponents, they did other things that were, and are, of considerable import. The situation is actually quite similar to the effects of the use of Tayloristic management strategies in industry. As a management technology for de-skilling workers and separating conception from execution, Taylorism was less than fully successful. It often generated slowdowns and strikes, exacerbated tensions, and created new forms of overt and covert resistance. Yet, its ultimate effect was to legitimate a particular ideology of management and control both to the public and to employers and workers.[18] Even though it did not succeed as a set of techniques, it ushered in and finally brought acceptance of a larger body of ideological practices to de-skill pink-, white-, and blue-collar workers and to rationalize and intensify their labor.

This too was one of the lasting consequences of these earlier curriculum "reform" movements. While they also did not completely transform the practice of teaching, while patriarchal relations of authority which paradoxically "gave" teachers some measure of freedom were not totally replaced by more efficient forms of organizing and controlling their day-to-day activity, they legitimated both new forms of control and greater state intervention using industrial and technical models and brought about a new generation of more sophisticated attempts at overcoming teacher "resistance." Thus, this new generation of techniques that are being instituted in so many states in the United States and elsewhere currently—from systematic integration of testing, behavioral goals and curriculum, competency-based instruction and prepackaged curricula, to management by objectives, and so forth—has not sprung out of nowhere, but, like the history of Taylorism, has grown out of the failures, partial successes, and resistances that accompanied the earlier approaches to control. As I have claimed, this is not only the history of the control of state employees to bring about efficient teaching, but a rearticulation of the dynamics of patriarchy and class in one site, the school.

Intensification and Teaching

In the first half of this chapter, we paid particular attention to the historical dynamics operating in the schools. I would like now to focus on more current outgrowths of this earlier history of rationalization and control.

The earlier attempts by state bureaucrats, industry, and others to gain greater control of day-to-day classroom operation and its "output" did not die. They have had more than a decade to grow, experiment, and become more sophisticated. While gender will be less visible in the current strategies (in much the same way that the growth of management strategies in industry slowly covered the real basis of power in factories and offices), as we shall see it will be present in important ways once we go beneath the surface to look at changes in the labor process of teaching, how some teachers respond to current strategies, and how they interpret their own work.

Since in previous work I have focused on a number of elements through which curricula and teaching are controlled—on the aspects of de-skilling and re-skilling of labor, and on the separation of conception from execution in teachers' work—here I shall want to concentrate more on something which accompanies these historically evolving processes: what I shall call *intensification.* First, let me discuss this process rather generally.

Intensification "represents one of the most tangible ways in which the work privileges of educational workers are eroded." It has many symptoms, from the trivial to the more complex—ranging from being allowed no time at all even to go to the bathroom, have a cup of coffee or relax, to having a total absence of time to keep up with one's field. We can see intensification most visibly in mental labor in the chronic sense of work overload that has escalated over time.[19]

This has had a number of notable effects outside of education. In the newspaper industry, for example, because of financial pressures and the increased need for efficiency in operation, reporters have had their story quotas raised substantially. The possibility of doing non-routine investigative reporting, hence, is lessened considerably. This has had the effects of increasing their dependence "on prescheduled, preformulated events" in which they rely more and more on bureaucratic rules and surface accounts of news provided by official spokespersons.[20]

Intensification also acts to destroy the sociability of non-manual workers. Leisure and self-direction tend to be lost. Community tends to be redefined around the needs of the labor process. And, since both time and interaction are at a premium, the risk of isolation grows.[21]

Intensification by itself "does not necessarily reduce the range of skills applied or possessed by educated workers." It may, in fact, cause them to "cut corners" by eliminating what seems to be inconsequential to the task at hand. This has occurred with doctors, for instance; many examinations now concentrate only on what seems critical. The chronic work overload has also caused some non-manual workers to learn or relearn skills. The financial crisis has led to shortages of personnel in a number of areas. Thus, a more diverse array of jobs must be done that used to be covered by other people—people who simply do not exist within the institution any more.[22]

While this leads to a broader range of skills having to be learned or relearned, it can lead to something mentioned earlier—the loss of time to keep up with one's field. That is, what might be called "skill diversification" has a contradiction built into it. It is also part of a dynamic of intellectual de-skilling[23] in which mental workers are cut off from their own fields and again must rely even more heavily on ideas and processes provided by "experts."

While these effects are important, one of the most significant impacts of intensification may be in reducing the *quality*, not the quantity, of service provided to people. While, traditionally, "human service professionals" have equated doing good work with the interests of their clients or students, intensification tends to contradict the traditional interest in work well done, in both a quality product and process.[24]

As I shall document, a number of these aspects of intensification are increasingly found in teaching, especially in those schools which are dominated by behaviorally prespecified curricula, repeated testing, and strict and reductive accountability systems. (The fact that these kinds of curricula, tests, and systems are now more and more being mandated should make us even more cautious.) To make this clear, I want to draw on some data from recent research on the effects of these procedures on the structure of teachers' work.

I have argued here and elsewhere that there has been a rapid growth in curricular "systems" in the United States—one that is now spreading to other countries.[25] These curricula have goals, strategies, tests, textbooks, worksheets, appropriate student response, etc., integrated together. In schools where this is taken seriously,[26] what impact has this been having? We have evidence from a number of ethnographic studies of the labor process of teaching to be able to begin to point to what is going on. For example, in one school where the curriculum was heavily based on a sequential list of behaviorally defined competencies and objectives, multiple worksheets on skills which the students were to complete, with pre-tests to measure "readiness" and "skill level" and post-tests to measure "achievement" that were given often and regularly, the intensification of teacher work is quite visible.

In this school, such curricular practice required that teachers spend a large portion of their time evaluating student "mastery" of each of the various objectives and recording the results of these multiple evaluations for later discussions with parents or decisions on whether or not the student could "go on" to another set of skill-based worksheets. The recording and evaluation made it imperative that a significant amount of time be spent on administrative arrangements for giving tests, and then grading them, organizing lessons (which were quite often standardized or pre-packaged), and so on. One also found teachers busy with these tasks before and after school and, very often, during their lunch hour. Teachers began to come in at 7:15 in the morning and leave at 4:30 in the afternoon. Two hours' more work at home each night was not unusual, as well.[27]

Just as I noted in my general discussion of the effects of intensification, here too getting done became the norm. There is so much to do that simply accomplishing what is specified requires nearly all of one's efforts. "The challenge of the work day (or week) was to accomplish the required number of objectives." As one teacher put it, "I just want to get this done. I don't have time to be creative or imaginative."[28] We should not blame the teacher here. In mathematics, for example, teachers typically had to spend nearly half of the allotted time correcting and recording the worksheets the students completed each day.[29] The situation seemed to continually push the workload of these teachers up. Thus, even though they tended to complain at times about the long hours, the intensification, the time spent on technical tasks such as grading and record-keeping, the amount of time spent doing these things grew inexorably.[30]

Few of the teachers were passive in the face of this, and I shall return to this point shortly. Even though the elements of curricular control were effective in structuring major aspects of their practice, teachers often responded in a variety of ways. They subtly changed the pre-specified objectives because they couldn't see their relevance. They tried to resist the intensification as well: first by trying to find some space during the day for doing slower-paced activities; and second by actually calling a halt temporarily to the frequent pre- and post-tests, worksheets and the like and merely having "relaxed discussions with students on topics of their own choosing."[31]

This, of course, is quite contradictory. While these examples document the active role of teachers in attempting to win back some time, to resist the loss of control of their own work, and to slow down the pace at which students and they were to proceed, the way this is done is not necessarily very powerful. In these instances, time was fought for simply to relax, if only for a few minutes. The process of control, the increasing technicization and intensification of the teaching act, the proletarianization of their work—all of this was an absent presence. It was misrecognized as a symbol of their increased *professionalism.*

Profession and Gender

We cannot understand why teachers interpreted what was happening to them as the professionalization of their jobs unless we see how the ideology of professionalism works as part of both a class and gender dynamic in education. For example, while reliance on "experts" to create curricular and teaching goals and procedures grew in this kind of situation, a wider range of technical skills had to be mastered by these teachers. Becoming adept at grading all those tests and worksheets quickly, deciding on which specific skill group to put a student in, learning how to "efficiently manage" the many different groups based on the tests, and more, all became important skills. As responsibility for designing one's own curricula and one's own teaching decreased, responsibility over technical and management concerns came to the fore.

Professionalism and increased responsibility tend to go hand in hand here. The situation is more than a little paradoxical. There is so much responsibility placed on teachers for technical decisions that they actually work harder. They feel that since they constantly make decisions based on the outcomes of these multiple pre- and post-tests, the longer hours are evidence of their enlarged professional status. Perhaps a quote will be helpful here.

> One reason the work is harder is we have a lot of responsibility in decision-making. There's no reason not to work hard, because you want to be darn sure that those decisions you made are something that might be helpful . . . So you work hard to be successful at these decisions so you look like a good decision maker.[32]

It is here that the concept of professionalism seemed to have one of its major impacts. Since the teachers thought of themselves as being more professional to the extent that they employed technical criteria and tests, they also basically accepted the longer hours and the intensification of their work that accompanied the program. To do a "good job," you needed to be as "rational" as possible.[33]

We should not scoff at these preceptions on the part of the teachers. First, the very notion of professionalization has been important not only to teachers in general but to women in particular. It has provided a contradictory yet powerful barrier against interference by the state; and just as critically, in the struggle over male dominance, it has been part of a complex attempt to win equal treatment, pay, and control over the day-to-day work of a largely female labor force.[34]

Second, while we need to remember that professionalism as a social goal grew at the same time and was justified by the "project and practice of the market professions during the liberal phase of capitalism,"[35] the strategy of professionalism has historically been used to set up "effective defenses against proletarianization."[36] Given what I said earlier about the strong relationship between the sexual division of labor and proletarianization, it would be not only ahistorical but perhaps even a bit sexist as well wholly to blame teachers for employing a professional strategy.

Hence, the emphasis on increasing professionalism by learning new management skills and so on today and its partial acceptance by elementary school teachers can best be understood not only as an attempt by state bureaucrats to de-skill and re-skill teachers, but as part of a much larger historical dynamic in which gender politics have played a significant role.

Yet the acceptance of certain aspects of intensification is not only due to the history of how professionalism has worked in class and gender struggles. It is heightened by a number of internal factors as well. For example, in the school to which I referred earlier, while a number of teachers believed that the rigorous specification of objectives and teaching procedures actually helped free them to become more creative, it was clear that subtle pressures existed to meet the priorities established by the specified objectives. Even though in some subject areas they had a choice of how they were to meet the objectives, the objectives themselves usually remained unchallenged. The perceived interests of parents and their establishment of routines helped assure this. Here is one teacher's assessment of how this occurs.

> Occasionally you're looking at the end of the book at what the unit is going to be, these are the goals that you have to obtain, that the children are going to be tested on. That may affect your teaching in some way in that you may by-pass other learning experiences simply to obtain the goal. These goals are going home to parents. It's a terrible thing to do but parents like to see 90's and 100's rather than 60's on skills.[37]

In discussing the use of the skills program, another teacher points out the other element besides parents that was mentioned: "It's got a manual and you follow the manual and the kids know the directions and it gets to be routine."[38]

Coupled with perceived parental pressure and the sheer power of routine is something else: the employment practices surrounding teaching. In many schools, one of the main criteria for the hiring of teachers is their agreement with the overall curricular, pedagogic, and evaluative framework which organizes the day-to-day practice. Such was the case in this study. Beyond this, however, even though some investigators have found that people who tend to react negatively to these pre-packaged, standardized, and systematized curricular forms often leave teaching,[39] given the depressed market for new teachers in many areas that have severe fiscal problems and the conscious decision by some school districts to hire fewer teachers and increase class size, fewer jobs are available right now. The option of leaving or even protesting seems romantic, though current teacher shortages may change this.

Gendered Resistance

At this point in my argument it would be wise to return to a claim I made earlier. Teachers have not stood by and accepted all this. In fact, our perception that they have been and are passive in the face of these pressures may reflect our own tacit beliefs in the relative passivity of women workers. This would be an unfortunate characterization. Historically, for example, as I shall demonstrate in the following chapter, in England and the United States the picture of women teachers as non-militant and middle-class in orientation is not wholly accurate. There have been periods of exceptional militancy and clear political commitment.[40] However, militancy and political commitment are but one set of ways in which control is contested. It is also fought for on the job itself in subtle and even "unconscious" (one might say "cultural") ways—ways which will be contradictory, as we shall now see. Once again, gender will become of prime importance.

In my own interviews with teachers it has become clear that many of them feel rather uncomfortable with their role as "managers." Many others are less than happy with the emphasis on programs which they often feel "lock us into a rigid system." Here the resistance to rationalization and the loss of historically important forms of self-control of one's labor has very contradictory outcomes, partly as a result of sexual divisions in society. Thus, a teacher using a curricular program in reading and language arts that is very highly structured and test-based states:

> While it's really important for the children to learn these skills, right now it's more important for them to learn to feel good about themselves. That's my role, getting them to feel good. That's more important than tests right now.

Another primary grade teacher, confronted by a rationalized curriculum program where students move from classroom to classroom for "skill groups," put it this way:

> Kids are too young to travel between classrooms all the time. They need someone there that they can always go to, who's close to them. Anyway, subjects are less important than their feelings.

In these quotes, discomfort with the administrative design is certainly evident. There is a clear sense that something is being lost. Yet the discomfort with the process is coded around the traditional distinctions that organize the sexual division of labor both within the family and in the larger society. The *woman's* sphere is that of providing emotional security, caring for feelings, and so on.

Do not misconstrue my points here. Teachers should care for the feelings and emotional security of their students. However, while these teachers rightly fight on a cultural level against what they perceive to be the ill-effects of their loss of control and both the division and the intensification of their labor, they do so at the expense of reinstituting categories that partly reproduce other divisions that have historically grown out of patriarchal relations.[41]

This raises a significant point: much of the recent literature on the role of the school in the reproduction of class, sex, and race domination has directed our attention to the existence of resistances. This realization was not inconsequential and was certainly needed to enable us to go further than the overly deterministic models of explanation that had been employed to unpack what schools do. However, at the same time, this literature has run the risk of romanticizing such resistances. The fact that they exist does not guarantee that they will necessarily be progressive at each and every moment. Only by uncovering the contradictions within and between the dynamics of the labor process *and* gender can we begin to see what effects such resistances may actually have.[42]

Labor, Gender, and Teaching

I have paid particular attention here to the effects of the restructuring of teachers' work in the school. I have claimed that we simply cannot understand what is happening to teaching and curriculum without placing it in a framework which integrates class (and its accompanying process of proletarianization) and gender together. The impact of de-skilling and intensification occurs on a terrain and in an institution that is populated primarily by women teachers and male administrators—a fact that needs to be recognized as being historically articulated with both the social and sexual divisions of labor, knowledge, and power in our society.

Yet, since elementary school teachers are primarily women, we must also look beyond the school to get a fuller comprehension of the impact of these changes and the responses of teachers to them. We need to remember something in this regard: women teachers often work in *two* sites—the school and then the home. Given the modification of patriarchal relations and the intensification of labor in teaching, what impact might this have outside the school? If so much time is spent on technical tasks at school and at home, is it possible that less time may be available for domestic labor in the home? Other people in the family may have to take up the slack, thereby partly challenging the sexual division of household labor. On the other hand, the intensification of teachers' work, and the work overload that may result from it, may have exactly the opposite effect. It may increase the exploitation of unpaid work in the home by merely adding more to do without initially altering conditions in the family. In either case, such conditions will lead to changes, tensions, and conflicts outside of the sphere where women engage in paid work.[43] It is worth thinking very carefully about the effects that working in one site will have on the other. The fact that this dual exploitation exists is quite consequential in another way. It opens up possible new avenues for political intervention by socialist feminists, I believe. By showing the relationship between the home and the job and the intensification growing in both, this may provide for a way of demonstrating the ties between both of these spheres and between class and gender.

Thinking about such issues has actually provided the organizing framework for my analysis. The key to my investigation in this chapter has been reflecting about changes in *how* work is organized over time and, just as significantly, *who* is doing the work. A clearer sense of both of these—how and who—can enable us to see similarities and differences between the world of work in our factories and offices and that of semi-autonomous state employees such as teachers.

What does this mean? Historically the major struggles labor engaged in at the beginning of the use of systematic management concerned resistance to speed-ups.[44] That is, the intensification of production, the pressure to produce more work in a given period, led to all kinds of interesting responses. Craft workers, for example, often simply refused to do more. Pressure was put on co-workers who went too fast (or too slow). Breaks were extended. Tools and machines suddenly developed "problems."

Teachers—given their contradictory class location, their relationship to the history of patriarchal control and the sexual division of labor, and the actual conditions of their work—will find it difficult to respond in the same way. They are usually isolated during their work, and perhaps more so now given the intensification of their labor. Further, machinery and tools in the usual sense of these terms are not visible.[45] And just as importantly, the perception of oneself as professional means that the pressures of intensification and the loss of control will be coded and dealt with in ways that are specific to that workplace and its own history. The ultimate effects will be very contradictory.

In essence, therefore, I am arguing that—while similar labor processes may be working through institutions within industry and the state which have a major impact on women's paid work—these processes will be responded to differently by different classes and class segments. The ideology of professional discretion will lead to a partial acceptance of, say, intensification by teachers on one level, and will generate a different kind of resistance— one specific to the actual work circumstances in which they have historically found themselves. The fact that these changes in the labor process of teaching occur on a terrain that has been a site of patriarchal relations plays a major part here.

My arguments here are not to be construed as some form of "deficit theory." Women have won and will continue to win important victories, as I will demonstrate in the following chapter. Their action on a cultural level, though not overtly politicized, will not always lead to the results I have shown here. Rather, my points concern the inherently *contradictory* nature of teachers' responses. These responses are victories and losses at one and the same time. The important question is how the elements of good sense embodied in these teachers' lived culture can be reorganized in specifically feminist ways—ways that maintain the utter importance of caring and human relationships without at the same time reproducing other elements on that patriarchal terrain.

I do not want to suggest that once you have realized the place of teaching in the sexual division of labor, you have thoroughly understood de-skilling and re-skilling, intensification and loss of control, or the countervailing pressures of professionalism and proletarianization in teachers' work. Obviously, this is a very complex issue in which the internal histories of bureaucracies, the larger role of the state in a time of economic and ideological crisis,[46] and the local political economy and power relations of each school play a part. What I do want to argue quite strongly, however, is the utter import of gendered labor as a constitutive aspect of the way management and the state have approached teaching and curricular control. Gendered labor is the absent presence behind all of our work. How it became such an absent presence is the topic of the next chapter.

Notes

1. Erik Olin Wright and Joachim Singelmann, "The Proletarianization of Work in American Capitalism," University of Wisconsin-Madison Institute for Research on Poverty, Discussion Paper No. 647–81, 1981, p. 38.
2. *Ibid.*, p. 43. See also Michael W. Apple, "State, Bureaucracy and Curriculum Control," *Curriculum Inquiry* 11 (Winter 1981), 379–388. For a discussion that rejects part of the argument about proletarianization, see Michael Kelly, *White Collar Proletariat* (Boston and London: Routledge & Kegan Paul, 1980).
3. De-skilling, technical control and proletarianization are both technical and political concepts. They signify a complex historical process in which the control of labor has altered—one in which the skills employees have developed over many years on the job are broken down into atomistic units, redefined, and then appropriated by management to enhance both efficiency and control of the labor process. In the process, workers' control over timing, over defining appropriate ways to do a task, and over criteria that establish acceptable performance are all slowly taken on as the prerogatives of management personnel who are usually divorced from the actual place in which the work is carried out. De-skilling, then, often leads to the atrophy of valuable skills that workers possessed, since there is no longer any "need" for them in the redefined labor process. The loss of control or proletarianization of a job is hence part of a larger dynamic in the separation of conception from execution and the continuing attempts by management in the state and industry to rationalize as many aspects of one's labor as possible. I have discussed this in considerably more detail in Michael W. Apple, *Education and Power* (Boston and London: Routledge & Kegan Paul, 1982). See also Richard Edwards, *Contested Terrain* (New York: Basic Books, 1979), and Michael Burawoy, *Manufacturing Consent* (Chicago: University of Chicago Press, 1979).
4. Erik Olin Wright, "Class and Occupation," *Theory and Society* 9 (No. 2, 1980), 182–183.
5. Apple, *Education and Power.*
6. Wright, "Class and Occupation," 188. Clearly race plays an important part here too. See Michael Reich, *Racial Inequality* (Princeton: Princeton University Press, 1981), and Mario Barrera, *Race and Class in the Southwest: A Theory of Racial Inequality* (Notre Dame: Notre Dame University Press, 1979).
7. Janet Holland, "Women's Occupational Choice: The Impact of Sexual Divisions in Society," Stockholm Institute of Education, Department of Educational Research, Reports on Education and Psychology, 1980, p. 7.
8. *Ibid.*, p. 27.
9. *Ibid.*, p. 45.
10. Gail Kelly and Ann Nihlen, "Schooling and the Reproduction of Patriarchy," in Michael W. Apple (ed.), *Cultural and Economic Reproduction in Education: Essays on Class, Ideology and the State* (Boston and London: Routledge & Kegan Paul, 1982), pp. 167–168. One cannot fully understand the history of the relationship between women and teaching without tracing out the complex connections among the family, domesticity, child care, and the policies of and employment within the state. See especially, Miriam David, *The State, the Family and Education* (Boston and London: Routledge & Kegan Paul, 1980).
11. For an interesting history of the relationship among class, gender and teaching, see June Purvis, "Women and Teaching in the Nineteenth Century," in Roger Dale, Geoff Esland, Ross Fergusson, and Madeleine MacDonald (eds.), *Education and the State, Vol. 2: Politics, Patriarchy and Practice* (Barcombe, Sussex: Falmer Press, 1981), pp. 359–375. I am wary of using a concept such as patriarchy, since its very status is problematic. As Rowbotham notes, "Patriarchy suggests a fatalistic submission which allows no space for the complexities of women's defiance" (quoted in Tricia Davis, "Stand by Your Men? Feminism and Socialism in the Eighties,") in George Bridges and Rosalind Brunt (eds.), *Silver Linings: Some Strategies for the Eighties* (London: Lawrence & Wishart, 1981), p.14. A history of women's day-to-day struggles falsifies any such theory of "fatalistic submission."
12. Jane Barker and Hazel Downing, "Word Processing and the Transformation of the Patriarchal Relations of Control in the Office," in Dale, Esland, Fergusson and MacDonald (eds.), *Education and the State, Vol. 2*, pp. 229–256. See also the discussion of de-skilling in Edwards, *Contested Terrain.*

13. For an analysis of how such language has been employed by the state, see Michael W. Apple, "Common Curriculum and State Control," *Discourse* 2 (No. 4, 1982), 1–10, and James Donald, "Green Paper: Noise of a Crisis," *Screen Education* 30 (Spring 1979), 13–49.
14. See, for example, Seymour Sarason, *The Culture of the School and the Problem of Change* (Boston: Allyn & Bacon, 1971).
15. Apple, *Education and Power*, and Susan Porter Benson, "The Clerking Sisterhood: Rationalization and the Work Culture of Sales Women in American Department Stores," Radical America 12 (March/April 1978), 41–55.
16. Roger Dale's discussion of contradictions between elements within the state is very interesting in this regard. See Roger Dale, "The State and Education: Some Theoretical Approaches," in *The State and Politics of Education* (Milton Keynes: The Open University Press, E353, Block 1, Part 2, Units 3–4, 1981), and Roger Dale, "Education and the Capitalist State: Contributions and Contradictions," in Apple (ed.), *Cultural and Economic Reproduction in Education*, pp. 127–161.
17. Dale, "The State and Education," p. 13.
18. I have examined this in greater detail in Apple, *Education and Power*. See as well Edwards, *Contested Terrain*, and Daniel Clawson, *Bureaucracy and the Labor Process* (New York: Monthly Review Press, 1980).
19. Magali Larson, "Proletarianization and Educated Labor," *Theory and Society* 9 (No. 2, 1980), 166.
20. *Ibid.*, 167.
21. *Ibid.* Larson points out that these problems related to intensification are often central grievances even among doctors.
22. *Ibid.*, 168.
23. *Ibid.*, 169.
24. *Ibid.*, 167.
25. Apple, *Education and Power*. See also Carol Buswell, "Pedagogic Change and Social Change," *British Journal of Sociology of Education* 1 (No. 3, 1980), 293–306.
26. The question of just how seriously schools take this, the variability of their response, is not unimportant. As Popkewitz, Tabachnick and Wehlage demonstrate in their interesting ethnographic study of school reform, not all schools use materials of this sort alike. See Thomas Popkewitz, B. Robert Tabachnick, and Gary Wehlage, *The Myth of Educational Reform* (Madison: University of Wisconsin Press, 1982).
27. This section of my analysis is based largely on research carried out by Andrew Gitlin. See Andrew Gitlin, "Understanding the Work of Teachers," unpublished Ph.D. dissertation, University of Wisconsin, Madison, 1980.
28. *Ibid.*, 208.
29. *Ibid.*
30. *Ibid.*, 197.
31. *Ibid.*, 237.
32. *Ibid.*, 125.
33. *Ibid.*, 197.
34. This is similar to the use of liberal discourse by popular classes to struggle for personal rights against established property rights over the past one hundred years. See Herbert Gintis, "Communication and Politics," *Socialist Review* 10 (March/June 1980), 189–232. The process is partly paradoxical, however. Attempts to professionalize do give women a weapon against some aspects of patriarchal relations; yet, there is a clear connection between being counted as a profession and being populated largely by men. In fact, one of the things that are very visible historically is the relationship between the sexual division of labor and professionalization. There has been a decided tendency for full professional status to be granted only when an activity is "dominated by men—in both management and the ranks." Jeff Hearn, "Notes on Patriarchy: Professionalization and the Semi-Professions," *Sociology* 16 (May 1982), 195.
35. Magali Larson, "Monopolies of Competence and Bourgeois Ideology," in Dale, Esland, Fergusson, and MacDonald (eds.), *Education and the State, Vol. 2*, p. 332.
36. Larson, "Proletarianization and Educated Labor," p. 152. Historically, class as well as gender dynamics have been quite important here, and recent research documents this clearly. As Barry Bergen has shown in his recent study of the growth of the relationship between class and gender in the professionalization of elementary school teaching in England, a large portion of elementary school teachers were both women and of the working class. As he puts it: Teaching, except at the university level, was not highly regarded by the middle class to begin with, and teaching in the elementary schools was the lowest rung on the teaching ladder. The middle class did not view elementary teaching as a means of upward mobility. But the elementary school teachers seemed to view themselves as having risen above the working class, if not having reached the middle class. . . . Clearly, the varied attempts of elementary teachers to professionalize constitute an attempt to raise their class position from an interstitial one between the working class and middle class to the solidly middle class position of a profession. See Barry H. Bergen, "Only

a Schoolmaster: Gender, Class, and the Effort to Professionalize Elementary Teaching in England, 1870–1910," *History of Education Quarterly* 22 (Spring 1982), 10.

37. Gitlin, "Understanding the Work of Teachers," p. 128.
38. *Ibid.*
39. Martin Lawn and Jenny Ozga, "Teachers: Professionalism, Class and Proletarianization," unpublished paper, The Open University, Milton Keynes, 1981, p. 15 in mimeo.
40. Jenny Ozga, "The Politics of the Teaching Profession," in *The Politics of Schools and Teaching* (Milton Keynes: The Open University Press, E353, Block 6, Units 14–15, 1981), p. 24.
41. We need to be very careful here, of course. Certainly, not all teachers will respond in this way. That some will not points to the partial and important fracturing of dominant gender and class ideologies in ways that signal significant alterations in the consciousness of teachers. Whether these alterations are always progressive is an interesting question. Also, as Connell has shown, such "feminine" approaches are often important counterbalances to masculinist forms of authority in schools. See R. W. Connell, *Teachers' Work* (Boston and London: George Allen & Unwin, 1985).
42. See Henry Giroux, "Theories of Reproduction and Resistance in the New Sociology of Education: A Critical Analysis," *Harvard Educational Review* 53 (August 1983), 257–293, even though he is not specifically interested in gender relations.
43. While I have focused here on the possible impacts in the school and the home on women teachers, a similar analysis needs to be done on men. We need to ask how masculinist ideologies work through male teachers and administrators. Furthermore, what changes, conflicts, and tensions will evolve, say, in the patriarchal authority structures of the home given the intensification of men's labor? I would like to thank Sandra Acker for raising this critically important point. For an analysis of changes in women's labor in the home, see Susan Strasser, *Never Done: A History of American Housework* (New York: Pantheon, 1982).
44. Clawson, *Bureaucracy and the Labor Process*, pp. 152–153.
45. In addition, Connell makes the interesting point that since teachers' work has no identifiable object that it "produces," it can be intensified nearly indefinitely. See Connell, *Teachers' Work*, p. 86.
46. Apple, *Education and Power*, and Manuel Castells, *The Economic Crisis and American Society* (Princeton: Princeton University Press, 1980).

16

The Paideia Proposal

Mortimer J. Adler

Democracy and Education

We are on the verge of a new era in our national life. The long-needed educational reform for which this country is at last ready will be a turning point toward that new era.

Democracy has come into its own for the first time in this century. Not until this century have we undertaken to give twelve years of schooling to all our children. Not until this century have we conferred the high office of enfranchised citizenship on all our people, regardless of sex, race, or ethnic origin.

The two—universal suffrage and universal schooling—are inextricably bound together. The one without the other is a perilous delusion. Suffrage without schooling produces mobocracy, not democracy—not rule of law, not constitutional government by the people as well as for them.

The great American educator, John Dewey, recognized this early in this century. In *Democracy and Education*, written in 1916, he first tied these two words together and let each shine light upon the other.

A revolutionary message of that book was that a democratic society must provide equal educational opportunity not only by giving to all its children the same quantity of public education—the same number of years in school—but also by making sure to give to all of them, all with no exceptions, the same quality of education.

The ideal Dewey set before us is a challenge we have failed to meet. It is a challenge so difficult that it is understandable, perhaps excusable, that we have so far failed. But we cannot continue to fail without disastrous consequences for all of us. For the proper working of our political institutions, for the efficiency of our industries and businesses, for the salvation of our economy, for the vitality of our culture, and for the ultimate good of our citizens as individuals, and especially our future citizens—our children—we must succeed.

We are all sufferers from our continued failure to fulfill the educational obligations of a democracy. We are all the victims of a school system that has only gone halfway along the road to realize the promise of democracy.

At the beginning of this century, fewer than 10 percent of those of an age eligible for high school entered such schools. Today, almost 100 percent of our children enter, but not all complete such secondary schooling; many drop out for many reasons, some of them understandable.

It has taken us the better part of eighty years to go halfway toward the goal our society must achieve if it is to be a true democracy. The halfway mark was reached when we finally managed to provide twelve years of basic public schooling for all our children. At that point, we were closer to the goal that Horace Mann set for us more than a century ago when he said: "Education is the gateway to equality."

But the democratic promise of equal educational opportunity, half fulfilled, is worse than a promise broken. It is an ideal betrayed. Equality of educational opportunity is not, in fact, provided if it means no more than taking all the children into the public schools for the same number of hours, days, and years. If once there they are divided into the sheep and the goats, into those destined solely for toil and those destined for economic and political leadership and for a quality of life to which all should have access, then the democratic purpose has been undermined by an inadequate system of public schooling.

It fails because it has achieved only the same quantity of public schooling, not the same quality. This failure is a downright violation of our democratic principles.

We are politically a classless society. Our citizenry as a whole is our ruling class. We should, therefore, be an educationally classless society.

We should have a one-track system of schooling, not a system with two or more tracks, only one of which goes straight ahead while the others shunt the young off onto sidetracks not headed toward the goals our society opens to all. The innermost meaning of social equality is: *substantially the same quality of life for all.* That calls for: *the same quality of schooling for all.*

We may take some satisfaction, perhaps, in the fact that we have won half the battle— the quantitative half. But we deserve the full development of the country's human potential. We should, therefore, be vexed that we have not yet gone further. We should be impatient to get on with it, in and through the schools.

Progress toward the fulfillment of democracy by means of our educational system should and can be accelerated. It need not and must not take another century to achieve uniform quality for all in our public schools.

There are signs on all sides that tell us the people want that move forward now. The time is ripe. Parents, teachers, leaders of government, labor unions, corporations—above all, the young themselves—have uttered passionate complaints about the declining quality of public schooling.

There is no acceptable reason why trying to promote equality should have led to a lessening or loss of quality. Two decades after John Dewey, another great American educator, Robert Maynard Hutchins, as much committed to democracy as Dewey was before him, stated the fundamental principle we must now follow in our effort to achieve a true equality of educational conditions. "The best education for the best," he said, "is the best education for all."

The shape of the best education for the best is not unknown to us. But we have been slow to learn how to provide it. Nor have we always been honest in our commitment to democracy and its promise of equality. A part of our population—and much too large a part—has harbored the opinion that many of the nation's children are not fully educable. Trainable for one or another job, perhaps, but not educable for the duties of self-governing citizenship and for the enjoyment of things of the mind and spirit that are essential to a good human life.

We must end that hypocrisy in our national life. We cannot say out of one side of our mouth that we are for democracy and all its free institutions including, preeminently, political and civil liberty for all; and out of the other side of our mouth, say that only some of the children—fewer than half—are educable for full citizenship and a full human life.

With the exception of a few suffering from irremediable brain damage, every child is educable up to his or her capacity. Educable—not just trainable for jobs! As John Dewey said almost a century ago, vocational training, training for particular jobs, is not the education of free men and women.

True, children are educable in varying degrees, but the variation in degree must be of the same kind and quality of education. If "the best education for the best is the best education for all," the failure to carry out that principle is the failure on the part of society—a failure of parents, of teachers, of administrators—not a failure on the part of the children.

There are no unteachable children. There are only schools and teachers and parents who fail to teach them.

The Same Course of Study for all

To give the same quality of schooling to all requires a program of study that is both liberal and general, and that is, in several, crucial, overarching respects, one and the same for every child. All sidetracks, specialized courses, or elective choices must be eliminated. Allowing them will always lead a certain number of students to voluntarily downgrade their own education.

Elective choices are appropriate only in a curriculum that is intended for different avenues of specialization or different forms of preparation for the professions or technical careers. Electives and specialization are entirely proper at the level of advanced schooling— in our colleges, universities, and technical schools. They are wholly inappropriate at the level of basic schooling.

The course of study to be followed in the twelve years of basic schooling should, therefore, be completely required, with only one exception. That exception is the choice of a second language. In addition to competence in the use of English as everyone's primary language, basic schooling should confer a certain degree of facility in the use of a second language. That second language should be open to elective choice.

The diagram depicts in three columns three distinct modes of teaching and learning, rising in successive gradations of complexity and difficulty from the first to the twelfth year. All three modes are essential to the overall course of study.

These three columns are interconnected, as the diagram indicates. The different modes of learning on the part of the students and the different modes of teaching on the part of the teaching staff correspond to three different ways in which the mind can be improved—(1) by the acquisition of organized knowledge; (2) by the development of intellectual skills; and (3) by the enlargement of understanding, insight, and aesthetic appreciation.

In addition to the three main Columns of Learning, the required course of study also includes a group of auxiliary subjects, of which one is physical education and care of the body. This runs through all twelve years. Of the other two auxiliary subjects, instruction in a variety of manual arts occupies a number of years, but not all twelve; and the third consists of an introduction to the world of work and its range of occupations and careers. It is given in the last two of the twelve years.

	COLUMN ONE	*COLUMN TWO*	*COLUMN THREE*
Goals	ACQUISITION OF ORGANIZED KNOWLEDGE	DEVELOPMENT OF INTELLECTUAL SKILLS—SKILLS OF LEARNING	ENLARGED UNDERSTANDING OF IDEAS AND VALUES
	by means of	by means of	by means of
Means	DIDACTIC INSTRUCTION LECTURES AND RESPONSES TEXTBOOKS AND OTHER AIDS	COACHING, EXERCISES, AND SUPERVISED PRACTICE	MAIEUTIC OR SOCRATIC QUESTIONING AND ACTIVE PARTICIPATION
	in three areas of subject-matter	in the operations of	in the
Areas of Operations and Activities	LANGUAGE, LITERATURE, AND THE FINE ARTS, MATHEMATICS AND NATURAL SCIENCE, HISTORY, GEOGRAPHY, AND SOCIAL STUDIES	READING, WRITING, SPEAKING, LISTENING CALCULATING, PROBLEM-SOLVING, OBSERVING MEASURING, ESTIMATING EXERCISING CRITICAL JUDGMENT	DISCUSSION OF BOOKS (NOT TEXTBOOKS) AND OTHER WORKS OF ART AND INVOLVEMENT IN ARTISTIC ACTIVITIES e.g., MUSIC, DRAMA, VISUAL ARTS

THE THREE COLUMNS DO NOT CORRESPOND TO SEPARATE COURSES, NOR IS ONE KIND OF TEACHING AND LEARNING NECESSARILY CONFINED TO ANY ONE CLASS.

17

The False Promise of the Paideia: A Critical Review of *The Paideia Proposal*

Nel Noddings

The Paideia Proposal is offered as an educational prescription for all of America's children. It is based on two major premises: that "the shape of the best education for the best is not unknown to us" (p. 7) and that "the best education for the best . . . is the best education for all" (p. 6). Surely no humane and decent person finds it easy to counsel against a proposal that promises to provide the "same quality of schooling to all," and thereby to educate all of our children to their fullest potential. Hard as it is, however, I believe that we should reject the recommendations in *The Paideia Proposal.* I will argue that "equality of quality" in education cannot be achieved by forcing all students to take exactly the same course of study, nor can the ideal of a democratic, classless society be actualized by establishing only one model of excellence.

The *Paideia*'s recommendations fall into two major categories: content and method. Those on method will be discussed at the end of this essay. The recommendations on content are encapsulated in this paragraph from the *Paideia*:

> The course of study to be followed in the twelve years of basic schooling should, therefore, be completely required, with only one exception. That exception is the choice of a second language. (Adler 1982, p. 21)

There is little use in arguing directly against the *Paideia*'s recommendations, because they follow inexorably from Mortimer Adler's two basic assumptions. But both of Adler's premises may be called into question as well as his strategy of persuasion: linking John Dewey and Robert Hutchins together as though no disagreement separated the two should cause thoughtful educators considerable uneasiness. I will start by examining that strategy, and then I will examine each of Adler's premises in turn.

1

The Paideia Proposal is dedicated to Horace Mann, John Dewey, and Robert Hutchins, "who would have been our leaders were they alive today." This is a lovely dedication, but Adler fails to mention that, if Dewey and Hutchins were alive today, they would almost certainly be engaged in the continuing battle of method and principle that they so vigorously mounted during their actual lifetimes. Mr. Hutchins would be an eloquent and outspoken advocate of the *Paideia*: Mr. Dewey would be a softer spoken but rigorously thoughtful opponent of the program. To suggest, even tacitly, that the *Paideia* fulfills the dreams and recommendations of both John Dewey and Robert Hutchins does a monumental disservice to John Dewey. The man and his educational thought deserve better. Further, Adler is thoroughly informed on the differences I shall point out, and one wonders why he chose to omit their discussion. Perhaps he believes that it is high time for reconciliation between Hutchins and Dewey and that this reconciliation holds promise for real improvement in the system of public education that both men loved (in some ideal form) and that is now so terribly beset with problems. Granted this generous motive, he still cannot responsibly attempt to effect reconciliation by assimilating a worthy opponent to the position of his adversary without even mentioning the problems that opponent would encounter in considering such a reconciliation.

Dewey and Hutchins are linked in Adler's arguments through their manifest interests in democracy and "equality of quality" in education. But their views on both concepts differed radically. Adler refers to Dewey's *Democracy and Education* when he says:

> A revolutionary message of that book was that a democratic society must provide equal opportunity not only by giving to all its children the same quantity of public education—the same number of years in school—but also by making sure to give to all of them, all with no exceptions, the same quality of education. (*Paideia*, p. 4)

Now, it is clear that Dewey did advocate a substantial "equality of quality" in education for all children. But his ideas on this were very different from those of Hutchins. In *The School and Society*, Dewey (1899, p. 3) said:

> What the best and wisest parent wants for his own child, that must the community want for all its children. Any other ideal for our schools is narrow and unlovely; acted upon, it destroys our democracy.

Clearly, we have to ask what Dewey meant when he referred to "the best and wisest parent." It is crystal clear at the outset, however, that he meant by "best" something very different from the "best" of Hutchins in the initial premises cited by Adler. Yet Adler throws them together in the same paragraph as though both were advocates of the program under construction. He says:

> There is no acceptable reason why trying to promote equality should have led to a lessening or loss of quality. Two decades after John Dewey, another great American educator, Robert Maynard Hutchins, as much committed to democracy as Dewey was before him, stated the fundamental principle we must follow in our effort to achieve a true equality of educational conditions. "The best education for the best," he said, "is the best education for all." (*Paideia*, p. 6)

Dewey would certainly challenge this premise if "best" is interpreted as "intellectually best"—as it surely is in the writings of Hutchins and Adler. Further, Dewey *did* challenge both premises in direct rebuttal of Hutchins. In a series of 1937 articles in *The Social Frontier*, Dewey (1937a, b) criticized the program of higher education that Hutchins proposed in *The Higher Learning in America*. Dewey made it clear in the ensuing exchange of views that, while he accepted and admired some of Hutchins' analysis, he rejected the proposed remedy. He said:

> The essence of the remedy . . . is emancipation of higher learning from . . . practicality, and its devotion to the cultivation of intellectuality for its own sake. (Dewey 1937a, p. 103)

Dewey's objections to the remedies suggested in *The Higher Learning* centered on two matters that he thought were at the heart of Hutchins' ideas: belief in "the existence of fixed and eternal authoritative principles" and the separation of "higher learning from contemporary social life." It is not an exaggeration to say that Dewey's voluminous writings over a lifetime of effort attacked these ideas again and again from a wide variety of perspectives. The separation of learning from contemporary social life was, indeed, a favorite target of his criticism. Exactly the same objections may be brought against the *Paideia*: It elevates intellectual life above that which it should serve (the social communion of human beings), and it assumes an essential sameness in human beings and values that suggests, logically, a sameness in education.

It would be fun (and instructive, too) to follow the Dewey-Hutchins debate further, but I cannot do that here. Suffice it to say that these two great educators did not really communicate with each other. Hutchins, indeed, began his rejoinder to Dewey by saying that he could not "in any real sense" respond to Dewey for

> Mr. Dewey has stated my position in such a way as to lead me to think that I cannot write, and has stated his own in such a way as to make me suspect that I cannot read. (Hutchins 1937, p. 137)

This sort of wit was a favorite gambit of Hutchins. He did not engage in *dialogue* with Dewey and continually side-stepped Dewey's most telling points, preferring to display verbal pyrotechnics and to persuade through rhetoric. The same charade is now being replayed. Adler offers us a tightly argued program based on rhetorical premises, themselves entirely unsupported by logical argumentation. Accept his premises and he has you, because he does not make errors in the logic of *developing* his program. What is sad is that so many educators are listening to Adler without a murmur of logical protest. He is right about one thing—and, paradoxically, it is working for him—the education of educators is not all that it should be.

2

Let me raise a murmur of logical protest. Put aside for the moment the premise that makes claims about the "shape of the best education," and let's concentrate on the other. The best education for the best is the best education for all.

The word "best" is used three times here. All three uses invite scrutiny, but the second deserves special attention. It is used elliptically as a noun. If we insist that the ellipsis be filled and that "best" be used as an adjective, what noun will it modify? It is clear that "best" is not meant to modify such nouns as "life" or "effort" or "performance" or the like. Both Hutchins and Adler are talking about *people* when they refer to "the best." Now what noun shall we insert: people? students? minds? It is eminently clear that Hutchins meant to refer to an *intellectually best* when he used the word and that an accurate filling in of the ellipsis would be, "The best education for the intellectually best students is the best education for all." Further, because the two premises have influenced each other historically, "intellectually best" has been narrowed to "academically best" in the traditional sense. Adler wants all children to receive an education that is, in content at least, the education designed for our academically best students.

Why should we consider doing this? Are the academically best the only group that should provide a model for school learning? Is the mission of the school to provide training or "education" only for the mind? Or are there many models of excellence that must be recognized in both society and school? In my own secondary schooling, I participated in a program very like the one Adler outlines. I loved it. I was completely captivated by Caesar's Gallic Wars, geometry, trigonometric identities, and even Cicero's essay on old age. It was not until years later that I learned about the utter misery most of my classmates endured in the "same" environment. Mr. Adler, to his great credit, would try to alleviate that misery by better classroom teaching and individual coaching, but he is mistaken in what he believes would be effected. No special effort or even genius in teaching would have brought most of my classmates into fair competition with me. Whatever they did, however they improved, I would have done more of it and at a higher level. It is not that I was "better" than they. I was *interested* in the sort of material the school wanted me to learn. Now one might claim a special benefit in this side effect: the academically able would be pushed through increased competition to surpass themselves. But then they would be engaged in academics (if they remained engaged) for largely the wrong reasons and with loss of the joy that accompanies doing what one has chosen out of love to do. We should consider the *Paideia*'s proposals, then, if we want this sort of effect.

Giving all of our children the *same* education, especially when that "sameness" is defined in a model of intellectual excellence, cannot equalize the quality of education. When parents and their children want the sort of education prescribed in the *Paideia*, it seems right to accommodate them, but to impose a plan such as this on all children in the name of equality is wrong. It proceeds in part from the stated assumption that we are "politically a classless society" and that we should, therefore, be an "educationally classless society." Mr. Adler has the cart before the horse. We are *not*, in any but the most technical sense, a classless society and to impose a uniform and compulsory form of education on all children is likely to aggravate an already unhealthy condition. When children must all study the same material and strive to meet the same standards, it becomes infinitely easier to sort and grade them like so many apples on a conveyor belt. Some children will be in the top quartile and some will be in the bottom quartile. Are we to say, then, that they all had an "equal chance" and that the "classes" thus established are, at least, objectivly and fairly established?

To put the horse properly before the cart, we would have to ask what education might do to help the society arrive at the classless ideal it has stated for itself. Many theorists insist that the schools can do very little to change the society: As institutions *of* the society, they are instruments for the reproduction of society as it is. We can certainly take a more hopeful view than this, but whatever view we take must be realistic at the outset. People in our society perform a huge variety of tasks, have hundreds of different interests, hold a variety of precious values. We do not offer equality when we ask them to model themselves after the traditional profile of an "intellectual best." What the schools need to do, instead, is to legitimize multiple models of excellence, e.g., mechanical, artistic, physical, productive, academic, and caretaking. Standing over all these should be the ethical, for what we need far more urgently than intellectual prowess is ethical goodness.

Many thoughtful planners shrink from the notion of "multiple models" of excellence because they believe the schools are already asked to accomplish too much. John Gardner, for example, in his influential *Excellence* (1961), lauded excellence in all its forms at the level of societal activity, but he charged the school with the task of promoting only academic excellence. It seems entirely right in a society such as ours to value "excellent plumbers above mediocre philosophers," but must we not also value the budding plumber—the youngster who will be a craftsman—while he or she is still a student? Gardner argued that the schools cannot do everything and that they are best organized to achieve *academic* excellence. The weakest part of his argument was revealed when he admitted that some youngsters (probably many) would not do well in a program so oriented. They would have to understand, he said, that the failure they had experienced in school was only *one form* of failure and that they might still achieve excellence in other enterprises. But I ask you this: How is a youngster who has been at the bottom of the heap for twelve years going "to understand" that his or her failure so far is only "one form" of failure? Surely, if we value plumbing, and farming, and dancing, and writing, and repairing electronic devices at the societal level, we can find ways of valuing the talents that lead to these occupations during school years. We really *have* to do this if our talk of equality is to be anything more than *mere* talk.

To be reasonable, however, we do have to consider Gardner's concern that demands on the schools have so proliferated that they cannot achieve any sort of excellence. I suggest that it is not subject and activity demands that have overburdened our schools but, rather, demands to solve the problems of a society unwilling to bear its burdens where they should properly be shouldered. A society unwilling to rid itself of racial prejudice asks the *schools* to achieve desegregation. A society unwilling to talk with its children about love, delight, and commitment asks the *schools* to teach sex education. A society unwilling to recognize the forms of excellence that Mr. Gardner identifies asks the *schools* to teach everyone algebra. The greatest burden of the schools, as a result, is trying to find some way to teach to adequately intelligent students things that they do not want to learn.

Acting on the *Paideia* would not produce a "classless education." The *Paideia* selects a form of education traditionally associated with an academically privileged class—"education for the best"—and prescribes it for all children, regardless of home influences, individual interests, special talents, or any realistic hope that all can participate in the sort of professional life that such an education has traditionally aspired to. Even if we were to deny the existence of classes in our current society, we would inevitably produce them under the *Paideia.* In this system, *everyone* is to be judged by the standards usually applied to the academically talented. I object to this. I object as a teacher, as a parent, and as a thoughtful human being. There is more to life, more to excellence, more to success, and more to devotion than can be captured in a single intellectual model of excellence.

To provide an equal quality of education for all our children requires, first, that we hold the variety of their talents and legitimate interests to be equally valuable. This does not mean that schools should provide no common learnings. Of course the schools should teach all children to read, write, and compute. But the schools should also teach all children how to operate the technical machinery and gadgets that fill our homes and offices; to care responsibly for living things; to develop their bodies for lifelong physical grace; to obtain and convey information; to use their hands in making and finishing things; to develop their receptive capacities in the arts; to develop a commitment to service in some capacity. This sounds like an impossible list—and it is almost certainly incomplete. But the beautiful truth is that when we take all of the valuable aspects of life into consideration and when we respect all of our children's legitimate interests in our educational planning, it becomes *easier* to teach the basic skills. They become obviously necessary to the satisfaction of real problems and actual tasks. The answer is not to spend more and more time on "basics" but to revitalize the basics in a broad scheme of general education that is laid out boldly along the entire continuum of human experience.

Now, I can imagine at least some of the advocates of *Paideia* saying: But that is exactly what we mean to do; that is what education for the best has traditionally done! It provides a broad, general education that aims to liberate the human mind; it conduces to the "examined life." It . . . "Whoa up!" I'd have to say. You are still talking about an essentially abstract and bookish sort of education. Consider this: Is it not at least possible that academic talent is *per se* a somewhat specialized talent? If it is, and I believe there is evidence to support the contention, then so long as our schooling is highly "intellectualized," we have a specialized curriculum no matter how many traditional subjects we force people to take in the name of breadth. Such a program can hardly meet the criteria for "equality of quality."

3

Now, consider the second premise. Adler claims that "the shape of the best education for the best is not unknown to us." If he means by this that we know what has been provided for an intellectually and socially privileged class in the past, the claim seems reasonable. The force of his argument would then be, "Let us now give all our children what we have given these privileged few in the past." But is the traditional "education for the best" really the "best" even for our academically most able students? On what grounds is it so judged? The *Paideia* aims at an education that will enable all children to earn a living in an intelligent and responsible fashion, to function as intelligent and responsible citizens, and to make both of these things serve the purpose of leading intelligent and responsible lives—to enjoy as fully as possible all the goods that make a human life as good as it can be (p. 18).

"To achieve these three goals," Adler writes (p. 18):

> basic schooling must have for all a quality that can be best defined, *positively*, by saying that it must be general and liberal; and *negatively*, by saying that it must be nonspecialized and non-vocational.

There are at least two difficulties here. One has to do with the word "vocational" and its uses. Another is the meaning of "nonspecialized." I have already argued that the sort of abstract and bookish education recommended by the *Paideia* is itself—in spite of its internal breadth—a specialized curriculum. It is designed for those whose further education will be academic, and there is little evidence that it will promote continued learning across other fields of endeavor. One could design a "mechanical-technical" education every bit as broad (internally) as the *Paideia*'s "liberal" education (thus avoiding the rapid obsolescence of skills), and most of us would still consider it too highly specialized to be used exclusively and for all our children. One can imagine, however, several such beautifully designed curricula, equally valuable, each characterized by internal breadth, offered on equal levels and freely chosen by well-informed students. This sort of plan might realistically avoid premature specialization. Further, the freedom of choice provided seems appropriate preparation for democratic life.

In its own effort to prepare children "equally" for participation in "democracy," the

Paideia sacrifices a first principle of democracy: In the pursuit of eventual freedom, it denies students any freedom whatsoever in the choice of their own studies.

The one-track system of public schooling that *The Paideia Proposal* advocates has the same objectives for all without exception (p. 15).

Further:

> All sidetracks, specialized courses, or elective choices must be eliminated. Allowing them will always lead a certain number of students to voluntarily downgrade their own education (p. 21).

Think what we are suggesting in making or accepting such a recommendation. Why should electives in cooking, photography, or science fiction constitute a "downgrading" of education? Is James Beard a failure? Is Edward Steichen? Is Ray Bradbury? Now I am not arguing for premature specialization. I am simply pointing out what John Dewey counseled again and again: Any subject freely undertaken as an occupation—as a set of tasks requiring goal-setting, means-ends analysis, choice of appropriate tools and materials, exercise of skills, living through the consequences, and evaluating the results—is educative. Cooking can be approached with high intelligence and elegant cultural interests or it can deteriorate to baking brownies and cleaning ovens: similarly, mathematics can be taught so as to require deep reflective and intuitive thinking or it can be taught as a mindless bag of tricks. It is not the subjects offered that make a curriculum properly a part of education but how those subjects are taught, how they connect to the personal interests and talents of the students who study them, and how skillfully they are laid out against the whole continuum of human experience.

We see in this discussion another area of great disagreement between John Dewey and the perennialists, and this involves the difficulty I mentioned concerning the word "vocational." It is true, as Adler points out, that Dewey argued against something called "vocational education." But Dewey was arguing against a narrow form of specialization that tended to downgrade the participants *as persons*. He was arguing against a form of schooling, not education at all, that labels some children fit only to do Vocation X, where X itself may be held in disdain. More importantly, however, he wanted all children to experience education *through* occupations or vocations more broadly construed. He said:

> A vocation signifies any form of continuous activity which renders service to others and engages personal powers in behalf of the accomplishment of results. (Dewey 1916, p. 319)

Dewey insisted that education could be conducted through occupations or vocations in the important sense we are considering here. He insisted upon the organic connection between education and personal experience and, thus, between education and contemporary social life. Students do not have to study exactly the same subject matter nor need they be deprived of choice in order to be truly educated. Dewey spoke favorably of Plato's fundamental principle of tailoring education to the abilities of students, but he drew back from the hierarchical evaluation connected with this form of education, saying:

> His [Plato's] error was not in qualitative principle, but in his limited conception of the scope of vocations socially needed: a limitation of vision which reacted to obscure his perception of the infinite variety of capacities found in different individuals. (Ibid. 1916, p. 309)

Dewey wanted us to avoid two equally pernicious ideas in education: first, that education must consist of a set of prespecified material to be transmitted to everyone regardless of personal interest: second, that education should consist of a hierarchically ordered set of curricula—the "highest" given to the "best," the "lowest" to the "least." To provide "equality of quality" in education for all our children requires that we start with equal respect for their talents and aspirations and that we help them to choose wisely within the domain of their interests.

My main aim in this section has been to cast doubt on Mr. Adler's claim that "the shape of the best education for the best is not unknown to us." On the contrary. I believe that far more reflection and responsible experimentation are required before we can support such a claim.

4

I promised at the beginning of this essay to say something about the recommendations the *Paideia* makes concerning methods of instruction. Three modes of teaching are prescribed, and they are all useful. Each mode of teaching is connected to a mode of learning: for the acquisition of organized knowledge, didactic instruction is recommended; for the development of intellectual skills, coaching is to be employed; and for the enlargement of understanding, insight, and aesthetic appreciation, "maieutic" or Socratic methods are to be used. All three methods, properly implemented, are sound and useful, and education would take a giant step forward if teachers were skilled in each of them.

But the methods as they are described are somewhat warped by the prescribed subject matter. There is no mention of the enormous skill required of teachers in setting the environment so that children will formulate purposes and thus *seek* to acquire segments of organized knowledge. Nor is the choice of coach or the relation between coach and student mentioned. These are oversights that I need not belabor. The attitude of which I complain pervades the *Paideia*: Students are treated as "minds" to be filled equally with the same quality material. Nowhere is there proper consideration of the *persons* who are, in their essential freedom and infinite diversity, central and instrumental in their own education.

References

Mortimer J. Adler. (1982). *The Paideia Proposal.* New York: Macmillan Publishing Co., Inc.
John Dewey. (1915). *The School and Society.* Chicago: The University of Chicago Press.
John Dewey. (1916). *Democracy and Education.* New York: The Free Press.
John Dewey. "President Hutchins' Proposals to Remake Higher Education," *The Social Frontier* 3 (1937a): 103–104.
John Dewey. "The Higher Learning in America," *The Social Frontier* 3 (1937b): 167–169.
John Gardner. (1961). *Excellence: Can We Be Equal and Excellent Too?* New York: Harper.
Robert Maynard Hutchins. "Grammar, Rhetoric, and Mr. Dewey," *The Social Frontier* 3 (1937): 137–139.

18

Implementation as Mutual Adaptation: Change in Classroom Organization

Milbrey Wallin McLaughlin

Most observers believe that the educational innovations undertaken as part of the curriculum reform movement of the 1950s and early 1960s, as well as the innovations that comprised the initiatives of the "Education Decade," generally have failed to meet their objectives.[1] One explanation for these disappointments focuses on the type of innovations undertaken and points out that until recently few educators have elected to initiate innovations that require change in the traditional roles, behavior, and structures that exist within the school organization or the classroom. Instead, most innovative efforts have focused primarily on technological change, not organizational change. Many argue that without changes in the structure of the institutional setting, or the culture of the school, new practices are simply "more of the same" and are unlikely to lead to much significant change in what happens to students.

Since 1970, however, a number of educators have begun to express interest in practices that redefine the assumptions about children and learning that underlie traditional methods—new classroom practices that attempt to change the ways that students, teachers, parents, and administrators relate to each other. Encouraged and stimulated by the work of such writers as Joseph Featherstone, Charles Silberman, and William Glasser, some local schoolmen have undertaken innovations in classroom organization such as open education, multiage grouping, integrated day, differentiated staffing, and team teaching. These practices are not based on a "model" of classroom organization change to be strictly followed, but on a common set of convictions about the nature of learning and the purpose of teaching. These philosophical similarities, which can be traced to the work of the Swiss psychologist Piaget, are based on a belief that humanistic, individualized, and child-centered education requires more than incremental or marginal change in classroom organization, educational technology, or teacher behavior.

Because classroom organization projects require teachers to work out their own styles and classroom techniques within a broad philosophical framework, innovations of this type cannot be specified or packaged in advance. Thus, the very nature of these projects requires that implementation be a *mutually adaptive process* between the user and the institutional setting—that specific project goals and methods be made concrete over time by the participants themselves.

Classroom organization projects were among the local innovations examined as part of Rand's Change-Agent Study.[2] Of the 293 projects surveyed, eighty-five could be classified as classroom organization projects; five of our thirty field sites were undertaking innovation of this nature. The findings of the change-agent study suggest that the experience of these projects should be examined in some detail. At the most general level, the change study concluded that implementation—rather than educational treatment, level of resources, or type of federal funding strategy—dominates the innovative process and its outcomes. The study found that the mere adoption of a "better" practice did not automatically or invariably lead to "better" student outcomes. Initially similar technologies undergo unique alterations during the process of implementation and thus their outcomes cannot be predicted on the basis of treatment alone. Further, the process of implementation that is inherent in classroom organization projects was found to describe effective implementation generally. Specifically, the change-agent study concluded that *successful implementation is characterized by a process of mutual adaptation.*

Contrary to the assumptions underlying many change strategies and federal change policies, we found that implementation did not merely involve the direct and straightforward application of an educational technology or plan. Implementation was a dynamic organizational process that was shaped over time by interactions between project goals and methods, and the institutional setting. As such, it was neither automatic nor certain. Three different interactions characterized this highly variable process.

One, *mutual adaptation*, described successfully implemented projects. It involved modification of both the project design and changes in the institutional setting and individual participants during the course of implementation.

A second implementation process, *cooptation*, signified adaptation of the project design, but no change on the part of participants or the institutional setting. When implementation of this nature occurred, project strategies were simply modified to conform in a pro forma fashion to the traditional practices the innovation was expected to replace—either because of resistance to change or inadequate help for implementers.

The third implementation process, *nonimplementation*, described the experience of projects that either broke down during the course of implementation or were simply ignored by project participants.

Where implementation was successful, and where significant change in participant attitudes, skills and behavior occurred, implementation was characterized by a process of mutual adaptation in which project goals and methods were modified to suit the needs and interests of participants and in which participants changed to meet the requirements of the project. This finding was true even for highly technological and initially well specified projects: unless adaptations were made in the original plans or technologies, implementation tended to be superficial or symbolic and significant change in participants did not occur.

Classroom organization projects provided particularly clear illustration of the conditions and strategies that support mutual adaptation and thus successful implementation. They are especially relevant to understanding the operational implications of this change-agent study finding for policy and practice not only because mutual adaptation is intrinsic to change in classroom organization, but also because the question of institutional receptivity does not cloud the view of effective implementation strategies afforded by these projects.

The receptivity of the institutional setting to a proposed innovation varied greatly among the projects we examined—from active support to indifference to hostility. The amount of interest, commitment, and support evidenced by principal actors had a major influence on the prospects for successful project implementation. In particular, the attitudes and interest of central administrators in effect provided a "signal" to project participants as to how seriously they should take project goals and how hard they should work to achieve them. Unless participants perceived that change-agent projects represented a school and district educational priority, teachers were often unwilling to put in the extra time and emotional investment necessary for successful implementation. Similarly, the attitudes of teachers were critical. Unless teachers were motivated by professional concerns (as opposed to more tangible incentives such as extra pay or credit on the district salary scale, for example), they did not expend the extra time and energy requisite to the usually painful process of implementing an innovation.

Classroom organization projects were almost always characterized by high levels of commitment and support for their initiation, both at the district and at the building level. This is not surprising when we consider the risk and difficulty associated with these projects; it is unlikely that a district would elect to undertake a project of this nature unless they believed strongly in the educational approach and were committed to attempting the changes necessary to implement it.

In fact, classroom organization projects possess none of the features traditionally thought to encourage local decision makers to adopt a given innovation:

1. Ease of explanation and communication to others.
2. Possibility of a trial on a partial or limited basis.
3. Ease of use.
4. Congruence with existing values.
5. Obvious superiority over practices that existed previously.[3]

Innovations that focus on classroom organization are at odds with all five of these criteria. First, since there is no specific "model" to be followed, it is difficult to tell people how these approaches operate. Advocates can only offer general advice and communicate the philosophy or attitudes that underlie innovation in classroom organization and activities.

Second, although open classroom or team-teaching strategies can be implemented slowly, and can be installed in just one or two classrooms in a school, it is generally not possible to be "just a little bit" open or just a "sometime" part of a team-teaching situation. The method is based on fundamental changes which are hard to accomplish piecemeal.

Third, change in classroom organization is inherently very complex. Innovations of this nature require the learning of new attitudes, roles and behavior on the part of teachers and administrators—changes far more difficult to bring about than the learning of a new skill or gaining familiarity with a new educational technology. Classroom organization changes also typically require new arrangements of classroom space, the provision of new instructional materials, and usually new school scheduling and reporting practices.

Fourth, strategies of open education or team teaching are a radical departure from the traditional or standard practices of a school, district, or teacher. Change in classroom organization means changing deeply held attitudes and customary behavior. These projects, by attempting to change organizational structure and goals, attempt to affect the fundamental nature of the organization and are therefore basically incongruent with existing values.

Fifth, although proponents argue that humanistic, child-centered education represents a big advance, the objective evidence is ambiguous. Most evaluations of informal classrooms conclude that participating children do better on affective measures, but there is little evidence of significant cognitive differences that could confidently be attributed to open classrooms themselves. An administrator contemplating a change in classroom organization is confronted with a complicated innovation that shows no clear advantage over existing practices—at least in the ways that often matter most to school boards, voters, and anxious parents.

Thus, given the complex, unspecified, and inherently difficult nature of these projects, they were rarely initiated without the active support and commitment of district officials and participants. Consequently, the insufficient institutional support that negatively influenced implementation in other projects and so made it difficult to obtain a clear picture of the strategic factors affecting project implementation (i.e., did disappointing implementation result from a lack of enthusiasm or from inadequate training?) generally was not a problem for classroom organization projects. Variance in the implementation outcome of classroom organization projects, consequently, can be attributed in large measure to the project's particular implementation strategy.

For classroom organization projects, as for other change-agent projects, *institutional receptivity was a necessary but not a sufficient condition for successful implementation.* Unless project implementation strategies were chosen that allowed institutional support to be engaged and mutual adaptation to occur, project implementation foundered. A project's particular implementation strategy is the result of many local choices about how best to implement project goals and methods. What seems to be the most effective thing to do? What is possible given project constraints? What process fits best with local needs and conditions? Decisions about the type and amount of training, the planning necessary, and project participants are examples of such choices. They effectively define how a proposed innovation is put into practice. Implementation strategies are distinguishable from project treatment. That is, the educational method chosen for a project (i.e., team teaching, diagnostic/prescriptive reading) is different from the strategies selected for implementing the method. No two reading projects, for example, employ quite the same process or strategy for achieving their almost identical goals.

Implementation Strategy

Each project employs its own combination of strategies that effectively defines its *implementation strategy*. Thus, in addition to identifying especially effective component strategies, it is meaningful to examine how and why the various individual strategies interact with each other to form a "successful" implementation strategy and to promote mutual adaptation. The experience of classroom organization projects suggests at least three specific strategies that are particularly critical and that work together to form an adaptive implementation strategy: local materials development; ongoing and concrete staff training; iterative, on-line planning combined with regular and frequent staff meetings.

Local Material Development

In almost all of the classroom organization projects, the staff spent a substantial amount of time developing materials to use in the project classrooms. These materials either were developed from scratch or put together from bits of commercially-developed materials. Although these activities were sometimes undertaken because the staff felt they couldn't locate appropriate commercial materials, the real contribution lay not so much in "better pedagogical products" but in providing the staff with a sense of involvement and an opportunity to "learn-by-doing." Working together to develop materials for the project gave the staff a sense of pride in its own accomplishments, a sense of "ownership" in the project. It also broke down the traditional isolation of the classroom teacher and provided a sense of "professionalism" and cooperation not usually available in the school setting. But even more important, materials development provided an opportunity for users to think through the concepts which underlay the project, in practical, operational terms—an opportunity to engage in experience-based learning. Although such "reinvention of the wheel" may not appear efficient in the short run, it appears to be a critical part of the individual learning and development necessary for significant change.

Staff Training

All the classroom organization projects we visited included both formal and informal, pre-service and in-service staff training. For example, one project's formal training took place in a two-week summer session before the project began; its informal development activities had been extensive, providing for almost constant interaction among project staff. Almost all of these projects provided pre-service training that included observations in operating classrooms. One open classroom project staff even participated in a trip to observe British infant schools. All projects also conducted regular workshops throughout the first three years of project implementation.

One-shot training, or training heavily concentrated at the beginning of the project, was not effective. Although such training designs have the virtues of efficiency and lower cost, they ignore the critical fact that project implementors cannot know what it is they need to know until project operations are well underway. This is generally true for all innovative efforts, but particularly salient in the case of amorphous classroom organization projects. There is just so much that a would-be implementor can be taught or can understand until problems have arisen in the course of project implementation, and solutions must be devised. Training programs that attempt to be comprehensive and cover all contingencies at the outset are bound to miss their mark and also to be less than meaningful to project participants.

Project staffs agreed that staff development and training activities were a critical part of successful implementation. They also agreed that some kinds of training activities were more useful than others. With few exceptions, visits by outside consultants and other outside "experts" were not considered particularly helpful. Teachers in all the change-agent projects we examined complained that most visiting consultants could not relate to the particular problems they were experiencing in their classrooms, or that their advice was too abstract to be helpful. Where outside experts were considered useful, their participation was concrete and involved working closely with project teachers in their classrooms or in "hands-on" workshops. However, it was unusual for outside consultants to have either the time or the inclination to provide assistance in other than a lecture format. Such expert delivery of "truth and knowledge," however, was seldom meaningful to participants, and foreclosed more powerful learning opportunities.

The sessions participants thought most useful were regular meetings of the project staff with local resource personnel in which ideas were shared, problems discussed, and support given. Materials development often provided the focus for these concrete, how-to-do-it training sessions. Visits to other schools implementing similar projects were also considered helpful; the teachers felt that seeing a similar program in operation for just a few hours was worth much more than several days of consultants delivering talks on philosophy.

Some commentators on the outcomes of planned change contend that where innovations fail, particularly innovations in classroom organization, they fail because their planners overlooked the "resocialization" of teachers. Even willing teachers have to go through such a *learning (and unlearning) process* in order to develop new attitudes, behaviors, and skills for a radically new role. Concrete, inquiry-based training activities scheduled regularly over the course of project implementation provide a means for this developmental process to occur.

Adaptive Planning and Staff Meetings

Because of their lack of prior specification, almost all classroom organization projects engaged in adaptive or on-line planning. Planning of this nature is a continuous process that establishes channels of communication and solicits input from a representative group of project participants. It provides a forum for reassessing project goals and activities, monitoring project activities, and modifying practices in light of institutional and project demands. Planning of this nature has a firm base in project and institutional reality; thus issues can be identified and solutions determined before problems become crises. Just as one-shot training activities can neither anticipate the information needs of implementors over time nor be comprehensible to trainees in the absence of direct experience with particular problems, neither can highly structured planning activities that attempt extensive prior specification of operational procedures and objectives effectively address all contingencies in advance or foresee intervening local conditions. Often problems arise and events occur during the course of implementation that are unexpected and unpredictable. As a result, project plans drawn up at one point in time may or may not be relevant to project operations at a later date. Planning activities that are ongoing, adaptive, and congruent with the nature of the project and the changing institutional setting are better able to respond to these factors.

Frequent and regular staff meetings were often used as a way to carry out project planning on a continuous basis. Projects that made a point of scheduling staff meetings on a frequent and regular basis had fewer serious implementation problems and greater staff cohesiveness. Staff meetings not only provided a vehicle for articulating and working out problems, but they also gave staff a chance to communicate project information, share ideas, and provide each other with encouragement and support.

Finding time for these meetings or planning activities was a problem that some districts were able to solve and others were not. One classroom organization project, for example, arranged time off one afternoon a week for meetings. Project participants almost universally singled out these meetings as one of the most important factors contributing to project success. Such time to share ideas and problems was, in the view of all classroom organization respondents, especially important in the rough and exhausting first year of the project. Where meetings were infrequent or irregular, morale was noticeably lower and reports of friction within the project were higher.

Past research on implementation is almost unanimous in citing "unanticipated events" and "lack of feedback networks" as serious problems during project implementation.[4] Routinized and frequent staff meetings combined with ongoing, iterative planning can serve to institutionalize an effective project feedback structure, as well as provide mechanisms that can deal with the unanticipated events that are certain to occur.

Two Open Classroom Projects[5]

The critical role that such elements of an adaptive implementation strategy play in project implementation and outcomes is best illustrated by describing the experiences of two open classroom projects that were similar in almost every respect—resources, support and interest, target group background characteristics—but differed significantly in implementation strategy and in implementation outcome. The Eastown open education project had extensive and ongoing staff training, spent a lot of staff time and energy on materials development, arranged for staff to meet regularly, and engaged in regular formative evaluation. This project was also well implemented, ran smoothly, and met its objectives. In fact, this project received validation as a national exemplary project in its second year—a year before it was theoretically eligible.

The very similar Seaside project, in contrast, did not employ such an implementation strategy. Because of late funding notification, there was little time for advance planning or pre-service training; project teachers were asked to implement a concept that they supported but that few had actually seen in operation. The planning that was done subsequently was mainly administrative in nature. The in-service training was spotty and was offered almost totally by "outside experts." The Seaside project did no materials development but instead tried to convert traditional materials to the goals of open education. This project has not only been less successful than hoped, but in our judgment, its central percepts and objectives are yet to be fully implemented. Teacher classroom behavior exhibits only a very superficial understanding of the rhetoric of open education; our observations led to the conclusion that teachers have yet to understand the practical implications of the tenets of open education, and have made only symbolic use of the more standard methods. For example, in many of the classrooms we visited, although the teacher had set up interest centers, these centers had not been changed in six or seven months. Thus they failed to serve their purpose of providing a continually changing menu of material for students. Teachers in the Seaside project had dutifully rearranged their classroom furniture and acquired rugs—as befits the open classroom—but even in this changed physical space, they continued to conduct their classes in a traditional manner. A student teacher commented that many of the teachers in this school conducted their class in the small groups or individualized manner appropriate to this educational philosophy only on visitors' day. In our judgment, many of the teachers in the school honestly wanted to implement open education, and many sincerely believed that they had accomplished that goal. But, in our view, implementation in this project was only *pro forma*—largely because of the absence of implementation strategies that would allow learning, growth, and development or mutual adaptation to take place.

Summary

In summary, overcoming the challenges and problems inherent to innovations in classroom organization contributes positively and significantly to their effective implementation. The amorphous yet highly complex nature of classroom organization projects tends to *require* or *dictate* an adaptive implementation strategy that permits goals and methods to be reassessed, refined and made explicit during the course of implementation, and that fosters "learning-by-doing."

The adaptive implementation strategies defined by effectively implemented local projects were comprised of three common and critical components—local materials development; concrete, ongoing training; on-line or adaptive planning and regular, frequent staff meetings. These elements worked together in concert to promote effective implementation. Where any one component was missing or weak, other elements of the overall implementation strategy were less effective than they might be. A most important characteristic these component strategies hold in common is their support of individual learning and development—development most appropriate to the user and to the institutional setting. The experience of classroom organization projects underlines the fact that the process of mutual adaptation is fundamentally a learning process.

General Implications

It is useful to consider the implications of the classroom organization projects and the general change-agent study findings in the context of the ongoing debate about the "implementation problem."

The change-agent study is not the first research to point to the primary importance of implementation in determining special project outcomes.[6] A number of researchers and theoreticians have come to recognize what many practitioners have been saying all along: Educational technology is not self-winding. Adoption of a promising educational technology is only the beginning of a variable, uncertain, and inherently local process. It is the unpredictability and inconsistency of this process that have generated what has come to be called the "implementation problem."

There is general agreement that a major component of the "implementation problem" has to do with inadequate operational specificity.[7] There is debate concerning *who* should make project operations more specific, *how* it can be done, and *when* specificity should be introduced.

One approach prescribes more specificity prior to local initiation. Adherents of this solution ask that project planners and developers spell out concrete and detailed steps or procedures that they believe will lead to successful project implementation. It is hoped that increased prior operational specificity will minimize the necessity for individual users to make decisions or choices about appropriate project strategies or resources as the project is implemented. This essentially technological approach to the "implementation problem"— exemplified at the extreme by "teacher-proof" packages—aims at standardizing project implementation across project sites. It is expected that user adherence to such standardized and well-specified implementation procedures will reduce local variability as project plans are translated into practice and so lead to predictable and consistent project outcomes, regardless of the institutional setting in which the project is implemented.

A second approach takes an organizational rather than a technological perspective and focuses primarily on the development of the user, rather than on the prior development of the educational treatment or product. This approach assumes that local variability is not only inevitable, but a good thing if a proposed innovation is to result in significant and sustained change in the local setting. This approach also assumes that the individual learning requisite to successful implementation can only occur through user involvement and direct experience in working through project percepts. Instead of providing packages which foreclose the necessity for individuals to make decisions and choices during the course of project implementation, proponents of this perspective maintain that implementation strategies should be devised that give users the skills, information, and learning opportunities necessary to make these choices effectively. This approach assumes that specificity of project methods and goals should evolve over time in response to local conditions and individual needs. This second solution to the "implementation problem," in short, assumes that mutual adaptation is the key to effective implementation.

The findings of the change-agent study strongly support this second perspective and its general approach to the "implementation problem." We found that *all* successfully implemented projects in our study went through a process of mutual adaptation to some extent. Even fairly straightforward, essentially technological projects were either adapted in some way to the institutional setting—or they were only superficially implemented and were not expected to remain in place after the withdrawal of federal funds. Where attempts were made to take short cuts in this process—out of concern for efficiency, for example—such efforts to speed up project implementation usually led to project breakdown or to only *pro forma* installation of project methods.

Viewed in the context of the debate over the "implementation problem," these findings have a number of implications for change-agent policies and practice. At the most general level, they suggest that adaptation, rather than standardization, is a more realistic and fruitful objective for policy makers and practitioners hoping to bring about significant change in local educational practice. Such an objective would imply change-agent policies that focused on implementation, not simply on adoption—policies that were concerned primarily with the development of users and support of adaptive implementation strategies. Specifically, the classroom organization projects suggest answers to the strategic issues of "who, how, and when" innovative efforts should be made operationally explicit, and how user development can be promoted.

Furthermore, the classroom organization projects, as well as other innovative efforts examined as part of the change-agent study, imply that the would-be innovator also must be willing to learn and be motivated by professional concerns and interests if development is to take place. Thus, change-agent policies would be well advised not only to address the user needs that are part of the implementation process *per se*, but also to consider the developmental needs of local educational personnel that are requisite to the initial interest and support necessary for change-agent efforts. It is not surprising that teachers or administrators who have not been outside their district for a number of years are less eager to change—or confident in their abilities to do so—than planners would hope. Internships and training grants for administrators, or travel money and released time for teachers to participate in innovative practices in other districts, are examples of strategies that may enable educational personnel to expand their horizons and generate enthusiasm for change.

The findings of the change-agent study and the experience of the classroom organization projects also have implications for the dissemination and expansion of "successful" change-agent projects. They suggest, for example, that an effective dissemination strategy should have more to do with people who could provide concrete "hands-on" assistance than with the transcription and transferral of specific successful project operations. It is somewhat ironic that staff of the "developer-demonstrator" projects who last year pointed to the central importance of local materials development are, in their dissemination year, packaging their project strategies and materials without a backward glance. Indeed, the change-agent findings concerning the importance of mutual adaptation and "learning by doing" raise a number of critical questions for educational planners and disseminators. For example, to what extent can this developmental process be telescoped as project accomplishments are replicated in a new setting? What kinds of "learning" or advice can be transferred? If adaptation is characteristic of effective implementation and significant change, what constitutes the "core" or essential ingredients of a successful project?

District administrators hoping to expand successful project operations face similar issues. Our findings suggest that—even within the same district—replication and expansion of "success" will require that new adopters replicate, in large measure, the developmental process of the original site. While there are, of course, general "lessons" that original participants can transfer to would-be innovators, there is much that the new user will have to learn himself.

In summary, the experience of classroom organization projects together with the general change-agent study findings suggest that adaptation should be seen as an appropriate goal for practice and policy—not an undesirable aberration. These findings suggest a shift in change-agent policies from a primary focus on the *delivery system* to an emphasis on the *deliverer*. An important lesson that can be derived from the change-agent study is that unless the developmental needs of the users are addressed, and unless project methods are modified to suit the needs of the user and the institutional setting, the promises of new technologies are likely to be unfulfilled. Although the implementation strategy that classroom organization projects suggest will be effective represent "reinvention of the wheel" to a great extent—an unpalatable prospect for program developers, fiscal planners, and impatient educational policy makers—the experience of these projects counsels us that a most important aspect of significant change is not so much the "wheel" or the educational technology but the process of "reinvention" or individual development. Though new education technologies are undoubtedly important to improved practices, they cannot be effective unless they are thoroughly understood and integrated by the user. The evidence we have seen strongly suggests that the developmental process mutual adaptation is the best way to ensure that change efforts are not superficial, trivial, or transitory.

Notes

1. This essay is a revision of a paper presented at the March 1975 American Educational Research Association meeting in Washington, D.C. It is based on the data collected for The Rand Corporation study of federal programs supporting educational change. However, the interpretation and speculations offered in this paper are my sole responsibility and do not necessarily represent the views of The Rand Corporation, or the study's sponsor, the United States Office of Education, or my colleague Paul Berman, who has been so helpful in formulating this paper.

2. The conceptual model, methodology, and results of the first year of the Rand Change-Agent Study are reported in four volumes: Paul Berman and Milbrey Wallin McLaughlin. *Federal Programs Supporting Educational Change, Vol. I: A Model of Educational Change.* Santa Monica, Calif.: Rand Corporation, R-1589/1-HEW, April 1975; Paul Berman and Edward W. Pauly, *Federal Programs Supporting Educational Change, Vol. II: Factors Affecting Change Agent Projects.* Santa Monica, Calif.: Rand Corporation, R-1589/2-HEW, April 1975; Peter W. Greenwood, Dale Mann, and Milbrey Wallin McLaughlin. *Federal Programs Supporting Educational Change, Vol. III: The Process of Change.* Santa Monica, Calif.: Rand Corporation, R-1589/3-HEW, April 1975; and Paul Berman and Milbrey Wallin McLaughlin. *Federal Programs Supporting Educational Change, Vol. IV: The Findings in Review.* Santa Monica, Calif.: Rand Corporation, R-1589/4-HEW, April 1975. Four technical appendices to Volume III describe in detail the federal program management approach, state education agency participation, and case studies for each of the programs in the study.
3. E. Rogers and F. Shoemaker. *Communication of Innovation.* New York, N.Y.: Free Press, 1962.
4. See for example, W. W. Charters et al. *Contrasts in the Process of Planning Change of the School's Institutional Organization, Program 20.* Eugene, Ore.: Center for the Advanced Study of Educational Administration, 1973; O. Carlson et al. *Change Processes in the Public Schools.* Eugene, Ore.: Center for the Advanced Study of Educational Administration, 1971; M. Fullan and A. Pomfret. *Review of Research on Curriculum Implementation.* Toronto, Ont.: The Ontario Institute for Studies in Education, April 1975; M. Shipman. *Inside a Curriculum Project.* London, Eng.: Methuen, 1974; N.C. Gross et al. *Implementing Organizational Innovations.* New York, N.Y.: Basic Books, 1971; and L.M. Smith and P.M. Keith. *Anatomy of Educational Innovations: An Organizational Analysis of an Elementary School.* New York, N.Y.: John Wiley, 1971.
5. Project and site names are fictitious.
6. See especially the analysis of this debate in Pullan and Pomfret, *op. cit.* See also E.C. Hargrove. *The Missing Link: The Study of the Implementation of Social Policy.* Washington, D.C.: The Urban Institute, 1975, paper 797–1; and W. Williams, "Implementation Analysis and Assessment," Public Policy Paper No.8, Institute of Governmental Research, University of Washington, February 1975.
7. See Pullan and Pomfret, *op. cit.*

Part Four

After a Century of Curriculum Thought: Change and Continuity

Introduction to Part Four

Our purpose in this last section of the *Reader* is to sample the contemporary field of curriculum studies. In doing so, we introduce a range of topics as we have found that focusing on recent scholarship is often a tricky business. A challenge that we did not face in summarizing the previous readings is that in our final section we lack the advantages of hindsight. As scholarship ages, its significance seems to emerge almost like the images in a developing photograph. But with contemporary work we are still guessing. What makes a given line of inquiry a part of the curriculum field? Or does it more properly belong to some other specialization? And if a line of scholarship is included within the broad category of curriculum studies, how central is it to the field? When do particular studies represent the influence of other fields, and when do they represent contributions? What counts as pioneering work, or work that is likely to make a difference in the next generation of curriculum scholarship? All of these questions are difficult and contested.

In selecting and organizing the particular articles that follow, we have sought to steer a general course by acknowledging both change and continuity in the field's contemporary landscape. All of the following articles are conceptually linked (in various ways) to the traditions represented in earlier sections of the *Reader*. This continuity is what gives the readings a family resemblance common to curriculum scholarship *per se*. At the same time, many of the readings either cross into other fields or signal new directions for previous work. On both counts, we looked for scholarship that did not simply follow the beaten path.

The inseparability of change and continuity is important for practical reasons. If we were concerned only with the field's responsiveness to political headlines, the following scholarship would represent little more than a survey of last season's curricular fashions. Veteran scholars know that today's hot topics in the educational press may well be tomorrow's forgotten curiosities. But if we were to take the other extreme, concerned solely with continuity, our selection would include just those authors who are undisputed "curriculum" scholars and only those readings that focus on developments internal to the field. To do so is to risk talking to only the select and relatively few scholars in our particular "discourse." And a preoccupation with who we are as curriculum scholars may detract from the influence of broader educational trends. On occasion it has seemed that our field has been caught unaware as contemporary movements marched over the horizon and out of sight, leaving us to play catch-up.

We hope our selections avoid both the extremes of faddism and intellectual stasis. The first chapter cuts through this tension. In an excerpt from *A Post-Modern Perspective on Curriculum*, William Doll Jr. argues that our role as scholars is to bring the curriculum field into our post-modern era. On the one hand, the need to update curriculum thought, to move it forward with the times, signals a break from the past, and especially a break from modernism (Miller, 2010). On the other hand, breaking from tradition is itself something of a tradition in the field following Bobbitt, Dewey, and Tyler. To group Doll with the likes of Bobbitt and Tyler may seem inappropriate, but regardless of how we categorize this author, Doll's alternative to the Tyler rationale opens up intriguing questions around the criteria he labels *Richness* (a curriculum's depth of meaning), *Recursion* (the complex structures that support critical reflection), *Relations* (the intersecting of curriculum and cultures), and *Rigor* (a commitment to exploration).

Whereas Doll seeks to supplant tradition, the second reading by Peter Hlebowitsh's sees current changes in the field as moderating. This author's argument is that the "new age for curriculum studies" differs from past reconceputalist thought by opening new possibilities for "centripetal" dialogue around the field's canon or disciplinarity. Hlebowitsh's argument is important because it addresses the question of what comes after reconceptualization. This question has been addressed before, perhaps most directly at a 2006 conference dubbed "Next Moments in Curriculum Studies" (Malewski, 2010). The best of intentions to explore post-reconceptualization somewhat fizzled in this context due largely to generational differences among the conference participants. Hlebowitsh's approach sides with many of the senior scholars at the 2006 conference in urging that we reconsider the field's need for greater coherence and synthesis across longstanding tensions between theory and practice as well as among ideological divides.

These tensions among curriculum theorists have unfolded during a lengthy period during which policymakers have again looked to top-down approaches to school reform. The next article, by Wayne Au, is titled "High-Stakes Testing and Curricular Control: A Qualitative Metasynthesis." It serves to introduce the broader trends related to testing, the standards movement, and school accountability as tools to coerce reform. For example, by the opening years of the twenty-first century, *No Child Left Behind* mandated testing and it was widely assumed that the curriculum would increasingly conform to what was tested: teachers would teach to the test. That is, the curriculum would narrow, thus reducing opportunities, for example, for curricular enrichment and individualization of instruction.

Through his analysis of 49 qualitative studies, Au concludes that generally the curriculum is narrowed by high-stakes testing with, for example, instructional emphasis on fragmented pieces of knowledge that are expected to appear on the test. He also concludes, however, that in a significant minority of cases high-stakes testing is associated with enriching curriculum through ways such as integration of knowledge. Thus the general effects of high-stakes testing need to be qualified in much the same way that research by Susan Stodolsky (1999) qualified the old saw that teachers teach by following the textbook: "Too little attention has been given," Stodolsky warned, "to the nature of the books in relation to their use" (p. 145).

The next chapter, by Christine Sleeter and Jamy Stillman, looks at curriculum control in California via content standards in reading/language arts and social studies. Adopting Basil Bernstein's constructs on how curriculum is classified (i.e. how knowledge boundaries and hierarchies are established) and framed (i.e. the degree to which teachers and students have authority use the curriculum to their own ends and in their own ways), they discern that content standards have been about far more than the declared aim of improving learning through standardizing subject matter. They charge that the standards have been used, for example, to "sanitize" ethnic conflict, value competence in English but not the first languages of English language learners, and, as Apple (this volume, Chapter 15) puts it, control the work of teachers. Given the breadth of their topic, Sleeter and Stillman inevitably must deal in generalizations about curriculum design, some of which readers might well question. Nevertheless, the weight of evidence clearly suggests their thesis cannot easily be dismissed.

While standards-based accountability, including recent common-core standards, have placed renewed emphasis on reading and mathematics, the next reading by Leslie Siskin focuses on how high school subjects "outside the core" have responded to this trend. Siskin's report is part of a larger study that examined how the standards movement has played out across various subjects, locations, and different types of schools. Siskin looks specifically at music. Like other subjects, music holds a particular status in the hierarchy of secondary school curricula, affecting how it garners resources. Music also differs from many subjects in its assessment strategies and in traditions. To explore how these concerns shape responses to high-stakes accountability, Siskin examines schools in Kentucky. This state is unlike most others in deciding to include music as a tested subject. With this decision, as Siskin notes, music teachers faced a number of practical challenges, not the least of which was finding agreement on what knowledge and skills across the wide scope of this subject would be appropriate for all students and thus what knowledge and skills should be required for a student to graduate.

In the next reading Elliot Eisner contends that we should know more about schools than simply how well their students score on a standardized test. Eisner has been a consistent voice deploring recent reforms for setting the educational bar too low and devaluing rather than capitalizing on individual differences. He asks us to think more deeply about what schools might accomplish by imagining a temporary halt to all testing. Without the scores, what questions would we ask to determine the quality of any given school? Some of Eisner's own questions include: What forms of thinking do school experiences invite? Are these experiences connected to life outside of school, and do they encourage multiple forms of literacy? Will these experiences help students form their own purposes, work cooperatively, cultivate their personal talents, and take an active part in assessing their own achievements? Eisner admits that these are difficult questions to answer, but he also contends that such questions are at the heart of what matters in schools.

The next four readings take up this theme of valuing diversity and the challenges this presents for curriculum design and implementation. The first reading is by Angela Valenzuela. She examines how dominant English-speaking culture affects schooling for children of Mexican descent. Valenzuela studied a large, comprehensive inner-city high school in Houston where virtually all the students are Mexican (45 percent immigrants and 55 percent U.S. born). Eighty-one percent of the teachers are non-Latino and 19 percent Latino.

Her thesis is that a process of "de-Mexicanization" was taking place, by which schools "subtract" cultural resources from students. Thus, although schooling is supposed to be "additive," for many of the students she observed the opposite happened. She sees two main reasons for this plight. First, students' culture and language, which are "consequential to their achievement and orientations toward school," are devalued by the school and education system more generally. Second, the school and the system see the students as unresponsive or even hostile to well-intentioned efforts to educate them. Regardless of the students' nativity, Valenzuela argues, education is understood in Mexican culture as more than just book knowledge but also "to live responsibly in the world as a caring human being, respectful of the individuality and dignity of others" (this volume, Chapter 25). Valenzuela finds this view of education to fit closely with Nel Noddings' theory of care. For Noddings, *authentic caring* is premised on *relation*, in this case between students and teachers or administrators. Thus, while the teachers charged that students don't *care about* their schoolwork, such caring is unlikely to happen until these students' expectations of being *cared for* are met.

The second reading in this group is authored by Elaine Chan who describes a study conducted in Canada. While the location differs, the themes in her article hold more than a passing similarity to the studies conducted in California by Sleeter and Stillman (this volume, Chapter 22) and Texas by Valenzuela (this volume, Chapter 25). Chan studied two teachers at a school in a Toronto neighborhood with a diverse population, many of whom were immigrants. The teachers tried to acknowledge the ethnic, linguistic, and religious diversity of their students and the community in their curriculum and teaching practices.

Chan's report focuses on the "complications and challenges" that arise in organizing a 4-day field trip for an outdoor education activity, which school personnel saw as holding strong educational potential. The two teachers soon found, however, that a number of parents did not wish their children to go on the trip. The reasons varied but all were related in one way or another to diversity of views and needs among the school's varied constituents. For example, one parent was opposed to the field trip because the student was needed at home as a caregiver for a younger sibling; another parent did not believe girls should go on such a trip; and so on. Chan underscores how diversity has layers of meaning affecting school communities that go beyond multicultural content or culturally sensitive pedagogy. It is no simple task, apparently, to respect diversities that may have contradictory tenets. Indeed, Chan ponders the question: "What does it mean for a school community to be "accepting" of diversity?" (this volume, Chapter 26).

In the next reading Dennis Sumara and Brent Davis argue that curriculum has an obligation to interrupt heteronormative thinking. They focus on two research projects that use queer theory to critically examine a number of curriculum issues. Queer theory has been an established sub-genre of educational research for over two decades. It draws on curriculum and educational traditions specifically to understand the socio-cultural and political constructions of desire and sexuality. Through the applications of queer theory, Sumara and Davis write, "the possibilities for what might count as knowledge are broadened—not just knowledge about sexuality, but knowledge about how forms of desire are inextricable from processes of perception, cognition, and interpretation. Queer theory does not ask that pedagogy *become* sexualized, but that it excavate and interpret the way it is already *is* sexualized" (emphasis in original).

Whereas Sumara and Davis raise possibilities for what might be, in the next reading Stephen Thornton looks at the silence surrounding what is. Thornton argues that although gay issues are a visible part of public life in the contemporary United States, they are avoided in schools and especially absent in social studies curricula. Not only can this absence be damning in itself, but it entirely dismisses the question of how sexual orientation should be represented, on what terms, and from whose perspective. Avoiding these questions leaves students in the hands of what Thornton calls "the hidden curriculum everyone sees." This is a curriculum that stigmatizes any deviance from heterosexual experience, which Thornton notes "is surely one of the most successful exercises in social training that schools perform" (this volume, Chapter 28).

The next two readings do not so much leave diversity as a theme but insert it in the issue of citizenship in times of globalization and post-communism. In the first of these articles, Peggy McIntosh looks at what gender means in education for citizenship in a globalizing world. Citizenship and education about it, she notes, has traditionally been gendered, with its very definition being centered fundamentally in male experience rather than a human experience. With vivid autobiographical detail McIntosh lays out what curriculum, and the essentials of teacher education to support it, for citizenship in a globalizing world might look like if women's experience was given equal weight with men's experience.

The next reading by Thomas Misco is concerned with the implementation of a Holocaust curriculum in the "overlapping historical, community, and political contexts" of post-communist Latvia. Misco uses McLaughlin's (this volume, Chapter 18) lens of "implementation as mutual adaptation" to explore this curriculum reform. He concludes that, in the complex circumstances, employing a mutual adaptation paradigm proved the only useful method of understanding what was happening. Simply looking for fidelity to the curriculum designers' intentions, Misco explains, would have been "fatuous" since it would not illuminate how the curriculum was used and why. On the other hand, merely focusing on classroom enactment of the curriculum would have failed to incorporate significant factors affecting implementation external to the classroom.

The next and final two readings, by Christy M. Moroye and by Nel Noddings, also relate to adapting curriculum to the new demands of changing times. Both Moroye and Noddings follow in the footsteps of Alfred North Whitehead (1929) when he spoke of "stretching" curriculum from within. That is, rather than simply displacing an existing curriculum re-designing it internally.

Moroye is alarmed by the growing ecological threat to the world. At the same time, she observes, environmental education has remained "on the fringe" of curriculum in American schools. While Moroye would prefer this was not so, she chooses for now to look at how some teachers *do* insert environmental lessons into the standard subjects of the curriculum such as English and geography. In this way, Moroye illuminates what she calls a "complementary ecological curriculum."

Finally, Noddings notes how the traditional disciplines of a hundred years ago still dominate the secondary-school curriculum. She contends that this curriculum fails in educating adolescents to lead satisfying lives. Nor does it, she maintains, feature the skills required for twenty-first-century occupations. While she would like to see the curriculum replaced by something else, she doubts this will happen. So, instead, she proposes how the traditional disciplines can be stretched from within. Noddings moves beyond the abstract and presents compelling suggestions for how school programs in English, science, and social studies might be redesigned to realize twenty-first-century goals.

References

Malewski, E. (2010). *Curriculum studies handbook: The next moment.* New York: Routledge.

Miller, J. L. (2010). Postmodernism. In C. Cridel (Ed.), *Encyclopedia of curriculum studies* (pp. 666–669). Thousand Oaks, CA: Sage.

Stodolsky, S. S. (1999). Is teaching really by the book? In M. J. Early & K. J. Rehage (Eds.), *Issues in curriculum* (pp. 141–168). Chicago: National Society for the Study of Education.

Whitehead, A. N. (1929). *The aims of education and other essays.* New York: Macmillan.

19

The Four R's—An Alternative to the Tyler Rationale

William E. Doll Jr.

The three R's of "Readin', 'Ritin', and 'Rithmetic" were late nineteenth- and early twentieth-century creations, geared to the needs of a developing industrial society. Reading was the functional reading of sales slips and bills of lading, combined with the inspirational stories of Horatio Alger and the moral aphorisms of McGuffey. Writing was literally penmanship, with the Palmer method introducing a ledger-oriented style in the first grade. Such cursive training had to begin early, for by the fifth grade half of those who had entered as first graders had left. Arithmetic, not mathematics, was essentially column addition and subtraction, with algorithmic multiplication and division coming in the later elementary years. Again, the emphasis was on store clerk functionalism, keeping the sales slips and ledgers accurate and neat. Problem solving was introduced as early as the second grade, but it was heavily, if not exclusively, associated with buying in an urban store.

Born in the early 1930s, I had my early elementary school training in these three R's. My word-lists for reading and spelling prepared me for the urban, industrial society my parents and I inhabited. The Palmer method was begun in the first grade, with an itinerant teacher brought in weekly to instruct us in the big O's and C's so distinctive of its style—flowing but clear. From Miss Wiley, Miss James, and Miss Thatcher—the maiden ladies who taught grades one, two, and three—I learned to keep my ten's column digits out of my hundred's column or my unit's column, and *always* beginning with the right column to "bring down" a single digit and to "carry" into the next column any digits left over. Miss Newcomb in the fourth grade made a small modification to this "consonant" method—namely, that with decimals it was the decimal points which needed to form a vertical, unbroken phalanx. Zeros were added to the right of the decimal point to keep the right column, the hundredths (often considered as pennies), in line.

Mr. Bartlett, our corner grocer, was not as good as my triumvirate of maiden teachers at keeping his columns straight. Further, he began his addition with the left, not the right column. When questioned he stated that he wished to make no mistakes with the dollars or dimes and this method assured him greater accuracy with those important columns. Worse, he grouped digits together either in his head or with small notations in combinations equal to ten. This method intrigued me. I passed on my newfound wisdom to Miss Thatcher (married women were not allowed to teach school). She, however, dismissed Mr. Bartlett's methods as heresy. In retrospect, I think Mr. Bartlett was more industrially oriented than Miss Thatcher and maybe even a better pedagogue. In dealing with my own elementary school classes, I have found that much columnar addition—at least of any practical type—has a better "feel" when it is done left to right, thus allowing intuition and estimation to come into play. Further, doing simple columnar work by grouping numerals into combinations of ten not only produces more accurate and quicker answers but also encourages structural and situational thinking—for example, doing 101–49 as 102–50, or maybe as 100–50 with two added on. Such "chaotic ordering" has been a hallmark of my students' *modus operandi* for many years now—before I read Whitehead or heard of postmodernism; it has generally served them well (Doll, 1977, 1989).

At first glance one does not see a connection between the Tyler rationale and the three R's. However, a pre-set functionalism underlies both. While Tyler's frame expands and broadens industrial functionalism beyond the sales slips and ledgers of the three R's, the assumption of pre-set goals still exists. In this frame, *goals* do not emerge—as Cvitanovi? suggests they should—by "playing with" experiences; rather, goals are pre-determined as are the *experiences* and *methods* for developing those experiences. All are firmly in place before any interaction with students occurs. *Evaluations* are designed to correlate the experiences only with the pre-set goals, not to explore what the students generate personally after reflecting on the experiences. In fact, as was pointed out earlier in the chapter, framing evaluation in terms of generation, reflection, transformation is virtually oxymoronic from a modernist perspective.

So what would serve as criteria for a curriculum designed to foster a post-modern view? What criteria might we use to evaluate the quality of a post-modern curriculum—a curriculum generated not predefined, indeterminate yet bounded, exploring the "fascinating imaginative realm born of God's laughter," and made up of an ever-increasing network of "local universalities?" I suggest the four R's of Richness, Recursion, Relations and Rigor might serve this purpose.

Richness. This term refers to a curriculum's depth, to its layers of meaning, to its multiple possibilities or interpretations. In order for students and teachers to transform and be transformed, a curriculum needs to have the "right amount" of *indeterminacy, anomaly, inefficiency, chaos, disequilibrium, dissipation, lived experience*—to use words and phrases already described. Just what is the "right amount" for the curriculum to be provocatively generative without losing form or shape cannot be laid out in advance. This issue is one to be continually negotiated among students, teachers, and texts (the latter having long histories and basic assumptions that cannot be neglected). But the issue of the curriculum needing disturbing qualities is not to be negotiated; these qualities form the problematics of life itself and are the essence of a rich and transforming curriculum. Another way to state this is to say that the *problematics, perturbations, possibilities* inherent in a curriculum are what give the curriculum not only its richness but also its sense of being, its *dasein.*

The main academic disciplines taught in schools have their own historical contexts, fundamental concepts, and final vocabularies. Hence, each will interpret richness in its own way. Language—including reading, writing, literature, and oral communication—develops its richness by focusing heavily (but not exclusively) on the interpretation of metaphors, myths, narratives. Saying this places language within a hermeneutic frame; it is to see language as integrated with culture, as one of the determinants of culture.

Mathematics—a subject in which computational arithmetic plays but a small part—takes its form of richness from "playing with patterns." Obviously, this can be done *par excellence* with computers—tools that any mathematically rich curriculum should possess—but computers are not a *sine qua non.* Patterns may be seen, developed; played with in simple number combinations (as with the Fibonnaci series) or with geometry of both a Euclidean and fractal sort. Breaking a square into right triangles is an example of the former; the Sierpinski triangle is an example of the latter. At all levels, from kindergarten through graduate school, mathematics can be dealt with meaningfully as "playing with patterns."

Science—including the biological and the physical—can be seen as intuiting, developing, probing, "proving" hypotheses concerning the world in which we live. This moves science beyond the collection of "facts"—with the assumption these facts are objective bits of reality—into the realm of manipulating, creating, working with facts or information in an imaginative and (thermo)dynamic manner. This view of science is obviously more Whiteheadian than Newtonian, more oriented toward Prigogine than Laplace. The social sciences—those multiple disciplines of anthropology, economics, history, psychology, and sociology—take their concept of richness from dialoguing about, or negotiating passages between, various (often competing) interpretations of societal issues. Here, probably more than in any other discipline, assumptions are questioned. It is these assumed givens that form the foundations of society's mores, norms, standards; and in a democratic society it is imperative these givens be open to dialogue.

Obviously these disciplines, their languages, and histories are not mutually exclusive. The concept of developing richness through dialogue, interpretations, hypothesis generation and proving, and pattern playing can apply to all we do in curriculum. Again, such ideas sound strange to those imbued with a modernist perspective, which helps explain why we need to transcend this perspective to a post-modernist one.

Recursion. From recur, to happen again,[1] recursion usually is associated with the mathematical operation of iteration. In iteration a formula is "run" over and over, with the output of one equation being the input for the next. In $y = 3x + 1$, a y of 4 (if the $x = 1$) becomes the next x, and the new y of 13 becomes the next x, and so on. In such iterations, there is both stability and change; the formula stays the same, the variables change (in an orderly but often nonpredictable manner). As was explained earlier, some interesting complex patterns develop with particular formulae and particular x, y variables.

However, when Bruner (1986) states that "any formal theory of mind is helpless without recursion" (p. 97)—and asserts the importance of recursion for epistemology and pedagogy—he refers less to mathematics and more to the human capacity of having thoughts loop back on themselves. Such looping, thoughts on thoughts, distinguishes human consciousness; it is the way we make meaning. As Bruner says:

> Much of the process of education consists of being able to distance oneself in some way from what one knows by being able to reflect on one's own knowledge. (p. 127)

This is also the way one produces a sense of self, through reflective interaction with the environment, with others, with a culture. As I pointed out earlier, such "recursive reflection" lies at the heart of a transformative curriculum; it is *the process* which Dewey, Piaget, Whitehead all advocate. In the 1960s Bruner made a beginning at defining a recursive curriculum with his "spiral curriculum" (1960) and his elementary school social studies program, "Man: A Course of Study" (1966). However, in our then-modernist mode both of these were mis-seen, attaining only popular approval and notoriety. Their power never became evident; the former got lost in the question of calculus for first graders, the latter in the issue of Bruner's patriotism.

In a curriculum that honors, values, uses recursion, there is no fixed beginning or ending. As Dewey has pointed out, every ending is a new beginning, every beginning emerges from a prior ending. Curriculum segments, parts, sequences are arbitrary chunks that, instead of being seen as isolated units, are seen as opportunities for reflection. In such a frame, every test, paper, journal entry can be seen not merely as the completion of one project but also as the beginning of another—to explore, discuss, inquire into both ourselves as meaning makers and into the text in question. This curriculum will, of course, be open not closed; like post-modernism itself, it is Janus-faced, eclectic, interpretive.

Recursion and repetition differ in that neither one, in any way, reflects the other. Repetition, a strong element in the modernist mode, is designed to improve set performance. Its frame is closed. Recursion aims at developing competence—the ability to organize, combine, inquire, use something heuristically. Its frame is open. The functional difference between repetition and recursion lies in the role reflection plays in each. In repetition, reflection plays a negative role; it breaks the process. There is a certain automaticity to repetition that keeps the same process going—over and over and over, as in flash card arithmetic drills or in ball machine tennis drills. In recursion, reflection plays a positive role; for thoughts to leap back on themselves, as in Dewey's secondary experience reflecting back on primary experience, or in Piaget's reflexive intelligence reflecting back on practical intelligence, it is necessary, as Bruner has said, to step back from one's doings, to "distance oneself in some way" from one's own thoughts.[2] Thus, in recursion it is a necessity to have others—peers, teachers—look at, critique, respond to what one has done. Dialogue becomes the *sine qua non* of recursion: Without reflection—engendered by dialogue—recursion becomes shallow not transformative; it is not reflective recursion, it is only repetition.

Relations. The concept of relations is important to a post-modern, transformative curriculum in two ways: in a *pedagogical* way and in a *cultural* way. The former might, naturally, be called pedagogical relations, referring to those within the curriculum—the matrix or network which gives it richness. The latter might, just as naturally, be called cultural relations, referring to those cultural or cosmological relations which lie outside the curriculum but form a large matrix within which the curriculum is embedded. Both relations are important; each complements the other.

In focusing on *pedagogical relations*, one focuses on the connections within a curriculum's structure which give the curriculum its depth as this is developed by recursion. Here the twin processes of doing and reflecting-on-doing are important, and through these processes the curriculum becomes richer with the passage of time. As Prigogine is fond of saying, time in a Newtonian frame is *reversible and unimportant*; in the dissipative structure frames he studies, it is *irreversible and important* (1988; with Stengers, 1984, Ch. 7). If the universe is already set, time does no more than give one the chance to "see" more of that universe. "Mastery learning" assumes this frame—the student is to take the time necessary to master the material presented to a certain, predetermined level of repetitious proficiency (Torshen, 1977). In a universe of and in process, time takes on a different, qualitative dimension; it acquires a transformative aspect, since development of one sort or another is always occurring. Conditions, situations, relations are always changing; the present does not recreate the past (though it is certainly influenced by the past) nor does the present determine the future (though it is an influencer). So, too, the curriculum frame operating at the beginning of the course is unavoidably different from the curriculum frame operating at the end of the course.

The issue is not difference but degree or quality of difference—whether the difference is a difference that makes a difference.

Recognizing the contingency of relations, and hoping that these relations will be positively and communally developed during the course of a semester, I organize my undergraduate and graduate university courses to enhance this development. Among the devices I use, one is to provide a syllabus that lists common readings for only two-thirds of the course; for the last third various groups choose their readings from a selected list. Class time is devoted not to summarizing these various readings but to interconnecting them to both the common readings and to each other. The quality of discussion improves as the semester *develops*; so, too, papers written early in the semester improve dramatically when rewritten and reframed after utilizing the insights gained. Sometimes the change is transformative.

In junior high classes, where I have often used a set text, I build time-oriented relationships by asking students to reframe the material presented, to choose from or reframe chapter questions, and to deal with the textual material on both a "what-if" (imaginary) basis and a "relate-it-to-yourself" (real) basis. In dealing with elementary school grades, I follow the same general procedures but use far more manipulative materials, story telling, projects, and dramatic presentations. The textbook, throughout all this, is seen as something to revise, not as something to follow. It is the base from which transformation occurs. Curriculum in a post-modern frame needs to be created (self-organized) by the classroom community, not by textbook authors.

It should be obvious in all these personal anecdotes that, in building a curriculum matrix with a rich set of relationships, I have been strongly influenced by Whitehead's (1929/1967) dictum to "not teach too many subjects" but to "teach thoroughly" what I do teach, and to let the main ideas "be thrown into every combination possible" (p. 2).

The concept of *cultural relations* grows out of a hermeneutic cosmology—one which emphasizes narration and dialogue as key vehicles in interpretation. Narration brings forward the concepts of history (through story), language (through oral telling), and place (through a story's locality). Dialogue interrelates these three to provide us with a sense of culture that is local in origin but global in interconnections. Thus, all our interpretations relate to local culture and interconnect with other cultures and their interpretations via a global matrix. Discourse (narration and dialogue) operates, then, within such a double-tiered cultural frame; it does this far more so than within the foundationalist, abstract, and privileged frame modernism posited. Discourse now becomes what Jim Cheney (1989) calls "contextualist" (p. 123)—bound always by the localness of ourselves, our histories, our language, our place, but also expanding into an ever-broadening global and ecological network. It is this double-tiered or dual-focused nature that makes cultural relations so complex.

Recognizing the contextualist nature of discourse helps us realize that the constructs of those participating frame all conversations, all acts of teaching. As teachers we cannot, do not, transmit information directly; rather, we perform the teaching act when we help others negotiate passages between their constructs and ours, between ours and others'. This is why Dewey says teaching is an interactive process with learning a *by-product* of that interaction.

Modernism has not adopted such an interrelational view; it has taken as one of its hallmarks movement beyond the local and contextual to the universal and abstract. Instead of the narrational, it has aimed for, indeed created, the *meta*narrational, the *grand écrit* Lyotard attacks. Teachers, fitting unconsciously into this paradigm—as we all do—have unwittingly carried on their discourses with students by speaking *ex cathedra*. Too often, teacher explanations have resounded with the authority of God; too rarely have meaningful, interactive, participating dialogues been held.

C.A. Bowers (1987; with Flinders, 1990) has tied the concept of cultural relationships to the ecological crises we face today. In doing this he draws our attention to modernism's overly strong sense of individualism. Individualism has tended to pit humanity against nature (civilization is defined as society improving on nature) and to believe that progress occurs through competition, not cooperation. This is one of modernism's myths founded on beliefs like Bacon's that we should *subject Nature to the hand of man*. This statement would be abhorrent, even sacrilegious, to pre-modern or tribal cultures such as the North American Indian.

But this belief in competition and the virtue of controlling the natural is part of our present day pedagogy and cosmology. Bowers, Griffin, and Oliver (also Lydon, 1992) are among the few curricularists who encourage us to rethink our concept of relations, who see that *cultural relationships* extend beyond our personal selves to include the ecosystem—indeed the cosmos in which we live. Only now, in the past decade or so, are we beginning to develop a cosmic and interrelational consciousness. The challenge of such recognition is twofold: on the one hand, to honor the localness of our perceptions and, on the other hand, to realize that our local perspectives integrate into a larger cultural, ecological, cosmic matrix. Our progress and our existence—as individuals, as communities, as a race, as a species, as a life form—depend on our ability to bring these two perspectives into complementary harmony.

Rigor. In some ways the most important of the four criteria, rigor keeps a transformative curriculum from falling into either "rampant relativism" or sentimental solipsism. In presenting transformation as an alternative to our current measurement frame, it is easy to see transformation as no more than anti-measurement or nonmeasurement. Here, transformation becomes not a true alternative but yet another variation on the very thing it tries to replace. This certainly happened in the progressive and open education movements. Dewey wrestled with the problem in the progressive education movement and wrote "Need for a Philosophy of Education" to explain why progressive education needed to be more than anti-traditional, why progressive education had to have its own foundation and frame. In contrasting his view of progressive education—developmental and transformative—with either the received progressive view (which he considered too romantic) or the established traditional view (which he considered too rigid), he said:

> This alternative is not just a middle course or compromise between the two procedures. It is something radically different from either. Existing likes and powers are to be treated as possibilities. (1934/1964, p. 8)

In such a transformative frame, with its emphasis on indeterminacy, shifting relationships, and spontaneous self-organization, rigor wears a very different set of clothes than it did in the modernist frame. Rigor began, at least in the scholastic sense, with the Jesuits' Q.E.D.—"Quod Erat Demonstrandum" (thus it is demonstrated)—from the deductive power of their Aristotlean-based logic. Descartes objected to this logic, replacing it with his own "clear and distinct" ideas—those which no reasonable person could doubt, those he received from God, but also ones he "saw" with his mind's eye. Rigor thus moved from Aristotlean-Euclidean logic to deeply felt perceptions and conceptions. The English empiricists wanted to move rigor yet again, away from subjective states, no matter how personally appealing, to the objective and observable. Here rigor entered a world that could be measured and manipulated. Our present twentieth-century concept of rigor has elements of all these strains—scholastic logic, scientific observation, and mathematical precision.

To think of rigor without these qualities is to call for a virtual redefinition of the concept. Rigor in a post-modern frame requires just this. It draws on qualities foreign to a modernist frame—interpretation and indeterminacy, to mention but two. In dealing with indeterminacy, one can never be certain one "has it right"—not even to the 95th or 99th percentile of probability. One must continually be exploring, looking for new combinations, interpretations, patterns. This is why, in his scientific methodology, Dewey (1933/1971) listed the fourth stage as "the mental elaboration of an idea" (p. 107), "developing the relations of ideas to one another" (p. 113), and "playing with concepts" (p. 182). Here we find echoes and presagings of statements made by Whitehead, Kuhn, Bruner—not to close too early or finally on the rightness of an idea, to throw all ideas into various combinations. Here rigor means purposely looking for different alternatives, relations, connections. Michel Serres does this well, as shown in his wolf and sheep essay, drawing together LaFontaine's fable and Descartes' right method.

In dealing with interpretation rigorously, one needs to be aware that all valuations depend on (often hidden) assumptions. As frames differ so do the problems, procedures, and valued results. Rigor here means the conscious attempt to ferret out these assumptions, ones we or others hold dear, as well as negotiating passages between these assumptions, so the dialogue may be meaningful and transformative. As Iser points out, dialogue between reader and text is a two-way process, each has a voice, and in this dialogue there is a combining of determinacy and indeterminacy. Indeterminacy here does not mean arbitrariness; rather, it "allows [for] a spectrum of actualization" (1978, p. 24)—better yet, it allows for a range of possibilities from which actualizations appear. Which actualization does appear for development depends on the interaction process itself, on mixing indeterminacy with determinacy.

So, too, rigor may be defined in terms of mixing—indeterminacy with interpretation. The quality of interpretation, its own richness, depends on how fully and well we develop the various alternatives indeterminacy presents. In this new frame for rigor—combining the complexity of indeterminacy with the hermeneutics of interpretation—it seems necessary to establish a community, one critical yet supportive. Such a community is, I believe, what Dewey thought a school should be.

Notes

1. It is interesting to note that *recursion* (as well as *recur*) is derived from the Latin *recurrere* (to run back). In this way recursion is allied with *currere* (to run), the root word for curriculum.
2. As I've said already, it is this distancing of oneself from one's actions and thoughts that is missing in Schön's concept of reflection.

References

Bowers, C.A. (1987). *Elements of a post-liberal theory of education.* New York: Teachers College Press. Bowers, C.A., & Flinders, D. J. (1980). *Responsive teaching.* New York: Teachers College Press.

Bruner, J. (1960). *The process of education.* Cambridge, MA: Harvard University Press.

——. (1986). *Actual minds, possible worlds.* Cambridge, MA: Harvard University Press.

Cheney, J. (1989). Post-Modern environmental ethics: Ethics as bioregional narrative. *Environmental Ethics, 11* (Summer), 117–134.

Dewey, J. (1964). Need for a philosophy of education. In R. D. Archambault (ed.), *John Dewey on education: Selected writings* (pp. 3–14). New York: Random House. (Original work published 1934.)

——. (1971). *How we think.* Chicago: Henry Regnery. (Original work published 1933.)

Doll, W. E., Jr. (1977). The role of contrast in the development of competence. In Alex Molner & John Zahorik (eds.), *Curriculum theory* (pp. 50–63). Washington, D.C.: Association for Supervision and Curriculum Development.

——. (1989). Complexity in the classroom. *Educational Leadership, 47,* 65–70.

Iser, W. (1978). *The act of reading.* Baltimore: Johns Hopkins University Press.

Lydon, A. (1992). Cosmology and curriculum. Unpublished dissertation, Louisiana State University.

Prigogine, I. (1988). The rediscovery of time. In Richard F. Kitchener (ed.), *The world view of contemporary physics: Does it need a new metaphysics?* (pp. 125–143). Albany: SUNY Press.

Prigogine, 1., & Stengers, I. (1984). *Order out of chaos: Man's new dialogue with nature.* New York: Bantam Books.

Torshen, K (1977). *The mastery approach to competency-based education.* New York: Academic Press.

Whitehead, A. N. (1967). *The aims of education.* New York: Free Press. (Original work published 1929.)

20

Centripetal Thinking in Curriculum Studies

Peter Hlebowitsh

In his celebrated essay, *The Hedgehog and the Fox*, Isaiah Berlin (1953/2008) asserted a divide between scholars who seek to understand the world by siding with a single discrete and widely explanatory idea and scholars who opt for divergence and for whom the world cannot be gainfully explained with the embrace of a single defining idea. Berlin's position was encapsulated in an aphorism taken from the 7th-century Greek poet Archilocus—"The fox knows many things, but the hedgehog knows one big thing." He used the distinction to put forward an intellectual history marked by those who seek synthesis (the hedgehogs) as they analytically vie against those who seek multiplicity and incommensurability (the foxes).

The field of curriculum studies has, of course, had its share of both hedgehogs and foxes. The early development of the field was largely a project that aimed to find a center of gravity for those thinking about schools and school reform—a center that was clearly associated with school administration efforts to exercise some control over the course of the school experience (Callahan, 1962; Cremin, 1961; Pinar & Grumet, 1981). The emerging center, however, was not uncontested. It was marked by different constructions of how administrative control should be exercised in the curriculum (Hlebowitsh, 1993; Kliebard, 2004) and by broader varieties of both subject-centered and child-centered school-based expressions. Efforts to find synthesis, however, eventually settled on the organizing idea of curriculum development, as it was embodied in the work of Franklin Bobbitt, Ralph Tyler, Hilda Taba, and later, Daniel and Laurel Tanner (Null, 2008). The hedgehogs, in this sense, had prevailed at both the early founding and later developmental years of the field, so much so that the possibilities for a paradigmatic configuration in the field began to be debated (Jickling, 1988; Tanner & Tanner, 1988).

Thus, only 30 years ago, if one secured a doctoral degree in the area of curriculum studies, it likely meant that the recipient was someone versed in school development concerns, in the historical literature attesting to those concerns, and in the main skills needed to design, implement, and ultimately understand the school experience. The reality was that the field was fundamentally a low-theory/high-practice endeavor. One of the key generational or vertical lines taught to aspiring curricularists was tied to understanding the school experience through the act of curriculum development (Hlebowitsh, 2005). In other words, the skill sets typically associated with curriculum development work (designing objectives, constructing instructional plans, and formulating evaluative mechanisms) were central to the education of curricularists. Consider the titles of some of the key texts: Franklin Bobbitt's (1924) *How to Build a Curriculum*; The

National Society for the Study of Education (NSSE) 26th Yearbook (1927), *Foundations of Curriculum-Making*; and Othanel Smith, William Stanley, and Harlan Shores's (1950) *Fundamentals of Curriculum Development.* Additionally, Hollis Caswell and Doak Campbell (1935), Hilda Taba (1962), and the Tanners (1975/2007), each wrote texts titled *Curriculum Development.* Even Eliot Eisner's (2002) well-known text, *The Educational Imagination*, considered by many as the creative departure from the traditional curriculum text, was subtitled "On the Design of School Programs." It is also important to note that various forms of instructional and evaluative design (including mental measurement techniques) made their way into the schools because of the influence of curricularists, most notably Ralph Tyler (1949), whose rationale has had some consequence in shaping school experiences. Thus generally speaking, curriculum scholars one generation removed, operated in the schools, knew something about the procedural elements of the school curriculum, and were taught an intellectual history that dealt with the various rationales used to justify school actions.

Today, however, such a generational line no longer centrally applies to the education of the curriculum studies scholar (Wraga, 1999). It has been offset by the reconceptualists' mission to build intellectual divergence. Indeed, by the late 1970s, the foxes had arrived with a vengeance, resulting in a new multifaceted view of curriculum studies, emerging mostly from the pen of William Pinar—one that went straight to the core of the field and set the wheels in motion for the creation of a new generation of thinkers whose views spun with centrifugal force (Pinar, Reynolds, Slattery, & Taubman, 1995). The age of the hedgehog had clearly turned and the old center gave way, creating something along the chasm that Berlin detailed in his famous essay . . . between, to use Berlin's (1953/2008) words:

> those, on one side, who relate everything to a single central vision, one system, less or more coherent or articulate, in terms of which they understand, think and feel—a single, universal, organizing principle in terms of which alone all that they are and say has significance—and, on the other side, those who pursue many ends, often unrelated and even contradictory, connected, if at all, only in some de facto way. . . . (p. 22)

The new curriculum field entertained ideas that were clearly centrifugal rather than centripetal in nature—not restricted to the lines of the school curriculum, moving along multiple epistemological levels, varied in orientation and pushing outward into the larger experience, with only nominal regard for the institutional or the normative. It is not that the school became irrelevant; it is simply that it had to give up quite a bit of space to other undertakings not historically or traditionally associated with curriculum work. This was, in fact, the main point of the reconceptualization—to broaden the project of the field and to shake it out of its preoccupation with the school. One early result was schism and dispute, a pulling apart of differences across the field that brought forward its share of critical responses, starting with Tanner and Tanner (1979) and Philip Jackson (1980) and later with William Wraga (1999) and Peter Hlebowitsh (1999a). A similar tension also surfaced in the early critiques of critical pedagogy (Bowers, 1991; Ellsworth, 1989).

Today, the academic discipline that we now call curriculum studies is in a queasy state of reorientation. Having left its place of comfort in the schools, the curriculum studies field has, in effect, become a kind of homeless adventurer—venturing far and wide on a journey to explore the world for new understanding. The effect has been enrichment on one side, especially on the point of theoretical vibrancy, and impoverishment on the other, especially as one considers the impotence of the field in relation to school-based concerns (Hlebowitsh, 1999a; Wraga, 1999). The question we face now is whether we are now prepared to make a home again. The foxes have certainly taken us out into the world, so now what?

Not surprisingly, some momentum is now building in the direction of stability and centeredness in the field, as a new discourse emerges that directly and unabashedly aims to look for some conceptual nucleus for the field, all with the consequence of putting the foxes in the role of the hedgehogs, and by implication, making the hedgehogs all the more aware that a new and perhaps uncomfortable synthesis might be in order. So, from my perspective at least, I find it heartening that some modest efforts are now under way to start what Pinar (the field's most famous fox) calls a discussion about disciplinarity (Pinar, 2008), which is indeed a new form of thinking in the curriculum field that looks for convergence (or even canon) in the quest for disciplinarity, bringing with it many newcomers into what is undeniably the realm of the hedgehogs.

Although the effort to find a canon may not yield hard principles, it might still yield enough of an answer for the field, in that some discourse over commonalities and differences may prove to be an effective lubricant for wider understanding. Such understanding can be conceived, to use Pinar's descriptors, both horizontally and vertically (Pinar, 2008). The vertical construction of the field speaks to its intellectual heritage and to a working sense of what curriculum professors should know about the field historically, while the horizontal construction of the field speaks to the manner in which diversifying perspectives are brought to bear upon current-day issues and concerns. These are useful ways to begin a discussion that pulls us inward. So, in the interests of advancing the project, I would like to offer a few thoughts to consider.

From the Poverty of the Divergent to the Beauty of the Diverse

I start with the question of how to manage diversity concerns in a discourse that admits centripetal force as its main pursuit. The proclaimed reconceptualization of the field, it should be noted, has largely been an exercise in divergence—that is, a systemic and fully bodied criticism of the historical basis of the field. Interestingly, scholarly commentary in the curriculum field has failed to make the important distinction between the concepts of divergence and diversity.[1]

Logically speaking, the historic (traditional, if you will) curriculum field has as much of a claim as the reconceptualized one on the point of diversity. Each, after all, makes its fair share contribution to the conceptual variance in the field. In this sense, diversity is an all-encompassing and diffuse concept. It puts all claimants on equal footing and clears out a space for as much variation as can be produced. Thus, the foxes, no matter how hard they may try, have difficulty arguing for diversity on the one hand and against the traditions of the field on the other. The contradiction is often glaring. Often those offering antagonistic commentary against the historic field, who criticize it for narrowness and its many modernist abuses, make a simultaneous claim to be working on the side of diversity. But the idea of diversity, in its purest sense, necessarily reaches out to perspectives that one is against.

The idea of divergence, on the other hand, is palliative in nature, looking to counter prevailing orthodoxies. It is moved by a curriculum version of Dadaism, at least in its open rejection of the prevailing standards of the field. It certainly carries some diversifying effects, but it is articulated in opposition to existing conventions. It is, by all accounts, a corrective. Asking for, say, divergence from the Tyler rationale without feeling compelled to support its equal standing on the diversity landscape is logical and without contradiction because the idea of divergence results in pushing new things in while pushing other (less desirable) things out. And while this is a more honest and less contradictory position than the one situated in diversity, it is still a deeply problematic one because much of the recent friction in the field has been an argument over what gets pushed out. Divergence, in this sense, has an solipsistic way about it; it can balkanize a field by creating friendship/enemy distinctions that carry the burden of party line loyalties. In this sense, the reconceptualist critique has never really embraced the idea of diversity; it embraced instead the idea of divergence.

If, however, we replace the idea of divergence with the idea (or principle) of diversity, the discourse changes because the fundamental premise of diversity is inclusiveness. Such a result, of course, creates different kinds of problems, in that it can diffuse a field. But given the inchoate nature of the field of curriculum studies, such worries might be premature. The field, it seems, has not yet identified centrally held tools and principles that could allow it to make these judgments. For reasons that I will explain, there is more possibility for our field in the idea of diversity than in the idea of divergence.

I came to this conclusion in an exchange I had with Handel Wright in 2005 on the pages of *Curriculum Inquiry.* Wright was keen to make a distinction between alternative versus corrective histories. The latter construction of history apparently made its claim on the landscape of the field side by side with the vast display of other ostensibly alternative (and traditional) histories, while the former made its claim on the same landscape with the intention of pushing others out. I very much liked the distinction because it afforded me an analytical device against which to understand the scholarship of divergence that has marked curriculum studies in recent decades. In short, it became clear to me that those who advocated from the position of divergence adopted an all-embracing corrective orientation while those who argued for diversity in the field worked more in the line of tolerance for difference and acceptable, if not harmonious, alternativeness.

Centripetal thinking works well with the construct of diversity because together they put the field on a pathway toward some working sense of mutuality. One of the interesting lessons of diversity for the curriculum field is accounting for the manner in which we can use it to adjust an argument in a way that pulls the field inward. This seems to be especially the case when the curriculum field offers criticism on school policy and practice. It strikes me that very good criticism of No Child Left Behind (NCLB), the American federal policy on school reform, can be drawn from the diverse elements of the field and still have a centered "curriculum studies" ring to it. Take, for instance, the manner in which scientifically based teaching, which NCLB is promoting for the teaching of reading in low-achieving schools, can be critically assessed. Believing that best methods of instruction are identifiable through experimental design, proponents of scientifically based teaching are prepared to identify such methods and encourage teachers to use them. The potential upshot here is that the discretionary space that teachers need to make responsive judgments in the classroom might be compromised by a desire (or possibility an insistence) to use only best methods. Such methods are, after all, certified by science.[2]

The curriculum studies community, however, had and continues to have something to say about this. For example, the hermeneutical analysis provided by Patrick

Slattery, Karen Krasny, and Michael O'Malley (2007) spoke to the need for teachers to embrace the ambiguous nature of the classroom—to accept the unanticipated question or strange tangent, as they put it, that emerges from the educational situation. We witnessed a practical extension of Slattery in Eisner (2002), who says something similar by advancing the idea of expressive outcomes in the classroom, which is the embrace of unanticipated goals as they materialize in the heat of classroom action, usually in response to some situational nuance. So we begin to think centripetally (and, in this case, horizontally) and can see how a teacher's decision to take a student, or more generally an entire classroom, in an unforeseen direction is part of her professional repertoire, influenced, in some combination, by intuition, felt need, and wider psychological as well as pedagogical considerations. Here, we can see how the personal and tangential can represent a hedge against preplanned instructional events and how the venture from routine can be an educative venture. This strikes me as something like a horizontal line of understanding.

But the possibilities also exist for vertical understanding on this point because of the centripetal forces of history. In John Dewey (1922/1988), for instance, we can find discourse not only on the possibilities of directing experience through goals, but also on deriving goals from experience. Aims, he declared "are not strictly speaking ends or termini of action. . . . They are terminals of deliberation and so turning points in activity" (p. 154). This was Dewey's way of saying that teaching should not be viewed as simply the means used to fulfill and complete ends. Teaching is indeed guided by goals, but it also produces its own goals from within.

So we begin to spin centripetally with Slattery, Eisner, and Dewey. Imagine what this could mean when the field begins to stare down problems such as the ill-conceived notion of scientifically based teaching, which argues that operational answers to teaching can be drawn from research studies that identify practices or methodologies believed to be transferable to all classrooms. Clearly, a vertical line of understanding in our field speaks to the support of the emergent judgments of teachers, who are naturally obligated to be apprised of the scientific research, but who also understand that the "right" decision in a classroom depends on weighing various factors related to the nature of the child, to available resources, to the defined purposes in the curriculum, to the subject matter at hand, and to a raft of other variables residing in the educational situation. Joseph Schwab (1983), joins in:

> There are thousands of ingenious ways in which commands on what and how to teach can, will and must be modified or circumvented in the actual moments of teaching. . . . Moments of choice of what to do, how to do it, and whom and at what pace, arise hundreds of times in a school day and arise differently every day and with every group of students. No command or instruction can be so formulated as to control that kind of artistic judgment and behavior, with its demand for frequent, instant choices of ways to meet an ever varying situation. (p. 245)

Support for the emergent decision-making powers of the teacher is centrally located in the field, largely because it has a sturdy embrace across diversifying perspectives.

Interestingly, the other side of emergent judgment (what we might call planned activity) is less decisively located in the horizontal construction of the field. But it still has a good argument from the vertical perspective. Anyone who has worked in the schools knows that the normative agenda of the curriculum, as articulated in the manifest curriculum, cannot be easily ignored, and any that decide to venture from it must be professionally rationalized. Teachers, for instance, do not have the right to not teach children how to read. Reading is normatively located and requires ongoing planning efforts. In fact, most classroom decisions must pass a vertically established test that actually has some legal underpinnings, a notion popularly known as "cause." Teacher judgment can be questioned on the grounds of incompetence, insubordination, and conduct unbecoming. The criteria used to sort out these challenges usually go to the age and maturity level of the student, some sense of professional ethics, and the general mission of the school. This is another way of saying that teachers are obliged to conduct themselves in a way that offer experiences that are responsive to the nature of the learner, that are within the purposeful and deliberately conceived educational scope of the school, and that satisfy a standing ethic of professionalism. The problem, of course, is that the manner in which such a test is used is itself subject to different interpretations—ranging from behaviorist views on what is best for children to romantic naturalist views. We may not have a clear-enough understanding about how such lines should be drawn yet, beyond what we might need to identify unprofessional behavior, but this is part of the excitement that could result as we look to draw from diversity to fashion some convergence of thought in curriculum studies.

Canon—The Knowing is in Doing the Knowing

In Plato's (1956) *Meno*, the work's two central characters, Socrates and Meno, are engaged in a focused discussion on the topic of human virtue. The dialogue first turns to the task of determining the essential definition of virtue, offered as a logical prerequisite to knowing whether virtue can be taught. Socrates pushes Meno to define virtue, but could only get Meno to identify various features and examples of it. Faced with examples of virtue but no good unifying definition of it, Socrates asks the big question: Is virtue many things or one big thing?

Eventually, we realize at the conclusion of the Plato's dialogue that no conclusive or clear agreement could be found on defining virtue. Socrates was looking for a hedgehog, but could only find fox-like responses. He wanted to find a unifying definition of virtue that accounted for its varied dimensions and instances in life. Instead, he got a list of virtue's main characteristics.

On balance, however, Plato taught us that the dialogue did, in fact, make some contribution to the participants' understanding of virtue because, if nothing else, the discussion itself, while leaving the participants somewhat disoriented nevertheless provided an experience in working the answer to the question it raised. In other words, Plato instructed us to judge the dialogue less by an expected or desired outcome than by the process it engaged. So, we ask: Was it Socrates' intention all along to pose questions that generated dialogue but no definitive answers? Was the master teacher creating a dialogue whereby the actual act of trying to define virtue was resulting in some argumentative idea on the definition of virtue? In other words, did Socrates understand that the knowing of virtue was ipso facto in doing the knowing of virtue (Chambliss, 1987)?

I believe that we can use Plato's dialogue as an analogue for the pursuit of canon or disciplinarity in curriculum studies. Faced with many representations of what is rationalized as curriculum studies, we ask: What is the one main thing that holds all of this varied work together? What makes the long list of different types of scholarship all identifiable as curriculum studies? What is virtuous curriculum work, and if it is many things, what is the one big thing that makes the many things all virtuous? Much like Socrates' hedgehog, ours will also likely prove to be elusive. But can we benefit from the same effect found in Meno, from understanding that our best answer will have more to do with trying to find an answer than delivering a definitive conclusion.

Plato's dialogue, of course, represents an early example of the kind of classic means/ends equation that Dewey later elucidated. When Socrates framed the discussion with Meno, he originally fixed the idea of knowing virtue into an end to pursue. The reader is convinced, from the onset of the dialogue, that an authoritative answer might be provided. But such an end, in this case, turns out to be a means of knowing as well. Plato shows us that the dialogue, in effect, comprises the main task of knowing. Using Dewey ends/means characterization, Hugh LaFollette (2000) makes the argument clear:

> Suppose Bob says he wants to become a good person. On the standard view, "being a good person" is a remote end Bob can achieve by acting in certain ways. However, doing good deeds is no mere means to becoming good; doing good deeds regularly constitutes making oneself a good person. There is no end "being a good person" out there that is separable from the activities constituting being a good person. (p. 411)

In the same way, to know virtue, as Socrates asks us to know it, is inseparable from the act of trying to know it.

I raise these questions because the curriculum field is now pursuing several hedgehog-like projects. In 2007, the American Association for the Advancement of Curriculum Studies (AAACS) endorsed The Canon project, putting William Schubert (2008) in charge of studying and potentially identifying a curriculum studies canon. Madeleine Grumet also has been examining the nature of the coursework offered and required in curriculum doctoral programs across the nation. Such projects carry all the main characteristics of Plato's dialogue. If curriculum studies can be taught, we first need to identify what it is. And our impulse will likely be the same as Meno's, which is to enumerate features of the scholarship that we can call curriculum studies, without being able to answer what holds these varied forms of understanding and inquiry together.

It is clear that the common basis for intellectual pursuit in curriculum studies is very much in flux. I have argued elsewhere that some restoration is in order for the field to regain its bearing (Hlebowitsh, 1999b), but that project never materialized and probably for good reason. The reality is that the curriculum studies community will have to instead retune the sound of its scholarship with an ear toward some of its more dissonant chords. It is clear that a new space has been made for the kind of curriculum work portrayed as dedicated to understanding rather than school development. And the main reason has to do with the fact that the new orientation in the field no longer aims to supplant the historical orientation toward development as much as to live with it. Horizontality, in fact, demands that we examine how different traditions can coexist or even enrich each other. This is, as indicated, the general spirit of embracing diversity, as opposed to divergence, in the field.

Inevitably, the struggle to identify a curriculum canon will center around disagreements over inclusions and exclusions. But if we could side with the idea of diversity of interpretation, and appreciate how the knowing of the canon is synonymous with trying to do the knowing of the canon, the result might finally generate some solid discourse on the struggle to better understand the field both horizontally and vertically. The idea of disciplinarity in curriculum studies is generally argumentative; it does not forgo our differences, but it might at least put them into a universe of common discourse. Schubert (2008) phrased The Canon project really in Socratic terms, as yielding "possible set of foci for wondering, pondering, speculating, discussing- . . . conceptions of the continuum in-between canon and anti-canon" (p. 1). Schubert, in fact, is the perfect choice for such an initiative because his work testifies to the mind of a hedgehog and the heart of a fox. The reality is that the idea of canon cannot be broached unless all of us take on a similar role.

I doubt that canonistic thinking will yield an identifiable framework (or even a body of required readings). Like Meno, we are likely to find such a task hopelessly inconclusive. But by insisting on having a conversation about a curriculum canon, we can conflate ends with means in a manner that allows us to find our way into a convergent exercise that may give us a dialogic sense of key principles, theories, and literature.

Paradigm Lost

Interestingly, no one has used the term *paradigm* in any of these centripetal discussions about the curriculum field. The idea of paradigm means, in the Kuhnian sense, that the anomalous work of the field has some common framework. Such a framework is expected to play a policing role in the field by filtering the scholarship *against* basic and commonly held assumptions, beliefs, theories, and knowledge. The idea of disciplinarity is clearly one that has some vibration with paradigmatic systems of understanding and belief. The struggle for disciplinarity will naturally need to be a shared undertaking that speaks broadly to a common intellectual history (vertically) and to a common (and broadly held) basis of skills and understandings (horizontality). Disciplinarity, in effect, becomes the general model for the membership in the community. But because curriculum studies is in a prescience condition, it is not likely to produce such a framework. And any premature effort to settle around a paradigm will likely produce scholarship proudly resistance to the settled form, which brings us back to the divergence problem described earlier.

The field of curriculum studies has taken a long journey from its birthplace in social efficiency concerns, through its early development in the laboratory schools to its growing maturity as an agency for the development of school experiences dedicated to normative causes. Wesley Null (2008) has characterized the evolution along the thematic idea of curriculum development, rightly interpreting even the iconoclastic views of Schwab as representing a continuing extension of the curriculum field's commitment to the institutional and to the deliberate and conscious design of school experiences. I made a similar point in arguing that curriculum development was indeed a tie that bound the historic field—that Schwab, for all of his argumentation about the breaking away from the status quo, had more of an intellectual vibration with the historical anchors of the field (Tyler and others) than with its many critics (Hlebowitsh, 2005). The Tanners, of course, conceive of a paradigm within the act of curriculum development.

Few can deny, however, that the arc of curriculum development has indeed been interrupted, if not broken, by the growing popularity of the reconceptualist's critique, which although varied in its many analytical sights, shares common disdain for the concept of development. The effect has been real, so that as the idea of curriculum development found its way out of favor among curriculum scholars, the field went asunder and exploded with new embryonic life in all directions.

But like a lost child, the idea of curriculum development found quick comfort and succor in the arms of others, notably scholars in both the mental measurement and educational administration communities and scholars working in what we might tentatively label as school-based instruction. Today, the best-selling book on the design of school experiences is written by two authors (Wiggins & McTighe, 2005), whose affiliation is much stronger to instructional- and practitioner-based groups, such as the Association of Supervision and Curriculum Development (ASCD), than to research-based and university-affiliated groups, such as the American Educational Research Association (AERA) and its subdivisions. The design of content standards, the alignment of standards of purposes, and the negotiation of assessments in the curriculum development process (all actions that are especially relevant to the lives of schoolteachers and schoolchildren) now have an easier place in the professional lives of psychometricians than they do in the lives of curricularists. The sad side effect of the curriculum field's experience with divergent scholarship has been an impoverished school profile. If the reconceptualist effort was a triumph for new theoretical strength in the field, the victory was Pyrrhic.

Although we have nothing like a paradigm to capture our field, the idea of curriculum development persists in the field. The recent publication of *The Sage Handbook of Curriculum and Instruction* (Connelly, 2008), for instance, has very much helped to burnish the image of curriculum development by putting it on equal footing with its theoretical counterparts. With sections dedicated to managing and making the curriculum, with a chapter expressly dedicated to the history of curriculum development and with an unabashed treatment of the normative conditions of schooling (via issues related to change, reform and implementation), the *Handbook* signals the comprehensive (and diverse) nature of the field.

If we think centripetally, we can at least start a discussion on how the concept of curriculum development can be conceived in the field without worrying about the implications of supporting a paradigm. And we might start by pointing to the theoretical (vertically articulated) isomorphism between Tyler, Taba, Dewey, and Schwab. For instance, what Tyler called screens, or what Dewey obliquely referred to as the fundamental processes (adumbrated as a regard for the nature of the learner, for the values of society and community, and for the contributions of specialized subject matter), look quite a bit like Schwab's commonplaces: teachers, subject matters, students, and milicu. Parallels here between the commonplaces (students, subject matter, and milieu) and Tyler's three screens still require conversation about why Schwab added the teacher to the conceptual framework, but they nonetheless provide a map for the field to return to the geography of the school. This geography could in fact constitute a subspecialization that exists in tension (but comity) with other specializations.

If the historic (and argumentative) paradigm that the Tanners' claimed for the field was a kind of Eden for those of us interested in curriculum development work, the paradigm (and the paradise) has been lost. But as in Milton's epic poem, we may yet find "A paradise within thee, happier far." To paraphrase Plato's question, if we ask what makes virtuous curriculum work virtuous, we might be able to better balance the relation between our discourse communities, between what Mikhail Bakhtin (1930s/1981) labeled as monologia and heteroglossia, which in the case of the former, unifies the language of a discourse community, and in the case of the latter, multiplies the modes of discourse. The important point to remember is that both heteroglossia and monologia are needed because a field is always marked by ideas that are simultaneously pulling inward and pulling outward.

The forces of monologia undoubtedly give us some center, something along the lines of what Pinar is calling through horizontal and vertical forms of understanding, while the forces of heteroglossia, acknowledge our differences and compel a level of understanding equal to what linguists might call code switching—the ability to jump in and out of various discourse communities. So, the paradox is that much of what we might seek in canon or disciplinarity sides with both centrifugal and centripetal forces. In other words, to be a hedgehog, one also has to be a fox. Our problem is that we have for too long been nothing but foxes.

Conclusion

The curriculum field is poised to engage in a new and largely unfamiliar conversation. After years of generating divergent approaches to scholarship, cast mostly as reactions against a historical orthodoxy, the curriculum studies community is now looking at a new dialectic—one marked by a physics that pull ideas inward toward some centripetal center. The tension between looking for grand unifying ideas as they articulate with a multiplicity of incommensurate ones has, in fact, marked the nature of scholarly thinking. Berlin personified such tension in his use of the Greek aphorism, "The fox knows many things, but the hedgehog knows one big thing." In recent years, the curriculum field has been dominated by foxes, which have largely resisted falling into the role of a hedgehog. But several projects have recently been launched in the field that might signal a new age for curriculum studies, as a new dialogue has been opened to consider the possibilities of finding some semblance of canon or disciplinarity in the field. Such a charge, as I explain, requires a centripetal form of thinking that embraces diversity (not divergence). Like Aristotle's and Meno's search for a unifying explanation of virtue, the search for canon or disciplinarity is less likely to yield a hard-and-fast verifiable outcome as much as an inconclusive discussion. But, as Plato reminds us, such a discussion is precisely the point because the knowing of canon is at its minimum doing the knowing of canon. This might fall short of the hedgehog response, but it puts the field on a new grounding that could begin to push it out of its pre-paradigmatic state.

Notes

1. The distinction between these two ideas was originally brought to my attention by my colleague Greg Hamot, who noted the tendency of university policies to be more committed to the goal of divergence (views marked as oppositional to established forms) than to diversity.
2. According to guidelines set down in NCLB, the education of public school children is now best served by compelling school districts and individual schools to use what are known as scientifically based programs and practices. The narrative of the NCLB Act includes repeated references to the term *scientifically based research* (SBR) and is unabashed in promoting SBR as a key principle for the reform of low-achieving schools. State and local education agencies are, in fact, required to use SBR to bring improvements to low-achieving schools targeted for assistance. The law also calls for a general commitment to school reforms that seek to "identify and implement professional development, instructional strategies, and methods of instruction that are based on scientifically-based research and that have proven effective in addressing the specific instructional issues that caused the school to be identified for school improvement" (NCLB Act, 2002, Title I, Part A, Section 1116). NCLB specifically authorizes funds "to provide assistance to State educational agencies and local educational agencies in establishing reading programs for students in kindergarten through grade 3 that are based on scientifically based reading research, to ensure that every student can read at grade level or above no later than the end of grade 3" (NCLB Act, 2002, 20 U.S.C.§ 6361).

References

Bakhtin, M. M. (1981). *The dialogic imagination: Four essays* (Michael Holquist, Ed.). Austin: University of Texas Press. (Original work published 1930s)

Berlin, I. (2008). *The fox and the hedgehog.* In H. Hardy & A. Kelly (Eds.), *Russian thinkers* (pp. 22–81). London: Penguin Classics. (Original work published 1953)

Bobbitt, J. F. (1924). *How to build a curriculum.* Boston: Houghton Mifflin.

Bowers, C. A. (1991). Some questions about the anachronistic elements in the Giroux/McLaren Theory of critical pedagogy. *Curriculum Inquiry, 21(2),* 239–252.

Callahan, R. E. (1962). *Education and the cult of efficiency.* Chicago: University of Chicago Press.

Caswell, H. L., & Campbell, D. S. (1935). *Curriculum development.* New York: American Book

Chambliss, J. J. (1987). *Educational theory as theory of conduct: From Aristotle to Dewey.* Albany: State University of New York Press.

Connelly, F. M. (2008). *The Sage handbook of curriculum and instruction.* Thousand Oaks, CA: Sage

Cremin, L. A. (1961). *The transformation of the school.* New York: Knopf.

Dewey, J. (1988). *Human nature and conduct.* Carbondale: Southern Illinois University Press. (Original work published 1922)

Eisner, E. (2002). *The educational imagination.* New York: Macmillan.

Ellsworth, E. (1989). Why doesn't this feel empowering? Working through the repressive myths of critical pedagogy. *Harvard Educational Review, 59(3),* 297–324.

Hlebowitsh, P. (1993). *Radical curriculum theory reconsidered: A historical approach.* New York: Teachers College Press.

Hlebowitsh, P. (1999a). The burdens of the new curricularist. *Curriculum Inquiry, 29(3),* 343–354.

Hlebowitsh, P. (1999b). The common unity and the progressive restoration of the curriculum field. In L. Behar-Horenstein & J. Glantz (Eds.), *Modern and postmodern perspectives in the curriculum field* (pp. 54–69). New York: Greenwood.

Hlebowitsh, P. (2005). Generational ideas in curriculum: A historical triangulation. *Curriculum Inquiry, 35(1),* 73–87.

Jackson, P. W. (1980). Curriculum and its discontents. *Curriculum Inquiry, 10(2),* 28–43.

Jickling, B. (1988). Paradigms in curriculum development: Critical comments on the work of Tanner and Tanner; A tough nut: A rejoinder to Robin Barrow and to Daniel and Laurel Tanner. *Interchange, 79(2),* 41–67.

Kliebard, H. (2004). *The struggle for the American curriculum, 1893–1958.* New York: Routledge Falmer.

LaFollette, H. (2000). *The Blackwell guide to ethical theory.* Oxford, UK: Blackwell.

Null, J. W. (2008). Curriculum development in historical perspective. In F. Michael Connelly, Ming Fang He, & J. Phillion (Eds.), *The Sage handbook of curriculum and instruction.* Thousand Oaks, CA: Sage.

Pinar, W. (2008). *Intellectual advancement through disciplinarity: Verticality and horizontality in curriculum studies.* Rotterdam, the Netherlands: Sense.

Pinar, W., & Grumet, M. (1981). Theory and practice and the reconceptualization of curriculum studies In M. Lawn & L. Barton (Eds.), *Rethinking curriculum studies: A radical approach* (pp. 20–42). New York: Wiley.

Pinar, W., Reynolds, W., Slattery, P., & Taubman, P. (1995). *Understanding curriculum.* New York: Peter Lang.

Plato (1956). *Protagoras and Meno* (W. K. C. Guthrie, Trans.). New York: Penguin.

Public Law 107–110, The No Child Left Behind Act of 2001. Retrieved December 18, 2007, from http:// www.ed.gov/ policyhttp://www.ed.gov/policy

Schubert, W. (2008, March 23). *The AAACS curriculum canon project: Divergent and convergent possibilities and evolutions.* Paper presented at the annual meeting of the American Educational Research Association, New York.

Schwab, J.J. (1983). The practical 4: Something for curriculum professors to do. *Curriculum Inquiry, 13(1),* 239–256.

Slattery, P., Krasny, K., & O'Malley, M. P. (2007). Hermeneutics, aesthetics, and the quest for answerability: A dialogic possibility for reconceptualizing the interpretive process in curriculum studies. *Journal of Curriculum Studies, 32(6),* 537–558.

Smith, B. O., Stanley, W. O., & Shores, J. H. (1950). *Fundamentals of curriculum development.* New York: Harcourt.

Taba, H. (1962). *Curriculum development: Theory and practice.* New York: Harcourt Brace.

Tanner, D., & Tanner, L. N. (1979). Emancipation from research: The reconceptualist prescription. *Educational Researcher, 8,* 8–12.

Tanner, D., & Tanner, L. N. (1988). The emergence of a paradigm in the curriculum field: A reply to Tickling. *Interchange, 19(2),* 41–67.

Tanner, D., & Tanner, L. N. (2007). *Curriculum development: Theory into practice.* New York: Macmillan. (Original work published 1975)

Tyler, R. W. (1949). *Basic principles of curriculum and instruction.* Chicago: University of Chicago Press.

Wiggins, G., & McTighe, J. (2005). *Understanding by design* (2nd ed.). New York: Prentice Hall.

Wraga, W. G. (1999). Extracting sun-beams out of cucumbers: The retreat from practice in reconceptu- alized curriculum studies. *Educational Researcher, 28*, 4–13.

Wright, H. (2005). Does Hlebowitsh improve on curriculum history? Reading a rereading for its political purpose and implications. *Curriculum Inquiry, 35(1)*, 103–117.

21

High-Stakes Testing and Curriculum Control: A Qualitative Metasynthesis

Wayne Au

With the advent of federally mandated high-stakes testing since the No Child Left Behind Act of 2001, many important questions have been raised regarding the implementation of this policy tool at the classroom level. In this article, I focus on one such question: What, if any, is the effect of high-stakes testing on curriculum? To answer this question, I begin by exploring the meanings of two key terms, "curriculum" and "high-stakes testing," and by offering a brief review of some of the literature regarding the relationship between the two. Then, using the method of qualitative metasynthesis, I undertake a comparative study of 49 qualitative studies of high-stakes testing to better understand testing's impact on curriculum.

Curriculum

There exists a wide range of definitions of the term "curriculum" (Beauchamp, 1982; Jackson, 1996; Kliebard, 1989). Historically, the word has its roots in the Latin word *currere*, which means a course to be run (Eisner, 1994), and was first used at the University of Glasgow in the 17th century to describe "a formal course of study that the students completed" (Harden, 2001, p. 335). This definition is perhaps the simplest and easiest for most to recognize because it is evident in the way schools are generally organized around a course of predetermined, required subject matter classes that students must pass to graduate. Thus most scholars and educators would at least recognize that curriculum encompasses a body of content knowledge to be learned in some way, shape, or form.

However, to stop at the level of content obscures other crucial aspects of curriculum because subject matter content within schools implies not only *selection* but also *transmission* of knowledge. As McEwan and Bull (1991) state,

> Subject matter is always an expression of a desire to communicate ideas to others. . . . Differences within the form and content of various expressions of subject matter reflect an understanding of differences in the backgrounds of potential audiences and the circumstances of the subject matter's formulation. (p. 331)

Indeed, all content is pedagogical. It implies the communication of ideas to an audience and does so through the structuring of knowledge (Segall, 2004a, 2004b). The concept of curriculum, therefore, also implicates the structure of knowledge embedded in curricular *form*—the form of how knowledge is organized and presented within a curriculum (Apple, 1995), as well as pedagogy—the intended form of communication of selected content. Thus the trilogy of (a) subject matter content knowledge, (b) structure or form of curricular knowledge, and (c) pedagogy are three defining aspects of "curriculum." This basic conception of curriculum is what I use for the present analysis.

High-Stakes Testing

A test is high-stakes when its results are used to make important decisions that affect students, teachers, administrators, communities, schools, and districts (Madaus, 1988). In very specific terms, high-stakes tests are a part of a *policy design* (Schneider & Ingram, 1997) that "links the score on one set of standardized tests to grade promotion, high school graduation and, in some cases, teacher and principal salaries and tenure decisions" (Orfield & Wald, 2000, p. 38). As part of the accountability movement, stakes are also deemed high because the results of tests, as well as the ranking and categorization of schools, teachers, and children that extend from those results, are reported to the public (McNeil, 2000).

The Research Debate

The question of whether high-stakes testing affects curriculum has been highly contested in the field of educational research. For instance, at a time when high-stakes testing policies were inconsistently implemented across individual states, Airasian (1987) and Madaus (1988) offered some of the earliest assertions that the tests would control classroom practice. M. L. Smith (1991) followed with one of the few early empirical studies, finding that high-stakes tests promote "multiple choice teaching." More recent research on high-stakes testing is more conflicted. Some research finds that high-stakes tests merely represent one limited factor, among others, influencing classroom practice (see, e.g., Cimbricz, 2002; Firestone, Mayrowetz, & Fairman, 1998; Grant, 2003), have little to no influence on what teachers do in the classroom (see, e.g., Gradwell, 2006; van Hover, 2006), or lead to improved learning experiences and positive educational outcomes (see, e.g., Braun, 2004; Williamson, Bondy, Langley, & Mayne, 2005). Other research challenges these claims, however, finding that high-stakes testing undermines education because it narrows curriculum, limits the ability of teachers to meet the sociocultural needs of their students, and corrupts systems of educational measurement (see, e.g., Amrein & Berliner, 2002a, 2002b; Lipman, 2004; McNeil, 2000; McNeil & Valenzuela, 2001; Nichols & Berliner, 2005, 2007; Watanabe, 2007). Given the wide range of research evidence, and given the ubiquity of high-stakes testing in education in the United States, the purpose of this study is to develop a broader, more complex understanding of the ways that these tests influence curriculum at the classroom level.

Method

For the purposes of this study I have chosen to analyze examples of qualitative research because of their focus on human interaction and attention to the day-to-day functioning of schools and classrooms (Valenzuela, Prieto, & Hamilton, 2007). To review the body of evidence reported in qualitative studies, I draw on the methodology of qualitative metasynthesis (DeWitt-Brinks & Rhodes, 1992; Noblit & Hare, 1988; Sandelowski, Docherty, & Emden, 1997; Thorne, Jensen, Kearney, Noblit, & Sandelowski, 2004), also referred to as qualitative meta-analysis (McCormick, Rodney, & Varcoe, 2003). Qualitative metasynthesis is part of a tradition of metaresearch that involves synthesizing the results of qualitative studies to gain a better understanding of the general nature of given phenomenon (DeWitt-Brinks & Rhodes, 1992; Thorne et al., 2004).

In this study I make use of a specific form of qualitative metasynthesis known as template analysis (Crabtree & Miller, 1999; King, 1998, 2006). In this form of thematic meta-analysis, textual data are coded using a template of codes designed by the researcher. These codes are often hierarchical in nature, starting with broad themes and moving toward more narrow or specific ones. In this case the textual data used are from the collection of qualitative studies gathered by the researcher. In template analysis the coding template is developed in two stages based on themes that arise from the body of textual data. In the first stage the researcher begins by developing an initial template based on a combination of a priori codes and an initial reading and coding of a subset of the textual data. In the second stage, the initial template is then applied to the whole data set, and codes are added to the template as new themes arise. This leads to the creation of the final template. The final template is then used to interpret the textual data set as a whole, and the findings are presented in some form (King, 1998, 2006).

Data Collection

The data set consists of 49 qualitative studies. These studies were gathered from a search completed in June of 2006 using the Educational Resources Information Center (ERIC), Academic Search, and Education Full Text databases, as well as the library book database at the University of Wisconsin, Madison. Initially, the search terms "high-stakes testing" and "state-mandated testing" were used to identify potential studies for use in my qualitative metasynthesis. This rather large initial pool was then narrowed to studies (a) based on original, scholarly research, (b) using qualitative methods, (c) taking place in the United States, and (d) specifically addressing the relationship between high-stakes tests and either curriculum or instruction, or both. Because this study focuses on the relationship between high-stakes testing and curriculum at the K-12 classroom level, the sample excludes studies that examine the relationship between high-stakes testing and retention, studies that focus on the role of high-stakes testing and access to teacher education programs (e.g., Praxis II), studies that focus on the tests themselves (e.g., discourse analyses of the actual test content), and policy studies that use qualitative methods to compare pressures between states. In addition, because of their ambiguous and complicated positions in school hierarchies, studies that focus on student teachers are also excluded.

Based on the self-identification of the researchers, the data gathered and analyzed from the 49 studies used in the qualitative metasynthesis performed here include at least 740 "teachers" identified as participants; 845 "educators" or "teachers and administrators" (not broken out into "teachers" alone) identified as participants; 96 schools identified as the focus of study; 38 districts identified as the level of focus of study; and covers at least 19 states (Arizona, Colorado, Florida, Illinois, Kansas, Kentucky, Maine, Maryland, Massachusetts, Michigan, Minnesota, New York, North Carolina, Ohio, Oregon, Texas, Vermont, Virginia, and Washington). In addition, of the 49 qualitative studies used in this metasynthesis, 15 focus on elementary education, 23 focus on secondary education, and 11 are K-12 analyses. Alternatively, while several of the included studies (23) are more general in focus, 14 are history/social studies-specific (3 elementary and 11 secondary), 9 are English/language arts-specific (1 elementary and 8 secondary), and 3 are math/ science-specific. (See Table 21.1 for a complete listing of the studies analyzed here.)

Table 21.1 Qualitative Metasynthesis Studies and Codes

Article	*Codes*[a]
Agee, 2004	SAC, PCT, KCF
Anagnostopolous, 2003a	SAC, SAE, PCT, KCF
Anagnostopolous, 2003b	SAC, PCT, KCF
Barton, 2005	SAE, KCI
Bol, 2004	PCT, KCF
Bolgatz, 2006	KCI
Booher-Jennings, 2005	PCT
Brimijoin, 2005	SAC, PCT
Clarke et al., 2003	SAC, SAE, PCT, PCS, KCI
Costigan, 2002	PCT
Debray, Parson, & Avila, 2003	SAC
Fickel, 2006	SAE, PCT, KCI
Firestone, Mayrowetz, & Fairman, 1998	SAC, PCT, KCF
Gerwin & Visone, 2006	SAC, PCT, KCF
Gradwell, 2006	No changes[b]
Grant, 2003	No changes[b]
Grant et al., 2002	SAC, PCT, KCF
Groves, 2002	SAC, PCT
Hillocks, 2002	SAC, KCF
Landman, 2000	SAC, PCT, KCF
Libresco, 2005	SAE, PCS, KCI
Lipman, 2002	SAC, PCT, KCF
Lomax et al., 1995	SAC, PCT, KCF
Luna & Turner, 2001	SAC, SAE, PCT, KCF
McNeil, 2000	SAC, PCT, KCF
McNeil & Valenzuela, 2001	SAC, PCT, KCF
Murillo & Flores, 2002	SAC
Passman, 2001	SAC, PCT, KCF
Perreault, 2000	SAC, PCT
Renter et al., 2006	SAC
Rex, 2003	SAC, PCT
Rex & Nelson, 2004	SAE, PCS, KCI
Salinas, 2006	SAE, SAC
Segall, 2003	SAE, SAC, PCT, KCF, KCI
Siskin, 2003	SAC
Sloan, 2005	SAC, PCT, KCF
Smagorinsky, Lakly, & Johnson, 2002	SAC, PCT, KCF
Smith, A. M., 2006	SAE, SAC, PCT, KCF
Taylor et al., 2001	SAC, PCT, KCF
Valenzuela, 2000	SAC, PCT, KCF
van Hover, 2006	SAC, KCF
van Hover & Heinecke, 2005	PCT, KCF
Vogler, 2003	SAC, SAE
Williamson et al., 2005	PCT
Wolf & Wolf, 2002	SAE, PCS, KCI
Wollman-Bonilla, 2004	SAE, PCS, KCI
Wright & Choi, 2005	SAC
Yeh, 2005	SAE, PCS, KCI
Zancanella, 1992	SAC, PCT, KCF

a See Table 21.2 and the text discussion of it for explanations of the codes.
b These two studies reported no curricular changes in response to high-stakes testing.

Data Analysis

For this study I tracked the citation information, research sites, scope, and methods of inquiry of the 49 qualitative studies, including the dominant themes in each study's findings. I then coded dominant themes using the above definition of curriculum as the framework for my initial template of analysis. Thus my thematic coding began with three broad categories: Subject Matter Content, Pedagogy, and Structure of Knowledge. Consistent with the template analysis methodological framework, the full elaboration of my coding template evolved during the course of the research. For instance, it has been widely asserted over the past 20-plus years that high-stakes tests cause a narrowing or contraction of nontested subject areas. I was aware of research substantiating this assertion prior to beginning the template analysis and thus assumed that I would need to code the studies that reported the theme of contraction of subject matter content. Based on my previous understandings and on an initial analysis of qualitative studies, I produced an initial template of codes. However, after I undertook the template analysis, for instance, in addition to finding the theme of narrowing/contraction of curriculum to align with high-stakes tests, I also encountered the theme of subject matter content expansion. This finding required the addition of a new thematic code. As I read and reread the 49 qualitative studies, I added thematic codes as the patterns emerged and used them to develop the final template of codes for metasynthesis.

The thematic codes in Table 21.2 can be explained as follows. The first set of thematic codes seeks to track whether teachers, as individual actors at the classroom level, aligned their classroom content to the high-stakes tests. If they did, the thematic codes then mark the nature of this alignment—either subject matter content expansion or subject matter content contraction. In looking for subject matter contraction, I studied the research findings for occurrences of teachers and schools reducing the amount of instructional time and course offerings in either tested or nontested subject areas. An example of findings being coded for content matter expansion can be found in the research of Renter and colleagues (Renter et al., 2006), who found that schools were reducing the amount of instruction in science and social studies because those subjects were not a focus of the high-stakes tests. Conversely, in looking for subject matter expansion, I analyzed the data for reports of teachers and schools increasing the teaching of either tested or nontested subjects in response to high-stakes tests. Vogler (2003) is an example of a study that was coded for test-related content expansion because he found that social studies teachers in his study added language arts/literacy instruction to their social studies curriculum in response to high-stakes tests, which tested for writing but not for social studies content knowledge.

Table 21.2 Qualitative Metasynthesis Code Template

Curriculum	*Code*
Content	SAC—Subject matter content alignment, contraction
	SAE—Subject matter content alignment, expansion
Knowledge form	KCF—Form of knowledge changed, fractured
	KCI—Form of knowledge changed, integrated
Pedagogy	PCT—Pedagogic change to teacher-centered
	PCS—Pedagogic change to student-centered

The second set of thematic codes tracked whether the high-stakes tests affected curricular knowledge forms. This theme was perhaps the most elusive of the three because it required that I follow how teachers organized the knowledge in their classrooms in relation to high-stakes testing. If a study reported that there was a shift in how teachers structured the knowledge they taught, I then coded for whether classroom knowledge forms became more fragmented and isolated into discrete, test-driven bits or became more expansive, inclusive in integrated wholes. As an instance of a study being coded for knowledge fragmentation, one study in this metasynthesis found that math and science were increasingly being taught as a collection of procedures and facts, as opposed to being taught as conceptual, thematic, and higher-order mathematic and scientific thinking (Lomax, West, Harmon, Viator, & Madaus, 1995). Such test-influenced instruction thus essentially fragmented the content knowledge into individuated and isolated procedures and facts for use on the high-stakes test. Other examples can be found where researchers reported that subjects such as social studies were broken up into collections of historical data (see, e.g., Grant et al., 2002) or subjects such as writing were reduced to the production of formulaic and procedural five-paragraph essays (see, e.g., Hillocks, 2002). Conversely, more integrated knowledge forms were coded in studies that found, for instance, some teachers focusing on more conceptual, higher-order thinking that sought to develop more holistic understanding of mathematics (see, e.g., Firestone et al., 1998) or studies that found language arts teachers focusing more conceptually on the process of writing as opposed to step-by-step procedural essay writing (see, e.g., Hillocks, 2002).

Third, I looked at the theme of teachers' pedagogy in response to high-stakes tests. If a study reported that teachers changed their instructional practice because of the testing, then I coded for the theme of teacher-centered instructional strategies or the theme of student-centered instructional strategies. In tracking these themes, I analyzed the studies' findings for evidence of teachers' increasing their use of direct instruction or increasing their use of more interactive pedagogies in response to the tests. For instance, in their research into high-stakes-testing-related social studies instruction, Gerwin and Visone (2006) found that teachers in their study showed dramatic increases in the amount of teacher-centered, fact-driven instruction in subjects included in state-mandated tests. Studies such as this were coded as demonstrating increased teacher-centered pedagogy. Studies reporting teachers' increasing the amount of student-centered, constructivist instruction in response to high-stakes tests, for example, some studies of language arts classrooms where teachers increased their use of interactional and student-led activities (see Wollman-Bonilla, 2004), were coded accordingly.

Once coding was completed, I analyzed the codes for patterns and anomalies on three levels. First, looking at the data as a whole collection, I tracked the predominant themes in terms of individual codes, essentially asking, what do these studies tell us about the overall effects of high-stakes testing on curriculum in terms of content, form, and pedagogy? Within this first level of analysis, I then sought to find relationships between the trends at the level of the single codes and other contextual variables found within the research, looking for overlaps between grade levels and subject areas and the trends found among individual themes.

At the second level I analyzed theme pairings. This involved tracking the number of times that particular codes appeared in corresponding pairs to determine if any relationships existed between changes in content, knowledge structures, and pedagogy. At this level of analysis, I also tracked whether the pairings corresponded to particular grade levels or subject areas.

Finally, at the third level, I analyzed theme triplets, seeking any potential connections between all three areas of content, pedagogy, and knowledge form in relation to the effects of high-stakes testing on classroom practice.

In addition to these three levels of analysis, I looked at the anomalies or weaker thematic relationships. Some studies simply came up with singular findings that did not match or support the trends and patterns of the larger metasynthesis; some groups of studies (such as are found within the social studies) were more conflicted in their findings.

Study Reliability

Reliability is a known issue within template analysis (King, 1998, 2006; Pawson, Greenhalgh, Harvey, & Walshe, 2005), and I have used two strategies to ensure the reliability of the findings of this study. First, to empirically determine the interrater reliability of my own coding, two colleagues independently coded findings of a sample subset of 10 studies. The findings of these coders were then checked against my own, resulting in the following interrater reliability percentages: subject matter content contraction, 86.7 percent; subject matter content expansion, 83.3 percent; knowledge fragmentation, 93.3 percent; knowledge integration, 96.7 percent; teacher-centered pedagogy, 90 percent; student-centered pedagogy, 86.7 percent. The overall interrater reliability for this study was 89.4 percent.

Second, reliability in template analysis is also improved when researchers are explicitly reflexive about both the process of their research and their positioning in relation to their study (King, 1998, 2006; Pawson et al., 2005). Thus it is important to explain my research orientation. I approach this study from within the critical realist tradition, which holds that a real world exists objectively outside human perception, that this world is to varying extents knowable through human cognition, and that this world is in fact changeable relative to our knowledge of it. Furthermore, critical realism recognizes human subjectivity in the understanding of the externally existing world, and as such views knowledge as a social process and as fallible. In these ways, critical realism simultaneously rejects both positivist objectivist *and* relativist subjectivist theories of knowledge in favor of an epistemology that in essence synthesizes aspects of both—an objectively existing world and a socially mediated understanding of that world (Benton & Craib, 2001; Bhaskar, 1989). Consequently, my use of template analysis combined with critical realism makes this study a form of realist review (Pawson et al., 2005).

My critical realist positioning also influences this study in that the use of the word "critical" points to a particular set of political commitments on the part of the researcher. Critical realists seek to understand the world to change it for the better, seek to reflexively understand social mechanisms to promote social equality (Benton & Craib, 2001; Bhaskar, 1989). A similar political commitment underlies the impetus for this study, because I, as a social justice educator, scholar, and activist, have sought to understand the relationship between education and power (see, e.g., Au, 2005, 2006; Au & Apple, 2004). As such, I am interested in the relationship between high-stakes testing and inequalities associated with race and socioeconomic status (see, e.g., Hunter & Bartee, 2003; Kim & Sunderman, 2005; Sirin, 2005). However, although ultimately inseparable from my overall research agenda, for the purposes of this study I have attempted to put my political commitments aside in favor of a focused empirical analysis of how high-stakes testing affects curriculum. Thus, although these effects may have implications for educational equality and social justice, I have made a conscious choice here to bracket those implications as beyond the scope of this specific study and analysis.

Study Limits

Before presenting the findings, it is important to recognize that this study has a specific focus and is therefore limited in at least two particular ways. First, in this metasynthesis I inquire into the frequency and types of curricular change induced by high-stakes testing. Consequently, my inquiry excludes instances where high-stakes testing does not affect the curriculum. As this study's findings will show, the body of research analyzed here focuses predominantly on test-related events, as opposed to test-related nonevents. In this regard, even though a handful of studies included here specifically focus on a lack of test-related instructional changes (see, e.g., Bolgatz, 2006; Gradwell, 2006; Grant, 2003), the findings of this qualitative metasynthesis are inherently skewed toward what the researchers in the majority of these studies chose to focus on in their research: class-room-level changes due to high-stakes tests.

A second way in which the findings of this qualitative metasynthesis are limited relates to the time periods reported on. The studies analyzed here report inconsistently on how curriculum changes in response to high-stakes testing relative to time. Thus some studies focus on periods of curricular change in the months, weeks, or days leading up to high-stakes tests, and others focus on test-related curricular change more generally. Consequently, it was difficult to ascertain whether high-stakes testing was affecting the curriculum all year or simply in time periods immediately preceding the tests. I would argue, however, that these two limits do not take away from the power of the findings presented here. Rather, the limits simply refine the focus of this qualitative metasynthesis, which provides a snapshot and general depiction of the types and frequency of changes made to curricula in high-stakes testing environments.

Findings

As Table 21.3 indicates, the findings of this study suggest that there is a significant relationship between the implementation of high-stakes testing and changes in the content of a curriculum, the structure of knowledge contained within the content, and the types of pedagogy associated with communication of that content. These changes represent three types of control that high-stakes tests exert on curriculum: content control, formal control, and pedagogic control.

Content Control

The dominant theme found in the qualitative research regarding high-stakes testing and curriculum is that of content alignment. More than 80% of the studies contained the theme of curricular content change, whether by contraction or expansion. Furthermore, as Table 21.3 shows, in an overwhelming number of the qualitative studies,

Table 21.3 Summary Findings: Effects of High-Stakes Testing on Curriculum

Curricular Change	*Number of Studies, N = 49*	*Percentage of Total*	*Exemplar of Dominant Theme*
Subject matter	41	83.7%	A Colorado teacher: "Our district has told us to focus on reading, writing, and mathematics. Therefore, science and social studies . . . don't get taught." Taylor et al., 2001, p. 30
Contraction	34	69.4%	
Expansion	14	28.6%	
Knowledge form	34	69.4%	A Massachusetts teacher: "You know, we're not really teaching them how to write. We're teaching them how to follow a format. . . . It's like . . . they're doing paint-by-numbers." Luna & Turner, 2001, p. 83
Fractured	24	49%	
Integrated	10	20.4%	
Pedagogy	38	77.6%	A Kansas teacher: ". . . I don't get to do as many fun activities, like cooperative learning activities or projects. . . . [T]his year I've done a lot more direct teaching than being able to do student-led learning. . . ." Clarke et al., 2003, p. 50
Teacher-centered	32	65.3%	
Student-centered	6	12.3%	

Note: Individual code totals do not necessarily equal the total for any one category because some studies exhibit multiple, even contradictory, codes; for example, subject alignment contraction and subject alignment expansion may appear in the same study.

participants reported instances of the narrowing of curriculum, or curricular contraction to tested subjects. This phenomenon was the most prominent way in which "teaching to the test" manifested in curricula, as nontested subjects were increasingly excluded from curricular content. A more detailed analysis finds that the narrowing of curricular content was strongest among participants in the studies that focused on secondary education, with the most narrowing found in studies of social studies and language arts classrooms. In addition, in another expression of curricular alignment, a significant minority of studies reported some form of content expansion as a result of high-stakes testing, with most of these coming from studies focusing on secondary education and social studies classrooms. As the above evidence suggests, whether in the form of content contraction or content expansion, high-stakes testing leverages a significant amount *content control* over curriculum.

Formal Control

Table 21.3 also indicates that, in a significant number of the qualitative studies, participants reported changes to the form that curricular knowledge took in response to high-stakes testing. The dominant theme in this category suggests that there is a relationship between high-stakes testing and teachers' increasing the fragmentation of knowledge. Such fragmentation manifested in the teaching of content in small, individuated, and isolated test-size pieces, as well as teaching in direct relation to the tests rather than in relation to other subject matter knowledge. However, it is important to note that, as shown in Table 21.3, a minority of studies found that high-stakes testing had led to the increased integration of knowledge in the classroom. Thus, within the body of qualitative research, a dominant theme is that, whether leading to fragmentation or integration of knowledge, high-stakes testing affects curricular form, that is, it leverages *formal control* over the curriculum.

Pedagogic Control

A third dominant theme that appears in the qualitative research is pedagogic change. As shown in Table 3, a significant number of participants in qualitative studies reported that their pedagogy changed in response to high-stakes tests and that a significant majority of the changes included an increase in teacher-centered instruction associated with lecturing and the direct transmission of test-related facts. In addition, as Table 21.3 indicates, a small but important number of studies exhibited the theme of increased student-centered instruction as an effect of high-stakes testing. Further analysis shows that, in this metasynthesis, a cluster of test-related, teacher-centered pedagogy exists surrounding instruction in both language arts and social studies classrooms. Whether in the form of increased teacher-centered instruction or increased student-centered instruction, the evidence suggests that high-stakes testing exerts significant *pedagogic control* over curriculum.

Theme Pairings

An analysis of theme pairings generally mirrors the above findings but also provides a more nuanced outline of potentially significant relationships between dominant themes.

As Table 21.4 indicates, the most prominent theme pairing suggests that there is a relationship between the narrowing of curriculum and an increase in teacher-centered instruction as teachers respond to pressures created by high-stakes testing environments. The next highest occurrence of theme pairing suggests that increased teacher-centered pedagogy and increased fragmentation of knowledge forms are likely to coincide in response to high-stakes testing. The third most frequent theme pairing suggests a relationship between curricular content narrowing and the fragmentation of knowledge forms, which are likely to occur together in response to high-stakes testing.

The findings further suggest that there are weaker but significant relationships between the expansion of subject matter and an increase of a more integrated structure of knowledge in response to high-stakes testing, as well as a contraction or narrowing of curricular content and a simultaneous content expansion. Three other significant theme pairings appear in the study, two of which are seemingly contradictory to the dominant trends outlined above. As Table 21.4 shows, theme pairing of curricular expansion and an increase in teacher-centered pedagogy in response to high-stakes testing was also

Table 21.4 Summary of Selected Theme Pairings

Theme Pairing	*Occurrence*
Content contraction/teacher-centered pedagogy	26/37 (70.3%)
Teacher-centered pedagogy/knowledge fragmentation	23/35 (65.7%)
Content contraction/knowledge fragmentation	22/34 (64.7%)
Content expansion/knowledge integration	9/34 (26.5%)
Student-centered pedagogy/knowledge integration	6/35 (17.1%)
Content contraction/content expansion	7/43 (16.3%)
Content expansion/teacher-centered pedagogy	6/37 (16.2%)
Content expansion/student-centered pedagogy	6/37 (16.2%)

found. Other findings showed increases in student-centered pedagogy paired with an increase in the integration of knowledge in response to high-stakes testing.

Theme Triplets

A total of 28 studies in this qualitative metasynthesis produced codes within each area of curriculum identified here. I now turn to the final level of analysis, examining these theme triplets to determine if there are any potential relationships between all three thematic areas. Overwhelmingly, the prevalent theme triplet in the qualitative research was the combination of contracting curricular content, fragmentation of the structure of knowledge, and increasing teacher-centered pedagogy in response to high-stakes testing. This theme triplet appears 21 times (75%) among the 28 studies that produced themes in all three areas, suggesting a relationship between the themes in response to high-stakes testing. The second most frequently occurring theme triplet, that of curricular content expansion, increasing integration of knowledge, and increasing student-centered instruction, appears 6 times (21.4%) in the study. This triplet is indeed the exact opposite of the dominant triplet.

Discussion

Despite some researchers' claims to the contrary, the findings of this study suggest that high-stakes tests encourage curricular alignment to the tests themselves. This alignment tends to take the form of a curricular content narrowing to tested subjects, to the detriment or exclusion of nontested subjects. The findings of this study further suggest that the structure of the knowledge itself is also changed to meet the test-based norms: Content is increasingly taught in isolated pieces and often learned only within the context of the tests themselves. Finally, in tandem with both content contraction and the fragmentation of knowledge, pedagogy is also implicated, as teachers increasingly turn to teacher-centered instruction to cover the breadth of test-required information and procedures. Thus I have identified three different, interrelated types of curricular control associated with high-stakes testing: *content, formal,* and *pedagogic.* The control over knowledge content and the form the knowledge takes are related to and associated with control of pedagogy as well.

As I noted in Tables 21.3 and 21.4, however, several less frequently occurring themes seemed to contradict the predominant findings of this study. The data suggest that in a small number of cases, high-stakes testing was associated with an increase in student-centered instruction, content integration, and subject matter expansion. For instance, there are seven simultaneous occurrences of the themes of content contraction and content expansion related to high-stakes tests, most of which come from secondary social studies and language arts (see, e.g., Anagnostopolous, 2003b; Luna & Turner, 2001; Segall, 2003; A. M. Smith, 2006; Vogler, 2003). In these cases, teachers are both adding some content to meet the demands of the tests and contracting content in other areas. In addition, because the stakes of state-mandated social studies testing vary greatly from state to state (Grant & Horn, 2006), the findings indicate that high-stakes-test-induced curricular expansion has taken place in social studies classrooms as teachers integrate reading-test-related literacy skills into their own social studies curricula (see, e.g., Vogler, 2003).

Indeed, this phenomenon of expanding curricular content due to the integration of test-required literacy skills or test-specific content accounts for the majority of the instances of curricular expansion (see, e.g., Barton, 2005; Clarke et al., 2003; Libresco, 2005; Rex & Nelson, 2004; Wolf & Wolf, 2002; Wollman-Bonilla, 2004; Yeh, 2005).

There appears to be a similar relationship regarding the small numbers of increases in student-centered pedagogies relative to high-stakes testing. Almost all occurrences of the theme of increases in student-centered pedagogy occur with instances of subject matter expansion. These cases revolve around teachers whose test-based instruction involves the development of critical literacy skills (see, e.g., Clarke et al., 2003; Libresco, 2005; Rex & Nelson, 2004; Wolf & Wolf, 2002; Wollman-Bonilla, 2004; Yeh, 2005). For instance, New York State's history exam involves a mix of multiple-choice questions and a document-based essay question (DBQ; Grant, 2003). Social studies teachers, in preparing students for DBQs, have the charge of teaching a specific critical literacy skill set instead of being forced to focus solely on a rigidly imposed collection of historical facts (see, e.g., Bolgatz, 2006; Clarke et al., 2003; Grant, 2003; Libresco, 2005). It is likely that teachers in these studies thus find the potential for increased flexibility in the content and pedagogy they use to teach social studies in their respective high-stakes environments. Furthermore, because social studies instruction figures prominently in the above contradictory findings, and because the only two studies to argue that testing does not influence any aspect of curriculum also focus on this subject area (Gradwell, 2006; Grant, 2003), it is also possible that social studies represents a special case in relation to high-stakes testing and curricular control (Au, in press).

The above discussion indicates a likely relationship between the construction of the high-stakes tests themselves and the curricular changes induced by the tests. Research supports the existence of such a relationship. As Yeh (2005) finds, teachers in Minnesota report that their pedagogy is not negatively affected by high-stakes tests because they feel the tests there are well designed and do not promote drill and rote memorization. Another example comes from Hillocks (2002), who analyzes the teaching of writing in relation to the writing examinations delivered in Texas, Illinois, New York, Oregon, and Kentucky. One of Hillocks's main findings is that states with poorly designed systems of writing assessment promote a technical, mechanical, five-paragraph essay form, and that teachers' pedagogy adapts to that form in those states. The findings of these studies suggest that test construction matters in terms of teachers' curricular responses to high-stakes tests (see also Clarke et al., 2003).

Conclusion

In this study, using a form of qualitative metasynthesis called template analysis, I have reviewed the findings of 49 qualitative studies addressing the impact of high-stakes testing on curriculum. As Tables 3 and 4 indicate, the evidence presented here strongly suggests that as teachers negotiate high-stakes testing educational environments, the tests have the predominant effect of narrowing curricular content to those subjects included in the tests, resulting in the increased fragmentation of knowledge forms into bits and pieces learned for the sake of the tests themselves, and compelling teachers to use more lecture-based, teacher-centered pedagogies. Another significant finding of this study is that, in a minority of cases, high-stakes tests have led to increases in student-centered pedagogy and increases in content knowledge integration. Combined, these findings indicate that high-stakes testing exerts significant amounts of control over the content, knowledge forms, and pedagogies at the classroom level.

The curricular control found in this study further suggests that high-stakes testing represents the tightening of the loose coupling between policymakers' intentions and the institutional environments created by their policies (Burch, 2007). This conclusion should not be surprising to educational researchers and practitioners because systems of educational accountability built on high-stakes, standardized tests are in fact intended to increase external control over what happens in schools and classrooms. As Moe (2003) explains, the rationale behind systems of high-stakes accountability is quite clear:

> The movement for school accountability is essentially a movement for more effective topdown control of the schools. The idea is that, if public authorities want to promote student achievement, they need to adopt organizational control mechanisms—tests, school report cards, rewards and sanctions, and the like—designed to get district officials, principals, teachers, and students to change their behavior. . . . Virtually all organizations need to engage in top-down control, because the people at the top have goals they want the people at the bottom to pursue, and something has to be done to bring about the desired behaviors.
>
> The public school system is just like other organizations in this respect. (p. 81)

The intentions of promoters of high-stakes test-based educational reforms are thus apparent in the policy designs, which are purposefully constructed to negate "asymmetries" between classroom practice and the policy goals of those with political and bureaucratic power (Wöþmann, 2003).

Given the central findings of this study, however, a crucial question is raised: Are test-driven curriculum and teacher-centered instruction good or bad for teachers, students, schools, communities, and education in general? Considering the body of research connecting high-stakes testing with increased drop-out rates and lower achievement for working-class students and students of color (see, e.g., Amrein & Berliner, 2002b; Groves, 2002; Madaus & Clarke, 2001; Marchant & Paulson, 2005; Nichols, Glass, & Berliner, 2005), the findings of this study point to the need for further analysis of how curricular control may or may not contribute to educational inequality.

Note

I would like to thank Diana Hess, Simone Schweber, Keita Takayama, Ross Collin, Eduardo Cavieres, Quentin Wheeler-Bell, the three anonymous *ER* reviewers, and *ER* editor Gregory Camilli for their invaluable feedback on this article.

References

References marked with an asterisk indicate studies included in the metasynthesis.

*Agee, J. (2004). Negotiating a teaching identity: An African American teacher's struggle to teach in test-driven contexts. *Teachers College Record, 106*(4), 747–774.

Airasian, P. W. (1987). State mandated testing and educational reform: Context and consequences. *American Journal of Education, 95*(3), 393–412.

Amrein, A. L., & Berliner, D. C. (2002a, December). *An analysis of some unintended and negative consequences of high-stakes testing.* Tempe, AZ: Educational Policy Studies Laboratory, Arizona State University. Retrieved February 12, 2006, from http://www.asu.edu/educ/epsl/EPRU/epru_2002_Research_Writing.htm

Amrein, A. L., & Berliner, D. C. (2002b). High-stakes testing, uncertainty, and student learning. *Education Policy Analysis Archives, 10*(18). Retrieved September 27, 2005, from http://epaa.asu.edu/epaa/v10n18

*Anagnostopolous, D. (2003a). The new accountability, student failure, and teachers' work in urban high schools. *Educational Policy, 17*(3), 291–316.

*Anagnostopolous, D. (2003b). Testing and student engagement with literature in urban classrooms: A multi-layered perspective. *Research in the Teaching of English, 38*(2), 177–212.

Apple, M. W. (1995). *Education and power* (2nd ed.). New York: Routledge.

Au, W. (2005). Power, identity, and the third rail. In P. C. Miller (ed.), *Narratives from the classroom: An introduction to teaching* (pp. 65–85). Thousand Oaks, CA: Sage.

Au, W. (2006, November). Against economic determinism: Revisiting the roots of neo-Marxism in critical educational theory. *Journal for Critical Education Policy Studies, 4*(2). Retrieved December 12, 2006, from http://www.jceps.com/?pageID=article&articleID=66

Au, W. (in press). Social studies, social justice: W(h)ither the social studies in high-stakes testing? *Teacher Education Quarterly.*

Au, W., & Apple, M. W. (2004). Interrupting globalization as an educational practice. *Educational Policy, 18*(5), 784–793.

*Barton, K. C. (2005). "I'm not saying these are going to be easy": Wise practice in an urban elementary school. In E. A. Yeager & O. L. Davis Jr. (eds.), *Wise social studies teaching in an age of high-stakes testing* (pp. 11–31). Greenwich, CT: Information Age Publishing.

Beauchamp, G. A. (1982). Curriculum theory: Meaning, development, and use. *Theory Into Practice, 21*(1), 23–27.

Benton, T., & Craib, I. (2001). *Philosophy of social science: The philosophical foundations of social thought.* New York: Palgrave.

Bhaskar, R. (1989). *Reclaiming reality: A critical introduction to contemporary philosophy* (2nd ed.). New York: Verso.

*Bol, L. (2004). Teachers' assessment practices in a high-stakes testing environment. *Teacher Education and Practice, 17*(2), 162–181.

*Bolgatz, J. (2006). Using primary documents with fourth-grade students: Talking about racism while preparing for state-level tests. In S. G. Grant (ed.), *Measuring history: Cases of state-level testing across the United States* (pp. 133–156). Greenwich, CT: Information Age Publishing.

*Booher-Jennings, J. (2005). Below the bubble: "Educational triage" and the Texas accountability system. *American Educational Research Journal, 42*(2), 231–268.

Braun, H. (2004). Reconsidering the impact of high-stakes testing. *Education Policy Analysis Archives, 12*(1). Retrieved March 29, 2006, from http://epaa.asu.edu/epaa/v12n1

*Brimijoin, K. (2005). Differentiation and high-stakes testing: An oxymoron? *Theory Into Practice, 44*(3), 254–261.

Burch, P. E. (2007). Educational policy and practice from the perspective of institutional theory: Crafting a wider lens. *Educational Researcher, 36*(2), 84–95.

Cimbricz, S. (2002). State testing and teachers' thinking and practice. *Education Policy Analysis Archives, 10*(2). Retrieved September 4, 2006, from http://epaa.asu.edu/epaa/v10n2.html

*Clarke, M., Shore, A., Rhoades, K., Abrams, L. M., Miao, J., & Li, J. (2003, January). *Perceived effects of state-mandated testing programs on teaching and learning: Findings from interviews with educators in low-, medium-, and high-stakes states.* Boston: National Board on Educational Testing and Public Policy, Lynch School of Education, Boston College. Retrieved March 20, 2006, from http://www.bc.edu/research/nbetpp/reports.html

*Costigan, A. T., III. (2002). Teaching the culture of high stakes testing: Listening to new teachers. *Action in Teacher Education, 23*(4), 28–34.

Crabtree, B. F., & Miller, W. L. (1999). Using codes and code manuals: A template organizing style of interpretation. In B. F. Crabtree & W. L. Miller (eds.), *Doing qualitative research* 2nd ed., (pp. 163–178). Thousand Oaks, CA: Sage.

*Debray, E., Parson, G., & Avila, S. (2003). Internal alignment and external pressure. In M. Carnoy, R. Elmore, & L. S. Siskin (eds.), *The new accountability: High schools and high-stakes testing* (pp. 55–85). New York: RoutledgeFalmer.

DeWitt-Brinks, D., & Rhodes, S. C. (1992, May 20–25). *Listening instruction: A qualitative meta-analysis of twenty-four selected studies.* Paper presented at the annual meeting of the International Communication Association, Miami, FL.

Eisner, E. W. (1994). *The educational imagination: On the design and evaluation of school programs* (3rd ed.). New York: Macmillan.

*Fickel, L. H. (2006). Paradox of practice: Expanding and contracting curriculum in a high-stakes climate. In S. G. Grant (ed.), *Measuring history: Cases of state-level testing across the United States* (pp. 75–103). Greenwich, CT: Information Age Publishing.

*Firestone, W. A., Mayrowetz, D., & Fairman, J. (1998). Performance-based assessment and instructional change: The effects of testing in Maine and Maryland. *Educational Evaluation and Policy Analysis, 20*(2), 94–113.

*Gerwin, D., & Visone, F. (2006). The freedom to teach: Contrasting history teaching in elective and state-tested course. *Social Education, 34*(2), 259–282.

*Gradwell, J. M. (2006). Teaching in spite of, rather than because of, the test: A case of ambitious history teaching in New York State. In S. G. Grant (ed.), *Measuring history: Cases of state-level testing across the United States* (pp. 157–176). Greenwich, CT: Information Age Publishing.

*Grant, S. G. (2003). *History lessons: Teaching, learning, and testing in U.S. high school classrooms.* Mahwah, NJ: Lawrence Erlbaum.

*Grant, S. G., Gradwell, J. M., Lauricella, A. M., Derme-Insinna, A., Pullano, L., & Tzetzo, K. (2002). When increasing stakes need not mean increasing standards: The case of the New York state global history and geography exam. *Theory and Research in Social Education, 30*(4), 488–515.

Grant, S. G., & Horn, C. L. (2006). The state of state-level history tests. In S. G. Grant (ed.), *Measuring history: Cases of state-level testing across the United States* (pp. 9–27). Greenwich, CT: Information Age Publishing.

*Groves, P. (2002). "Doesn't it feel morbid here?" High-stakes testing and the widening of the equity gap. *Educational Foundations, 16*(2), 15–31.

Harden, R. M. (2001). The learning environment and the curriculum. *Medical Teacher, 23*(4), 335–336.

*Hillocks, G., Jr. (2002). *The testing trap: How state writing assessments control learning.* New York: Teachers College Press.

Hunter, R. C., & Bartee, R. (2003). The achievement gap: Issues of competition, class, and race. *Education and Urban Society, 35*(2), 151–160.

Jackson, P. W. (1996). Conceptions of curriculum and curriculum specialists. In P. W. Jackson (ed.), *Handbook of research on curriculum: A project of the American Educational Research Association* (pp. 3–40). New York: Simon & Schuster Macmillan.

Kim, J. S., & Sunderman, G. L. (2005). Measuring academic proficiency under the No Child Left Behind Act: Implications for educational equity. *Educational Researcher, 34*(8), 3–13.

King, N. (1998) Template analysis. In G. Symon & C. Cassell (eds.), *Qualitative methods and analysis in organizational research: A practical guide* (pp. 118–134). London: Sage.

King, N. (2006, October 23). *What is template analysis?* University of Huddersfield School of Human and Health Sciences. Retrieved April 27, 2007, from http://www.hud.ac.uk/hhs/research/template_analysis/whatis.htm

Kliebard, H. M. (1989). Problems of definition in curriculum. *Journal of Curriculum and Supervision, 5*(1), 1–5.

*Landman, J. (2000, January 7). *A state-mandated curriculum, a high-stakes test: One Massachusetts high school history department's response to a very new policy context.* Doctoral qualifying paper, Harvard Graduate School of Education, Cambridge, MA. (ERIC Document Reproduction Service No. ED440915)

*Libresco, A. S. (2005). How she stopped worrying and learned to love the test . . . sort of. In E. A. Yeager & O. L. Davis Jr. (eds.), *Wise social studies teaching in an age of high-stakes testing* (pp. 33–49). Greenwich, CT: Information Age Publishing.

*Lipman, P. (2002). Making the global city, making inequality: The political economy and cultural politics of Chicago school policy. *American Educational Research Journal, 39*(2), 379–419.

Lipman, P. (2004). *High stakes education: Inequality, globalization, and urban school reform.* New York: RoutledgeFalmer.

*Lomax, R. G., West, M. M., Harmon, M. C., Viator, K. A., & Madaus, G. F. (1995). The impact of mandated standardized testing on minority students. *Journal of Negro Education, 64*(2), 171–185.

*Luna, C., & Turner, C. L. (2001). The impact of the MCAS: Teachers talk about high-stakes testing. *English Journal, 91*(1), 79–87.

Madaus, G. F. (1988). The influence of testing on the curriculum. In L. N. Tanner (ed.), *Critical issues in curriculum: Eighty-seventh year-book of the national society for the study of education* (pp. 83–121). Chicago: University of Chicago Press.

Madaus, G. F., & Clarke, M. (2001). The adverse impact of high-stakes testing on minority students: Evidence from one hundred years of test data. In G. Orfield & M. L. Kornhaber (eds.), *Raising standards or raising barriers? Inequality and high-stakes testing in public education* (pp. 85–106). New York: Century Foundation Press.

Marchant, G. J., & Paulson, S. E. (2005, January 21). The relationship of high school graduation exams to graduation rates and SAT scores. *Education Policy Analysis Archives, 13*(6). Retrieved February 8, 2006, from http://epaa.asu.edu/ epaa/v13n6/

McCormick, J., Rodney, P., & Varcoe, C. (2003). Reinterpretations across studies: An approach to meta-analysis. *Qualitative Health Research, 13*(7), 933–944.

McEwan, H., & Bull, B. (1991). The pedagogic nature of subject matter knowledge. *American Educational Research Journal, 28*(2), 316–334.

*McNeil, L. M. (2000). *Contradictions of school reform: Educational costs of standardized testing.* New York: Routledge.

*McNeil, L. M., & Valenzuela, A. (2001). The harmful impact of the TAAS system of testing in Texas: Beneath the accountability rhetoric. In G. Orfield & M. L. Kornhaber (eds.), *Raising standards or raising barriers? Inequality and high-stakes testing in public education* (pp. 127–150). New York: Century Foundation Press.

Moe, T. M. (2003). Politics, control, and the future of school accountability. In P. E. Peterson & M. R. West (eds.), *No child left behind? The politics and practice of school accountability* (pp. 80–106). Washington, DC: Brookings Institution Press.

*Murillo E. G., Jr., & Flores, S. Y. (2002). Reform by shame: Managing the stigma of labels in high-stakes testing. *Educational Foundations, 16*(2), 93–108.

Nichols, S. L., & Berliner, D. C. (2005, March). *The inevitable corruption of indicators and educators through high-stakes testing* (No. EPSL-0503-101-EPRU). Tempe; AZ: Education Policy Studies Laboratory, Arizona State University. Retrieved September 27, 2005, from http://www.asu.edu/educ/epsl/EPRU/documents/EPSL-0503-101-EPRU-exec.pdf

Nichols, S. L., & Berliner, D. C. (2007). *Collateral damage: How high-stakes testing corrupts America's schools.* Cambridge, MA: Harvard Education Press.

Nichols, S. L., Glass, G. V., & Berliner, D. C. (2005, September). *High-stakes testing and student achievement: Problems for the No Child Left Behind Act* (No. EPSL-0509-105-EPRU). Tempe, AZ: Education Policy Studies Laboratory, Arizona State University. Retrieved September 27, 2005, from http://www.asu.edu/educ/epsl/EPRU/documents/EPSL-0509-105-EPRU.pdf

Noblit, G. W., & Hare, R. D. (1988). *Meta-ethnography: Synthesizing qualitative studies* (Vol. 11). Newbury Park, CA: Sage.

Orfield, G., & Wald, J. (2000). Testing, testing: The high-stakes testing mania hurts poor and minority students the most. *Nation, 270*(22), 38–40.

*Passman, R. (2001). Experiences with student-centered teaching and learning in high-stakes assessment environments. *Education, 122*(1), 189–199.

Pawson, R. Greenhalgh, T., Harvey, G., & Walshe, K. (2005). Realist review: A new method of systematic review designed for complex policy interventions. *Journal of Health Services Research & Policy, 10*(1), 21–84.

*Perreault, G. (2000). The classroom impact of high-stress testing. *Education, 120*(4), 705–710.

*Renter, D. S., Scott, C., Kober, N., Chudowsky, N., Joftus, S., & Zabala, D. (2006, March 28). *From the capital to the classroom: Year 4 of the No Child Left Behind Act.* Washington, DC: Center on Education Policy. Retrieved March 28, 2006, from http://www.cep-dc.org

*Rex, L. A. (2003). Loss of the creature: The obscuring of inclusivity in classroom discourse. *Communication Education, 52*(1), 30–46.

*Rex, L. A., & Nelson, M. C. (2004). How teachers' professional identities position high-stakes preparation in their classrooms. *Teachers College Record, 106*(6), 1288–1331.

*Salinas, C. (2006). Teaching in a high-stakes testing setting: What becomes of teacher knowledge. In S. G. Grant (ed.), *Measuring history: Cases of state-level testing across the United States* (pp. 177–193). Greenwich, CT: Information Age Publishing.

Sandelowski, M., Docherty, S., & Emden, C. (1997). Qualitative meta-synthesis: Issues and techniques. *Research in Nursing & Health, 20*(4), 365–371.

Schneider, A. L., & Ingram, H. (1997). *Policy design for democracy.* Lawrence: University of Kansas.

*Segall, A. (2003). Teachers' perceptions of the impact of state-mandated standardized testing: The Michigan Educational Assessment Program (MEAP) as a case study of consequences. *Theory and Research in Social Education, 31*(3), 287–325.

Segall, A. (2004a). Blurring the lines between content and pedagogy. *Social Education, 68*(7), 479–482.

Segall, A. (2004b). Revisiting pedagogical content knowledge: The pedagogy of content/the content of pedagogy. *Teaching and Teacher Education, 20*, 489–504.

Sirin, S. R. (2005). Socioeconomic status and student achievement: A meta-analytic review of research. *Review of Educational Research, 75*(3), 417–453.

*Siskin, L. S. (2003). Outside the core: Accountability in tested and untested subjects. In M. Carnoy, R. Elmore, & L. S. Siskin (eds.), *The new accountability: High schools and high-stakes testing* (pp. 87–98). New York: RoutledgeFalmer.

*Sloan, K. (2005). Playing to the logic of the Texas accountability system: How focusing on "ratings"—not children—undermines quality and equity. In A. Valenzuela (ed.), *Leaving children behind: How "Texas-style" accountability fails Latino youth* (pp. 153–178). Albany: State University of New York.

*Smagorinsky, P., Lakly, A., & Johnson, T. S. (2002). Acquiescence, accommodation, and resistance in learning to teach within a prescribed curriculum. *English Education, 34*(3), 187–213.

*Smith, A. M. (2006). Negotiating control and protecting the private: History teachers and the Virginia standards of learning. In S. G. Grant (ed.), *Measuring history: Cases of state-level testing across the United States* (pp. 221–247). Greenwich, CT: Information Age Publishing.

Smith, M. L. (1991). Put to the test: The effects of external testing on teachers. *Educational Researcher, 20*(5), 8–11.

*Taylor, G., Shepard, L., Kinner, F., & Rosenthal, J. (2001, September). *A survey of teachers' perspectives on high-stakes testing in Colorado: What gets taught, what gets lost.* Boulder, CO: CRESST/CREDE/University of Colorado at Boulder. Retrieved February 24, 2006, from http://education.colorado.edu/epic/COStdRprts/COstdrpreptitle.asp

Thorne, S. E., Jensen, L., Kearney, M. H., Noblit, G. W., & Sandelowski, M. (2004). Qualitative metasynthesis: Reflections on methodological orientation and ideological agenda. *Qualitative Health Research, 14*(10), 1342–1365.

*Valenzuela, A. (2000). The significance of the TAAS test for Mexican immigrant and Mexican American adolescents: A case study. *Hispanic Journal of Behavioral Sciences, 22*(4), 524–539.

Valenzuela, A., Prieto, L., & Hamilton, M. P. (2007). No Child Left Behind and minority youth: What the qualitative evidence suggests. *Anthropology & Education Quarterly, 38*(1), 1–8.

*van Hover, S. D. (2006). Teaching history in the old dominion: The impact of Virginia's accountability reform on seven secondary beginning history teachers. In S. G. Grant (ed.), *Measuring history: Cases of state-level testing across the United States* (pp. 195–219). Greenwich, CT: Information Age Publishing.

*van Hover, S. D., & Heinecke, W. (2005). The impact of accountability reform on the " 'wise practice" of secondary history teachers: The Virginia experience. In E. A. Yeager & O. L. Davis Jr. (eds.), *Wise social studies teaching in an age of high-stakes testing* (pp. 89–105). Greenwich, CT: Information Age Publishing.

*Vogler, K. E. (2003). An integrated curriculum using state standards in a high-stakes testing environment. *Middle School Journal, 34*(4), 10.

Watanabe, M. (2007). Displaced teacher and state priorities in a high-stakes accountability context. *Educational Policy, 21*(2), 311–368.

*Williamson, P., Bondy, E., Langley, L., & Mayne, D. (2005). Meeting the challenge of high-stakes testing while remaining child-centered: The representations of two urban teachers. *Childhood Education, 81*(4), 190–195.

Wößmann, L. (2003). Central exit exams and student achievement: International evidence. In P. E. Peterson & M. R. West (eds.), *No child left behind? The politics and practice of school accountability* (pp. 292–324). Washington, DC: Brookings Institution Press.

*Wolf, S. A., & Wolf, K. P. (2002). Teaching *true* and *to* the test in writing. *Language Arts, 79*(3), 240.

*Wollman-Bonilla, J. E. (2004). Principled teaching to(wards) the test? Persuasive writing in two classrooms. *Language Arts, 81*(6), 502–511.

*Wright, W. E., & Choi, D. (2005, December). *Voices from the classroom: A statewide survey of experienced third-grade English Language Learner teachers on the impact of language and high-stakes testing policies in Arizona.* Tempe, AZ: Educational Policy Studies Laboratory, Arizona State University. Retrieved February 12, 2006, from http:// www.asu.edu/educ/epsl/EPRU/epru_2005_Research_Writing.htm

*Yeh, S. S. (2005, October 28). Limiting the unintended consequences of high-stakes testing. *Education Policy Analysis Archives, 13*(43). Retrieved February 8, 2006, from http://epaa.asu.edu/epaa/v13n43/

*Zancanella, D. (1992). The influence of state-mandated tessting on teachers of literature. *Educational Evaluation and Policy Analysis, 14*(3), 283–295.

22

Standardizing Knowledge in a Multicultural Society

Christine Sleeter and Jamy Stillman

Introduction

> Curriculum in any time and place becomes the site of a battleground where the fight is over whose values and beliefs will achieve the legitimation and the respect that acceptance into the national discourse provides. (Kliebard, 1995, p. 250–251)

Across the United States, in an attempt to raise standards for student learning, states have developed curriculum standards that specify what students are to learn. Raising standards has become synonymous with standardizing curriculum. This study critically examines two sets of current curriculum standards document in California. There, very detailed curriculum standards were developed during the 1990s in history-social science, reading/ language arts, mathematics, natural science, and visual and performing arts. In 2001, state legislation created a seamless web specifying not only subject matter content in every discipline for K-12, but also disciplinary subject matter university coursework for teacher preparation. Standards for teacher credentialing were also aligned to K-12 content standards, making the main role of teacher education preparation to teach state-adopted curriculum. The purpose of this article is to examine standards in two disciplines in order to explore their connection with broader power relationships.

Theoretical Framework

For over a century, curriculum in the United States has periodically surfaced as a lightening rod for debate about what schools should do, and more broadly, about basic values and beliefs about how young people should view society, and what adults expect of them as they enter the adult world. Like Kliebard (1995), Bernstein and Solomon (1999) argued that in any society, groups struggle for the means to control consciousness of people, and that education develops the consciousness of children and youth: "The pedagogic device, the condition for the materializing of symbolic control, is the object of a struggle for domination, for the group who appropriates the device has access to a ruler and distributor of consciousness, identity, and desire" (p. 268).

To examine the legitimation of power and control in two disciplines in California, we used Bernstein's (1975) theory of codes of power in curriculum. Bernstein suggested that codes of power can be uncovered by examining how curriculum is classified and framed. *Classification* refers to the degree to which curriculum contents are separated and bounded—for example, the strength of boundaries among disciplines, or between school knowledge and everyday knowledge. "Where classification is strong, contents are well insulated from each other by strong boundaries" (p. 88). Bernstein distinguished between two basic types of curriculum in relationship to classification: a collection code curriculum, and an integrated code curriculum. A *collection code* reflects strong classification; the stronger the classification, the more hierarchical the structure of knowledge, the more status academic knowledge has over everyday knowledge, and the greater degree to which teaching moves sequentially from basic facts toward the deep structure of a given discipline. An *integrated code* curriculum is weakly classified, boundaries are blurred, and knowledge is viewed much less hierarchically. Curriculum tends to be organized around themes and emphasizes the knowledge construction process rather than accumulation of disciplinary facts and concepts. Bernstein suggested that movements away from collection to integrated code curricula may reflect broader social movements that attempt to "alter power structures and principles of control" (p. 111). Conversely, movements that attempt to reestablish collection code curricula may reflect broader movements to reestablish traditional power hierarchies.

Frame refers to "the degree of control teacher and pupil possess over the selection, organization, pacing and timing of the knowledge transmitted and received in the pedagogical relationship" (Bernstein, 1975, p. 89). Under strong framing, teachers and students learn to work within a set of received knowledge; under weak framing, they are encouraged to use their own sense-making process. Curriculum that has strong framing offers little decision-making power to teachers or students; curriculum that has weak framing encourages classroom decision-making. "Framing regulates the form of socialization into the category system, that is, into the positional structure, and into the form of the power relationships which constitute, maintain and reproduce the structure" (p. 179). In other words, teachers and students learn their place in hierarchical power relationships through the degree of power they have over selecting, organizing, and teaching or learning curriculum.

These codes are constructed and play out within structural relationships, which include relationships among teachers (grade level, subject area), between teachers and administrators, and among students (particularly how students are grouped in school). Ultimately, Bernstein was interested in how young people are inducted into a stratified and segmented society. Because he viewed education as a primary regulator of society, he saw classification and framing as tools for examining how regulation is imposed and, at times, disrupted.

The standards movement in the United States followed a period in which power relations in the broader society had been disrupted. The civil rights movement had spawned various movements to redistribute power, which in education took forms such as school desegregation, multicultural education, and bilingual education. To what extent can the standards movement be understood as an attempt to restore earlier power relations? Bernstein's framework enables us to examine this question as it is reflected in curriculum documents. Below, we develop and situate the standards movement in an historic context, then report our analysis of a set of content standards documents.

From Civil Rights to Standardization

Beginning with the civil rights movement in the 1960s, the ethnic studies movement, the women's movement, and other democratically based equity movements challenged collection code curricula that had defined academic knowledge of Europeans and European Americans as superior to other knowledge systems. When schools were initially desegregated, parents and community leaders of color began to demand that the curriculum reflect their communities, and that teachers expect the same level of academic learning of their children as they did of white children (Gay, 1995; Weinberg, 1977). Historically disenfranchised communities argued that textbooks and other sources of curriculum were too often culturally irrelevant to students of color, and inaccessible to students of non-English language backgrounds. Particularly on college campuses, youth demanded ethnic studies courses that related to their own experiences. Ethnic studies and women's studies scholarship burgeoned; faculty hired to teach such courses found themselves needing to unearth subjugated knowledge to construct new curricula (Gay).

By the 1980s, models and approaches to multicultural and bilingual curriculum had been created; they tended to follow integrated curriculum codes and weakened framing in that many of the models emphasized teachers' and students' power over the knowledge construction process. For example, Watkins's (1993) six black curriculum frameworks and Tetreault's (1989) phases of the integration of women into curriculum dislodged classifications within traditional academic knowledge. Ladson-Billings's (1994) and Gay's (1995) research on culturally relevant pedagogy, along with bilingual education research, demonstrated how essential it is for all students, and especially second-language learners to build their academic skills on everyday life experiences and family-based knowledge (e.g., Cummins, 1996; Gutierrez et al., 2002; Ruíz, 1995; Tharp et al., 2000). Bilingual education research demonstrated that primary language literacy among English learners supports second language acquisition, and that fluency in multiple languages is superior to fluency in only one (e.g., Cummins, 1996; Dicker, 1996; Hakuta, 1986; Thomas & Collier, 1999).

More general conceptions of language learning and language arts instruction also shifted. In particular, more holistic and integrated approaches to reading and writing instruction emerged and began to challenge traditional pedagogical models of language arts instruction (Emig, 1971, 1982; Goodman & Goodman, 1979; Graves, 1982; Gutierrez, 2001). Scholarship that argued for a more social and cultural notion of language learning followed (e.g., Heath, 1983), and influenced the development of and research about language arts instructional models that showed effectiveness for culturally and linguistically diverse children. In particular, researchers came to considerable consensus about the most helpful instructional principles and processes, emphasizing the importance of contextualized rather than skill-driven instruction, and the connections between language, thinking, values, culture, and identity (Center for Research on Education, Diversity and Excellence, 2002; Gibbons, 2002; Wink & Putney, 2002).

Social science was also a subject of debates. One view was that the main purpose of social studies is to prepare citizens. That view conflicted with the more traditional view of social science as discipline based, with curriculum drawing from discipline-specific content. Yet a third view defined social science as a process of reflective inquiry (Brophy & VanSledright, 1997); for example, Wineberg (2001) suggested teaching students to think historically and to analyze historical texts as artifacts of human production in specific contexts, rather than delivering historian-constructed interpretations of the past.

The mid-1980s ushered in the standards movement, which viewed the main purpose of schooling as bolstering the U.S. economy and its national sovereignty and security (Coles, 2000; Engels, 2000). Its genesis is often traced to the publication of *A Nation at Risk* in 1983 (National Commission on Excellence in Education). Subsequent reform reports expressed concerns of the business community: that technological advances and global restructuring were transforming the nature of production and work, and that the United States would need to develop many, many more workers for demands of this new economy. These new workers would need to master "technological visualization; abstract reasoning, mathematical, scientific, and computer expertise; knowledge of specific technologies and production techniques; individual initiative; and so forth" (Berliner & Biddle, 1995, p. 141). On the heels of these reform reports came a barrage of highly visible conservative critiques of multiculturalism and bilingual education (e.g., Bloom, 1989; Ravitch, 1990; Schlesinger, 1992), which targeted curricular changes and policies that had been instituted in schools and universities. They charged that multiculturalism was damaging education and social cohesion, and that multicultural and bilingual curricula were intellectually weak, addressing minority student achievement in damaging ways by appealing mainly to self-esteem rather than hard work and intellectual challenge.

The reform reports and the conservative critiques of multiculturalism depicted schools, and U.S. society generally, as being in a state of crisis. In response; beginning in the 1980s, states began to construct disciplinary content standards. By the mid-1990s, most states had content standards in place and were designing or beginning to implement statewide systems of testing based on them. No Child Left Behind, passed by Congress and signed into law in 2001, mandates that states receiving federal funding implement accountability systems, with annual testing in reading and math.

The specificity, user-friendliness, and prescriptiveness of content standards vary from state to state. In some states, they are highly detailed and specific, leaving fairly little room for local decision-making, while in others, they are very broad and general. For example, in their analysis of 14 states' language arts standards documents, Wixson and Dutro (1999) compared the structure of standards in Texas and California, both of which serve diverse students. While California's language arts standards comprise three volumes, only one of which explicitly addresses how to teach English language learners (ELLs), Texas includes both standards and instructional guidelines in one accessible and user-friendly document that integrates strategies throughout for tailoring instruction to ELLs.

Within the standards movement, the general paradigm shifted from integrated code curricula to collection code curricula, and from weak framing to strong framing, using science to justify certain pedagogies. State and federal governments define science to mean studies that claim to be value-neutral and rely heavily on quantitative methods. Reading and language arts particularly were affected by the seminal "scientific" study supporting phonics instruction, commonly called *The Foorman Study* (Foorman et al., 1998) and sponsored by the National Institute of Child Health and Human Development (NICHD).[1] Across the country, "alignment" has become a watchword as schools and school districts have worked to align their curriculum with state standards and state testing.

Standardizing Curriculum in California

California has a highly diverse student population. In academic year 2002–2003, students in California public schools were 45 percent Hispanic, 34 percent non-Hispanic White, 8 percent Black, 8 percent Asian, 3 percent Filipino 1 percent American Indian/Alaskan Native, and 1 percent Pacific Islander (Educational Demographics Office, 2004). Over 25 percent of the students came to school speaking a first language other than English. One out of every four students was an ELL, and one in three elementary school students was considered to have limited English proficiency (Gándara et al., 2003).

California is often cited as having led the nation's standards movement by drafting curriculum frameworks in the early 1980s, which became the cornerstone of its standards-based reform program. For all content areas, the State Board of Education, appointed by the governor, makes curriculum decisions. Subject-matter decisions are made by committees that report to the Curriculum Commission. Members of the Curriculum Commission are appointed by the State Board of Education, the governor, and the Speaker of the House of the Assembly. Commission recommendations go to the State Board of Education, which then flow down to the colleges and the counties, then to districts, then to schools. In other words, the decision-making structure is decidedly top-down.

Content standards guide adoption of textbooks for grades one through eight by the State Board of Education and construction of state achievement tests. The Public School Accountability Act of 1999 established a system of achievement testing based on curriculum standards, and on rewarding high-performing schools and sanctioning low-performing schools. The 2002 Master Plan for Education, which outlines recommendations for education from preschool through university, makes frequent reference throughout to aligning curriculum and teacher preparation to the state's content frameworks and standards.

Our main question, then, is this: Given the historic context of struggles over curriculum, how has the standards movement reconfigured codes of power as manifest in curriculum, and in whose interests?

The Standards Documents

We conducted a content analysis of the following California frameworks and standards.

- *History-Social Framework and Standards for California Public Schools* (California Department of Education, 2001)
- *English-Language Arts Content Standards for California Public Schools* (California Department of Education, 1997)
- *Reading/Language Arts Framework for California Public Schools* (California Department of Education, 1999b)
- *English Language Development Standards* (California Department of Education, 1999a)

Content standards in both disciplines were initially adopted in 1987. The *History-Social Science Framework and Standards* document, which was readopted three times with only minor updates, describes what should be taught in the social studies curriculum in considerable detail for every grade except ninth. (For ninth grade, there are suggested units, but local decision-making over curriculum is allowed.) Its initial adoption was highly controversial and was contested vigorously by numerous educators, community groups, and scholars, particularly African American scholars. The main objection was that it had been written primarily by European American scholars working within a European American perspective that conceptualizes everyone within an immigrant paradigm. In so doing, it ignores perspectives that arise from nonimmigrant historical experiences, such as those of Native Americans and African Americans (see Cornbleth & Waugh, 1995; King, 1992). These concerns were never addressed. In fact, the preface to the newest edition says that "a consensus existed in the field for the framework" (p. viii). Ultimately, several school districts (notably San Francisco, Oakland, and Hayward) rejected the adopted texts or recommended that they be used only with substantial alternatives.

In 1997, California adopted a new set of reading/language arts standards and frameworks to replace those adopted in 1987. These new documents embody a distinctly different theoretical orientation from those issued previously by shifting away from a constructivist, literature-based approach to reading instruction to a direct instruction approach. This shift is evident throughout all three of the reading/language arts documents that we analyzed, mainly in the authors' tendencies to make theoretical claims reminiscent of the previous framework, and then offer content standards and practical guidelines from the direct instruction approach.

Introductions to the documents in both disciplines address California's diverse students, especially the increasing number of students who are not proficient in English. The authors make clear their dedication to the academic success of such students and their perception that the content frameworks and standards are based upon consensus about what California's students need to know. What does an analysis of how curriculum is classified and framed reveal?

Methodology

We used two main processes to analyze these documents. First, we read them for themes, keeping systematic notes on each theme. For the reading/language arts documents, we read for themes reflecting a sociocultural perspective (operationalized through terms such as contextualization, scaffolding, primary language instruction, bilingual, and bicultural) and a skill-based perspective (operationalized through terms such as decode, phonics, phonemic awareness, and phoneme). For the history-social science document, we read for themes reflecting multicultural content (such as depiction of African American history, depiction of women, depiction of European immigration) and pedagogical approaches (such as interdisciplinarity, use of student-generated historical analysis, use of expert-generated historical analysis)

Second, we counted words and items in each document that reflected patterns related to our thematic analysis. We counted the demographic characteristics of people named for study in the history-social science document, but not the reading/language arts documents, which did not name people for study. There, we counted terms representing pedagogical approaches, and references to ELLs.

Results of Analysis

Below, we describe how curriculum is classified and framed, according to Bernstein's analytical framework.

Classification

Our analysis of classification addresses how knowledge boundaries and hierarchies are established. The boundaries we identified include those between disciplines and languages. We also noted distinct patterns in sequencing and structuring knowledge in each discipline.

The standards solidify disciplinary boundaries. Separate disciplinary committees prepared the standards, and even though the covers of the documents are similar, their overall internal structure is not. The English-language arts standards for every grade level are organized into four areas: reading, writing, written, and oral English language conventions, and listening and speaking. Standards and substandards are then organized into each of these four areas. In history-social science, the standards and substandards are organized mainly according to theme, time period, and geographic location, which differ from one grade level to the next. For example, second grade is organized around the theme of "people who make a difference"; it includes five standards that have up to four substandards. Eighth grade is organized chronologically around U.S. history; 12 standards each have between three and nine substandards. That each discipline's standards are organized according to a different internal logic would tend to discourage constructing interdisciplinary curriculum.

The English-Language Arts Content Standards (ELA) mandates *what* all students must learn. The *Reading/Language Arts Framework* details *how* and *in what order* teachers must introduce language arts material. These two documents separate what students must learn from pedagogy and instructional decision-making.

The three reading/language arts documents solidify language boundaries and the primacy of English. The English Language Development Standards (ELD) are mapped against the English-Language Arts Content Standards to help California's ELLs to " 'catch up' to the state's monolingual English speakers" (California Department of Education, 1997, p. 1). The ELA standards are named 130 times as *the* instructional objectives of the ELD standards. Learning in English is given clear primacy over learning reading, writing, and other language arts skills in any other language. The documents ignore language arts proficiencies that students might have in a language other than English. For example, while the introduction to the ELD standards document acknowledges research supporting the value of primary language literacy, the standards themselves encourage teachers to tap students' primary language knowledge only with reference to students' familiarity with English phonemes.

The standards set up a complex structure of knowledge for each discipline. In both, knowledge derived from students' experience is subordinated to school knowledge. For example, the ELA standards refer to students' familiar experiences and interests primarily with reference to their selection of topics in which to practice oral presentation. Otherwise, there is little reference to students' interests and experiences. The history-social science standards refer to students' community and local area in the primary grades, but from fourth grade onward, detail content to learn without reference to students' lived experiences. In the remainder of this section, we examine how disciplinary knowledge is constructed within each of the two disciplines.

Language arts is hierarchically structured into a learning sequence, leading toward classification of students based on mastery of that sequence. Students are to learn skills first, and build meaning on skills. This emphasis on sequence is premised on the assumption that "a comprehensive program ensures that students master foundational skills as a gateway to using all forms of language as tools for thinking, learning and communicating" (California Department of Education, 1999b, p. 4). The authors emphasize their commitment to a *balanced* literacy program, but also state that "balanced does not mean that all skills and standards receive equal emphasis at a given point in time. Rather, it implies that the overall emphasis accorded to a skill or standard is determined by its priority or importance relative to students' language and literacy levels and needs" (p. 4). Further, the standards embrace balance mainly when addressing the learning needs of native English speakers. They relegate students who are still learning English to a "back-to-basics" program until they master foundational skills.

This is not to preclude a well-trained teacher from delivering high-quality reading/language arts instruction to ELLs. Nonetheless, following the standards' sequencing with fidelity may lead teachers who have received little or no training in this area to a very imbalanced program, particularly for ELLs. The *Reading/Language Arts Framework* contends that "simplified texts should be used only with students with weak proficiency in English," and that "students who use the simplified text need intensive English language instruction to enable them to catch up with their peers" (California Department of Education, 1999b, p. 76). In other words, California's reading/language arts standards enable balanced instruction more for students who read English at or above grade level than for others.

All three reading/language arts documents are heavily weighted toward phonics instruction and construct literacy largely as word analysis, particularly in the early grades. The words "phonemes," "phonics," and "phonemic awareness" are mentioned 200 times in these documents collectively. They are mentioned only 22 times in the 84-page ELA document (14 of which are in the glossary), but 66 times in the 93-page ELD document (only two of which are in the glossary). Further, the ELD standards emphasize it from kindergarten through the 12th grade, while in the ELA standards, most references to phonics-driven instruction appropriately diminish after the fourth grade. Thus, the ELD standards treat phonics mastery as a gatekeeper for English learners through the 12th grade.

As a result, language minority students may be precluded from engaging in literary analysis and other intellectual activities that would prepare them for admission to higher education institutions. And although the standards at times suggest to teachers that optimal student learning happens when skill instruction is embedded in authentic texts, discrete skill instruction is consistently separated from comprehension or literary analysis by requiring that activities such as literature-based instruction be introduced only *after* students demonstrate their discrete skill mastery.

Literature is further separated from skills instruction by being developed in yet a fourth document. Each time the authors of the reading/language arts documents suggest using literature, they advise teachers to refer to the state-sponsored list, *Recommended Literature: Kindergarten Through Grade Twelve* (California Department of Education, 1996). None of the titles is integrated into the standards documents.

The *History-Social Science Framework and Standards* document gives clear primacy to history as "a story well told" (California Department of Education, 2001, p. 4). The story around which the standards are structured develops over about 10 grade levels. Its central idea is that, as an immigrant society, the United States has always been multicultural; students need to "understand the special role of the United States in world history as a nation of immigrants" (p. 21). At the same time, "its institutions were founded on the Judeo-Christian heritage, the ideals of the Enlightenment, and English traditions of self-government" (p. 64). Its unfinished story tells "the historic struggle to extend to all Americans the constitutional guarantees of equality and freedom" (p. 21). Much of its content revolves around the political system of the United States as outlined in the Constitution, and is developed primarily through the conceptual tools of chronology and geography, as its introduction states.

The dominant storyline revolves around European and European Americans, particularly men. For example, we counted representation of people. Of the 96 Americans named for study, 82 percent were male and 18 percent were female. They were 77 percent white, 18 percent African American, 4 percent Native American, 1 percent Latino, and 0 percent Asian American. Authors of the history-social science framework recommend integrating children's literature with history (a break in the otherwise strong classification system) and gave specific suggestions. We tallied the racial and gender composition of the 88 authors of recommended children's literature. Fifty-seven percent were male, and 35 percent were female; we were unable to identify the gender of 8 percent. Sixty-two percent were European or European American, 19 percent were African or African American, 1 percent (one author) was Native American, 7 percent were Asian or Asian American, and none was Latino or South American; we were unable to identify the background of 10 percent. We saw a noticeable effort to include stories about diverse European ethnic groups, including Swedish, Irish, and Russian immigrants.

Because history-social science was constructed mainly as a story of immigration, stories of conquest were filtered through that paradigm using the tools of timelines and maps. Students first study European colonialism briefly in fourth grade in the context of California history. In fifth grade, they meet European explorers largely through map study, and then they study English settlements in North America. In seventh grade, they examine different world regions, concluding with a unit on "the Age of Exploration to the Enlightenment." European exploration and conquest are mentioned, but political ideals of the Enlightenment receive at least as much attention. This is important because it casts colonialism not as the taking of land, life, and sovereignty, but rather as the spread of reason, ideas, and liberty. In eighth grade, students encounter "the extension of the United States beyond its borders" (California Department of Education, 2001, p. 106), but relationships between the United States and Puerto Rico, the Philippines, or islands in the Pacific and Caribbean are not mentioned. In tenth grade, there is some review of "the worldwide expansion that was fueled by the industrial nations' demand for natural resources and markets and by their nationalist aspirations," presented as map study in which students survey colonial possessions of several European nations and the United States (California Department of Education, 2001, p. 126). Thus, it is possible to graduate from high school with only a fuzzy idea of European and United States histories of conquest and exploitation.

The conquests of northern Mexico and indigenous peoples are marginalized and sanitized. In third grade, students briefly study indigenous people of the past, then move on. In fourth grade, when studying the history of California, they briefly study American Indian nations in California's past. In fifth grade, students begin to study U.S. history, starting with a unit devoted to pre-Columbian indigenous people. After that unit, indigenous people appear only sporadically, and in relationship to the story of the westward movement of European Americans. Students study the conquest of Mexico in fourth, fifth, and eighth grades, but do so mainly as map study and timelines. Given that California used to be part of Mexico, and became a part of the United States through conquest, this casting of history negates family knowledge of many students of Mexican and indigenous descent.

To summarize, the documents set up strong classification, solidifying a collection code. With the exception of the history-social science framework's recommendation to connect history with children's literature, the disciplines are treated as distinctly separate, each having its own internal and hierarchical structure of knowledge. Reading/language arts is conceptualized as an accretion of skills acquired sequentially and in English. As a result, ELLs may well have less access to higher-order thinking than native English speakers, because thinking and literary analysis in a student's first language do not count. History-social science is constructed as a detailed story, sequenced over several grade levels, and organized around historically dominant groups' perspectives, experiences, and ways of seeing the world. The high degree of detail in both disciplines and the differing organizational systems that structure them would discourage interdisciplinary teaching or development of other integrated code curricula. Further, the privileging of English and use of English proficiency as a gatekeeper and the privileging of a European American immigration story as the backbone for academic content in the social sciences establish knowledge of white English speakers as dominant.

Framing

Framing refers to the degree to which teachers and students have authority to bring their own questions, points of view, organization, and pacing to the curriculum. We found reading/language arts to be more strongly framed than history-social science.

Compliance with the standards is enforced mainly through testing and textbooks. This alignment is more direct in reading/language arts than in history-social science. Each year, all public school students in grades 2–11 are required by state law to take standardized tests, which focus heavily on reading. For grades K-3, schools can choose between only two reading series, both of which are heavily skills based and scripted. Teachers at higher grade levels have a little more choice; for example, fourth-grade teachers can select from six reading texts, and eighth-grade teachers can select from among eight texts.

Although some of California's few remaining bilingual education programs are permitted to administer standardized tests in languages other than English, these tests merely supplement English standardized tests and are not used, as the English tests are, to determine class placement, grade promotion, or a school's ranking on the scale used to determine a school's funding and state intervention efforts. Because California's Public School Accountability Act uses English tests as the *only* outcome measures in its school ranking system, it is increasingly difficult for teachers to stray from the reading/language arts standards even if their own professional experience leads them to believe that doing so would benefit their students.

Compliance with the history-social science content standards is enforced at the elementary level mainly through the state's textbook adoption process. Elementary students are not yet tested on mastery of this content. However, at grades 8, 10, and 11, social studies is part of the state's standardized testing program; the eighth-grade test is designed to cover the curriculum for grades six through eight. Secondary teachers have more latitude than elementary teachers to choose texts, but are held accountable through student testing.

Both disciplines are strongly framed through the degree to which content and skills are minutely specified, and through use of disciplinary expertise and science to support the standards. The reading/language arts documents mask ideological debates about literacy by using rhetoric of science. For example, the introduction to the *Reading/Language Arts Framework* document states, "reading/language arts and related disciplines are the beneficiaries of an abundance of converging research that produces a professional knowledge base related to fostering and sustaining competence in the language arts, particularly beginning reading" (California Department of Education, 1999b, p. 3). The authors name a study sponsored by the National Research Council (1998) as "most important" because of its claim that "there is [now] a convergence of evidence to guide instruction in the language arts" (p. 3). All three documents rely heavily on this research to substantiate their emphasis on phonics instruction and phonemic awareness, but there is a notable absence of references to studies that support alternative approaches to reading instruction, particularly sociocultural approaches that may be more effective than phonics-driven methods, especially for diverse students.

We examined the documents for the extent to which they frame how teaching is to occur, particularly given the diverse students teachers have. Content in reading/language arts is highly prescribed. At several points in the ELD and ELA documents, the authors mention the "special needs" of ELLs and suggest that teachers modify their instruction to better meet them. Paradoxically, neither document suggests how to do this. In fact, neither document mentions the terms "scaffold," "specially designed academic instruction in English (SDAIE)," or "contextualize," all of which are commonly used in literature that details effective ways of teaching second-language acquisition.

The *Reading/Language Arts Framework*, on the other hand, mentions the word "scaffold" many times in the section entitled "Universal Access." This section, featured throughout the document, is broken down into three subsections in an effort to address the needs of (1) students with reading difficulties or disabilities, (2) ELLs, and (3) advanced learners. A universal access section is offered at each of the early grade levels, but it is included less frequently at the higher grades. At each grade level, only a few standards are mentioned and discussed in detail; teachers are then given suggestions for adapting the standards to meet their students' needs. For example, project extension guidelines are offered for advanced learners, and scaffolding interventions are offered for English learners. To the extent that the universal access section suggests that teachers tailor their instruction to their students, it could be seen as weakening the framing of curriculum by inviting teacher judgment. At the same time, we found the 300-plus-page *Reading/ Language Arts Framework* so unwieldy, it was difficult to imagine a teacher finding the time or wherewithal to study these suggestions. Overall, the three reading documents language arts taken together specify so many skills (English-Language Arts Content Standards for California Public Schools, Reading/Language Arts Framework for California Public Schools, and English Language Development

Standards) to teach and the order in which they are to be introduced, that one could see drill on the standards as the best way to get through everything.

In addition, the universal access section of the *Reading/Language Arts Framework* emphasizes using students' scores ("standard deviations") on the language arts portion of the state's standardized test to "diagnose" students' gaps in learning. Accordingly, teachers are then urged to integrate test preparation into their intervention efforts (California Department of Education, 1999b, pp. 226–229). Closely tying the standards documents to standardized tests raises questions about the degree to which teachers have the latitude to implement the standards as they deem most effective, particularly for special needs students such as ELLs and learning disabled students.

The language arts' emphasis on sequencing similarly strengthens the framing of the language arts curriculum, particularly for English learners and their teachers. For example, the *Reading/Language Arts Framework* suggests that when students demonstrate persistent difficulty in mastering the language arts standards for their grade level, teachers should be "differentiating curriculum and instruction, using grouping strategies effectively, and implementing other strategies" in order to meet the needs of these students (California Department of Education, 1999b, p. 226). In principle, this would allow for a weaker framing of the curriculum by affording teachers the chance to exercise their own professional judgment about instructional delivery. Yet, the *Framework* also encourages teachers to deliver instruction for special needs students that is even more sequential than for other students (p. 229). This sequential format, which reads like a list of skills and instructional activities, would most easily be aligned with a scripted skill-driven program, leaving little room for modification.

The *History-Social Science Framework and Standards* encourages higher-order thinking and active teaching processes throughout the grade levels. The document acknowledges that historians construct history, and that students should become aware of debates among them. For instance, a standard for 11th grade requires that students "evaluate major debates among historians concerning alternative interpretations of the past" (California Department of Education, 2001, p. 142). And occasionally the *History-Social Science Framework* mentions how historians work and that they often disagree with each other. But the main learning process that the *History-Social Science Framework* authorizes is consumption of an interpretation of the past prepared by someone else, rather than learning to construct an interpretation using the tools of historical thinking. The standards are largely content driven, spelling out conclusions that students should reach. For example, the term "analyze" is used repeatedly to describe what students should do: "At the same time students should analyze periodic waves of hostility toward newcomers and recognize that the nation has in different eras restricted immigration on the basis of racial, ethnic, or cultural grounds." (p. 10). But the authors have already constructed a general analysis for students; their task is to comprehend analysis rather than learn to construct an original analysis based on historic data. The authors recommend using a variety of teaching strategies such as debates, simulations, role-play, narratives, and video so that students will become engaged in learning the material. It is possible for teachers to alter how they construct their history or social studies curriculum, but because the curriculum as a whole is packed, it is simply easier for teachers to follow what they are given.

California's new teacher credential standards also strengthen the framing of the curriculum. As discussed elsewhere (Sleeter, 2003), the teacher credential standards explicitly define teacher education as preparation to deliver the state's academic content standards. The phrase "state-adopted academic content standards" appears 34 times in California's new Professional Teacher Preparation document, and 26 times in its Professional Teacher Induction Program document. By contrast, the phrases "culturally relevant," "multicultural," and "justice" appear in neither one. Disciplinary content preparation for teachers is also tied to the content standards; disciplinary programs must be approved by the state as being aligned to the content standards for certification programs to be authorized. In this way, what teachers learn in the university should match with what is in the standards, lessening the possibility that teachers will bring to the classroom ideas that conflict.

To summarize, the state standards strongly frame curriculum in both reading/language arts and history-social science. In the reading/language arts documents, the emphasis on sequence, the prescriptive nature, and the strict compliance enforced by high-stakes standardized testing ensures that a back-to-basics reading/language arts curriculum will be implemented across the state, and will be the most strictly enforced with special needs children. In addition, the dearth of instructional strategies for teachers of English learners and the inaccessibility of guidelines that are included discourage straying from or expanding upon the curriculum, even in the interest of meeting the needs of individual students. Further, because of the theoretical contradictions present throughout all three reading/language arts documents, a teacher may be given the impression that he or she can implement a literature-based and linguistically responsive reading/language arts program, but then be limited from doing so simply because of a lack of available instructional time, and/or state and district pressure to "teach to the test." The *History-Social Science Framework and Standards* are content driven, although filled with suggestions for student activities. Teachers have more latitude for deciding how to teach history and social studies than reading, but the curriculum is so packed and backed up by state-adopted texts that it is an effort to not follow the standards.

Discussion and Implications

Given the context of California and the historic context of struggles over curriculum, how has the content standards movement reconfigured codes of power, and in whose interests?

Our analysis of the way that the standards classify curriculum shows that they reassert disciplinary boundaries and boundaries between traditional academic knowledge in English versus knowledge in languages other than English, as well as knowledge from home and community. In both reading/language arts and history-social science, the content standards specify a structure of knowledge and sequence for teaching it. In reading/ language arts, the structure builds higher-order thinking on discrete skills, and in so doing, makes higher-order thinking more accessible to English-speaking students with average or above average reading skills than to everyone else. Further, the reading/language arts documents consistently refer to California's non-white, non-English speaking students as "these students" and "they" instead of one of "us." History-social science is structured largely as a story of European immigration and the construction of a nation around Judeo-Christian values and European political institutions. Implicitly, in an attempt to reduce the significance of the growing demographic diversity of California students, the content standards set up a we/they perspective in which "we" are of European, Judeo-Christian heritage and English-speaking, and "they" are not.

Ideologically, the curriculum in both disciplines rests most comfortably on historically dominant groups' perspectives, language, and ways of seeing the world.

Framing examines the place that teachers and students are expected to take within this structure, and the degree of latitude they have for defining that place. Our analysis of the standards shows that, particularly in reading/language arts, teachers and students are expected to follow the state's prescription. Compliance is enforced mainly through statewide standardized testing in English, and through the textbook adoption process. Compliance is also enforced through the sheer prescriptiveness of a packed curriculum, particularly at the elementary level. Further, compliance in the way that reading/language arts is taught is to be enforced mainly in schools that score low on standardized tests, and with students designated as having special needs.

Although the content standards in both disciplines rest within a specific ideology, they are presented as if there were no serious ideological debates to consider. Both present a detailed curriculum outline, and both give enough verbal recognition to cultural, racial, and linguistic diversity that teachers without a deep understanding of diverse intellectual funds of knowledge, diverse ideological perspectives, and effective pedagogy for diverse students might see the standards as fully inclusive. The use of disciplinary "experts" as curriculum document writers and the use of "scientific" research about reading encourage compliance. Although the documents occasionally suggest use of project- and literature-based teaching, the prescriptiveness of the standards, limited availability of instructional time, and adoption of a mandatory scripted reading program steer teachers toward a back-to-basics curriculum. In the top-down curriculum-making structure of California, teachers and students have little recognized power.

This standards-based curriculum planning process hearkens back to that described by Cubberley almost a century ago, when he characterized schools as "factories in which the raw products (children) are to be shaped and fashioned into products to meet the various demands of life" (cited in Beyer & Liston, 1996, p. 19). Like a century ago, curriculum is being organized scientifically for efficiency, deriving learning objectives from social and economic needs and casting teachers as managers of the process of producing student achievement scores. But both sets of standards, and particularly those in reading/language arts, deflect attention from their ideological underpinnings by virtue of being situated within a testing movement. Rather than asking whose knowledge, language, and points of view are most worth teaching children, teachers and administrators are pressed to ask how well children are scoring on standardized measures of achievement.

Our analysis suggests that California's curriculum standards fit within a political movement to reconfigure power relations among racial, ethnic, language, and social class groupings. This is not simply about trying to improve student learning, but more important, about reasserting who has a right to define what schools are for, whose knowledge has most legitimacy, and how the next generation should think about the social order and their place within it.

Note

1. This use of science may explain why the current standards go largely unquestioned (Shannon, 2001). A growing body of research is beginning to demonstrate that *The Foorman Study* was flawed and even deliberately manipulated

to attain particular results (Coles, 2000; Taylor, 1998), and that subsequent advocacy of phonological reading strategies has been overstated (Swanson et al., 2003).

References

Berliner, D. C., and B. J. Biddle. (1995). *The manufactured crisis.* Cambridge, MA: Perseus Books.

Bernstein, B. (1975). *Class, codes and control.* (Rev. ed.) London: Routledge and Kegan Paul.

Bernstein, B., and J. Solomon. (1999). Pedagogy, identity, and the construction of a theory of symbolic control: Basil Bernstein questioned by Joseph Solomon. *British Journal of Sociology of Education* 20 (2): 265–280.

Beyer, L., and D. Liston. (1996). *Curriculum in conflict.* New York: Teachers College Press.

Bloom, A. C. (1989). *The closing of the American mind.* New York: Simon & Schuster.

Brophy, J., and B. VanSledright. (1997). *Teaching and learning history in elementary schools.* New York: Teachers College Press.

California Department of Education. (1996). *Recommended literature: Kindergarten through grade twelve.* Sacramento, CA: Author. Available at http://www.cde.ca.gov/ci/literature.

——. (1997). *English-language arts content standards for California public schools.* Sacramento, CA: Author.

——. (1999a). *English language development standards.* Sacramento, CA: Author.

——. (1999b). *Reading/language arts framework for California public schools.* Sacramento, CA: Author.

——. (2001). *History-social science framework and standards for California public schools.* Sacramento, CA: Author.

Center for Research on Education, Diversity, and Excellence. (2002). *Research evidence: Five standards for effective pedagogy and student outcomes.* Technical Report No. Gl, March 2002. University of California, Santa Cruz. Available at http://crede.ucsc.edu/pdf/evidence_gl.pdf.

Coles, G. (2000). *Misreading reading: The bad science that hurts children.* Portsmouth, NH: Heinemann.

Cornbleth, C., and Waugh, D. (1995). *The great speckled bird: Multicultural politics and education decision-making.* New York: St. Martin's Press.

Cummins, J. (1996). *Negotiating identities: Education for empowerment in a diverse society.* Ontario, CA: California Association for Bilingual Education.

Dicker, S. (1996). *Languages in America: A pluralist view.* Clevedon, UK: Multilingual Matters.

Educational Demographics Office. (2004). *Enrollment in California public schools by ethnic designation, 1981–82 through 2002–03.* Sacramento: California Department of Education. Available at http://goldmine.cde.ca.gov/demographics/reports/index.html.

Emig, J. (1971). *The composing process of twelfth graders.* NCTE Research Report No. 13. Urbana, IL: National Council of Teachers of English.

——. (1982). Inquiry paradigms and writing. *College Composition and Communication* 33: 64–75.

Engels, M. (2000). *The struggle for the control of public education: Market ideology vs. democratic values.* Philadelphia: Temple University Press.

Foorman, B. R., Francis, D. J., Fletcher, J. M. and Scatschneider, C. (1998). The role of instruction in learning to read: Preventing reading failure in at-risk children. *Journal of Educational Psychology* 90: 37–55.

Gándara, P., Rumberger, R., Maxwell-Jolly, J., and Callahan, R. (2003). English learners in California schools: Unequal resources, unequal outcomes. *Education Policy Analysis Archives* 11, no. 36. Available at http://epaa.asu.edu/epaa/vl1n36/.

Gay, G. (1995). Curriculum theory and multicultural education. In J. A. Banks and C. A. M. Banks (eds.), *Handbook of research on multicultural education,* 25–43. New York: Macmillan.

Gibbons, P. (2002). *Scaffolding language, scaffolding learning: Teaching second language learners in the mainstream classroom.* Portsmouth, NH: Heinemann.

Goodman, K., and Goodman, Y. (1979). Learning to read is natural. In L. Resnick and P. Weaver (eds.), *Theory and practice of early reading,* vol. 1, 137–154. Hillsdale, NJ: Erlbaum.

Graves, D. (1982). How do writers develop? *Language Arts* 59 (2): 173–79.

Gutierrez, K. (2001). So what's new in the English language arts: Challenging policies and practices, ¿y que? *Language Arts Journal* 78 (6): 564–69.

Gutierrez, K., Asato, J., Swantos, M., and Gotanda, N. (2002). Backlash pedagogy: Language and culture and the politics of reform. *The Review of Education, Pedagogy, and Cultural Studies* 24 (4): 335–51.

Hakuta, K. (1986). *Mirror of language: The debate on bilingualism.* New York: Basic Books.

Heath, S. B. (1983). *Ways with words: Language, life, and work in communities and classrooms.* Cambridge, UK: Cambridge University Press.

King, J. E. (1992). Diaspora literacy and consciousness in the struggle against mis-education in the black community. *Journal of Negro Education* 61 (3): 317–340.

Kliebard, H. M. (1995). *The struggle for the American curriculum.* 2nd ed. New York: Routledge.

Ladson-Billings, G. (1994). *The dreamkeepers.* New York: Jossey-Bass.

National Commission on Excellence in Education. (1983). *A nation at risk.* Washington, DC: U.S. Government Printing Office.

National Research Council. (1998). *Preventing reading difficulties in young children.* Washington, DC: National Academy Press.

Ravitch, D. (1990). Diversity and democracy: Multicultural education in America. *American Educator* 14 (1): 16–20, 46–68. Ruiz, N. T. (1995). The social construction of ability and disability: Optimal and at-risk lessons in a bilingual special education classroom. *Journal of Learning Disabilities* 28: 491–502.

Schlesinger, A. M., Jr. (1992). *The disuniting of America.* New York: Norton.

Shannon, P. (2001). What's my name? A politics of literacy in the latter half of the 20th century in America. In P. Shannon (ed.), *Becoming political, too: New readings and writings on the politics of literacy education,* 112–141. Portsmouth, NH: Heinemann.

Sleeter, C. E. (2003). Reform and control: An analysis of SB 2042. *Teacher Education Quarterly* 30(1): 19–30.

Taylor, D. (1998). *Beginning to read and the spin doctors of science: The political campaign to change America's mind about how children learn to read.* Urbana, IL: National Council of Teachers of English.

Tetreault, M. K. T. (1989). Integrating content about women and gender into the curriculum. In J. A. Banks and C. A. M. Banks (eds.), *Multicultural education: Issues and perspectives,* 124–144. Boston: Allyn & Bacon.

Tharp, R., Estrada, P., Dalton, S. S., and Yamauchi, L. A. (2000). *Teaching transformed: Achieving excellence, fairness, inclusion and harmony.* Boulder, CO: Westview Press.

Thomas, W., and Collier, V. (1999). *School effectiveness for language minority students.* Washington, DC: National Clearinghouse for Bilingual Education, George Washington University.

Watkins, W. H. (1993). Black curriculum orientations: A preliminary inquiry. *Harvard Educational Review* 65 (3): 321–338.

Weinberg, M. (1977). *A chance to learn: The history of race and education in the United States.* Cambridge, UK: Cambridge University Press.

Wineberg, S. (2001). *Historical thinking and other unnatural Acts.* Philadelphia: Temple University Press.

Wink, J., and Putney, L. (2002). *A vision of Vygotsky.* Boston: Allyn & Bacon.

Wixson, K. K., and Dutro, E. (1999). Standards for primary-grade reading: An analysis of state frameworks. The Elementary School Journal 100 (2): 89–100.

23

Outside the Core: Accountability in Tested and Untested Subjects

Leslie Santee Siskin

Standards-based accountability policies entered the public schooling system at the end of the twentieth century as a major reform effort, one that has the potential to dramatically change the face and function of the comprehensive high school. For the past hundred years, the pattern of high school change has mainly been one of enrollment growth. In the middle of that period, the Conant Report (1959) posed the primary challenge to high school organization: could high schools accommodate the "horde of heterogeneous students that has descended on our secondary schools" (p. 602)? To do so, high schools would grow not only in size but in structure, offering a widely differentiated array of courses aimed at the "heterogeneous" tastes and talents of diverse students, and organizing teachers and content into discrete departments.

Conant argued that high schools would also have to develop differentiated expectations. Some courses would "maintain high standards" for those of high ability, while others, by necessity, would have "another standard." Just what those standards would be, however, were not specified by reformers nor standardized by policy makers. Instead, they were quietly and locally negotiated—classroom-by-classroom, track-by-track, subject-by-subject. The American high school grew, as Powell, Farrar, and Cohen (1985) vividly described it, into a version of a "shopping mall" with something for everyone, where "some [students] shop at Sears, others at Woolworth's or Bloomingdale's" (p. 8)—but where not every neighborhood was likely to attract a Bloomingdale's.

It is against that pattern of practice that current reformers press, arguing for high standards that will be the same for all schools, and for all students within a school. But when policies directed at the whole school hit the high school, they collide with that differentiated structure, refracting at different angles through different departments, bending and even reconstituting different subjects. Through establishing standards, choosing which subjects (and what content) will be tested, and then attaching stakes to achievement scores on those tests, the states materialize what kinds of knowledge count, and how much. In some cases, policy makers explicitly quantify how much.

Kentucky, which includes music (or at least humanities) among the tested subjects, counts performance in that area as worth 7.13 percent of the school's total score. Performance in English, on the other hand, counts for 14.25 percent directly. But, recognized as a basic skill needed for performance in other subject areas, English is understood to count much more. An English teacher in Kentucky talked of how the state standards have made teaching her subject more central to the work of the whole school: "Now, it's not just up to the English teachers. It's up to everybody in the school." Those subjects outside the core, less central to achieving a good score, are likely to see their value go down. As the pressure for schools to perform on accountability tests rises, and resources are reallocated to provide extra time to students in the tested areas, teachers in untested subjects wonder what will become of their subjects, and whether their jobs are at stake under high-stakes accountability policies.

To understand how high schools are responding to new state accountability policies (or why they are not), we need to take account of the internal differentiation which characterizes the comprehensive high school. We need to examine the ways in which different subjects and departments receive and respond to the call for common standards and standardized tests. To understand the kinds of changes that are taking place under this policy shift, we also need to look to evidence at the level of the subject and the department. Even large changes taking place at this level may be lost if data are aggregated or averaged to the level of the school.

Drawing on interview data gathered over two years of fieldwork though the CPRE project on accountability and the high school, this essay examines the case of one subject "outside the core"—music. To do so, I adapt, to the level of subject departments, a framework that has emerged out of our analyses of school-level responses to accountability. That framework suggests that to understand school response we need to consider three distinct but interrelated factors: the initial position of the school, relative to the policy; the internal conditions already present—the organizational structures, internal accountability systems, and collective expectations; and then, within that context, the strategic choices and actions of those within it.

In applying this framework to subject departments, we distinguish between the *subject* as a knowledge category that extends across schools and the *department* as an organizational sub-unit within a school. Thus, we need to analyze:

- The initial position of the *subject* relative to the policy;
- The internal conditions of the *department*—the structure, internal accountability system, and collective expectations; and then
- The strategic choices and actions of those within them.

Initial Position

Even before the accountability reform kicks in, some subjects start out positioned favorably within the schooling system. They have high status and high levels of agreement on what the subject is, what should be taught, and even, in some subjects, how the subject should be taught (Goodson 1993; Siskin 1994). Math, for example, commands a relatively high status position, and is considered to have a relatively tight paradigm (agreement and coherence about what counts as knowledge). As one math teacher explained, "every math teacher" across the country knows what should be known in algebra II: "Algebra II, you have to do certain things, and every math teacher knows that when you're done with Algebra II you know these things."

Moreover, math content is considered highly stable, and the sequencing of what topics are to be covered is firmly established—so much so that past reforms have found it almost impossible to dislodge (Leinhart and Smith 1985; Siskin 1994; Stodolsky 1993). When high stakes accountability has encountered a subject that begins from this position, the problem has not been figuring out what should be on the test, but rather how to get students into the sequence so they get to algebra II and "know these things" before they take the test.

English may also be part of the academic core but it does not command the same status or demonstrate the same tightness in its paradigm, stability in its curriculum, or solidified sequence. Coming to consensus on what things a student should know at the end of tenth grade English, and therefore what the state can reasonably expect its testing to assess, is a different problem.

Music, as a subject, occupies a position that, as one Massachusetts teacher explained to me, "has pretty high status; it's somewhat elite, but also . . . marginalized." Music is not typically considered a core subject, or a top contender for the lists of "what every high school student should know and be able to do" that are central to accountability policy. One science teacher in New York, for example, argued that there should be high standards and testing for (almost) all students—but only in some subjects: "For the majority? Yes, there should be, certainly, the English standards, and the social studies standards, and the math standards. I actually disagree on the science standards for some, and I'm a science teacher." He did note, however, that there should be some standards in science for everyone, since "everybody should know how their body works, so they can make informed medical decisions." But the possibility of standards for everyone in the arts does not even enter the conversation.

Among music teachers, however, the contention is widely made that they do have standards, and that they have had them since long before the terminology of standards-based accountability came into vogue: "We tend, I think—and I'm speaking generally—I think as musicians, we've always tended to be sort of standards-based without knowing it." In almost all the interviews, teachers talked of how they have "always" had standards, "for a long time," or "for centuries." A Vermont teacher described the lineage of a discipline with a well-established history of shared standards: "I think we've always had a standard. My joke in front of the staff and the audiences here in [Garrison] has been that standards for us were established over five hundred years ago. Bach in the 1600s developed the equal temperament, and that's how we've been tuning our pianos ever since. Pythagoras came up with the original scale that we use. So we can go a long ways back for the standards."

For these teachers, it's not simply that there are standardized instruments and scales, but that there are widely shared standards about what should be taught in music, and even about what the order is for learning the essentials. A Kentucky teacher explained that "you can't skip levels. I guess it's sort of like math." A Vermont colleague concurred that "for a long, long, time music has always been taught sequentially." Teachers can be quite precise about just what it is that students need to know to meet these standards: "They need to know note value . . . Quarter note, eighth note, sixteenth note. They need to know note value. They need to know the letter names of notes, lines, and spaces. They need to know rhythm, be able to identify rhythm . . . Name it; perform it. They need to be able to sing, that's a category. You need to be able to sing alone and in a group. . . . You should be able to know music terminology, basic music terminology . . . Dynamics . . . Degrees of loud and soft . . . Vivace, which means lively, fast . . . Allegro, which is also a form of fast. It's not as fast as vivace . . . Be able to recognize grande, or dolce."

Mixed in with the lists of standards for what students need to be able to "recognize" or to "know" are the verbs for what they need to be able to *do*—to sing, to "perform." For, as teachers across the schools and states consistently point out, music as a subject has "for centuries" been not only standards-based, but performance-based. Ultimately, it is the performance of their students that counts: "I realize I've got to teach these students how to play their instruments. Bottom line."

Especially in group-performance oriented subjects, such as band or orchestra, the essential importance of having shared standards becomes immediately and concretely apparent. After all, explained one teacher, "to tie it all together consistently, we're all using the same evaluation pieces. So I know when the flutes come in to join the band rehearsal, they've had the same material as the clarinets and the trumpets." One of the remarkable aspects of music in this area is that the need to "tie it all together" so that students can "join" in for a group performance operates not only within the school, but also across schools. Several teachers describe preparing students to go out to regional and state-level performances where they may perform all together in a larger orchestra, or compete against other groups performing the same piece. The need to have everyone on the same page—to know and to be able to perform the same material in concert—transmits and reinforces the establishment of common standards throughout the musical community.

That focus on performance to a commonly shared standard, on the skills students need to be able to "tie it all together" to perform a musical piece, has put music teachers ahead of their colleagues in shifting to standards-based accountability. As three music teachers told us:

> One thing that we always found interesting was that music and fine arts are performance-based. We have products. We have outcomes. And they tried to take what we do and move us out of the performance area so they could put us back in. And instead of looking at what we have done through the centuries . . . a lot of the other areas have not bought in to this idea that we are where they want to be.
>
> We didn't have to change the way we taught. We didn't have to change the curriculum. We didn't have to change anything. It's like, now everyone is catching up with what music has been doing all along, which is really interesting. We've been performance-based all along. How we grade is how you perform.
>
> I think the folks who have been in the arts have been on the front edge of this for many, many years . . . And when I've gone to different classes and so forth, on how to use rubrics and things, we've had instructors that have said, "you folks in the arts always seem to be so far ahead. You already know what it is you want to assess, you know what you want for results." And so for me, the biggest thing is learning this new language of "how do we want to assess kids?" And once we came up with a rubric, it was pretty easy to just go ahead.

State rubrics and standards seem "pretty easy" in part because they don't introduce accountability into the field. Instead, music teachers have long seen themselves as accountable to their communities for the performance of their students—not on tests, but in the public arena. As two teachers told us:

> If I teach the [state] standards, well, maybe they'll be able to think about music better, which is good. But when we're at a basketball game, and when they're playing a song and it sounds awful, everybody's going to say, well, that's a bad band director.
>
> [That's what my] role as a teacher is, and that's to have these students play when I'm no longer around. And they can't do that unless they learn certain skills. And that's what I'm accountable to. The community has had a great deal of pride, even though it's a very small school . . . concerts are always well attended here, basketball games, football games.

And unlike the state accountability system, in this kind of arena, the stakes can be very high, and attach directly to individual teachers:

> So, yeah, the theory behind having the test, those questions—the theory behind the [state] standards, [the district] standards, is great. But the real practical aspect is, I've got to get those kids to learn how to play these instruments. If I don't do that, the band will sound awful; therefore my job can be on the line.

The subject of music thus provides a certain anchoring in a culturally valued and long established discipline, one where standards are widely shared, where the work is highly performance-based, and where that performance is embedded in a system of public accountability which predates, and may even compete with, new state accountability policies. But to understand why this teacher's job would be "on the line" and why that would be so consequential, we also need to look to the conditions of music as a department within the current organization of the high school.

Internal Conditions of the Department

In the complex organization of the comprehensive high school, teachers are likely to identify themselves, not only as subject specialists, but as members of a particular department that provides them with the primary social, political, and intellectual context for their work (Siskin 1994). These departments, especially in large high schools, can be like different worlds, where English teachers may never have met their science colleagues, and have little or no structured opportunity to see themselves as part of the same collective professional community, to develop shared expectations about student work, or about what teaching should be (Siskin 1991). The distances between departments and the "two worlds phenomenon" tend to be even more pronounced between teachers in the "core" academic departments and those in the "special" subjects like vocational education or the arts (Little 1993; see also Goodson 1993; Siskin 1994).

In this study music teachers also described feeling like they were in a different world from their academic colleagues: "Nothing against the school, but it seems that we're kind of in a world of our own. The choral department, the band, and the orchestra." Even when there was an effort to have the whole faculty focus on state tests, teachers had a hard time "relating" to the work of their distant colleagues: "There has [been discussion of how the school is doing]. And the way I work, it's hard for me to relate to things, or students, or student bodies that I don't know about. Or if they're talking math, or English, you know, there's no point of reference for me personally."

Another teacher we asked about school discussions of state tests (in Vermont, where music is not tested) believed that such discussions probably were taking place, but ". . . not that I'm aware of. I'm sure it takes place within the academic communities who are mandated to reaching [those scores]. And since we're not, we kind of fall by the wayside and in the cracks, and don't really . . . aren't really part of that circle."

The distance between the "two worlds" is not simply one of physical or social geography, but often takes the form of material difference. Some departments have more status and more resources; some, like music, may derive cultural status from their discipline, but little material resource or political support for their organizational status. Resources, even the basic resource of *having* a job, can be hard to come by. A music teacher in Vermont noted that "we have three music teachers in our district." Not in the school, but in the entire district. Another, in New York, explained that: "Music positions are not very easy to come by. Most of the teachers who have music or art positions, they hold on to them for life because the chances of them finding another job are pretty much zero. It's not easy to find a music opening."

Moreover, the positions that music teachers do find are in many cases quite different from the jobs of their colleagues in other subjects. Across the schools we studied, these three teachers described positions that cross school boundaries:

> I'm here every day, last block, but I also go to four elementary schools, and a middle school.
>
> Well, this year, they started this vertical teaming, and I'm actually assigned to elementary now. So, since we have set up here on a block schedule and you have A days and B days, on my B days, I go twice a day to the elementary and I teach there.
>
> This is my home school, and then I have eight elementary schools.

The assignment to nine different schools mentioned by this teacher may be an extreme case, but part time assignments across multiple buildings are not unusual. As the nine-school teacher also told us, that can make organizational accountability a complex and difficult issue: "To figure out with all the principals, whose schedule you are on, who you're responsible to, and that kind of thing . . . Every principal thinks you work for them, and each school has a different music program, so you've got to go in and figure out what they want, what's expected of you, what you can expect from them. Trying to figure out who, indeed, you do answer to, and who, indeed, you don't answer to." Each school may have a different music program (although in our sample, one school does not have a music program or music teacher), but each school does not have a different music department.

Instead, when it comes to departmental status, music is often in the position of the transient stepchild, put into the arts family in one school, for example, or into the English department in another. But while that might make bureaucratic sense, given the small numbers of music teachers, it creates a "problem" when departments are expected to be the site for substantive conversation about working toward standards: "The principal has told us to take a couple of hours in our department meetings to talk about the standards and how to use them. The problem is, they're always putting me with foreign language and arts teachers. And I guess they kind of group us all together in the arts." As that teacher continued, the "best thing" the school could do would be to have "all the band directors from across the county get together, and we could talk about the standards, and we could wrestle with them." Wrestling with English teachers, or foreign language teachers, however, doesn't seem to help. Nor can many of these music teachers turn to their department heads for substantive support. When we asked one teacher, in Kentucky, about department support, he replied that the person he would go to is another music teacher—but not his chair: "But again, being with the arts and humanities, we answer to, actually, a French teacher. Well, not answer to, but that is our department chair."

What it means to "answer to" a chair in such a multidisciplinary department illustrates one weakness of internal school accountability systems with regard to subjects like music. For when asked if he has been evaluated in this workplace, this same teacher replied, "I have not. Well, not to my knowledge." And when he described what he thought that evaluation would look like, it seemed unlikely that it would actually inform his practice: "I mean, you probably know; in any workplace that they seem to pick out the least important things, and make the most of them. For the most part."

At the one school in our study that does have a strong, single-subject music department, there are other reasons why teachers still feel outside the core—in this case literally, since they are housed in a separate building. Even at this physical distance, however, they view themselves as part of the school community and as an essential part of school pride—at least as long as they keep doing well in regional, state, and even national competitions. They turn to that other public accountability system—external to the school but integral to the field of music—for meaningful evaluation, for professional support, and even for fiscal resources.

As a department, as a sub-unit of the school, music does have a claim to a share of the school budget. As one teacher there explained, the school does honor that claim, but the amount is minimal: "the school gives up $2,800 a year . . . I don't do anything but buy a computer or a piece of equipment with that." Music is an expensive subject, especially when students need, not only equipment, but funding to travel to the essential competitions or stage performances at home that will bring public support: instruments, costumes, sets and scenery—costs that this teacher estimates at over $400 for a student in chorus, over $700 for one in band: "Then we find a way to earn it. Then we do a show, and we have 2,000 seats in the auditorium. We do $10 a seat. We pack the house several times. Do the math. We clear $40,000 a show. Our budget is just under half a million dollars every year. And it all comes from fundraising and performances." Although music teachers often describe feeling "outside the circle" of the school's departmental system, it is not clear that they really want to move into it, or that they feel themselves accountable to it. The principal doesn't have time to evaluate them, the department chair is not in their field, but they do have strong ties to, shared expectations with, and accountability mechanisms developed among the other music teachers in their district, region, and professional community. Like other teachers in the arts studied by Sikes, Measor, and Wood (1985), these teachers see (or hear) themselves as active participants in their field, not just as subject teachers but as practitioners and performers of music: music teachers are musicians in a way that physics teachers are not physicists.

To Test or Not to Test

Music teachers are concerned about being pushed further outside the technical core of schooling by standards-based accountability actions of the state and by the predictable responses of their schools. From the vantage point of the Kentucky music department, teachers relate how, as a department and as a subject group, they received and responded to the shift in policy. They responded early, with direct action, and with unanticipated results.

Once it seemed clear that the state of Kentucky was moving to a new testing system, and that testing would be the new measure of school success, music teachers recognized the shift as a direct threat to their survival. Jobs might be lost altogether, or music turned into more of a "dumping ground" to relieve the "real" teachers of the discipline problems that interfered with their academic work: "For so long, music teachers were thought of [as if] the only reason we existed was to give the real teacher an off period. And we're still dealing with that issue, and it's tacky . . . but it's a real issue all across this country. Music teachers are not real teachers. But we are." Under this new wave of accountability policy, to be real is to be tested. So these music teachers, and others across the state, joined together to orchestrate a movement to have their subject count.

While music might be weak in terms of departmental status, as a subject it has significant strengths. Teachers were able to unite their forces through powerful cross-institutional professional connections (music teachers across our states are remarkable in the number and intensity of references to subject associations), to invoke national standards (widely shared), to mobilize parents who saw in the subject knowledge to be valued in and of itself, for its connections to adult life after school, or for its ability to connect students, who might otherwise be disengaged from high school (and any high school or district official can testify to the latent power of band parents). They were able to successfully lobby to have music on the agendas of state accountability policy makers.

They were not, however, able to convince policy makers that all high school students should know and be able to demonstrate the kinds of standards embodied in the national standards for music—and it is almost impossible to imagine a policy system that could agree that every student in the state should really be able to read, compose, and perform to any meaningful standard. So what Kentucky adopted was a required standard for the humanities, including music, but including it along with other arts.

There are two profound and problematic consequences of this compromise. First, music as a tested subject had to become something new, something that all students could be expected to do (although many students had never been music students) and that could be "done" on a paper and pencil test. That entails a major shift within the subject, one that many music teachers see as both a transformation and a lowering of the centuries-old standards of the discipline: "It makes it real difficult when we're in performance mode with all the competitions and performances coming up . . . when we're doing so much performance, it's a little difficult to have them talking about the rhythms and the Brandenberg concertos, as opposed to getting out there playing."

Second, the act created a new subject—humanities—that no teacher had ever taught and no student had ever taken: "Some of it is music, some of it is art. Some of it deals with historical-type things as far as art, how it's related, and dance. There's some dance. And what I found phenomenal about the dance part, is there are only select schools that teach dance. And the PE teachers are supposed to teach dance . . . I haven't seen any of those teachers teach that in the ten years I've been teaching."

Across Kentucky, teachers scrambled to construct new curricula, to identify places in the existing curriculum where the required knowledge might fit, and to compose a new subject—one that crosses both disciplinary and departmental boundaries:

> My first year, we had no one teaching humanities . . . and basically we rotated the kids [the juniors] two weeks before they were to take the test. So we had all the juniors lumped together, and we divided them, thirty each, divided them amongst five different majors [PE, dance, history, art, and music]. So we divided those kids between all five of us, because some of those kids had never had music. In all the years they had been in school, they'd never had music. Meaning if there was a music question on the test, they would never understand what a treble clef was . . . so that's how we did it the first year I was here. We split them into groups of thirty and rotated them every thirty minutes. Then we filled them with as much knowledge as we could fill them with.

That kind of new subject, in which established disciplines are truncated into two-week bursts, decontextualized and disconnected from the performance standards that have long characterized the field, changes not only the knowledge of the subject but the nature of teaching. One music teacher noted the irony in that now "we're embracing the fact that we're going to become reading and writing teachers who also teach music."

The example of music dramatically illuminates one of the major problems confronting high-stakes accountability at the high school level. Once we move beyond (or arrive at) required standards for reading and writing, is there actually agreement on what all high school students should know and be able to do to earn a high school diploma? Are high standards possible across all subjects? Will we expect all students to achieve high standards in chemistry or to "know how their body works, so they can make informed medical decisions"? To perform the *Gloria Vivaldi* or to correctly label the kind of dance illustrated by a picture of dancers in poodle skirts and flat tops? In transforming subjects into something all students need to be able to demonstrate on a test, do we inadvertently lower performance standards, weaken existing professional accountability systems, or lose knowledge outside the core altogether?

The knowledge that standards are supposed to measure—to ensure that the next generation receives it intact—is being altered by the act of measuring itself. In an irony that Heisenberg would have appreciated, accountability policies may well be held accountable for changing the very disciplines they were devised to perpetuate.

References

De Brabander, C. J. (1993). Subject conceptions of teachers and school culture. In F. K. Kievet and R. Vandenberghe (eds.), *School culture, school improvement, and teacher development*, 77–107. Leiden: DSWO Press.

Goodson, I. F. (1993). *School subjects and curriculum change.* (3rd ed.) London: Falmer Press.

Kliebard, H. (1986). *The struggle for the American curriculum, 1893–1958.* London: Routledge and Kegan Paul.

Leinhart, G., and Smith, D. A. (1985). Expertise in mathematics: Subject matter knowledge. *Journal of Educational Psychology* 77: 247–271.

Little, J. W. (1993). Professional community in comprehensive high schools: The two worlds of academic and vocational teachers. In J. W. Little and M. W. McLaughlin (eds.), *Teachers' work: Individuals, colleagues, and contexts*, 137–163. New York: Teachers College Press.

McNeil, L. M. (2000). *Contradictions of school reform.* New York: Routledge.

Powell, A. G., Farrar, E., and Cohen, D. K. (1985). *The shopping mall high school: Winners and losers in the educational marketplace.* Boston: Houghton Mifflin.

Sikes, P., Measor, L., and Woods, P. (eds.) (1985). *Teacher careers: Crises and continuities.* London: Falmer Press.

Siskin, L. S. (1991). Departments as different worlds: Subject subcultures in secondary schools. *Educational Administration Quarterly* 27: 134–160.

Siskin, L. S. (1994). *Realms of knowledge: Academic departments in secondary schools.* London and New York: Falmer Press.

Stodolsky, S. S. (1993). A framework for subject matter comparisons in high schools. *Teaching and Teacher Education* 9: 333–346.

Young, M. F. D. (ed.) (1971). *Knowledge and control.* London: Collier-Macmillan.

24

What Does it Mean to Say a School Is Doing Well?

Elliot W. Eisner

Driven by discontent with the performance of our schools, we are, once again, in the midst of education reform, as we were in 1983 with *A Nation at Risk*, in 1987 with *America 2000*, and a few years later with *Goals 2000*. Each of these reform efforts was intended to rationalize the practice and performance of our schools. Each was designed to work out and install a system of measurable goals and evaluation practices that would ensure that our nation would be first in science and mathematics by the year 2000, that all our children would come to school ready to learn, and that each school would be drug-free, safe, and nonviolent.[1]

The formulation of standards and the measurement of performance were intended to tidy up a messy system and to make teachers and school administrators truly accountable. The aim was then, and is today, to systematize and standardize so that the public will know which schools are performing well and which are not. There were to be then, and there are today, payments and penalties for performance.

America is one of the few nations in which responsibility for schools is not under the aegis of a national ministry of education. Although we have a federal agency, the U.S. Department of Education, the 10th Amendment to the U.S. Constitution indicates that those responsibilities that the Constitution does not assign explicitly to the federal government belong to the states (or to the people). And since the Constitution makes no mention of education, it is a responsibility of the states.

As a result, we have 50 departments of education, one for each state, overseeing some 16,000 school districts that serve 52 million students in more than 100,000 schools. In addition, each school district has latitude for shaping education policy. Given the complexity of the way education is organized in the U.S., it is understandable that from one perspective the view looks pretty messy and not altogether rational. Furthermore, more than a few believe that we have a national problem in American education and that national problems require national solutions. The use of highly rationalized procedures for improving schools is a part of the solution.

I mention the concept of rationalization because I am trying to describe the ethos being created in our schools. I am trying to reveal a world view that shapes our conception of education and the direction we take for making our schools better.

Rationalization as a concept has a number of features. First, it depends on a clear specification of intended outcomes.[2] That is what standards and rubrics are supposed to do. We are supposed to know what the outcomes of educational practice are to be, and rubrics are to exemplify those outcomes. Standards are more general statements intended to proclaim our values. One argument for the use of standards and rubrics is that they are necessary if we are to function rationally. As the saying goes, if you don't know where you're headed, you will not know where you have arrived. In fact, it's more than knowing where you're headed; it's also knowing the precise destination. Thus the specification of intended outcomes has become one of the primary practices in the process of rationalizing school reform efforts. Holding people accountable for the results is another.

Second, rationalization typically uses measurement as a means through which the quality of a product or performance is assessed and represented. Measurement, of course, is *one* way to describe the world. Measurement has to do with determining matters of magnitude, and it deals with matters of magnitude through the specification of units. In the United States, the unit for weight is pounds. In Sweden or the Netherlands, it is kilograms. It's kilometers in Europe; it's miles in the United States. It really doesn't matter what unit you use, as long as everyone agrees what the unit is.[3]

Quantification is believed to be a way to increase objectivity, secure rigor, and advance precision in assessment. For describing some features of the world, including the educational world, it is indispensable. But it is not good for everything, and the limitations of quantification are increasingly being recognized. For example, although initial discussions about standards emphasized the need for them to be *measurable*, as standards have become increasingly general and ideological, measurability has become less salient.

Third, the rationalization of practice is predicated on the ability to control and predict. We assume that we can know the specific effects of our interventions, an assumption that is questionable.

Fourth, rationalization downplays interactions. Interactions take into account not simply the conditions that are to be introduced in classrooms or schools but also the kinds of personal qualities, expectations, orientations, ideas, and temperaments that interact with those conditions. Philosophical constructivists have pointed out that what something means comes both from the features of the phenomenon to be addressed and from the way those features are interpreted or experienced by individuals.[4] Such idiosyncratic considerations always complicate assessment. They complicate efforts to rationalize education as well. Prediction is not easy when what the outcome is going to be is a function not only of what is introduced in the situation but also of what a student makes of what has been introduced.

Fifth, rationalization promotes comparison, and comparison requires what is called "commensurability." Commensurability is possible only if you know what the programs were in which the youngsters participated in the schools being compared. If youngsters are in schools that have different curricula or that allocate differing amounts of time to different areas of the curriculum, comparing the outcomes of those schools without taking into account their differences is extremely questionable. Making comparisons between the math performance of youngsters in Japan and those in the United States without taking into account cultural differences, different allocations of time for instruction, or different approaches to teaching makes it impossible to account for differences in student performance or to consider the side effects or opportunity costs associated with different programs in different cultures. The same principle holds in comparing student performance across school districts in the U.S.

Sixth, rationalization relies upon extrinsic incentives to motivate action; that's what vouchers are intended to do. Schools are likened to businesses, and the survival of the fittest is the principle that determines which ones survive. If schools don't produce effective results on tests, they go out of business.

In California and in some other parts of the country, principals and superintendents are often paid a bonus if their students perform well on standardized tests: payment by results. And, of course, such a reward system has consequences for a school's priorities. Are test scores the criteria that we want to use to reward professional performance?

The features that I have just described are a legacy of the Enlightenment. We believe our rational abilities can be used to discover the regularities of the universe and, once we've found them, to implement, as my colleague David Tyack titled his book, "the one best system."[5] We have a faith in our ability to discover what the U.S. Department of Education once described as "what works." The result is an approach to reform that leaves little room for surprise, for imagination, for improvisation, or for the cultivation of productive idio-syncrasy. Our reform efforts are closer in spirit to the ideas of René Descartes and August Compte than to those of William Blake. They are efforts that use league tables to compare schools and that regard test scores as valid proxies for the quality of education our children receive.[6] And they constitute an approach to reform that has given us three major educationally feckless reform efforts in the past 20 years. Are we going to have another?

What are the consequences of the approach to reform that we have taken and what should we pay attention to in order to tell when a school is doing well? First, one of the consequences of our approach to reform is that the curriculum gets narrowed as school district policies make it clear that what is to be tested is what is to be taught. Tests come to define our priorities. And now we have legitimated those priorities by talking about "core subjects." The introduction of the concept of core subjects explicitly marginalizes subjects that are not part of the core. One of the areas that we marginalize is the arts, an area that when well taught offers substantial benefits to students. Our idea of core subjects is related to our assessment practices and the tests we use to determine whether or not schools are doing well.

Because those of us in education take test scores seriously, the public is reinforced in its view that test scores are good proxies for the quality of education a school provides. Yet what test scores predict best are other test scores. If we are going to use proxies that have predictive validity, we need proxies that predict performances that matter outside the context of school. The function of schooling is not to enable students to do better in school. The function of schooling is to enable students to do better in life. What students learn in school ought to exceed in relevance the limits of the school's program.

As we focus on standards, rubrics, and measurement, the deeper problems of schooling go unattended. What are some of the deeper problems of schooling? One has to do with the quality of conversation in classrooms. We need to provide opportunities for youngsters and adolescents to engage in challenging kinds of conversation, and we need to help them learn how to do so. Such conversation is all too rare in schools. I use "conversation" seriously, for challenging conversation is an intellectual affair. It has to do with thinking about what people have said and responding reflectively, analytically, and imaginatively to that process. The practice of conversation is almost a lost art. We turn to talk shows to experience what we cannot do very well or very often.

The deeper problems of schooling have to do with teacher isolation and the fact that teachers don't often have access to other people who know what they're doing when they teach and who can help them do it better.[7] Although there are many issues that need attention in schooling, we search for the silver bullet and believe that, if we get our standards straight and our rubrics right and make our tests tough enough, we will have an improved school system. I am not so sure.

The message that we send to students is that what really matters in their education are their test scores. As a result, students in high-stakes testing programs find ways to cut corners—and so do some teachers. We read increasingly often not only about students who are cheating but also about teachers who are unfairly helping students get higher scores on the tests.[8] It's a pressure that undermines the kind of experience that students ought to have in schools.

Perhaps the major consequence of the approach we have taken to rationalize our schools is that it ineluctably colors the school climate. It promotes an orientation to practice that emphasizes extrinsically defined attainment targets that have a specified quantitative value. This, in turn, leads students to want to know just what it is they need to do to earn a particular grade. Even at Stanford, I sometimes get requests from graduate students who want to know precisely, or as precisely as I can put it, what they need to do in order to get an A in the class.

Now from one angle such a request sounds reasonable. After all, it is a means/ends approach to educational planning. Students are, it can be said, rationally planning their education. But such planning has very little to do with intellectual life, where risk-taking, exploration, uncertainty, and speculation are what it's about. And if you create a culture of schooling in which a narrow means/ends orientation is promoted, that culture can undermine the development of intellectual dispositions. By intellectual dispositions I mean a curiosity and interest in engaging and challenging ideas.

What the field has not provided is an efficient alternative to the testing procedures we now use. And for good reason. The good reason is that there are no efficient alternatives. Educationally useful evaluation takes time, it's labor intensive and complex, and it's subtle, particularly if evaluation is used not simply to score children or adults but to provide information to improve the process of teaching and learning.

The price one pays for providing many ways for students to demonstrate what has been learned is a reduction of commensurability. Commensurability decreases when attention to individuality increases. John Dewey commented about comparisons in a book that he wrote in 1934 when he was 76 years old. The book is *Art as Experience.* He observed that nothing is more odious than comparisons in the arts.[9] What he was getting at was that attention to or appreciation of an art form requires attention to and appreciation of its distinctive features. It was individuality that Dewey was emphasizing, and it is the description of individuality we would do well to think about in our assessment practices. We should be trying to discover where a youngster is, where his or her strengths are, where additional work is warranted. Commensurability is possible when everybody is on the same track, when there are common assessment practices, and when there is a common curriculum. But when students work on different kinds of problems, and when there is concern with the development of an individual's thumbprint, so to speak, commensurability is an inappropriate aim.

What have been the consequences of the rationalized approach to education reform that we have embraced? Only this: in our desire to improve our schools, education has become a casualty. That is, in the process of rationalization, education—always a delicate, complex, and subtle process having to do with both cultural transmission and self-actualization—has become a commodity. Education has evolved from a form of human development serving personal and civic needs into a product our nation produces to compete in a global economy. Schools have become places to mass produce this product.

Let us assume that we impose a moratorium on standardized testing for a five-year period. What might we pay attention to in schools in order to say that a school is doing well? If it is not higher test scores that we are looking for, what is it? Let me suggest the kind of data we might seek by raising some questions that might guide our search.

What kinds of problems and activities do students engage in? What kind of thinking do these activities invite? Are students encouraged to wonder and to raise questions about what they have studied? Perhaps we should be less concerned with whether they can answer our questions than with whether they can ask their own. The most significant intellectual achievement is not so much in problem solving, but in question posing. What if we took that idea seriously and concluded units of study by looking for the sorts of questions that youngsters are able to raise as a result of being immersed in a domain of study? What would that practice teach youngsters about inquiry?

What is the intellectual significance of the ideas that youngsters encounter? (I have a maxim that I work with: If it's not worth teaching, it's not worth teaching well.) Are the ideas they encounter important? Are they ideas that have legs? Do they go someplace?

Are students introduced to multiple perspectives? Are they asked to provide multiple perspectives on an issue or a set of ideas? The implications of such an expectation for curriculum development are extraordinary. To develop such an ability and habit of mind, we would need to invent activities that encourage students to practice, refine, and develop certain modes of thought. Taking multiple perspectives is just one such mode.

In 1950 the American psychologist J.P. Guilford developed what he called "the structure of intellect," in which 130 different kinds of cognitive processes were identified.[10] What if we used that kind of structure to promote various forms of thinking? My point is that the activities in which youngsters participate in classes are the means through which their thinking is promoted. When youngsters have no reason to raise questions, the processes that enable them to learn how to discover intellectual problems go undeveloped.

The ability to raise telling questions is not an automatic consequence of maturation. Do you know what's the biggest problem that Stanford students have in the course of their doctoral work? It is not getting good grades in courses; they all get good grades in courses. Their biggest obstacle is in framing a dissertation problem. We can do something about that before students get to the doctoral level. In a school that is doing well, opportunities for the kind of thinking that yields good questions would be promoted.

What connections are students helped to make between what they study in class and the world outside of school? A major aim of education has to do with what psychologists refer to as "transfer of learning." Can students apply what they have learned or what they have learned how to learn? Can they engage in the kind of learning they will need in order to deal with problems and issues outside of the classroom? If what students are learning is simply used as a means to increase their scores on the next test, we may win the battle and lose the war. In such a context, school learning becomes a hurdle to jump over. We need to determine whether students can use what they have learned. But even being able to use what has been learned is no indication that it will be used. There is a difference between what a student can do and what a student will do.

The really important dependent variables in education are not located in classrooms. Nor are they located in schools. The really important dependent variables are located outside schools. Our assessment practices haven't even begun to scratch that surface. It's what students do with what they learn when they can do what they want to do that is the real measure of educational achievement.

What opportunities do youngsters have to become literate in the use of different representational forms? By representational forms, I mean the various symbol systems through which humans shape experience and give it meaning.[11] Different forms of human meaning are expressed in different forms of representation. The kinds of meaning one secures from poetry are not the kinds of meaning one secures from propositional signs. The kinds of meanings expressed in music are not the meanings experienced in the visual arts. To be able to secure any of those meanings, you have to know how to "read" them. Seeing is a reading. Hearing is a reading. They are processes of interpreting and *construing* meaning from the material encountered; reading text is not only a process of decoding, it is also a process of encoding. We *make* sense of what we read.

What opportunities do students have to formulate their own purposes and to design ways to achieve them? Can a school provide the conditions for youngsters, as they mature, to have increased opportunity to set their own goals and to design ways to realize them? Plato once defined a slave as someone who executes the purposes of another. I would say that, in a free democratic state, at least a part of the role of education is to help youngsters learn how to define their own purposes.

What opportunities do students have to work cooperatively to address problems that they believe to be important? Can we design schools so that we create communities of learners who know how to work with one another? Can we design schools and classrooms in which cooperating with others is part of what it means to be a student?

Do students have the opportunity to serve the community in ways that are not limited to their own personal interests? Can we define a part of the school's role as establishing or helping students establish projects in which they do something beyond their own self-interest? I want to know that in order to know how well a school is doing.

To what extent are students given the opportunity to work in depth in domains that relate to their aptitudes? Is personal talent cultivated? Can we arrange the time for youngsters to work together on the basis of interest rather than on the basis of age grading? Youngsters who are interested in ceramics might work in depth in ceramics; those interested in science might work in depth in science. To make these possibilities a reality, we would need, of course, to address the practical problems of allocating time and responsibility. But without a conception of what is important, we will never even ask questions about allocating time. A vision of what is educationally important must come first.

Do students participate in the assessment of their own work? If so, how? It is important for teachers to understand what students themselves think of their own work. Can we design assessment practices in which students can help us?

To what degree are students genuinely engaged in what they do in school? Do they find satisfaction in the intellectual journey? How many students come to school early and how many would like to stay late? The motives for such choices have to do with the "locus of satisfactions." Satisfactions generate reasons for doing something. Basically, there are three reasons for doing anything. One reason for doing something is that you like what it feels like and you like who you are when you do it. Sex, play, and art fall into this category. They are intrinsically satisfying activities.

A second reason for doing something is not because you like doing it, but because you like the results of having done it. You might like a clean kitchen, but you might not enjoy cleaning your kitchen. The process is not a source of enjoyment, but the outcome is.

A third reason for doing something is not because you like the process or even the outcome, but because you like the rewards. You like the grades you earn. You like the paycheck you receive. That's what Hannah Arendt described as labor.[12] There is too much labor in our schools—and not enough work. Work is effort from which you derive satisfaction. We ought to be paying attention to the joy of the journey. This is easy to say but difficult and challenging to do. Nevertheless, we ought to keep our minds focused on it as a goal.

Are teachers given the time to observe and work with one another? To what degree is professional discourse an important aspect of what being a teacher means in the school? Is the school a resource, a center for the teacher's own development? Is the school a center for teacher education?

The center for teacher education is not the university; it is the school in which the teacher works. Professional growth should be promoted during the 25 years that a teacher works in a school—not just during the year and a half that he or she spends in a teacher education program. Can we create schools that take the professional development of teachers seriously? And what would they look like? Schools will not be better for students than they are for the professionals who work in them.

All of us who teach develop repertoires. We all have routines. We all get by. We get by without serious problems, but getting by is not good enough. We need to get better. And to get better, we have to think about school in ways that address teachers' real needs. And when I say, "addressing teachers' real needs," I don't mean sending them out every 6,000 miles to get "inserviced" by a stranger.

Are parents helped to understand what their child has accomplished in class? Do they come to understand the educational import of what is going on? Very often children's artwork is displayed in the school, with the only information provided being the student's name, the grade, and the teacher's name, all in the lower right-hand corner. Then the best student work is posted more formally. What we do, in effect, is use a gallery model of exhibition. We take the best work, and we display it. What we need to create is an educationally interpretive exhibition that explains to viewers what problems the youngsters were addressing and how they resolved them.[13] This can be done by looking at prior work and comparing it with present work—that is, by looking at what students have accomplished over time. I am talking about interpretation. I am talking about getting people to focus not so much on what the grade is, but on what process led to the outcome.

What is my point? All my arguments have had to do with creating an educationally informed community. We need to ask better questions.

Can we widen what parents and others believe to be important in judging the quality of our schools? Can we widen and diversify what they think matters? Can those of us who teach think about public education not only as the education of the public in the schools (i.e., our students), but also as the education of the public outside of our schools (i.e., parents and community members)? Can a more substantial and complex understanding of what constitutes good schooling contribute to better, more enlightened support for our schools?

Can a more informed conception of what constitutes quality in education lead to greater equity for students and ultimately for the culture? Educational equity is much more than just allowing students to cross the threshold of the school. It has to do with what students find after they do so. We ought to be providing environments that enable each youngster in our schools to find a place in the educational sun. But when we narrow the program so that there is only a limited array of areas in which assessment occurs and performance is honored, youngsters whose aptitudes and interests lie elsewhere are going to be marginalized in our schools. The more we diversify those opportunities, the more equity we are going to have because we are going to provide wider opportunities for youngsters to find what it is that they are good at.

And that leads me to the observation that, in our push for attaining standards, we have tended to focus on outcomes that are standard for all youngsters. We want youngsters to arrive at the same place at about the same time. I would argue that really good schools increase variance in student performance. Really good schools increase the variance *and* raise the mean. The reason I say that is because, when youngsters can play to their strengths, those whose aptitudes are in, say, mathematics are going to go faster and further in that area than youngsters whose aptitudes are in some other field. But in those other fields, those youngsters would go faster and further than those whose aptitudes are in math. Merely by conceiving of a system of educational organization that regards productive variance as something to be valued and pursued, we undermine the expectation that everybody should be moving in lockstep through a series of 10-month years in a standardized system and coming out at pretty much the same place by age 18.

Part of our press toward standardization has to do with what is inherent in our age-graded school system. Age-graded systems work on the assumption that children remain more alike than different over time and that we should be teaching within the general expectations for any particular grade. Yet, if you examine reading performance, for example, the average range of reading ability in an ordinary classroom approximates the grade level. Thus at the second grade, there is a two-year spread; at the third grade, a three-year range; at the fourth grade, a four-year range. Consider how various the picture would be if performance in four or five different fields of study were examined. Children become more different as they get older, and we ought to be promoting those differences and at the same time working to escalate the mean.

Does more enlightened grasp of what matters in schools put us in a better position to improve them? I hope so. What I have argued here is intended to divert our focus away from what we normally use to make judgments about the quality of schools and redirect it instead toward the processes, conditions, and culture that are closer to the heart of education. I am unabashedly endorsing the promotion of improvisation, surprise, and diversity of outcomes as educational virtues that we ought to try to realize through our teaching.

The point of the questions I have raised is to provide something better than the blinkered vision of school quality that now gets front-page coverage in our newspapers. Perhaps this vision serves best those in positions of privilege. Perhaps our society needs losers so it can have winners. Whatever the case, I believe that those of us who wish to exercise leadership in education must do more than simply accept the inadequate criteria that are now used to determine how well our schools are doing.

We need a fresh and humane vision of what schools might become because what our schools become has everything to do with what our children and our culture will become. I have suggested some of the features and some of the questions that I believe matter educationally. We need reform efforts that are better than those we now have. The vision of education implicit in what I have described here is just a beginning.

Notes

1. The document that most directly expresses this view is National Commission on Excellence in Education, *A Nation at Risk: The Imperative for Educational Reform* (Washington, D.C.: U.S. Government Printing Office, 1983).
2. Donald Schon describes the process of rationalization of behavior as "technical rationality." See Donald Schon, *The Reflective Practitioner: How Professionals Think in Action* (New York: Basic Books, 1983). Nor is this the first time technically rational approaches to planning and assessment have dominated schooling. The efficiency movement in American schools—from about 1913 to about 1930—is one example. The behavioral objectives and accountability movements of the 1960s and 1970s are two more.
3. For a discussion of issues pertaining to the quantification and use of standards, see Elliot W. Eisner, "Standards for American Schools: Help or Hindrance?," *Phi Delta Kappan*, June 1995, pp. 758–764.
4. One of the foremost philosophical constructivists is John Dewey. The concept of interaction was a central notion in his philosophy of mind and in his conception of the educational process. For a succinct view of his ideas pertaining to education, see John Dewey, *Experience and Education* (New York: Macmillan, 1938).
5. David Tyack, *The One Best System* (Cambridge, Mass.: Harvard University Press, 1974).
6. League tables not only affect the priorities of the school, they are a major influence on real estate values. The value of houses is influenced significantly by perceptions of the quality of the schools in a neighborhood, and test scores are the indices used to determine such quality.
7. For a full discussion of the processes of observation and disclosure as they pertain to teaching and its improvement, see my book *The Enlightened Eye: Qualitative Inquiry and the Enhancement of Educational Practice* (New York: Macmillan, 1991).
8. For an insightful and lucid discussion of the pressures secondary school students experience in the high-stakes environment that we have created in schools, see Denise Pope, "Doing School" (Doctoral dissertation, Stanford University, 1998).
9. John Dewey, *Art as Experience* (New York: Minton, Balch and Company, 1934), especially chap. 13.
10. J.P. Guilford, *The Nature of Human Intelligence* (New York: McGraw-Hill, 1967).
11. Elliot W. Eisner, "Forms of Understanding and the Future of Educational Research," *Educational Researcher*, October 1993, pp. 5–11. Also see my book *Cognition and Curriculum Reconsidered* (New York: Teachers College Press, 1994).
12. Hannah Arendt, *The Human Condition* (Chicago: University of Chicago Press, 1958).
13. For a discussion and illustration of what I call educationally interpretive exhibitions, see Elliot W. Eisner et al. *The Educationally Interpretive Exhibition: Rethinking the Display of Student Art* (Reston, Va.: National Art Education Association, 1997).

25

Subtractive Schooling, Caring Relations, and Social Capital in the Schooling of U.S.-Mexican Youth

Angela Valenzuela

Schools subtract resources from youth in two major ways. The first involves a process of "de-Mexicanization," or subtracting students' culture and language, which is consequential to their achievement and orientations toward school. The second involves the role of caring between teachers and students in the educational process. De-Mexicanization erodes students' social capital (Coleman 1988, 1990; also see Stanton-Salazar, 1997), by making it difficult for constructive social ties to develop between immigrant and U.S.-born youth. By *social capital*, I mean the social ties that connect students to each other, as well as the levels of resources (like academic skills and knowledge) that characterize their friendship groups. This dynamic is of special consequence to regular-track, U.S.-born Mexican youth, who often lack a well-defined and effective achievement orientation.

Regarding caring, teachers expect students to *care about* school in a technical fashion before they *care for* them, while students expect teachers to *care for* them before they *care about* school. By dismissing students' definition of education—an orientation thoroughly grounded in Mexican culture and advanced by caring theorists (e.g., Noddings, 1984, 1992)—schooling subtracts resources from youth.

After describing the study I undertook at Seguín High School,[1] I explain how I derived the concept of "subtractive schooling." This description incorporates my concerns about current theorizing (especially see Portes, 1995) that narrowly casts achievement differences between immigrant and U.S.-born youth as evidence of "downward assimilation." I then elaborate on how culture and caring relations are involved in the process of subtractive schooling. Throughout, I draw selectively on both quantitative and qualitative evidence that lends support to my thesis.

The Seguín High School Study

Seguín High is a large, comprehensive, inner-city high school located in the Houston Independent School District. Its 3,000-plus student body is virtually all Mexican and generationally diverse (45 percent immigrant and 55 percent U.S. born).[2] Teachers, on the other hand, are predominantly non-Latino. Currently, 81 percent are non-Latino, and 19 percent are Latino (mostly Mexican American).

Seguín's failure and dropout rates are very high. In 1992 a full quarter of the freshman class repeated the grade for at least a second time, and a significant portion of these were repeating the ninth grade a third and fourth time. An average of 300 students skip daily. Between 1,200 and 1,500 students enter the 9th grade each year and only 400 to 500 students graduate in any given year. Low expectations are virtually built into this school: Were students to progress normally from one grade to the next, there would be no space to house them. As things stand, Seguín's 3,000-plus student body is crammed into a physical facility capable of housing no more than 2,600. Because of the school's high failure and dropout rates, the freshman class makes up more than half of the school population.

An ethnic brand of politics that has focused on problems in the school has made for a contentious relationship between Seguín and its surrounding community. Although local community activists have historically supported numerous causes, including legal challenges against segregation during the early 1970s, a massive student walkout in October 1989, and a number of school reforms such as site-based management, little has changed to significantly alter its underachieving profile. Seguín is locked in inertia. Steeped in a logic of technical rationality, schooling centers on questions of how best to administer the curriculum rather than on why, as presently organized, it tends to block the educational mobility of huge segments of its student body. Excepting those located in the privileged rungs of the curriculum—that is, honors classes, the magnet school program, and the upper levels of the Career and Technology Education (CTE) vocational program[3]—the academic trajectories of the vast majority are highly circumscribed. Because as a group, 9th graders are especially "at risk," I tried to talk to as many of them as possible and to incorporate their voices and experiences into this ethnographic account.

Although my study makes use of quantitative data, the key modes of data collection are based on participant observation and open-ended interviews with individuals and with groups of students. Group interviews enabled me not only to tap into peer-group culture but also to investigate the social, cultural, and linguistic divisions that I observed among teenagers at Seguín. Before elaborating my framework, I will first address relevant survey findings that pertain to parental education, schooling orientations, and generational differences in achievement.[4]

First, students' parental education levels are very low, hovering around nine years of schooling completed for third-generation students.[5] Though higher than the average for parents of first-generation respondents (i.e., six years of schooling), a "high" of nine for the U.S.-born population means that parents have little educational "advantage" to confer to their children (Lareau 1989). That is, most parents have either no high school experience or a negative one to pass on to their progeny. Rather than aberrant, this finding is consistent with Chapa (1988), who found that third-generation Mexican Americans in the state of Texas complete an average of 9.3 years of education and that the dropout rate is 56 percent.[6]

These data indicate that with such low average attainment levels, the major responsibility for education falls on the school by default. School officials, however, tend not to see it this way. They tend to blame the students, their parents, their culture, and their community for their educational failure. This tendency on the part of teachers and administrators to blame children, parents, and community has been amply observed in ethnographies of minority youth in urban schools (Fine, 1991; Peshkin, 1991; Yeo, 1997; McQuillan, 1998).

Complicating matters—and reinforcing many teachers' and other school officials' opinion that students "don't care" about school—is that a significant proportion of students, mostly U.S. born, have become adept at breaking school rules. For example, they skip class and attend all three lunch periods knowing that the numbers are on their side and that they are unlikely to get processed even if they get spotted by school officials. A common scenario is the presence of several administrators in the school cafeteria alongside scores of students whom they know are skipping class. The sheer amount of time, paperwork, and effort that would be required to process every offender discourages massive action. In short, violations of school policies are so common that they outstrip the administration's capacity of address them, making Seguín a capricious environment that minimizes many students' sense of control, on the one hand, and their respect toward authority, on the other. Despite the fact that certain types of students, discussed shortly, consistently succeed, the prevailling view is that students "don't care."

Another finding from survey data corroborated in the ethnographic account is that immigrant youth experience school significantly more positively than do their U.S.-born peers. That is, they see teachers as more caring and accessible than do their U.S.-born counterparts, and they rate the school climate in more positive terms as well. They are also much less likely to evade school rules and policies. These students' attitudes contrast markedly with those of their second- and third-generation counterparts, whose responses in turn are not significantly different from one another. Particularly striking is how generational status—and not gender or curriculum track placement—influences orientations toward schooling.

Because of its relevance, I interject at this point how ethnographic evidence additionally reveals that immigrant, more than U.S.-born, youth belong to informal peer groups that exhibit an esprit-de-corps, proschool ethos. Immigrants' collective achievement strategies, when combined with the academic competence their prior schooling provides, directly affect their level of achievement. Academic competence thus functions as a human-capital variable that, when marshaled in the context of the peer group, *becomes* a social-capital variable (Coleman, 1988, 1990). This process is especially evident among females in Seguín's immigrant student population (see Valenzuela, 1999). In contrast, and borrowing from Putnam (1993, 1995), regular-track, U.S.-born youth are "socially decapitalized." Through a protracted, institutionally mediated process of de-Mexicanization that results in a de-identification from the Spanish language, Mexico, and things Mexican, they lose an organic connection to those among them who are academically oriented. U.S.-born youth are no less solidaristic; their social ties are simply devoid of academically productive social capital.

Finally, quantitative evidence points to significantly higher academic achievement among immigrants than among U.S.-born youth located in the regular track. Though not controlling for curriculum track placement, other scholars have observed this tendency among Mexican and Central American students (Buriel, 1984; Buriel & Cardoza, 1988; Matute-Bianchi, 1991; Ogbu, 1991; Suárez-Orozco, 1991; Vigil & Long, 1981). This finding has been primarily interpreted from an individual assimilationist perspective rather than from a critical analysis of assimilating institutions.

Invoking a generational analysis of change, classic assimilation theory (Gordon, 1964) suggests that achievement should improve generationally if assimilation worked for Mexicans in the way that it has worked for European-origin immigrant groups in the United States. Though unintended, this generational model encourages a construction of U.S.-born youth as "deficient" and as fundamentally lacking in the drive and enthusiasm possessed by their immigrant counterparts. Drawing on several works that examine the phenomenon of oppositionality among minority youth (Fordham &

Ogbu, 1986; Matute-Bianchi, 1991; Ogbu, 1991), Portes and Zhou (1993, 1994) conclude that U.S.-born minority youth are members of "adversarial cultures" (or "reactive subcultures"). They convey the imagery of a downward achievement spiral that accompanies the assimilation process, culminating, often by the second generation, in a devaluation of education as a key route to mobility. Sorely lacking in their account is an understanding of the myriad ways in which powerful institutions such as schools are implicated in both the curtailment of students' educational mobility and, consequently, in the very development of the alleged "adversarial culture" about which Portes and Zhou express concern.

My data show that institutionalized curricular tracking is a good place to begin assessing the academic well-being of the would-be socially ascendant. That is, the previously observed pattern of higher immigrant achievement vis-à-vis U.S.-born underachievement is *only* evident among youth within the regular, noncollege-bound track. In other words, as one would expect, location in the college-bound track erases these differences. At Seguín, however, the vast majority of youth are located in the regular academic track. Only between 10 and 14 percent of the entire student body is ever located in either honors courses, the magnet school program, or the upper-levels of the Career and Technology Education (CTE) vocational program (see Oakes, 1985; O'Connor, Lewis, & Mueller, this volume; Olsen, 1997).

To categorically characterize U.S.-born Mexican youth as emanating from cultures that do not value achievement is to at once treat them as if they were a monolith and to promote an invidious distinction. Key institutional mechanisms such as tracking—and, as I shall shortly argue, subtractive schooling—mediate and have always mediated achievement outcomes. That most minority youth, however, are not located in the college-bound track should not keep us from recognizing the power of such placement: It is there where they acquire privileged access to the necessary skills, resources, and conditions for social ascendancy within schools, and ultimately, within society.

Beyond the "blind spot" in the assimilation literature overlooking the significance of tracking, the limitations of assimilation theory to account for differences in achievement between immigrant and U.S.-born youth becomes further apparent through a close examination of the subtractive elements of schooling. The theoretical question that emerges from the framework I have elaborated is not whether we bear witness to "downward assimilation," as Portes (1995) suggests, but rather *how schooling subtracts resources from youth.*

The Concept of Subtractive Schooling

I derive the concept of "subtractive" in the phrase *subtractive schooling* from the sociolinguistic literature that regards assimilation as a non-neutral process (Cummins, 1981, 1986; Gibson, 1988; Skutnabb-Kangas & Cummins, 1988). Schooling involves either adding on a second culture and language or subtracting one's original culture and language. An additive outcome would be fully vested bilingualism and biculturalism. Whenever Mexican youth emerge from the schooling process as monolingual individuals who are neither identified with Mexico nor equipped to function competently in the mainstream of the United States, subtraction can be said to have occurred.

There is no neutral category for schooling because the status quo is subtractive and inscribed in public policy: the Texas Bilingual Education Code is a transitional policy framework.[7] The state's English as a Second Language (ESL) curriculum is designed to impart to non-native English speakers sufficient verbal and written skills to effectuate their transition into an all-English curriculum within a three-year time period. Under these circumstances, maintaining and developing students' bilingual and bicultural abilities is to swim against the current.

Though "subtractive" and "additive bilingualism" are well-established concepts in the sociolinguistic literature, they have yet to be applied to either the organization of schooling or the structure of caring relationships. Instead, the bulk of this literature emphasizes issues pertaining to language acquisition and maintenance. Merging these concerns with current evidence and theorizing in the nascent comparative literature on immigrant and ethnic minority youth—as I do in this chapter—is fruitful, broadening the scope of empirical inquiry. Currently, the literature addresses differences in perceptions and attitudes toward schooling among immigrant and ethnic minority youth, as well as the adaptational coping strategies they use to negotiate the barriers they face in achieving their goals (e.g., Gibson, 1988, 1993; Matute-Bianchi, 1991; Suárez-Orozco & Suárez-Orozco, 1997). While I address this in my work as well, it is also worthwhile to investigate how the organizational features of schooling relate to the production of minority status and identities, on the one hand, and how these productions relate to achievement and orientations toward schooling, on the other.

I derive the concept of "schooling" in "subtractive schooling" from the social reproduction literature, which views schools as actually "working"—that is, if their job *is* to reproduce the social order along race, class, and gender lines (e.g., Callahan, 1962; Giroux, 1988; Olsen, 1997). Academic success and failure are presented here more as products of schooling than as something that young people do. Of course, the manifest purpose of schooling is not to reproduce inequality, but the latent effect is that with which we must contend.

Segregated and generationally diverse, Seguín proved to be a natural laboratory for investigating reproduction theory. One can see what students are like when they enter school as immigrants and what they look like after having been processed. The combined terms "subtractive" and "schooling" thus bring the school into greater focus than has much of the previous literature on ethnic minority, but especially Mexican, schooling.

The Process of Subtractive Schooling

Language and Culture

"No Spanish" rules were a ubiquitous feature of U.S.-Mexican schooling through the early 1970s (San Miguel, 1987). They have been abolished, but Mexican youth continue to be subjected on a daily basis to subtle, negative messages that undermine the worth of their unique culture and history. The structure of Seguín's curriculum is typical of most public high schools with large concentrations of Mexican youth. It is designed to divest them of their Mexican identities and to impede their prospects for fully vested bilingualism and biculturalism. The single (and rarely taught) course on Mexican American history aptly reflects the students marginalized status in the formal curriculum.

On a more personal level, students' cultural identities are systematically derogated and diminished. Stripped of their usual appearance, youth entering Seguín get "disinfected" of their identifications in a way that bears striking resemblance to the prisoners and mental patients in Goffman's essays on asylums and other "total institutions" (1977). ESL youth, for example, are regarded as "limited English proficient" rather than as "Spanish dominant" and/or as potentially bilingual. Their fluency in Spanish is construed as a "barrier" that needs to be overcome. Indeed, school personnel frequently insist that once "the language barrier" is finally eliminated, Seguín's dismal achievement record will disappear as well. The belief in English as the panacea is so strong that it outweighs the hard evidence confronting classroom teachers every day: The overwhelming majority of U.S.-born, monolingual, English-speaking youth in Seguín's regular track do not now, have not in the past, and likely will not in the future prosper academically.

Another routine way in which the everyday flow of school life erodes the importance of cultural identity is through the casual revisions that faculty and staff make in students' names. At every turn, even well-meaning teachers "adapt" their students' names: *Loreto* becomes *Laredo; Azucena* is transformed into *Suzy.* Because teachers and other school personnel typically lack familarity with stress rules in Spanish, surnames are especially vulnerable to linguistic butchering. Even names that are common throughout the Southwest, like Martinez and Perez, are mispronounced as MART-i-nez and Pe-REZ. Schooling under these conditions can thus be characterized as a mortification of the self in Goffman's terms—that is, as a leaving off and a taking on.

Locating Spanish in the Foreign Language Department also implicates Seguín in the process of subtraction. This structure treats Mexicans as any other immigrant group originating from distant lands and results in course offerings that do not correspond to students' needs. Because Spanish is conceived of as similar to such "foreign languages" as French and German, the majority of the courses are offered at the beginning and intermediate levels only. Very few advanced Spanish-language courses exist. Rather than designing the program with the school's large number of native speakers in mind, Seguín's first- and second-year Spanish curriculum subjects students to material that insults their abilities.

Taking beginning Spanish means repeating such elementary phrases as "Yo me llamo María." (My name is María.) "Tú te llamas José." (Your name is José.) Even students whose linguistic competence is more passive than active—that is, they understand but speak little Spanish—are ill served by this kind of approach. A passively bilingual individual possesses much greater linguistic knowledge and ability than another individual exposed to the language for their first time. Since almost every student at Seguín is either a native speaker of Spanish or an active or passive bilingual, the school's Spanish program ill serves all, though not even-handedly. To be relevant, the curricular pyramid would have to be reversed, with far fewer beginning courses and many more advanced-level courses in Spanish.

Subtraction is further inscribed in Seguín's tracking system. That is, the regular curriculum track is subdivided into two tracks—the regular, English-only, and the ESL track. This practice of nonacademic "cultural tracking" fosters social divisions among youth along cultural and linguistic lines and limits the educational mobility of all youth. A status hierarchy that relegates immigrant youth to the bottom gets established, enabling the development of a "politics of difference" (McCarthy, 1993). That is, immigrant and U.S.-born youth develop "we-they" distinctions that sabotage communication and preclude bridge building.

The sharp division that exists between immigrant and U.S.-born youth is a striking feature, particularly when one considers that many of the U.S.-born students have parents and grandparents who are from Mexico. However, such divisions have been observed among Mexican adults as well (Rodriguez & Nuñez, 1986). This discussion should not be taken to mean that immigrants should not be accorded their much-needed, and often deficient, language support systems. I simply want to express that the broader Mexican community's collective interest to achieve academically gets compromised by a schooling process that exacerbates and reproduces differences among youth.

Regarding mobility, time-honored practices make it virtually impossible for ESL youth to make a vertical move from the ESL to the honors track. Never mind that many immigrant youth attended *secundaria* (known more formally as *educación media*) in Mexico. Since only 16.9 percent of the total middle school-age population in Mexico attends *secundaria*, any *secundaria* experience is exceptional (Gutek, 1993). Though members of an "elite" group, they are seldom recognized or treated as such by school officials, including counselors who either do not know how to interpret a transcript from Mexico or who are ignorant about the significance of a postprimary educational experience. Such negligent practices helped me understand immigrant youth who told me, "I used to be smarter." "I used to know math."

Ironically, the stigmatized status of immigrants—especially the more "*amexicanados*"—endures vis-à-vis their Mexican American peers, enhances their peer group solidarity, and protects them from the seductive elements of the peer group culture characteristic of their U.S.-born counterparts. Immigrant students' proschool, esprit-de-corps ethos (that explains their ESL teachers' affectionate references to them as "organized cheaters") finds no parallel in the schooling experiences of U.S.-born youth. Immigrants' collective achievement strategies, when combined with the academic competence their prior schooling provides, translate into academically productive social capital.

Disassociation and deidentification with immigrant youth and Mexican culture have no such hidden advantage for Mexican American youth. The English-dominant and strongly peer-oriented students who walk daily through Seguín's halls, vacillating between displays of aggressiveness and indifference, are either underachieving or psychically and emotionally detached from the academic mainstream. Hence, for U.S.-born youth, to be culturally assimilated is to become culturally and linguistically distant from those among them who are academically able. Thus eroded in the process of schooling is students' social capital. Within a span of two or three generations, "social decapitalization" may be said to occur. Under such conditions, teachers become highly influential and even necessary gatekeepers. Hence the significance of caring relations.

Caring Relations

Regardless of nativity, students' definition of education, embodied in the term *educación*, gets dismissed. Interestingly, the concept of "*educación*" approximates the optimal definition of education advanced by Noddings (1984) and other caring theorists. Being an educated person within Mexican culture carries with it its own distinctive connotation (Mejía, 1983; Reese, Balzano, Gallimore, & Goldenberg, 1991). *Ser bien educado/a* (to be well educated) is to not only possess book knowledge but to also live responsibly in the world as a caring human being, respectful of the individuality and dignity of others. Though one may possess many credentials, one is poorly educated (*mal educado/a*) if deficient in respect, manners, and responsibility toward others, especially family members.

Following from students' definition of education is the implicit notion that learning should be premised on *authentic* caring, to use Noddings' (1984) terminology. That is, learning should be premised on *relation* with teachers and other school adults having as their chief concern their students' entire well-being. In contrast to their teachers' expectations, Seguín youth prefer to be *cared for* before they *care about* school, especially when the curriculum is impersonal, irrelevant, and test driven. U.S.-born students, in particular, display psychic and emotional detachment from a schooling process organized around *aesthetic*, or superficial, caring. Such caring accords emphasis to form and nonpersonal content (e.g., rules, goals, and "the facts") and only secondarily, if at all, to their students' subjective reality.

The benefit of profound connection to the student is the development of a sense of competence and mastery over worldly tasks. In the absence of such connectedness, students are not only reduced to the level of objects; they may also be diverted from learning the skills necessary for mastering their academic and social environment. Thus, the difference in the ways in which students and teachers perceive school-based relationships can have direct bearing on students' potential to achieve.

Caring becomes political, however, when teachers and students hold different definitions of caring and the latter are unable to insert their definition of caring into the schooling process because of their weaker power position. Mexican American youth frequently choose clothing and accessories such as baggy pants and multilayered gold necklaces that "confirm" their teachers' suspicions that they really do not care about school. Withdrawal and apathy in the classroom mix with occasional displays of aggression toward school authorities. This makes them easy to write off as "lazy underachievers."

U.S.-born youth indeed engage in what Ogbu calls "cultural inversion" whereby they consciously or unconsciously oppose the culture and cognitive styles associated with the dominant group (Fordham & Ogbu, 1986). However, they do so mainly in the realm of self-representation. In contrast to what Fordham and Ogbu (1986) and Matute-Bianchi (1991) have observed among African American and Mexican American youth in their studies, strong achievement orientations among youth at Seguín are never best interpreted as attempts on their part to "act white." Instead, proschool youth are simply dismissed as "nerdy" or "geeky." Rather than education, it is *schooling* they resist—especially the dismissal of their definition of education.

Some of the most compelling evidence that students do care about education despite their rejection of schooling lies with the great number of students who skip most classes chronically but who regularly attend that one class that is meaningful to them. Without exception, it is the teacher there who makes the difference. Unconditional, authentic caring resides therein.

Seguín's immigrant students often share their U.S.-born peers' view that learning should be premised on a humane and compassionate pedagogy inscribed in reciprocal relationships, but their sense of being privileged to attend secondary school saps any desire they might have to insert their definition of education into the schooling process. Immigrant students therefore respond to the exhortation that they "care about" school differently from U.S.-born youth. Immigrant students acquiesce and are consequently seen by their teachers as polite and deferential. Their grounded sense of identity further combines with their unfamiliarity with the Mexican American experience to enable them to "care about" school without the threat of language or culture loss or even the burden of cultural derogation when their sights are set on swiftly acculturating toward the mainstream. U.S.-born youth in Seguín's regular track, on the other hand, typically respond by either withdrawing or rebelling. *Caring about* threatens their ethnic identity, their sense of self.

Frank's story illustrates one student's resistance to schooling, the productive potential of a caring relationship at school, and the debilitating effects of a curriculum that fails to validate his ethnic identity. He is an unusually reflective ninth-grader. As a "C-student," he achieves far below his potential. His own alienation from schooling accounts for his poor motivation:

> I don't get with the program because then it's doing what *they* [teachers] want for my life. I see *mexicanos* who follow the program so they can go to college, get rich, move out of the *barrio*, and never return to give back to their *gente* (people). Is that what this is all about? If I get with the program, I'm saying that's what it's all about and that teachers are right when they're not.

Frank resists caring about school not because he is unwilling to become a productive member of society, but rather because to do so is tantamount to cultural genocide. He is consciously at odds with the narrow definition of success that most school officials hold. This definition asks him to measure his self-worth against his ability to get up and out of the *barrio* along an individualist path to success divorced from the social and economic interests of the broader Mexican community. With his indifference, this profoundly mature young adult deliberately challenges Seguín's implicit demand that he derogate his culture and community.

Frank's critique of schooling approximates that of Tisa, another astute U.S.-born, female student whom I came across in the course of my group interviews. When I ask her whether she thinks a college education is necessary in order to have a nice house and a nice car and to live in a nice neighborhood, she provided the following response: "You can make good money dealing drugs, but all the dealers—even if they drive great cars—they still spend their lives in the 'hood. Not to knock the 'hood at all. . . . If only us *raza* (the Mexican American people) could find a way to have all three, money . . . *clean* money, education, and the 'hood."

In a very diplomatic way, Tisa took issue with the way I framed my question. Rather than setting up two mutually compatible options of being successful and remaining in one's home community, Tisa interpreted my question in *either/or terms*, which in her mind unfairly counterposed success to living in the 'hood. That I myself failed to anticipate its potentially subtractive logic caused me to reflect on the power of the dominant narrative of mobility in U.S. society—an "out-of-the-*barrio*" motif, as it were (Chavez, 1991).

Thus, for alienated youth such as Frank and Tisa to buy into "the program," success needs to be couched in additive, both/and terms that preserve their psychic and emotional desire to remain socially responsible members of their communities. These findings bring to mind the ethos that Ladson-Billings (1994) identifies as central to culturally relevant pedagogy for African American youth. Specifically, effective teachers of African American children see their role as one of "giving back to the community." For socially and culturally distant teachers, such discernment and apprehending of "the other" is especially challenging and can only emerge when the differential power held by teachers of culturally different students is taken fully into account (Noddings, 1984, 1992; Paley, 1995; Ladson-Billings, 1994).

Conclusion

Schools such as Seguín High School are faced with a special challenge. To significantly alter the stubborn pattern of underachievement, they need to become authentically caring institutions. To become authentically caring institutions, they need to at once stop subtracting resources from youth and deal with the effects of subtraction. Although it is up to each school to determine what a more additive perspective might entail, my study suggests that an important point of departure is a critical examination of the existing curriculum.

The operant model of schooling structurally deprives acculturated, U.S.-born youth of social capital that they would otherwise enjoy were the school not so aggressively (subtractively) assimilationist. Stated differently, rather than students failing schools, schools fail students with a pedagogical logic that not only assures the ascendancy of a few but also jeopardizes their access to those among them who are either academically strong or who belong to academically supportive networks.

Although the possession of academically productive social capital presents itself as a decided advantage for immigrant youth, analytical restraint is in order here as well. However "productive" it may be, social capital is still no match against an invisible system of tracking that excludes the vast majority of youth. Strategizing for the next assignment or exam does not guarantee that the exclusionary aspects of schooling will either cease or magically come to light. Even should it come to light, the power to circumvent regular-track placement remains an issue, especially for the more socially marginal. Most sobering is the thought that in some ultimate sense, schooling is subtractive for all.

Notes

This chapter is based on a talk that the author gave at the University of Texas at Austin on February 25, 1998. The presentation was sponsored by the Center for Mexican American Studies and the Department of Curriculum and Instruction. It originally appeared as Angela Valenzuela. "Subtractive Schooling: U.S.-Mexican Youth and the Politics of Caring." *Reflexiones 1998: New Directions in Mexican American Studies* (Austin: Center for Mexican American Studies, University of Texas).

1. All names used herein are pseudonyms.
2. I use the term *Mexican*, a common self-referent, to refer to all persons of Mexican heritage when no distinction based on nativity or heritage is necessary.
3. My extensive observations of Seguin's CTE program have led me to conclude that the acquisition of work skills is compatible with students' college-going aspirations because it reinforces the academic curriculum. The CTE program is effective because the teachers enjoy higher salaries, small class sizes, access to career counselors, and, in the higher level courses, the ability to select their students.
4. I administered a questionnaire to all 3,000 students in November 1992. It included questions about students' family background. English and Spanish language ability, generational status, school climate, teacher caring, and academic achievement. With a 75 percent response rate, a sample of 2,281 students for analysis resulted.
5. My study adopts a conventional generational schema. First-generation students were, along with their parents, born in Mexico. Second-generation students were born in the United States but had parents born in Mexico. Students were classified as third generation if they and their parents were born in the United States. I use the self-referent *Mexican American* and the term *U.S.-born* to refer to second- and third-generation persons. (Fourth-generation youth [i.e., those whose parents and grandparents were born in the United States] were combined with third-generation youth because of their resemblance in both the quantitative and qualitative analyses.)
6. The comparable figures for Mexicans in California and the nation are 11.1 and 10.4 years of schooling completed and dropout rates of 39 and 48 percent, respectively. Mexicans from Texas are thus faring even more poorly than their underachieving counterparts nationwide (Chapa 1988).

7. The Texas Bilingual Education Code (Sec. 29.051 State Policy) rejects bilingualism as a goal: "English is the basic language of this state. Public schools are responsible for providing a full opportunity for all students to become competent in speaking, reading, writing, and comprehending the English language."

References

Buriel, R. (1984). Integration with traditional Mexican-American culture and socio-cultural adjustment. In J. L. Martinez, Jr., & R. Mendoza (eds.), *Chicano Psychology* (2nd ed.). Orlando, FL: Academic.

Callahan, R. E. (1962). *Education and the cult of efficiency*. Chicago, IL: University of Chicago Press.

Chapa, J. (1988). The question of Mexican American assimilation: Socioeconomic parity or underclass formation? *Public Affairs Comment, 35*(1), 1–14.

Chavez, L. (1991). *Out of the barrio: Toward a new politics of Hispanic assimilation*. New York: Basic Books.

Coleman, J. S. (1988). Social capital in the creation of human capital. *American Journal of Sociology, 94*, 95–120.

Coleman, J. S. (1990). *Foundations of social theory*. Cambridge, MA: Harvard University Press.

Cummins, J. (1981). The role of primary language development in promoting educational success for language minority students. In California State Department of Education (ed.), *Schooling and language minority students: A theoretical framework*. Los Angeles, CA: Evaluation, Dissemination, and Assessment Center, California State University.

Cummins, J. (1986). Empowering minority students: A framework for intervention. *Harvard Educational Review, 56*, 18–36.

Fine, M. (1991). *Framing dropouts: Notes on the politics of an urban public high school*. Albany, NY: State University of New York Press.

Fordham, S., & Ogbu, J. U. (1986). Black students' school success: Coping with the burden of acting white. *Urban Review, 18*(3), 176–206.

Gibson, M. A. (1988). *Accommodation without assimilation: Sikh immigrants in an American high school*. Ithaca, NY: Cornell University Press.

Giroux, H. A. (1988). *Schooling and the struggle for public life: Critical pedagogy in the modern age*. Minneapolis, MN: University of Minnesota Press.

Goffman, E. (1977). *Asylums: Essays on the social situation of mental patients and other inmates*. Garden City, NY: Anchor.

Gordon, M. M. (1964). *Assimilation and American life: The role of race, religion and national origins*. New York: Oxford University Press.

Gutek, G. L. (1993). *American education in a global society: Internationalizing teacher education*. White Plains, NY: Longman.

Ladson-Billings, G. (1994). *Dreamkeepers: Successful teachers of African American children*. San Francisco, CA: Jossey-Bass.

Lareau, A. (1989). *Home advantage: Social class and parental intervention in elementary education*. London; New York: Falmer.

Matute-Bianchi, M. E. (1991). Situational ethnicity and patterns of school performance among immigrant and nonimmigrant Mexican-descent students. In M. A. Gibson & J. U. Ogbu (eds.), *Minority status and schooling: A comparative study of immigrant and involuntary minorities*. New York: Garland.

McCarthy, C. (1993a). Beyond the poverty of theory in race relations: Nonsynchrony and social difference in education. In L. Weis & M. Fine (eds.), *Beyond silenced voices: Class, race, and gender in United States schools*. New York: State University of New York Press.

McCarthy, C. (1993b). Multicultural approaches to racial inequality in the United States. In L. Castenell, Jr. & W. F. Pinar (eds.), *Understanding curriculum as racial text: Representations of identity and difference in education* (pp. 225–246). Albany, NY: State University of New York Press.

McQuillan, P.J. (1998). *Educational opportunity in an urban American high school: A cultural analysis*. Albany, NY: State University of New York Press.

Mejía, D. (1983). The development of Mexican American children. In G. J. Powell (ed.), *The psychosocial development of minority group children*. New York: Brunner/Mazel.

Noddings, N. (1984). *Caring: A feminine approach to ethics and moral education*. Berkeley, CA: University of California Press.

Noddings, N. (1992). *The challenge to care in schools: An alternative approach to education*. New York: Teachers College.

Oakes, J. (1985). *Keeping track: How schools structure inequality.* New Haven, CT: Yale University Press.
Ogbu, J. (1991). Immigrant and involuntary minorities in comparative perspective. In M. A. Gibson & J. U. Ogbu (eds.), *Minority status and schooling: A comparative study of immigrant and involuntary minorities.* New York: Garland.
Olsen, L. (1997). *Made in America: Immigrant students in our public schools.* New York: New Press.
Paley, V. G. (1995). *Kwanzaa and me: A teacher's story.* Cambridge, MA: Harvard University Press.
Peshkin, A. (1991). *The color of strangers the color of friends: The play of ethnicity in school and community.* Chicago, IL: University of Chicago Press.
Portes, A., & Zhou, M. (1993). The new second generation: Segmented assimilation and its variants. *Annals of the American Academy of Political and Social Sciences,* 530, 74–96.
Portes, A., & Zhou, M. (1994). Should immigrants assimilate? *Public Interest, 116,* 18–33.
Putnam, R. D. (1993). The prosperous community: Social capital and public life. *American Prospect, 13* (spring), 35–42.
Putnam, R. D. (1995). Bowling alone: America's declining social capital. *Journal of Democracy, 6*(1), 65–78.
Reese, L., Balzano, S., Gallimore, R., & Goldenberg, C. (1991, November). *The concept of* educación: *Latino family values and American schooling.* Paper presented at the Annual Meeting of the American Anthropological Association, Chicago, IL.
Rodriguez, N. P., & Nuñez, R. T. (1986). An exploration of factors that contribute to differentiation between Chicanos and indocumentados. In H. Browning & R. de la Garza (eds.), *Mexican immigrants and Mexican Americans: An evolving relation.* Austin, TX: CMAS Publications, Center for Mexican American Studies, University of Texas at Austin.
San Miguel, G. (1987). *"Let all of them take heed": Mexican Americans and the campaign for educational equality in Texas, 1910–1981.* Austin, TX: University of Texas Press.
Skutnabb-Kangas, T., & Cummins, J. (1988). *Minority education: From shame to struggle.* Clevedon, Canada: Multilingual Matters 40.
Stanton-Salazar, R. (1997). A social capital framework for understanding the socialization of ethnic minority children and youths. *Harvard Educational Review, 67,* 1–39.
Suárez-Orozco, M. M. (1991). Hispanic immigrant adaptation to schooling. In M. A. Gibson & J. U. Ogbu (eds.), *Minority status and schooling: A comparative study of immigrant and involuntary minorities.* New York: Garland.
Valenzuela, A. (1999). *Subtractive schooling: U.S.-Mexican youth and the politics of caring.* Albany, NY: State University of New York Press.
Vigil, J. D., & Long, J. M. (1981). Unidirectional or nativist acculturation: Chicano paths to school achievement. *Human Organization, 40,* 273–277.
Yeo, F. L. (1997). *Inner-city schools, multiculturalism, and teacher education: A professional journey.* New York: Garland.

26

Teacher Experiences of Culture in the Curriculum

Elaine Chan

Preamble

Cultural and linguistic diversity are among the characteristic features describing the Canadian landscape. Eighteen percent of the total population was born outside the country, and 11 percent of the population identify themselves as members of a visible minority group (Statistics Canada 1998, 2003). Not surprisingly, multi-culturalism has been seen as a key educational issue. Yet, despite the importance of multi-culturalism, there are all too few examinations of the interaction of culture and curriculum in school contexts.

There is a wealth of normative prescription about the acknowledgement of culture. Cummins (1996), Igoa (1995), and Wong-Fillmore (1991a, b) have highlighted the academic, emotional, and societal importance of acknowledging diversity by engaging students in learning about their home cultures and languages. Banks (1995) has highlighted the importance of the inclusion of culture in the curriculum as a means of developing positive attitudes among racial and/or ethnic minorities. Rodriguez (1982), Kouritzin (1999), and McCaleb (1994) have explored the dangers of the failure to acknowledge the cultural knowledge of students of ethnic minority backgrounds. Ada (1988) has discussed a project in which the families of students of minority background were engaged in bilingual literacy projects. Paley's (1995) "integrated" curriculum had parents and children discussing values, rituals, and cultural experiences through family stories in order to foster a sense of community within the classroom.

However, although there is much discussion outlining the importance of "information and awareness of the cultural backgrounds of pupils in order to better diagnose strengths, weaknesses, and differences in cognitive styles" (Moodley 1995: 817), there is a lack of consensus about how best to acknowledge this diversity in a school context. In this paper, I examine the challenges and complications that two middle-school-level teachers encountered as they attempted to implement a curriculum event.

Introduction

> The students came into Room 42 after lunch today with all kinds of questions about their upcoming field trip to Boyne River. They wanted to know when they would be leaving, when they would be returning, what they should bring, whether it would be cold at Boyne River, what they would eat, where they would sleep, and so on. They seemed very excited about the trip.

> William answered their questions . . . [but] when he asked for a show of hands of students from those who would be participating, I was surprised to see that many students did not put their hands up. Sahra, who was sitting directly in front of William, did not put her hand up.
>
> "My father won't let me go" Sahra said. She explained that she could not go on field trips where they would be spending the night. Sahra's family is South Asian and her parents, especially her father, are very strict about the kinds of school activities they allow her to take part in.
>
> "Do you want me to talk to him?" William asked her. "You should be able to go."
>
> I asked some of the students sitting near me whether they would be going on the field trip.
>
> "It's against my religion for girls to go out" Zeynab said.
>
> "I can't. I need to go with my father to the hospital, to help translate for him."
>
> "I need to pick my sister up from school and get my brother from daycare—my parents have to work."
>
> "I work at my family's tea store, and sometimes I need to help them [i.e. my parents] with the forms."
>
> (Field note: November 2000)

I present this field-note documenting student responses to a school field-trip in order to introduce the complexities that two middle-school teachers at Bay Street School, William and Dave, faced as they attempted to acknowledge their students' ethnic, linguistic, and religious diversity in their curriculum and their teaching practices. The field trip to Boyne River, an outdoor-adventure centre, provides a context for examining the intersection of diverse beliefs and values at Bay Street School.[1] This intersection is at the core of the work done by teachers in Canada, and in particular in Toronto, as representatives, and members, of a receiving culture that has a reputation for welcoming immigrants. However, they work with students and families whose values and beliefs about education, and ways of interacting with others, may differ significantly from their own.

In Fall 2000, William and his colleague Dave were preparing to take their combined classes of 71 grade-8 students on a 4-day field trip to Boyne River. I centre this discussion on the planning of this trip, one of many activities and events that occurred during the 3.5 years I spent as a participant observer at Bay Street School.[2]

Despite William's willingness to address issues of diversity in conversations with his colleagues and students, and to be culturally-sensitive in his practices and in his curriculum, there were differences in perspective around the Boyne River trip, and other school activities. Thus, William and Dave found that there were a few parents who did not seem to support activities they undertook; there were tensions between members of ethnic groups in some interactions; and students sometimes did not seem especially interested in sharing aspects of their own cultures, or learning about the cultures of their peers. Given that the teachers at Bay Street School seemed to recognize the value of acknowledging culture by accommodating for differences in the curriculum, these tensions were always surprising.

I use Schwab's (1973) commonplaces of teacher, learner, subject matter, and milieu to explore how differences in perspective around a single curriculum event—the subject matter—were shaped by experiences that teachers, learners, their families, and other members of the school community brought with them to the school milieu.

Research on teachers' professional knowledge landscapes (Clandinin and Connelly 1996, Connelly and Clandinin 1999), the role of schooling in shaping a sense of ethnic identity (Wong Fillmore 1991a, b, Cummins 1996, Kouritzin 1999), experience and education (Dewey 1938, Connolly and Clandinin 1988), and narrative inquiry (Clandinin and Connelly 1994, 2000, Phillion 2002) form the theoretical framework for this study. Given Dewey's (1938) philosophy of the inter-connectedness between education and experience, I see all that the students' encounter in their school context, as well as all that occurs in their school, home, and neighbourhood, as experience with the potential to contribute to their learning about what a sense of ethnic identity may mean to them. This broad base of potentially-influential interactions highlights the power of schooling experiences, and further reinforces the importance of recognizing and celebrating the diversity that students bring to a school context.

The Boyne River Field Trip

Bay Street School had been placed on a list at the outdoor-education centre to be contacted if another school cancelled their booking. When a call came from Boyne River, the staff at Bay Street School began work to make arrangements in order for their students to participate. They developed an information package complete with translations of notices and waiver forms in different languages, made bookings for buses and supply teachers, and arranged for the teachers remaining in the school to cover the classes of those who would be accompanying the students to Boyne River. These arrangements were made within 3 days of receiving the call; for the teachers at Bay Street School, the field trip was a valuable activity.

Other members of the school community also supported the Boyne River trip. The community-development worker viewed the field trip as an opportunity for students who might not otherwise be able to participate in this kind of outdoor education activity to do so. He spoke about the importance of equality of access for children whose families might not be able to support learning opportunities of this kind outside of a school context.

Dave was the only one of the three grade-8 teachers who was to accompany the students to Boyne River. He spoke of the field trip as an opportunity to interact with the students in a way different from their regular in-school and in-class interactions. His own experience as a camp counsellor and outdoor-education teacher reinforced his personal philosophy in the value of interaction with individual students while participating in outdoor activities.

Marla, the special education teacher who worked with William and Dave, viewed the field trip as an opportunity for the students to gain experiences that were outside of the academic curriculum. She did not understand the unwillingness of some of the parents to send their children: she thought that the field trip was an especially important way for students who were not academically-inclined to excel in a different area. She pointed to one student in particular who had difficulty sitting still, and who struggled academically, and stated that he would likely enjoy something like an outdoor-adventure trip.

Bay Street School Context

William responded to Sahra's statement that she would not be able to participate in a class field trip by offering to speak to her father—to convince him of the value of the field trip and to emphasize to him the importance of female students having educational opportunities equal to those available to male students.

Such criticism by teachers of the unwillingness of some of the parents to permit their children to participate in the Boyne River field trip may suggest a lack of sensitivity to the backgrounds that the students were bringing to the school context. However, throughout my years of work in Bay Street School I saw examples of the teachers' willingness to learn about the cultures of their students, and to accommodate for different practices. William included discussions on cultural diversity and racism in social studies classes, addressing the injustice and prejudice that Native Canadians suffered in New France as his students learned about settlement in Canada. He read passages featuring the experiences of members of the Black community in Canada during Black History Month, and continued to incorporate information about the Black community. He had his students interview their parents in order to write about their childhood in their home countries before immigrating to Canada; he gave his students a family-studies project that involved the preparation of recipes translated from their parents' home language into English. During his first year at Bay Street School, he fasted during Ramadan along with his South Asian students. He supported the integrated international languages classes that are a part of the curriculum at Bay Street School, and demonstrated his desire to learn about the cultures and languages of his students by asking them about specific practices or about vocabulary or expressions in Chinese, Vietnamese, and Spanish.

William and Dave's recognition of the backgrounds of their students was also set in the context of a school community with a history of diversity that began with its establishment over 125 years ago (Connelly *et al.* 2003); the present student population at Bay Street School is highly diverse (Chan and Ross 2002). The school is in a neighbourhood where immigrants settle[3]—in a city identified by the UN as the most culturally-diverse in the world.

In other words, the members of the school community at Bay Street School seemed to be doing what is seen as important in creating a culturally-sensitive curriculum and school context. Nonetheless, the implementation of curriculum events was met with resistance by some students and parents. The difficulties that the teachers encountered as they attempted to be sensitive to the needs of their diverse student population can be explored in terms of Clandinin and Connelly's (1996: 25) distinction between *cover stories, sacred stories,* and *secret stories* about multicultural education and a culturally-sensitive curriculum. Thus, the secret stories of what is actually lived on the school landscape and in classroom are often not presented or explored because they counter a public need to believe that schools are meeting the needs of a culturally-diverse student population. However, these secret stories recognize that the process of acknowledging culture in the curriculum is complicated: good intentions may be misconstrued, or individuals may bring to the school context experiences that shape their interpretations of school events in ways that differ significantly from what was intended.

Differing Student Perspectives

Although the teachers and administrators at Bay Street believed in the value of the field trip to Boyne River, problems around its perceived value became clear when many of the students' parents did not grant permission for their children to participate.

Twenty-six of the 71 students did not go on the trip. The reasons were varied. A Pakistani student told me that she needed to accompany her father to the hospital to act as an interpreter; an East Indian student, who had only recently joined the class, did not attend because her parents did not feel comfortable letting her go. Many of the Chinese students did not participate because they had family responsibilities. Kevin was not able to attend because he was responsible for picking up his younger brother from daycare and his sister from school while his parents worked. Bing could not participate because he worked in his family's tea store and was sometimes called upon to complete customs forms and other documents.

I had assumed that the students would want to participate in the field trip, and that those students left behind would feel resentful. The students with whom I spoke, however, did not seem especially resistant to their parents' refusal to allow them to participate. When I shared an earlier draft of this paper with her, a colleague commented that perhaps the sense of self-esteem gained from contributing in important ways to the well-being of the family contributed to their sense of identity in a more significant way than the freedom to take part in a school trip.

Of the Chinese students who participated, Mandy, Elsa, and Annie said that, although they were not usually permitted to attend sleep-overs at their friends' homes, they were permitted to go on school-sponsored field trips: "if it's for school, it's okay!" (Field note: November 2000). They spoke of how their parents had a high regard for school and for their teachers, and school-sponsored activities were viewed in a different light than those initiated outside of school. Nevertheless, although the activities were part of the curriculum and were supported by their teachers, their parents did not show the same commitment to the school's athletic, artistic, or outdoor-education activities as they showed for academic subjects such as science, mathematics, or English.

Teacher Perspectives Interacting with Parent Perspectives

> It's against my religion for girls to go out. (Field note: November 2000)

Sahra was resigned to the fact that she would not be permitted to take part in the field trip. In fact she did not feel that she could even raise the issue with her father since she felt quite certain that such a request would not only be likely to be refused, but would also anger her parents. William offered to speak with her father but, after some consideration, Sahra declined his offer. She explained that her parents had permitted her to participate in an outdoor-education overnight field trip 2 years earlier, but that it had been an exception. Her father had stated explicitly that her participation then had been a one-time exception and that she was not to ask again.

My discussion with William suggested that acknowledging the cultural diversity of his students around the trip by supporting the beliefs and values of their parents conflicted with his personal and professional knowledge. He felt strongly that his students should have the opportunity to take part in school-sponsored events, regardless of gender. It was difficult to support the wishes of some of his students' parents that girls not participate in some school activities and events. And, in the days prior to the departure for Boyne River, it became evident that many of the South Asian girls were not permitted to go. William pointed out that the younger brother of one of his students had been permitted to attend, but that because his student was female, she was not allowed to.

A colleague with whom I discussed this incident responded in a way that was similar to William's reaction. She did not know how a public school could accommodate such differences in perspective around the rights and privileges of the female South Asian students—she is the parent of two daughters. Her husband also felt very strongly that the girls were having their rights infringed upon: as citizens in a democratic society, it is among our responsibilities to protect the rights of the girls and ensure that children are not denied learning opportunities because of their gender.

Thus, the interaction between William and Sahra highlighted the potential for tensions to develop when differences in perspective about the value of specific curriculum events arise. When William offered to speak to Sahra's parents, he hoped he could convince them to permit her to participate in the field trip. He was not aware of the history of Sahra having negotiated permission from her parents to take part in an earlier school field trip, nor was he aware of her agreement not to ask for permission to participate in subsequent overnight field trips.

Nor did William[4] realize the extent to which the parents of some of the South Asian students at Bay Street School are relatively strict with respect to their children's participation in school-sponsored activities away from the school's premises. In the 3 years since this incident, both William and I have learned about some of the practices of the students' families. We are now not surprised when a South Asian student tells us that he or she is not permitted to take part in swimming in physical education classes or go on a field trip. We know how many of the South Asian students fast for a month during the fall, how some of the students and their families regard structured prayer times as a very important aspect of their daily lives, and how some students engage in elaborate washing rituals prior to the prayers held in the library at the school on Friday afternoons. We know—from what some of the female South Asian students in William's class have said—that, with respect to *some* of the South Asian parents, male children are more likely than female children to be permitted to participate in the full range of school activities.

The teachers at Bay Street School realize that their beliefs about curriculum sometimes differed from those of the parents of their students—to the point of conflicting—and that they were faced with the dilemma of how to "accommodate" for such vastly different views. Thus, William was aware that the cultural and social narratives guiding his practices might differ from those guiding the parents of his students, and he was committed to acknowledging the diversity of his students. However, he had not anticipated that his professional identity would come in conflict with values held by some of his students' parents. The Boyne River field trip highlighted the extent to which the implementation of curricular practices seemed to conflict, at times, with his, and his colleagues', beliefs about the "needs" of their students of ethnic minority background. However, it was not until he was faced with a situation where the differences hindered the implementation of an activity he supported that the differences became problematic. When differences in perspective did not have an effect on practice, supporting these differences did not challenge his beliefs, or involve high stakes.

Regardless of the reasons for the parents not wishing their children to participate, we must ask how appropriate it is for a teacher to attempt to influence these decisions. Thus, William had the best of intentions when he offered to speak to Sahra's parents about the Boyne River field trip; he recognized the value of the field trip and wanted to instill in Sahra and his other students an appreciation for the importance of equality of opportunity regardless of gender. He had not realized the potential that his intervention might have to create conflict between Sahra and her parents.

William's offer could also be viewed in terms of his rights and his role as Sahra's teacher in relation to the rights and roles of Sahra's parents as they worked to instill in Sahra the beliefs that they valued. In a situation where her parents and her teachers agreed about the values they would like to instill, Sahra would have had the support of both her parents and her teacher. However, William wanted Sahra to have the opportunity to experience an outdoor-education centre while her parents did not think such a field trip would be appropriate for a young woman. Sahra was caught in the middle: she was a child growing up in an immigrant family whose values differed significantly from those supported in her Canadian school context.

William did not approach Sahra's parents. However, what should teachers do in situations of this kind? What is the formal framework pertaining to student participation in school activities, in general and at Bay Street School in particular? What are the ethics of introducing beliefs and ideas, and engaging students to support these perspectives, when their parents would be opposed to them? Is suggesting to parents that they permit their children to participate in activities they do not value an instance of crossing ethical and professional boundaries? In attempting to convince parents to reconsider their decisions about school activities, are teachers conveying to students, and their parents, that they are more appropriate guides for the development of values and choice of practices than their parents? By stating, openly or tacitly, that they do not support the specific values guiding parents' decisions, are teachers putting students in the middle? A culturally-sensitive curriculum is sine qua non of contemporary schooling; the issues around the Boyne River field trip highlight the complexity of these issues.

Differences in opinion around the appropriate behaviour of and towards female students also surfaced on another occasion. After hearing from some of the female students in his class that a grade-7 boy from an adjourning classroom had been behaving inappropriately with them, William scolded them for not telling him about it sooner. He then emphasized to them that they had a right to expect to be treated with respect. As I watched the interaction, I was reminded that some of his students lived such different realities between home and school with respect to ideas about the role of women in society. The students were standing at the door of the classroom, wearing head coverings, preparing to return home to families where they lived with codes of behaviour that define the position of women in the home and society as very different than that of males. Their teacher was telling them that "no one has the right to make you feel less of a person!" (Field note: March 2002). I wondered whether their parents would have encouraged them to take such a stance, or to do so in the way William was suggesting.

The intersection of cultures also became apparent as students and their parents negotiated ways in which their home culture would be adhered to in their school context. As I have indicated, many of the female, South Asian students at Bay Street School wear a head covering, a hijab, when they are outside of the home. I found it interesting that many of the girls who usually wear hijab to school did not wear them for their graduation ceremony, photos, or the party afterwards.

I noticed one day that Miriam, who did not usually wear the hijab, had begun wearing one. She explained that her South Asian friends in her home-room class had pressured her into wearing it because it was Ramadan, the holy month during which many members of the South Asian community at Bay Street School fast during daylight hours. I looked around and indeed all of the South Asian girls in William's class that year were wearing hijab. Miriam said that her mother was not strict about her wearing the hijab and had left it to her to decide whether or not to wear it. She had decided against it; but when her friends started to pressure her, she wore it. She continued to wear the hijab to school, and from that day until one day towards the end of her grade-8 year, I did not see her hair again because it was always covered. She did not, however, wear the hijab for her graduation photos or for her class photos.

Sahra and Miriam told me that wearing the hijab is a serious responsibility. The girls and their families decide whether or not to wear the hijab when the girls are young; once they reach puberty, it is a responsibility that is expected of them. Moreover, once they begin to wear the hijab, they are not to stop. Mrs Mohamed, a teacher at Bay Street School, told me that her older daughter had chosen on her own to wear the hijab when she was very young. "I didn't want her to. I told her, 'Once you start wearing it, you cannot stop'. But she wanted to wear it, and since she was 8, she has always worn the hijab. She was the first of all her friends to wear it." I thought I detected a hint of pride in her voice, which I did not quite understand.

I have been told by members of the Bay Street School community (and read) that some South Asian women find wearing the hijab to be liberating: It provides protection from unwanted attention when out in the streets, and is worn with pride. I had not realized until I began writing about this incident that (I think) I had seen the hijab as a reminder that some opportunities were available to South Asian men but not to South Asian women. I had not understood how it could be liberating to be told to wear something because someone else deemed it appropriate. I might even have believed that those who were wearing the hijab would be more likely to adhere to traditional practices that define the role of women in more restrictive ways than that of men.

In my discussions with William, he also indicated that he sees wearing the hijab as a form of oppression of women. He reasoned that, since women are wearing them because they are being told, or required to, rather than out of freedom of choice, it cannot be a form of liberation. He further argued that if men are not required to wear hijab while women are, then it cannot be viewed as a form of liberation for women. William also indicated how he views South Asian women as having less freedom within their culture than do men: he does not see the need for a man to accompany his wife, or mother, or sister when they are doing errands outside the home, as he sees some of the South Asian men in the community do. As a response to these observations, William's teaching colleague, Lina, suggested that "Maybe it's for their protection"; to which William responded, "If it's the men that are harassing the women, then they are the problem, not the women. Don't you think that it would be a burden, to have someone accompanying you all the time?"

As with the Boyne River field-trip situation, the tensions with respect to the practice of wearing the hijab highlight dilemmas. Thus, William believed that individuals have the right to choose what they will wear, and that the practice of wearing the hijab discriminated against women. At the same time, he wanted to support the parents' attempts to instill their ethnic and religious values in their children. Here we have an interaction of beliefs and values within an individual teacher: He would like to instill in his students values he supports; he also realizes that he may not agree with some of the practices supported by the parents of his students. In a larger sense, there is a tension in that the rights of the individual conflict with the rights of a school to put in place practices and support behaviours that reflect the values respected in the school context but which may conflict with the right of parents to raise their children in ways they deem appropriate.

Confronting Personal Biases to Meet on Landscapes of Difference

The importance of teachers making curriculum decisions and interacting with students and their parents in ways free from bias is a quality that is appreciated in a culturally-diverse society. What is not often acknowledged, however, is that as humans whose beliefs and values have been shaped by prior experiences and interactions, teachers come to teaching with strong views about some aspects of teaching. These strong views may also be interpreted as "biases" in some situations.

For example, I had thought of myself as relatively accepting of difference and tolerant of cultural diversity. However, as I reflected upon how I had written about the role of women in the South Asian community at Bay Street School and about what William and I thought wearing the hijab meant, I realized—with a fair amount of discomfort—that I had judged these practices using my own perceptions of their meaning. I was presenting the practice of wearing a hijab and of "serving men" as examples of ways in which women are valued less than men in South Asian culture, and interpreting in a stereotypical way the role of women in the South Asian community as submissive to that of the men.

I also realized that I was making assumptions about practices without understanding the reasons individuals accepted them, and then judging them by my own beliefs. I overlooked things that I did know that suggested that I needed to reconsider my interpretations. An example: one South Asian woman who works at Bay Street School built a new life in Canada for her three school-aged children and herself after her husband died suddenly shortly after their arrival in Toronto. I also overlooked that Mrs Mohamed, whom I had been judging as very "traditional" in her attitudes—I had heard from William's teaching colleague that she had placed an ad in the local South Asian newspaper in search for an appropriate husband for her 19-year-old daughter—was an architect before immigrating to Canada, and that she supported her daughter's plans to study medicine. She had also raised four children on her own when she had arrived in Canada a few years before her husband was able to emigrate. Thinking about this reminded me that there is much that I do not know about South Asian communities, and that I need to be cautious about judging their practices.

Thus, as I have reflected on the interaction of personal and professional beliefs and values as teachers, students, and parents at Bay Street School live the curriculum, I have to realize the potential of these values and beliefs to shape the work of teachers—as well as their potential role in shaping the work of researchers who undertake research with teachers. I was making generalizations based on an assumption that the behaviours and practices of members of the South Asian community would be uniform. Thus, while I have been contending that Chinese culture cannot be defined by specific traits, characteristics, or practices, I was making assumptions about members of the South Asian community based on generalizations. I was also troubled that my perception of myself as accepting and tolerant was being challenged, and I wondered—and worried about—what this might mean for someone who works with diverse school communities.

Were my feelings similar to those experienced by Dave in the weeks that followed a disagreement during a School Council meeting?[5] Dave felt that he was being perceived as racist when he publicly disagreed with the views of a Black parent about how a Black child who had not complied with school regulations had been disciplined. From conversations with Dave, and from observations of him interacting with students and teaching lessons in which he demonstrated a willingness to address issues of diversity, racism, injustice, I perceived Dave to be supportive of the causes of members of ethnic minority groups. When he expressed an opinion different from that of a Black parent in the School Council meeting, however, he was perceived as racist. Dave expressed frustration at this label, and was indignant that he could not have views that differed from those of someone of an ethnic background different from his own without worrying about offending them. He worried that, as a male of European background, if he took a firm viewpoint, he would be perceived of as representing a privileged position. My reflection upon the incident, and my conversations with members of the school community, lead me to wonder whether his positive attitude towards diversity and willingness to learn about the languages and cultures of his students were sufficient. Sensitivity and tolerance for difference are admirable traits, but they need not be at the expense of the freedom to express differences in opinion without fear that these differences would be interpreted as racist or discriminatory.

This Council meeting led to months of discussion among some teachers at Bay Street School about diversity, racism, school policies pertaining to diversity, and their role as teachers in modelling appropriate behaviours and attitudes. These conversations in turn led me to reflect upon the tensions among the members of the School Council. I have heard individual members of the Council speak with conviction about their commitment to working together to create as positive a learning environment as possible for the sake of the children in the school. In my experience of interacting with members of the School Council, I have found them to be sensitive and supportive of the diversity in the Bay Street School community. However, I wondered what the disagreement meant to the individuals who had been directly involved.

Thus, the difficulties in accommodating for the diverse perspectives and beliefs of those involved in the lived experience of curriculum highlight the need to explore in greater detail what it means to develop, and implement, a "culturally-sensitive curriculum". With respect to the implementation of the Boyne River field trip, the teachers were demonstrating sensitivity to differences in values and beliefs as they sought to accommodate the parents who did not want their children to participate in the activity.[6] However, while it may be perceived as "culturally-sensitive" to accommodate for the parents' wishes, it may also be perceived as culturally-sensitive to raise the awareness of the students involved by highlighting and addressing the differences in perspective. This approach might be likened to Ali's (2004) argument for the importance of acknowledging potentially sensitive issues by raising them such that they may be explored and discussed.

In other words, reflection upon the responses of the teachers, including myself, highlights the complexity of the issues involved in sensitivity to ethnic, religious, and linguistic diversity in a school context, and reinforces the extent to which we are, as the receiving culture, unprepared to deal with some of the issues that arise.

Conclusion

Interaction among students of diverse ethnic backgrounds in a supportive school environment provides a context where positive attitudes towards race and ethnicity may develop (Banks 1995). This approach reinforces the importance of schools in creating opportunities for exposure to, and interaction with, individuals of diverse backgrounds. However William and Dave's experiences of working with their ethnically-, linguistically-, and religiously-diverse students reveals the extent to which mere exposure, and even good intentions and specific ideas about ways in which culture may be acknowledged through school practices, are insufficient and leave some important questions unresolved.

Thus, William's experience around the Boyne River field trip shows how acknowledging cultural diversity can be a challenge. What does it mean for a school community to be "accepting" of diversity? How does a knowledge and an acceptance of differences affect the teaching of values that are normative in the larger community while, at the same time, supporting practices that are important to parents, but may not accord with the larger community's values? While it may be possible to achieve tolerance, how do teachers acknowledge and incorporate conflicting values? Would William, in accommodating for the values of his South Asian students, be indirectly expressing a lack of support for a majority group whose values differ significantly from those of the minority? If he accommodated for a group whose values he does not support, is he nonetheless supporting those values by conceding?

Teachers bring to their teaching beliefs and values shaped by their own experiences of teaching, and being taught. Cohen (1989, see Ball 1990: 274) sees teaching practices and beliefs as "deep-seated dispositions, simmered over the years of a teacher's experience and seasoned by cultural assumptions about and images of teaching and learning". Given the role of experience in shaping perceptions of curriculum, we can expect that teachers' practices and beliefs about incorporating culture in the curriculum would be shaped by their own experiences of culture in their school curriculum. Difficulties arise, however, when we realize that many teachers do not have such curricular experiences to draw on.

Cohen and Ball (1990: 352) raise the question, "How can teachers teach a mathematics that they never learned, in ways that they never experienced?" in their examination of teachers' experiences of mathematics curriculum reform. A similar question emerges around the implementation of a culturally-sensitive curriculum. The changing demographic composition of communities in North America, Europe, and Australia implies that teaching is vastly different than it was 40, or even 20, years ago—when today's teachers experienced schools themselves as students. Teachers working in settings such as Bay Street School are faced with the challenges of acknowledging in a positive way diverse cultures, but many are doing so without a professional knowledge-base, or the personal experience of having themselves lived school contexts of this kind.

In addition, while teachers' beliefs and practices are "simmered over the years of a teacher's experience and seasoned by cultural assumptions about and images of teaching and learning" (Cohen 1989, see Ball 1990: 274), the parents of the students they teach also bring their own "deep-seated dispositions" to the curriculum landscape, simmered over years of schooling in their own cultures, shaped by the interaction of the cultural and social narratives unique to their own situations. These experiences in turn shape their values and beliefs about curricula they interpret as appropriate. In some instances, as with the Boyne River field trip, the beliefs that some families bring to the school context differ in significant ways from the values guiding the practices of others—to the extent that they are in conflict.

These are no easy answers to these questions. However, it is clear that even the teachers who work at Bay Street School—with its tradition of accepting diversity—and who demonstrate a willingness to learn about diverse cultures and languages, and believe in equality and equity for their students regardless of cultural backgrounds and gender need to address and discuss the events that may arise as diverse cultures intersect on their school landscapes, to identify issues of relevance to the particular ethnic communities involved.

The teacher, student, and parent responses to the Boyne River field trip highlight the extent to which the receiving cultures of immigrants need to explore ways of accommodating for this diversity in school contexts. We have the expectation that children of ethnic minority background need to "adapt" to "our" school communities, but we may overlook that, as a host country for immigrants, we also need to explore the extent to which this relationship may be reciprocal. We need to explore ways of accommodating for diverse cultures in ways that are respectful of the differences. At the same time, we need to provide as rich an experience of "our" schooling as possible for the children involved. By addressing potentially sensitive issues, we begin the process of uncovering the "secret stories" (Clandinin and Connelly 1996: 25) that may hinder our ability to meet the needs in our school communities. For example, is a belief in the rights of girls that may lead us to disrespect the views of conservative South Asian parents who are living in another world an example of a secret story that needs to be raised for discussion. Sensitivity to such stories also allows us to explore our role in facilitating the acculturation of individuals of ethnic-minority background through the curricula we implement.

Acknowledgements

I would like to express my heartfelt thanks to F. Michael Connelly of the Ontario Institute for Studies in Education, the University of Toronto and to D. Jean Clandinin of the University of Alberta for their contribution to my research and graduate student experience.

This study was generously supported by a Social Sciences and Humanities Research Council (SSHRC) of Canada Doctoral Fellowship.

Notes

1. This research was part of a larger study examining the ethnic identity of first generation Canadians in a multicultural school context (Social Sciences and Humanities Research Council (SSHRC) Doctoral Fellowship 752–2001–1769), which was in turn embedded in F. M. Connelly and D. J. Clandinin's long-term SSHRC- supported programme of research examining the diverse cultural landscapes of experience that students, parents, and educators bring to the professional knowledge landscape of an elementary school (Standard Research Grants—"Landscapes in Motion; Landscapes in Transition"; "Landscapes in Transition; Negotiating Diverse Narratives of Experience"; and "Intersecting Narratives: Cultural Harmonies and Tensions in Inner-City Canadian Schools"). As I worked at Bay Street School, my observations and interactions with the teachers were guided by the following kinds of questions: What kinds of curriculum events and activities did the teachers plan? How do the teachers understand the home cultures of the students? How do they accommodate for the diversity of their students in their everyday interactions?
2. To learn about William and Dave's experiences of culture in the curriculum on this multicultural school landscape, I interacted with them over the course of hundreds of hours of school visits. I began observations at the school during

the spring of 2000, and continued until the spring of 2003 for the larger project of which this study is part. Field notes for this study were written during the 2000–2001 school year I spent with William and his teaching colleague, Dave, and their combined classes of 71 grade-8 students at Bay Street School. I wrote field notes following school visits, staff meetings, field trips, classroom observations, school assemblies, and interaction with members of the school community at events such as Multicultural Night, Curriculum Night and School Council meetings. These field notes, along with interview transcripts, researcher journals, and theoretical memos, were filed in an existing project archival system. I also collected documents such as school notices, announcements of community and school events, notices posted on bulletin boards and classroom walls, agendas and minutes from School Council meetings, newspaper clippings of local media coverage, and samples of student work to learn about ways in which the interaction of diverse cultures played out in the school context.

3. The neighbourhood community from which the student population is drawn reflects immigration patterns of recent immigrants into Toronto. Families who have recently immigrated to Canada settle in the community (Makhoul 2000) before moving to suburban communities as they become more established.
4. He was just a few months into his first year of teaching at the time.
5. School Councils were established by the provincial ministry and local school boards, in part, to facilitate the process of parents and teachers working together (Ministry of Education and Training 2004a, b).
6. Although teachers may not have much choice in this matter, since teachers at Bay Street School seem to accept parental decisions about whether their children are permitted to participate in specific curriculum activities or not, the students whose parents did not grant them permission were deprived of the enjoyment and educational value of the activity.

References

Ada, A. F. (1988) The Pajaro Valley experience: working with Spanish-speaking parents to develop children's reading and writing skills through the use of children's literature. In T. Skutnabb-Kangas and J. Cummins (eds.), *Minority Education: From Shame to Struggle*, Clevedon, UK: Multilingual Matters, 223–238.

Ali, N. (2004) Meaning-making for South Asian immigrant women in Canada. Doctoral dissertation, University of Toronto.

Ball, D. (1990). Reflections and deflections of policy: the case of Carol Turner. *Educational Evaluation and Policy Analysis*, 12(3), 263–275.

Banks, J. A. (1995) Multicultural education: its effects on students' racial and gender role attitudes. In J. A. Banks and C. A. M. Banks (eds.), *Handbook of Research on Multicultural Education*, Toronto, ON: Prentice-Hall, 617–627.

Chan, E. and Ross, V. (2002) Report on the ESL survey: sponsored by the ESL Workgroup in collaboration with the OISE/UT Narrative and Diversity Research Team, Toronto: Centre for Teacher Development, Ontario Institute for Studies in Education of the University of Toronto.

Clandinin, D. J. and Connelly, F. M. (1994) Personal experience methods. In N. K. Denzin and Y. S. Lincoln (eds.), *Handbook of Qualitative Research in the Social Sciences*, Thousand Oaks, CA: Sage, 413–427.

Clandinin, D. J. and Connelly, F. M. (1996) Teachers' professional knowledge landscapes: teacher stories—stories of teachers—school stories—stories of schools. *Educational Researcher*, 25(3), 24–30.

Clandinin, D. J. and Connelly, F. M. (2000) *Narrative Inquiry: Experience and Story in Qualitative Research*, San Francisco, CA: Jossey-Bass.

Cohen, D. K. (1989) Teaching practice: plus ça change. In P. W. Jackson (ed.), *Contributing to Educational Change: Perspectives on Research and Practice*, Berkeley, CA: McCutchan, 27–84.

Cohen, D. K. and Ball, D. L. (1990) Policy and practice: an overview. *Educational Evaluation and Policy Analysis*, 12(3), 347–353.

Connelly, F. M., and Clandinin, D. J. (1988) *Teachers as Curriculum Planners: Narratives of Experience*, New York: Teachers College Press.

Connelly, F. M. and Clandinin, D. J. (1999) Stories to live by: teacher identities on a changing professional knowledge landscape. In F. M. Connelly and D. J. Clandinin (eds.), *Shaping a Professional Identity: Stories of Educational Practice*, London, ON: The Althouse Press, 114–132.

Connelly, F. M., Phillion, J. and He, M. F. (2003) An exploration of narrative inquiry into multiculturalism in education: reflecting on two decades of research in an inner-city Canadian community school. *Curriculum Inquiry*, 33(4), 363–384.

Cummins, J. (1996) *Negotiating Identities: Education for Empowerment in a Diverse Society*, Ontario, CA: California Association for Bilingual Education.

Dewey, J. (1938) *Experience and Education*, New York: Simon & Schuster.

Igoa, C. (1995) *The Inner World of the Immigrant Child*, New York: St. Martin's Press.

Kouritzin, S. G. (1999) *Face(t)s of First Language Loss*, Mahwah, NJ: Lawrence Erlbaum Associates.

Makhoul, A. (2000) *Ryerson Community School—Where You Belong*. Caledon Institute of Social Policy. Available online at: http:www.caledoninst.org, accessed 5 May 2005.

McCaleb, S. P. (1994) *Building Communities of Learners: A Collaboration among Teachers, Students, Families and Community*, New York: St. Martin's.

Ministry of Education and Training (2004a) *About the OPC: History and Role of the OPC*. Available online at: http://www.ontarioparentcouncil.org/about_the_opc/default.asp?load=contributions1, accessed 14 September 2004.

Ministry of Education and Training (2004b) *School Councils*. Available online at: http://www.ontarioparentcouncil.org/school_councils/Default.asp?language=English, accessed 14 September 2004.

Moodley, K. A. (1995) Multicultural education in Canada: historical development and current status. In J. A. Banks and C. A. M. Banks (eds.), *Handbook of Research on Multicultural Education*, Toronto, ON: Prentice-Hall, 801–820.

Paley, V. G. (1995) *Kwanzaa and Me: A Teacher's Story*, Cambridge, MA: Harvard University Press.

Phillion, J. (2002) Becoming a narrative inquirer in a multicultural landscape. *Journal of Curriculum Studies*, 34(5), 535–556.

Rodriguez, R. (1982) *Hunger of Memory: The Education of Richard Rodriguez*, Boston, MA: David R. Godine.

Schwab, J. J. (1973). The practical 3: translation into curriculum. *School Review*, 81(4), 501–522.

Statistics Canada (1998) 1996 Census: Ethnic origin, visible minorities. Available online at: http://www.statcan.ca/Daily/English/980217/d980217.htm, accessed 19 September 2005.

Statistics Canada (2003) *Census of Population: Immigration, birthplace and birthplace of parents, citizenship, ethnic origin, visible minorities and Aboriginal peoples*. Available online at: http://www.statcan.ca/Daily/English/030121/ d030121a.htm, accessed 19 September 2005.

Wong-Fillmore, L. (1991a) When learning a second language means losing the first. *Early Childhood Research Quarterly*, 6(3), 323–346.

Wong-Fillmore, L. (1991b) language and cultural issues in the early education of language minority children. In S. L. Kagan (ed.), *The Care and Education of America's Young Children: Obstacles and Opportunities*. 90th Yearbook, Part 1, of the National Society for the Study of Education, Chicago: University of Chicago Press, 30–50.

27

Interrupting Heteronormativity: Toward a Queer Curriculum Theory[1]

Dennis Sumara and Brent Davis

In the first volume of his *History of Sexuality*, Foucault[2] explains how Western culture has fashioned an entangled relationship between knowledge and sex. Following Foucault, Sedgwick[3] has further explained that because sexuality has been expressive of both identity *and* knowledge, it has become the centering force of the heterosexism and of the generalized and pervasive homophobia that continues to exist. This homophobia is difficult to unravel because, as Britzman explains, "every sexual identity is an unstable, shifting, and volatile construct, a contradictory and unfinalized *social relation*."[4]

Understanding sexuality as a relational construct underpins recent work in queer theory. As a form of cultural study, queer theory acknowledges the polyvalent ways in which desire is culturally produced, experienced, and expressed. As Morton suggests, "Queer theory is seen as making an advance by opening up a new space for the subject of desire, a space in which sexuality becomes primary."[5] Following Sedgwick, this means universalizing sexuality as an analytic category.[6] Elaborated by Britzman, this process begins by interrupting commonsense understandings of what constitutes sex, sexuality, pleasure, desire, and the relationships among these and the technologies for learning about and enacting their differences.[7]

Bridged to the work of curriculum theory, queer theory asks that the forms of curriculum and the relations of pedagogy by appropriated as sites to interpret the particularities of the perceived differences among persons, not merely among categories of persons. "Queer" is not meant as a signifier that represents gay, lesbian, bisexual, and transgendered identities. Rather, "queer" functions as a marker representing interpretive work that refuses what Halley has called "the heterosexual bribe"—that is, the cultural rewards afforded those whose public performances of self are contained within that narrow band of behaviors considered proper to a heterosexual identity. In so doing, the possibilities for what might count as knowledge are broadened—not just knowledge about sexuality, but knowledge about how forms of desire are inextricable from processes of perception, cognition, and interpretation. Queer theory does not ask that pedagogy *become* sexualized, but that it excavate and interpret the way it already *is* sexualized—and, furthermore, that it begin to interpret the way that it is explicitly heterosexualized. Moreover, rather than defining queer identities in strict reference to particular bodily acts and aberrant or quirky lifestyles, queer theory asks that the continued construction of narratives supporting that unruly category "heterosexual" be constantly interrupted and renarrated.

In this article, we refer to our involvement in two research projects to enter into a critical inquiry of what queer theory might offer curriculum theory. Both projects were developed around shared readings of literary texts. One project involved a group of gay, lesbian, and transgendered teachers; another project involved teachers and children in grades 5 and 6. Positioning ourselves in the wake of feminist theories that have identified gender as an analytic category in curriculum studies,[9] we follow the work of queer theorists whose explicit aim is to do the same with sexuality. Rather than understanding the study of sexuality as something that is parallel to studies of curriculum, we believe that studies of sexuality must become intertwined with all questions relating to the study of curricular relations.

Identifications

Elspeth Probyn argues that childhood must not be considered as a prototype of adulthood.[10] Our experience working in communities with those who identify as gay, lesbian, bisexual, and transgendered supports Probyn's contention, suggesting to us that there really is no more common ground among the experience of queer adults' childhoods than among any others. There are, as Sedgwick argues, queer kids who do not become queer adults and kids who were not queer that do.[11] This has led us to believe that autobiographical and biographical work that attempts to create interpreted bridges between currently lived identities and memories of experience may, paradoxically, support the belief that if one could control childhood experiences, one might be able to create more predictable and suitable identities.

Although we acknowledge the importance of the "coming out of the closet" literature and the work it accomplishes,[12] we worry that it continues to participate in the ongoing subjugation, through representation practices of differentiation, of those identities that do not identify as ones that are structured by opposite-sex desire. At the same time, we understand that these literatures function, in important ways, to unveil what Sedgwick has called the "open secret"—that is, to demonstrate there *are* identities other than those structured by opposite-sex desire that successfully exist, that contribute to the ongoing production of knowledge, and that do not depend upon particular bodily acts and particular forms of social organization for their existence.[13] We wonder, however, about the continued examination of queer identities in the absence of critical inquiries into heterosexual ones. Although it is becoming increasingly clear to us that what constitutes experiences of heterosexuality are incredibly varied, there remains a generalized set of cultural myths about what constitutes the quintessential heterosexualized identity. As Foucault[14] explains in his *History of Sexuality*, and as Barbara Gowdy brilliantly shows in her novel, *Mister Sandman*,[15] heterosexual identities continually experience dissonance between lived experiences of pleasure and desire and culturally sanctioned expressions of heterosexuality. This means that, like those who identify as queer, heterosexual identities must exist in a particular "closet"—a well-defined and restrictive *heterosexual closet*. In our recent work, we have become particularly interested in not only learning about queer closets but, as well, about heterosexual closets and the unruly lines that articulate what it means to identify as heterosexual and what it means to identify as queer. To do so, we have developed some research practices that, we believe, create opportunities to learn about these usually transparent experiences.

In our current research into the relationship between sex and pedagogy, we use shared readings of literary texts as sites for critical inquiry. These reading activities require that readers form literary identifications with characters and situations that challenge and expand remembered and currently lived experiences. By working with our fellow reading researchers to interpret these literary identifications, moments of insight occur that often interrupt the transparent structures of our perceptions and our thinking. For us, these shared responses to literary texts create possibilities for an interesting "literary anthropology"—an interpretive activity where the relationships among memory, history, and experiences of subjectivity are made available for analysis.[16]

In one research project, we invited eight gay, lesbian, and transgendered teachers to respond, during all-day meetings, to various works of literature. Although most of these literary texts were written by authors who identify as queer, and featured a number of characters who identify as such, our purpose in reading them was not to consolidate or affirm our experiences as queer teachers but, rather, to wonder what we might learn by critically examining our experienced identifications to and interpretations of these texts. Because we all read the same texts, we predicted that our responses would be similar. Of course, this proved not to be the case.

In reading and responding to Audre Lorde's *Zami: A New Spelling of My Name*,[17] for example, we discovered that no two members of our group identified similarly. Not only were the responses noticeably structured by learned gender differences, they were also clearly influenced by the members' racial and ethnic backgrounds (all members were Caucasian, whereas the characters depicted in this book are, for the most part, Caribbean American). As well, because none of us had had histories of "coming out" as queer in the fifties and sixties in urban America, there was tremendous dissonance between group members' remembered and reported lived experiences and those of the characters described in the book.

Some of the responses, particularly among several male members of the group, were puzzling, in that they seemed unable to acknowledge that anger and frustration was very much part of the experience of women depicted in the book. As Jim explained:

> I just don't understand why the main character is always so angry. Surely, things were not as bad for women as is suggested. Even if they were, I think that maybe some of what she is experiencing she is bringing on herself.

Here it became clear that, although some male members of the group expressed the need for "queers to unite" under the banner of same-sex identification, many of their responses were structured by a profound and largely unnoticed (by them) misogyny. The women in the group, however, did notice, and, for them, these responses confirmed past experiences with gay men. As Jan explained:

> I guess I shouldn't be surprised by some of the things I hear from the men in the group. I mean, that's one of the reasons that lesbians must have their own communities. Gay men can be just as sexist as straight men.

While one might think, based on these sexist interpretations, that male members of our group might rally round a reading of a novel that depicts gay male experience, this did not prove to be so. In reading Edmund White's *A Boy's Own Story*,[18] for example, there was less literary identification among the men in our group with the main character than we expected. For some members, the book interrupted certainties about what constituted the experience of gay children. Confirming Probyn's theorizing, our discussion of the book made it clear that the trajectory of sexual identification in adulthood could not be predicted by one's childhood experiences. As John explained:

> I grew up in a small, farming community. Not only can I not identify with what the character in this novel has experienced, I can't remember thinking about sex in the ways he did. It's not just because things are different in Canada and the United States, or that things are different in rural and urban locations. It has more to do with a different understanding of what was and is sexually interesting and pleasurable to me. I can't identify with what this character finds sexually arousing, even though we both call ourselves gay.

This curious blend of identifying/not identifying continued in our reading and discussion of Pat Califia's story, "The Surprise Party,"[19] where we learned that personally familiar erotic identifications can become surprised by literary identifications. This story, which depicts group sex among a lesbian and several gay men, prompted strong erotic identifications among most group members. As Karla explained:

> After reading this story, I had some vivid dreams that included sex of the kind the characters had. I find that I'm both drawn to these new fantasies and I'm repulsed by them. Mostly, I'm curious about how unexpected my responses were to the story. I didn't think that I could become interested in that kind of sex.

What do these responses to literary fictions suggest about the relationships between expressed and experienced identities, forms of sociality, and experiences of pleasure and desire? Although it is obvious that humans experience events of identification and of pleasure that are not necessarily understood as proper heterosexual conduct, the various technologies of regulation around gender and sexuality force open secrets about what constitutes both identification and pleasure. And, although "the closet" is usually understood as the place where queer identities simultaneously hide and make themselves comprehensible to themselves, following Sedgwick and Britzman,[20] we suggest that the closet's boundaries must be understood to include the polymorphous ways in which identification and pleasure are produced. If sexuality is understood as a category of experience that emerges from various and overlapping technologies of self-formation and reformation, then the cultural mythologies around what constitutes the category of "heterosexual" must be called into question.

This idea is elaborated by Fuss[21] who argues that sexuality should be understood as one of the intertwining valences of what constitutes the experience of identity and the activity of identification. Subjectivity is not so much a matter of how one acts if one is *this* or *that* identity but, rather, how one becomes (and comes to be known as) *this* or *that* identity. Eschewing causal relationships between identities and identifications, Fuss points to the need to come to more complex understandings about, for the human species at least, what it might mean to be male or female, queer or straight.

It must be remembered that, as Foucault[22] has shown, it is only recently that sexuality has been primarily associated with a particular kind of identification called "sexual orientation"—which, in turn, is complexly linked with attraction to same or opposite sex. Sex, in this usage, is synonymous with the distinction made between male and female and, hence, has become understood as gender. But, of course, sex is also understood as that which is chromosomally determined. And so, sex announces both acts and bodies that act. Sexuality is generally used to signify the larger experience of the way in which sex *and* one's identified sex collapse to form a particular way of expressing physical pleasure or, we might say, participation in an agreed-upon set of sexualized event structures.

What would happen if sex and sexuality were not understood as discrete actions of particular male and/or female identities but, rather, as sets of social relations that produce physical, emotional, and psychic pleasures? And what if one's identification with one form of attraction/desire over another were understood to coevolve with the constantly shifting relations that comprise all aspects of human subjectivity, including those experiences we have come to call sex?

The responses of members of our reading group to works of literary fiction point to the complex ways in which gendered identities and sexualities are complexly formed and reformed through ongoing acts of remembered and fantasized acts of relationality. Not only does this suggest the inextricability of knowledge about oneself and knowledge about one's sexuality (and their polymorphous possibilities), it further suggests what Foucault and Sedgwick have insisted about the perceived and interpreted identities of human subjects: They shift along with the specific topography of experience. This does *not* mean to suggest that sexuality is *chosen* or that it may be *altered* by changing one's circumstances or one's mind about things. Rather, it suggests that there is a complex and ever-evolving relationship between the biological and the phenomenological, a relationship that always shifts with context over the course of one's lifetime. One's sexuality, from this perspective, is always structured by the various narratives and experiences of gender, race, ethnicity, access to resources, physical capacities, and so on. At the same time, one's experienced sexuality, in part, functions to restructure those things that participate in its own creation. Experiencing same-sex attraction or opposite-sex attraction—or both—or neither—is both informed by and informs one's perceptions, identification and representation practices, and interpretations.

Our work in the Queer Teachers Study Group continually challenged us to revise and reinterpret our understandings of the complex ways in which sexuality was structured and experienced. Although we continued to believe that these collaborative experiences would both affirm and help us to better understand our common experience of identifying as queer, we found ourselves continually surprised at the very different ways in which we became positioned by our literary identifications. Most important, these surprising responses interrupted, for us, certainties about what might constitute a queer identity. As Sedgwick suggests, "People are different from one another."[23] Lives are not lived as stereotypes or as categories. As became evident over the two years of our shared work, the particular identifications each of us made could not be confined to what might constitute the quintessential queer identity. In fact, it seemed that, rather than finding convergence on the basis of our explicit queerness, we continued to locate points of radical difference among ourselves. Lived and experienced identities, as reported in the group—particularly as these were disclosed in response to involvement with works of literature—suggested to us that Sedgwick is correct in her contention:

> [T]he sister or brother, the best friend, the classmate, the parent, the child, the lover, the ex-: our families, loves and enmities alike, not to mention the strange relations of our work, play, and activism, prove that even people who share all or most of our own positionings along these crude axes may still be different enough from us, and from each other, to seem like all but different species.[24]

Most surprising to us, then, was not so much that our literary identifications revealed identities that interrupted our understanding of who we imagined ourselves to be, but that these identifications suggested that we needed to refuse to believe that we could use identifying signifiers such as "gay," "lesbian," or "transgendered" as if we knew precisely what they meant. Further, we needed to understand the complex ways in which cultural mythologies about sexuality/identity collected within these categorical signifiers and, most importantly, of the experiences that we had that existed, rather untidily, outside these signifiers. Acknowledging the ways in which identities and sexualities were complexly situated within remembered, lived, and fantasized experiences and expressions meant rejecting the minoritizing view that "queer" could become a signifier that captures the various identities of those who do not identify as heterosexual. Instead, it helped us to understand "queer" as a collecting signifier for the notion that, just as knowledge cannot be in control of itself, experiences of sex and expressions of sexuality cannot be in control of themselves. They are always more than can be captured by the language used to describe them.

What might these interpretations contribute to an understanding of schooled readings and the identities that participate in them?

Stirrings

As part of a larger research project with a group of teachers from a small urban inner-city school, we took part in a two-month teaching project with one teacher and her grade 5/6 class. This teaching unit was developed around readings and responses to Lois Lowry's book, *The Giver.*[25] Decidedly Orwellian, this novel presents the reader with a futuristic society where all historical memory is lost to the general population and is retained by one person, designated the "receiver of memories," whose task it is to use this knowledge, when necessary, to advise political leaders. The general population exists in state-controlled and regulated family units comprised of two adults, one male and one female, and one or two adopted children. Reproduction is accomplished by "birth mothers," and the biological origin of the children is not known by the parents. Sexual feelings, or "stirrings," are forbidden—and, when they arise in adolescent children, they are quickly extinguished with daily doses of medication. The onset of stirrings is detected by parents through the daily practice of "dream telling," which is a required activity for all members of each family unit. The principal character in the novel is Jonah, who, like all twelve-year-olds in the community, has been assigned his life's work—in his case, the very honorable position as the new "receiver of memories." In preparation for his new role, Jonah must meet with the current "receiver"—newly renamed the "giver"—who, by laying his hands on Jonah's bare back transmits, in installments, all historical cultural memories, including memories of color, pain, and pleasures to which no other citizens have access.

In interesting ways this literary fiction demonstrates how knowledge about "things" cannot be dissociated from knowledge about historical forms and knowledge about oneself. As Jonah learns about the pain of war and the pleasures of seeing a color and riding a sleigh, for example, he becomes aware that his identity is changing. As well, new knowledge about how "unacceptable" babies are euthanized casts the identity of his father—"nurturer of babies"—in a new light. Although access to knowledge is exciting for Jonah, it is also exceedingly painful, as he is not only forced to reconsider what he knows, he is compelled to reinterpret past relations with his parents and other community members and to make new decisions about who he thinks he is. Additionally, because he has been directed to refuse the medication that controls his sexual feelings (his stirrings), he must now learn to understand the complex way in which desire and knowledge intertwine with experiences of identity.

Prior to reading the novel with the children, we participated in two reading group discussions: one with teachers from the school, and one with teachers from the school and a number of parents who also had read the book. The first discussion occurred as part of a planned research strategy to inquire into teachers' understandings of the function of the literary imagination in school settings; the second discussion emerged from the teachers' fears, voiced in the first discussion, that parents in this community would be offended if this particular novel were used as part of the elementary school curriculum.

The shared reading of this novel with teachers and parents of school-aged children created an opportunity for us to consider, with them, important issues related to the surveillance and regulation of knowledge and sexuality. Curiously, it was these discussions—ones that asked adults to interrupt the transparency of their current lived experiences—that prompted their strong desire for their children to become involved. Because the plot made explicit the relationship between identity and sexuality, it was generally believed that reading it with schoolaged children would create situations such as those their parents and teachers had recently experienced in our discussion groups. This, of course, was quite surprising to us, as we were convinced, along with the teachers in this school, that parents would be reluctant to invite their children into reading experiences that might challenge common beliefs about the relationship between knowledge about sex and knowledge about other matters. When later questioned about this, the parents suggested that, although they were uncomfortable with the prospect of their children becoming involved in the thinking sponsored by this novel, they felt that it was likely an important experience for them to have. Because they were not prepared to offer their children this experience at home, however, it was believed that it ought to be presented, within the context of literary study, at school.[26]

Although all of the two months of this teaching event was interesting, most fascinating to us were the focus group discussions involving several groups of the children, their teacher, and one of us (Sumara) that were conducted at the end of the project. Organized to create another critical space for continued inquiry into the ongoing interpretations that we and the children were making to our readings of *The Giver*, these discussions focused on the way in which particular knowledge generated complex changes in one's experienced and expressed identity—and, further, in one's perceptions and interpretations of others' identities.

A key topic in our discussions was the suppression of "the stirrings." Referring to her own experience of learning about sexuality, Gina suggested that information had not come directly from her parents, but through such media as books and videos that they provided for her. For Gina, discussion of the stirrings was uncomfortable because, as she explained, "My family's really weird around that subject and now I think that I'm weird around it too." Although it was clear to Gina that knowledge about sexuality was, in some way, part of the expressed identities of her parents and of herself, this knowledge always was mediated by the artifacts given to her by her parents in the absence of any discussion. And, although one might imagine that this pedagogical shortcoming might be overcome in school, it was clear during our discussion that, like at home, knowledge about sexual feelings was also mediated by forms—in this case, curriculum artifacts such as the "you're growing up" films shown in health class. Because these curriculum artifacts were (as is typical of these forms) presented as information rather than as beginning places for critical inquiry into what might constitute experiences of sexuality and sex, Gina (and a number of her classmates) seemed unable to represent anything other than the usual cultural myths about sex and sexuality—particularly myths about what counts as sex (only intercourse, it seems) and as sexual partners (opposite sex only).

Margaret, on the other hand, although generally quiet and withdrawn in class during our work with *The Giver*, discussed sexuality at length in our focus group interview. Her knowledge seemed, in part, to have emerged from her family's habit of "building up conversations around books":

> My mum, my brother, and I like to build up conversations around books. One of the things from this book we talked about was stirrings. We even told some of our own stirrings. Talking about them helps us to learn more about each other.

Margaret continued to reveal the complex way in which her knowing about her own and her parents' sexualities was related to her knowing about other matters—most specifically, matters about relations among her peers at school. When Trent, during the same interview, indicated that he did not understand the significance of stirrings with the confession, "I don't have stirrings," Margaret responded by explaining:

> Don't worry, you'll have them soon. Girls usually get them before boys. Most of the girls in our class have stirrings, but hardly any of the boys do. I'm just starting to have stirrings.

The most interesting question emerging from this frank disclosure of "just starting to have stirrings" is not so much the disclosure but, rather, what we imagined was being disclosed. What, for Margaret, constitutes a sexual stirring? What, for that matter, constitutes a sexual stirring for anyone? Although it is clear that Margaret's comment emerges, in part, from cultural myths about the advent of adolescence and the awakening of sexual desire, the question of what might constitute preadolescent stirrings is obscured. Trent's comment, "I don't have stirrings," is perhaps the most helpful here, for it exposes a general ignorance that, as Sedgwick suggests, necessarily exists alongside any expression of knowledge:

> Insofar as ignorance is ignorance *of* a knowledge—a knowledge that may itself, it goes without saying, be seen as either true or false under some other regime of truth—these ignorances, far from being pieces of the originary dark, are produced by and correspond to particular knowledges and circulate as part of particular regimes of truth.[27]

What ignorance is presented when Margaret suggests that she has stirrings and Trent suggests that he doesn't have them? Following Britzman's argument that sexuality education must become more interested in what structures the production of knowledge about sexuality (not just in providing information about sex),[28] we must wonder how curriculum might begin to insert itself into the tangled web of ignorance that currently exists in and around discourses about sexuality.

What was most fascinating to us about this matter-of-fact exchange of information about sexual feelings among these children was not so much that they were having it, but, rather, the cultural mythologies around what constituted a sexual feeling that were being reproduced in their narratives. Although there was considerable evidence to suggest that their sexuality education had been, at best, sporadic and flimsy, it was clear that they had formed very definite opinions about what constituted a sexual feeling, about when this feeling might occur, about which sex achieved these feelings first, and about how these feelings were to manifest themselves. And, although it may seem that it was the discussion in and around the stirrings that created the most interest for these readers, it became clear that this was, for them, rather mundane when read alongside various other specific events associated with the deliberate suppression of historical and cultural memory.

When adults (that is, parents and teachers) and young readers were pressed to describe what they imagined a stirring to be, or what kind of situation might create the experience of a stirring, predictable responses were given. Stirrings, it seemed, were always associated with feelings one imagines one might have when in the presence of a certain someone of the opposite sex, particularly if there were some promise of a specific sort of sexual activity—namely, intercourse. When asked whether stirrings could be, say, the pleasure of chocolate, a good book, or a roller coaster ride, both children and adults, although considering the possibilities, insisted on demarcating stirrings as something that was contained within a specific narrative of heterosexuality. Although passing mention was made by one of the parents that, of course, "there are those who *do* have sexual feelings for the same sex," this was contextualized as an aberrant possibility.

Because neither the "giver of memories" nor Jonah (the new "receiver of memories") was permitted to take the medication that suppressed sexual desire, the question of what they *do* with this desire emerged. Since biological reproduction occurred outside human acts of copulation, rendering it unnecessary for survival of the species, we wondered, with the children and the adults, how stirrings might weave their way through each of the character's lived experiences. Most of the conversation around this topic was rather mundane, emphasizing discourses of suppression and redirection. Eleven-year-old Gina's response, however, was most interesting:

> I think that stirrings means something different for Jonah and the Giver because they have memories of other things. They can see other things—like color. And they know things that other people don't know—like the stuff about the killing of old people and babies. So, I think that—I'm not sure why—that stirrings are different for them.

If, following Foucault, we believe that knowledge about sexuality becomes the primary link to all other knowledges, all other forms of knowing,[29] then it seems that Gina's intuition about different experiences of stirrings is profoundly correct. Learning to see differently, learning to see what not previously noticed, does not merely add a layer of information to what is already known. Rather, as an act of (re) cognition, the self that knows freshly understands itself differently and, as a consequence, understands the world differently. What might constitute a stirring for one who can see the color red might not for one who cannot.[30] And, of course, as Sedgwick and Britzman have suggested, people are different and experience sex differently.

Stirrings, then, as Gina brilliantly interpreted, are not *objects*, but *relations* that depend upon particular forms of knowledge and interpretation. Given this understanding, we may question one of the most fundamental aspects of the plot of *The Giver*—the very possibility for sexual stirrings to even occur when historical and cultural memory is non-existent. If sexual stirrings emerges from the complex relations of memory, of presently lived experience, and of fantasy, could stirrings even occur without memory? If so, what then does memory do to attraction and how is memory changed by continued experience?

These were some of the questions announced by the curriculum forms created by our shared readings of literary fiction with our Queer Teachers Study Group and of *The Giver* with adults and with schoolaged children. While the specifics, of course, differed in our conversations with our Queer Teachers Study Group and with the ten- and eleven-year-old children, these interpretive sites became, for us, a curriculum that was noticeably altered. Our continued participation in and interpretation of these shared reading and interpretation activities events has helped us better understand how heteronormativity in educational settings might be interrupted.

Interruptions

Michael Warner uses the term "heteronormativity" to refer to the complex ways in which "Het[erosexual] culture thinks of itself as the elemental form of human association, as the very model of intergender relations, as the indivisible basis of all community, and as the means of reproduction without which society wouldn't exist."[31] "Normal" and "heterosexual" are understood as synonymous. This means that all social relations and all forms of thinking that exist with these relations are heteronormative. To put it crudely, heteronormativity creates a language that is "straight." Living within heteronormative culture means learning to "see" straight, to "read" straight, to "think" straight.

These normalized forms, we have suggested, can be interrupted. As educators, it *is* possible to attend to Britzman's interdiction to "stop reading straight."[32] Similar to Toni Morrison's challenge to interrupt the Whiteness of the literary imagination,[33] queer curriculum theorists and practitioners are interested in interrupting heteronormative thinking. Whereas this desire is, in part, impelled by the desire to eliminate the destructive homophobia and heterosexism that pervades all social forms, it is also spurred by the desire to create more interesting forms for thinking. If we believe that all forms of expression are intimately connected, then we must come to agree that heteronormative structures are limiting. Interrupting heteronormativity, then, becomes an important way to broaden perception, to complexify cognition, and to amplify the imagination of learners.

Whereas this article has been developed around a general interest in issues of culture and curriculum, it has been focused specifically on trying to understand the developing relationship between queer and curriculum theories. Not surprisingly, queer theorists have suggested that, as a necessary participant in cultural studies, queer theory has some work to do. This is aptly put by Warner who insists:

> For academics, being interested in queer theory is a way to mess up the desexualized spaces of the academy, exude some rut, reimagine the public from and for which intellectuals write, dress, and perform. Nervous over the prospect of a well-sanctioned and compartmentalized academic version of "lesbian and gay studies," people want to make theory queer, not just to have a theory about queers.[34]

Although, as Warner suggests, the word "queer" has recently been used to collect studies of the relations among sexuality, perception, cognition, interpretation, and their attendant identities and practices, it is important to remember that there have been, for many years, curriculum theorists who have attended to these complex relations. Whereas these writers have not necessarily identified themselves as queer theorists or as interested in queer theory, they most certainly have attempted to "make theory queer" and to "mess up the desexualized spaces of the academy."[35] Following this important curriculum scholarship, we have attempted—in our research, our teaching, and our writing—to begin to understand what might constitute a queer curriculum theory. And, following Warner, we are *not* interested in promoting queer curriculum theory as a theory about queers but, rather, are interested in showing how *all* educators ought to become interested in the complex relationships among the various ways in which sexualities are organized and identified and in the many ways in which knowledge is produced and represented. The interpretations we have included in this article represent the ways in which some of our emergent theoretical understanding of what might characterize queer curriculum theory has informed our research, teaching, and thinking practices.

But, of course, this is not sufficient. Following Said,[36] it is our conviction that the products of scholarly activity and thinking must, in some way, become represented in ways that are interesting and useful to others. This is always risky, for it means locating words that must, however imperfectly, begin to account for thinking that is, of course, never fully known or representable. Despite this, we conclude by offering our preliminary understandings of what, for us, constitutes queer curriculum theory. It is important to state that we do *not* list these as principles or characteristics or requisites but, instead, as placeholders that, we hope, will help to collect a deeper understanding of what it might mean to interrupt the heteronormative relations of curriculum. As we readily admit that these conceptual placeholders are, for us, tentative, we imagine that they might become useful *beginning* places for continued exploration of how the spaces of pedagogy can become more attentive to the complex relations of sex and knowledge.

First, we suggest that curriculum theory might continue to work toward a deeper understanding of the forms that curriculum can take so that sexuality is understood as a necessary companion to all knowing. The character of this sort of curriculum was announced by Britzman when she asked the provocative question, "What might it mean for educators to explore the dynamics of sexual subordination and sexual pleasure in ways that require the involvement of everyone?"[37] We believe that the interpretive work accomplished by our Queer Teachers Study Group and the work done by teachers, parents, and elementary age children around shared readings of *The Giver* accomplished some of this work. By attempting to interpret the complex relations among knowledge, desire, and identities (and not just queer identities), these interpretive sites yielded complex understandings of the ways in which knowledge/ignorance, queer/straight, and male/female always are articulated in and through one another. Further, as we hope that some of our interpretations have shown, the continued wondering about how ignorance is always already a part of knowledge created situations where as researchers and teachers we were able to generate locations for the rearticulation of the lines of knowing and identity.

Second, we believe that rather than focusing on the elaboration and interpretation of queer identities, curriculum theory might begin to wonder about the unruly heterosexual closet and seek to render problematic the always known but usually invisible desires and pleasures that circulate throughout it. Curriculum forms that do this work are *not* those that ask persons to identify identifications that are aberrant to what is understood to be "proper" heterosexual conduct. Rather, they are forms that invite persons to participate in structures that create surprising (and often troubling) moments of contact and revelation.[38] Particularly, they are curriculum forms that function to call into question the very existence of heterosexuality as a *stable* category.

Third, we suggest that curriculum theory ought to be more interested in understanding and interpreting differences among persons rather than noting differences among categories of persons. Whereas curriculum theory must continue to attend to queer identities, it must continue to wonder what circumstances lead to different identification experiences. And, although curriculum theory should continue to be concerned with the complex relations among past, present, and imagined experiences, it ought to reject the still-pervasive belief that events during childhood are prototypical for events in adulthood. Instead, curriculum theory might become more intrigued by the ways in which identities are topographically arranged and by the remarkable ways they continually shift.

Fourth, we believe that curriculum theory should continue to be curious about experiences of desire, of pleasure, and of sexuality. Most important, curriculum theory ought to wonder how human subjects might continue to interrupt common beliefs of what constitutes each of these experiences so that the necessary relationships among them might become better understood. When identity-and-identification is conceptualized as a complex relation, it becomes less surprising, for example, that one would experience an unexpected erotic pleasure, for in this formulation pleasure has less to do with the object of identification than with the way in which the identifications and identities are intertwined. This suggests that the forms known as curriculum might become less interested in reporting on existing knowledge and more interested in inquiring into the ways knowledge becomes available, the ways knowledge is structured, and the ways identities are continually formed through curriculum identifications.

Of course, these theoretical ruminations necessarily lead to the question of application: How might educators think about structuring curriculum that accomplishes some of this needed work?

We believe educators might begin by creating curriculum events that are "heterotopic." As explained by Foucault,[39] a heterotopia is an event structure in which things not usually associated with one another are juxtaposed, allowing language to become more elastic, more able to collect new interpretations and announce new possibilities. In our Queer Teachers Study Group, for example, heterotopic events occurred when readers' remembered experiences were juxtaposed with their literary identifications. During readings of *The Giver* with elementary school children and adults, heterotopic event structures were created when science fiction illuminated the usually transparent structure of contemporary Western culture.

Although the creation of heterotopic forms does not depend upon the inclusion of engagements with literary texts, because these texts require that the reader become complicit in generating the literary experience, they often create possibilities where familiar structures that limit perception become available for interpretation.[40] We are *not* suggesting that heteronormative thinking can become erased through literary engagement. Our experience in these research projects, however, suggests that it can become interrupted. Not only do these interruptions to heteronormative thinking assist in the important work of eliminating homophobia and heterosexism in society, but they also create some conditions for the human capacity for knowing and learning to become expanded.

Acknowledgment

The research that supported the writing of this article was funded by The Social Sciences and Humanities Research Council of Canada (Grant #410-96-0686).

Notes

1. The first part of the title ("Interrupting Heteronormativity") deliberately parallels the title of Magda Lewis's groundbreaking essay "Interrupting patriarchy: Politics, resistance, and transformation in the feminist classroom," *Harvard Educational Review* 60 (Winter 1990), 259–268. We borrow her construction to make explicit the necessary relation between critical feminist work and queer theory. Most particularly, with this copied syntax, we acknowledge the complex and important ways in which our theorizing about pedagogy and our pedagogical practices have been influenced by this work.
2. Michel Foucault, *The history of sexuality: An introduction* (New York: Vintage, 1990).
3. Eve Sedgwick, *Epistemology of the closet* (Berkeley, CA: University of California Press, 1990).
4. Deborah Britzman, "What is this thing called love?" *Taboo: The Journal of Cultural Studies and Education* 1 (Spring 1995): 65–93, p. 68, original emphasis.
5. Donald Morton, editor of *The material queer: A LesBiGay cultural studies reader* (Boulder, CO: Westview Press, 1996), p. 11.
6. Sedgwick, *Epistemology of the closet.*
7. Britzman, "What is this thing called love?"
8. Janet Halley, in her essay "The Construction of Heterosexuality" (in *Fear of a queer planet: Queer politics and social theory*, edited by Michael Warner, 82–102. Minneapolis: University of Minnesota Press, 1993), explains the "heterosexual bribe" as the situation that occurs when the class "homosexual" becomes deviant by constructing it with reference to particular bodily acts—acts in which, presumably, not-homosexuals do not participate. Whereas homosexuals can be clearly defined by these bodily acts, the unruly class of "not-homosexuals," because they are only defined as those who exist outside this regulated category, cannot. This has particularly privileging consequences, for as Halley argues, "Both their epistemological privilege and their exemptions are contingent, however, on their continued silence about the heterogeneity and fabricatedness of their class—on their acceptance of what I have called the 'bribe' " (p. 97).
9. See, for example, Lewis, "Interrupting patriarchy"; Leslie Roman and Linda Christian-Smith, editors of *Feminism and the politics of popular culture* (London: Falmer, 1988).
10. Elspeth Probyn, *Outside belongings* (New York: Routledge, 1996).
11. Sedgwick, *Epistemology of the closet.*
12. Here we are specifically referring to those works that present autobiographical and biographical representations of the lived experiences of gay, lesbian, bisexual, and transgendered persons.
13. Sedgwick, *Epistemology of the closet.*
14. Foucault, *The history of sexuality.*
15. Barbara Gowdy, *Mister Sandman* (Toronto, ON: Somerville House, 1995).
16. Wolfgang Iser first announces this idea in *Prospecting: From reader response to literary anthropology* (Baltimore: The Johns Hopkins University Press, 1989) and elaborates this thinking in *The fictive and the imaginary: Charting literary anthropology* (Baltimore: The Johns Hopkins University Press, 1993). Dennis Sumara has applied some of these ideas to research in curriculum in *Private readings in public: Schooling the literary imagination* (New York: Peter Lang, 1996).
17. Audre Lorde, *Zami: A new spelling of my name* (Freedom, CA: The Crossing Press, 1982).
18. Edmund White, *A boy's own story* (New York: Dutton, 1982).
19. Pat Califia, "The surprise party" (in *Forbidden passages: Writings banned in Canada*, edited by Pat Califia and Janine Fuller, 110–124, San Francisco, CA: Cleis Press, 1995).
20. Sedgwick, *Epistemology of the closet*; Deborah Britzman, "On becoming a 'little sex researcher': Some comments on a polymorphously perverse curriculum." *Journal of Curriculum Theorizing* 12 (Summer 1996): 4–11.
21. Diana Fuss, *Identification papers* (New York: Routledge, 1995).
22. Foucault, *The history of sexuality.*
23. Sedgwick, *Epistemology of the closet*, p. 22.
24. Ibid.
25. Lois Lowry, *The giver* (New York: Bantam Doubleday, 1993).
26. It is worth noting that, in our view, this agreement for children to participate in such thinking had much to do with the fact that this pedagogy was to be structured around a literary text. Although most literary theorizing now accepts that literary experience can be as influential as any experiences (see Iser's *The fictive and the imaginary* and Sumara's *Private readings in public*), this belief has not yet become commonplace among those experienced readers who continue to believe that knowledge produced through literary experience is not as influential as knowledge produced in other ways.

27. Sedgwick, *Epistemology of the closet*, p. 8 (original emphasis).
28. Britzman, "On becoming a 'little sex researcher.'"
29. Foucault, *The history of sexuality*.
30. See Oliver Sacks's essay "The Colorblind Painter," in his *An anthropologist on Mars* (Toronto: Alfred A. Knopf, 1995), for an interesting discussion of the effects of altered sensorial abilities and its relation to "knowing" "identity" and "sexuality."
31. Michael Warner, *Fear of a queer planet*, p. xxi.
32. Deborah Britzman, "Is there a queer pedagogy? Or stop reading straight." In *Educational Theory* 45 (Spring 1995): 151–165.
33. Toni Morrison, *Playing in the dark: Whiteness and the literary imagination*. (Cambridge, MA: Harvard University Press, 1992).
34. Warner, *Fear of a queer planet*, p. xxvi.
35. See, for example, Mary Aswell Doll, *To the lighthouse and back: Writings on teaching and living* (New York: Peter Lang, 1995); Deborah Britzman, *Lost subjects, contested objects: Toward a psychoanalytic inquiry of learning* (Albany, NY: State University of New York Press, 1998); Madeleine Grumet, *Bitter milk: Women and teaching* (Amherst, MA: University of Massachusetts Press, 1988); Pinar, *Autobiography, politics and sexuality* (New York: Peter Lang, 1994); and James Sears, *Sexuality and the curriculum* (New York: Teachers College Press, 1992). Suzanne de Castell and Mary Bryson, "Don't ask; don't tell: 'Sniffing out queers' in education" (in *Curriculum: Toward new identities*, edited by William F. Pinar, 233–252, New York: Garland, 1998).
36. Edward Said, *Representations of the intellectual* (New York: Vintage Books, 1994).
37. Britzman, "What is this thing called love?", p. 68.
38. See Mary Bryson and Suzanne de Castell, "Queer pedagogy: Praxis makes im/perfect." *Canadian Journal of Education* 18 (3), 285–305, for critical analysis of resistance to queer pedagogy in university contexts.
39. Michel Foucault, *The order of things* (New York: Vintage, 1973), p. xviii.
40. We understand that not all literary forms have the potential to interrupt the familiarity of the reader's experience. We do suggest, however, that because fiction requires that readers simultaneously identify with characters represented in the text and with memories of other lived experiences they have had, the experience of literary engagement has the potential to complicate, in productive ways, the reader's world.

References

Aswell Doll, Mary. *To the lighthouse and back: Writings on teaching and living*. New York: Peter Lang, 1995.

Britzman, Deborah. 1995. "Is there a queer pedagogy? Or stop reading straight." In *Educational Theory* 45 (Spring): 151–165.

Britzman, Deborah. 1995. "What is this thing called love?" *Taboo: The Journal of Cultural Studies and Education* 1 (Spring): 65–93.

Britzman, Deborah. 1996. "On becoming a 'little sex researcher': Some comments on a polymorphously perverse curriculum." *Journal of Curriculum Theorizing* 12 (Summer): 4–11.

Britzman, Deborah. 1998. *Lost subjects, contested objects: Toward a psychoanalytic inquiry of learning*. Albany, NY: State University of New York Press.

Bryson, Mary and Suzanne de Castell. 1993. "Queer pedagogy: Praxis makes im/perfect." *Canadian Journal of Education* 18 (3), 285–305.

Califia, Pat. 1995. "The surprise party." In *Forbidden passages: Writings banned in Canada*, edited by Pat Califia and Janine Fuller, 110–124. San Francisco, CA: Cleis Press.

de Castell, Suzanne and Mary Bryson. 1997. "Don't ask; don't tell: 'Sniffing out queers' in education." In *Curriculum: Toward new identities*, edited by William F. Pinar, 233–252, New York: Garland.

Foucault, Michel. 1973. *The order of things*. New York: Vintage.

Foucault, Michel. 1990. *The history of sexuality: An introduction*. New York: Vintage.

Fuss, Diana. 1995. *Identification papers*. New York: Routledge.

Gowdy, Barbara. 1995. *Mister sandman*. Toronto, ON: Somerville House.

Grumet, Madeleine. 1988. *Bitter milk: Women and teaching*. Amherst, MA: University of Massachusetts Press.

Halley, Janet. 1993. "The construction of heterosexuality." In *Fear of a queer planet: Queer politics and social theory*, edited by Michael Warner, 82–102. Minneapolis: University of Minnesota Press.

Iser, Wolfgang. 1989. *Prospecting: From reader response to literary anthropology*. Baltimore: The Johns Hopkins University Press.

Iser, Wolfgang. 1993. *The fictive and the imaginary: Charting literary anthropology.* Baltimore: The Johns Hopkins University Press.

Lewis, Magda. 1990. "Interrupting patriarchy: Politics, resistance, and transformation in the feminist classroom." *Harvard Educational Review* 60 (Winter): 259–268.

Lorde, Audre. 1982. *Zami: A new spelling of my name.* Freedom, CA: The Crossing Press.

Lowry, Lois. 1993. *The giver.* New York: Bantam Doubleday.

Morrison, Toni. 1992. *Playing in the dark: Whiteness and the literary imagination.* Cambridge, MA: Harvard University Press.

Morton, Donald (Ed.). 1996. *The material queer: A LesBiGay cultural studies reader.* Boulder, CO: Westview Press.

Pinar, William F. 1994. *Autobiography, politics, and sexuality: Essays in curriculum theory,* 1972–1992. New York: Peter Lang.

Probyn, Elspeth. 1996. *Outside belongings.* New York: Routledge.

Roman, Leslie and Linda Christian-Smith (Eds.). 1998. *Feminism and the politics of popular culture.* London: Falmer.

Sacks, Oliver. 1995. *An anthropologist on Mars.* Toronto: Alfred A. Knopf.

Said, Edward. 1994. *Representations of the intellectual.* New York: Vintage Books.

Sears, James. 1992. *Sexuality and the curriculum.* New York: Teachers College Press.

Sedgwick, Eve. 1990. *Epistemology of the closet.* Berkeley, CA: University of California Press.

Sumara, Dennis J. 1996. *Private readings in public: Schooling the literary imagination.* New York: Peter Lang.

Warner, Michael (Ed.). 1993. *Fear of a queer planet: Queer politics and social theory.* Minneapolis: University of Minnesota Press.

White, Edmund. 1982. *A boy's own story.* New York: Dutton.

28

Silence on Gays and Lesbians in Social Studies Curriculum

Stephen J. Thornton

Imagine, as was once the case, that today's social studies curriculum measured all else against a standard of being male, Protestant, and Anglo-Saxon.[1] Women, African Americans, Catholic and Eastern Orthodox Christians, Jews, and Muslims, not to mention other religious, ethnic, and racial groups, would react with righteous outrage. With justification, we can claim that today's social studies curriculum has become more inclusive of a range of groups and perspectives within and beyond the United States.

Although still imperfect, the contemporary K-12 social studies curriculum has moved away from the tacit equating of "American" with, for example, Protestant, or Christian for that matter. At least one major exception to this legitimation of diversity persists: it is still tacitly assumed that everyone is heterosexual until proven otherwise. Despite striking growth in social, political, legal, and media presence of gays in American life, especially in the past decade,[2] few social studies materials appear to have substantive treatment of gay history and issues. Indeed, many of these materials fail to even mention such words as homosexual, straight, or gay. It is as if the millions of gay inhabitants of the United States, past and present, did not exist. Although scholarship studied in colleges is now sometimes rich with gay material, Americans who do not attend college—and the least educated are precisely those who are most inclined to be prejudiced against gay people[3]—are unlikely to hear of such scholarship.

The belief that the archetypal human is straight is called *heteronormativity*. It belies an inclusive curriculum. Moreover, it encourages stereotypes. As James Banks has warned, using a "mainstream" benchmark against which group differences are measured promotes "a kind of 'we-they' attitude among mainstream students and teachers."[4] Banks's observation about multiethnic education seems equally applicable to the study of homosexuals: "Ethnic content should be used to help students learn that all human beings have common needs and characteristics, although the ways in which these traits are manifested frequently differ cross-culturally."[5]

Heteronormativity goes basically unchallenged in teaching materials for K-12 social studies. Unless children are raised in a limited number of locales or have teachers who go beyond what the textbook provides, they may graduate from high school being none the wiser that heteronormativity paints an inaccurate picture of social life and perpetuates intolerance, sometimes with tangibly destructive consequences such as harassment and physical violence.[6]

Curricular Limitations of Current Inclusion

The social studies curriculum, because it must make some attempt at describing the world as it is, has always dealt with "difference." The debate, as Margaret Smith Crocco shows, has centered on what the differences are and how they have been dealt with.[7] The common failure even to mention the existence of lesbians and gay men (let alone bisexual and transgender persons) clearly clashes with gay matters today being a visible part of the public landscape in most of America. Thus, a first step that social studies educators need to take is frank acknowledgment that differences in sexual orientation (and other taboo subjects such as religion) exist in America.[8] To put it another way, educators must answer the question, Does everybody count as human?[9]

One current and widely used U.S. history high school textbook is illustrative of the current failures. In its treatment of postwar African American novelists, James Baldwin is described as writing about "patterns of discrimination" directed toward blacks. This point is placed as a precursor to the struggle against racial injustice in the civil rights era.

The text is silent, however, about Baldwin's being both African American and homosexual. He wrote eloquently of "patterns of discrimination" directed toward gay men. For example, in *Giovanni's Room* and in *Another Country*, which were written in the same postwar and civil rights period of American history, Baldwin explores how young gay men fled prejudice in family and community in the United States for the relative anonymity of Paris.[10]

This silence on homosexual expatriate writers stands in stark contrast to the treatment of heterosexual expatriate writers. U.S. history textbooks routinely discuss the "lost gener- ation" of the 1920s, the group of literary artists such as Hemingway and Scott Fitzgerald who, disillusioned with American materialism, traveled to Paris searching for meaning. Their fictional characters and the motives of these characters are frequently canonized in high school history textbooks, while Baldwin's fictional gay characters and the motives of his characters go unmentioned.

The same silences that characterize the American history curriculum appear in global history and geography. Take the subject of human rights. There has been a great deal of attention, especially since September 11, 2001, to the oppression of Afghan women by the harsh, extremist brand of Islam embraced by the Taliban. Properly, this denial of basic human rights to women has widely stood condemned both in the West and in the Islamic world. But no such condemnation of systematic persecution of gay men (or allegedly gay men) in parts of the Islamic world, such as recently in Egypt, appears in the curriculum although, as with Afghan women, the persecution rests on these men simply for being who they are.

Social studies courses most directly devoted to citizenship, such as government and civics, routinely extol the freedoms Americans enjoy because they are Americans. That such freedoms still extend only to some people and not to others, however, is likely to go unmentioned in textbooks. For example unlike important allies such as the United Kingdom, of whose armed forces in Afghanistan and the Persian Gulf we have heard so much recently, U.S. armed forces legally discriminate against lesbians and gay men. Although American youngsters will certainly study American freedoms in social studies courses, they may never be told or question that other closely associated nations also extend freedoms to gays that are denied them in the United States. American history and government texts justifiably vaunt our belief in self-evident rights dating back to at least 1776; they omit that some of these rights are selectively available depending on a person's sexual orientation.

The limitations of the current curriculum, however, run deeper than exclusion from history and other courses. Although acknowledgment of the humanity of gay people and democratic tolerance for them should be fundamental, these aims fail to strike at the heart of heteronormativity. While it is generally acknowledged that the social studies should prepare young people for citizenship, gay people are vulnerable to the way freedom to participate fully in the affairs of the state is defined. At present, as Nel Noddings writes, it seems that "to improve their status, the vulnerable must either become more like the privileged or accept some charitable form of the respect taken for granted by those acknowledged as full citizens."[11] In other words, even if gay people were identified as gay people in the curriculum, this begs the question of what should be said about them and from what perspectives.

The Hidden Curriculum Everybody Sees

The hidden curriculum of schools rigidly patrols the boundaries of sex role behavior. Homophobia is common in American schools.[12] Although unmentioned in the publicly announced curriculum, all young people learn that sex role deviance, actual or perceived, exacts a heavy price. It is surely one of the most successful exercises in social training that schools perform. Moreover, this unannounced curriculum functions in practically all schools regardless of racial and ethnic composition, social class, and so forth. Indeed, young people who are themselves oppressed by poverty, crime, or racial mistreatment frequently become oppressors of peers perceived to be gay.[13]

Whether by choice or neglect, school professionals are implicated in patrolling sex role boundaries.[14] In corridors and classrooms, for example, few if any taunts are more com- mon than "fag," and embedded in history textbooks are messages about what it means to behave in a "masculine" fashion.[15] In other parts of school grounds such as parking lots, bathrooms, and locker rooms, where youngsters are frequently unsupervised by adults who know them, sex role deviations sometimes meet with physical violence.

There seems to be a variety of motives for how teachers respond to all of this. Some teachers may be afraid of being labeled "gay" if they correct students for bigoted behavior. Disturbingly, some teachers appear to agree with condemnations of perceived departures from "normal" sex roles; girls must be "feminine" and boys must not be "effeminate." They may ignore, and sometimes even encourage, harassment of students perceived to be gay. Administrators and teachers may counsel harassed students to avoid "flaunting" their allegedly deviant behavior, in effect, blaming the victim.[16]

What is clear is that administrators and teachers are not being neutral or impartial when they ignore this hidden curriculum. Silence, far from neutral, implicitly condones continuation of the persecution. Studies have long shown that depression and suicide are far more common among youngsters who are gay than among their straight peers.[17] School professionals—classroom teachers, administrators, counselors, and librarians—are frequently the only responsible adults to whom these at-risk children can turn for both needed support and equal educational opportunities.

Toward More Inclusive Curriculum

It is too easy for educators to feel absolved of responsibility because authorities have frequently omitted gay people and gay issues from curriculum documents and materials. Moreover, censorship of gay material is commonplace. Ominously, these forms of neglect exist alongside a persistent countermovement. Every step forward for the well-being of gay students and a curriculum more inclusive of lesbian and gay experience has been doggedly challenged by anti-gay groups.[18]

Teachers have choices. All teachers are curricular-instructional gatekeepers—they largely decide the day-to-day curriculum and activities students experience.[19] How teachers enact curriculum, even with today's constraints such as standards and high-stakes tests, still matters both practically and ethically. Opportunities to incorporate at least some gay material into the standard curriculum exist; in many instances, all that is required is the will to call attention to aspects of standard subject matter that heretofore went unmentioned.

Quite a few inclusion opportunities in mainstay secondary school courses such as U.S. history, world history, and geography present themselves. No U.S. history survey textbook that I have seen, for instance, omits Jane Addams. She is rightly portrayed as one of the nation's greatest social and educational thinkers and activists, not to mention her formidable work for world peace. Addams never married. She chose to spend her adult life among a community of women and had a long-time special relationship with one woman.[20] This may raise ample opportunities for properly directed class discussion: What did it mean that a considerable number of educated women of Addams's means and generation chose to forsake marriage and pursue careers beyond domesticity? Were they models for gender equity for later generations of women's rights and equity advocates?

Note, we have not directly addressed Addams's sexual orientation. (The evidence, in any case, seems inconclusive.) Perhaps more important than a rush or need to judge, however, is to ask if this woman's accomplishments would be diminished or enhanced by such knowledge. Or a primary educational objective could be to understand how Addams, who rejected some gender conventions for her day, helped shape her times and her legacy for today. Her significance, in this scheme, incorporates the complexities and controversial aspects of her life as well as speaking to different but nonetheless related questions today.

Other topics such as the ancient world in global history courses provide different path-ways to incorporate the gay experience. Again, let me underscore that we are still working with standard material in the curriculum. No new instructional materials are required. Specialist knowledge, while as desirable as ever, is unessential.

Take the topic of Alexander the Great. One high school world history textbook I exam- ined, for example, shows how, through his military genius and statesmanship, Alexander built a "multicultural" empire. Although adjectives such as "multicultural" (and "gay" for that matter) are anachronistic here, the point for today's readers seems plain enough: Alexander was a leader, probably before his time, in building what we might call today an inclusive society.

Here we might pause to challenge how inclusive (or "multicultural") this textbook treatment is. No mention is made of Alexander's homosexuality. Teachers, however, could readily place Alexander's homosexuality in its cultural and temporal context. In those terms, his sexual orientation was relatively unremarkable. Sensitively approached, such a perspective may lead students to rethink stereotypes of both warriors and homosexuals.

Classical Greece provides numerous opportunities to explore beyond the information given. Textbooks routinely feature photographs of idealized male images such as Greek athletes and actors. Why did the Greeks so prize the male form? What does it reveal about their culture? How does it relate to today's notions of athleticism and the arts? How is the ideal of male community perpetuated by today's college campus fraternities?

Of course, gay materials may also be an instructional focus rather than ancillary to the main part of a lesson or unit. In U.S. history courses, a unit on the civil rights struggle of the 1950s and 1960s is standard. These days a wide range of groups in addition to African Americans are often featured in this unit, such as Latinos, women, Native Americans, and so forth. But seldom does this extend to gay people. Such a unit could be made more genuinely inclusive if it also included a lesson devoted to a turning point in civil rights for gay people, such as the 1969 Stonewall riots in Greenwich Village, New York City.

Although much more the exception than the rule, teachers in some parts of the country have designed instructional sequences on gay topics longer than a lesson or two. One civics teacher, for example, as part of a nine-week unit on "Tolerance and Diversity," included a two-week mini-unit on "Homophobia Prevention." He has written of the experience and materials he used.[21]

Current events instruction is also a ready site for dealing with gay material. By way of illustration, recently published secondary school American history textbooks are silent on the "history" of former U.S. President Bill Clinton's "don't ask, don't tell" policy for gays in the military. Teachers, however, could still treat this rights topic in the classroom because the media report on it with some regularity. A good issue for critical thinking might be why the number of persons discharged from the armed forces for their homosexuality has continued to rise in the decade since the supposed implementation of the policy.[22]

Conclusion

Even concerned and willing educators face some significant obstacles to incorporating gay material in the curriculum. Many veteran teachers may never have studied gay material during their preservice teacher education programs, either in academic or professional courses. As noted, this situation has changed somewhat in the academy today in courses in history, the social sciences, and literature. In teacher education, too, the situation has altered. "Student sexual diversity guidelines for teachers" now appear in some teacher education textbooks, for instance.[23] Furthermore, explicit training for and sensitivity to inclusion is now common in teacher education programs in diverse regions of the nation. We probably shouldn't expect, however, in-service workshops devoted to gay subject matter to arise everywhere in the nation any time soon. But nearly everywhere the legal realities of protecting the rights of gay students, if nothing else, may compel some staff development.[24]

Heteronormativity is also a concern because many students in our schools now have parents who are gay or lesbian. These children have the same rights to an equal education as do their peers whose parents are heterosexual. About ten years ago, however, a storm of controversy erupted in New York City when it was suggested that the children's book *Heather Has Two Mommies* even be allowed as an option to be included on a several- hundred-page list of curriculum ideas on diversity from which teachers might choose.[25]

Although it is now most noticeable in large cities, many schoolchildren across the nation have lesbian or gay parents. Yet only "traditional" families tend to be included in the curriculum. Despite *Heather's* apparent sensitivity to appropriate treatment for the intended age group, this failed to prevent its being removed from the list of suggested (not mandated) books. However, at least some more encouraging reports of teachers addressing the issue of nontraditional families have appeared more recently. For example, one New York City teacher reported on positive outcomes from teaching a novel to middle school students that concerned a boy coming to terms with his father's being gay.[26]

If we are to be inclusive in the social studies curriculum, then the kinds of changes I have sketched here are vital first steps. The alternative, if many educators perpetuate heteronormativity, is that most young people will continue to learn about homosexuality through a popular prejudiced lens.

Notes

1. Frances FitzGerald, *America Revised: History Schoolbooks in the Twentieth Century* (New York: Vintage, 1980).
2. Suzanna Danuta Walters, *All the Rage: The Story of Gay Visibility in America* (Chicago: University of Chicago Press, 2001).
3. Patricia G. Avery, "Teaching Tolerance: What Research Tells Us," *Social Education* 66, no. 5 (2002): 270–275.
4. James A. Banks, *Multiethnic Education* (Boston: Allyn and Bacon, 1988), 177.
5. Ibid., 175.
6. Human Rights Watch, *Hatred in the Hallways: Violence and Discrimination against Lesbian, Gay, Bisexual, and Transgender Students in U.S. Schools* (New York: Human Rights Watch, 2001).
7. Margaret Smith Crocco, "Dealing with Difference in the Social Studies: A Historical Perspective" *International Journal of Social Education* (in press).
8. Rahima Wade, "Diversity Taboos: Religion and Sexual Orientation in the Social Studies," *Social Studies and the Young Learner* 7, no. 4 (1995): 19–22.
9. Stephen J. Thornton, "Does Everybody Count as Human?" *Theory and Research in Social Education* 30, no. 2 (2002): 178–189.
10. See James Baldwin, Giovanni's Room (New York: Modern Library, 2001) and Another Country (New York: Dial Press, 1962).
11. Nel Noddings, "Caring, Social Policy, and Homelessness," *Theoretical Medicine* 23 (2002): 441.
12. For an analysis of this state of affairs, see Margaret Smith Crocco, "The Missing Discourse about Gender and Sexuality in the Social Studies," *Theory into Practice* 40, no. 1 (2001): 65–71 and "Homophobic Hallways: Is Anyone Listening?" *Theory and Research in Social Education* 30, no. 2 (2002): 217–232.
13. Kevin C. Franck, "Rethinking Homophobia: Interrogating Heteronormativity in an Urban School," *Theory and Research in Social Education* 30, no. 2 (2002): 274–286.
14. Human Rights Watch, op. cit.
15. Jeffrey J. Kuzmic, "Textbooks, Knowledge, and Masculinity: Examining Patriarchy from Within," in *Masculinities at School*, ed. Nancy Lesko (Thousand Oaks, CA: Sage, 2000).
16. Perry A. Zirkel, "Courtside: Gay Days," *Phi Delta Kappan* 84, no. 5 (2003): 412–413.
17. Human Rights Watch, op. cit., 75.
18. See, for example, People for the American Way, "Right Wing Watch: Back to School with the Religious Right," www.pfaw.org/pfaw/general/default.aspx?oid=3652, accessed February 4, 2003.
19. For elaboration of this point, see Stephen J. Thornton, "From Content to Subject Matter," *The Social Studies* 92, no. 6 (2001): 237–242 and "Teacher as Curricular-Instructional Gatekeeper in Social Studies," *Handbook of Research on Social Studies Teaching and Learning*, ed. James P. Shaver (New York: Macmillan, 1991).

20. Jean Bethke Elshtain, *Jane Addams and the Dream of American Democracy: A Life* (New York: Basic Books, 2002).
21. Brian K. Marchman, "Teaching about Homophobia in a High School Civics Course," *Theory and Research in Social Education* 30, no. 2 (2002): 302–305.
22. David Harris has developed a scoring rubric for classroom discussions of controversial issues, in which he uses this issue as the running example. See David Harris, "Classroom Assessment of Civic Discourse," in *Education for Democracy: Contexts, Curricula, and Assessments*, ed. Walter C. Parker (Greenwich, CT: Information Age, 2002).
23. See, for example, Myra Pollack Sadker and David Miller Sadker, *Teachers, Schools, and Society* (Boston: McGraw Hill, 2000).
24. Zirkel, op. cit.
25. Leslea Newman and Diana Souza, *Heather Has Two Mommies* (Boston: Alyson Publications, 1989).
26. Greg Hamilton, "Reading 'Jack,' " *English Education* 30, no. 1 (1998): 24–39.

29

Gender Perspectives on Educating for Global Citizenship

Peggy McIntosh

Defining Global Citizenship

The 21st century requires us to think about citizenship as extending far beyond the "city" from which the word derives, and the state and the nation with which it has also been associated. Throughout the history of the United States, the matter of what citizenship entails has been contested. But a citizen is generally defined as a person having duties, rights, responsibilities, and privileges within a political unit that demands loyalty from that person and extends protection in return. Since we are living on a shrinking planet and are made contiguous with others by technology, commerce, conflicts, international networks, and the environment, the question arises of how citizenship could be redefined if one of its dimensions were felt membership in a political and social unit that is the whole globe.

The very definitions of citizenship need to be changed before the political and social unit can be conceived of as the globe itself. Political definitions of citizenship would need to be augmented by more affective definitions. The ideas of loyalty, protection, duties, rights, responsibilities, and privileges would need to be expanded and multiplied to the point where one's loyalty and expectation of protection come not only from such units as the living place, province, or nation, but also from a sense of belonging to the whole world. Within this vast world, the marks of citizenship would need to include affection, respect, care, curiosity, and concern for the well-being of all living beings.

What would it take to be global citizens? I can answer only from my own experience and perceptions. I associate the idea of a global citizen with habits of mind, heart, body, and soul that have to do with working for and preserving a network of relationship and connection across lines of difference and distinctness, while keeping and deepening a sense of one's own identity and integrity.

I associate global citizenship first with several capacities of mind: 1) the ability to observe oneself and the world around one, 2) the ability to make comparisons and contrasts, 3) the ability to "see" plurally as a result, 4) the ability to understand that both "reality" and language come in versions, 5) the ability to see power relations and understand them systemically, and 6) the ability to balance awareness of one's own realities with the realities of entities outside of the perceived self. These capacities of mind may be developed through daily life anywhere and fostered in many ways. They do not require literacy. But in our technologically interconnected world—and through experience in reading, writing, imagining, and traveling—such mind capacities can become well developed. They do not fit well with the world of formal education as it is carried on in the United States. But for me, they are key constituents of global awareness and they point toward values of transglobal communication and peaceful coexistence.

I also associate global citizenship with several capacities of heart: 1) the ability to respect one's own feelings and delve deeply into them, 2) the ability to become aware of others' feelings and to believe in the validity of those feelings, 3) the ability to experience in oneself a mixture of conflicting feelings without losing a sense of integrity, 4) the ability to experience affective worlds plurally while keeping a gyroscopic sense of one's core orientations, 5) the capacity to wish competing parties well, 6) the ability to observe and understand how the "politics of location" affect one's own and others' positions and power in the world, and 7) the ability to balance being heartfelt with a felt knowledge of how culture is embedded in the hearts of ourselves and others. These heart capacities can, I believe, be strong in many people who are not literate, and I observe that they are often quite weak in people who have a great deal of formal education. It is as though strengthening the muscles that allow one to compete in the economic realms of the capitalist world weakens the muscles needed for entertaining multiple emotional connections balancing many complexities of life.

I further associate global citizenship with related capacities of the physical body and the spiritual soul. The global citizen knows his or her body not as a tool for mastery or beauty, but as a body in the body of the world. We have both unique individuality and intricate, inevitable connection with other bodies in the local and global habitats we share. Knowledge of self and other, comparison and contrast between the self and others, plural understanding of the integrity of all beings, and a sense of balance between dependence and interdependence in the physical world are all elements in the development of a global citizen's sense of inhabiting and using a body. Knowledge of our mortality, knowledge that being born entails dying, is part of the wisdom of the body. Respect for our own and others' physical needs is part of the wisdom of the body.

I feel that the soul needs a certain sweetness to be that of a global citizen. Observing turbulence and stillness, comparing and contrasting the outcomes of various kinds of human desire and behavior, I think that the global soul seeks the nondestructive as it seeks to preserve the bodies that house souls. Yet I also see souls of global citizens taking part in the dangerous conflicts of the contentious world, engaging rather than withdrawing, in order that the personality may be put in the service of something larger than itself, and that danger and suffering may be alleviated.

What I have sketched here goes beyond most discussions of citizenship and bears the strong marks of my own experience working with women and doing research on gender relations. It seems to me that many of the qualities that I am defining as essential to global citizenship are qualities that are gender-related. That is, they have been especially delegated to, conditioned in, and rewarded in women. When females bring forth children or do the caretaking that is expected of us, we are automatically placed in obvious relation to other beings and must develop many capacities for plural seeing and feeling: capacities for comparison and contrast, hearing more than one voice, understanding more than one version of self-interest, being empathic persons who have the capacity to hold and to internalize, as our own, more than one version of reality. Women have been charged with caring about the decent survival of all. This charge deeply affects our development.

I do not know, and other researchers do not know, the extent to which these capacities in women are biologically based, and it is very hard to find this out through empirical research. Some must be, in part, biologically based. But if we observe changes over the last century in women's and men's lives in the industrialized world, it is possible to conclude that many forms of gender socialization in the past were based on invented notions of what is appropriate to males and females. Experimentation has shown that these notions can change. Only continuing experimentation can tell us now what the actual limits of male and female capacity are. I do not feel that the capacities for global citizenship and plural competency that I am describing are the purview of women alone, or that they should be. In U.S. society, this openness is, for example, common in small boys before the society delivers messages to them such as "boys don't cry," which weakens their sense of self-knowledge and undermines their ability to feel empathy or acknowledge vulnerability.

In any case, women's ascribed roles in all societies especially require attentiveness to others, and the capacity to hear and take in many voices, stories, and versions simultaneously. Without these capacities women cannot do well the tasks of caretaking they have been assigned. They entail what Jean Baker Miller terms "the emotional housekeeping of the world," and they are crucial to human survival (Miller 1976).

I believe that the transpersonal care and understanding that women have been asked to do is central to history and to citizenship. It is not, however, central to the discussion of citizenship that focuses on rights, responsibilities, and public duties. Insofar as the public world has been assigned to men, as men's definitions of what citizenship is about have prevailed in its definitions. Within patriarchy, male definitions of reality trump female experience. Behind the scenes of what is presented to us as "history," women make and mend the fabric of society. "Lower-caste" men are likewise expected to make and mend the fabric. Those who wield the most public power are seen to be the leaders of citizens, but in fact the alternative fabric of day-by-day maintenance of citizens exists in a world more or less out of sight of public discussion. This lateral work requires a patience and sensibility focused on "getting through" and "getting on," rather than "getting ahead." The nurturance of each generation depends on this lateral, ongoing way of sustaining life in the world.

Educating Global Citizens

I feel that in order to educate global citizens, we need to give young people in school training and support in the little-named skills of what Miller once called, in an unpublished talk, "finding one's development through the development of others," that is, the skills of working for, and wanting, the commonweal, the well-being of all. Young people need rewards for and experiences of caring as a vital part of citizenship and a vital aspect of themselves. In other words, they all need to respect and develop qualities in themselves and in the culture as a whole that were conditioned into women or lower-caste men, who were expected to make and mend the fabric of the society behind the scenes. For the whole point of making and mending the fabric is to keep the self and the habitat, social or ecological, alive and whole.

When the emphasis is put on making and mending the social fabric as a central value for all citizens, then the emphasis can shift, as I feel it should, away from "rights" to "needs" as the basis for local and global policy and care. I feel that "rights" are an invention by 18th-century European thinkers and are not biologically demonstrable. The hand of the Creator did not descend and present us with rights. Human needs, on the other hand, are empirically verifiable and are in all of us. Water, food, clothing, shelter, and meaningful connection with other human beings are basic needs without whose fulfillment we die. The ethos of global citizenship, I believe, must start with providing, and caring about providing, these basic human necessities, and the protections for the sustaining ecosystems that humans depend on.

Can U.S. educators muster the character needed to widen the sense of loyalty and care in themselves and in students beyond the units of family, team, class, school, town, city, state, and nation? At present, most teachers and their students have not been educated to think that good character might require thinking or feeling so broadly or plurally. For most, the United States as a nation is the outermost ring of the series of concentric loyalties suggested above. Beyond this national margin are other peoples and nations mostly seen as competitors, threats, or unknowns, none of them measuring up to the United States. Technology, however, insistently reminds us of our commonalities with others beyond our borders. The national values have not yet caught up.

Another obstruction to bringing what I see as empathetic and plural-minded global citizenship into education is that many educators and parents today in the United States would see compassionate values as undermining the society by undermining the innate nature of boys and men. A myth persists that male and female are "opposite" sexes, and a patriarchal conviction persists that male and female are not equally valuable. In fact, the sexes overlap; in many ways men and women are similar physiologically and psychologically. Either sex can be shown to demonstrate an edge in ability and capacity. Nevertheless, the myths of oppositeness and of male superiority require that males be protected from developing attributes that have been projected onto women. These attributes are seen to undermine, and even to contaminate, masculinity. Males, especially young males, may have strong competencies in the caring, the relationality, and the plural seeing that I think are essential for global citizenship. What is rewarded in them, however, is solo risk-taking and individualism, and if they are white males, a go-it-alone and "damn-the-torpedoes" kind of bravery without a balanced regard for, or awareness of, the outcomes for other people of one's behaviors. Resistance against the kind of global education that I favor is to be expected in the United States in this day and age, since it seems to undermine the values of white male individualism. I favor, however, a balance in all citizens between virtues that have been projected differentially onto people of different groups, on the theory that all of our human virtues carry some validity, and that relational aspects of our personalities are needed in everyone because our world needs plural-minded citizens with capacities for concern and compassion in every citizen.

Gender Roles and Global Education

It is my opinion that both men and women hold within them the capacities that have been projected onto those of the "opposite sex," or "opposite" races or ethnic groups. These capacities in and of themselves are neither negative nor positive. For example, in terms of gender among white people in the United States, individuation and bravery are important human qualities that both sexes would do well to cultivate, as both may be needed at some time in one's life and in the life of one's community. But patriarchy and white supremacy are strong societal frameworks in the United States. Each keeps rules, perceptions, standards, definitions, and control in the hands of a dominant group. Whether or not the members of the dominant group are nice people has no bearing on these dynamics. Within patriarchy, white supremacy, or any other hierarchical system, a power imbalance is inevitable; the attributes projected onto and rewarded in the dominant group count for more than the attributes projected onto and rewarded in members of a subordinate group. Roles projected onto and expected of women—like being attentive to and protective of vulnerable things—are not valued alongside of valor and acquisition of power for the self, as projected onto men, especially white men, in the United States. Cultural restrictions on developing into "whole" persons interfere with the development of global citizens who have individual integrity as well as cosmopolitan attentiveness to the existence and well-being of others. This balance, though I see it as wholeness, would be seen by many as "not strong enough, not male enough" within a U.S. context. So I see a need within school curricula to explore strength and courage more broadly and deeply, to offset the individualistic presentation of heroism, as it is frequently studied in our schools, with the study of goodness and strength in making and mending the fabrics of culture.

A related difficulty in educating global citizens in the United States may reside in the tepid response of many Americans to the idea of citizenship itself. The concept of leadership has had more appeal, as something muscular, tough, interesting, stimulating, and rewarding. And although patriotism has been a very strong emotion in the nation since September 11, 2001, I think that citizenship still has less appeal, being associated with obligations, docility, obedience, and good behavior. It could be that in the popular white mind, citizenship is to women as leadership is to men. Citizenship is not necessarily heroic, expressive, or creative. It is seen as involving responsibilities, duties, and what must be done without the status of social reward. Leadership is seen to enable individuality and special status, whereas citizenship is seen as a social leveler. The United States government prides itself on global leadership, on being out in front as the sole superpower. But in my view, as the 21st century begins, the administration of George W. Bush shows no capacity for, nor understanding of, global citizenship; that is, of belonging within an entity larger than the nation itself. It is hard to press for education of global citizens in a nation whose government is acting out the role of the independent, dominant, unapproachable, individualistic, lone power whose self-interest is seen as the ethos that should prevail throughout the world.

Despite the dominant cultural values of U.S. society and education, many valiant teachers have construed education more broadly and have attempted to do global teaching in the light of their own understandings of intelligence, growth and development for their students. I received some formal global schooling myself in the 1950s that is illuminating for me to think back on now. Remembering both its content and my resistance to the content sheds light on dynamics that I believe persist in the minds and hearts of many white U.S. citizens. This global education occurred because my parents were appalled when the United States dropped the atomic bombs on Hiroshima and Nagasaki in 1945. They became Quakers and pacifists and transferred me to a Quaker school when I was 15 years old. I thought that the plural and gender-fair education I received there was annoying and ridiculous. For example, I had a weird teacher by the name of Mr. Cleveland who taught World Religions, with an "s." It seemed to me that Mr. Cleveland wasted our time. He taught about Buddhism, Hinduism, Islam, Taoism, and Confucianism. I was in school to learn about "the best." I felt that he diluted the class with extraneous books and people. I was filled with scorn when he said there were many paths up the mountain of religious belief. I felt he should take an interest only in "the right path."

Having inflicted comparative religions on us, i.e., comparative "seeing" of a kind that I now believe that global citizens need, Mr. Cleveland went on to teach Semantics, which I also resisted intellectually and emotionally. In fairness, I should empathize with the self I was in those days. World War II had just ended, a war that may be considered a simpler war, morally, for the United States than any subsequent war we have been involved in. I was in a bipolar mode of thinking: win/lose, right/wrong. Mr. Cleveland complexified all that simplicity with the study of semantics. It upset me to be told that "what I say" may not be "what you hear." I believed there was or should be a direct transfer from one mind to another, and that given two different interpretations of what had been said, only one of the two could be right. And if we were right in World War II and the Germans and Japanese were wrong, why on earth did this teacher and his colleagues at my new school hold work camps in Germany and invite Japanese students to attend the school?

Another problem with Mr. Cleveland was that he introduced us to Theories of History. I wanted to hear only one theory, which went approximately this way: People encounter problems in their climb toward perfection. Wars and depressions are such problems, or setbacks. We are now in a post-Depression and postwar time and are making progress toward the millennium, when history will be further along toward perfection. Mr. Cleveland, however, gave us bizarre alternative versions: pendulum theories, spiral theories, progress theories, and descent theories. He said we could think about history as "coming down through the ages" or "coming up through the ages," and that each was a different conceptualization and that the differences were interesting. I was so impatient with this man's attention to differences!

The crowning stupidity, I thought, came when our class put on a play and instead of directing it himself, as head of the Drama Department, he appointed a student director. Though I was the student director, I thought this was a result of the fact that Mr. Cleveland simply didn't know what he was doing. John Dewey might have given several years of his life to know that teachers would actually do this kind of teaching in which students' growth and development are placed at the center of instruction. And I am now aware that his decision to empower a girl in the role of director was unusual in its time.

Moreover, the school had a policy of coeducation in all student offices. A boy and a girl must hold each office. This radical policy enforced coeducational sharing of power. It delivered a message that the school assumed boys and girls should have equal power, and that the school would be better if they did. As it happens, the Quaker Meeting for Worship, a one-hour silent meeting each week at which anyone might speak, had a correspondingly power-sharing feel to it. I found it a rather homespun event, since there was no pulpit and no male authority to preach to us as there had been at the other places of worship I had attended. I remember my particular embarrassment when women stood and spoke in Meeting. What did they know?

The pattern that I see here is that of a representative 1950s small-town, small-minded white middle-class "good girl" challenging everyone who was trying to give her a democratic and, in fact, a global education. Through internalized sexism and classism, I was rejecting teaching that offered us lateral answers to the question of who was competent, who was important, who had knowledge. The answer was everybody. Mr. Burton, the physics teacher, put it in so many words when he said, on the first day of class, "Physics is nothing but common sense wrapped around things you've seen all of your life. Ever since you were a baby hitting balls around your playpen, you have understood inertia and momentum. I just give you the names." So we were already in physics, and it was already in us. He made it seem as though we could all "do physics," because we already had. He also had us build batteries before we studied electricity, on the theory that in this way the boys would not feel they started out ahead of the girls, with a male affinity for science.

Mr. Burton seemed to me "too nice" for a Physics teacher. I heard that in another school a physics teacher said, "Physics is like Mt. Everest. Only a few of you will make it." I thought that made sense. Physics required heroism, and only a few survivors would live to tell the tale. In that other school students indeed fell off the mountain of physics, and if they lived to tell the tale, they compared their wounds, slings, casts, and scars, but they didn't love physics. Mr. Burton had a way of producing students who entered math and science fields, and my very shy lab partner, Ken Wilson, went on to win the Nobel Prize in Physics. It was not Mr. Burton's aim to produce Nobelists, but to be enabling for all of us. Everybody should be engaged and everybody should know that they brought to physics the authority of their own experience, even their infant experience, in the physical world. Now when I hear continual top-down comparisons made between industrialized nations and other nations, or between technological cultures and more indigenous cultures, I remember how the strong base of knowledge in all people was recognized by my Quaker teachers in a way that was impressive and exemplary for global education.

The Challenge for Teachers

This kind of education need not be confined to private schools. What it requires is the professional development of teachers who have cultivated a global sensibility or, in some cases, merely been given permission to bring their global sensibilities into school. Will this nation's domestic culture dare to produce students and teachers who practice thinking and connecting laterally? I think it is possible. It takes courage and imagination to bring to schooling more than we were taught to bring. But I feel that our current crises call for repair of a system that has settled for solipsism and a narrowly functional definition of citizenship that produces people who are employable and do not ask broader questions.

Moreover, I have found that teachers suffer from the same confinements that their students do. Many long to repair the damage done to them by the requirement that they leave their whole selves at home each day and teach from a very narrow segment of their perceptions and capacities, which too often means preparing students for standardized tests and unspeculative, normative ways of thinking. Though it may be hard to change schools and educational ideals, I have found through my experience that it is not so hard for teachers themselves to change if they feel they are recovering something they lost: their human breadth and their longing to help shape a world that is not torn apart.

For the last two decades, I have been working on professional development of teachers from my base at the Wellesley College Center for Research on Women. My main work is with the National SEED Project on Inclusive Curriculum, which I founded 17 years ago and have been codirecting with Emily Style since 1987. SEED stands for Seeking Educational Equity and Diversity. The program establishes teacher-led seminars in K-12 schools. Each seminar involves 10 to 20 committed teachers who meet each month to discuss questions like "What are we teaching?" and "What messages does our teaching deliver with regard to gender, race, class, culture, region, nation, and the world? What outcomes do we want of education? What works for students' and our own growth and development? Can we give our students a more complete picture than we were given ourselves, of the self and the world in their many dimensions? How can we make school climate, teaching methods, and curricula more gender-fair, multicultural, and global?" SEED seminars are powerful, and teachers are deeply changed by them. In some ways they resemble the format and assumptions of Quaker Meeting about the worth of all participants. They create space in which everybody speaks. There is no leading authority and there are no required texts, though there are piles of resources of many kinds. Teachers bring the authority of their own experience. They bring their life stories. The facilitators, whom we prepare for these seminars, receive many books and materials and videos, but it is up to them whether they want to use any of these. When teachers are in lateral spaces psychologically and are allowed to have their own conversations about what they know without outside pressure, then I think SEED replicates some elements of my Quaker schooling: comparative curriculum, reflective listening, and empowering assumptions about where knowledge resides.

But SEED seminars do not depend on any one spiritual tradition, and they improve on my own Quaker experience by teaching systemic seeing. They counter the usual U.S. ideology of individualism, in which the individual is seen as the unit of society, and the belief is that whatever one ends up with is what one wanted, worked for, earned, and deserved. SEED seminars acknowledge systems of power working both within our psyches and in the world outside us. They call forth participants' own deep experience of power. In the balance between testifying to one's own experience and hearing the testimony of others, those qualities that I define as belonging to a capacity for global citizenship are brought forth. The technique that I have named Serial Testimony is particularly relevant to global perspectives. Each member of a group speaks in turn, within a set amount of time, very often 1 minute, or at most 3 minutes. During a serial testimony there is no interruption, no "cross-talk." After a serial testimony there is no debate. The aim is to speak and to listen, to hear and be heard, to compare, contrast, and deepen one's understanding of oneself and others. The modes of Serial Testimony undercut politics-as-usual. For educators, they provide a rare and welcome relief from faculty meetings and other forums in which the talkers talk, the listeners listen, and a general feeling of malaise prevails.

SEED seminars have now been led in the United States, Canada, Latin America, and 10 Asian countries, and may be led in any language with any materials. Many international schools that had an entirely U.S.-based curriculum before teachers engaged in SEED seminars have developed curricula, including language study, that are respectful of their host countries. On the more immediate level, within the seminar, the respectful interactive mode includes everyone of every nationality and cultural group as an authority on his or her own experience. Cultural chasms are bridged in SEED seminars. By balancing what codirector Emily Style calls "the scholarship on the shelves" with "the scholarship in the selves," they do inner and outer work. The program was devised by women and bears the imprint of our plural socialization. It reflects the balance of self and other that is asked of all people doing relational tasks. In another metaphor of Emily Style, the curriculum is like an architectural structure built around students. Ideally it provides a balance of "windows" out to the experience of others and "mirrors" of the students' own reality and validity. When curriculum serves as both "window" and "mirror," students are helped to become whole-souled, complex people. I imagine them as potential citizens of the world, having developed both identities of their own and interconnectedness with others. We have found that when the curriculum serves students as both "window" and "mirror," their alienation and anger decrease, together with their violence toward themselves and others.

Interactive Phases and Global Citizenship Education

United States educational institutions merely replicate the power relations of the rest of U.S. society unless we intervene with correctives. One corrective lens that SEED seminars often use is a Phase Theory I developed in 1983. It is a typology called "Interactive Phases of Curricular and Personal Re-Vision." I devised it after observing changes in college faculty members as they brought Women's Studies perspectives into their liberal arts courses.

I saw that traditionally trained white faculty members in any discipline were likely to move from what I called a Phase I frame of mind, which is womanless and all white, to a Phase II frame of mind, which admits "exceptional others" to the discipline, but only on the terms already laid down. Both frames of mind are challenged by what I identified as Phase III thinking, in which all women, and men of color, are seen as a problem, anomaly, absence, or victim, both in the academic world and in the aspect of the world that the discipline encompasses. Phase III is about coming to see systemically, and to understand local and global issues of, racism, sexism, classism, homophobia, anti-Semitism, nationalism, militarism, colonialism, and other kinds of power dynamics.

I see Phase III as an improvement on the womanless and all-white Phase I and the "exceptional others" flavor of Phase II. It is far wider and more accurate than teaching based on the ideology of individualism. It observes power systems and brings in issues of justice and care. It calls for and inspires action, including intellectual action. But Phase III can be polarizing and get arrested in victim studies. It can reduce people who suffer into mere cyphers with deficit identities. The systemic vision of Phase III makes an important advance into analysis of global problems, injustices, and mal-distribution of goods and resources. But its stories can all sound the same, as in oppressor/oppressed; victims/victimizers; winner/losers.

Phase III improves when it partakes of, and rests on, the detailed narratives, the moving, grounded, daily, and plural stories of Phase IV, the phase of experience, everyone's experience, anywhere in the world. In Phase IV everyone is a knower. Everyone's daily life is history, politics, literature, drama, economics, psychology, and ecology. Within Phase IV, binary thinking is seen as too simple.

The four first interactive phases point toward an eventual Phase V: a version in which the world of knowledge is redefined and reconstructed to include us all, which I consider will take us 100 to 200 years to conceive, depending on the political choices the world makes in this and coming decades. I feel that we desperately need thinking that goes back and forth across the interface between Phase III issues and Phase IV experience, that is, in the interface between systemic issues of power and policy, seen abstractly, and the actual poignant stories of human beings' textured, relational, and interdependent lives as makers and menders of the fabric of life.

Most of education in the United States at present is stuck in Phases I and II. Standardized testing has intensified the value placed on womanless and all-white versions of reality, with a few "exceptions" allowed in. Phase I is about studying government, management, laws, wars, and winners, whether in the arts, sciences, or social sciences. Phase I courses ignore almost all of the world's population. In Phase II, the standardized textbooks bring in a few "others" who are seen as unlike their kind and therefore worth studying. The standardized tests bring in Frederick Douglass or Harriet Tubman, neither as living the actual daily life of an enslaved person, and each seen as modeling heroism in a way that more of their people "should have done." Though the United States in the last three decades paid lip service to critical thinking as a skill to be developed in students, and though it relates to what I see as the need for minds that can compare and contrast evidence from many sources, in recent years the call has been for basic literacy, with no attention paid at all to developing analytical minds, which of course might turn countercultural. Preparation for standardized testing squeezes out both the Phase III critical faculties and the Phase IV method in which student voices may be heard bringing in their own experience. These suppressions are no accident within an administration working toward centralized control. For if students or teachers are encouraged to tell what they know, their deep memories will lead them away from single and simple loyalties and right/ wrong views of the world.

As I have written in my interactive Phase Theory, stories told by those who go back to their early childhood reveal that the multicultural globe is interior; the multicultural worlds are in us as well as around us. Early cultural conditioning trained each of us as children to shut off awareness of certain groups, voices, abilities, and inclinations, including the inclination to be with many kinds of children. Continents we might have known were closed off or subordinated within us. The domains of personality that remain can and do fill the conceptual space like colonizing powers. But a potential for pluralized understanding remains in us; the moves toward reflective consciousness come in part from almost-silenced continents within ourselves. Greater diversity of curriculum reflects not just the exterior multicultural world but the interior self that in early childhood was aware of, and attuned to, many varieties of experience. Recovery of that connectedness is a powerful aid to global citizenship. It can be a source of disorientation and anxiety, even shock, when one first remembers early connectedness that we were made to break off, as our educations or families shaped us for narrower class, race, and ethnic lives than our hearts inclined to.

Phase IV teaching dares to bring students' experience into the classroom and to derive new understanding from hitherto excluded or overlooked sources. Phase IV is the only frame of mind within the first four in my typology in which the student's own life counts. In its ability to educate and engage students, Phase IV goes far beyond the top-down oppressiveness of Phase I, the "exceptional others" framework of Phase II, and the focus on disembodied issues and polarities of Phase III.

Most traditionally trained white teachers started and continue to teach within the framework in which they were themselves taught: Phase I mono-culturalism, in which U.S. white culture is the chief reality. In this frame of mind a teacher is oblivious of the racial and gender elements in his or her actual life, and ignores her/his Phase III issues and Phase IV relational experience while doing his or her paid work. Most teachers teach about conflict and wars, and accept bullying on the playground, or sexual harassment in the hallways, while they think of themselves as desiring peace. There is a gap between the avowed ideals of being peaceful and the actual practice of teaching, with teachers operating as if vertical conflict were inevitable and hierarchical competition were the only logical framework within which schooling could occur. Jane Roland

Martin's call for the three C's of care, concern, and connection to balance the three R's of reading, writing, and 'rithmetic has scarcely been answered.

In SEED seminars, when we ask teachers to remember vivid vignettes from their own schooling as children and teenagers, nearly all of the memories are negative, and nearly all involve competition, loss, humiliation, and mortification. When the exercise shifts and we request that they recall positive moments from their own schooling, what they usually remember is working together, in connection, on projects, or sitting in peaceful places, talking. Their positive memories rarely involve beating others or winning, but they do sometimes involve pushing oneself beyond one's usual limits. If educators learn from such testimony and wish to work for a world that is peaceful, they will arrange to balance the win-lest-you-lose paradigm that schooling now takes for granted as "normal" with a paradigm emphasizing students' growth and development in connection. Most schoolchildren testify that they like to work on collaborative projects more than they like to work alone. Recently many schoolchildren have been greatly interested in Internet hookups with children of other countries. They are responding to global education.

Hope for the Future

Writing this chapter during the spring of 2003 is very taxing because of the disconnect I feel between the ideal of educating U.S. students for global citizenship and the behavior of the U.S. government. To me, U.S. citizenship does not feel equated with God's particular approval. I see the United States as a place with a rare and wonderful dream of unity in diversity and a promise of the good life that has not yet been realized within its boundaries. I see the "American Dream" as set back severely by the acts of the Bush administration. It has enforced white, male-led Euro-American power and class dominance, when we need more global unity in diversity to hold the international fabric together. I feel that the Iraq war and its many costs do violence to the daily work of upkeep and maintenance everywhere, even in the United States. I fear that the United States's "good vs. evil," "us against them" thinking has weakened global cohesiveness over the long term, disrespecting men and women all over the world, rupturing the fabric of trust and the hope of more tolerant life between differing religions and cultures. It assumes the top-down, either/or Phase I model of life as War: every warrior for himself; every group of warriors for themselves; women and children can deal with their terrors and trials alone, while being expected to take care of daily provisioning for all of us behind the scenes. Though some women are in the U.S. armed services, these are wars conceived by and led by men. The U.S. media present women in the armed services as borrowed from their families; the media do not present generals as borrowed from their families.

While the situation in the United States in the first few years of the 21st century feels like living with an abusive, unbalanced, controlling father who is a bully at home and a bully in the neighborhood, I take hope from numerous sources. One is the interest of many U.S. citizens in wisdom from indigenous and non-Western cultures, including Asian cultures. Learning from people of color in the United States and learning from Asian people in Asia has given me a feeling of hopefulness, as they teach from a less exclusive base of thinking and acting. There is not such a sense of spiritual or social loneliness, nor such stratification based on money and possessions. Acquisition and greed are not such prime values, and the sense of community seems to me far stronger than in the communities of white capitalism that I know best, in which "community" was and still seems to me an empty, disembodied idea. In U.S. African-American, Latino, Native, and Asian-American cultures, I feel that the sense of community is stronger than in my white worlds. The United States has had increasing opportunities to study and learn from more plural value systems and skills, as the schools and the society have become more diverse in their populations. Usually the differences I see in cultures less powerful than my own correspond to values I was taught to hold as a woman in my particular part of patriarchal white U.S. culture. In doing multicultural study I am both revising what I see I am and recovering some of what I was encouraged to give up to fit into the place designated for me in U.S. social and gender structures.

Another source of hope for me is the change toward global education that has slowly but very surely occurred at Wellesley College, where I work. Though Wellesley is not very self-conscious or even verbal about its changes, they are remarkable to me. Nearly half of the students are U.S. students of color or international students who come from some 40 nations. Courses are offered in many languages. Eight or nine religious faiths from around the world are mentioned in the weekly calendar of events. Performance groups and social organizations have many cultural bases. Consultants, lecturers, and visitors come from around the world. New faculty members are hired from outside the United States. Curricula have become more and more international, cross-cultural, and serious about women. Women's Studies is thriving. The values of the college have shifted over the last 50 years, from promoting education for women who would marry powerful white men to promoting the development of students who will matter to themselves and to others in the world. I would not claim that the students are global citizens in the sense that I have defined global citizenship. The values of soloistic behavior, materialism, and personal power once conditioned chiefly into men are strong in the sensibilities of the female students I work with. But they are being educated to know that there is more out in the world than their individual ambitions will encompass or affect for the better. I think their frames of reference and values will widen in later years, as mine did, in part because those teachers of my 15-year-old self did not give up on me. I take as a given, now, that I should not give up on young people even if they do not want to become global citizens. Neither did I.

I was also very heartened by a poem and the woman who wrote it at the time of the inauguration of William Jefferson Clinton as President of the United States in 1992. It seemed wonderful to me that Clinton asked Maya Angelou to write the inaugural poem, which she entitled *On the Pulse of the Morning*. The poem's global dimensions were spiritually uplifting to me. I remembered Robert Frost reciting his sonnet "The Gift Out-right" at the time of John Kennedy's inauguration. Beautiful though it seemed to me, I found it on rereading to be deeply racist in its assumption that this land was empty until English people arrived. I saw Frost's poem as ignorant: in a characteristic U.S. history textbook way. Its language was intricately filled with legalistic double meanings about deeds and ownership of the land. By contrast, Maya Angelou used as her primary metaphors The Rock, The River, and The Tree, which are in all lands and speak to all people. She invoked all of the peoples who live or lived in the United States and in every other culture in the world. She recognized deep suffering and inhumanity, and also looked to a new morning. That a poem of such reach and power would grace the inauguration of a U.S. president gave me and others whom I spoke with a great surge of hope in the future of the world.

Another source of hope for me has been the four U.N. Women's conferences of 1975, 1980, 1985, and 1995. The sharp divisions between the two sections of each signals to me that change is possible. In the official U.N. conference, women represent their nations' governments, or are represented by men in those governments, and the arguments and contentions are predictable and orchestrated by rules, rights, privileges, and responsibilities of membership in one's nation and in the conference. But in the Nongovernmental Forum, women come together with much more of a sense of a shared and global agenda. In 1995 thirty thousand women came to the Forum in Beijing. I would trust them to run the world far more than I trust our present leaders, and to devise global education that would help us to live together better. Of course the women contend and fight, but the underlying plural sense of holding and being held in the midst of complexities is there. Our deep training is against either/or thinking and the violence it leads to. Since women and our dependents are the majority of any population and have had at least half of the world's lived experience, with responsibility for so many beyond ourselves, I feel we could in the aggregate be decent global judges of wise distribution of assets. Our policy concerns and skills have certainly been visible at these United Nations conferences. I used to scorn, as inefficient, the bureaucratic U.N. processes of inching toward a plural and multicultural agreement. Now I wonder how the world will survive without these U.N. processes and the empowerment of women's perspectives within them, which was started off so many years ago by the plural imagination and inclusive vision of Eleanor Roosevelt.

That we as a nation moved, for a while, into more global thinking than we had 50 years ago, before the U.N. was founded, is a source of hope for me despite the Bush administration's incapacity and disregard for plural understanding and its lack of intercultural skill. Its ignorance of other cultures reminds me of a more benign moment in the 1950s when my retired uncle from Middlebury, Connecticut, invited me to join him and his wife for a meal at the stately Savoy Hotel in London on the way home from their first trip outside the United States. In a booming voice heard all over the red-velvet Victorian dining room, my uncle proclaimed, "I've been all over Europe, seen seventeen capitals in twenty one days, and I don't think they've improved on us in any way, shape, or from!" His wife sat silently. He seemed to me a stunningly ignorant, loud, rich, blind American. He was very badly educated. The White House today is not about lessening arrogance, ignorance, greed, chauvinism, or patriarchy through education. But educators themselves can still choose to change the mindset and heartset of the system that produced my uncle and his silent wife. They can, among other efforts, work to bring out her voice, so that a man does not speak for both parties. In her voice I think I would have heard at the very least that beyond her husband there were other people in those 17 capitals of Europe.

I remember my schoolteachers' fears of the House Committee on Un-American Activities in the 1950s. Citizens accused of having communist leanings were blacklisted and lost jobs and public protection. Many teachers who refused to take loyalty oaths to the United States were fired. At the time I did not know why my teachers were quite so upset. In response to many policies of the Bush administration, the forces for repression of dissent are strong, and once again many college students seem to be ignorant of why any of their professors are upset about silencing of academic discussion of our foreign policy, and about the silencing of commentary on the Iraq war's local and international race, gender, and class dimensions. Most students have trouble seeing the war or U.S. government policy globally or systemically. In this regard they are good students of what the culture at large has taught them: that there are no large power systems in or around us. I feel that to educate global citizens we will need to support teachers to prepare students and themselves not only for what the United States has considered "standard," but also for "nonstandard" awareness and appreciation of the connected global ecosystems we are in, and the many ways in which human beings can make meaning of our lives without killing each other.

Global travel can be a great introduction or reinforcement to global awareness, though it has class parameters and limitations. Closer to home, even travel down the road can pluralize the mind and heart. In this technological age, much vicarious experience can be had through Internet travel and international exchanges. But students need to develop critical faculties with which to see, and heartfelt connections with which to feel what they are traveling into. In school, sometimes it is the heartfelt trust of a teacher in the worth of a student in a completely local situation that produces a faith within the student that he or she is connected to the world in a way that matters, and that the world is worth caring about. Often it is the day-by-day exchanges that open our capacities to care about, seek to understand, and work for that which is beyond our immediate view, that which is larger than us, but includes and holds us. The global sense for belonging and making spaces for all to belong can be developed close to home by teachers bringing the wholeness of their emotions and capacities into classrooms, unafraid to help students also to develop the plural capacities and the wide-ranging awareness that caretakers absolutely depend on when they work for the decent survival of all.

Reference

Miller, J. B. (1976). *Toward a new psychology of women.* Boston: Beacon Press.

30

Moving Beyond Fidelity Expectations: Rethinking Curriculum Reform for Controversial Topics in Post-Communist Settings

Thomas Misco

This study explores the implementation of a Holocaust curriculum designed for Latvian schools five years after its enactment. In 2004, teachers, curriculum writers, and historians from the Republic of Lativia, the United States, Israel, and Sweden produced a new Holocaust education curriculum within the *Teaching the Holocaust in Latvian Schools Project* (THLSP) in response to perceived historical silences on this topic within Latvian schools and society. To construct the curriculum, this project employed the method of curriculum deliberation (Schwab, 1970/1978), which empowers teachers, curricularists, and historians in a deliberative forum to solve practical curricular problems. The grant project ultimately produced and disseminated 1,000 teacher books and 10,000 student books throughout Latvia (Hlebowitsh, Hamot, & Misco, 2006). Because the implementation effects of curriculum projects of this kind are largely undocumented, this study sought to understand the ways in which teachers enacted, modified, or ignored the new curriculum.

Given the problem of unknown outcomes, I decided to explore the conditions that provided fertile ground for teacher use of the curriculum and the extent to which materials from the curriculum deliberation project responded to obstacles to curriculum use. Therefore, the pragmatic research question guiding this study focused on curriculum use:

Are teachers using the curriculum? To what extent is it used? Are some components utilized more than others? What serves to inhibit or invite use of materials? To what extent were the materials responsive to the curricular problem that guided the grant activities?

By exploring the ways in which Latvian educators employed this new curriculum over the past five years, this study offers a knowledge base regarding the successes and failures of curriculum deliberation. This study also moves beyond curriculum deliberation as a curriculum writing method and attends to its application to a particular controversial topic in a post-communist state, which may help future curriculum projects—those conducted cross-culturally and within country—make refined plans for the recruitment of writers, publication of materials, dissemination, and a wide range of other variables.

Conceptual and Theoretical Framework

I was fundamentally interested in the challenges and pathways to curriculum implementation—specifically, curriculum produced to help students and teachers address a controversial topic within a post-communist setting. I conceptualize implementation as the "actual use of an innovation or what an innovation consists of in practice" (Fullan & Pomfret, 1977, p. 336). The implementation of a new curriculum certainly requires supporting actions for teachers, identification of facilitation responsibility, and an understanding that change takes time, sometimes years, to see any sense of implementation (Hord & Huling-Austin, 1986). By examining the kinds of instructional change and different forms of evidence suggesting change (Fullan, 2008), this study explores multiple variables, such as clarity and quality, influencing implementation (Fullan, 2001). Given the Latvian curriculum writers' commonly held sentiment that Latvians are Holocaust fatigued (Misco, 2007a), I looked to disentangle individual teacher content preferences from the perceived strengths and weaknesses of the curriculum. In addition, the delicate balancing of old and new in post-communist curriculum development has a tremendous impact on implementation (Laanemets, 2003), which prompted constant consideration of this dialectical interplay.

If we think about implementation simplistically, we might imagine curricularist *x* creating materials *y*, which are adopted by teacher *z*, culminating in the precise and exact use of the curriculum in the classroom *as envisioned by the curricularist* without modification. The *fidelity* paradigm offers this congruence of what is intended and achieved, which fits within a producer-consumer model (Aoki, 1984). In the main, this view of implementation is uncomplicated and unproblematic—there is little need to describe processes of fidelity implementation because it is either largely "successful" or it is not (Leithwood, 1990). Although largely discredited (Aoki, 1984), the *fidelity* paradigm is distinct from the main competing paradigm, *mutual adaptation*, which takes into account local contexts, honors the professionalism of the teacher, and assumes diverse realities, meanings, and agents adapting curriculum in different ways. Criticisms of the fidelity versus adaptation distinction include a finding of teachers who actually engage in curriculum adaptation, yet claim fidelity. Moreover, the fidelity versus adaptation distinction assumes that fidelity implementation is a deliberate decision, when it may be an issue of undeveloped professional expertise and curriculum literacy (Ben-Perentz, 1990). A third paradigm also exists, *curriculum enactment*, the antipode of the fidelity paradigm, which emphasizes teachers and students as the designers and implementers of a curriculum and discounts many normative concerns external to the classroom (Hlebowitsh, 2005).

I chose to use the mutual adaptation paradigm as a lens for this study, primarily because the fidelity approach does not allow for teacher modification of the curriculum, which in the context of Latvian schools, with this particular topic, would be a fatuous expectation. Moreover, a fidelity lens sharpens our attention to the extent the curriculum was implemented as is, rather than understanding the process of how teachers used the curriculum and what factors played into their decision making. Finally, the curriculum enactment paradigm does not encompass the full complement of variables external to a classroom-based curriculum design that were integral to the curriculum deliberation design of the Holocaust curriculum under study, including overlapping historical, community, and political contexts.

In contrast to the fidelity and curriculum enactment paradigms, mutual adaptation emphasizes the "complexity of the context in which change takes place" (Cho, 1998, p. 3) and the reduction of space between "what is" and "what should be" through a series of tradeoffs. Within this paradigm, we cannot explore the teacher's role as "resisting" curricular changes—resistance is really a part of the fidelity lexicon. Nor can we think of materials as "teacher proof." Instead, within a mutual adaptation framework, we view practitioners as having authority and autonomy as curricularists with full decision making capacities and expertise. Part and parcel of this paradigm is relying on the " 'the wisdom of the practice' that is situational and implicit within the context in which a pedagogical judgment should be made by the teacher" (Cho, 1998, p. 20). For example, in this particular study, the context of Latvian classrooms is one of post-communism, nascent democratic government, little instructional time devoted to history, and a lack of a social studies tradition that leverages history to meet citizenship aims and goals. This is what Guba and Lincoln (1994) called "modified dualism" (p. 109), whereby the user (teacher) needs to transform curriculum into a unique context. Honoring of local context inherent in mutual adaptation dovetails with curriculum deliberation, which was the design theory that guided the curriculum-making process. Both curriculum deliberation (design) and mutual adaptation (implementation) are involved in a "dialectical relationship" among teachers, students, and subject matter (Aoki, 1984, p. 114).

Mutual adaptation takes into account the "slippages" that occur as teachers in all national educational systems deviate from "official" curricular policies, including time and topic allocations (Benavot & Resh, 2003, p. 172). Because implementation in this paradigm is not about compliance, but rather about balancing the normative and emergent while being responsive to the needs of children and society within the judgment of the teacher (Hlebowitsh, 2005), curriculum becomes filtered, rendered, and owned *by* the teacher, *for* the students, and *within* a local context. When designing curriculum with mutual adaptation in mind, it does not necessarily mean that the materials should be entirely open and devoid of structure. Although it would seem that offering procedural specification in the curriculum might be more closely related to fidelity expectations, offering some structure and specifications as to how it might unfold acts as a point of departure for the internal dialogue teachers need to have concerning the what, when, how, and why of their teaching role in relation to the innovation (Van Den Akker, 1988).

The curriculum deliberation writing process was designed in response to the challenges implementers face (Fullan, 1982). The use of the curriculum deliberation model was to act as a foil for many of these issues, beginning with teachers as curriculum authors, for only they know what can be implemented (Hlebowitsh, 2005). The main work of curriculum deliberation involves what Schwab (1973/1978) called the "juxtaposition of incommensurables" (p. 383). Values of commonplaces (teacher, students, subject matter, and milieu) are continually set aside and returned to through the evaluation and revaluation of incompatible ideas concerning what should be done to resolve the curricular problem. Parker (2003) likened the conclusion of this process to "forging together the alternatives and making a decision" (p. 105). Dewey (1922/1976) described it as a problem of wanting "things that are incompatible with one another; therefore, we have to make a choice of what we *really* want" (p. 134). In group deliberations, where part of the judgment, choice, and action concern what people value, the problems of making and exercising judgments are magnified (Reid, 1999). The *THLSP* achieved a diverse membership of deliberators, including teachers, historians, curricularists, administrators, and teacher educators. After months of writing and research, both domestically and abroad, the members of the deliberative team finally agreed on the set of topics and learning experiences that would enter into the middle school and high school project textbooks. Choice and action represented a final phase in the deliberative process but not *finality*, which is illusory given the tentative nature of decisions concerning practical problems. New data, evidence, and changes in reality or commonplaces might, quite quickly, demand a reconceptualization of the problem and command renewed deliberations.

Country and Curriculum Context

In the case of Latvia, the Holocaust *as it occurred* in Latvia, the overlapping historical contexts of dual occupation, Latvian collaboration in the Holocaust, decades of Soviet occupation, and nascent democracy collectively provide context for this study. These overlapping contexts influence which historical narratives are silenced or neglected, to be sure, but also how schools engage in citizenship education through these narratives.

Prior to the outbreak of war in Europe, Nazi Germany and the Soviet Union signed the furtive Molotov-Ribbentrop Pact (1939), which divided Poland, the Baltic States, and other territory into spheres of Soviet and German influence. During the Soviet occupation of Latvia (1940–41) thousands of Latvians were deported and murdered, some suggesting that these acts constituted genocide or crimes against humanity (Cimdina, 2003; Sneidere, 2005). The murder of the Jews in Latvia, during Nazi occupation, was the gravest crime and tragedy in the history of Latvia (Erglis, 2005; Stranga, 2005). Soon after Nazi Germany abrogated the treaty and occupied Latvia (1941), Germans and native collaborators murdered over 70,000 Latvian Jews, as well as 20,000 Jews from other territories under Nazi German control. The history of the Holocaust in Latvia is an extremely complicated and controversial history, one which involved numerous responses among Latvian individuals and institutions within the context of multiple occupations (Misco, 2009).

In response to a perceived pervasive historical silence surrounding this history, the *THLSP* produced and disseminated 1,000 teacher books and 10,000 student books, conducted a national conference to showcase the new curriculum, and offered a series of teacher trainings. The new curriculum included 38 lesson plans, designed through curriculum deliberation, which cover topics ranging from local Holocaust history in Krustpils (Latvia) to Latvian rescuers, perpetrators, and collaborators.

An additional contextual layer concerns the relationship of Latvians and Russians. The majority of Latvian residents speak the official language of Latvian, and Russian-speakers constitute the largest minority language plurality. Ethnic Latvians constitute 58% of the population (Central Intelligence Agency, 2010) and the proximity of Latvia to Russia has resulted in economic opportunities for those knowing the Russian language. The Latvian government has tended to focus on ties to the East, however, evident in Latvia's accession to the European Union and the North Atlantic Treaty Organization (NATO). Yet given the tension stemming from Russia's past occupations of Latvia, and the current claims of discrimination against ethnic Russians within Latvia, a general acrimony between ethnic Russian and ethnic Latvians exists.

Given the large plurality of ethnically Russian, but Latvian citizens (30%), contentious parallel schooling systems based on language of instruction have persisted (Crawford, 2002). For example, when a large proportion of Russian parents began sending children to Latvian-speaking schools, officials responded by suggesting the undesirability of "mixed" schools due to the potential "negative effects" for Latvian students (Silova, 2002, p. 466). Fearful of the 'mixing' effects associated with increased enrollment of Russian students in Latvian-speaking schools, policy makers decided to increase the Latvianization of minority schools, thereby providing Latvian language skills but maintaining separate institutions (Batelaan, 2002).

Relevant Literature

Most of our understanding of the implementation effects of curriculum deliberation design when applied to controversial problems in cross-cultural and post-communist settings is anecdotal. However, a number of studies demonstrate the promises and challenges of the method in U.S. contexts. For example, in a study of doctoral programs, Page (2001) found the curriculum deliberation process of particular value because it combined normative curriculum questions with a deliberative process directed toward practical problems. In Page's study, the faculty engaged in pragmatic reasoning with an eye toward establishing common ground that affirmed diversity and variation of thought, thereby placing differences in a harmonious context. Another study pointed to a university's successful employment of curriculum deliberation to more effectively address special education and inclusion (Poetter, Everington, & Jetty, 2001). Yet, there are insufficient data describing the process of implementation and implementation paradigms (Cho, 1998; Carless, 1998; Fullan, 2008), and the longitudinal studies on implementation of any sort of curriculum do not examine how cross-cultural curriculum projects in post-communist states fare. In addition, research is needed that illuminates how curriculum designs and teacher requirements influence the process of implementation (Penuel, Fishman, Yamaguchi, & Gallagher, 2007). Therefore, this study also seeks to fill a gap in the curriculum deliberation knowledge base by examining a large-scale project in a post-communist setting five years after the curriculum's distribution.

Curriculum Implementation

A facile approach to a study of this kind might explore the extent to which teachers are *using* the new curriculum. But implementation is not this straightforward—it means different things to different people and this variability is compounded within different ontological eras of curriculum theory. For example, only since the 1970s have we witnessed more wide-ranging thought about what implementation might mean (Fullan, 1982). Prior to that time, implementation primarily focused on outcomes of learning in terms of the intended curriculum instead of the *process* leading to a variety of possible realities, and thus leading to an array of educational experiences (Leithwood, 1990).

A purely utilitarian approach to implementation might look for the "actual use of an innovation or what an innovation consists of in practice" (Fullan & Pomfret, 1977, p. 336). This view was eventually criticized for its simplicity in constructing implementation as the delivery of an innovation (Hord & Huling-Austin, 1986). Some have taken a more expansive approach to implementation, thinking of it as "not an event but a change process," which is highly dependent on context (Cho, 1998, p. 29). In this sense, those features informing curricular change within a particular context include the teacher, the curriculum, the curriculum developer's intentions, strategies used, and pupil responses (Carless, 1998, p. 353). Other curricularists focused on implementation as an *event* where teachers learn new roles and unlearn old roles. These events are marked by changes in behavior, attitudes, and beliefs (Van Den Akker, 1988).

We might also think of implementation as getting curriculum to do *what we want it to do* in terms of "congruence between purpose and action," which includes teachers as curricularists exercising judgment and where implementation serves as a "point of departure" (Hlebowitsh, 2005, pp. 217–18). This last view embraces the idea of many possible outcomes, variables, and processes involved in implementation. If implementation is about what needs to change for an innovation to be employed, then we need to keep in mind that implementation can be nonexistent, superficial, partial, substantive, or occur in some other form (Fullan, 2007).

Conditions Leading to Implementation

By examining the kinds of instructional change and different forms of evidence suggesting change (Fullan, 2008), I actively pursued any factor that might influence implementation, with an eye toward the three categories and nine critical factors Fullan (2007) advanced:

1. Characteristics of change (need, clarity, complexity, quality)
2. Local characteristics (district, community, principal, teacher)
3. External factors (government and other agencies)

Each of these factors informed interview questions (Appendix), and the resulting data helped to answer each research question.

In terms of a priori expectations, the literature suggests that implementation is strengthened by developing materials locally, providing a regimen of ongoing training, and holding regular staff meetings dedicated to the curricular change (McLaughlin, 1976). The key feature for implementation is the teacher (Cho, 1998), and having collaborative colleagues at a school site helps to facilitate implementation through momentum and generativity (Hord & Huling-Austin, 1986; McLaughlin, 1993; Penuel et al., 2007). Curriculum reforms that fail often do so because they have ignored local context and culture. They are incomplete because they place too much emphasis on planning and not enough on action, or they are not open to the multiple realities that exist (Fullan, 2007).

The particular problem of silenced and controversial issues in curriculum implementation, such as the Holocaust in Latvia, naturally entails the problem of changing teaching behavior. In this case, a finding of weak or limited implementation may very well be more an issue of the planning and coordinating of the curriculum project and less an issue of dogmatic resistance (Fullan, 2007). In short, due to teacher time constraints and limited endorsement from central education authorities, teachers often lack the incentives and the time to change behavior. Sometimes the critical obstacle hinges on the "social and political winds" that blow through the school and "grab hold of the curriculum in a way that limits the range of expression that can emerge" (Hlebowitsh, 2005, p. 222). This challenge and others can ultimately be diluted by supportive school administrators and principals (Benavot & Resh, 2003), as well as teachers and community members.

Generally, it is difficult for teachers to change their roles, especially with new instructional strategies and lack of background knowledge on the topic (Van Den Akker, 1988). In addition, time becomes an expensive price to pay for implementation (Hord & Huling-Austin, 1986). Trainings and support are important to mitigate these challenges (Carless, 1998), but single trainings are not as effective as serial trainings designed specifically in response to perceived challenges (McLaughlin, 1976). Ideally, there is monitoring, coaching, and professional development that dovetail with what teachers currently do in order to release the potential of adaptive work (Penuel et al., 2007).

Schooling is supposed to challenge local traditions (Hlebowitsh, 2005), but this is often easier said than done. Even those ebullient about change can be disillusioned if there is insufficient support (Carless, 1988). In order for change to occur, teachers need to have a good understanding of the proposed curricular change because people will "always misinterpret and misunderstand some aspect of the purpose or practice of something that is new to them" (Fullan, 1991, p. 355). Too often, curriculum planning fails in implementation because we do not take into account local context enough or we are too unaware of the challenges teachers face (Fullan, 2007).

Another key undermining element is the lack of time to plan for implementation (Penuel et al., 2007), which is certainly the case in Latvia as teachers are woefully underpaid and overworked (Soros Foundation, 2001). Because the intention of the curriculum writers was to unleash a more substantive treatment of the topic, we hoped students would have the opportunity to ask questions and engage in protracted discussions, essential forms of inquiry to be sure, but also the result of teachers being more comfortable with the topic (Penuel et al., 2007). Having comfort with topics comes about through greater knowledge, but this depends on teachers having the time to explore the curriculum. Again, a central issue around implementation is the issue of teacher planning time.

Another key issue is that teachers do not exist *sui generis* in implementation. The essence of change relies upon the development of meaning—meaning in terms of people working together and of ideas and individuals enjoying connections (Fullan, 2007). Given the importance context plays in implementation, the post-Soviet residue very much informs the reality that "teachers transform curriculum materials into learning experiences available to the students by means of teachers' personal knowledge, shaped by previous experiences and their belief systems" (Cho, 1998, p. 25). Historical and intellectual heritage are part of the meaning that teachers make about education, curricular expectations, and the role of history.

Assumptions and Expectations

A great deal of sagacious advice from implementation theory and practice scholars helps to frame the assumptions and expectations of this study. Chief among the tocsins are to not "be seduced into looking for the silver bullet" (Fullan, 2007, p. 125) and to be skeptical of the "façade of change," whereby some form of implementation appears to have occurred, but with very little actual impact (Carless, 1998, p. 353). In addition, Fullan (2007) offered the following assumptions for consideration:

1. Do not assume your version of change should be the one that is implemented—engage others in their realities.
2. Assume that any innovation requires implementers to make their own meaning because implementation is really a "process of clarification" (p. 123).
3. Assume conflict is inevitable and part of successful change.

4. Assume people need pressure to change but change depends on other factors too.
5. Assume effective change takes time—it may take 2–3 years.
6. Do not assume the reason for lack of implementation is a rejection of the values of the change—there are many possible reasons for lack of implementation.
7. Do not expect all or most people to change.
8. Assume you will need a plan based on these assumptions.
9. Assume that change depends not only on knowledge but political and institutional context.
10. Assume that changing the culture is the real agenda, not implementing single innovations.

Given what we know about a nuanced view of implementation within the paradigm of mutual adaptation, just what might we consider to be successful implementation? Clearly this will depend on who is making the judgement and deciding on the parameters of success. Because gauging success is such a normative and slippery affair, success through the lens constructed here may very well be different from success viewed through other lenses; much depends on what is elevated as desirable and important (Hord & Huling-Austin, 1986).

For example, we could look at the conditions leading to implementation, the problems teachers faced, strategies for resolution, feasibility, capabilities, policy changes needed, or other factors (Leithwood, 1990). Instead, I chose to eschew this sort of evaluation in favor of understanding the processes taking place within multiple realities, with the primary purpose of informing future curriculum projects dealing with controversial issues. Therefore, the research questions and analyses do not attempt to judge teachers or community contexts, but rather better understand the practices and phenomena that are desirable for leading to the kind of implementation that releases the full and ready use of the curriculum to prepare democratic citizens. These questions also seek to identify what needs to be done to make implementation realized and describe teacher practices in relation to the stages of implementation (Leithwood, 1990). This approach moves beyond the exactness of the teachers' implementation, which would fit more closely within a fidelity paradigm study (Cho, 1998), and instead squarely focuses on the generative value for future projects.

I also explored the degree to which incentives, encouragement, and discouragement played out between administrators and teachers, both within schools and districts. The curriculum writers in the grant project consciously considered students, teachers, historians, governmental officials, pedagogical experts, packaging, utility, methodology, standards, representation of Latvians, and a number of other stake-holders and variables. This study offers a sense of the actual extent and scope of implementation.

Methodology

This study employed qualitative methods primarily because they are well-suited for addressing research problems concerning norms, structures, conditions, and processes (Glaser & Strauss, 1967), features that are at the heart of this study's research questions. Moreover, these questions contain normative elements and assume a constructivist ontology, which undergirds qualitative methods and asserts that there is not one reality, but rather multiple interpretations and renderings of the world (Merriam, 2001).

In addition to exploring individual teachers and districts as case studies within a qualitative paradigm, I drew upon understandings gained through an earlier ethnographic study (Misco, 2007a), which included the history of the community, as well as the attitudes of community members, parents, educators, citizens, policy makers, and students. Because cultural context also involves shared beliefs, values, attitudes, and behavior patterns that inform what is and what should be (Patton, 1990), this study sought out the constructed meanings of educational commonplaces, including students, teachers, and subject matter (Schwab, 1973/1978). In addition, given the mutual adaptation paradigm informing this study, I was keenly interested in the implementation in terms of "discovering underlying assumptions, interests, values, motives, perspectives, root metaphors, and implications for action to improve the human condition" (Aoki, 1984, p. 117), all of which fit within post-positivistic inquiry (Lincoln & Guba, 1985).

During the course of this study I collected interview responses and field notes. I invited 60 teachers within the city-centers, suburbia, and outskirts of two Latvian cities: Liepāja and Riga and 40 of those (67%) chose to participate in semi-structured interviews. The *THLSP* had shipped textbooks to all 60 potential respondents, whose contact information was retrieved and in some cases updated by a Latvian interpreter I hired for the course of the study. In spite of the dissemination efforts, four of the respondents never actually received the curriculum.

I conducted five of the interviews in group form, one of which included three teachers, while the others were teacher pairs. The individual interviews lasted between 45 and 90 minutes and most group interviews were well over an hour in length. Although I intended to conduct all interviews individually, in these cases the teachers preferred to be interviewed with colleagues. The remaining 29 interviews were conducted in an individual format. Because schools within Latvia are conducted in either Russian or Latvian as the language of instruction, within each of these city regions I sought variance by conducting interviews in both Russian and Latvian schools, with experienced teachers as well as novices, and with teachers in schools representing all strata of socioeconomic environments. Of the 40 respondents, 15 were from Liepāja, including 5 from Russian-speaking schools. The 25 respondents from the Riga area included 17 teachers from Latvian-speaking schools and 8 from Russian-speaking schools.

The type of sampling I chose to use was therefore purposive as it sought out the typical cases of those teachers who received and enacted the curriculum (Miles & Huberman, 1994; Patton, 1990). Because a case can be a person, event, organization, program, or community, I decided to view the curriculum implementation in Latvia as a case, which was comprised of individual teachers who constitute sub-cases. Because of logistical and translation miscommunication, two teachers I interviewed received the curriculum but chose not to employ it. Finally, these "typical cases" may also be considered somewhat extreme or anomalous as many teachers in Latvia did not receive the curriculum and many of the teachers contacted reported that they either did not use the curriculum, did not receive the curriculum, or that they did not want to be interviewed. Many of the teachers declining an interview indicated that they had too much work to do and did not have time to participate in an interview. One in particular thought the research was "a waste of time," and that as teachers "[we] do not benefit from such things."

I recorded field notes of conversations with other individuals who have a stake in Latvian education, and also of classroom and school visits. I kept descriptive notes of various contextual features concerning the milieu, such as Russian beliefs about Latvian discrimination directed towards them, economic challenges affecting schools, students, and teachers, and political maneuverings outside the classroom door. When used in concert with the interviews, these two data streams helped record teacher beliefs and contextual nuance within a thick description of practices and processes, an approach that fits well with implementation studies (Leithwood, 1990).

Rather than apply analytical tools *a priori*, I drew from the suggestions of numerous qualitative methodologists, as well as the data, to inform my emergent approach. I reduced data in ways that allowed for interpretations through a process of dissecting, dividing, and reassembling data into understandable forms (LeCompte & Schensul, 1999), while attempting to retain conceptuality and not dilute thick description into thin description (Steiner-Khamsi, Torney-Purta, & Schwille, 2002). I engaged in simultaneous data analysis through multiple musings of the data during, immediately after, and in days following the interviews. As much as possible, I attempted to adhere to the guidelines set forth by Bogdan and Biklen (1992) that suggest writing observer comments during the process, memos to self, and a general cognizant attunement to all facets of the research process and the subjects' point of view.

In order to include discrepant data and to ensure the correct representation of codes that symbolized the variety of data collected, I engaged in multiple readings, meditations, and annotations of interview data. For purposes of credibility and accuracy, I reached and cut across multiple interview data sources (Merriam, 2001; Miles & Huberman, 1994). I went about analysis by locating concepts that "help us to make sense of what is going on in the scenes documented by the data" (Hammersley & Atkinson, 1995, p. 209), a process that works dialectically with data collection. Data analysis did not therefore start when data collection ended, but rather it enjoyed constant interplay between conceptualizing meaning and redirecting subsequent data collection. The analysis led to a recurring comparison of incidents and inductively conceived categories (Merriam, 2001).

Ultimately this study was responsive to the call for synthesizing multiple implementation studies (Penuel et al., 2007), with the hope that this and other projects can determine features that ultimately *work* for mutual adaptation. All instances of data collection and analysis were therefore aimed at producing grounded understandings in order to inductively arrive at transferability for future trends and situations (Misco, 2007b). Although findings in one context are not necessarily applicable to another context, they have the potential to generate hypotheses for other current or future contexts and can inform policy and practice implications not only for the context under study, but for similar contexts as well (Hahn & Alviar-Martin, 2008; Schofield, 1990).

Findings

Each emerging theme in this study fits within the Schwabian (1973/1978) curriculum deliberation framework of students, teachers, and subject matter. The categories and related themes inform the nature of implementation in a variety of Latvian schools, including the obstacles, variables, pathways, challenges, and nuanced features that collectively provide some sense of what happened to the curriculum.

Students

Teacher perceptions of students. The respondents were keenly aware of students as they engaged in their curriculum decision making. For example, one respondent overheard prejudical and anti-Semitic remarks among youth in the community and therefore decided to provide a more substantive treatment of the Holocaust, outside of the Ministry of Education's planned curriculum. Although respondents cautioned that students do not typically encounter these attitudes, many clearly wanted to use the space of the public school to ensure the only source of Holocaust historical knowledge for students was not outlying public opinion. One history teacher in a Russian-speaking school in Riga also cited examples of students encountering Holocaust deniers and others students who "don't feel comfortable with the topic" because of their relatives' role in the event. A teacher in a Latvian-speaking school in Riga commented on student knowledge at the beginning of a course as being either erroneous or inadequate, including "anti-Holocaust" as "Holocaust denial voices are growing." In these cases, respondents counter other sources of knowledge with rational consideration in the classroom. The perceived lack of knowledge (or actual lack of knowledge) among students provides motivation for some respondents to discuss this topic in classes.

Part of the limited knowledge base is attributed to parents, who in some cases "don't know anything—yet they provide the history." A teacher in a rural Latvian-speaking school outside of Liepāja explained that students are not resistant to the topic but "they will take what you offer—they are blank slates. If we talk about personal experience and the 20th century and the cooperative farming, that is much more interesting and that's what they know about. The Holocaust doesn't touch their family. Other topics relate more, cooperative farming and the like."

One frustration teachers expressed during the interviews was students' lack of knowledge about the Holocaust, evident in one 12th grade student's statement in Riga, who "thought the Holocaust was a bachelor." In general, student knowledge of local and general Holocaust history very much "depends upon the family and what the attitude is among family members for instructing their kids prior to grade 9." When students are exposed to the topic in schools, many are shocked. A beginning teacher in a Latvian-speaking school in Liepāja noted that they "don't realize something like that can happen—it is a shocking moment."

The teacher in the rural Latvian-speaking school suggested her students have "no idea what it is [Holocaust]—some thought it was a big hill or mountain. In our town some families were deported. There was not a passing on of this history here—there is nothing positive to share." Another teacher from Liepāja recalled how families used to provide more of this history for their kids, but "now they don't talk about it at home. So, oftentimes the information they know is smaller and shallower than it used to be, leaving stereotypes to arise from a lack of knowledge and information."

Student interest. Respondents located implementation of the topic broadly, including the *THLSP* curriculum, in terms of student interest. If students are interested in the topic, and discussion develops, then "we can do more. It all depends." But a teacher in a

Russian-speaking school in Riga noted that her 12th grade students' "lack of communication skills" ultimately means "they can't work in groups," an important instructional approach for teaching the topic. Cooperative learning discussions, document analysis, and presentations all hinge on the successful interaction of students. As a result, she found that students "simply get to know that there was a Holocaust" and very seldom do they ask "why Jews?"

Another teacher from a Russian-speaking school in Riga asserted her 12th grade students were reading at 4th grade levels and the only topics or mediums that resonate with them "involve computers." The students "hate books" and "starting four years ago they became completely different; even if I give them a computer task they seem to have ADD." The Riga respondents from a Russian-speaking school who do not use or did not receive the curriculum suggested many materials seem "too complicated for middle school students; they need some more background in order to move into some of the complexities . . . need to focus more on the basics." Beliefs that children "do not want to read," which for some of these non-implementing respondents meant a reliance on movies and PowerPoint slideshows in an attempt to use modern mediums that attract student interest, was certainly a sub-theme.

Some students also brought documents to class "proving the Holocaust did not happen." Others exhibited insatiable interest on the topic, asking questions such as "Why here? How did it develop? and why Jews?" Although one Russian-speaking teacher from Riga admitted that the topic "is not very popular in Latvia," she found that students will often advance their own curiosities and pursue the topic in tangentially related classes, other course topics, or during their project weeks if they do not fully satisfy their curiosity during regular class time.

In most cases, teachers determined the extent of coverage, and therefore implementation of the curriculum, based on student interest. As a teacher from a Latvian-speaking school in Riga remarked, "it all depends on the kids and if there are children who are interested it is very good additional material I can give, but that doesn't happen every year." The criterion of student interest transferred to the curriculum and the use of materials, whereby teachers acted on the basis of "what they need or want" and "it really depends on the kids." If teachers were not actively attuned to student interest and were disinterested themselves, then the topic and the curriculum had very little hope for treatment in the classroom.

Teachers

Academic freedom. Both *perceived* and *actual* academic freedom help explain the degree and kind of implementation of the curriculum. For example, two different respondents from Russian-speaking schools in Riga remarked that "I can choose what I need" and "nothing is influencing this treatment; nothing limits." This freedom worked both ways, however, in terms of teachers feeling liberated to employ materials and teachers having the freedom to choose not to teach the topic at all. A teacher from a Latvian-speaking school in Liepāja indicated, "nobody says 'don't talk about it'—it's very individual for the teacher; it all [treatment of the topic] depends on the teacher."

Yet when I asked if they would be able to restructure the curriculum design of the course, to perhaps make a history course thematically based or taught in reverse, most respondents indicated this would be problematic and thought they would be unable to exert that level of control over the direction of the curriculum. Similar to the situation of teachers in the United States, whose curricular freedom is limited by calibration and curriculum mapping movements, the freedom of teachers in Latvia is, in the main, localized to topics. They either have or perceive to have the freedom to use whatever materials they wish and teach with whatever methods they choose, but within the parameters of an epoch or specific topic. Conversely, teachers also have the freedom to quickly move through the topic in cursory ways. These liberties and freedoms were certainly expressed by many respondents who do not go beyond two or three 40-minute lessons on the Holocaust in a course, primarily because "there is too little time for this; sometimes I have to stop them asking questions because we must go on to discuss other subjects; there is not enough time for that [the Holocaust].

One teacher from a Russian-speaking school in Riga noted the "complete freedom" of her position and the "lack of negative influence" on the topic from anyone within or outside of her school. She indicated that "the longer I work at the school the more flexibility I give myself." Interviews also revealed that the curriculum is more attractive to teachers who perceive themselves to have academic freedom and it is also responsive to one of the common limitations to academic freedom—the time to prepare new lessons. One teacher from a Latvian-speaking school in Liepāja highlighted this feature as "it means teachers don't have so much time to gather resources and make classes better and interesting and innovative." As a result, she noted that the curriculum:

> Wasn't a waste of money and resources but it wasn't used cover to cover; the reality is that teachers can draw on what they want and take what they want and use it in the classroom. A very important fact—they were available for schools and in the right amount needed. If they had to make copies, plan how many students, it's more work. All the extra work means you don't do it. In this case, it's a big help, these materials, they are ready to go and ready to use. It's all about making things easy and ready for use on day one.

Teachers who did not experience enough planning time or had little interest in the topic, and consequently did not put forth energies for uncovering it within the courses, were among those with little or no implementation of the curriculum. As a teacher in a Russian-speaking school on the fringe of Liepāja noted,

> if I would stick to the [national curriculum] standards, I would not teach it [the Holocaust] at all. But I know the right way to manipulate the program; if there is a checkup on sticking to the standards, that's ok, I can prove I'm doing it the right way. As a teacher, you find ways to manipulate the program.

This respondent is at the end of his career and views himself as an empowered and somewhat subversive agent. If not, he said teaching would be "boring." These kinds of teachers, who are willing to view responsibilities and professional judgment outside the codified parameters of the school or Ministry of Education, were those who engaged in the most comprehensive implementation of the curriculum. These teachers were willing to sacrifice other topics—giving them less attention in order to allocate more instructional time for the Holocaust.

Many of the high implementation teachers I found were in Russian-speaking schools, where I noticed a great deal more perceived liberty and willingness to employ the curricular materials as compared to Latvian-speaking schools. Part of this difference might be attributed to a general disconnection from state policies, which would cohere with their resistance of state-mandated instructional time allocations of the Latvian language in Russian schools, as well as less of a connection to the Latvian nation-state. It may also be attributed to more comfort with the topic because the curriculum implicates Germans and Latvians, not Russians.

Another emergent theme concerning academic freedom entails teachers who have administrators explicitly endowing them with the freedom to teach the Holocaust. As a teacher from a Russian-speaking school in Riga noted, there is a schedule for the topics, and "the Holocaust is not on there, but there are topics on totalitarianism, international politics, etc., so it gets included in different topics. There is no definite topic on the Holocaust, rather integrating it into the existing structure." Although a teacher from a Latvian-speaking school in Riga remarked that "there is a lot to teach—we have to teach according to the school programs and there are no exceptions to this case," those with administrators actively supporting their efforts, as well as citizenship goals, generally enjoyed more discretion for employing the curriculum.

Finding other places in the macrocurriculum. In addition to academic freedom, the respondents demonstrated extensive use of the curriculum when they were willing and able to find other places in the macrocurriculum for the topic to fit. A teacher from a Russian-speaking school in Liepāja felt that "there is nothing holding me back to teach it—only the standards—and I have the obligation and opportunity to find ways to use it." A teacher from a Russian-speaking school in Riga also reported having success integrating "the lessons from the curriculum with the textbook—fascism, totalitarianism, anti-Semitism, Holocaust—this is all one unit—lots to cover in WWII. We start from Poland, and then to Baltic States, all the while discussing anti-Semitism." Others found opportunities when working with teachers in other disciplines, such as language arts teachers who cover issues of xenophobia and tolerance.

The most widespread implementation was found among history teachers who teach other subjects. For example, a teacher in a Russian-speaking school in Riga was limited to teaching about the Holocaust using the *THLSP* curriculum "in four lessons," but found she was also able to address it in the political science class she teaches, as well as when covering "topics of discrimination, xenophobia—I take it and use it for all these things. I take this book [the curriculum] and I have examples." Because the curriculum contains "ready to use sources with broad appeal" teachers are able to use it when discussing "laws, power, distribution of power, etc." This approach to seeking points of contact within the larger curriculum, both within history and outside the social sciences, seemed to make a significant difference for time allotted to Holocaust history. As one teacher from a Latvian-speaking school in Riga suggested, "if we view it strictly in terms of the prescribed curriculum, then [I teach] one or two lessons; when also teaching other courses (political science) and hitting topics of some relation (Genocide, Cambodia)—then we can get this curriculum in as well." But "as to the basic requirement, I can only talk about it for 40 minutes for one study year" and this is typically in grades 9 and 12.

Similar to "homeroom" in the United States and "upbringing hour" in the former USSR, the "class masters" course was another entry point for the curriculum. If history teachers serve as the primary instructor of this course, there is an opportunity for implementation given the absence of a regular formal curriculum. For example, one teacher from a Latvian-speaking school in Liepāja who teaches this course claimed to use the curriculum anytime "good and evil come up." Another way teachers implement the curriculum into other instructional spaces is within "project week." Typically dedicated to one week in the spring semester, this is an opportunity for students to create culminating projects on topics of their choosing. Though rare, some students select the Holocaust or the Holocaust in Latvia for this project and the teacher provides them with the curriculum as a resource. Also, students who take a special interest in the topic can access the curriculum for exploratory and enrichment ends.

Collaboration. Another distinguishing characteristic of teachers and schools providing substantive implementation of the curriculum has to do with the professional interaction found in the department, school, or larger education community. Collaboration with other teachers, administrators, or educational stakeholders is foundational to teachers adapting the curriculum to their unique educational spaces, and moving implementation beyond partial fidelity.

For example, in one Russian school I visited, three teachers were fully committed to the topic and the curriculum. For them, teaching about the Holocaust and using this curriculum very much rested upon collegiality—they would share teaching ideas, tests, videos, and a common materials room. They also enjoyed an administration that actively encouraged Holocaust education in order to deflate a growing sense of nationalism and xenophobia in the local community. Other characteristics of this close-knit group's teaching included the use of guest speakers, field trips to both local and European memorials and camps, a rich school library, and a diverse student and faculty population. These teachers have won national teaching awards and the school enjoys more monetary resources than other schools due to their size (1,500 students). In short, this particular school was anomalous but it represented the best case scenario of implementation opportunity, primarily due to collaboration within the school, and the culture of the history department in particular.

Another common thread among those implementing the curriculum with a sense of autonomy and judgment was their regular attendance at professional development conferences. For example, a teacher in a Russian-speaking school in Riga recalled going "even as far as Daugavpils [230 kilometers] to hear a famous history teacher who gathers materials about survivors and rescuers." One teacher in a Latvian-speaking school in Liepāja and her colleague, an art teacher, decided to respond to the invitation to receive the *THLSP* curriculum and training primarily because they knew the Latvians who wrote the curriculum. Given their past experiences with these individuals, respondents found their reputations to be a "big draw." Another group of teachers from Liepāja who habitually seek out professional development opportunities noted that any materials from "Soros and IAC [aforementioned NGO]," was worthwhile. Therefore, the extent to which teachers are active, connected, professional, and vibrant life-long learners serve as indicators of their willingness not only to consider new curricula, but also to implement it with thoughtful judgment.

Similar to the reputation of curriculum project personnel, a teacher from a Latvian-speaking school in Liepāja also remarked on how important the trainings were in shaping implementation:

> If they [other teachers] have been in the seminar and tried; if they go through the same process, they have a connection in their mind, then there is security; they know it works and that it's cool. If you just give it to a different teacher, it's different; you don't rely that it will come out good and have the same results you would like to see.

During some of the trainings with other curriculum projects, "people would just read the paper," but the *THLSP* curriculum trainings brought forth an atmosphere that one teacher "really appreciated" and he was "truly engaged and developed a wonderful feeling about the curriculum." In short, the recurring theme I found at schools adapting the curriculum to their needs with a great sense of integrity and thoughtfulness enjoyed a synergy brought on by relationships, collegiality, and meaning.

Changes in behavior. As a result of this study's purposeful sampling, the respondents I interviewed represented the implementation segment of the larger population of Latvian history teachers. Yet, perhaps the only commonality among these teachers in terms of the way they implemented the curriculum is that of variance: The teachers' responses reflected different effects on their teaching and planning of Holocaust education. For example, a teacher in a Russian-speaking school in Liepāja commented that "at first it seemed there wouldn't be much to use, but as I read more, I found topics that would be applicable for multiple classes." Part of this open-mindedness stemmed from being ready at this particular time in Latvia's history to address the past, as well as dissatisfaction with the way in which textbooks portray this and other topics with "numbers and just basic facts." Textbooks do treat the Holocaust and the Holocaust as it occurred in Latvia, but suffer from both selective and cursory coverage (Klišāne, Goldmane, Klaviaņa, Misāne, & Straube, 2007).

One of the hopes expressed by curriculum writers during the design process was that the curriculum would have collateral effects for democratic pedagogy. In other words, not only would the curriculum lead to more provocative treatment of the topic, but that it would also develop and strengthen the instructional side of Latvian classrooms—not just for the Holocaust, but for other topics as well. Although respondents indicated that there was really "no change to teaching strategies" as the "methods are not new," the curriculum did seem to reinforce some of the more interactive and engaging ways of teaching they had exposure to. For example, many respondents indicated their fondness for photographs, political cartoons, statistical data tables, reference sources, discussion questions, and cooperative learning activities in the curriculum. One teacher from a Russian-speaking school in Riga indicated that although the ways of teaching are not new, the:

> Ministry of Education doesn't offer such good materials to us because, in fact, the materials of this and Soros—these are the two things we can use in addition to the school book and what the problem is here is that there is no institution in Latvia that is concerned with methodology of teaching . . . it helps me a lot to really teach, in terms of methods . . . I feel the Ministry does not work to help teachers become good teachers.

Another teacher from a Russian-speaking school in Riga stated that the "methodology is very different in the book—it's very different for me," the difference is that it "helps students think, not just feel" and "these discussion techniques fit not only for these lessons but others as well."

A younger teacher in a Latvian-speaking school in Liepāja reported that the "older teachers believe it is lecture only—this material encourages cooperative learning, expressing opinions, listening to others, thinking critically and the older ones are not using it." This respondent cited the positive nature of the visual materials and how "students connect better with these; interactive, student-centered, constructivist . . . in the university everything was taught in lecture form" and "reading materials is not very appealing for students." For those utilizing more interactive methods, they ultimately found themselves having more time on "life before the Holocaust and the life of children . . . not just historical context, but also giving the students the understanding of what the German attitude was and how it developed." Although "most Latvian teachers during the last year have had lots of training on interactive teaching and know a lot of these methods," "only a small portion of them use them as everyday strategies in their classrooms." The main reason for this is not a lack of knowledge of *how* to teach, but because "they are still thinking they cannot put knowledge into students to be successful in exams [by using interactive teaching] . . . It means they don't use these strategies very often."

Eclectic use. Another hallmark of mutual adaptation is the eclectic use of the curriculum. There are 38 total lessons in the curriculum. Some teachers decided to try each lesson in different years, given the time restrictions within a class. One teacher in a Russian-speaking school in Liepāja taught "every lesson in the middle school book with the exception of three." Others found that the coverage of Jewish resistance in the textbook is inadequate, so their primary use is of the data tables in the middle school book as a supplement. Another respondent used the curriculum to help students understand discrimination, in its ultimate form during the Holocaust, from "not 6 million but to individual stories." One teacher from a Russian-speaking school in Riga expressed appreciation for the design of the curriculum as separate lessons because this provides "the freedom to select what I think is important and also adapt for my needs. It helps to also develop discussion and group work." A teacher in a Latvian-speaking school in Riga implemented the curriculum by having students compare it to their regular school textbook, while her colleague had students explore the "reference sources, which are not found in a school book." Another teacher from a Latvian-speaking school in Riga focused on "provoking discussions and we can't always predict reactions. With school books, they read certain materials and then it stops." Generally speaking, within a mutual adaptation paradigm, respondents commented on how they like to "experiment" with their teaching and how they used the lessons eclectically because they "don't like scripted things."

In addition to instructional strategy changes and the eclectic use of the materials, respondents also expressed how their knowledge of this period of history changed as a result of the curriculum and how this ultimately transferred to a change in comfort level with the topic. Consequently, they allocated more time to the Holocaust in their course curriculum. Similar to the promise of implementation cited earlier (Penuel et al., 2007), a teacher from a Latvian-speaking school in Riga experienced "very much a change in comfort, due to a change in knowledge," and another found that before the curriculum they were "speaking more about anti-Semitism and the definition of the Holocaust. Now, we focus more on the actual event—how and why it happened." In such cases the curriculum has served more as an informational tool and does not necessarily change methodological practice but results in teachers being more knowledgeable. One respondent found that this topic is new for students and another suggested "they [students] know nothing about this time." Another teacher from a Latvian-speaking school in Riga found students learned a great deal about the local Holocaust history and that the curriculum revealed that students "can't be ignorant about it."

However, four respondents in Latvian-speaking schools indicated very little or no marked change in teaching practice as a result of the curriculum. One Riga teacher felt it had "no profound impact for me, but it's good to have another material." A teacher from Liepāja positioned herself in defensive ways to not changing practice or devoting more time to the topic:

> The subject about equality is very important at all times. If we look at materials they should be generally spread out—teach about equality, not just the Holocaust; we are just so into the Holocaust—we are taught to never repeat it, but Latvians have never been the aggressive people—do we need to worry about this nation of Latvians doing something like that?

Two respondents from Liepāja directed my attention "to the period 1940 to 1950" and how "we have more important events [in that decade] to talk about." Moreover, because there is "nothing in exams" on the topic, these teachers both provide one lesson in high school and one in middle school. One of these respondents decided not to move beyond the study of rescuers, which often overemphasizes this portion of the population when compared to bystanders and perpetrators, while the other proclaimed that the curriculum contained "nothing very new—similar to what we received earlier."

The Subject Matter

Curricular need. The original formulation of the curriculum project did not contain a provision for a comprehensive needs assessment. In the years preceding the *THLSP*, two other Holocaust education curricula were distributed to some Latvian schools. The Museum of Occupation in Riga authored *Holokausts*, which contains a great deal of primary source documents on placards. The other, *Tell Ye Your Children*, is more of a narrative book outlining the Holocaust in broad strokes. The *THLSP* attempted to advance this effort by providing ready-to-use lesson plans on a variety of Holocaust topics.

It was therefore not surprising to find respondents who felt that they had sufficient materials to guide their planning and enactment of Holocaust-related learning experiences. This belief was especially common among respondents who viewed the curriculum as a rigid directive from the Ministry and did not choose to manipulate time allotments for topics. One respondent simply stated: "I have everything [I need] and it is only two classes." Another teacher from Riga echoed this sentiment by indicating "we have so many materials" and some defended their school's ability to construct the appropriate lessons, claiming "we have very creative people here; we use many innovative materials. So honestly, no, we have enough literature on the Holocaust." One teacher from a Latvian-speaking school in Riga proposed a solution to the time and materials issue:

> Having two lessons in the program for the Holocaust but all these big books of lessons . . . Perhaps it would be good to have that as well as a smaller version for one or two or three lessons for the teacher who would like to but is afraid of the time limitations. Maybe [producing] two lessons—"the best of."

However, this approach is clearly a fidelity one, whereby the Ministry of Education or some other agency would judge two lessons to be of supreme value, teachers would ultimately implement them, and the topic would be "covered" without allowing individual teachers in unique contexts to decide on the ideal content, strategies, scope, and sequence for their classes.

A prominent theme among those who felt the existent materials were sufficient concerned the internet and the sources available through that medium. One teacher from a Latvian-speaking school in Riga who was sent the curriculum but did not receive it indicated that "we have had lots of curriculum" and she did not think additional materials were needed. Those who did not receive the materials suggested "there is so much concerning this on the internet." Another teacher from a Russian-speaking school in Riga who did receive the curriculum but rarely employed it asserted that:

> there are too many books, perhaps you should save paper—too much material—there is also much accessible online . . . we all get more than enough information through the internet and it's easily accessible and we copy it and make handouts of whatever is needed.

In some ways finding content on the internet represents an iterative step toward a full and open treatment of the topic in classrooms, for to use the internet to supply lessons rests on the assumption that teachers want to teach the topic and they are able to discern which content and sources are appropriate for their students. In short, teachers are exercising professional judgment on a historical topic that was once fraught with misinformation, ignorance, and avoidance. Alternatively, this may be a historian-focused route to accessing documents in order to produce lessons leading primarily to content mastery and missing the democratic citizenship components of addressing controversies, as well as a controversial history though more student-centered constructivist lessons.

Yet, 36 of the 40 respondents indicated that any addition of Holocaust curriculum materials is beneficial. One teacher from a Latvian-speaking school in Liepāja recalled that when she first received it "there was a lot available, but then I decided to pick up certain parts from this material." The willingness to try new curricula, even when other material exists, ties back to the open-mindedness and professionalism cited earlier. For another teacher from a Latvian-speaking school in Liepāja, the curriculum was seen as an improvement on the earlier work not only "because there are different children who could have more interest" but because *Tell Ye Your Children* is a "horror story" and *Holokausts* is "more of a document collection." Instead, the *THLSP* curriculum "has lesson plans—it's very flexible and evolving."

Other positive responses for the new curriculum included a teacher in a Latvian-speaking school in Riga who "did not know anything about the Holocaust" but after recent coursework and employing our curriculum feels quite comfortable teaching the topic. Respondents reflected on how we are still responding to the deficiencies of the 1990s when "there was a serious lack of materials" and some commented on how the more sources available, the more teachers can choose what to use and when to use it.

Finally, the omnipresent issue of time constantly surfaced in conjunction with need for curriculum materials. A teacher in a Latvian-speaking school in Liepāja suggested that because 20th century history is only covered in the 12th grade with a maximum of three lessons on the topic, "was it necessary to make all of these when the outlet is so limited? Was it worth it to go through all this?" She felt that if time would allow they would "read it cover to cover, but there is the time limit" and "if there were more time she would like to use it more . . . it's just difficult to get to everything; so much material about the topic and even the 12th graders lack so much knowledge." The issue of time, both to explore the new curriculum and actually employ it seemed a bit onerous, resulting in responses such as "it is too detailed and too vast for everyday use at school" and "I did a couple of these lessons but I was unable to cover it all—it's impossible to cover it."

Curriculum attributes. Respondents also commented on the structure and arrangement of the curriculum, which ultimately influenced the ways and extent to which they implemented the curriculum. One recurring problem related to this theme was the nature of curriculum and materials produced by the Ministry of Education and state-run agencies. A number of respondents commented on how the *THLSP* curriculum allowed them to select what to teach, but that:

> This is not always the case with materials developed in Latvia. Formerly, textbooks were written by those who don't teach in schools and they didn't know methodologies for schools, and there is still this problem . . . I can tell this curriculum was written by people who know schools and know the needs of schools.

A variety of curricula in Latvia are designed by historians and for teachers, prompting a number of respondents to comment on how the new Holocaust curriculum was noticeably different—that is, "prepared by teachers" and is therefore more "flexible and durable for changes in the standards." In addition, respondents realized that the curriculum presented "a uniqueness to different approaches to the problem. Each author seems to show unique ways of looking at history. It was not a single person who prepared the methods—lots of variety and that's unique."

Respondents also commented on the nature and medium of the content included in the curriculum. For example, one respondent from a Latvian-speaking school in Riga felt that schools "do not have enough visuals" and that "it's very hard to get maps." Another teacher from a Russian-speaking school in Riga stated that she "went to the archives, but they resist me" and noted that "I never had these maps before . . . this book helps make the story the teacher tells improved." Having the "cartoons and being shown how to use them," as well as "the glossary, pictures, maps, charts" were dominant themes throughout the interviews. Rather than employing meaningful activities, using analytical tools, and engaging students with provocative sources, teachers find that too often they only have text-based passages that lack seductive quality for students. Of the items teachers wished there were more of, even within the new curriculum, were visuals, cartoons, photographs, and graphic organizers. The use of such tools brought forth remarks that they enable students to "evaluate history themselves and draw conclusions on their own."

The general ease of instruction constitutes another emergent theme. For example, teachers commented on how the design of the curriculum positioned them to "prepare handouts—just Xerox pages and hand them out." A teacher from a Russian-speaking school in Liepāja remarked on how "even if the teacher could not prepare for the lesson, they could take it and go." One teacher from a Latvian-speaking school in Liepāja likes "having students fill in the data tables" and how she "does not need to prepare anything extra." In short, "it makes it very easy for the teacher; they don't have to look at many sources. Each class is different and there is enough material to present this information so you can broach the topic how you want, which is great for differentiated instruction." At times, respondents made fidelity-related remarks, such as "it was very well thought out, nothing was random—it was a good way to plan lessons without spending a lot of time to think of what to do." The curriculum offered these opportunities primarily because it is "very concrete—much more so than other curriculum I've seen—it doesn't contain unnecessary things."

Respondents also found the curriculum accessible, especially in terms of vocabulary whereby it "corresponds to the level of the school." Because the "books from the state are complicated" and this curriculum was primarily formulated by teachers, the biggest advantage teachers found was how "understandable" everything was for the kids and how the "content is very clear." One benefit of this clarity is the ability to position students to "feel that they are in the ghetto—feel these things." This prompted a number of complimentary statements directed toward the curriculum, including the fact that there "is no other book that is as well developed as this one. There are such books by different authors and other topics, but they are not so detailed."

Another accessibility issue concerned language. As both Russian-and Latvian-speaking schools exist, it was important for the curriculum to be in both languages, which the *THLSP* project was able to do for the middle school version, but not for high school version. Although the high school text is only in Latvian, one respondent found that Russian-speaking children "have no problem with this, but I myself sometimes have difficulty with this book" and that in middle school how important it is in Russian "since this book addresses ethics and feelings, this really needs to be in your mother tongue." Others had divergent perspectives, in one case suggesting the Russian students "can't read it because it's in Latvian. Even for Latvians the language might be too complicated."

In spite of the positive remarks on the physical nature of the materials, many responses made it seem as though a resource book of content and pedagogy might have been a more efficient approach to design and layout. After all, respondents claimed to rarely use the lessons "as is" and although this expectation is part of the fidelity paradigm, perhaps module lesson plans only complicated modification and enactment. The curriculum could still be attractive and respond to teacher preferences for many viewpoints and complex evidence to enable students to "come away with their own conclusions" in another format. The questions for discussion following each lesson were a tremendous contribution and the curriculum as a whole is, as one respondent suggested, "saturated with sources" and offers "multiple points of views" and "lots of first-person accounts" that "strong and weak pupils" alike can access. Respondents appreciated the connections to other tragedies in other countries, thereby providing the connective tissue to other topics, though many wished they had an electronic version and perhaps a format that could be "spread out" in classrooms if a teacher did not possess a full set of student books.

Perhaps the best justification for having lesson plans instead of sourcebooks and pedagogy books ties back to the fundamental tenet of mutual adaptation. Although teachers would rarely teach a lesson from start to finish, except in the class master course, the assembly of content, skills, dispositions, and assessments in a packaged discrete lesson allowed teachers to critically explore what they should do given their time limits and local needs—not a terminal lesson to be scripted, but a turning point from which subsequent lessons and adaptations could be built.

Conclusion and Implications

This study sought to understand the implementation of a controversial topic in a post-Soviet context, designed using the method of curriculum deliberation, five years after dissemination. The research questions framing this study focused on the extent to which the curriculum is being used, the factors inhibiting and inviting its use, and whether curriculum deliberation worked in the sense of teachers engaging in mutual adaptation. The findings, organized along Schwabian commonplaces of students, teachers, and subject matter reveal the complexity of change, local characteristics of change, and external factors Fullan (2007) emphasized. Collectively, these findings provide some descriptive guidance for future curriculum projects aimed at enhancing the treatment of controversial topics in nascent democratic societies.

The findings demonstrate that students very much influence teacher decisions about the implementation Holocaust education within Latvia. Because some students hold beliefs that appear to be uninformed, due to parental influence or some other source of knowledge, teachers often found this phenomenon to be a motivating factor for devoting more time and energy to the topic. Teachers were also keenly aware of student interest and their "emotional void." Responding to student needs on a local level is certainly a hallmark of mutual adaptation, but it also represents a risk when students have no interest, especially if the teacher shares that disposition. Given the larger societal and citizenship benefits of employing the curriculum, curricular decision-making based on students seems to suggest a platform for preservice and inservice training within Latvia. In short, providing more philosophical complexity on the issue of how teachers should respond to student needs and interests may be a beneficial conversation for current and future teachers to engage in. It also represents the first of many points of entry for future curriculum projects to attend to.

Similar to Cho's (1998) findings, the gravitational center for implementation, when weighed against other commonplaces, is certainly the teacher. As a number of societies face intense challenges of transitioning from totalitarian to democratic educational paradigms, the teacher is uniquely positioned as the fulcrum for this transformation. The opportunity for students to learn about controversial issues is a democratic imperative, as is the need for citizens to be able to critically examine the history of their country. These larger aims, which are consonant with studies seeking to understand teaching practices, may be advanced by employing the curriculum deliberation design found in this curriculum project. The findings revealed that teachers' perceptions of academic freedom very much dictate the extent to which they are interested in and perceive themselves as able to use new curriculum materials that do not necessarily correspond closely to standards and exams. Academic freedom, as a point of entry for curriculum implementation, is again tied back to teacher training and development. Promoting an enhanced vision of the teacher as gatekeeper (Thornton, 2005) and as professional within these educational spaces could very well assist in the future employment of curricula. Application of this freedom can ultimately promote the circumspection of the macrocurriculum to find, as many teachers successfully did, other curricular spaces that can accommodate this essential topic.

Although this curriculum project included a provision for two professional development trainings, which included roughly 80 history teachers, the findings reveal the importance of teacher participation in trainings (McLaughlin, 1976). Cultivating these relationships and exposure to curriculum can act as a catalyst for generativity among colleagues, and to an extent, with regard to pedagogical habits (Hord & Huling-Austin, 1986; Penuel et al., 2007). Because some of teachers who declined to be interviewed indicated they do not use the curriculum, teacher training is another point of entry that demands serious consideration as future projects grapple with how best to inform and prepare teachers to implement a new curriculum.

Finally, within the teacher commonplace, changes in behavior appear to be tied to other emergent themes, including academic freedom and collaboration. The teachers who demonstrated mutual adaptation did so in a wide variety of ways predicated on a sense of instructional autonomy. The eclectic approach to using content and strategies resulted from an open-mindedness to new materials, but also from a realization of the topic's importance, a view of Ministry standards and exams as something less than the final arbiter of what should be done to prepare future citizens, and an increased knowledge base on the topic (Penuel et al., 2007). Although teachers perceived that changes in their pedagogical behavior as a result of the curriculum were minimal, the enduring value of reinforcing interactive teaching methods was certainly a recurring finding among teachers.

The perceived need (Fullan, 2007), or lack thereof, for the curriculum raises a critical point for subsequent curriculum projects. Because this curriculum project did not include a comprehensive needs assessment, what teachers already had available to them and what they felt they needed in order to teach the Holocaust in a deep and complex manner was unknown. The majority of teachers indicated that more materials on the topic are beneficial, and that *THLSP* materials were particularly helpful given their unique composition of discrete lesson plans with provocative visuals, tables, maps, and discussion questions. But providing a more solid justification, based on evidence, for teachers serves as a caveat and point of entry for future projects of this ilk.

In Latvia, the normative entrepreneurs have largely come and gone. The Soros Foundation, the Center for Civic Education, and U.S. governmental resources have largely dried up, with attention instead directed toward more nascent and fragile democracies. But as one teacher indicated, "totalitarianism has roots" and "here in this society it is kind of rooted . . . especially if there are new tendencies—the young people are always inclined to listen to it. Democracy here is not very strong." Latvia's economic and political challenges are directly linked to its educational system. The ability of future citizens to grapple with controversial issues and make informed and reasoned decisions was a hope for this curriculum project and in many cases this was realized. But a great number of students are learning history within schools that focus primarily on content knowledge acquisition and do not include a full complement of reflective thinking accorded to these topics. The beliefs and "supposed forms of knowledge" (Dewey, 1933, p. 9) in every democracy require persistent subjection to reason and reflection. It is this ultimate aim that implementation hopefully strengthened and one that future projects are obligated to consider.

Appendix: 2009 Implementation Study Interview Protocol

About the curriculum:

1. Tell me about your reaction when you received the curriculum. Had you heard anything about the project prior to receiving it? Did you attend any conferences or trainings that dealt specifically with this curriculum? Did you use it the first year? This year? Do you think this is the case in other schools?
2. What do you like or dislike about the curriculum in terms of content?
3. What do you like or dislike about the curriculum in terms of methods and strategies?
4. To what extent is this curriculum innovative or new? In what ways is it different from traditional curriculum? In what ways is it different than curriculum in the Soviet era (if applicable)?
5. In what ways, if any, is it different from other curricula, on any topic, that you use? Which topics?

6. To what extent do you use the THLSP curriculum? Lessons/days per semester/ year?
7. Which lessons do you find yourself using? Are some better than others?
8. To what extent do you use other curricula on this topic? Lesson per year?
9. Does anything serve to limit your use of this curriculum?
10. In what ways has this curriculum changed the way in which you teach about the Holocaust?
11. In what ways has this curriculum changed the way you teach other topics?
12. Would you like to see other historical and social topical curricula follow the model of this curriculum?
13. Please comment on the following attributes of the curriculum:
    Clarity
    Appropriateness of content
    Complexity
    Quality
    Practicality
14. Please comment on how the following institutions or agents influenced your implementation of the curriculum in terms of incentives, encouragement, and discouragement:
    Students
    Parents
    School District
    Community Perceptions
    Administrators/Principals
    Ministry of Education
    Nongovernmental Organizations (NGOs)
    History Teachers' Association
15. In what ways might teaching about the Holocaust be controversial for your students, in your school, or in your school district?
16. Please comment on the extent to which there is a desire in class to focus on the Soviet crimes against Latvia instead of the Nazi crimes against Latvian Jews.
17. This curriculum attempted to be innovative and responsive to a topic not always discussed with great depth in schools. Could you please offer a general evaluation of the extent to which this goal was met?
18. To what extent were you comfortable teaching about this topic before you received this curriculum?
19. To what extent were you comfortable teaching this topic as a result of this curriculum? In short, was there in any change in your comfort level with the content? Do you think the curriculum was needed?
20. Finally, does this curriculum discourage or encourage your desire to address this topic or provide it with more or less instructional time? Does this ultimately happen (more instructional time as a result of the curriculum)? In what ways?

Note

The author would like to thank Ms. Sheila Johnson Robbins; Miami University's School of Education, Health, and Society; and the Philip and Elaina Hampton Fund for their generous support of this research. Thanks are also due to Victoria Shaldova and Marta Tuna for ably interpreting teacher interviews.

References

Aoki, T. (1984). Towards a reconceptualization of curriculum implementation. In D. Hopkins and M. Wideen (Eds.) *Alternative perspectives on school improvement* (pp. 107–118). New York: The Falmer Press.

Batelean, P. (2002). Bilingual education: The case of Latvia from a comparative perspective. *International Education, 13*(4), 359–374.

Ben-Peretz, M. (1990). *The teacher-curriculum encounter.* Albany, NY: SUNY Press.

Benavot, A., & Resh, N. (2003). Educational governance, school autonomy, and curriculum implementation: A comparative study of Arab and Jewish schools in Israel. *Journal of Curriculum Studies, 35*(2), 171–196.

Bogdan, R. C. & Biklen, S. K. (1992). *Qualitative research for education.* Boston: Allyn and Bacon.

Carless, D. R. (1998). A case study of curriculum implementation in Hong Kong. *System, 26*, 353–368.

Central Intelligence Agency. (2010). *The world factbook: Latvia.* Updated January 15, 2010. Retrieved February 8, 2010, from https://www.cia.gov/library/publications/the-world-factbook/geos/lg.html

Cho, J. (1998). *Rethinking curriculum implementation: Paradigms, models, and teachers' work.* Presented at the Annual Meeting of the American Educational Research Association, San Diego, CA. (ERIC Document Reproduction Service No. ED 421 767).

Cimdina, A. (2003). *In the name of freedom: A biography of Vaira Vike-Freiberga* (K. Streips, Trans.). Riga, Latvia: Jumava.

Crawford, A. N. (2002). Bilingual education in the United States: A window on the Latvian situation. *Intercultural Education, 13*(4), 375–389.

Dewey, J. (1933). *How we think.* Lexington, MA: D.C. Heath & Company.

Dewey, J. (1976). Social purposes in education. In *The middle works of John Dewey*, 1923–1924, v. 15. Carbondale: Southern Illinois University Press. (Original work published in 1922)

Erglis, D. (2005). A few episodes of the Holocaust in Krustpils: A microcosm of the Holocaust in occupied Latvia. In V. Nollendorts & E. Oberlander (Eds.), *The hidden and forbidden history of Latvia under Soviet and Nazi occupations 1940–1991* (pp. 175–187). Riga, Latvia: Institute of the History of Latvia.

Fullan, M. (1982). *The meaning of educational change.* New York: Teachers College Press.

Fullan, M. (1991). *The new meaning of educational change* (2nd ed.). New York: Teachers College Press.

Fullan, M. (2007). *The new meaning of educational change* (4th ed.). New York: Teachers College Press.

Fullan, M. (2008). Curriculum integration and sustainability. In F. M. Connelly, M. F. He, & J. Phillion (Eds.), *The Sage handbook of curriculum and instruction* (pp. 113–121). Thousand Oaks, CA: Sage.

Fullan, M., & Pomfret, A. (1977). Research on curriculum and instruction implementation. *Review of Educational Research, 47*(1), 335–397.

Glaser, B. G., & Strauss, A. L. (1967). *The discovery of grounded theory.* Chicago: Aldine.

Guba, E. G., & Lincoln, Y. S. (1981). *Effective evaluation.* San Francisco: Jossey-Bass.

Hahn, C. L., & Alviar-Martin, T. (2008). International political socialization research. In L. S. Levstik & C. A. Tyson (Eds.), *Handbook of research in social studies education* (pp. 81–108). New York: Routledge.

Hammersley, M., & Atkinson, P. (1995). *Ethnography.* New York: Routledge.

Hlebowitsh, P. S. (2005). *Designing the school curriculum.* Boston: Allyn & Bacon.

Hlebowitsh, P. S., Hamot, G. E., & Misco, T. (2006). *The development of Holocaust education materials for two curriculum forms in the Latvian schools: A final report.* Unpublished grant report.

Hord, S. M., & Huling-Austin, L. (1986). Effective curriculum implementation: Some promising new insights. *The Elementary School Journal, 87*(1), 96–115.

Klišane, J., Goldmane, S., Klaviņa, A., Misane, I., & Straube, L. (2007). *Vesture Pamatskolai: Jaunakie Laiki* [History for primary school: 20th Century Latvia]. Riga, Latvia: Zvaigzne ABC.

Laanemets, U. (2003). Learning for the future in Estonia: Content revisited and reconceptualized. In W. F. Pinar (Ed.). *International handbook of curriculum research* (pp. 285–300). Mahwah, NJ: Lawrence Erlbaum.

LeCompte, M. D., & Schensul, J. J. (1999). *Designing and conducting ethnographic research.* Walnut Creek, CA: AltaMira.

Leithwood, K. A. (1990). Implementation evaluation. In T. Husen & T. N. Postlethwaite (Eds.), *International encyclopedia of education research and studies* (pp. 295–299). New York: Pergamon.

Lincoln, Y. S., & Guba, E. G. (1985). *Naturalistic inquiry.* Beverly Hills, CA: Sage.

McLaughlin, M. W. (1976). Implementation as mutual adaptation: Change in classroom organization. *Teachers College Record, 77*(3), 339–351.

McLaughlin, M. W. (1993). What matters most in teachers' workplace context? In J. W. Little & M. W. McLaughlin (Eds.), *Teachers' work: Individuals, colleagues, and contexts* (pp. 79–103). New York: Teachers College Press.

Merriam, S. B. (2001). *Qualitative research and case study applications in education.* San Francisco: Jossey-Bass.

Miles, M. B., & Huberman, A. M. (1994). *Qualitative data analysis.* Thousand Oaks, CA: Sage.

Misco, T. (2007a). Holocaust curriculum development for Latvian schools: Arriving at purposes, aims, and goals through curriculum deliberation. *Theory and Research in Social Education, 35*(3), 393–426.

Misco, T. (2007b). The frustrations of reader generalizability and grounded theory: Alternative considerations for transferability. *Journal of Research Practice, 3*(1), Article M10. Retrieved April 3, 2009 from http://jrp.icaap.org/index.php/jrp/article/view/45/136

Misco, T. (2009). Teaching the Holocaust through case study. *Social Studies, 100*(1), 14–22.

Page, R. N. (2001). Reshaping graduate preparation in educational research methods: One school's experience. *Educational Researcher, 30*(5), 19–25.

Parker, W. C. (2003). The deliberative approach to education for democracy: Problems and possibilities. In J. J. Patrick, G. E. Hamot, & R. S. Leming, (Eds.), *Civic learning in teacher education* (pp.99–115). Bloomington, IN: ERIC Clearinghouse for Social Studies/Social Science Education. (ERIC Document Reproduction Service No. ED475824)

Patton, M. Q. (1990). *Qualitative evaluation and research methods.* Newbury Park, CA: Sage.

Penuel, W. R., Fishman, B. J., Yamaguchi, R., & Gallagher, L. P. (2007). What makes professional development effective? Strategies that foster curriculum implementation. *American Educational Research Journal, 44*(4), 921–958.

Poetter, T. S., Everington, C., & Jetty, R. (2001). Curriculum deliberation in action: Preparing school leaders for inclusion. *Journal of Curriculum and Supervision, 16*(2), 162–182.

Reid, W. (1999). *Curriculum as institution and practice.* Mahwah, NJ: Lawrence Erlbaum Associates.

Schofield, J. W. (1990). Increasing the generalizability of qualitative research. In E. W. Eisner & A. Peshkin (Eds.), *Qualitative inquiry in education* (pp. 171–203). New York: Teachers College Press.

Schwab, J. J. (1978). The practical: A language for curriculum. In I. Westbury & N. J. Wilkof (Eds.), *Science, curriculum, and liberal education* (pp. 287–321). Chicago: University of Chicago Press. (Original work published in 1970)

Schwab, J. J. (1978). The practical: Translation into curriculum. In I. Westbury & N. J. Wilkof (Eds.), *Science, curriculum, and liberal education* (pp. 365–384). Chicago: University of Chicago Press. (Original work published in 1973)

Silova, I. (2002). Bilingual education theater: Behind the scenes of Latvian minority education reform. *Intercultural Education, 13*(4), 463–476.

Sneidere, I. (2005). The first Soviet occupation period in Latvia 1940–1941. In V. Nollendorts & E. Oberlander (Eds.), *The hidden and forbidden history of Latvia under Soviet and Nazi occupations 1940–1991* (pp. 33–42). Riga, Latvia: Institute of the History of Latvia.

Soros Foundation, (2001). A Passport to social cohesion and economic prosperity: Report of education in Latvia 2000. *Peabody Journal of Education, 76*(3&4), 159–174.

Steiner-Khamsi, G., Torney-Purta, J., & Schwille, J. (2002). Introduction: Issues and insights in cross-national analysis of qualitative studies. In G. Steiner-Khamsi, J. Torney-Purta, & J. Schwille (Eds.), *New paradigms and recurring paradoxes in education for citizenship: An international comparison* (pp. 1–36). London: Elsevier.

Stranga, A. (2005). The Holocaust in occupied Latvia: 1941–1945. In V. Nollendorts & E. Oberlander (Eds.), *The hidden and forbidden history of Latvia under Soviet and Nazi occupations 1940–1991.* Riga, Latvia: Institute of the History of Latvia.

Thornton, S. J. (2005). *Teaching social studies that matters.* New York: Teachers College Press.

Van Den Akker, J. J. (1988). The teacher as learner in curriculum implementation. *Journal of Curriculum Studies, 20*(1), 47–55.

31
Complementary Curriculum: The Work of Ecologically Minded Teachers

Christy M. Moroye

Introduction

Public interest in global environmental issues has surged. From newspaper cover stories to political causes to sitcom story-lines, 'green' perspectives and conversations are becoming more commonplace. Both formal and non-formal education has, since the 1970s, been asked to respond to this growing concern (International Union for the Conservation of Nature and Natural Resources/UNESCO 1970, United Nations Conference on Environment and Development 1992), and, to that end, researchers, practitioners, government agencies, and communities have worked to implement environmental and ecological education models. However, these initiatives remain largely on the fringes of schooling, particularly in the US. The purpose of this study is not to elaborate on why environmental education remains on the 'outside', but rather to offer another perspective—from inside the schools themselves. That perspective comes from ecologically-minded teachers who work in traditional US public schools and who teach 'non-environmental' curricula,[1] that is, teachers who are not explicitly engaged in teaching about the environment or in environmental education programmes.

Environmental education is a collective, broad term encompassing many facets of earth-inclusive education. 'Traditional' environmental education has roots in nature study, conservation education, and outdoor education, and is often found in supplementary programmes and activities that occur in addition to the 'regular' curriculum (Heimlich 2002). A more recent movement has emerged toward 'ecological education' (see Orr 1992, Jardine 2000), which Smith and Williams (1999: 3) define as 'an emphasis on the inescapable embeddedness of human beings in natural systems'. Other models include place-based education (Sobel 2004, Noddings 2005, Smith 2007), eco-justice education (Bowers 2001, Martusewicz 2005), education for sustainability (Sterling 2001), and education for sustainable development (Jickling and Wals 2007), to name a few. Jickling and Wals (2007) point out that this last model, education for sustainable development, while somewhat contested, 'has become widely seen as a new and improved version of environmental education, most visibly at the national policy level of many countries' (p. 4), although such policies remain absent in the US. While myriad models exist, Gruenewald and Manteaw (2007: 173) note that environmental education continues to be 'marginalized, misunderstood as mainly about science, and in many places totally neglected'.

There may be many reasons for environmental education's neglect or 'failure' (Blumstein and Saylan 2007), but certainly, if we look to the future success of environmental education in any of the above models, we must consider the work of teachers. To that end, many researchers have investigated a variety of aspects of the roles of teachers in environmental education. Cutter-Mackenzie and Smith (2001) looked at teachers' environmental knowledge or 'eco-literacy', and their related beliefs about the importance of attitudes toward, rather than knowledge about, the environment. Robertson and Krugly-Smolska (1997) report on three sources of the 'gap' between environmental education theory and practice: (1) 'the practical', in terms of variables such as time, materials, and schedules, (2) 'the conceptual', referring to 'conflicting ideas and resources that (make it difficult) for teachers to understand what the task of environmental education really is'; and (3) 'teacher responsibility', referring to the idea that 'teachers are not completely certain that they are permitted to do many of the things that are necessary to accomplish the lofty social and political goals of environmental education' (p. 316). Other studies (Dillon and Gayford 1997, Cotton 2006a, b) discuss teachers' beliefs and actions related to controversial environmental issues in the curricula. These and other studies illustrate that environmental education is no easy task for teachers.

While other studies, such as the ones described above, have focused on teachers in sanctioned environmental education settings, I focus on teachers in traditional US public schools who happen to be ecologically-minded, but whose curricular responsibilities do not necessarily include environmental topics. I selected teachers in social studies and English/language arts for two reasons. First, social studies and language arts are largely unexplored environmental education territory (Heimlich 2002). Secondly, while environmental science and technology may play an important role in mediating the environmental crises we face, many suggest that cultural values play at least an equal part (see, e.g. Bowers 1993, Blumstein and Saylan 2007, Gruenewald and Manteaw 2007). Subject areas like English/language arts and social studies, which contribute to transmitting and transforming cultural values, may have an important role in environmental and ecological education reform.[2]

By studying the intentions and actions of ecologically-minded teachers in public schools, I was able to discern themes that emerged naturally as a result of teachers' strongly held beliefs. One such theme is a new term I argue for as an addition to the curricular lexicon, the *complementary curriculum.* This is not an attempt to redefine curriculum—it already has many definitions (see Connelly *et al.* 2008); instead, it is an attempt to call attention to a particular type of curriculum and, by so doing, offer the potential for expanding ecological perspectives in schools. I start, therefore, with the broad definition of curriculum offered by He *et al.* (2008: 223):

> Curriculum for us is a dynamic interplay between experiences of students, teachers, parents, administrators, policy-makers, and other stakeholders; content knowledge and pedagogical premises and practices; and cultural, linguistic, sociopolitical, and geographical contexts.

Within this definition the complementary curriculum is situated in the kinds of experiences teachers provide for students, as well as in the 'pedagogical premises and practices' that result from the teachers' beliefs.

In his discussion of the 'curriculum shadow', Uhrmacher (1997) argues for the use of a variety of terms to specify different curricula. He distinguishes, for example, the shadow curriculum and the null and hidden curricula. The *shadow curriculum* identifies a 'disdained' or neglected curriculum that could in fact improve the pedagogy at hand

(Uhrmacher 1997). As an example Uhrmacher points to a social studies teacher who, in the name of order and efficiency, lectured on the US Constitution rather than encouraging discussion, which could be considered a more democratic means of learning.

The *null curriculum* (Flinders *et al.* 1986, Eisner 2002) describes what is missing. It includes intellectual processes and subject matter (Eisner 2002), as well as affect (Flinders *et al.* 1986). The null curriculum might include singular topics or perspectives as well as entire fields of study.[3] The *hidden curriculum* identifies the norms of schooling. Thus, Jackson (1968) distinguishes the official curriculum from the associated skills required to master it, skills such as putting forth effort, completing homework, and understanding and operating within institutional norms. Together these and other 'unofficial' aspects of what is taught in schools constitute the hidden curriculum.

Of the three terms discussed here, the *complementary curriculum* is most closely associated with the hidden curriculum. However, there are at least two key differences between the two. First, the hidden curriculum has its origins in something more ominous, or at the very least more negative; that is, in Jackson's original definition, it referred to the processes of schooling that were not explicitly taught but were required for success. In contrast, the complementary curriculum is an addition that may enhance or hinder the school experience, and students are not required to master any related skills. The second difference between the hidden and the complementary curriculum is the source. The hidden curriculum emerges from a variety of places, such as the school structure, the bell schedule, furniture, administrative decisions, textbooks, paint colours, etc. The complementary curriculum has one source: the teacher.

These (and other) terms, Uhrmacher (1997) argues, help curricularists make distinctions that may otherwise go unnoticed. This is, I believe, the case with complementary curriculum, which I describe as the embedded and often unconscious expression of a teacher's beliefs. In the study described here, focused upon ecological beliefs, it may include the teacher's use of examples, personal stories, vocabulary, and pedagogical practices that relate to or emerge from ecological ideas, even though the curriculum does not necessarily include information *about* an earth-based idea like watershed or ecosystem health. Adding this term to our curricular lexicon, I argue, brings to light pathways to understanding and improving curriculum and instruction, particularly from an ecological standpoint.

Method of Inquiry

The study was designed to respond to two questions:

- What are the intentions of ecologically minded teachers? and
- How are those intentions realized (or not realized) in a teacher's practice?

In order to describe and interpret the potentially subtle manifestations of the participants' beliefs and intentions, I used the methods of educational connoisseurship and criticism (Flinders 1996, Eisner 1998, 2002, see also Barone 2000, Uhrmacher and Mathews 2005).[4]

This study has a particular focus on ecological themes, and, while educational criticism is a broad term defining the research methodology, *eco-educational criticism* is the term I use to specify the particular ecological lens through which I filtered my observations and interpretations. By 'ecological' I mean situations, ideas, and issues that address the inescapable embeddedness between and among humans and the natural environment including but not limited to issues of relationship (Smith and Williams 1999), care (Noddings 2005), decision-making (Heimlich 2002), and sustainability and global equity (Smith and Williams 1999). I was specifically seeking to understand how ecological concepts and themes emerged in non-ecological[5] contexts.

In this paper I provide educational criticisms in the form of vignettes with the intention to bring to light the manifestations of teachers' ecological beliefs in the classroom. In a previous study (Moroye 2005) I also used eco-educational criticism to describe teachers who did not necessarily hold to ecological beliefs, but whose practices could be described by ecological themes. In future studies this method could be used to draw forth additional ecological themes, as well as to analyse a variety of educational contexts and models for their ecological implications.

Two large US public high schools, Seneca Lake High School[6] (SLHS) and Highline High School (HHS),[7] served as the sites for my research. The three participants discussed here are US public high school teachers; two of the three teach English, and one teaches social studies. I first conducted an individual formal interview using a protocol in which the questions referred to the teachers' intentions, their ecological beliefs, and their educational practice in general. Next, I observed each teacher for 3–6 weeks. I concluded with a follow-up interview, which often synthesized the connection between the teachers' ecological beliefs and their practices. Working with one teacher at a time afforded me the opportunity to immerse myself in their work and to better understand the architecture of their practice. I then wrote accounts of each teacher that included the four aspects of an educational criticism: description, interpretation, evaluation, and thematics (Eisner 2002). Portions of those criticisms are included here in the form of vignettes.

Findings

As stated above, two questions guided this study: What are the intentions of ecologically minded teachers? How are those intentions realized in a teachers practice? As Eisner (1988) points out, the intentional dimension of schooling is important because intentions 'influence the kind of opportunities students will have to develop their minds . . . and intentions tell the young what adults think is important for them to learn; they convey our values' (p. 25). While Eisner was speaking about the school's intentions, the idea works for teachers as well. Intentions guide, among other things, curricular choices, emphases, and omissions. Here I look at the intentions of individuals with common values that were not directly related to schooling and I explore how, if at all, their practice was affected by these values. It is important to note that I asked teachers about their ecological beliefs, as well as their intentions for their students. I was seeking to understand the teachers' ways of connecting the two.

To that end, I interviewed each participant both prior to and after conducting classroom observations. One purpose of the interview was to understand the teachers' intentions for their students and whether or not they thought their ecological beliefs were linked to those intentions. Mr Rye, the first participant, explained the connection in this way:

> I can't walk in and give daily lessons on drilling in the [Arctic National Wildlife] Refuge, and I can't walk in and talk on a daily basis about treatment of animals or of the natural world. But I can talk about [students'] treatment of other human beings, their view of their own lives, and the values and principles upon which they base their own lives.

As Mr Rye points out, his ecological beliefs are somewhat at odds with his teaching. As an English teacher he is not charged with the role of teaching environmental education. However, including ecological ideas in the classroom is important to him, so he chooses to infuse his practice with a broader principle that, for him, is connected to an ecological ethic. That principle is *integrity*:

> I think that, at the core of environmental issues is personal integrity, [which guides whether] we exploit something or choose not to exploit something. And what I want to do with my students on a daily basis is to have them examine and, hopefully, develop their integrity.

Mr Rye also alludes to his own sense of integrity and that he tries to live his personal and professional lives in such a way that they are in alignment with his beliefs. He does so, however, with awareness that he does not want to alienate his students. 'I try not to project myself as an environmentalist as much as just a human being who loves nature and who considers [the environment in making decisions].' Furthermore, he wants his students to live 'authentic' lives: 'My deep concern is about the type of lives these guys are going to live, and are they going to live lives that are individual and interesting and somehow sacred, or . . . lives that are frighteningly generic?'

Mr Rye appears sensitive to either the real or perceived limits imposed upon him by the formal curriculum, as well as by the potential negative reactions of his students. Therefore, he discusses his intentions for his students in broad terms with 'integrity' and 'authenticity' at the heart of his goals for them. So how do these ideals play out in practice? Consider the following vignette and notice how his beliefs are woven into the lesson:

> 'I want this project to rock!' Mr Rye shouts in a pep talk to his senior [i.e. Year 12] English class. He is preparing them to write their autobiographies as their final senior paper. This class is considered 'remedial' for students performing below grade level, and many in the class are staffed in special education.
>
> 'You need AT LEAST four sheets of paper. Not very environmental, I know.' Mr Rye roars at his students, 'HOORAY! You don't have to write essays!' A student asks if they will have assignments that tell them what to write about. 'You are prophetic! We're gonna break it down—b-b-b break it down!' Mr Rye and the class erupt in laughter at his failed attempt at rap music.
>
> Mr Rye then begins to explain the first writing assignment. 'FOOD in 2005 is fascinating! Why am I asking you to write about food? This isn't health class. But studies show that food is the single most determining factor about how long you will live and the quality of your life.' Mr Rye explains that writing about food is really writing about their lives. He talks about the history of humankind and how it is easy to predict what people would eat based upon where they lived. 'What would people in Colorado eat? Buffalo, corn, wheat, potatoes, carrots. They didn't go to Whole Foods to pick up sushi. If you weren't able to import everything you wanted, you lived with what the land gave you.
>
> 'In our era it is unparallelled! You can choose to be a vegan and still have variety. You can choose to be a vegetarian. In this day and age it is fascinating to explore individuality because you have so much choice! You can go to a 7–11 [i.e. a convenience store] and get lunch. Now you can even get stuffed sausages—kinda scary! It's a crazy world. In 10 minutes from SLHS you can get Thai and Chinese.' He continues noting that within minutes of their school students can taste the world.

Mr Rye gives students 8 minutes to write about food as he buzzes about from student to student helping them brainstorm and encouraging their writing. 'Have some fun. Be spontaneous! Believe it or not, the power of life is in the details. If you want to stay on the surface with this project, I can't stop you. But this is your life and it's so much more interesting than that!' Mr Rye cheers as he hands out skinny slips of blue paper that say the following:

Life Signifiers: Uncovering the Reality of You

You and . . .

1. Food—what you eat and why where you eat; what you cook yourself; what your parents cook for you; guilty pleasures—stuff you eat but know you should not eat; what you will not eat and why; your typical day: . . . your food philosophy: what food means to you.

A student asks, 'Can I just list my allergies?'

'Yes! What a great feature!' he says again. Mr Rye puts a few strong student examples up on the overhead and discusses how interesting they are. One example deals with a student's Jewish religion and culture and their implications on the food she eats. As each student shares his or her responses, Mr Rye calls each by name, affirms his or her answer, and finds humour in almost every statement.

Remember that Mr Rye has two overarching intentions for his students: integrity and authenticity. These intentions come to life in several ways. The writing prompt itself values self-awareness, which for Mr Rye is connected to integrity and authenticity. So in that regard, his intentions are manifested in the explicit or stated curriculum. However, we may also see a more complex force, Mr Rye's beliefs, permeating the lesson.

First, the written handout details the first of several writing prompts for the students' autobiographies. The handout is a thin slip of paper that signifies reduced paper consumption. Secondly, Mr Rye remarks on the number of sheets of paper (four) students will need saying, 'Not very environmental, I know'. Thirdly, Mr Rye's elaboration on the history of food indicates his own understanding of the relationship between food and human existence, which did not always include a quick stop at a convenience store for a hot dog.

Separately, these three examples may not mean much. However, taken together they form a subtle curriculum. That subtle curriculum is the manifestation of Mr Rye's ecological beliefs. Throughout my observations of all participants, I noticed that their beliefs often emerged in understated ways, such as in the examples they used, personal stories about their lives, certain emphases, and even in their common vocabulary. While they were often not explicitly 'teaching' an ecological concept or idea, they were simply showing that their ecological beliefs are just below the surface, that they are part of who they are and how they teach. Because their beliefs are not separate from their practice, are not compartmentalized into a different section of their lives, are integral to who they are in the classroom, I refer to this type of subtle curriculum as the *complementary curriculum.*

A second and related vignette further illustrates the complementary curriculum in Mr Rye's practice. His ecological beliefs again emerge in his explanation of the written curriculum. In particular, Mr Rye asks students to consider the history of humans' need for drinking liquids, and he takes them through a brief story contrasting the use of local resources to the present-day beverage industry. Another teacher could simply ask students to think about their favourite beverages; Mr Rye offers a more ecological perspective in which he urges students to think about what humans really need, not just what they desire.

> After the students list their favourite foods and other food quirks, Mr Rye launches into the next topic—beverages. The next writing prompt he distributes, which is again on a small slip of blue paper, prompts students to explore the drinks they consume.
>
> 'What was "drink" for the history of humankind? WATER! Wine if you were lucky enough to live near grapes. Milk if you were lucky enough to have a willing cow. But check out a 7–11 [convenience store]! What drink options do you have? Five varieties of Slurpees, Gatorade—like 20 varieties, Powerade, Energy drinks—at least 10 of those, bottled water, sparkling water—what *is* that? How do they make it sparkle? Iced tea, soda—which doesn't quench your thirst—juice, and so on! And how do they get things to taste like that? This is the only culture in which we drink more liquids *other* than water, and we pay more money for bottled water even though [tap water in the US] is cleaner than water in almost any other country—even in toilets it's cleaner! Now we have flavoured water—no—it's *INFUSED*, not just flavoured!
>
> 'I want you to see how completely foreign this is to humankind—drink has never been a factor of individuality before. Maybe you choose different drink for different reasons—your concern for your health, your concern for the environment. That is what makes *you* interesting!'
>
> As class time draws to a close, Mr Rye prepares them for the next day by discussing 12 signifiers of individuality. 'This is how we measure and show and understand individuality. The next signifier is clothing—you'll find this interesting at SLHS. We see clothes and they say something. For example, look at girls with tie dyes. Does she love the earth? Does she love animals? Did she have a paint explosion? Your clothing is a great measure of who you are, at least in this country. Did you know that the average world citizen owns FIVE items of clothing—TODAY! So tomorrow we will talk about your clothing and you.

In the previous two vignettes, we might apply several different curricular terms, each revealing something different about this teacher's practice. We could analyse the formal or written curriculum, which is exhibited in Mr Rye's writing activity, and determine if such an activity were useful to his students and perhaps to others. We could also comment on the null curricula, what is missing, and note that perhaps Mr Rye did not place enough emphasis on editing or grammar. Selecting from a variety of terms provides us with a starting point for analysis and potential improvement. Additional terms such as complementary curriculum may provide additional and useful points of analysis.

In the second scenario, the complementary curriculum is expressed in Mr Rye's explanation of the assignment. He emphasizes to students that beverages have not always come from refrigerated coolers at convenience stores. He draws the connection between what the land could provide and what humans could consume. He notes for students that not only are they able to get drinks from around the world regardless of local agricultural limits, but also that the beverages now available have an air of absurdity about them. In a sense, he points out how far away from 'natural' the beverage industry has strayed. However, Mr Rye doesn't simply point out the state of this industry; he connects it to student choice. He is helping them to see that they do have choices that express their individuality, and that those choices say something about how they live in the world. He does not condemn them for drinking 'infused' water, but points to a perspective they may want to consider, and that perspective requires that they consider the origins of the products they consume. This consideration is a new paradigm for many students (and adults) comfortable with their present consumption patterns. Then at the close of class, Mr Rye tells them that the average world citizen owns only five pieces of clothing. He again includes a broad global perspective, albeit brief, that students may consider as they write their own autobiographies.

Is the complementary ecological curriculum here valuable? From an ecological perspective, we might wonder if Mr Rye's comments in the first vignette about the use of paper will have any meaning to students. Does merely mentioning the environmental insensitivity of using too much paper result in environmental stewardship in his students? Probably not. Perhaps Mr Rye's comments merely show his students that environmental ideas are on his mind, and that may lead them to ask him questions about the environment later. Mr Rye notes that while his students don't often bring this up, he is 'deeply gratified by the fact that it does occur'. However, perhaps his discussion of food and drink provides his students with a different perspective, one which allows them a window into a kind of ecological thinking, one that considers the origins of the products we consume. Considering consumption patterns is a key cultural component to addressing the ecological crisis, so in this regard, the complementary curriculum supplements the formal curriculum with a much needed focus on connections between consumption and production.

However, some environmental education scholars might question whether Mr Rye's attention to individuality is actually counterproductive to certain ecological ideas (see Bowers 1993). A more ecological perspective might focus more on the balance of individual and community needs (see Bowers 2003). This critique points to a difficult issue when discussing complementary curriculum; it may lead to an evaluation of teachers' personally held beliefs. This difficulty is compounded by Mr Rye's sensitivity to his students. He says, 'I'm aware . . . as a teacher not to alienate some of my kids because if they see me "an environmentalist" will they tune out [other lessons]?' Mr Rye therefore chooses to focus on self-awareness and personal integrity instead of other potential ecological ideas. These two areas of focus also serve as a proxy for explicit ecological perspectives in Ms Snow's practice.

While Mr Rye's ecological beliefs as expressed through the complementary curriculum are apparent in the way he explains and elaborates upon the explicit curriculum, it is much more behind the scenes for Ms Snow, an English teacher at Highline High School. Outside of school Ms Snow is a Native American minister,[8] and therefore she talks about spiritual beliefs in connection with ecological principles. She explains her ecological beliefs and related intentions for her students in this way:

> The core of my ecological beliefs has to do with relationship . . . relationship with self, relationship with others, [and] respect for self and respect for others . . . It also has to do with taking responsibility. We take responsibility for how we conduct ourselves in relationship to how we use resources on the earth, for instance. And because I believe that we must act with the spirit of integrity to preserve those resources for seven generations on down, then I think that learning things about the self and individuation and alchemy and the archetypes and all of those things really *is* in deep alignment [with my ecological beliefs].

Ms Snow feels constrained by the requirements of the courses she teaches; the English curriculum does not allow for reading environmental writing and in-depth discussion of issues. As Robertson and Krugly-Smolska (1997) point out, teachers—even in sanctioned environmental education settings—share similar concerns about what they are 'allowed' to do because they feel limited by what is expected in the formal curriculum. Instead, through studying texts like *Demian*, Ms Snow is addressing ecological ideas as she defines them. '*Demian*, Jungian psychology, [the] search for self and individualization, and being true to an inner voice . . . [all] have to do with relationships. Relationship with self, relationship with others.'

Ms Snow's discussion of her beliefs and intentions for students has a similar ring to that of Mr Rye. Each seeks to develop self-awareness and integrity in students. Ms Snow's intentions are apparent in the following vignette as she guides her students to think about what makes them unique and how they will share that uniqueness with the world. We also see how she addresses each student with care and respect, which facilitates thoughtful discussion in the class.

> The humming overhead reads, 'Most men lead lives of quiet desperation and go to the grave with the song still in them'. Respond to this famous quote by Henry David Thoreau. Do you think that this is a true assessment?' Ms Snow looks out over her senior [i.e. year 12] Humanities seminar class . . . They lean over notebooks occasionally glancing up at the overhead to reread Thoreau's words.
>
> 'Looks like you all had a lot to say about this one', Ms Snow smiles. 'Let's pick up with *Zelig*[9] and connect the ideas', she suggests, referring to a Woody Allen film they had recently viewed. They discuss the fear of being seen for whom we truly are and the risk we take when we allow ourselves to be real with others. 'Let's keep building on this. I know you're more awake than I am.'
>
> 'I think a lot of people might do that because they are afraid of what society might brand them. Like Martin Luther King, Jr. He took a risk,' one female student offers.
>
> 'Do you think he died with a song still in him?' Ms Snow asks.
>
> 'No. He lived it', she responds.
>
> 'A lot of it has to do with fear. Like if you let your true self out', another student says.
>
> 'Yeah. Isn't it about taking risks?' Ms Snow asks as she sits down in a chair in the front of the room. 'What if you do sing your song and people don't accept it?'
>
> 'No one expects anything more than mediocrity', a third student says.
>
> 'I don't agree with that', replies another.
>
> 'Okay. Good. Let's come back to that. I want to hear what Tracy has to say.'
>
> Tracy says, 'I think society wants you to strive. They want you to be the best. WE have to run this world.'
>
> 'Okay!' Ms Snow praises. 'We are getting some great responses here. Let's hear from Stacy, then Sarah.'
>
> 'The simplest things can be made so hard. It's like they expect you to work at a fast-food restaurant. Especially minorities. It's like minorities are still looked down upon—since you're Native American, you're just going to be a drunk. So just go back to the reservation', Stacy, an African American girl says.
>
> 'Stacy's goin'!' Ms Snow cheers. 'Let's hear from Sarah.'
>
> 'I think fear of society is only half of it. People are lazy. They have that quiet desperation in themselves, but they don't do anything about it. They just watch TV.'
>
> Ms Snow wraps up the conversation and then addresses the whole class:
>
>> I want to ask you a question, but I don't want you to answer it. We are reading Socrates and watching *Pleasantville* to find out who you are in the world. The question I want to ask you is—what is your song and how will you sing it? You are about to walk across a bridge—many of you into higher education. I am going to show you something; it's called 'An Invitation' written by a white woman. You don't have to be trapped in that moment of quiet desperation. Those moments can make us fight to sing that song. You are going to write a senior credo. You will like it!

> Students read 'The Invitation' and consider it silently. The first stanza reads, 'It doesn't interest me what you do for a living. I want to know what you ache for, and if you dare to dream of meeting your heart's longing.' Then, in silence, Ms Snow puts on the video of *Pleasantville*, a story of a teenager who wants to break out of his black-and-white sit-com world.

While the natural world and consumption patterns do not filter into this discussion as they did in Mr Rye's classroom, Ms Snow's stated intentions, which emanate from her ecological beliefs, include helping students examine their lives in order to take responsibility for their relationships. While it is apparent that the above vignette is in alignment with Ms Snow's intentions for students, it also shows that to Ms Snow, as well as to Mr Rye, self-awareness is a building block of integrity, and one who has consciously developed integrity, they believe, will be more likely to consider ecological perspectives. They do not include explicit ecological curriculum, but instead focus on what they consider to be a related ecological principle.

In contrast, the third participant, Mrs Avila, does tend to include more explicit ecological ideas, and she, like Mr Rye, does so through her elaboration of the written or stated curriculum. Mrs Avila's beliefs lead her to cover some subjects in more depth and with a particular perspective; for her it is a matter of emphasis. However, unlike Mr Rye, Mrs Avila feels very comfortable infusing her ecological beliefs:

> In geography, we talk about population, which is a pretty common topic, . . . [but] I feel totally comfortable deciding . . . to talk about not just where does population grow, where does it shrink and why, but also the impact of population growth, depending on whether it is a society that is resource-intense . . . I feel totally comfortable choosing to introduce the kids to that.

The following vignette illustrates this ecological emphasis as well as an extended, spontaneous discussion with her students about recycling. Notice the stated agenda and what actually occurs. Although lengthy, the vignette does illustrate a real situation in which the teacher uses questioning to guide the students' understanding away from a common line of thinking that ecological responsibility is inconvenient toward a more connected way of thinking about personal choice and action.

> Mrs Avila's 9th grade World Geography students are greeted by her friendly demeanour and an overhead that has the Geography Agenda with the Colorado state geography standards for the day:
>
> 6.1. Students know how to apply geography to understand the past.
> 6.2. Students know how to apply geography to understand the present and plan for the future.
>
> Today's activities
>
> 1. Complete presentations.
> 2. Discuss population's impact.
> 3. What causes population to grow or shrink?
> 4. Population pyramids in Lab A.
>
> The starter has a picture of a population pyramid, which looks like an isosceles triangle with horizontal stripes. The starter tells them that this is a population pyramid and asks students to explain what it might mean. 'Guessing is okay!' Mrs Avila tells them.
>
> Mrs Avila takes responses, and one student surmises that those at the bottom of the pyramid don't have a lot of money. 'Good thinking!' Mrs Avila responds. 'Ian, what did you put?'
>
> 'Nothing', Ian replies.

'What *will* you be writing down?' Mrs Avila asks again.

'I think maybe the bars show age.'

'Terrific thinking!' Mrs Avila praises. They then move on to student presentations. 'Who's the environment group?'

The group of four students makes their way to the front, and they discuss how we need clean air and water to live. They say that we as humans take more for ourselves, leaving little for other species, and they give specific examples about deforestation.

'Pause there,' Mrs Avila interjects. 'What was Brad talking about with BIODIVERSITY? What are we using up? Where are we getting 50% of our prescription drugs?'

'The Rainforest', a student in the audience answers.

'So biodiversity refers to plants and animals that exist. So do we benefit from biodiversity?'

'Yes, like with prescription drugs', another student responds.

'But what was Alice talking about? It's not only about us, is it?'

'No.'

'It is about the plants and animals—they become extinct! For example, let's think about egg-shells. In order for them to be made of what they need—calcium—birds eat snails; snails eat plants; and plants get calcium from soil. But why is calcium not in soil anymore?'

'ACID RAIN!' a student shouts.

'Acid rain caused by?'

'Burning of fossil fuels', the student responds.

Mrs Avila moves to stand near two talkative boys, but does not scold them. 'So when we get in our cars, do we say, "We're going to kill some birds today!"? No! But the unintended consequences are just as serious as the intended consequences.' As the discussion unfolds, Mrs Avila questions individual students about resource-use and -consumption patterns, and eventually turns to a discussion of waste.

'Where is this place called trash? Has anyone ever visited this place called trash?' Mrs Avila asks.

'You mean like a landfill?'

'Yeah. How long does the toothpaste tube stay there?'

'Forever?' one student guesses.

Mrs Avila prompts, 'How long are you planning to live? 100 years? I'm planning on 105, so you'll be taking care of me when I'm old. Will the tube be there when Armando is 100 years old?' Students shrug, and some say no, some yes. 'The tube I use is metal—it's recyclable.'

'What kind do you use?'

'Tom's of Maine.' [i.e. brand name]

'Oh. That organic stuff.'

'Yeah. So how long does it take for the toothpaste tube to dissolve? Thousands of years! Students gasp. 'The vast majority of my furniture is used—from the 1930s and 1950s. I make a conscious effort to recycle and to buy things that can be recycled.'

'Why?' a student asks.

'Because it's not just about me. I think about you guys when you are 105. I want you to have a planet worth living on. What we're talking about with global warming—300 scientists, the top in their field—say the earth's temperature is rising a couple degrees. Glaciers that have been in Greenland for thousands of years are melting. Penguins and polar bears are dying because they can't get their food. So guys, are these [population pyramids] just about the number of people growing?'

'No', several students respond.

'NO. It's about what?'

'How we use our resources and create junk and stuff,' one student says.

Mrs Avila then addresses a student with a plastic Coke bottle. 'Evan, what will you do with that Coke bottle?'

'Throw it away,' Evan says.

'Why? Why won't you recycle it?' Mrs. Avila asks.

'No recycle bins.'

'Okay! Why at HHS do we not have many recycle bins? There is an area of the school with recycle bins, but students can't go there. Is that a problem? Shana is drinking juice—and we're glad because juice is far better than Coke, no offence, Evan. But when you're done, will you ask me to recycle it for you?'

'No. You should have a recycle bin in here', Shana says.

'So it's up to me?' Mrs Avila asks.

'We should have a recycle day. All the students who get in trouble should pick up trash and recycling,' another student offers.

'They should have recycle bins,' another student says.

'Who is this "they"? Do *you* care?'

'It's more of a habit,' Shana says.

'How could we get you to change that habit? Do you all agree that if more recycle bins were available, you would recycle?' About eight students raise their hands to say yes.

'But we have to overcome laziness!' Shana says.

'Who needs to organize this movement?' Mrs Avila asks Shana.

'Everybody. Students.'

'Why students? Would some people listen to *you*? *You* personally? Armando, would you be willing to work with other students to increase the number of recycling bins?'

'Maybe.'

'What would make you more likely?'

'To know that students will use them,' Armando says.

'Did you know we used to have a recycling club?' Mrs Avila asks.

'No!' many students respond, shocked.

'It faded away because students stopped coming. Mr Hepner might be willing to do this again, but could this be student-driven?'

'Yes,' many respond.

'What would need to happen?'

'Talk to Ms Wright,' Shana says referring to the activities director.

'Is anyone willing?'

'Yes! I will!' Shana volunteers.

'Is this a big change in the scheme of things?'

'No. We are only one school', a student says.

'But maybe it will encourage other schools!' Shana offers.

> Class is ending, and Mrs Avila encourages students to think about their conversation today. 'Who will follow through?' she asks as they leave. Several students stay after the bell to talk further with her about the recycling club and various other ideas.

The written curriculum as evidenced by the agenda does not accurately reflect what actually occurred in the classroom.[10] While Mrs Avila certainly did 'discuss population's impact', she did so in a way that elicited thinking in her students that, for some, led to action and for others to increased overall engagement in the class. I asked Mrs Avila in our second interview if anyone had followed up on offering more recycling in the building.[11]

> They haven't had action yet, but they are still talking about it. And, actually Shana, one of the girls who volunteered, is talking to me more in class now and even turned in some late work . . . She was certainly not doing well [before this lesson], but I am hoping that she is feeling a little more tied in.

I asked Mrs Avila why she thinks that the lesson resonated in particular with Shana:

> I have some ideas that maybe it was because I totally trusted that she would do it and that I was very enthusiastic when she volunteered. I am hoping that she at least sees that I do believe in her. I am not sure that she believes in herself a whole bunch.

The complementary curriculum in Mrs Avila's case is not only expressed in the stories and examples of her own life, but also in the types of thinking she elicited in students through a series of questions and statements in the impromptu discussion about recycling. To elicit that thinking, she employed a pedagogical technique of questioning which is similar to strategies discussed by Cotton (2006b) in her study of three geography teachers in the UK. Cotton identified three strategies teachers use to discuss controversial environmental education topics: 'Strategy 1: Eliciting students' personal views . . .; Strategy 2: Enabling students to discuss their own views . . .; and Strategy 3: Challenging students' views' (p. 227).

Cotton's study and this study are similar in that both identify 'real', not 'ideal' practices. However, the contexts are different in that all three of Cotton's participants were actively engaged in teaching environmental issues as part of the formal curriculum. Still, the strategies discussed (and in particular Strategies 1 and 3) are evident in Mrs Avila's practice and offer another example of this pedagogy at work.

Furthermore, Mrs Avila appears more focused on uncovering the origins of students' individual behaviours. She spends a lot of time eliciting students' rationales for their own behaviour. ('Evan, what will you do with that bottle when you are done with it?'). This fourth strategy of considering the rationale for one's own behaviour could be considered useful in contexts in which teachers are focused on action, or in which the focus is on habits of mind that affect behaviour ('Why won't you recycle it?'). While the teachers in Cotton's study were more engaged in debating complex and abstract issues (such as the governance of Antarctica), Mrs Avila and her students were dealing with seemingly simple and concrete behavior—recycling. Discussing this immediate and daily behaviour highlighted the locality and immediacy of personal choice for students. This strategy, or pedagogical practice, emerged from deeply-held beliefs and the lifestyle of Mrs Avila, and it took place in the context of the caring classroom community she consciously orchestrated. It may be difficult for other teachers to emulate, but in this case, the pedagogical practice that characterizes the complementary curriculum in Mrs Avila's work led some students to reflect upon their own behaviour and to ultimately reorganize the Environment Club at Highline.

Implications for Teaching: Toward an 'Environmentally-Sustainable Pedagogy'

Mrs Avila's pedagogical choices help her to guide students to a more ecological frame of mind; she does so by expanding upon the formal social-studies curriculum. However, many ecological curriculum theorists suggest that environmentally-sustainable education should be characterized by a transdisciplinary curriculum (Van Kannel-Ray 2006). This kind of curriculum requires a communal effort and, I would argue, a whole-school reform effort.[12] The participants in the present study, however, did not have the benefit of working within whole-school curriculum framework, or even with like-minded others. Indeed, each teacher worked alone and in a single discipline. Therefore, to ask whether or not they are realizing a new model of ecological education is neither fair nor appropriate, but we may perhaps glean some aspects of what *environmentally-sustainable pedagogy* could look like:

> environmentally sustainable pedagogy as a theory of teaching can inform how to hold the individual and the community in relationship . . . It can offer a new identity to teachers as teaching with a moral imperative, as helping students to become more responsibly embedded in the natural world. (Van Kannel-Ray 2006: 122)

She suggests that pedagogical practices should emerge from the overarching ecological principles of 'intergenerational responsibility', 'organic perception', and 'sustainable outcomes' (p. 117). Each teacher from the present study contributes to a vision of these pedagogical practices through either intergenerational responsibility or organic perception (the present study is limited in understanding the effects on sustainable outcomes).

Intergenerational responsibility deals with balancing the individual's needs with the needs of the past and the future. Mr Rye begins to help weave this tale of balance in his writing exercises with students. He urges them to write in detail about their own individuality, but couches that uniqueness and related consumption in a broader perspective so as to avoid seeing 'the individual as the epicentre of the universe' (Bowers 1995: 7). Furthermore, this type of focus seems to be in line with Bonnett's (2002) discussion of education for sustainability as a frame of mind which seeks to 'reconnect people with their origins and what sustains them *and* to develop their love of themselves' (p. 271). Reminding them that until recently water was the predominant drink for humankind, and that also until recently humankind relied upon local food sources, Mr Rye brings a deeper awareness of the connections between humans and their environments to his students and highlights students' understandings of their own choices. Mr Rye does not, however, ask students to change their behaviours or to even consider the environmental or social ramifications of their choices. On the other hand, Mrs Avila does urge students to consider the effects of their choices, particularly the ways they handle trash and recycling. Her efforts seem particularly fruitful in that the Recycling Club gained renewed membership and activity.

Organic perception is an indication of an individual's perceived connection with the natural world (Van Kannel-Ray 2006). Seeing oneself as connected, or as Ms Snow puts it 'in relationship', limits our tendencies to exploit others, both human and other-than-human. Therefore, Ms Snow's work may also make a contribution to environmentally-sustainable pedagogy in her cultivation of a caring community. Not only does Ms Snow have a deep commitment to fostering relationships with her students, she facilitates students' relationships with each other through encouragement, creating space for students to have their voices heard, and by making it safe for them to discuss different ideas with each other, even in a very diverse setting. This is done in the context of individual purpose and a discussion of each student's 'song'. The learning community becomes a place that fosters organic perception.

Complementary curriculum, the embedded and often unconscious expression of one's beliefs, is the manifestation of a teacher's wholeness or completeness, of his or her integrity.[13] In his essay 'The heart of a teacher: identity and integrity in teaching', Palmer (1997) discusses the importance of teachers' awareness and development of identity and integrity in teaching. By identity Palmer means 'an evolving nexus where all the forces that constitute my life converge in the mystery of self . . . Identity is a moving intersection of the inner and outer forces that make me who I am' (p. 17). By integrity Palmer means 'whatever wholeness I am able to find within that nexus as its vectors form and re-form the pattern of my life. Integrity requires that I discern what is integral to my selfhood, what fits and what does not' (p. 17). For Palmer, a teacher's identity and integrity—not technique and method—are what make them great teachers:

> My ability to connect with my students, and to connect them with the subject, depends less on the methods I use than on the degree to which I know and trust my selfhood—and am willing to make it available and vulnerable in the service of learning. (p. 16)

Complementary curriculum is the expression of this identity and integrity, of what Palmer (1997: 16) calls the 'integral and undivided self'. As illustrated in the vignettes presented above, this expression might emerge in a variety of planned or spontaneous ways, often dependent upon the particular moment and context as orchestrated by the teacher. This is what makes complementary curriculum different from the myriad of other terms in our curricular lexicon: the source of complementary curriculum comes uniquely from the teacher and her personal passions and beliefs.

While the focus of this study is on the expression of ecological beliefs and therefore complementary *ecological* curriculum, this idea might be applied to other beliefs or passions, such as an artistic sensibility or commitment to social justice. In order to explore and understand the complementary curriculum of such beliefs, the researcher would need to first interview the teacher so that she may articulate her beliefs and passions. Next, the researcher would observe the teacher's work to see how if at all the beliefs are infused in practice. For example, these passions might be expressed through the use of music or stories of artistic encounters, or through a biographical study of social activists, or first-hand accounts of participating in social change. It is important to note that the teachers' beliefs may emerge intentionally or unintentionally, consciously or not. Therefore, a follow-up interview with the teacher can foster a discussion of the teacher's intentions and beliefs with the researcher's observations. The researcher is then better able to evaluate how the expression of that teacher's beliefs—the complementary curriculum—influences pedagogy, curriculum, assessment, class structure, or other dimensions of schooling.

In addition to conducting a follow-up interview, sharing the educational criticisms (or observations) with the teachers may illuminate for them previously unseen connections between their beliefs and practice. Such was the case in the present study, and after I shared the educational criticisms with each teacher, I was struck by their responses. Ms Snow writes:

> I learned about how our internal belief systems shape the teaching process. Before I understood the nature of [your] study, I could not accurately articulate why I had sometimes been very happy and other times very unhappy with teaching. Now I understand the very necessary and intrinsic core of how our ecological belief systems and (for me, at least) a corresponding spiritual belief system shapes the art of our relationships with our wonderful students. (Personal communication, 8 September 2006)

While this study looks particularly at ecological beliefs, having a similar dialogue with teachers about their particular beliefs and then illustrating for them how those beliefs come to light in their practice may lead to a more developed sense of their teaching integrity, and further research could also explore how the complementary curriculum affects students directly.

Implications for Ecological Teacher Education

Because of the skills, beliefs, and knowledge required to implement environmental education curricula, many point to the importance of ecological perspectives in teacher education programmes (Tilbury 1996, Oulton and Scott 1997, Corcoran 1999b). Some teacher educators have investigated the lives of ecologically-minded teachers and what factors caused them to become ecologically aware. Corcoran (1999b) details the process of writing an environmental autobiography, through which he guides his undergraduate pre-service teachers. Corcoran affirms the belief that environmental education in teacher education is the 'priority of priorities' (Tilbury 1996, cited in Corcoran 1999b: 179).

Corcoran says that environmental autobiographies can help us identify what makes humans want to live sustainably, an issue at the heart of environmental education. Corcoran says, 'A desire to protect the natural world arises from a deep sense of affinity with the land and nonhuman beings' (p.179). He terms this '*biophilia*', or a love for other living beings, which Corcoran believes is 'central to our nature as humans' (p. 180). This is where he begins with environmental educators—with this innate sense of connection explored through environmental autobiography.

Corcoran (1999a) also completed a study of environmental educators in which he sought to understand the significant childhood life-experiences that led environmental educators to feel a strong connection with the natural world. Mirroring a previous study in the UK by Palmer (1993), he surveyed 510 US teachers about their experiences in nature as children. The narratives have recurring themes such as parents and grandparents as environmental educators and role models; fear of the effects of environmental problems; world-view, faith, and spirituality; childhood time outside; and hope (Corcoran 1999a: 211–217). Corcoran believes that teachers who have had these significant life experiences will provide similar opportunities for their students to develop their own affinity for the natural world. The present study, in combination with those discussed and cited above, builds evidence that attention to the ecological beliefs of pre-service and in-service teachers may play an important role in the expansion of environmental and ecological education, whatever form they may take.

Complementary ecological curriculum also may have import for students. In the case of ecological education, Corcoran (1999a) notes that many who hold ecological beliefs trace the origins of those beliefs to a role model they had in childhood. Perhaps ecologically-minded teachers may become one of those role models as they demonstrate to students through the complementary curriculum that their ecological beliefs are just below the surface and guide their decisions and ways of being. It illustrates to students that ecological issues and ideas are connected to a variety of aspects of our lives, and that they are integral in the minds of the ecologically-minded teachers. These issues and ideas comprise parts of the teachers' identities, and they inform aspects of personal and global decisions. Complementary ecological curriculum reinforces the notion that the environment and ecological issues are not separate or supplemental; they are part and parcel of our everyday lives. Smith (2004) notes a similar phenomenon in his study of the Environmental Middle School. Teachers did not 'check their ideals at the door. They instead brought those ideals into every dimension of their work' (p. 77). Both studies indicate that teachers' ecological beliefs inform their practice, and therefore what students may experience.

Conclusion

In his discussion of educational criticism, Eisner (2002) considers whether or not we can generalize from such research. While criticism cannot predict outcomes, it can, Eisner argues, create 'forms of anticipation by functioning as a kind of road map for the future' (p. 243):

> Once having found that such and such exists in a classroom, we learn to anticipate it in other classrooms that we visit. Through our experience we build up a repertoire of anticipatory images that makes our search patterns more efficient. (p. 243)

This is the case, I believe, with complementary curriculum, ecological or otherwise. As critics, teacher educators, curricularists, and researchers, we can enter a classroom anticipating various expressions of teachers' personal beliefs. This recognition adds a layer to our understanding and evaluation of what is happening in a classroom, or to what could or should be happening. In this way, identifying, understanding, and evaluating the complementary curriculum is not only useful to teachers themselves, but also to those who aim to support teachers and schools in their efforts, particularly those important and difficult efforts to 'green' our schools.

Acknowledgment

I am grateful to Bruce Uhrmacher of the University of Denver and Peter Hlebowitsh of the University of Iowa for their thoughtful and constructive feedback on drafts of this paper.

Notes

1. By 'non-environmental' I simply mean educational contexts and models that are not explicitly focused on teaching environmental themes and ideas, such as a traditional school or an English classroom focused on the Western canon. Certainly all contexts can be considered ecological, although Orr (1992: 90) has said that 'all education is environmental education,'. In other words, it is impossible to separate humans and our constructed worlds from the planet on which we live.
2. It is important to note that many environmental education reforms call for integration of disciplines (see Orr 1992, Smith and Williams 1999, Jardine 2000). While this may indeed be an appropriate and necessary recommendation, the current reality of public schooling is that most US secondary schools are structured with disciplinary separation.
3. The current war in Iraq (Flinders 2006), some religious concepts, and in some cases evolution are all examples of what is not taught in US schools.
4. Eisner (1998) developed educational connoisseurship and criticism (henceforth called educational criticism) as method of qualitative inquiry intended to improve education. Connoisseurship is the art of appreciation and criticism the art of disclosure (Eisner 2002). Therefore, connoisseurship requires that the researcher have enough educational knowledge to be able to observe the subtleties and intricacies of the educational setting. The criticism, then, illuminates the connoisseur's perspective with the aim of educational improvement in mind.
5. See note 1.
6. The campus of SLHS boasts a collegiate setting with four separate buildings, three cafeterias, a variety of outdoor spaces to congregate, and extensive sports facilities. The school is situated on 80 acres adjacent to a large state park, and several of its classrooms overlook the reservoir. Students have a generous amount of autonomy. Of the 3700 students, approximately 86% are White, 2% are African American, 7% are Asian, and 5% are Hispanic.
7. HHS lies on 32 acres near a large public park and wetlands refuge. The single, more traditional high-school building has been recently remodelled to include an Academic Success Centre, a new athletic area, and refurbished entrances. Of the approximately 2000 students at Highline, 1% is Native American, 32% are African American, 6% are Asian, 16% are Hispanic, and 45% are White. Furthermore, students speak 52 home languages and come from 110 countries. Both schools have an average class size of about 25 students. SLHS and HHS participate in their district's large-scale curriculum implementation project in which all classes provide an opportunity to learn certain essential components in the core areas (English, mathematics, social studies, and science). Teachers are provided with extensive curriculum binders, but in most cases are not directed how to teach the essential core content. The formal curriculum is a compilation of the state of Colorado's standards as well as university-preparatory skills, and a major focus of the district is to improve performance on standardized state tests.
8. Ms Snow was trained by Native American teachers in various ceremonies for a number of years. For purposes of confidentiality, I have eliminated all other identifying details.
9. *Zelig* is the story of a man who transforms himself to be like those who surround him in order to gain approval.
10. Eisner (2002: 32–34) described that which actually happens in a classroom as the 'operationalized curriculum'.
11. After the conclusion of this study, HHS did resurrect the Environment Club. Many members came from Mrs Avila's class.
12. See, for example, the Portland Environmental Middle School (Smith 2004).
13. `Complementary' literally means 'forming a complement, completing, perfecting' or 'of two (or more) things: mutually complementing or completing each other's deficiencies' (*Oxford English Dictionary* 1989). We might think of complementary angles, which when paired together make a right angle. We might also think of complementary colours, 'which, in combination, produce white or colourless light' (*Oxford English Dictionary* 1989).

References

Barone, T. (2000) *Aesthetics, Politics, and Educational Inquiry: Essays and Examples* (New York: Peter Lang).

Blumstein, D. T. and Saylan, C. (2007) The failure of environmental education (and how we can fix it). *PLoS Biology*, 5(5), e120. Available online at: http://www.pubmedcentral.nih.gov/articlerender.fcgi?artid=1847843, accessed 12 November 2008.

Bonnett, M. (2002) Education for sustainability as a frame of mind. *Environmental Education Research*, 8(1), 265–276.

Bowers, C. A. (1993) *Education, Cultural Myths, and the Ecological Crisis: Toward Deep Changes* (Albany, NY: State University of New York Press).

Bowers, C. A. (1995) *Educating for an Ecologically Sustainable Culture: Rethinking Moral Education, Creativity, Intelligence, and Other Modern Orthodoxies* (Albany, NY: State University of New York Press).

Bowers, C. A. (2001) *Educating for Eco-justice and Community* (Athens, GA: University of Georgia Press).

Bowers, C. A. (2003) *Mindful Conservatism: Rethinking the Ideological and Educational Basis of an Ecologically Sustainable Future* (Lanham, MD: Rowman & Littlefield).

Connelly, F. M., He, M. F. and Phillion, J. (2008) *The SAGE Handbook of Curriculum and Instruction* (Los Angeles, CA: Sage).

Corcoran, P. B. (1999a) Formative influences in the lives of environmental educators in the United States. *Environmental Education Research*, 5(2), 207–220.

Corcoran, P. B. (1999b) Environmental autobiography in undergraduate educational studies. In G. A. Smith and D. R. Williams (eds), *Ecological Education in Action: On Weaving Education, Culture, and the Environment* (Albany, NY: State University of New York Press), 179–188.

Cotton, D. R. E. (2006a) Implementing curriculum guidance on environmental education: the importance of teacher's beliefs. *Journal of Curriculum Studies*, 38(1), 67–83.

Cotton, D. R. E. (2006b) Teaching controversial environmental issues: neutrality and balance in the reality of the classroom. *Educational Research*, 48(2), 223–241.

Cutter-MacKenzie, A. and Smith, R. (2003) Ecological literacy: the 'missing paradigm' in environmental education (Part one). *Environmental Education Research*, 9(4), 497–524.

Dillon, P. J. and Gayford, C. G. (1997) A psychometric approach to investigating the environmental beliefs, intentions, and behaviours of pre-service teachers. *Environmental Education Research*, 3(3), 283–297.

Eisner, E. W. (1988) The ecology of school improvement. *Educational Leadership*, 45(5), 24–29.

Eisner, E. W. (1998) *The Enlightened Eye: Qualitative Inquiry and the Enhancement of Educational Practice* (Upper Saddle River, NJ: Merrill).

Eisner, E. W. (2002) *The Educational Imagination: On the Design and Evaluation of School Programs*, 3rd ed. (New York: Macmillan).

Flinders, D. J. (1996) Teaching for cultural literacy: a curriculum study. *Journal of Curriculum and Supervision*, 2(4), 351–366.

Flinders, D. J. (2006) We can and should teach the war in Iraq. *Education Digest*, 71(5), 8–12.

Flinders, D. J., Noddings, N. and Thornton, S. J. (1986) The null curriculum: its theoretical basis and practical implications. *Curriculum Inquiry*, 16(1), 33–42.

Gruenewald, D. A. and Manteaw, B. O. (2007) Oil and water still: how No Child Left Behind limits and distorts environmental education in US schools. *Environmental Education Research*, 13(2), 171–188.

He, M. F., Phillion, J., Chan, E. and Xu, S. (2008) Immigrant students' experience of curriculum. In F. M. Connelly, M. F. He and J. Phillion (eds), *The SAGE Handbook of Curriculum and Instruction* (Los Angeles, CA: Sage), 219–239.

Heimlich, J. E. (ed.) (2002) *Environmental Education: A Resource Handbook* (Bloomington, IN: Phi Delta Kappa Educational Foundation).

International Union for the Conservation of Nature and Natural Resources (IUCN)/UNESCO (1970) *Final Report on an International Working Meeting on Environmental Education in the School Curriculum—International Union for the Conservation of Nature and Natural Resources in Cooperation with UNESCO as Part of UNESCO's International Education Year* (Gland, Switzerland: IUCN).

Jackson, P. W. (1968) *Life in Classrooms* (New York: Holt, Rinehart & Winston).

Jardine, D. W. (2000) '*Under the Tough Old Star*': *Ecopedagogical Essays* (Brandon, VT: Foundation for Educational Renewal).

Jickling, B. and Wals, A. (2007) Globalization and environmental education: looking beyond sustainable development. *Journal of Curriculum Studies*, 40(1), 1–21.

Martusewicz, R. (2005) Eros in the commons: educating for eco-ethical consciousness in a poetics of place. *Ethics, Place and Environment*, 8(3), 331–348.

Moroye, C. M. (2005) Common ground: an ecological perspective on teaching and learning. *Curriculum and Teaching Dialogue*, 7(1.2), 123–137.

Noddings, N. (ed.) (2005) *Educating Citizens for Global Awareness* (New York: Teachers College Press).

Orr, D. W. (1992) *Ecological Literacy: Education and the Transition to a Postmodern World* (Albany, NY: State University of New York Press).

Oulton, C. R. and Scott, W. A. H. (1997) Linking teacher education and environmental education: a European perspective. In P. J. Thompson (ed.), *Environmental Education for the 21st Century: International and Interdisciplinary Perspectives* (New York: Peter Lang), 45–57.

Oxford English Dictionary (1989) (Oxford: Oxford University Press).

Palmer, J. (1993) Development of concern for the environment and formative experiences of educators. *Journal of Environmental Education*, 24(3), 26–30.

Palmer, P. J. (1997) The heart of a teacher: identity and integrity in teaching. *Change*, 29(6), 15–21.

Robertson, C. L. and Krugly-Smolska, E. (1997) Gaps between advocated practices and teaching realities in environmental education. *Environmental Education Research*, 3(3), 311–326.

Smith, G. A. (2004) Cultivating care and connection: preparing the soil for a just and sustainable society. *Educational Studies*, 36(1), 73–92.

Smith, G. A. (2007) Place-based education: breaking through the constraining regularities of public school. *Environmental Education Research*, 13(2), 189–207.

Smith, G. A. and Williams, D. R. (1999) *Ecological Education in Action: On Weaving, Education, Culture, and the Environment* (Albany, NY: State University of New York Press).

Sobel, D. (2004) *Place-based Education: Connecting Classrooms & Communities* (Great Barrington, MA: The Orion Society).

Sterling, S. (2001) *Sustainable Education: Re-visioning Learning and Change* Schumacher Briefing, No 6 (Foxhole, UK: Green Books).

Tilbury, D. (1996) Environmentally educating teachers: the priority of priorities. *Connect*, 15(1), 1.

Uhrmacher, P. B. (1997) The curriculum shadow. *Curriculum Inquiry*, 27(3), 317–329.

Uhrmacher, P. B. and Matthews, J. (eds) (2005) *Intricate Pallette: Working the Ideas of Elliot Eisner* (Upper Sadle River, NJ: Pearson).

United Nations Conference on Environment and Development (earth Summit) (1992) *Agenda 21: Chapter 36: Promoting Education, Public Awareness and Training*. Available online at: http://www.un.org/esa/sustdev/documents/agenda21/english/agenda21chapter36.htm, accessed 3 November 2008.

Van Kannel-Ray, N. (2006) Guiding principles and emerging practices for environmentally sustainable education. *Curriculum and Teaching Dialogue*, 8(1/2), 113–123.

32

Curriculum for the 21st Century

Nel Noddings

1 Introduction

Virtually all over the world, the school curriculum is organized into courses centered on the traditional disciplines. Other courses appear occasionally. In the United States, when a problem arises, the standard response is to add a course. Thus we may see courses in sex education, driver safety, everyday nutrition, or moral education. However, these courses rarely count toward college admission. For this purpose, the disciplines remain sacred.

The practice of emphasizing the traditional disciplines has actually hardened in recent years with the growth of participation in Advanced Placement courses and International Baccalaureate programs. In addition, more cities and states in the United States now require virtually all secondary school students, regardless of their talents, to take standard academic courses. This requirement is defended in the name of equality of opportunity, but some of us believe that it is demonstrably unfair to force students into courses they hate and deprive them of courses (or programs) better suited to their talents and interests (Noddings, 2007).

The question to be explored here is this: Is curriculum for the 21st century best organized around the traditional disciplines or is there a more promising alternative?

2 Goals and Aims in Education

There is little discussion of aims in the United States today. It is as though the whole matter were long ago decided, and the problem to be addressed is how to get all students successfully through the standard curriculum. Twin economic aims are implicit: to produce students who will be economically successful as individuals and to maintain the economic supremacy of the nation.

Educators and policymakers have not always embraced such narrow aims. In 1918, the National Education Association produced a report, *Cardinal Principles of Secondary Education* (NEA, 1918), that suggested seven aims: health, command of fundamental processes, worthy home membership, vocation, citizenship, worthy use of leisure, and ethical character. The report was thought by some to presage a healthy transformation of secondary education, but it was condemned by others as the beginning of the end—the downfall—of American education. Those who have spoken in condemnation of the broader curriculum introduced by the comprehensive high school ignore the fact that the introduction of new courses and tracks made it possible to increase enrollment in secondary schools from barely 7% in 1900 to well over 50% by the middle of the 20th century. That is a remarkable achievement.

Although the aims recommended by the *Cardinal Principles* are rarely mentioned today, they may be more important now than they were in 1918. Families and home life have changed significantly. Often both parents work outside the home, and much time at home is spent watching television or communicating via computer. Little time may be spent working together on household tasks, and even less time may be devoted to the kinds of discussions that contribute to the education of whole persons. Indeed, 21st century schools may be called upon to take over many of the functions once assigned to homes.

We should note that these aims—with occasional exceptions—are not best pursued directly as specific learning objectives. Instead, they provide a lens through which we select topics, pedagogical methods, organizational features of our schools, and by which we evaluate what we are doing. As we plan, teach, and evaluate, we ask how our work is or is not promoting growth toward each of these aims.

Today, there are again a few voices raised in praise of efforts such as the *Cardinal Principles* and in opposition to the present trend to over-emphasize academic courses for all students. But this time, a question is raised whether a traditional program of studies in discrete disciplines is the best course of study for anyone. In the 21st century, even specialists may need a broader education than one provided by narrowly defined disciplines. Such an education may require substantial reorganization of the curriculum. At the least, it will require stretching the disciplines from within and blurring the lines between them. The biologist, E. O. Wilson remarks:

> There is, in my opinion, an inevitability to the unity of knowledge. It reflects real life. The trajectory of world events suggests that educated people should be far better able than before to address the great issues courageously and analytically by undertaking a traverse of disciplines. We are into the age of synthesis, with a real empirical bite to it. (2006, p. 137)

Some argue for a synthetic organization around themes, subordinating the disciplines to great social problems (Noddings, 2005a). Others, largely in agreement with the first group, argue for greater emphasis on attitudes, values, and social skills (Cheng, in press). What are these new aims, and what would the new forms of organization look like?

3 Educational Aims for a Changing World

As we consider educational aims for the 21st century, perhaps the first move should be to reaffirm aims of the sort set out in the *Cardinal Principles.* There was then, and there still is, a need to educate whole persons. It is not impossible to do this through the traditional disciplines, but it is difficult. Early in the 20th century, Alfred North Whitehead criticized the "fatal disconnection of subjects which kills the vitality of our modern curriculum." He went on to say:

> There is only one subject-matter for education, and that is Life in all its manifestations. Instead of this single unity, we offer children—Algebra, from which nothing follows; Geometry, from which nothing follows; Science, from which nothing follows; History, from which nothing follows; a Couple of Languages, never mastered; and lastly, most dreary of all, Literature,

> represented by plays of Shakespeare, with philological notes and short analyses of plot and character to be in substance committed to memory. (1967, pp. 6–7)

This is a devastating criticism of early 20th century curriculum. Today the problem Whitehead discussed may be even worse. Many more facts have been amassed in the disciplines, and territorial lines are drawn even more tightly. Mathematics teachers are neither prepared nor encouraged to discuss literature, and tenth grade literature teachers may be forbidden to teach literature prescribed for the eleventh grade. Moreover, the emphasis on preparation for standardized tests discourages the exploration of matters that cross disciplinary lines and reach into life itself.

Whitehead, a first-rate mathematician, was not arguing against the study of quantity, nor am I. He wrote:

> Elegant intellects which despise the theory of quantity, are but half developed. They are more to be pitied than blamed. The scraps of gibberish, which in their school-days were taught to them in the name of algebra, deserve some contempt. (1967, p. 7)

In our current zeal to teach all children—regardless of their own interests and talents—"algebra," the scraps of gibberish have grown into volumes, and more universal aims are neglected. Inner city teenagers, exposed to phony algebra, do not understand basic matters of quantity such as how they are cheated by check-cashing outfits.

In addition to the aims directed at satisfying personal lives, we now must prepare students for the new occupational structures of a post-industrial world. The work world, like that of home and family, has changed substantially. More workers are employed in relatively small organizations instead of the huge manufacturing plants characteristic of the early 20th century. Many work-places are not as hierarchically organized as they once were, and workers are evaluated by their peers as well as their bosses. Team work is required. Moreover, many jobs now require means-ends planning, diagnosis of problems, and cooperation in the search for solutions. Mindless, repetitive work has not disappeared, but it is no longer the norm. Then, too, few workers will devote their whole working life to one employer; most will change jobs, and many will make dramatic mid-career changes.

Aims for this new occupational world include:
Ability to communicate effectively
Ability to work as a team member
Flexibility
Preparedness to face changes and challenges
Preparedness to identify and solve problems
Skill in analysis and conceptualization
Capacity and willingness to learn new things
Ability to question, challenge, and innovate
Willingness and capacity to assume personal responsibility
Capacity for self-reflection and self-management (adapted from Cheng, in press).
These aims are required by demonstrable changes in the world of work.

Combined with aims directed at a satisfying life as an individual and citizen, a justifiable agenda for education in the 21st century bears little resemblance to the dull, grinding labor of attaining higher scores on standardized tests of narrowly defined subject matter.

4 Taking the New Aims Seriously

It is highly unlikely that the curriculum for secondary education will be reorganized around categories different from the traditional disciplines. Even if pre-college educators were enthusiastic about such a move, the colleges and universities would block it. The organization of their own curriculum and their criteria for admission ensure the continued emphasis on the disciplines as preparation for college.

However, the cause of curricular transformation is not hopeless. Thoughtful educators at both college and pre-college levels take seriously a call for more connections among subjects and for increased attention to the qualities required of 21st century workers. If the disciplines will remain as the nominal heart of the curriculum, their characterization and isolation may change.

Again, the new aims, like those named in the *Cardinal Principles*, should not be treated as specific learning objectives. We cannot design a set of lessons on "team membership" and expect that, at its conclusion, everyone will pass a test on teamwork. Instead, we have to ask how our selection of topics and teaching methods may contribute to the development of these attitudes and skills. Surely the search for real-life meaning is fundamental in learning to communicate, in developing the willingness to face changes and engage in analysis, self-reflection, and problem solving. A curriculum that demands relentless memorization and continual preparation for standardized tests is unlikely to promote such development.

It may help to give several examples of the sort of changes that are feasible. In the subject called *English* (or substitute the native language of other countries), literature plays a central role. But the literature selected for the curriculum could be chosen for its relevance to various existential and social questions. The usual way of selecting literary works is to list authors who should be read and then select those works that seem appropriate for a given age group. Sometimes, because those works are truly timeless, existential and social themes are paramount, but they are often ignored in favor of discussion of literary style, use of metaphor, and vocabulary. With deliberate emphasis on problems central to real life, teachers would be encouraged to discuss these themes and to connect what is read to discussions in other classes.

We should note also that the list of master-works—candidates for a canon—has grown so large that it is difficult to agree on which authors should be included. This is another reason for rejecting this method of selection. Of course, we would like our students to appreciate the power and beauty of great writing, but we would also like them to see literature as a contribution to their search for meaning in their own lives.

For example, students interested in their own reasons for learning—for achieving an education—might find much to dicuss in John Knowles, *A Separate Peace*, Charles Dickens, *Hard Times*, William Golding, *Lord of the Flies*, Muriel Sparks, *The prime of Miss Jean Brodie*, George Orwell, "Such, such were the Joys," and parts of Thomas Hardy, *Jude the Obscure*. Several of these works already appear in the American curriculum but, because they are not chosen as exemplars of a theme, students may not make the connection to "life itself."

In *A Separate Peace*, the narrator, Gene, looks back on his days as a student in a prestigious boys' school. Highly competitive as a student, Gene identified the great weakness of Chet, his nearest rival for academic honors. Chet was genuinely interested in some of what was taught, and this genuine interest distracted him from the pursuit of high grades in all subjects. Gene, in contrast, treated all subjects and all ideas alike.

This is a sad and important message for today's teenagers, many of whom are under enormous pressure to achieve high grades (Pope, 2001). Is there no room for genuine love of learning?

Hard Times describes a father, Thomas Gradgrind, who forbids his children to imagine or speculate. They must stick to the facts, and the novel's headmaster, M'Choakumchild, insists on the same approach in his teaching. The students are filled with trivial, mostly irrelevant facts, although they are longing for emotional connection and meaning in life. This story also echoes life in too many of today's schools.

Reading *Lord of the Flies* with an emphasis on education, students should consider whether a different form of education might have prevented Jack from becoming a cruel tyrant and perhaps have helped Ralph to foresee the tragic events that took place. Or is it possible that children (through at least their early teens) need careful adult supervision?

In reading *The Prime of Miss Jean Brodie*, students have an opportunity to examine the motives of teachers. Do all teachers have the best interests of their students at heart, or are some motivated by the desire for power and admiration? What about the students who betray their peers to curry the favor of a teacher?

We are encouraged to think of schooling as a benefit, but many students suffer in school. Orwell's "Such, such were the Joys," is a moving account of such suffering.

If education is accepted as a theme, teachers might want to add further biographical material. For example, reading about Winston Churchill's school experience yields an opportunity not only to criticize the curriculum that Whitehead found stifling but also to connect literature to history.

Teachers in different cultures will, of course, choose different literature. However, the basic idea remains intact. Existential themes are universal. Choose a theme that matters, and pursue it in some depth. Themes to consider include love of place, war and peace, our relation to nonhuman animals, religion and spirituality, virtue and vice, friendship, and romance. It may be especially important to do this today in countries, such as the United States, where the curriculum has been widely criticized as "a mile wide and an inch deep."

Consider another example, this time from science. In the United States, there are those who would like to include "creationism" or "intelligent design" as well as evolution in biology classes. In most places, this move has been blocked on the grounds that these alternatives are not science, but religion. This seems undeniably right. However, many of us believe that the debate itself and its fascinating history should be part of every student's education. Agreeing that creationism and its variants are not science and that they should not be presented *as* science, we still believe that the social problems of this debate should be explored.

In science class? This challenge illustrates the dilemma faced by those who would transform curriculum for the 21st century. The sharp division of subject matter along traditional disciplinary lines continually prevents wide-ranging and relevant exploration. My own answer is yes, of course, the discussion should take place in science class and in any other class where related questions arise. The division of subject matters is today preventing the pursuit of aims associated with genuine education.

But if we relax disciplinary lines and discuss topics in history, literature, religion, biography (the life of Charles Darwin), and politics in biology, how can we possibly cover the material required by the course of study? We cannot, and it can be argued that we should not "cover" so much material. Our aim is to *educate*, to encourage careful thinking (Noddings, 2006), critical examination of information, a commitment to examine all sides, and to allow time for genuine interest—perhaps even enthusiasm—to develop. We must have time to push back the boundaries of the disciplines

There is a related problem in the science curriculum, and higher education bears much responsibility for it. Colleges require "real" science—technical biology, physics, and chemistry—and they scorn what is called "popular science." But intelligent non-scientists depend regularly on popular science to inform us about matters of health, the natural environment, the effects of various drugs, progress in space, and technology. We may not be able to name the amino acids that construct proteins or the precise constitution of DNA, but we know that certain traits and dispositions can be traced to certain genes—their presence, absence, or mutation, and we know that the analysis of DNA has provided the evolutionary evidence once sought through fossil remains.

Too many teenagers today are forced to take courses in technical science—courses designed to prepare them for further courses in sciences, not for full, healthy adult lives. When we look carefully at the material chosen for college preparatory courses, we see that, too often, "nothing follows" from it except for those few who eagerly look forward to further courses in the same subject. To provide for these students is a difficult and complex problem that must be addressed. Its details are beyond the scope of this brief article, but its importance should not be denied.

We should look at one more example of ways in which to stretch the disciplines from within. The case of *social studies* is instructive. First, the 20th century change from history, civics, and geography as separate subjects to social studies is an early example of trying to push back the boundaries of discrete disciplines. The new area was to incorporate not only the three basic subjects but also some economics, politics, sociology, and perhaps psychology. It is a sign of what transformationists are up against that there are still vigorous opponents of the move away from history and civics, and even those of us who approve the change deplore the loss of geographical topics in the curriculum. However, we believe that elements of geography conforming to 21st century aims can be incorporated into a vital new curriculum (Thornton, 2007).

In the United States, critics of the move to social studies cite surveys that reveal the shocking ignorance of our citizens on basic facts of American history and government. A cry heard repeatedly is that the schools must return to teaching these essential facts. But the schools *do* teach these facts! The facts are simply lost in volumes of information that may be retained until a test is passed and then forgotten. Most people who answer the survey questions successfully are not responding with information retained from their school days but with knowledge continually gathered and interpreted through their on-going interest in public affairs. It is this attitude of continuing interest and the skills acquired through its exercise that the 21st century curriculum should promote.

Of all the school subjects, social studies is perhaps the easiest to transform in the direction discussed here, because it has already sought to unify several disciplines. Its successes and failures should be studied carefully. If the American trend toward an increase in the use of standardized tests as the main measure of achievement continues, we can predict a deterioration of social studies into discrete studies of history, economics, civics (or government), and geography.

Such fragmentation would be unfortunate in an age when attention must be given to the problems of resources (especially water), environmental preservation, religious understanding, peace, world health, technology, post-industrial work, the condition of minorities, and globalization (Noddings, 2005b). Notice that, in tackling these problems, the aims suggested for a 21st century curriculum are vital. People must work together, communicate effectively, be willing and able to solve problems without undo self-interest, and be flexible in the face of change.

Again, I do not mean to underestimate the problems involved in attempting this transformation of curriculum. It is easy to talk about skills associated with the values we recommend. But what, exactly, are these skills, and how are they best promoted? We have to ask not only what *all* students need to learn and be able to do but also what students with specialized interests need. What role should schools play in preparing future specialists? Which of the aims can be addressed in virtually all courses offered in our schools? Which require special attention? How might the organization of our secondary schools affect the promotion of our aims? What role is played, for example, by extra-curricular activities? How do our methods of evaluation enhance or detract from our efforts at the unification of knowledge? How can teachers be prepared for such large changes?

5 Conclusion

I have offered a tentative and preliminary answer to the question posed at the beginning of this article: Is curriculum for the 21st century best organized around the traditional disciplines of is there a more promising alternative? Because it seems likely that the disciplines will continue to serve as the organizing rubric for the curriculum, I have suggested that they be stretched from within, that we push back the boundaries between disciplines and ask how each of the expanded subjects can be designed to promote new aims for the 21st century.

References

Cheng, Kai-ming. (in press). Education for all, but for what? In Joel E. Cohen & Martin B. Malin (Eds.), *The wise child.*(Manuscript in preparation).

National Education Association (1918). *Cardinal principles of secondary education: A report of the commission on the reorganization of secondary education*, Washington, D. C.: U. S. Government Printing Office.

Noddings, Nel.(2005a). *The challenge to care in schools*, 2nd ed, New York: Teachers College Press.

—— (Ed.). (2005b). *Educating citizens for global awareness*, New York: Teachers College Press.

—— (2006). *Critical lessons: What our schools should teach*, New York: Cambridge University Press.

—— (2007). *When school reform goes wrong*, New York: Teachers College Press.

Pope, Denise Clark.(2001). *"Doing school": How we are creating a generation of stressed out, materialistic, and miseducated students*, New Haven: Yale University press.

Thornton, Stephen.(2007). Geography in American history courses, *Phi Delta Kappan*, March.

Whitehead, Alfred North.(1967). *The aims of education*, New York: Free Press. (Original work published 1929)

Wilson, E. O.(2006). *The creation: An appeal to save life on earth*, New York: W. W. Norton.

Permissions

"Scientific Method in Curriculum-Making" by Franklin Bobbitt. Public Domain, Preface and Chapter VI in Franklin Bobbitt, *The Curriculum*. Cambridge, MA: The Riverside Press, 1918.

From The Montessori Elementary Material: The Advanced Montessori Method by Maria Montessori © Bentley Publishers, 1734 Massachusetts Avenue, Cambridge, MA 02138. www.BentleyPublishers.com. Reprinted with permissions.

Dewey, John. "My Pedagogic Creed," *Journal of the National Education Association*, Vol. 18, No. 9, pp. 291–295, December 1929. Reprinted by permission of the National Education Association.

Addams, Jane. "The Public School and the Immigrant Child." *Journal of Proceedings and Addresses*, 1908, pp. 99–102. Reprinted with permission from the National Education Association.

"Dare the School Build a New Social Order" by George S. Counts. Chapters 3 and 4, in George S. Counts, *Dare the School Build a New Social Order?* New York: John Day, 1932. Copyright renewed 1959 by George S. Counts. Reprinted by permission of Martha L. Counts.

From Ralph W. Tyler, *Basic Principles of Curriculum and Instruction*, 1949: pp 1–7, 16–19, 25–33. Reprinted with permission by University of Chicago Press

Kliebard, Herbert M. "The Rise of Scientific Curriculum-Making and it's Aftermath," from *Curriculum Theory Network*, V. 5, #1, 1975, pp. 27–38. Reprinted with permission by Blackwell Publishing.

"A Man: A Course of Study" reprinted by permission of the publisher from *Toward a Theory of Instruction* by Jerome S. Bruner, pp. 73–101, Cambridge, Mass: The Belknap Press of Harvard University Press, Copyright © 1966 by the President and the Fellows of Harvard College.

Popham, James W. "Objective." Public domain, Chapter 2 from James W. Popham, *An Evaluation Guidebook: A Set of Practical Guidelines for the Educational Evaluator*. Los Angeles: The Instructional Objectives Exchange, 1972.

Eisner, Elliot W., "Education Objectives-Help or Hindrance." Reprinted by permission of the University of Chicago Press, from *School Review*, Vol. 75, No. 3, 1967: pp. 250–260. Copyright University of Chicago Press.

"The Daily Grind" Reprinted by permission of the Publisher. From Phillip W. Jackson, *Life in Classrooms*, New York: Teachers College Press, © 1990 by Teachers College, Columbia University. All rights reserved.Greene, Maxine. "Curriculum and Consciousness," Teachers College Record, Vol. 73, No. 2, 1971. pp. 253–270. Reprinted with permission.Pinar, William E. "The Reconceptualization of Curriculum Studies" *Journal of Curriculum Studies*,Vo. 10: 3 (1978), pp. 205–214. Taylor & Francis Ltd, http://www.informaworld.com, reprinted by permission of the publisher.

Excerpts from Paulo Freire, *Pedagogy of the Oppressed*. New York: Continuum, ©1970, 1993 by Paulo Friere: pp. 75–86, 95–100. Reprinted with permission of the publisher, The Continuum International Publishing Group.

"The Paideia Proposal" reprinted with the permission of Scribner, an imprint of Simon & Schuster Adult Publishing Group, from *The Paideia Proposal: An Educational Manifesto* by Mortimer J. Adler. Copyright © 1982 by the Institute for Philosophical Research. All rights reserved.

Noddings, Nel. "The False Promise of the Paideia: A Critical Review of the Paideia Proposal," from *Journal of Thought*, Vol. 18, No.4, 1983, pp. 81–91. Reprinted by permission of Caddo Gap Press.

McLaughlin, Milbrey Wallin. "Implementation as Mutual Adaptation: Change in Classroom Organization," *Teachers College Record*, Vol. 77, No. 3, 1976. pp. 339–351. Reprinted with permission. "The Four R's-An Alternative to the Tyler Rational." Reprinted by permission of the Publisher. From William E. Doll, *A Postmodern Perspective on Curriculum*, New York: Teachers College Press, © 1993 by Teachers College, Columbia University. All rights reserved.

Apple, Michael W. "Controlling the Work of Teachers" from *Teachers and Texts*, by Michael W. Apple. New York: Routledge & Kegan Paul, 1986, pp. 31–53. Reprinted with permission of Routledge, a member of Taylor & Francis Books.

Hlebowitsh, Peter. "Centripetal Thinking in Curriculum Studies" from *Curriculum Inquiry*, V. 40, No. 4 (2010), pp. 503–530. Reprinted with permission by Blackwell Publishing."High-Stakes Testing and Curriculum Control: A Qualitative Metasynthesis" by Wayne Au from *Education Researcher* Vol. 36, No. 5, June/July 2007, pp 258–267. Copyright 2007 by Sage Publications Inc. Journals. Reproduced with permission of Sage Publications Inc. Journals in the format Textbook via Copyright Clearance Center.

Sleeter, Christine and Jamy Stillman. "Standardizing Knowledge in a Multicultural Society," from *Curriculum Inquiry* V. 35, #1, Spr. 2005, pp 27–46. Reprinted with permission by Blackwell Publishing.

Siskin, Leslie. "Outside the Core: Accountability in Tested and Untested Subjects" from *The New Accountability: High Schools and High-Stakes Testing*, edited by Martin Carnoy, Richard Elmore, and Leslie Santee Siskin. New York: Routledge, 2003, pp. 87–98. Reprinted with permission of Routledge, a member of Taylor & Francis Books.

Eisner, Elliot W. "What Does it Mean to Say a School is Doing Well?" from *Phi Delta Kappan*, Vol. 82, No. 5, 2001, pp 367–372. Reprinted by permission of Phi Delta Kappa International.

Valenzuela, Angela. "Subtractive Schooling, Caring Relations, and Social Capital in the Schooling of U.S. Mexican Youth." Reprinted by permission from *Beyond Silenced Voices: Class, Race, and Gender in United States Schools, Revised Edition* edited by Lois Weis and Michelle Fine, the State University of New York Press ©1999, State University of New York. All rights reserved.

Chan, Elaine. "Teacher Experiences of Culture in the Curriculum" *Journal of Curriculum Studies*,Vo. 38: 2 (2006), pp. 161–176. Taylor & Francis Ltd, http://www.informaworld.com, reprinted by permission of the publisher.

Sumara, Dennis and David, Brent. "Interrupting Heteronormativity: Toward a Queer

Curriculum Theory" from *Curriculum Inquiry*, Vol. 29, No. 2 (Summer, 1999), pp. 191–208. Reprinted with permission by Blackwell Publishing.

"Silence on Gays and Lesbians in Social Studies Curriculum" from *Social Education*, vol. 67, No. 4, 2003, pp. 226–230. National Council for the Social Studies. by Stephen J. Thornton. © National Council for the Social Studies. Reprinted by permission.

McIntosh, Peggy. "Gender Perspectives on Educating for Global Citizenship." Reprinted by permission of the Publisher. From Nel Noddings, Editor, *Educating Citizens for Global Awareness*, New York: Teachers College Press, © 2005 by Teachers College, Columbia University. All rights reserved.

Misco, Thomas. "Moving Beyond Fidelity Expectations: Rethinking Curriculum Reform for Controversial Topics in Post-Communist Setting." From *Theory and Research in Social Education*. Vol. 38, No. 2, 2010, pg. 182–216. Taylor & Francis Ltd, http://www.informaworld.com, reprinted by permission of the publisher.

Moroye, Christy M. "Complementary Curriculum: The Work of Ecologically Minded Teachers." From the *Journal of Curriculum Studies*. Vol. 41, No. 6, 2009, pp. 789–811. Taylor & Francis Ltd, http://www.informaworld.com, reprinted by permission of the publisher.

Noddings, Nel. "Curriculum for the 21st Century" from *Educational Studies in Japan: International Yearbook*. No. 2, 2007, pp. 75–81. Reprinted with permission by the Japanese Educational Research Association.

Index

AAACS (American Association for the Advancement of Curriculum Studies) 229
Abrams, M. H. 128
academic knowledge 169–70
accountability 211, 247, 256, 269–77, 280; departments 270; initial position of subject 270–3; internal conditions of department 273–5; subjects 270; to test or not to test 275–7
activity analysis 70, 74, 75
Adams, James Truslow 48
Addams, Jane 7–8, 41–3, 334
adequacy criteria 99
Adler, Mortimer 145, 183–6, 187, 188–90, 192, 193, 194
adulthood, preparation for 70–1
AERA *see* American Educational Research Association
affective domain 102, 103–4, 110
age-graded systems 286
agricultural education 16–17
Airasian, P. W. 236
Ali, N. 310
alignment 256
America 2000 279
American Association for the Advancement of Curriculum Studies (AAACS) 229
American Dream 48
American Educational Research Association (AERA) 152, 231
American Historical Association 9
analysis 102, 103
Angelou, Maya 350
anthropology 19
Aoki, T. 355, 361
Apple, M. W. 153; *see also* teachers, controlling the work of
application 103
Arendt, Hannah 285
arithmetic 215–16
art as school subject 66–7
assessment *see* testing
Association for Supervision and Curriculum Development (ASCD) 150, 151, 154, 231
Atkinson, P. 362
attending 103
Au, Wayne *see* high-stakes testing and curriculum control
authenticity 383–8, 393

Baker, Eva 100
Bakhtin, M. M. 231
Baldwin, James 332
Ball, D. L. 311
banking method of education 145, 159, 160–1
Banks, J. A. 301, 331
Barton, George 110
basic principles of curriculum and instruction 56, 59–68; contemporary life studies 62–4; educational purposes 59–61; learners as a source of educational objectives 61–2; subject specialisms 64–8
Beard, Charles A. 9
behavioral objectives 96
Bergen, Barry H. 180n36
Berlin, I. 223, 224
Berliner, D. C. 256
Bernstein, B. 253–4
Bernstein, R. J. 7, 155
Biddle, B. J. 256
Biklen, S. K. 362
bilingual education 255, 256; California curriculum 262; Mexican youth 292–3, 294
Bloom, Benjamin 102, 110
Bobbitt, Franklin 4–6, 11–18, 69–72, 73, 76, 110, 223
Bode, Boyd 69, 70, 71–2, 73, 74, 77
Bogdan, R. C. 362
Bonnett, M. 392
Bowers, C. A. 220, 392
Britzman, Deborah 315, 318, 322, 323, 324, 325
Bruner, Jerome S. *see* Man: A Course Of Study (MACOS)
Bull, B. 235
Bush (G.W.) administration 349, 351
Bushmen 86, 88

Califia, Pat 318
Campbell, D. S. 224
Canada *see* culture in the curriculum
The Canon project 229, 230
Caswell, H. L. 224
CBTE (competency-based teacher education) 75
centripetal thinking 210, 223–32; the knowing is in doing the knowing 228–30; paradigm lost 230–2; poverty of the divergent to beauty of the diverse 225–8
Chan, Elaine *see* culture in the curriculum
Chapa, J. 290
characterization by value 104
Charters, W. W. 14, 69, 70, 75–6
Chavez, L. 297
Cheney, J. 219
child rearing 86–7
Cho, J. 354, 355, 357, 359, 374
choice 72, 143
Churchill, Winston 403
citizenship *see* global citizenship
Clandinin, D. J. 304, 312
classification 254, 259–62
classroom organization *see* implementation as mutual adaptation
classroom routines 58
Clinton, W. J. 350
cognitive domain 102, 103, 110
cognitive processes 283
Cohen, D. K. 311
collaboration 284, 367–8
collection code curriculum 254
commensurability 280, 282
Commission on the Social Studies 9
Committee of Ten 56, 64, 65
Commonwealth Teacher-Training Study 70, 75–6
community service 284
comparison 280, 282
competency-based teacher education (CBTE) 75
complementary curriculum 213, 379–96; definitions 380, 396n13; eco-educational criticism 381–2, 394, 395; ecological education 379; environmental education 379–80; findings 382–92: (integrity and authenticity 383–8, 393; self-awareness 384–92; spiritual beliefs 386, 394); hidden curriculum 381; implications for ecological teacher education 394–5; implications for teaching: environmentally-sustainable pedagogy 392–4; intergenerational responsibility 392; method of inquiry 381–2; null curriculum 381; organic perception 392–3; shadow curriculum 380–1
complex overt response 104
comprehension 103
compulsion 121–2
Conant Report (1959) 55, 269
Connelly, F. M. 231, 304, 312
consciousness and curriculum 58, 127–39; alternative views 131–2; disclosure, reconstruction, generation 129–31; learning-mode of orientation 132–5; literary criticism 127–9; making connections 135–8
contemporary life studies 62–4
conversation 281; *see also* dialogue
Corcoran, P. B. 394–5
Cotton, D. R. E. 391
Counts, George S. 8–9, 45–51
Cremin, L. 150
critical thinking 159, 161
Crocco, Margaret Smith 332
cultural relations 219
culture in the curriculum 211, 301–13; Bay Street School context 303–4; Boyne River Field trip 303; personal biases and landscapes of difference 309–10; student perspectives 304–5; teacher and parent perspectives 305–8
culture of immigrant children 41–2; *see also* culture in the curriculum; subtractive schooling
Cummins, J. 301
curriculum: definitions 13, 235–6
curriculum for the 21st century 213, 399–405; educational aims for a changing world 400–1; goals and aims in education 399–400; taking the new aims seriously 402–5
curriculum reform movement 55
curriculum standards 143–4, 210–11, 253–67; California 257–66: (classification 259–62; framing 262–5; methodology 258; standards documents 257–8); from civil rights to standardization 255–6; classification 254; framing 254; structural relationships 254; theoretical framework 253–4; discussion and implications 265–6
Cutter-MacKenzie, A. 380

the daily grind 58, 117–26; compulsion 121–2; crowds 120, 122–3; discipline 124; environment 119–20; familiarity 117–18; hidden curriculum 123–4; personality 124–5; power 122–3; praise 122–3; ritualistic and cyclic quality 121; scholarship 125; social context 120; time 118–19
Dale, Roger 171
Davis, Brent *see* queer curriculum theory
de-skilling 167, 173, 175, 179n3
democracy 49–51, 183–5, 187–9, 193–4, 375
desks, scientific 26–7
devices 92
Dewey, John 8, 218, 220, 221, 231; on art 129; on comparisons 282; on criticism 112–13, 114; on curriculum 9, 127, 355; on democracy and education 183, 185, 187–9, 193–4, 375; on goals 227; pedagogic creed 6–7, 33–40, 71; on schools 48
dialogue 157–60, 161, 218, 219–20, 228–9
Dickens, Charles: *Hard Times* 403
disciplinarity 225, 228, 229–30, 399–401; *see also* classification
discipline 124, 309–10

discourse 219–20, 231
divergence 225–6, 232n1
diversity 225, 226, 232n1; *see also* culture in the curriculum; culture of immigrant children; subtractive schooling
documentaries 92–3
Doll, William E., Jr. *see* the four R's
domains 102
Dow, P. B. 57
Dutro, E. 256

eco-educational criticism 381–2, 394, 395
ecological education *see* complementary curriculum
economic issues 46–7, 50
education: Dewey's pedagogic creed 6–7, 33–40, 71; method 37–9; psychological basis 33–4; and social progress 39–40; sociological basis 33–4; subject matter of 36–7
education for sustainable development *see* complementary curriculum
educational connoisseurship and criticism 381–2, 395, 396n4
educational equity 285–6
educational objectives 57, 59–61, 95–108; affective domain 102, 103–4, 110; all, or nothing at all? 97–8; behavioral objectives 96; choice 72, 143; cognitive domain 102, 103, 110; constructing *vs.* selecting objectives 104–8; from contemporary life studies 62–4; content generality 99–100; help or hindrance? 57–8, 109–15; learners as a source of 61–2; limitations of theory 111–14; measurability and clarity 95–7; performance objectives 96; proficiency levels 100–2; psychomotor domain 102, 104; selected and constructed learner responses 98–9; specificity of objectives 71–2, 110, 113; specificity of transfer 109–10; from subject specialists 64–8; taxonomies 102–4; terminology 95; test item equivalence 100
Eisner, Elliot 224, 227, 396n10; on educational connoisseurship and criticism 381, 382, 395, 396n4; on educational objectives 57–8, 109–15; on schools 211, 279–87
Eliot, T. S. 127–8
English *see* language curriculum; literature
English language learners (ELLs): California 256, 257, 258, 259, 260, 262, 263; Mexican youth 292–3, 294, 295
entry behavior and proficiency levels 101
environment 119–20, 122–3
environmental education *see* complementary curriculum
Eskimos 84–5, 86, 87, 88, 89–90
ethnicity 255; and discipline 309–10; and gender 305–8
evaluation 103
evolution 84
exhibitions, educationally interpretive 285
Experimental Psychology 21

familiarity 117–18
family life 42–3
Fitzgerald, F. Scott 332
Flinders, D. J. 220, 381; et al. 381
The Foorman Study 256
Fordham, S. 296
Foucault, Michel 315, 316, 318, 319, 323, 326
the four R's 209–10, 215–16; recursion 217–18; relations 218–20; richness 216–17; rigor 220–1; the three R's 215–16
framing 254, 262–5
Freire, Paulo 130, 135; *see also* pedagogy of the oppressed
Frost, Robert 350
Fullan, M. 354, 357, 358, 359–60, 374
Furter, Pierre 159, 160
Fuss, Diana 318

games 81, 86, 90
Gardner, John 190–1
Gay, G. 255
gays and lesbians in social studies curriculum 212, 331–7; curricular limitations of current inclusion 332–3; the hidden curriculum 333; toward more inclusive curriculum 334–5; *see also* queer curriculum theory
gender: and culture 305–8; and curriculum 255; girls' education for parenthood 42–3; and global education 342–5; *see also* gays and lesbians in social studies curriculum; global citizenship; queer curriculum theory; teachers, controlling the work of
Gerwin, D. 240
Gitlin, A. 175(n32), 176(n37), 180n27
global citizenship 213, 339–52; the challenge for teachers 345–7; definitions 339–41; educating global citizens 341–2; gender roles and global education 342–5; hope for the future 349–52; interactive phases and global citizenship education 347–9; National SEED Project on Inclusive Curriculum 345–7, 349
goals 227, 284, 399–400
Goals 2000 279
Goffman, E. 294
Golding, William: *Lord of the Flies* 403
Gowdy, Barbara 316
Greene, Maxine *see* consciousness and curriculum
Gruenewald, D. A. 379
Grumet, M. 229
Guba, E. G. 355
guided response 104
Guilford, J. P. 283

Halley, Janet 315
Hammersley, M. 362
Hamot, Greg 232n1
Harden, R. M. 235
He, M. F. et al. 380
Heath and Nielson (1974) 77
Hemingway, Ernest 332

Herrick, Virgil 110
heteroglossia 231, 232
heteronormativity 324, 331; *see also* gays and lesbians in social studies curriculum
heterotopia 326
hidden curriculum 123–4, 333, 381
high-stakes testing and curriculum control 210, 235–47; cheating 282; content control 242–3; data analysis 239–41; data collection 237–8; definitions 235–6; discussion 245–6; findings 242–5; formal control 243; method 236–7; pedagogic control 244; pedagogy 235–6, 240; the research debate 236; structure of knowledge 235, 240; study limits 242; study reliability 241–2; subject matter 235, 239; theme pairings 244–5; theme triplets 245
Hillocks, G., Jr. 246
history curriculum 226, 404; California 261–2, 263, 264; *see also* Holocaust curriculum: implementation
Hlebowitsh, Peter 358; *see also* centripetal thinking
Holocaust curriculum: implementation 213, 353–76; assumptions and expectations 359–60; conceptual and theoretical framework 353–6; conditions leading to implementation 358–9; country and curriculum context 356–7; curriculum enactment 354; curriculum implementation 357–8; fidelity implementation 354; findings 362–73; implementation study interview protocol 375–6; methodology 360–73; mutual adapatation 354–5; relevant literature 357–60; students: (interest 363–4; teacher perceptions of 363–4); subject matter: (curricular need 370–1; curriculum attributes 371–3); teachers: (academic freedom 364–6; changes in behavior 368–9; collaboration 367–8; eclectic use 369–70; finding other places in macrocurriculum 366–7; professional development 367–8); conclusion and implications 373–5
House Committee on Un-American Activities 351
Huebner, D. 151
Hull House, Chicago 7–8
human rights 332, 341
humanism 160–1
Hutchins, R.M. 145, 184, 187–9

Igoa, C. 301
immigrant child, public school and the 41–3
implementation as mutual adaptation 146–7, 195–205; adaptive planning and staff meetings 200–1; cooptation 196; general implications 202–4; implementation strategy 198; institutional receptivity 196–8; local material development 198–9; mutual adaptation 196; nonimplementation 196; open classroom projects 201; staff training 199–200; *see also* Holocaust curriculum: implementation
incentives 280–1
individualism 220
industrialism 50, 74
industry 42
Ingram, H. 236
Instructional Objectives Exchange (IOX) 105, 106–7
integrated code curriculum 254
integrity 383–8, 393
intellect 283
interactions 280
Interactive Phases of Curricular and Personal Re-Vision 347–9
Iser, W. 221

Jackson, P. W. 224, 381; *see also* the daily grind
James, William 87
Jickling, B. 379
job analysis 70, 74, 75

Kafka, Franz 133–6
Kennedy, J. F. 350
Kliebard, Herbert M. 56, 69–77, 150, 253
knowledge 102, 103; academic knowledge 169–70; the knowing is in doing the knowing 228–30; structure of knowledge 235, 240
Knowles, John: *A Separate Peace* 402–3
Kouritzin, S. G. 301
Krathwohl, David et al. 102, 110
Krugly-Smolska, E. 380, 386

labor 285
Ladson-Billings, G. 255, 297
LaFollette, H. 229
Lagemann, Ellen Condliffe 7
language curriculum 255; California 258, 259, 262, 263–4; and culture 289, 293–5; English as study of language 65; grammar curriculum 14–15; in MACOS project 80–3, 90; spelling 15; standards 269–70, 271
Lareau, A. 290
Larson, M. 175(n35–6)
Latvia *see* Holocaust curriculum: implementation
league tables 281
Leakey, Louis 84, 90
learner responses, selected and constructed 98–9
learning, transfer of 283
Lévi-Strauss, Claude 87–8
liberty 25, 27
Lincoln, Y. S. 355
literary criticism 127–9
literature 65–6, 402
Lomax, R. G. et al. 240
Lorde, Audre 317
Lowry, Lois 320

McCaleb, S. P. 301
McCarthy, C. 294
Macdonald, J. B. 150, 154

MacDonald, James B. 113
McEwan, H. 235
McIntosh, Peggy *see* global citizenship
McKinney, W. L. 153
McLaughlin, M. W. *see* implementation as mutual adaptation
McTighe, J. 231
Madaus, G. F. 236
Malraux, André 164n7
Man: A Course Of Study (MACOS) 55, 56–7, 79–93, 217; child rearing 86–7; form of the course 91–2; language 80–3, 90; pedagogy 89–91; social organization 85–6; structure of the course 79–80; teacher training 93; tool making 83–5; try-out and shaping 93; world view 87–9
Mann, Horace 184
Manteaw, B. O. 379
Mao Tse-Tung 164–5n10, 164n7
Martin, Jane Roland 348–9
materials 92, 93
mathematics 215–17, 270
Matute-Bianchi, M. E. 296
measurement 95–7, 280
mechanism 104
Merleau-Ponty, Maurice 129–31, 133–4, 137, 138
Merton, Robert 153
method, nature of 37–9
Mexican youth *see* subtractive schooling
Miller, J. B. 341
Misco, Thomas *see* Holocaust curriculum: implementation
model exercises 92
Moe, T. M. 247
monologia 231, 232
Montessori, Maria 5–6, 19–31
Moodley, K. A. 301
morality 30
Moroye, Christy M. *see* complementary curriculum
Morrison, Toni 324
Morton, Donald 315
multiculturalism 256; *see also* culture in the curriculum
music curriculum: departments 273–4; standards 269, 271–2, 274; to test or not to test 275–7
myths 88–9

narration 219
A Nation at Risk 256, 279
National Academy of Sciences 56
National Council of English Teachers 65
National Council of Mathematics Teachers 65
National Council of Social Studies Teachers 65
National Defense Education Act 170
National Education Association 56, 399–400
National Institute of Child Health and Human Development (NICHD) 256
National Science Foundation 55
National SEED Project on Inclusive Curriculum 345–7, 349
National Society for the Study of Education (NSSE) 224
natural phenomena, interest in 23–4
needs 6, 7–8, 42, 61–2, 67, 73; *see also* culture in the curriculum; English language learners (ELLs); subtractive schooling; teacher education
New Guinea 84–5
No Child Left Behind Act (NCLB) 226, 232n2, 235, 256
Noddings, Nel 8, 143, 146, 187–94, 295, 296, 333; *see also* curriculum for the 21st century
Novak, Michael 137
null curriculum 381
Null, J. W. 230

Ogbu, J. U. 296
organization 104
Orwell, George: "Such, such were the Joys" 403
outcomes 111, 279–80, 286

Page, R. N. 357
Paideia Proposal, The 145–6, 183–6; critical review of 146, 187–94; democracy and education 183–5; modes of teaching and learning 185–6, 194; the same course of study for all 185
Paley, V. G. 301
Palmer, George Herbert 65
Palmer, J. 394
Palmer, P. J. 393
paradigms 230
parent education 285
Parker, W. C. 355
patterns 216–17
PBTE (performance-based teacher education) 75
Pedagogical Anthropology 20, 21
Pedagogical Hygiene 21
pedagogical relations 218–19
pedagogy: definition 235–6; Dewey's pedagogical creed 6–7, 33–40, 71; in high-stakes testing 240; in MACOS project 89–91; and modern science 19–31
pedagogy of the oppressed 144–5, 157–65; activism 157; banking method of education 145, 159, 160–1; co-investigators 163; critical thinking 159, 161; dialogue 157–60, 161; domination 158; faith in man 158–9; generative themes 161–3; hope 159; humanism 160–1; humility 158; love 158; naive thinking 159–60; naming 157; praxis 157, 162; thematic investigation 162–4; trust 159; verbalism 157; words 157
perception 104
performance-based teacher education (PBTE) 75
performance objectives 96
personal talent and interests 284
personality 124–5
Peters, R. S. 131

Phenix, Philip H. 131, 132
philosophy 87–8
Piaget, Jean 129, 134, 218
Pinar, William E. 224, 225, 232; *see also* reconceptualization of curriculum studies
Pinter, Harold 133
Plato 193, 228–9, 231
Plochmann, G. K. 137
Poetter, T. S. et al. 357
policy design 236
Pomfret, A. 354, 357
Popham, W. James 57, 95–108
Portes, A. 292
Posner, G. J. 152
post-instruction behavior 97
Powell, A. G. et al. 269
power 45–6, 122–3, 143, 253–4
praise 122–3
prediction 280
presentism 63–4
Prigogine, I. 218
prizes 28–30
Probyn, Elspeth 316, 317
proficiency levels 100–2
programmed instruction 95
progress 29
Progressive Education Association 64–5
Progressive movement 3, 4, 48, 110
proletarianization 167–9, 179n3
psychomotor domain 102, 104
public school and the immigrant child 41–3
punishment 28–9, 30
Putnam, R. D. 291

quantification 280
queer curriculum theory 212, 315–28; identifications 316–20; interruptions 324–6; stirrings 320–4; *see also* gays and lesbians in social studies curriculum
queer theory 315
queries and contrasts 92

Rand Change-Agent Study 195–6
rationalization 279–80
receiving 103
reconceptualization of curriculum studies 144, 149–56; bureaucratic model 150; conceptual-empiricists 151–3; reconceptualists 153–5; traditionalists 149–51
recursion 217–18
reflection 218
Reid, W. A. 152, 153, 154
Renter, D. S. et al. 239
repetition 218
Report of the Committee on Science in General Education, The 67
representational forms 284
repression 30
responding 104
Review of Educational Research 152
richness 216–17
rigor 220–1
Robertson, C. L. 380, 386
Roosevelt, Franklin D. 9
rubrics 279–80
Rugg, Harold 8, 9

Said, Edward 325
Sartre, Jean Paul 127, 128–9
satisfactions 284–5
SBR (scientifically-based research) 232n2
Schneider, A. L. 236
scholarship 125
schools: Dewey's view 48; doing well 211, 279–87; educational purposes 59–61; and the immigrant child 41–3; limitations of 73–4; as social institution 35–6; and social progress 39–40
Schubert, W. 229, 230
Schutz, Alfred 131–2, 135, 137
Schwab, J. J. 55, 151, 152, 227, 230, 231, 301, 355, 362
science 19–31, 217, 256; functions of school subject 66, 67, 403–4; standards 271
Science in General Education 67
scientific curriculum-making 69–77; agricultural education 16–17; analyzing human activity 74–5; of Bobbittt 4–5, 11–18, 69–70; Bode as prophet 69, 77; of Charters 70; choice of objectives 72; contemporary aftermath 76; definition of curriculum 13; directed and undirected training 13–14; grammar curriculum 14–15; limitations of the school 73–4; preparing for adulthood 70–1; specificity of objectives 71–2; spelling 15; standard for living 73; in teacher education 75–6; teaching as technology 76–7; vocational curriculum 15–16
Scientific Pedagogy 5–6, 19, 20, 21, 25–6
scientifically-based research (SBR) 232n2
scientifically-based teaching 226, 227
Sedgwick, Eve 315, 316, 318, 319, 322, 323
self-assessment 284
self-awareness 384–92
self-consciousness 131
Sergi, Giuseppe 19–20, 21, 31
Serres, M. 221
set 104
shadow curriculum 380–1
Sikes, P. et al. 275
Silverman, D. 155
Siskin, Leslie Santee 211, 269–77
Slattery, P. et al. 226–7
slavery 27–8
Sleeter, Christine *see* curriculum standards
Smith, B. O. et al. 224
Smith, G. A. 379, 395
Smith, M. L. 236
Smith, R. 380
social capital 289, 291

social class 167–8
social liberty 25, 27
social order 45–51
social organization 85–6
social progress 39–40
social reconstructionism 9
social studies curriculum 9, 255, 404; California 261–2, 263, 264; in MACOS project 85–6, 89; *see also* gays and lesbians in social studies curriculum
Solomon, J. 253
Spark, Muriel: *The Prime of Miss Jean Brodie* 403
Spencer, Herbert 62, 73
spinal curvature 26–7
spiritual beliefs 386, 394
standards: and critical judgments 112–13; and rationalization 279–80; *see also* curriculum standards
Starr, Helen Gates 7
state departments of education 279
Stillman, Jamy *see* curriculum standards
Stodolsky, Susan 210
Strike, K. A. 152
structure of knowledge 235, 240
Style, Emily 345, 346
subject matter 36–7, 235, 239
subject specialists as a source of objectives 64–8
subtractive schooling 211–12, 289–99; caring relations 289, 295–7; concept 292–3; language and culture 289, 293–5; process 293–7; Seguín High School study 289–92; social capital 289, 291
Sumara, Dennis *see* queer curriculum theory
symbolic systems 88
synthesis 103

Taba, H. 224
Tanner, D. 224, 230, 231
Tanner, L. N. 224, 230, 231
Taylorism 171–2
teacher credentials 264–5
teacher education: *Commonwealth Teacher-Training Study* 70, 75–6; environmental education 394; in MACOS project 93; professional development 367–8; school as center for 285; scientific curriculum-making 75–6
teachers: and global citizenship 345–7; identity 393; integrity 383–8, 393; isolation 273–5, 281; peer review 285; power of 45–6; *see also* teachers, controlling the work of
teachers, controlling the work of 145, 167–81; academic knowledge and curricular control 169–71; de-skilling 167, 173, 175, 179n3; gendered resistance 176–7; intensification and teaching 172–4; labor, gender and teaching 177–9; legitimating intervention 171–2; profession and gender 174–6; proletarianization: class and gender 167–9, 170–1, 179n3; the state 171
teaching as technology 76–7
technical control 169, 179n3
technological rationality 154
technology 88; in MACOS project 83–5; teaching as 76–7
terminology 3
testing: and accountability 275–7; alternatives to testing 283–4; cheating 282; commensurability 280, 282; incentives 280–1; league tables 281; measurement 280; and narrowing of curriculum 281; and quality of education 281; self-assessment 284; test item equivalence 100; *see also* accountability; high-stakes testing and curriculum control
Tetrault, M. K. T. 255
Thorndike, E. L. 72, 109–10
Thornton, Stephen *see* gays and lesbians in social studies curriculum
thought: cognitive domain 102, 103, 110; cognitive processes 283; critical thinking 159, 161; and language 161; naive thinking 159–60; questioning 283; *see also* centripetal thinking
the three R's 215–16
time 118–19
Toffler, Alvin 132
transfer of learning 283
Tyack, David 281
Tyler, Ralph W. 110, 149, 150, 210, 216, 224, 231; *see also* basic principles of curriculum and instruction

Uhrmacher, P. B. 380–1
U.N. Women's conferences 351
unit materials 91–3

Valenzuela, Angela *see* subtractive schooling
value complex 104
valuing 104
Van Kannel-Ray, N. 392
Van Manen, M. 154
Visone, F. 240
vocational curriculum 15–16
Vogler, K. E. 239

Walker, D. F. 144, 152–3, 154
Wals, A. 379
Waples, Douglas 75–6
Warner, Michael 324
Watkins, W. H. 255
Wellesley College 345, 350
Westbury, I. 153
White, Edmund 317–18
Whitehead, A. N. 213, 400–1
Wiggins, G. 231
Williams, D. R. 379
Wilson, E. O. 400
Wineberg, S. 255–6
Wixson, K. K. 256

Wong-Fillmore, L. 301
work 285
world view 87–9
Wraga, W. G. 224
Wright, E. O. 167
Wright, H. 226

Yeh, S. S. 246

Zaret, E. 154

#0111 - 230916 - C0 - 254/178/23 [25] - CB - 9780415520768